D0113707

DISCOURSE PROCESSING

ADVANCES
IN
PSYCHOLOGY
8

Editors

G. E. STELMACH

P. A. VROON

NORTH-HOLLAND PUBLISHING COMPANY
AMSTERDAM · NEW YORK · OXFORD

DISCOURSE PROCESSING

Edited by

August FLAMMER
Department of Psychology
University of Fribourg
Switzerland

and

Walter KINTSCH
Department of Psychology
University of Colorado
Boulder, Colorado, USA

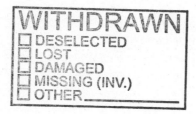

1982

NORTH-HOLLAND PUBLISHING COMPANY
AMSTERDAM · NEW YORK · OXFORD

© North-Holland Publishing Company, 1982

ISBN: 0 444 86515 2

Publishers:
NORTH-HOLLAND PUBLISHING COMPANY
AMSTERDAM · NEW YORK · OXFORD

Sole distributors for the U.S.A. and Canada:
ELSEVIER SCIENCE PUBLISHING COMPANY, INC.
52 VANDERBILT AVENUE
NEW YORK, N.Y. 10017

PRINTED IN THE NETHERLANDS

PREFACE

Research on discourse (or text) processing has only recently come into its own. It builds, of course, on the work on text analysis which has a long and distinguished history; but modern developments in psychology (e.g., memory research), artificial intelligence, linguistics and philosophy have contributed to its emergence in the last decade as a lively and promising research area.

As yet, however, the domain of discourse processing still has flexible boundaries and lacks a stable profile. One of the purposes of the International Symposium on Text Processing in Fribourg 1981 was to probe whatever consensus was beginning to emerge in that research domain, and to take a look at that field now that the groping first steps have been taken and a more mature and orderly stage of development has been reached. A second purpose of the Symposium, the importance of which became fully clear only during the actual conference itself, was to bring together researchers on discource processing from different nationalities. The event took place in Switzerland; half of the contributors were European from various linguistic backgrounds, a few were from Asia and Australia, and the rest came from North America. Several of us, the old-timers and experts included, were surprised to find out how much valuable and interesting research is being carried out in heretofore unsuspected places. Thus, the most important function of this book might be to permanently open up channels of communication across the barriers of continents and language.

Bringing the people together is one thing; publishing their contributions in a common language is another. We regret that a large proportion of the papers given at the Symposium had to be excluded from this publication, though the abstracts of these papers as well as the addresses of their authors are reprinted here. Thus, the final book contains 46 contributions, grouped topically into eight chapters. The grouping was made according to problem area and not according to methodology with the intent to thereby focus on the important issues in the field of discourse processing, and to show how diverse approaches contribute to a better understanding of the problems involved.

Obviously, this book is merely the final stage of a major enterprise which started in 1978 when the decision to launch the Symposium was made. Many people have made substantial contributions to this undertaking though only a few insiders may be able to spot their traces in the book itself. François Stoll, Zürich, president of the Swiss Psychological Association, which backed the Symposium, has helped us in numerous ways on many occasions. On the scientific committee for the Symposium we enjoyed the collaboration of Urs Aeschbacher, Fribourg; Beat Keller, Fribourg; François Stoll, Zürich; and Marianne Tauber, Fribourg.

The bulk of the organisational work was done by Ruth Lüthi, Fribourg, whom we cordially thank for the careful and reliable planning, execution and debugging of a thousand operations. Warm thanks are also extended to Kerrie Oeuvray, Ruth's second hand, and their helpers there: Irene Weber, Stefanie

Stadler, André Kaiser, and Raymond Geismar. For special services before and
during the Symposium we thank those staff members of the Fribourg Department
of Psychology who willingly assumed an extra workload: Anita Büttiker,
Christiane Schroeter, Ulla Werren, Hansruedi Kaiser.

Besides all this, the Symposium needed money, rooms and facilities. We
acknowledge the financial help of our sponsors, the Swiss Academy of Human
Sciences, the State, the City and the University of Fribourg, Siemens AG,
Zürich, the Swiss Psychological Association, and the Swiss Federal Office
of Education and Sciences. We are grateful for the moral and material
assistance of Bernhard Schnyder, Rector of the University of Fribourg,
Pascal Ladner, Vice-Rector, and Hans Brülhart, Administrative Director.

Above all, of course, we thank our authors for their collaboration, their
enthusiasm and their patience. Our special appreciation goes to those
whom we had to ask to write their contributions in a foreign language, in
the interest of international communication. All papers are now in English,
the common language of the Symposium. Yet, it is hard to see how this would
have been possible without the most effective contributions of Eileen
Kintsch, who acted as text editor and very often as text reviser for the
papers which were more or less close approximations to formal English.

We are also grateful for the efficient and flexible assistance of
Dr. K. Michielsen, North-Holland Publishing Company, Amsterdam. On site,
the bulk of the work was done by Anita Büttiker, Ulla Werren and Vinzenz
Morger, Fribourg, and Perle Bochet, Boulder, Colorado. Both editors are
happy to acknowledge the support of research sponsors who made some of this
work possible: the Swiss National Science Foundation (Grant No. 1.714-0.78),
the National Institute of Mental Health (Grant No. 15872), and the Center
for Advanced Study in the Behavioral Sciences (supported by NIMH Grant
No. 5T32 MH14581-06 and the Spencer Foundation) which provided shelter and
a congenial atmosphere to finish this project.

Fribourg and Boulder   August Flammer
30 June, 1982   Walter Kintsch

TABLE OF CONTENTS

TEXT STRUCTURE

DISCOURSE PROCESSING
A. Flammer and W. Kintsch (eds.)
© *North-Holland Publishing Company, 1982*

PLANS AND GOALS IN UNDERSTANDING EPISODES

Gordon H. Bower

Department of Psychology
Stanford University
Stanford, California

People's judgments about important elements in
narrative episodes were studied. Subjects chose
the protagonist's goal as most important, then
actions, outcomes, complications, and lastly background and modifiers. A statement's importance
correlated with its likelihood of recall and inclusion in a summary. Relating episodes to a Plan
schema, further experiments found that readers take
longer to comprehend an action in light of a goal
the greater the "distance" between them in a goal
hierarchy. Furthermore, the time to comprehend a
character's action increases the more independent
goals the reader is monitoring for that character.

INTRODUCTION

This symposium is concerned with how people understand texts, recall them,
paraphrase them, summarize them, and answer questions about them. The fact
that this symposium is being sponsored by a Psychology Department attests
to the progress being made in cognitive psychology. Psychologists'
concern with text processing is relatively recent. Eight years ago a symposium like this could not have taken place because there simply was not
enough research on the topic. But since 1974 there's been an increasing
stream of research on text processing, attested to by conferences and
specialized research journals.

Several years ago when I first began studying text comprehension with my
student, Perry Thorndyke (see Bower, 1976; Thorndyke, 1977), we adopted the
story-grammar approach then proposed by Dave Rumelhart (1975) and Tuen van
Dijk (1972). I have come to realize over the ensuing years that my
interest is not so much in stories as in how people understand episodes and
action sequences. Stories have episodes, of course, and the telling of the
episodes is arranged so as to arouse suspense, surprise, mystery, humor, or
irony, thus to entertain and hold the reader's attention. But I have not
been studying these affective, entertaining features of stories; rather,
I've studied only how people understand and remember episodes and event
sequences.

It turns out that the central part of story grammars is the way they
analyze simple episodes. Nearly all the story grammars assume that an
interesting episode must have at least four parts: a goal for the protagonist, some obstacle or complication to attainment of that goal, some
actions designed to overcome those obstacles, and some outcome of these

actions. Another way to say this is that an episode consists of a problem
and its resolution. The problem can be characterized as stemming from the
protagonist's goal plus a complication or obstacle; the resolution is comprised of the protagonist's action plan plus its outcome. To describe
these elements more fully, the complications typically arise either from
physical obstacles, or from the conflict of several goals within the same
individual, or the conflict of goals between two competing individuals or
teams. The resolution of an episode describes either the winning, losing,
or compromising of a goal, abandoning it, or regaining a lost state of
bliss. In order for the episode to be interesting, the problem must be
significant and the resolution must be novel or unexpected. Dull episodes
deal either with small problems or ones which have routine, familiar solutions.

The story grammars assume that people have acquired an implicit schema or
prototype about episodes. This schema has various uses. One function of
the schema is as a source of questions for readers. In his theory of
question-asking, August Flammer (1980) suggests that people ask questions
about gaps or critical slots in the episode schema that are not filled in
by, or inferable from, the text. It is further assumed that the schema
helps readers identify the critical elements of a text. If episode
schemas are used in analyzing texts and in parsing episodes into significant constituents, then subjects should be able to reliably identify these
allegedly important elements from a mass of text. Certainly, if naive
readers do not agree with the story grammars about what are the essential,
important elements in an episode description, then we all have surely
been following the wrong leads. After a brief survey of the relevant
literature, however, I was unable to find much direct empirical study of
which parts of episodes readers consider to be important and necessary.

IDENTIFYING EPISODE CONSTITUENTS

The question I asked is whether college readers will identify as important
those elements of narrative episodes which story grammars claim to be
critical. Furthermore, I wondered whether people would summarize the
episode and recall it largely in terms of these same critical elements. As
I noted, the elements are the problem (with constituents of goal and complication) and the resolution (with constituents of actions and outcome).
In order to study reader's intuitions, we wrote two six-episode narratives
and had people read them, judge them, and recall them.

The six distinct episodes were printed one per page in a booklet. Each
episode was written to set forth a distinct goal, complication, action-
plan, and outcome, these comprising four sentences. Among these we mixed
four further statements which set forth descriptive information, giving
background or elaborating on the properties of the other constituents.
From the viewpoint of story grammars these descriptive elaborations were
inessential fillers, although they tended to make the prose somewhat more
readable and natural.

One of the stories was about a male university student, Paul, and his
problems in paying for his schooling, getting good grades, holding down a
part-time job, and having an active social life. Here, for example, is
the first episode in the Paul story.

```
           (Goal)   Paul wanted to go to college.
          (Filler)  He decided on a university in California.
    (Complication)  But he didn't have enough money for expenses.
          (Filler)  He had only $535 in a savings bank.
          (Action)  He applied for a football scholarship.
          (Filler)  He had played halfback in high school.
         (Outcome)  After reviewing his case, the coaches granted him an award
                    enabling him to go to school.
          (Filler)  Paul hoped he could play first string.
```

The second story was about a female university student, Gail, who had a conventional set of problems--making friends, losing wieght, getting more exercise, breaking up with a boyfriend.

We had two groups of 30 college students read these stories. Some subjects simply read the stories, at 45 seconds per episode, then 15 minutes later recalled both stories when cued with the characters' names. Other subjects rank-ordered the eight statements in each episode according to their importance or significance within the episode. After they'd so ranked all statements, they re-read them and wrote a summary of each episode in two or three sentences, using less than 15 content words. They were instructed to imagine composing a telegram to relay the essential gist of the episode in as few informative phrases as possible while remaining faithful to the literal events. (This instruction prevented people from composing abstract morals as summaries.)

These two groups of subjects thus assessed each statement for its importance ranking within the episode, its likelihood of inclusion in a summary for that episode, and its likelihood of recall within the entire story. The text grammar hypothesis claims that the statements within each episode can be divided into two sets, those that are irrelevant or not essential versus those that are essential parts of any episode that has a point-namely, the goal, complication, planned action, and outcome. The hypothesis does not predict whether elements within the "essential" set will vary in importance.

The main results of this study are shown in Table 1 giving the average importance ranking, probability of being included in a summary, and probability of recall for each type of statement, averaged over the six episodes within each story. The four background fillers were combined in these statistics. Table 1 contains several interesting findings. First, the descriptive elaborations were indeed judged as irrelevant and unimportant, were least likely to be recalled, and least likely to be included in summaries of the episodes. Thus, subjects' intuitions about what are essential elements in an episode agree with our theory of the episode schema.

A second consistent finding is that subjects usually rate the goal statement as the most important statement in the episode. This average ordering arose for eleven of the twelve episodes (two stories each with six episodes). This is not simply a "first sentence" effect: half the episodes had some background fillers before the goal, yet even in those cases subjects still rated the goal highest in importance.

Table 1

Importance ranking, probability of inclusion in a summary, and probability
of recall by statement type, averaged over the six episodes in each story.
Importance scaled from 1 (most important) to 8 (least)

		Goal	Complication	Action	Outcome	Fillers
			STATEMENT TYPE			
PAUL STORY	Importance Rank	1.75	2.82	3.83	3.62	5.57
	Summary Inclusion	.57	.51	.50	.83	.10
	Free Recall	.65	.66	.79	.76	.53
GAIL STORY	Importance Rank	1./1	4.33	3.85	3.81	5.57
	Summary Inclusion	.74	.18	.67	.63	.16
	Free Recall	.82	.63	.79	.59	.54

A third finding is that the importance ordering of the complication, action, and outcome varied across the two stories. Thus, the data do not
support theories which assign importance to these elements simply on the
basis of their role in the episode structure.

In reviewing our two stories, I noticed another factor that seemed critical
in determining the importance rating subjects gave to the non-goal elements
of the episode. This other factor was how informative, nonredundant, or
unusual a given statement was in the context of the character's goal. Some
Complications or Actions were very routine and expected; stating them
conveyed little new information beyond what one could already infer from
the context. Consider a few of our Complications: an example of an informative Complication is that Paul's playing football frustrates his goal of
doing well in his classes; an example of a routine, redundant Complication
is that Gail lacked motivation to get more exercise; another is that Gail
didn't know what to do to become less shy, so she asked a friend who suggested an assertiveness class. Among American college students Gail's
"Complications" are so standard and routine that they are hardly worth
mentioning.

I thought that this redundancy factor would influence the importance
people assigned to the essential episode elements. So I had some new subjects rate the elements within each episode on a scale of informativeness
or unpredictability in context. This enabled us to separate the episode
elements somewhat more. Thus, Complications judged to be "informative" had
earlier received mean importance rankings of 2.93 (recall, 1 is the most
important) whereas Complications judged as more predictable and redundant
had received average importance rankings of 5.08, which is significantly
lower. A similar difference in importance rankings was found for Actions
rated as informative (3.60) versus those rated as redundant (4.17) with the
Goal or Complication. Outcomes did not differ often enough in redundancy
ratings for us to compare the importance assigned to high vs. low redundant
outcomes.

The conclusion from this post-hoc analysis is that the importance assigned
to a Complication or Action will usually be higher the more unexpected and
informative it is in light of the goal and the other elements.

Consider now the likelihood that different episode elements are included in the telegraphic summaries (see lines 2 and 4 of Table 1). Irrelevant fillers hardly appear at all in summaries; Actions, Complications, and Outcomes are likely to appear, but their exact ordering varies. For example, Complications appear in summaries of the Paul story but hardly ever in summaries of the Gail story. This difference probably reflects again   the predictable versus unpredictable nature of the complications in the two stories. Across the two stories, Complications rated as highly informative were included in episode summaries 74 percent of the time, whereas Complications judged to be redundant and predictable were included only 15 percent of the time. Thus, deletion of predictable Complications in summaries seems to follow Grice's Conversational Postulate--that is, one should be brief and not say what your audience can readily infer.

Table 1 also shows that free recall percentages were related to the impor-tance ranking of the elements of the episode. We computed the Spearman correlation coefficient among the three variables--recall, summary, and importance--across the five categories and two stories (so N=10). The results show moderately strong correlations: importance correlates .72 with likelihood of inclusion in a summary and .62 with free recall; and the likelihood of inclusion in a summary correlates .70 with likelihood that the statement will be recalled. While much common variance is being cap-tured by these measures, the variance unaccounted for still always exceeds 50 percent. Some of this is due to uncontrolled differences in content, in redundancy of the structural elements of the several episodes, and so on. However, perhaps we should be satisfied with the conclusion that to a first approximation, readers may be viewed as identifying and assigning greatest importance to statements stipulating the goal, the complications encountered, the actions undertaken, and the outcome, whereas they devalue and skip over background statements, descriptive elaborations, and details. Readers then use these structurally critical elements they've identified in order to reconstruct the text in recall.

EPISODES ELABORATE UPON PLAN SCHEMATA

One may notice that the constituents of episodes which we have identified are almost the same as the elements of a Plan schema underlying intentional actions. Plans have goals, actions, outcomes, and may encounter complica-tions. Thus, people's knowledge of narrative episodes certainly includes their knowledge about Plans. In this view, readers use their general Plan schema to understand intentional action sequences, and the Plan organizes behaviors according to their goals. Studies by John Black and I (1980) and Edward Lichtenstein and William Brewer (1980) have found that action Plans have a hierarchical structure, that goal-directed actions at higher-levels of the goal-tree are remembered better than non-goal-directed actions at lower, more detailed levels. Also, people do best at processing and recalling a text when it mentions the Plan elements in their stereotypic order.

I want to examine more closely now how plans and goals are used by readers in processing narratives. This topic is discussed in detail in the book by Roger Schank and Bob Abelson, (1977) and their student, Bob Wilensky, (1978), wrote a computer simulation program which understands plan-based stories. The program was called PAM, the initials standing for Plan Applying Mechanism. The basic assumption is that people understand events or statements in narratives by trying to explain them. Thus, actions are

to be understood by reference to the actor's plan; plans are understood by
reference to the goal they serve; goals are understood by reference either
to a superordinate goal, or a state or theme that gives rise to the goal.

Wilensky's PAM program follows a specific algorithm in understanding each
event as it occurs. First, it checks whether the action satisfies an
on-going expectation--for example, whether it fits into a known plan for
the actor. If so, then that's the explanation of the event and it is thus
incorporated into the reader's developing representation of the story.
Second, if the immediate predictions fail for this action, then the reader
tries to infer a plan which includes this action, then checks to see
whether this plan serves a known goal. Third, if a goal is stated or inferred, the reader supposedly checks whether it is consistent with a higher
goal or theme the actor has.

THE DISTANCE EFFECT IN GOAL-ACTION PAIRS

You might have noticed that some actions will be psychologically close to a
given goal but farther away from other goals. That is, a given action may
relate to its goal either directly or indirectly through several intermediate steps or sub-goals. This intuitive notion of the logical distance
between a goal and an action can be explained using the idea of a goal-
subgoal hierarchy or a goal-reduction tree. A goal reduction tree decom-
poses a top-level goal into subgoals, and those into further subgoals or
actions that can be performed. Figure 1 illustrates part of a goal reduction tree for someone's knowledge about how to steal money, which can be
done, let's say, through embezzlement, armed robbery, or stealthy burglary.
To carry out armed robbery, one should have a gun, a get-away plan, and
select a suitable target like a bank. To rob a bank requires that you get
information about the bank's cash reserves, what kind of security systems
they have, and so on.

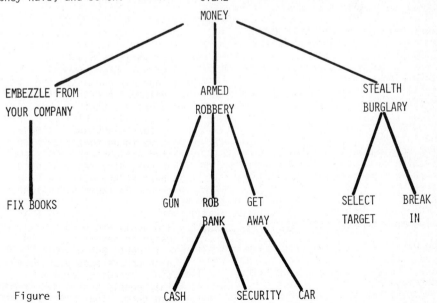

Figure 1

In such a goal-reduction tree, "understanding an action in light of a goal" would mean finding or computing a connecting link of the correct kind between the two elements in the tree. Notice that certain goal-to-action pairs are quite close in the tree whereas others are farther away. When someone thinks about this plan or goal-reduction tree, it would not be available in active memory all at once; rather, it would be retrieved piecemeal from long-term memory. We may think of the links in this figure as a set of one-step productions in memory which encode rules of the form "IF you want to achieve goal G, THEN do subgoals or actions A, B, and C." Thus, if one wants to find a connection between a goal and some action, the productions starting from that goal will be fired, entering its subgoals into active memory, and these in turn will fire their productions, entering their subgoals into active memory. If in this expanding activation process the specified action is encountered, then a connection has been found, so we can say that the reader has understood the action in terms of the plan.

If the retrieval and activation of each link in the goal-tree takes time, then comprehension or interpretation time should take longer for those action-goal pairs that are farther apart in the network. For instance, an action like "John checked out the security guards at the bank" would be understood quickly when preceded by a Near goal like "He wanted to rob a bank" but more slowly when preceded by a Far goal like "He wanted to steal some money".

DISTANCE EFFECT WITH NATURAL GOAL TREES

A Stanford student, Carolyn Foss, and I performed an experiment to see whether this analysis was worthwhile. First, we had to make up many pairs of goals and actions which were psychologically Near or Far from one another according to a plausible goal-reduction tree. Unfortunately these materials could only be chosen informally, by guessing about prototypical goal trees for many standard plans of our subjects. A principled way to select Near versus Far goal-action pairs is to choose three elements along a goal-reduction chain, as in the example above of a top-goal ("stealing"), a subgoal ("armed robbery"), and a lower action ("check out security guards"). In our experiment, we fixed the action and then preceded it either with a Near subgoal or with a Far, higher goal. Thus, the Near subgoal-action pair was nested within the Far goal-action pair, with a shorter distance.

Subjects were timed as they read each statement within a number of four-line episodes. They read for comprehension and had to answer a question after reading each episode. The subject pressed a button to present himself with each successive statement of the text on a CRT. Subjects were not aware that they were being timed for line-by-line reading. The time between button-presses presumably measures the time the subject required to read the statement, comprehend it, and integrate it into his interpretation of the text. We expect that actions will be understood faster when they follow Near rather than Far goals.

I've discussed only the case where the goal precedes the action, and where we measure the time required to understand the action. However, if understanding simply requires connecting up a goal with an action, then one might expect a similar distance effect when the goal follows the action and we measure the time required to comprehend the goal and its connections to that prior action. Thus, the subject would be timed on the second sentence

as he read the Near sequence "John decided to rob a bank. He wanted to
steal some money" versus the Far sequence "John checked out the security
guards at the bank. He wanted to steal some money." Presumably, when the
action is stated first, the person infers a plan and goal for it; then when
the target goal is read, it will produce either a relatively direct match
to the predicted goal in the Near case or will require several steps of
inference in order to link up through subordinate goals in the Far case.
Therefore, we predicted that the effect of distance on comprehension would
be about the same whether the subject were comprehending the action in
light of the goal, or vice versa. To test this, we had our subjects read
four-line episodes where the middle lines were equally often in the action-
goal order and in the goal-action order.

The results of this experiment are shown in Figure 2, which depicts the
average time required to comprehend a target sentence. The top line depicts

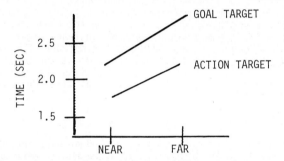

Figure 2

the time to understand a goal following a Near or Far action; the bottom
line is the time to understand an action following a goal.

The first conspicuous result is that a target sentence that is Near to its
preceding context sentence is comprehended about one-third second faster
than are targets that are Far from their preceding context. So, this is
the distance effect we were seeking.

A second result in Figure 2 is that readers are about one half second
faster in understanding an action following a goal than in understanding a
goal following an action. This goal-then-action sequence is, of course,
the prototypical as well as causal order of these elements in the Plan
schema. Thus, we may conclude that people more quickly understand statements when they occur in the same order as the slots in the schema used to
encode the sequence.

Figure 2 shows no interaction between the order of the goal and action, and
the distance between them. The two factors have additive effects on comprehension time.

DISTANCE EFFECT WITH SPECIALLY TRAINED GOAL TREES

Although this experiment succeeded in demonstrating distance effects,
Carolyn Foss and I were bothered that we had no measure of the distance
between a goal and action except our intuitions, which at best provide only
an ordering of more or less distance within a given goal-subgoal chain.
Our intuitive guesses might be wrong about the goal tree of many of our
subjects. Also, it's not clear to what extent the intuitive sense of

goal-action distance we were using was just associative strength of connection between the two predicates. Thus, to take just one example, "steal"
and "rob bank" are more closely associated than are "steal" and "gun". To
counter-argue this point, if one accepts the idea that people store plans,
then "associations" are just the consequence of the causal order of these
events in the Plan.

For such reasons, we decided to stop using naturalistic materials of unknown organization and instead have the subject learn a novel goal hierarchy which we could specify precisely. Therefore, Carolyn Foss and I ran
a second experiment in which we first had subjects read a text describing a
novel procedure; then, after they had thoroughly learned the goal-tree of
that procedure, subjects made a number of timed judgments using their
knowledge of this tree.

The text the subjects studied described the procedure for joining a fictitious Top Secret Club. The goal-hierarchy implicit in the text is shown in
Figure 3 below.

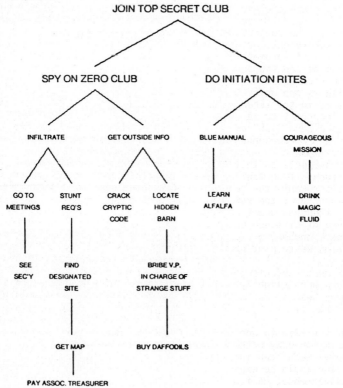

FIGURE 3
GOAL-STRUCTURE FOR EXPERIMENT 2

Thus, in order to join the Top Secret Club, the candidate must spy on its enemy, the Zero Club, and perform several initiation rites. To spy on the Zero Club, the candidate has to infiltrate the club and also get some outside information about it. To get that required that he crack a cryptic code and locate their treasury in a hidden barn, and so on. This goal-tree consists of 16 subgoals nested along six branches. It was rendered into prose resembling instructions for imaginary games like "Dungeons and Dragons" or "Startrek" with which most of our subjects were familiar. The subjects never saw the goal tree as set forth in Figure 3. Rather, they studied the text until they learned it well before the testing phase began.

For the test phase, subjects were told that some CIA agents had found burned and shredded copies of the procedure for joining the club, and they were trying to piece together the original complete procedure. These agents would formulate a plan and submit it for evaluation to the subject, since he was the expert; he was to decide quickly whether or not the proposed plan was well formed. The proposed plans were formatted as two separate clauses: first, a clause would appear on the CRT such as "In order to (infiltrate the Zero Club)"; after the person read that, he pushed a button which showed the second clause, something like "John had to see the secretary". The subject had to decide whether the action in the second clause was a subordinate or descendant of the goal mentioned in the first clause. Thus, it is proper to say that "In order to infiltrate the Zero club, John had to see the secretary"--that is a correct plan because the action in the second clause falls below the goal in the first clause. An Incorrect plan is one where the second clause refers to an action that is either above it in the tree or on a side branch from the first clause. Thus, it is incorrect to say that "In order to see the secretary, John infiltrated the Zero Club" or "In order to infiltrate the Zero Club, John had to carry out a courageous mission".

Training our subjects on this novel goal hierarchy provides several theoretical advantages. Importantly, we know what the goal structure is, and know that it's roughly the same for each subject. Also we know that the degree of learning of the various links in the tree is about the same, so associative strengths won't be varying randomly. Finally, we now have a simple measure of distance between any two nodes in the network as well as the amount of branching or fanning that occurs between two nodes. This measure enables us to plot parametric functions.

In the experiment subjects judged 56 plans once, then repeated the test series. There were slightly more Correct than Incorrect plans, and half of each type were Near or Far goal-action pairs. The basic result is shown in Figure 4.

Importantly, the time to decide that a goal-action plan is correct increased nearly linearly with the number of steps between the elements in the hierarchy. Each step increased reaction time by about half a second. Such a function would be expected if the person searched links downward from the goal at about half a second per step.

Second, Figure 4 shows that subjects answer quicker the second time through the tests. This would occur either if the subject is strengthening and facilitating the same links he'd used before, or if he is learning distant goal-action dependencies, accessing them directly, and by-passing derivation of their relationship the second time.

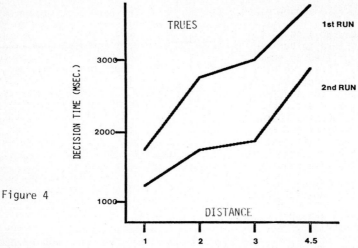

Figure 4

A third effect not shown in Figure 4 was an interference or fan effect of
slower search due to branching: for a given step-distance between the goal
and action, the decision time was longer the greater the branching along
the path connecting them.   This would result if the link-searching process
is slowed by dividing its resources at branching points.

Turning to the False judgments, we were surprised to find no difference
whatsoever between Near, Far, or Lateral False pairs. Mean RT for the
Near, Far, and Lateral falses were 2212, 2162, and 2132, respectively.
These do not differ significantly.   A downward search algorithm for the
goal-tree implies no difference for these cases.   Downward search means to
start from the goal in the first clause and retrieve its descendants below
in successive generations; if any of them matches the action in the second
clause, respond "Correct"; if none of the descendants match, respond
"False".   This downward search algorithm explains the lack of differences
among the Near, Far, and Lateral falses because in this experiment they all
had the same average number of descendants.   However, I should point out
that this was not a planned or controlled comparison in this experiment, so
we are not certain about our conclusions regarding False decisions.

As noted, we can represent the procedural hierarchy in this experiment as a
set of one-step productions in memory that link goals to subgoals.   The
process of searching through the graph structure would then be simulated by
the firing of productions, whereby a goal activates its immediate descendants, which fire their productions, activating their descendants.   Thus
will activation spread across generations.   This is one way to implement
the node-search procedure that is so familiar in semantic networks.

To summarize, we've found that the time to decide that an action is plausible in light of a goal increases almost linearly with the derivational
distance between the two in the goal tree.   Branching slows down the
search, and repetition of particular pathways strengthens them and speeds
up the search.

FURTHER EXPERIMENTS ON GOAL-HIERARCHIES

This experiment with a novel goal hierarchy has yielded orderly results on the time people take to perform memory search and verification. The technique can be exploited to examine a number of questions, some of which we plan to pursue. First, we plan to look at reading time for the second clause rather than decisions regarding proper plans; reading comprehension should be quicker for shorter goal-action pathways. Second, the goal-tree itself can be varied structurally so that one can study more systematically the effects of branching in the goal tree. Third, the test could list a conjunction of actions and ask the subject to decide whether all of them were necessary and sufficient to achieve some superordinate goal. Fourth, in the Foss experiment, the subject learned one large goal-tree and the tests checked the time required to retrieve different segments of the tree; no novel compositions or arrangements were required. The request for novelty in planning suggests further experiments in which we first teach the subject several pieces of disjoint plan hierarchies, and then measure how long he takes on tasks that require him to retrieve and assemble the plan-pieces in a particular order.

CURRENT EXTENSIONS ON GOAL MONITORING

I will briefly describe two extensions of our goal-action research. One project concerns how the reader monitors several goals for the actor. Imagine that the opening of a story describes several separate, independent goals that the actor wants to achieve as the opportunities arise. We conceive of this as the reader setting up a goal-list for that character in short-term memory, and then monitoring for an action relevant to any of these active goals. Later when the text describes an action, we imagine that to understand it, the reader tries to connect it up to some one of the active goals for this character. We may liken this process to Sternberg's memory-scanning task in which the subject searches for a probe digit amongst a memory list. Therefore, one predicts a set-size effect: that is, the more independent goals one has to keep in mind for a character, the longer it should take to decide that an action fits into a plan for some one of these goals.

The materials of this experiment are illustrated in Figure 5. The experimental subject reads many small vignettes in which a list of 1, 3, or 5 goals is introduced, then 0 or 3 irrelevant interpolated sentences occur to produce differing amounts of de-activation, then an action statement occurs. The subject decides as quickly as he can whether the test action is plausibily consistent with some one of the goals. Figure 5 illustrates a trial with 3 goals, with 3 interpolated sentences, and shows an example of a True action as well as a False action (only one would be presented per trial).

So far the results are confirming expectations. Decision time for an action increases with the number of active goals, and the slope (increase per goal) is less for True than for False action probes. The steeper slope for Falses would arise if each goal-action comparison takes much longer to decide mismatch than to decide match due to searching for ever more remote connections between mismatching elements. We are also finding that the interpolated material slows down all decision times and increases errors; this was predicted since interpolated material deactivates the goal elements, so time is needed to reactivate the goals to compare to the action probe.

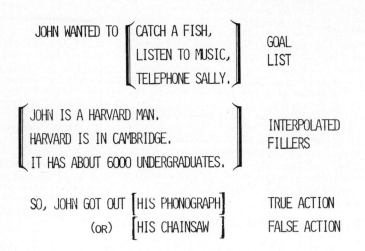

Figure 5

In sum, this experiment seems to be working rather well, with results as
expected. We plan to extend it to study the effects of keeping track of
two characters' goal lists, deleting goals from the list as they're
achieved, using action probes that simultaneously satisfy several of the
goals, and so on. The experimental paradigm seems useful for answering
many questions about how people track multiple goals and up-date the active
goal-list for particular characters in a story.

A second extension Carolyn Foss and I are currently exploring is to measure
comprehension and decision time using goal-hierarchies in the context of
actual stories. Unfortunately, most of the fairy tales Carolyn examined
had very shallow goal-trees, which are not ideal for investigating causal
distance effects. One story that is notorious for having a long chain of
subgoals is "The Old Farmer and His Stubborn Donkey" (Rumelhart, 1975), so
we are using that in a current experiment. The experimental subjects are
being timed while deciding the truth of causal implications of the form
"In order to achieve X, the farmer did Y". As before, the basic question
is whether decision time will increase with the distance between the goal
and the action in the hierarchy. I'm hoping that the results of this study
will confirm our earlier findings but with a goal hierarchy the subject has
learned within a real story.

CONCLUDING REMARKS

It is time that I bring this paper to a close. I have been discussing
episodes and the plan-goal analysis of actions, and have investigated how
people comprehend actions in light of goals, or goals in light of actions.
The guiding theme is that readers search for explanations of narrative
events, and that the difficulty of comprehension, and hence reading time,
increases the greater the derivational distance between a goal and a relevant action in a planning space. Also, tracking the goals of a character

can be thought of as maintaining those goals in active memory as explanatory sources for later events, with the time to find a given goal-to-action linkage depending on how many goals are active, how long is the link up, how activated are the correct versus incorrect goals, and so on.

These findings are not especially surprising given the theoretical analysis of the comprehension tasks in terms of goal hierarchies and memory search through activated elements in short-term memory. But the power of such ideas from cognitive psychology is their ability to explain different phenomena. The value of a theoretical framework is sometimes just to enable us to think systematically about certain phenomena and to frame questions about them in such manner that the answers seem almost obvious. Interestingly, researchers' feeling of understanding events in nature by substantiating their theoretical expectations runs almost exactly parallel to readers' feeling of understanding story events because they substantiate predictions they're made about the characters. This seems entirely fitting since both the scientist and the comprehender are just trying to explain events that engage their attention.

FOOTNOTE

Research reported here was supported by a grant MH-13905 to the author from the United States N.I.M.H.

REFERENCES

Black, J. B. & Bower, G. H. Story understanding as problem-solving. Poetics, 1980, 9, 223-250.

Bower, G. H. Experiments on story understanding and recall. Quarterly Journal of Experimental Psychology, 1976, 28, 511-534.

Flammer, A. Toward a theory of question-asking. Research Bulletin, Nr. 22, University of Fribourg, Psychologisches Institut, Fribourg, CH. 1980.

Lichtenstein, E. H. & Brewer, W. F. Memory for goal-directed events. Cognitive Psychology, 1980, 12, 412-445.

Rumelhart, D. E. Notes on a schema for stories. In: D. Bobrow and A. Collins (Eds.), Representation and understanding. New York: Academic Press, 1975, Pp. 237-272.

Schank, R. C. & Abelson, R. P. Scripts, plans, goals, and understanding. Hillsdale, N.J.: Erlbaum. 1977.

Thorndyke, P. W. Cognitive structures in comprehension and memory of narrative discourse. Cognitive Psychology, 1977, 9, 77-110

van Dijk, T. Some aspects of text grammars. The Hague: Mouton. 1972.

Wilensky, R. Understanding goal-based stories. Ph.D. Dissertation, Research Report #140, Computer Science Dept., Yale University, 1978.

DISCOURSE PROCESSING
A. Flammer and W. Kintsch (eds.)
© North-Holland Publishing Company, 1982

WHAT MAKES A GOOD STORY?
Towards the production of conversational narratives[+]

Uta M. Quasthoff and Kurt Nikolaus

Freie Universität Berlin
Fachbereich Germanistik
Habelschwerdter Allee 45
1000 Berlin 33

This paper presents linguistic criteria for the
evaluation of conversational narratives. These
criteria are derived from a theory of narrative
texts which is based on a descriptive mapping of
the process of planning and producing a non-fic-
tious story in conversation. The theory includes
not only aspects of discourse structure, but also
situational and functional variables. The empirical basis of the study is a large tape-recorded
corpus of everyday stories in natural conversation (in German).

1. PRODUCTION OF CONVERSATIONAL NARRATIVES

Though well in line with the tradition derived from Bartlett (and others),
our own approach to text processing differs from mainstream cognitive science in three major respects:

a) Since discourse production is logically prior to discourse comprehension, we deal with the former aspect of processing rather than the
   latter.
b) Since written texts rely on basic forms encountered in everyday communication, we focus on oral discourse. (Moreover, written language
   is subject to a higher degree of normative rigidity, whereas everyday
   speech is much more variable and flexible.)
c) Since laboratory experiments do not provide an easy basis for genera-
   lizing to "normal" life, we try to investigate discourse production in
   natural settings.

1.1. The notion of "conversational narrative"

As linguists, we focus on the sometimes subtle structural differences between different kinds of texts. So we tend to limit our subject to rather
specific discourse units: i.e., we shall deal only with what we have called
"conversational narratives".

[+]This research was supported by a grant of the Volkswagen-Stiftung for our
research project "Kognitive und sprachliche Entwicklung am Beispiel des
Erzählens in natürlichen Interaktionssituationen". The criteria were developed to enable the ranking of children's narratives.

A conversational narrative is an orally realized discourse unit, which
emerges spontaneaously in conversation. It is a communicative way of forming experience and coping with it. It is constrained by the following semantic and formal conditions:

Semantic conditions:

- The referent of the narrative discourse is some fragment of reality in the
  past, in our culture, a sequence of actions and/or events. This referent
  is called "episode".
- The episode is uniquely identifiable by a certain point in time and a
  certain place. It is not a habitual happening or behavior.
- The episode is reportable (Labov and Waletzky 1967 and Labov 1972). The
  reportability of an episode is the result of an at least minimal unusualness relative to the expectations of the participant in the episode and/
  or expectations that are based on general norms or frames.
- The narrator is identical with one of the participants ("characters") in
  the episode (agent, patient, observer...).

Formal conditions:

Compared to other forms of representing past experience (e.g., the report)
the conversational narrative is a vivid replaying (Goffman, 1974) rather
than a matter-of-fact presentation of the episode. As a consequence of this
form of representation, the following linguistic means are typical of conversational narratives:

- Evaluative and expressive linguistic forms
- Direct speech, including imitation of the characters' voices (accent,
  pitch, intonation + speech rhythm)
- A high degree of detail in presenting the story, "atomization" of the continuum of actions and events (at least in some parts of the narrative)
- The use of historical present (at least in the atomized part of the
  narrative).

Please note that the term "episode" - in contrast to the term "narrative" -
is used to refer to a non-linguistic, non-mental, non-fictitious, real-
world entity; whereas narratives consist of utterances, episodes are by definition made up of states, events, and actions. (Following v. Wright
(1963), we take an event to be the transition from one state of affairs to
another and an action to be the intentional bringing about or preventing of
an event.)

1.2. Production schema

Since 1974, we have been collecting a large corpus of (German) conversational narratives as defined above. Setting out from purely observational data
such as these, we tried to develop a descriptive model of how conversational narratives are produced by a narrator on a particular occasion (see
Figure 1). Our production schema rests on the following assumptions:

a) Discourse production is a cognitive process that consists in the formation and realization of cognitive plans. We use the concept of "plan" as
   proposed by Miller, Galanter & Pribram (1960), without presupposing any
   conscious intentions.

Figure 1: PRODUCTION SCHEMA FOR CONVERSATIONAL NARRATIVES

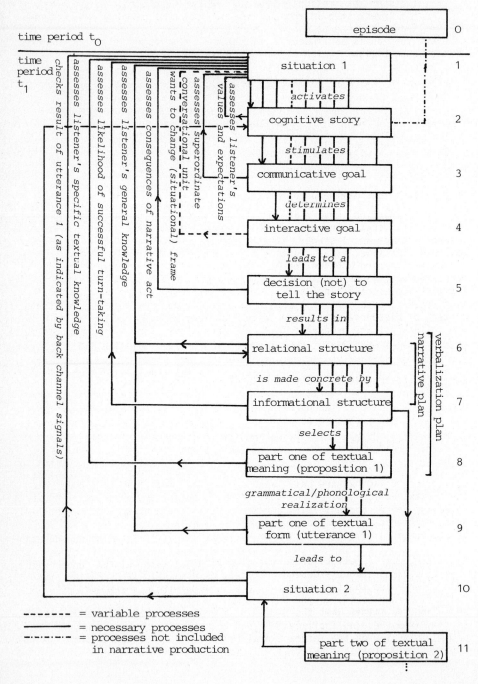

b) This planning process can be described as a series of decisions on several levels of information processing that are hierarchically ordered,
   such that every step in this process is both controlled by the higher-
   level steps and exerts control over the lower-level ones.
c) Every subplan is continuously monitored so as to conform to the pragmatic context within which the narrative is being told. This context includes both the social situation (assumptions about listener's knowledge, status, personality etc.) and the aims and intentions of the
   speaker.

Figure 1 provides a crude visualization of the production of narratives,
steps being denoted by rectangals and processes by arrows. The sequence of
steps and processes is logical rather than psychological or temporal. The
overall coherence of the production process is provided by means of feedback loops (some of which have been omitted for the sake of simplicity).

Some explanations may help in reading the diagram:

The term "situation" covers all the pragmatic aspects of language use (social context, spatio-temporal surroundings, personal and social relations
between speaker and listener, their mutual knowledge, and the like). You
may read this label as a kind of dummy symbol for any kind of information
that may be needed for the reconstruction or interpretation of a particular
narrative act. (Some situational aspects are specified as names of the
feedback loops connecting "situation" with the other steps of the production schema.) Each and every aspect of narrative production (or, for that
matter, of discourse production in general) depends on, is influenced by,
and influences many pragmatic factors. Since these effects, unfortunately,
are not easily controlled in experiments on text processing, they are
usually neglected.

Secondly, by "cognitive story" we wish to refer to whatever mental representation of the real-world episode is retrieved (or reconstructed) from
memory at the time of the narration. This reflects the distinction between
what the narrator recalls about what happened and what really happened; it
also reflects the distinction between what the narrator recalls and what
he/she actually tells.

As far as the distinction between communicative and interactive function/
goal is concerned, we are well aware of the fact that this terminology is
a bit awkward; for lack of anything better, we will use these terms in the
following sense: Communicative functions rely on the content of a narrative,
whereas interactive functions rely on its linguistic form, i.e., the type
of discourse unit itself (for example, "report" vs. "narrative").

Obviously, some functions of conversational narratives - like argumentation
or self-aggrandizement - depend primarily on what is told in the particular
story. These are the functions that are subsumed under the heading of "communicative functions". On the other hand, the very act of conversational
narration (no matter what the subject is) may serve the function of creating an atmosphere of intimacy and thus help the narrator to express and
promote his view of the interactional relation, namely "We're engaged in an
informal context with a relatively close personal relationship". Therefore,

we call this latter function of a conversational narrative and the corresponding intention of the narrator "interactive".

The intended function(s), the cognitive story, and their appropriateness
must be constantly checked against one another and the situation; this finally results in a decision to tell a particular story (or to refrain from
doing so). Once this decision has been achieved, every bit of information
about the episode that is accessible in the memory store is retrieved (and
missing links are reconstructed). This recall is guided by narrative schemata that are probably culture-specific. The process of recalling finally
results in an informational structure which is embedded in a relational net,
the details of which cannot be given here.

This complex semantic structure then is serialized: i.e., a tiny fragment
at a time is selected, verbalized, and finally uttered. Of course, even the
planning of the linguistic form of the utterance(s) is dependent on all the
preceding steps in the production schema. With the realization of the first
utterance and listener reactions, a new situation is created so that the
planning cycle starts all over again.

In our reconstruction of conversational narration, we have emphasized the
integration of both structural and functional aspects of linguistic behavior. However, our production schema does not yet include explicit criteria
for evaluating narratives. From our descriptive modeling of the production
process, we can derive such criteria on a theoretical basis and in a non-
normative way. Our basic hypothesis is that structures and functions have
to correspond, and be appropriate with regard to the situation.

2. CRITERIA FOR EVALUATING CONVERSATIONAL NARRATIVES

2.1. Pragmatic criteria

The basic criteria for "good" narratives can be explained in terms of those
steps in our production schema that precede the narrator's decision to tell
a particular story. These criteria specify what story (if any) is going to
be told, in contrast to how it's going to be told. Essentially, the narrator's task in this stage of the production process is to coordinate the
cognitive story he has in mind, the function(s) he intends to be fulfilled
by the narrative, and the definition of the situation held by himself and
the listener (steps 1-4 of Figure 1).

2.1.1. Appropriateness of the conversational narrative to the social
       situation

Of course, one of the basic criteria for good conversational narratives has
to be situational appropriateness:

1. Production of conversational narratives requires that both speaker and
   listener be at ease (in a leisurely mood), must know something about
   each other, and are not busy otherwise.

Examples of violations:

Trying to tell a conversational narrative to a stranger who is chasing a
bus violates all three aspects of criterion 1; or take a witness in court
who tells a long conversational narrative evaluating his observations and
expressing his personal opinions instead of giving a genuine short report.

This last violation shows that a relaxed mood is particularly important: It
is this criterion that makes conversational narratives inadequate in insti-
tutionalized contexts. There are a few exceptions to this rule, however.
Conversational narratives will be encouraged if (and only if) a personal relationship has been or is being established between the representative of
an institution and a client. This is the case in therapeutic sessions.

If the situation does not fulfill the above-mentioned requirements, it does
not favor the production of conversational narratives. To a certain degree,
however, story telling may be used as a device for redefining and changing
the situation; we habe labeled this as one of the interactive functions of
conversational narratives.

2.1.2. Suitability of the cognitive story for the intended function(s)

The cognitive story selected for narration must be compatible with the func-
tion(s) intended by the narrator. Among the communicative functions, we differentiate between the following kinds:

a) functions that are primarily speaker oriented (such as psychological or
   communicative unburdening and self-aggrandizement)
b) functions that are primarily hearer oriented (such as amusement/enter-
   tainment and giving information)
c) functions that are primarily context oriented (such as supporting an argument or providing an explanation).

Normally, these functions do not occur in isolation, but in combination
(with one of them clearly dominating in most cases). For most of the functions, the restrictions on the kind of episode to be related (hence the
cognitive story that represents the episode) are abvious:

2. a) In the case of self-aggrandizement, the episode must contain elements
      which would enhance the (positive) image of the narrator/agent.
   b) In the case of entertainment, the episode must be at least mildly
      amusing with regard to the expectations of the addressee; this im-
      plies that it is not too shocking, tragic, etc.
   c) When the function of the narrative is to give information, it must
      at least add details to the listeners' previous knowledge.
   d) When supporting an argument or providing an explanation, the point of
      the episode must lend plausibility to the claim being supported or
      explain the behavior at stake.

Examples of violations are obvious, though rare.

As far as unburdening is concerned, this function is somewhat different
from the rest: Its fulfillment is guaranteed by the act of story-telling
itself, no matter what the listener's reactions may be. Since narratives
with that function are purely subjectively motivated, they allow for any

kind of episode that affected the emotional well-being of the narrator. Personal experiences that are accompanied by strong emotions always tend to result in conversational narratives with an unburdening function; if the corresponding emotions are very strong, they may even overcome social and contextual constraints and result in narratives that seem out of place, thus violating criterion 1, situational appropriateness.

2.1.3. Reportability of the episode

Apart from the communicative functions, any episode that is to be related must satisfy certain general conditions:

3. a) The episode must be reportable and interesting (i.e., something unexpected must have happened). Furthermore, it must not violate any cultural taboos.
   b) In addition, the cognitive story as a representation of the episode must be complete (i.e., it can be molded into a narrative structure to be discussed below).

Example of a violation:

A story that is trivial according to the expectations of the listener and/ or of which essential parts have been forgotten.

Please note that a story is not interesting by itself, but becomes so only with respect to a particular addressee in a particular context (see criterion 1). This context may serve as a recall cue for retrieving from long-term memory the episodes that are momentarily relevant.

2.1.4. Compatibility between functions and situations

Certain communicative functions are restricted to certain kinds of conversational contexts:

4. a) Narratives with the context-oriented functions of explanation or argumentation are embedded in larger discourse segments (e.g., discussions); for that reason, any narrative designed to fulfill these functions must be thematically relevant to the topic that is being discussed.
   b) Amusement/entertainment is relatively independent of the surrounding discourse, but it does require a sociable situation.
   c) Psychological and communicative unburdening require special circumstances, namely a close personal relationship between narrator and listener, as has already been noted.
   d) Self-aggrandizement, by contrast, is not subject to any such restrictions; it is an aspect encountered in almost any conversational narrative where the narrator is a protagonist in the episode.

Examples of violations:

A narrative about a holiday in Switzerland as part of a discussion about the progress of linguistics in America; or telling funny stories at a burial.

In the case of the context-oriented functions, some of the characters or actions contained in the story must belong to an already established "universe of discourse" (i.e., they must have already been mentioned). The speaker-oriented and the hearer-oriented functions, however, allow for a shift in topic much more than the context-oriented functions do.

For a narrative to be "good" or "bad", it is a necessary (but not sufficient) condition that it must not violate any of these pragmatic requirements, otherwise it is less likely to fulfill the intended function(s). So communicative efficiency is a valuable criterion for judging how "good" a narrative is. The means, however, are at least as important as the ends; so now we shall turn to the details of the verbalization process in which the particular content of the story has to be communicated, its structure marked and its function indicated in a way that is comprehensible to the addressee.

2.2. Interaction between pragmatic and structural factors

This section deals with the interrelationship between steps 1 to 4 of the production schema - subsumed under the heading of "pragmatic factors" - and steps 6 to 9, called "structural factors". Please note that our concept of structure is a dynamic one, which includes the semantic structure of the narrative as well as the linguistic surface. Agreement between the pragmatic factors and the different structural aspects is considered a criterion for a good conversational narrative.

2.2.1. Correspondence between pragmatic factors and relational structure

The relational structure, i.e., the relationally ordered narrative schema, classifies narratives into three semantic types, distinguished according to three types of unusualness (cf. Quasthoff 1980) and the definition of conversational narrative given above:

a) agent reacts to unexpected actions/events;
b) observer witnesses unusual actions/events;
c) agent performs actions unusual according to general norms.

The relational structure includes semantically and pragmatically oriented relations; the realization of the pragmatic relations is optional and depends, for instance, on the speaker's assumptions about the listener's knowledge, expectations, etc. - in short, on the narrator's interpretation of part of the situation. So we can describe the first pragmatic-structural correspondence as follows:

5. The relational structure includes listener orienting parts, if and only if listener lacks necessary information about setting and background of the episode.

Examples of violations:

Narrator fails to give information about time, place, characters, and "background" of the episode, although listener's episodic memory or inferential capacity do not activate this information.

The opposite case, in which the given information is already available to the listener, is also a violation.

Accordingly, correlations can be assumed between the other pragmatic steps of the production schema and the relational structure. This structure contains a central element - the relation PLAN DISRUPTION. This relation refers to actions and/or events which are unexpected with regard to the "plan" of the narrator/observer/"generalized other", (depending on the semantic type of the narrative). Thus, the cognitive story corresponds to the relational structure in two ways:

6. The cognitive story must involve a PLAN DISRUPTION.

Example of a violation:

The description of a chain of actions which follows the "normal course of events" would be a violation of this correspondence rule ("Yesterday I got up, brushed my teeth, had breakfast, left for work..." is not a good story).

7. The narrator must be involved in the cognitive story in one of the three ways which distinguish semantic narrative types, and which are reflected in the relational structure.

Example of a violation:

The telling of a movie would not be a conversational narrative in the defined sense.

The correspondence between the communicative goal and the relational structure connects the specific communicative function of a narrative with the semantic type of the narrative and the pragmatically oriented parts of the relational structure:

8. The semantic type of the narrative and its communicative function must be compatible.

Example of a violation:

The communicative function of self-aggrandizement normally cannot be performed in a narrative of the observer type in which the narrator's role is restricted to mere observation.

9. Orienting and evaluative parts of the relational structure have to select or qualifiy the given information according to the communicative function.

Example of a violation:

A narrative which is intended to serve as evidence for a certain fact should not give information that could be judged as counterevidence for this particular fact. If such information is given, it has to be qualified in a way that prevents such an interpretation (e.g., as an exception).

The interactive goal governs the specific discourse pattern in which a particular fragment of reality is verbalized. Since narratives and reports

have different relational structures, it is the combination of situation
and interactive goal that triggers the narrative-specific relational
structure as a whole:

10. If the definition of the situation does not favor or even excludes the
    verbal activity of telling a narrative, the relational structure of a
    narrative can still be evoked if the speaker intends (and is able) to
    change the definition of the situation.

Example of a violation:

In a bureaucratic encounter, someone engages in telling conversational narratives instead of giving a report, with no intention of changing the formal relationship with his interlocutor to a more personal one.

For lack of space, we will not present examples from our corpus.

2.2.2. Correspondence between pragmatic factors and informational structure

The informational structure of a narrative is the set of propositions
which the text (explicitly) contains or (implicitly) entails. This set of
propositions is ordered by the relational structure. The informational
structure differs from the cognitive story in two important respects:

a) The cognitive story is restricted by mode and capacity of cognitive information processing. The informational structure, on the other hand,
   is dependent on the narrator's assumptions about the situation and the
   (communicative and interactive) functions of the narrative. So the information in the cognitive story will normally be selected (or even altered) to form the informational structure.
b) The order in which information is stored and activated is primarily a
   psychological one for the cognitive story, about which we know relatively little. The order of components of the informational structure is
   primarily a linguistic one, and can be specified in terms of the dis-
   course-specific relational structure.

Please note that both sets of information are not conceived of as being in
a linear order. The informational structure is ordered relationally without the implication of a fixed sequence. Consequently, the elements of the
informational structure have to be serialized for verbalization in later
phases of the planning process.

The hierarchical order of the informational structure can be conceptualized in terms of different layers of information which represent different
degrees of detail. The underlying chain of actions and/or events can be
chopped up in large or small units ("John sold his car" vs. "John put an
ad in the paper, talked to several potential buyers on the phone, made
arrangements for meeting with Mr. X, Y and Z..."). An inappropriate degree
of detail in a narrative results either in incomprehensibility or in an
absolutely boring narrative. A more important violation is presented by
those narratives which do not vary the degree of detail in accordance with
the relational structure. So we can formulate the following pragmatic-
structural correspondence as a maxim for a good narrative:

11. Don't be more or less detailed than is required by listener's knowledge
    and inferential capacity, your communicative and interactive goals and
    the relational structure of the narrative.

Examples of violations:

Narratives which are too detailed will usually not be finished because of
interventions of the listener.

Narratives in which the setting contains details that are not relevent to
the main parts of the story are bad narratives. They are even worse when
the narrator proceeds to give very little information in the complication
section.

2.2.3. Correspondence between cognitive planning and verbalization

It is only in this "last" part of the production schema (steps 8 and 9)
that the actual wording and the sequential order of the narrative is established. As stated above, our structural description of discourse, which
is semantically based, has to include serialization rules (cf. Bartsch &
Vennemann 1972). Since application of these rules is highly dependent on
the conversational context, they have to be conceptualized as variable
rules (Labov 1969; Cedergren & Sankoff 1974). One of the principles underlying this serialization process, for example, is the principle "sequence
of utterances maps sequence of events", which was so important to Labov &
Waletzky (1967). In our version, this categorical principle becomes a variable rule:

> "Sequence of utterance should map sequence of events,
> unless embedding in the conversational context, liste-
> ner interventions, building up the point of the story
> etc. advise otherwise."

This transformation from categorical principles into variable rules is considered to be a transformation from normative to descriptive analysis of
narratives.

In order to generate a narrative text from the relational and informational
structure, the narrator not only has to serialize information. He also has
to structure the linguistic surface of his narrative (and mark this structure as well). For the speaker himself, the serialized order of the utterances is derived from the underlying semantic structures and thus well
ordered. But the listener has to reconstruct these underlying semantic
structures on the basis of the surface of the incoming text, so this surface has to give indications as to the underlying semantic structures.
These indications are normally given in the form of discourse markers
(Wald 1978) or contextualization cues (Gumperz 1978).

Thus a criterion for a good narrative is not only:

12. Serialize your utterance according to the variable serializing rules;

but also:

13. Be sure to mark your narrative structure with relevant discourse mar-
    kers and contextualization cues.

Examples of violations:

Relating several episodes within a single narrative without clearly delimi-
ting them; or relating out-of-the-ordinary events as if they were ordinary
ones, without commenting on their unusualness.

3. PRINCIPLES FOR EVALUATING NARRATIVES

We have shown how a detailed, non-normative description of the production
of narrative discourse can be transformed into the formulation of criteria
for good narratives. For the practical evaluation of everyday conversational narratives, however, we still need to rank these criteria along the
dimension "more important - less important".

The significance of the criteria relates to our production schema in a very
simple way: The lower the violation in the production schema, the less severe it is (and the easier to repair in conversation). To make this ranking plausible, here are just a few examples: The wrong sequence of two
utterances, with respect to the serialization rules, does not turn an
otherwise good narrative into a bad one. This minor error is easily re-
paired locally. But if the knowledge of the listener is underestimated by
the narrator, the whole narration can fail. Possible repair is at least
very complicated.

Two sources of narrative evaluation provided the empirical basis for the
ranking of our criteria:

a) Ratings of 10 conversational narratives by independent naive raters.
   Agreement among raters was high (coefficient of consistency $r_{tt} = .94$),
   thus confirming our own intuitive judgment.
b) Conversational analysis of listeners' activities during and after conversational narration. These listener activities (like laughing, interruptions, questions, evaluations, etc., cf. Quasthoff 1981) always explicitly or implicitly judge the narrative.

What remains to be done is to provide manageable operationalizations for
the criteria proposed above. This work is still in progress, and would require an additional paper.

REFERENCES :

Bartsch, R. & Vennemann, T. Semantic structures. A study in the relation between semantics and syntax. Frankfurt a.M.: Athenäum, 1972.

Cedergren, H. & Sankoff, D. Variable rules. Performance as a statistical reflection of competence. Language, 1974, 50, 333-355.

Goffman, E. Frame analysis. An essay on the organization of experience. New York: Harper & Row, 1974.

Gumperz, J. Sprache, soziales Wissen und interpersonale Beziehungen. In: U. Quasthoff (Ed.), Sprachstruktur - Sozialstruktur. Kronberg/Ts.: Scriptor, 1978.

Labov, W. Contraction, deletion and inherent variability of the English copula. Language, 1969, 45, 715-762.

Labov, W. The transformation of experience in narrative syntax. In: W. Labov, Language in the inner city. Studies in the Black English Vernacular. Philadelphia: Univ. of Pennsylvania Press, 1972.

Labov, W. & Waletzky, J. Narrative analysis: Oral versions of personal experience. In: H. Helm (Ed.), Essays on the verbal and visual arts. Seattle/London, 1967.

Lienert, G. Testaufbau und Testanalyse. Weinheim: Beltz Verlag, 1961.

Miller, G., Galanter, E. & Pribram, K. Plans and the structure of behavior. New York: Holt, Rinehart & Winston, 1960.

Quasthoff, U. Erzählen in Gesprächen. Linguisitsche Untersuchungen zu Strukturen und Funktionen am Beispiel einer Kommunikationsform des Alltags. Tübingen: Gunter Narr Verlag, 1980.

Quasthoff, U. Zuhöreraktivitäten beim konversationellen Erzählen. In: Jahrbuch 1980 des Instituts für deutsche Sprache. Düsseldorf: Schwann, 1981.

Wald, B. Zur Einheitlichkeit und Einleitung von Diskurseinheiten. In: U. Quasthoff (Ed.), Sprachstruktur - Sozialstruktur. Kronberg/Ts.: Scriptor, 1978.

v. Wright, G.H. Norm and action.A logical enquiry. London: Routledge & Kegan Paul, 1963.

DISCOURSE PROCESSING
A. Flammer and W. Kintsch (eds.)
© *North-Holland Publishing Company, 1982*

TEXT DIVISIONS AND STORY GRAMMARS

Hans Christoph Micko

Institute of Psychology
University of Technology
Braunschweig, F.R. Germany

Text divisions are investigated as tests for
the predictive value of story grammars.

PROSPECTS AND PROBLEMS OF THE TEXT DIVISION PARADIGM.

When subjects divide a text into chapters, sections, subsections, sub-subsections etc., they impose a hierarchical tree structure on the text or rather
derive it from the text. Different subjects may produce different trees but
some uniformity can be expected due to the inherent structure of the text.
Whether uniform or different, text divisions are a most direct source of information about how subjects organize a text. Moreover the information is
detailed and obtainable at low cost. Apparently subjects consider text
division to be an interesting and easy task although sometimes it may turn
out to be quite difficult.

Two text division paradigms can be envisaged: (1) Subjects may be asked to
make a disposition of the text from memory in the form of a table of contents. That procedure is similar to the summarizing paradigm, putting weight,
however, more on memory of structure than of content. (2) Subjects may be
asked to partition a text while it is presented, either with or without time
pressure and possibly followed by the request to find titles for the sections
and subsections. The formulation of section-headings is a means of making
subjects aware of the fact that their text division is non-optimal and
should be corrected .

Text division may be of interest in itself. Most of its attractiveness,
however, derives from the possibility of using that paradigm as a means of
studying text memory structure. It is not more than an assumption, of course,
that text divisions are able to represent text memory structures. It is a
tempting assumption, however, since text memory structures are frequently
conceived as hierarchical tree structures, such as text divisions are by
nature. We may combine that assumption with another familiar assumption,
known as the level of hierarchy rule of recall (Kintsch, 1974; van Dijk, 1975;
Thorndyke, 1977). That would make it possible to test the level of hierarchy
rule independently of the choice of some general story grammar from which to
determine the hierarchy level of propositions. Reformulated in terms of
text divisions, the rule predicts that propositions from less frequently
subdivided sections are better recalled than propositions from sections
which are more often partitioned and repartitioned. Thus the hierarchy level
of a proposition is determined from the text division data of individual
subjects, not from one or another general, and fallible, story grammar.

It may turn out, of course, that text division trees differ fundamentally
from story grammar trees. Even in that case an inspection of the difference
may help to shed light on the way memory works.

In this paper, instead of predicting memory structures directly from text
division trees, we compare the latter with tree structures derived from
story grammars. Presumably it was never claimed that story grammars predict
text divisions. However, since both are supposed to predict story memory
structures, (Black, 1978) they should correlate as well; and obviously a
story grammar that is able to predict text division data would be preferred
to a grammar that does not - if not from a linguist's point of view then at
least from that of a psychologist.

When predicting text division trees from story grammar trees we assume the
following for any hierarchy level of the text division tree: Two successive
propositions are the more likely to fall into different (identical) sections
the higher up (further down) in the story grammar tree the lines from the
respective terminal nodes merge. In other words, we assume that subjects mark
a boundary between superordinate sections of a story in the space between
successive propositions whose lines from the terminal nodes merge high up
in the story grammar tree. An intersection between subordinate sections is
placed between propositions the lines of which merge somewhat further down
in the grammar tree, and no intersection is placed between propositions
which are already merged on the lowermost level.

Three specifications or supplements to the above general assumption are
required in order to predict text division trees from story grammar trees
precisely:

(1) We cannot expect text division trees to match story grammar trees perfectly. Many or most terminal nodes of story grammar trees represent propositions which are not explicitly stated in the story because they are
of minor importance or because they can be inferred. Moreover, some or many
hierarchy levels may be redundant in the sense that they represent rewrite
rules which do not impose a finer partition on the set of explicit propositions by themselves. Such rewrite rules only serve as a link for further
rewrite rules. Each successive inferior level of a story division tree, on the
other hand, represents a finer partition of the set of explicit propositions.
Therefore, we prefer to compare reduced story grammar trees with story
division trees. In a reduced story grammar tree all terminal nodes are
omitted which do not represent explicit propositions of the story. Similarly,
all nonterminal nodes are omitted which do not result in a finer partition of
the explicit story on the immediately subordinate level. Figure 1 gives an
example.

(2) Story grammars suffer from a certain ambiguity since they define only a
partial ordering of the nodes within a tree. We cannot compare the hierarchy
levels of propositions or subordinate text units across superordinate units,
i.e.,we do not know whether subordinate units within one part of the story
merge into superordinate units higher up or further down in the hierarchy
than units in another part of the story. (Compare,e.g.,the set of propositions
(1,2) with the set (3,4,5) in Figure 1a. The reduced trees of Figures 1b,
2a and 2b are equivalent representations of van Dijk's story grammar.)

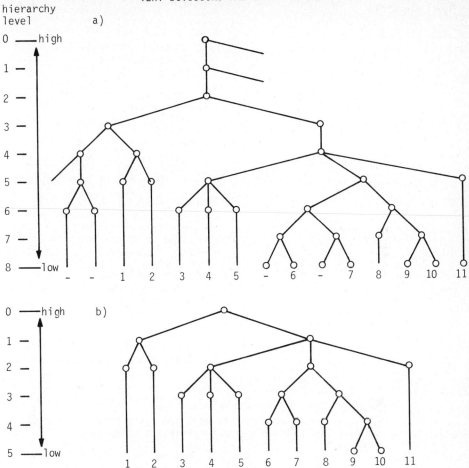

Figure 1
Complete (a) and reduced (b) story grammar tree
representing the analysis of the dog-story according to van Dijk's story grammar. (Hyphens denote
implicit and numbers explicit propositions of the
story. Lines without terminal nodes represent
optional story elements, missing in the dog-story.)

If the number of hierarchy levels in different branches of a story grammar
tree is the same, we expect only minor misrepresentations of the grammar
when simply defining nodes of equal rank within their branches to be of
equal rank in the tree (see e.g., the nodes which represent the roots of
subtrees ((-,6), (-,7)) and ((8), (9,10)) in Figure 1a). Usually, however,
story grammars produce trees with more hierarchy levels for some parts of
the story than for others. In Figure 1a e.g., more levels are required for
the representation of an episode than for that of a setting (episode:
((3,4,5),(((-,6),(-,7)),((8),(9,10))),11) vs. setting (1,2)). In that case
the ambiguity cannot be overcome by a simple definition.

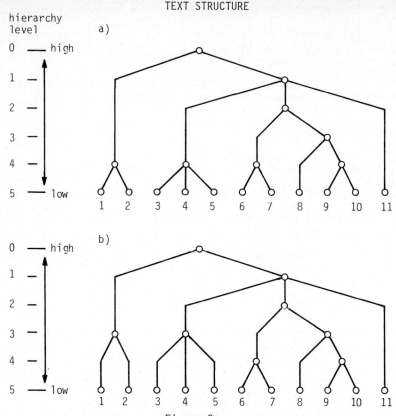

Figure 2
Reduced trees equivalent to that of Figure 1b
as determined by the (a) extreme and (b) compromise rule for predicting text divisions.

For predicting recall probabilities the representation of Figure 1a is
appropriate because, according to the level of hierarchy rule, the hierarchy
level of a proposition is defined as the number of rewrite rules necessary
to identify the function of a proposition in the story. That number is equal
to the hierarchy level of the respective terminal node. The rank order of
these hierarchy levels, after omitting redundant nodes, is preserved in the
reduced tree of Figure 1b.

For the prediction of text division data, the equivalent representation of
Figure 2a is likely to give a better fit than that of Figure 1b. That is
true at least in connection with our experimental procedure of asking subjects to separate subordinate sections of a text by a vertical line and
superordinate sections by two or more lines. Figure 2a differs from that of
Figure 1b in the hierarchy level on which lines merge. This level is chosen
as near to the terminal nodes as possible in Figure 2a and as near possible
to the root of the tree in Figure 1b. The former choice implies the prediction that subjects mark intersections by as few lines as possible, the latter
choice predicts intersections to be marked by as many lines as possible. In
the absence of counterevidence it appears more realistic to assume that

subjects put two successive propositions into one subordinate or at least superordinate section rather than into different ones.

In large story grammar trees, the number of hierarchy levels may vary considerably from one branch to another. In that case we may wish to have a rule that compromises between the extreme rules of letting lines merge as near to the tree root and as near to the terminal nodes as possible. That rule can be stated as follows:

Let $0,1,2,\ldots,i,\ldots,n_k$ denote the rank order, from top to bottom, of the nodes linking the root of a reduced tree with its k-th terminal node. Consider the subtree setting out from some node I of rank i and let $0,1,2,\ldots,n_1$ denote the rank order of the nodes linking node I with the 1-th terminal node within the subtree considered. Obviously $n_1<n_k$ if $i>0$ for any terminal node within the subtree. We now assign to node I the new rank i', which is the nearest integer to the term $(\max(n_k)\cdot i)/(\max(n_1)+i)$. This procedure spaces the nodes linking I an 1-th terminal node in roughly equal intervals over the hierarchy levels between ranks i and $\max(n_k)$. Figure 2b results if the compromise rule is applied to the reduced tree of Figure 1b: For all terminal nodes we obtain $i_{n_k}=(5\cdot n_k)/(o+n_k)=5$, for node $(9,10)$ we obtain $i'(9,10)=(5\cdot4)/(1+4)=4$, and so forth, $i'(6,7)=(5\cdot3)/(1+3)+0,25=4$, $i'(1,2)=(5\cdot1)/(1+1)+0,5=3$, $i'(3,4,5)=(5\cdot2/(1+2)-0.33=3$, $i'(8,9,10)=(5\cdot3)/(2+3)=3$, $i'(6,7,\ldots,10)=(5\cdot2)/(3+2)=2$, $i'(3,4,\ldots,11)=(5\cdot1)/(4+1)=1$, $i'(1,2,\ldots,11)=(5\cdot0)/(5+0)=0$.

The difference between the rules from which the trees of Figure 1b, 2a and 2b have been determined can be recognized most easily by comparing the hierarchy levels of the respective nodes $(1,2)$.

Perhaps more appropriate methods for abolishing the ambiguity of story grammars can be found if the content of rewrite rules is taken into account as well. In that case, however, different rules have to be defined for different story grammars. Here, we prefer the simplicity of general rules to the complications associated with procedures that may not yield more realistic predictions.

(3) Story grammar trees differ from text division trees fundamentally by the fact that the latter necessarily preserve the sequence of propositions within a text, while the former do not. Some story grammars consider semantic relations between constituents of a rewrite rule, e.g., event A enables event B, or action C results in event D. They cannot predict, however, the sequence in which these events and actions are reported in a story, because almost any content can be presented in various alternative sequences of propositions, more than one of which may be optimal or nearly optimal for understanding. As a consequence we may encounter story grammar trees, the terminal nodes of which are arranged in an order different from that of the respective propositions within the story. Therefore an additional rule for predicting story division trees from story grammar trees is required, a rule that handles inverted proposition sequences.

Apparent discrepancies between the proposition sequences in the story and story grammar tree need not be real since story grammar trees are invariant under changes of the sequence of lines which set out from one node. Therefore an admissible rearrangement of those lines may already result in a tree which represents the story grammar and preserves the proposition sequence of the story as well. Consider, e.g., the story grammar tree (a) in Figure 3. Its terminal nodes represent either propositions or larger units. In the

latter case the terminal nodes represent the roots of subtrees which are
not depicted. Let the sequence of letters A,B,C,D denote the temporal
sequence of the four propositions or units of the story. The story grammar
tree (a) predicts the same text division whether its terminal nodes are
labelled A,B,C,D or A,B,D,C, since the lines ending at C and D can be ex-
changed without altering the grammar tree. Moreover, the trees (b), (c) and
(d) of Figure 3 are equivalent to (a) since they also differ from (a) only
in the sequential arrangement of lines setting out from one node. Any story
grammar that predicts one of these trees predicts the others as well, each
in combination with a particular sequence of the story units: The equivalent
tree (b) preserves the order A,B,C,D, if the terminal nodes of (a) are
labelled A,D,B,C or A,D,C,B in succession. Similarly tree (c) is order
preserving if tree (a) is labelled D,A,B,C or D,A,C,B and (d) if (a) is
labelled D,C,A,B or D,C,B,A.

No order preserving equivalent tree can be found by admissible rearrange-
ments if a story grammar assigns to some superordinate unit two subunits,
which are separated in the story by another subunit which is assigned to
a different superordinate unit. Consider e.g.,the story grammar tree (a)
of Figure 3 with terminal nodes labelled B,C,A,D from left to right. From
that tree the units A and D would be predicted to fall into a common section
of a text division, at least more likely so than any other pair of units. In
the narration sequence, however, units A and D are separated by the units B
and C which the grammar predicts to fall rather into different sections.

The simplest and most natural rule for predicting text divisions from such
grammar trees states that subjects do not mark any intersection between story
units the order of which is inverted in the grammar tree. In other words, if
two units belong together according to the story grammar, they are assumed
to be placed into the same section, together with everything that may be
narrated in between. Of course, each of the units may be subdivided if
appropriate.

An alternative, less radical rule demands some sophistication in its application since minor trial and error manipulations of the story grammar tree
have to be performed. The rule requires one or another node, superordinate
to the disarrayed series of subunits, to be ignored or to be merged with
the immediately subordinate dependent nodes,respectively. In this way one
obtains a larger set of lines setting out from the combined node. These
lines may then be rearranged and possibly yield the correct sequence. If
the procedure is successful, some intersections of lower order will be
predicted from the manipulated grammar tree while the former rule lumps all
propositions together into one section. The result is a compromise between
the structure represented by the story grammar tree and the undifferentiated
structure resulting from the more radical rule.

Consider again the story grammar tree (a) in Figure 3 with terminal nodes
labelled B,A,C,D or B,A,D,C. The correct sequence A,B,C,D cannot be obtained
with any of the equivalent trees. A merger of the root and the intermediate
nonterminal node of tree (a) results in tree (e). That tree is somewhat but
not very different from tree (a) and it permits the desired rearrangement.
The predicted story division is fairly similar to that predicted from tree
(a), only the section common to the units A, C, D is lost. This cannot be
avoided since in the story sequence unit B is located between units A and
C,D. If the nodes of tree (a) are labelled C,D,A,B or C,D,B,A, an analogous
manipulation of the equivalent tree (d) results in tree (f), which again

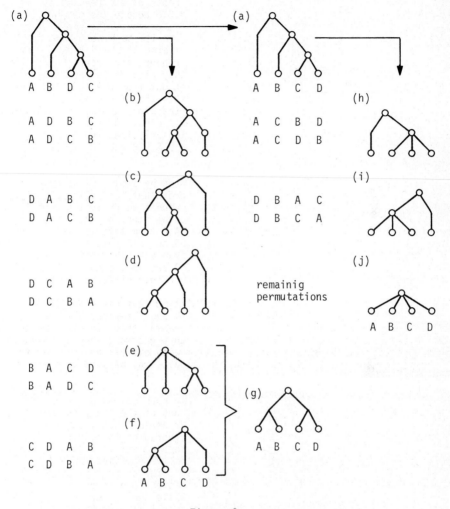

Figure 3
Modifications of story grammar tree (a) which
permit the rearrangement of inverted sequences
of story subunits. Equivalent trees (b,c,d) and
trees obtained by the node-merging rule (e,f),
lump-together rule (g) and both rules (h,i,j).

permits a rearrangement of the units to yield the correct sequence A,B,C,D.
According to the radical lumping rule tree (g) would be the predicted text
division tree in all four cases. It obviously differs more from the original
grammar trees (a) and (d) than the compromise trees (e) and (f) respectively.

If the terminal nodes of tree (a) are labelled A,C,B,D or A,C,D,B, a merger
of the intermediate and lowermost nonterminal nodes of tree (a) yields tree
(h) which permits the appropriate rearrangement. The same result is obtained,
however, by the radical rule as well, since inversions occur only in the
triad B,C,D which is lumped together by both rules. In the case of the
terminal nodes of tree (a) being labelled D,B,A,C or D,B,C,A an analogous
manipulation transforms tree (c) or (d) into tree (i) which allows the
appropriate rearrangement of lines.

The remaining eight permutations of the sequence A,B,C,D which may be associated with tree (a) require all four units to be lumped together as in
tree (j) in order to enable a successful rearrangement. In all cases the
unit represented by the left terminal node of tree (a) is located in the
story between the two units represented by the two terminal nodes to the
right. Therefore no partition except that predicted from tree (j) makes
sense. Tree (j) is obtained with both rules, the straightforward lump to-
gether-rule as well as the compromise rule which has to be applied twice
before the order A,B,C,D can be obtained.

THE COMPARISON OF STORY GRAMMAR TREES WITH TEXT DIVISION TREES.

We restrict our present considerations to story grammars which are defined
by rewrite rules. They impose on suitable stories a hierarchical tree
structure the terminal nodes of which represent the stated or inferred
propositions of the story. Grammars of this kind have been proposed by
Rumelhart (1975, 1977), van Dijk (1975), Thorndyke (1977), Mandler and
Johnson (1977), and Stein and Glenn (1977). For the time being, we will ignore
story grammars of Kintsch (1974), Schank (1975), Black (1978), and Glowalla
(1981) because they require the specification of different or additional,
more complicated rules for the prediction of text division data.

The grammars investigated were applied to three stories taken from Black
(1978): "The Dog and his Shadow" (11 propositions), "The Little Boy" (19
propositions), and "The Old Farmer and his Donkey" (32 propositions).
Reduced story grammar trees were derived for the first two stories, from
the complete trees of Black (1978). For the farmer story they were
constructed by the author. Inverted proposition sequences occurred in the
grammar trees of the farmer story only. They were remedied by the choice of
an equivalent tree in case of the Mandler and Johnson grammar and by applying
the less radical rule described in the preceding section in all other cases.
Two trees were considered for each grammar, one in which lines merged as
closely to the root, and one in which they merged as closely to the terminal
nodes as possible. In the majority of cases the trees obtained with the
latter rule yielded a better fit and were chosen, therefore, to represent
the grammar. This choice does not affect the results. The compromise formula
was not applied since the trees constructed by the extreme rules differed
only moderately. The stories and story grammar trees are presented in Micko
(1982).

METHOD

Subjects. 40 students of the University of Technology, Brunswick, were
assigned at random to an "experienced" or "unexperienced" group.

Materials. The results of a pilot experiment gave rise to the suspicion that
propositions are likely to be assigned to the same section if they are
formulated as super- and subordinate clauses in one sentence. Such an assignment is less likely if the propositions are stated in separate main clauses.
Therefore the stories employed in the present study were reformulated so
that all propositions were represented by a main clause.

The revised versions of the stories were printed on a separate sheet of paper
each. Three spacings instead of one were left between successive clauses for
subjects to mark intersections. Sufficient space was provided for the formulation of headings. Two copies were made of every sheet, one for making
and one for correcting the division if necessary. All instructions were
given in writing, either on top of the working sheets or on separate sheets
placed in front of the working sheets. At the bottom of most pages, space
was reserved for noting the time of the page being turned over in order to
begin with the subsequent task. The sheets were made up into a booklet
together with additional sheets for writing and partitioning recall protocols.
The booklets for the experienced and unexperienced group differed to the
extent necessary to account for the different temporal arrangements of tasks.

Procedure. Students sitting in the reading room of the university library
were exposed to a written request for participation in the experiment.
Volunteers were assigned at random to the experimental conditions and given
the respective booklet. Subjects of the experienced group were asked in the
written instruction to memorize the first story, then to memorize the second
and then the third. After that, the stories had to be recalled and recounted
in the same sequence. In a third step subjects gained experience in text
division by partitioning their recall protocols one after another. They were
also instructed to find a heading for every super- and subordinate section of
their recall protocols. Finally, subjects were asked to find the most appropri
division of the original stories. These could be divided either into equivalent sections or into sections, subsections, sub-subsections, etc. Intersections were to be marked by one or more vertical lines, the number of lines
depending on whether more or less superordinate sections were to be separated.
In the instructions the following examples were given, each pair of points
representing a proposition:

(1) ^{1}.. .. .. ..$|^{2}$.. .;.$|^{3}$..$|^{4}$.. ..$|^{5}$.. .. ..$|^{6}$..
    $_{1}$ $_{2}$ $_{3}$

    1.1 1.2   2.1
                           2.1.1 2.1.2 2.2.1   2.2.2 2.2.3
(2) ..$|$ .. ..$|||$.. ..$|$ ..$|||$.. ..$|$ ..$|$.. .. .. ..$|||$..

Again subjects were required to formulate headings for each super- or subordinate section, and they were allowed to correct text divisions which they
considered nonoptimal.

Subjects of the unexperienced group were given the task of dividing the
original stories first. Only afterwards were they unexpectedly required to
recall the stories and to partition the recountings. Instructions were the
same as those for the experienced group, subject to appropriate variations
to account for the different temporal sequence of tasks.

All subjects were free to use as much time as they pleased for the completion
of each task. Usually 60 - 90 minutes were required altogether. Subjects were
paid 10.DM. An additional bonus of 20.DM was promised to those six

subjects who produced the best performance according to some unspecified
composite criterion.

RESULTS AND DISCUSSION

The predominant impression conveyed by the raw data of the experiment is
the large variability of the partitions produced. Within the unexperienced
group, one division occurred four times and three divisions twice. Within
the experienced group, only one partition occurred twice. The remaining
170 divisions were all different from each other within groups. A comparison
across groups would hardly have changed that picture. Of course, many partitions were similar, but others were quite different from each other.

Any of the following assumption accounts for the diversity of partitions:
(1) There exists a particular, subjectively most satisfactory, partition
for each story. The interindividual variability is due to random deviations
from that partition. (2) There exists a limited number of typical partitions,
representing different styles of dividing a text. The interindividual
variability partly represents differences between styles and partly random
deviations from typical partitions. (3) There exists a multitude of subjectively satisfactory partitions of the stories. Interindividual variability just reflects that fact.

With the second assumption in mind a nonhierarchical cluster analysis was
performed in order to identify the partitions of stories which are characteristic of particular text division styles. The (dis)similarity of partitions
was assessed by computing distances between the respective text division
trees according to the unweighted r_D-metric on ranked trees proposed by
Boorman and Olivier (1973). The index D in r_D represents the PAIRBONDS-
metric on partitions discussed in Arabie and Boorman (1973). The choice of
r_D minimizes the unavoidable arbitrariness of any choice of a tree metric,
because (1) text division trees are ranked trees and r is the only tree-
metric available for ranked trees, (2) equal weighting of all hierarchy
levels is the least arbitrary weighting and (3) PAIRBONDS is the partition-
metric for which more favourable properties have been established than for
any other partition metric, from a theoretical as well as from an empirical
point of view.

Standard nonhierarchical clustering methods represent clusters as centres
of gravity of the elements within a cluster. The centre of gravity, however,
is a meaningless concept in the case of discrete spaces such as that of
ranked trees. We therefore represent a cluster by its most central element,
i.e., by the tree of smallest average distance to all other trees of the
cluster. That procedure has the additional advantage that surprisingly often
central elements of clusters remain invariant over a large range of number
of clusters considered.

Two cluster analyses were computed for each story, one for the 20 trees
produced by the experienced group and one for the 20 trees of the unexperienced group. The small number of trees to be clustered permitted a systematic
search for the representative trees of a one-, two-, and so forth up to a
seven-cluster solution. The solution was defined as that tree, pair,
triple,..., seven-tuple of trees that minimized the sum of distances within
clusters, after the remaining trees were assigned to the cluster represented
by the nearest member of the n-tuple. Details of the analysis are presented
in Micko (1982).

Table 1

S t o r y   G r a m m a r s[1]

	R 75	vD	Th	M&J	S&G	R 77
Dog-story						
Number of best fits	-	2	4	6	14	14
Distribution[2,3] of distances						
C_{25}	10.6	8.0	9.7	8.2	7.3	6.7
C_{50}	11.6	8.8	11.2	9.6	8.3	8.9
C_{75}	13.4	9.8	12.7	10.8	10.0	10.3
Distance to[3] compos. tree	13.7	7.8	14.6	9.9	9.2	7.2
Boy-story						
Number of best fits	-	4	4	15	2	15
Distribution[2,3] of distances						
C_{25}	37.7	21.0	31.4	20.5	20.5	17.0
C_{50}	41.7	33.5	35.3	27.0	28.7	29.0
C_{75}	43.2	39.0	38.5	33.0	36.6	37.2
Distance to[3] compos. tree	33.6	17.4	33.1	15.5	17.3	13.4
Farmer-story						
Number of best fits	5	25	-	2	8	-
Distribution[2,3] of distances						
C_{25}	14.5	11.4	18.0	16.0	14.4	17.0
C_{50}	16.4	14.0	20.3	18.3	15.8	19.0
C_{75}	18.7	16.3	23.7	21.7	18.0	21.3
Distance to[3] compos. tree	12.8	10.5	16.7	16.8	13.7	15.2

1) R 75, R 77 = Rumelhart (1975, 1977)   2) Median and Quartiles of the
   vD   = van Dijk (1975)   distribution of distances
   Th   = Thorndyke (1977)   between individual story
   M&J   = Mandler and Johnson (1977)   division trees and the respec-
   S&G   = Stein and Glenn (1977)   tive story grammar tree.

3) Units of measurement differ across stories.

Two to four clusters were obtained for each set of data on the basis of
standard break-off criteria. The significance of the clusters and their representative trees, however, is in doubt because only once was a characteristic tree found in the experienced as well as in the unexperienced group.
The remaining characteristic trees were found in one of the experimental
groups but not replicated in the other. Moreover, there was no indication
of consistent personal story division styles discriminating different types
of subjects, because the composition of clusters changed completely across
stories. From this lack of stability in the results avross texts and minor
changes of experimental conditions we conclude (1) that the clusters represent more or less random similarities of story divisions, (2) that the representative trees are artefacts, and (3) as a consequence, that the attempt
to identify a few predominant styles of partitioning a story has failed.

In spite of the diversity of individual story divisions, some locations in
the text were chosen by many or most subjects for marking an intersection
and others by few or very few. This indicates a certain degree of commonality.
It was decided therefore to construct a composite text division tree by
adding up the markings (1,2,.... vertical lines) of all 40 subjects in each
of the intervals between two successive propositions. This procedure does
not differ in principle from the method of constructing a tree from sorting
data. The obtained tree was reduced to a ranked tree by considering different
frequencies of marking intersections to be equal if they did not differ
significantly at the .05 level on the sign test. That procedure may lead to
inconsistencies, but in our case only one minor ambiguity had to be resolved.

Reduced story grammar trees were tested against the reduced composite tree
as well as against all individual text division trees. Distances computed
according to the r_D-metric served as the measure of (dis)similarity. Three
related criteria for the goodness of fit were considered: (1) The number of
text division trees to which a story grammar tree is most similar (number
of best fits). (2) The median distance of a story grammar tree from the
40 individual text division trees, supplemented by the 1st and 3rd quartile
as indicators of the spread of the distance distribution. (3) The distance
of a story grammar tree from the composite story division tree. The results
are shown in Table 1.

The predictive values of the story grammars investigated differ neither
markedly nor consistently. In most cases the predictions of the Rumelhart
(1975)- and the Thorndyke-grammar are somewhat inferior to those of the
other four grammars considered. The partitions of the dog story are predicted
about equally well by the grammars of van Dijk, Stein and Glenn, and Rumelhart (1977), those of the boy story by the grammars of Mandler and Johnson,
and Rumelhart (1977). Van Dijk's grammar is the best predictor of the farmer-
story trees. On that story the Rumelhart (1977)-grammar does worse than
the other grammars exept Thorndyke's and thus does live up to its promising
performance on the dog and boy story. The Stein and Glenn-grammar is the
most reliable one, its predictions usually come out second best.

It cannot be the ultimate objective of the text division paradigm to enable
evaluations of existing story grammars, particulary since all of them must
be regarded as proposals to be revised on the basis of experimental evidence.
Since text division data are easy to obtain, story grammars may be improved
most economically by first revising rewrite rules that bring about false
predictions of story partitions. The predictions of expensive memory data
may be put to test somewhat later. These tasks, however, are beyond the scope
of the present investigation.

REFERENCES

Arabie, P., and Boorman, S. Multidimensional scaling of measures of distance between partitions. Journal of Mathematical Psychology, 1973, 10, 148-203.

Black, J. Theories of story memory structure. Preliminary draft of a manuscript. Psychology Department, Stanford University.

Boorman, S., and Olivier, D.C. Metrics on spaces of finite trees. Journal of Mathematical Psychology, 1973, 10, 26-59.

Van Dijk, T.A. Recalling and summarizing complex discourse. Unpublished manuscript. University of Amsterdam, Amsterdam, The Netherlands, 1975.

Glowalla, U. Der rote Faden, ein handlungstheoretisches Modell zur Text-verarbeitung· Ph.D.thesis, University of Technology, Braunschweig, 1981.

Kintsch, W. The representation of meaning in memory. Hillsdale, N.J., Lawrence Erlbaum Associates, 1974.

Mandler, J.M., and Johnson, N.S. Remembrance of things parsed: Story structure and recall. Cognitive Psychology, 1977, 9, 111-151.

Micko, H.C. Text divisions, story grammars and story recall: Materials and data. Braunschweiger Berichte - Reports from the Institute of Psychology, University of Technology, Braunschweig, 1982/1.

Rumelhart, D. E. Notes on a schema for stories. In: D.G. Bobrow and A. Collins (Eds.) Representation and understanding: Studies in cognitive science. New York, Akademic Press, 1975.

Rumelhart, D.E. Understanding and summarizing brief stories: In: D. LaBerge and J. Samuels (Eds.) Basic processes in reading and comprehension. Hillsdale, N.J. Lawrence Erlbaum Associates, 1977.

Schank, R.C. The structure of episodes in memory. In: D.G. Bobrow and A. Collins (Eds.) Representation and understanding: Studies in cognitive science. New York, Academic Press, 1975a.

Schank, R.C. Conceptual information processing. New York, North-Holland, 1975b.

Stein, N.L., and Glenn, C.G. An analysis of story comprehension in elementary school children. In: R. Freedle (Ed.) Multidisciplinary perspectives in discourse comprehension. Hillsdale, N.J., Lawrence Erlbaum Associates, 1977.

Thorndyke, P.W. Cognitive structures in comprehension and memory of narrative discourse. Cognitive Psychology, 1977, 9, 77-110.

DISCOURSE PROCESSING
A. Flammer and W. Kintsch (eds.)
© *North-Holland Publishing Company, 1982*

CHILDREN'S KNOWLEDGE OF SOCIAL ACTION:
EFFECTS ON COMPREHENSION AND RECALL OF SIMPLE STORIES[*]

Hans Strohner, Gert Rickheit, and Rüdiger Weingarten

Fakultät für Linguistik und Literaturwissenschaft
Universität Bielefeld
D-4800 Bielefeld
West Germany

Nursery school children and Grade 5 school children listened to one of four versions of four episodes. The episodes
were either complete or one of three combinations of two
parts of the episodes. Young nursery school children with
high reproduction scores showed a tendency to complete the
incomplete versions of the texts. In the Grade 5 children
there was a negative relationship between reproduction and
completion performance. The results are discussed within
the framework of the problem-solving theory of text processing.

Story comprehension may be thought of as a two-fold problem-solving process
for the following reasons:
(1) The listeners or readers generally have to cope with the problem of
making sense out of texts which are to some degree incoherent and elliptical (Clark, 1978; de Beaugrande, 1980; Voss, Vesonder, & Spilich, 1980).
(2) In stories they have to trace the problem-solving actions of the characters in order to put these actions together to form a causal chain or
critical path (Black & Bower, 1980; Schank, 1975).
In many story comprehension situations a strong interaction between these
two levels of problem solving is observed (e.g. Anderson, 1978; Bower,
1978; Bruce, 1980).

Black (1978) has proposed a story memory theory, the Hierarchical State
Transition (HST) theory, which comprises of two different procedures for
solving problems. One of these procedures is called the "problem reduction
method". This method represents the problem-solving process as a hierarchy
of related actions. The actions lower in the hierarchy are more detailed
and specific than those higher up in the hierarchy. The other problem-solving representation is called "state-transition network" und represents
the problem-solving process as a series of states and actions. These actions change one state into another.

[*]The study was supported by grant No. 2365 from the University of Bielefeld.
We are grateful to the children, parents, and teachers of the Kindergarten
Dorfen and the Laborschule Bielefeld for their kind co-operation. We are
indebted to Helga Buurman, Reinhard Fiehler, Brigitte Gremse, Walther Kindt,
Gisela Klann-Delius, Horst Kock, Geoffrey Macpherson, Dietrich Meutsch,
Marcus Stein, and Roswitha Strohner for practical support and valuable
comments on earlier versions of the paper.

Several studies have focussed on the effects of the first part of the HST theory on the comprehension and recall of texts about action sequences (e. g. Black & Bower, 1979; Graesser, 1978; Graesser, Robertson, Lovelace, & Swinehart, 1980; Lichtenstein & Brewer, 1980). Essentially these studies have demonstrated better recall achievement for more superordinate statements in the problem-solving hierarchy than for more specific information. In the comprehension process subjects seem to infer relevance relationships between the various actions. It seems to be these relationships which also guide the retrieval of the actions.

The second part of the HST theory is also well investigated (e.g. Black & Bern, 1981; Bower, Black, & Turner, 1979; Kintsch, Mandel, & Kozminsky, 1977; Lichtenstein & Brewer, 1980). It can be concluded from these studies, that subjects rely on their knowledge of the structure of naturally occurring sequences of behavioural events in order to reconstruct them in a recall task.

Another main characteristic of a story, if seen under the perspective of problem solving, is the degree of completeness or explicitness of the information that is relevant for the current problem-solving processes (Black & Bower, 1980). If, for example, the problem-solving process is divided into the three stages namely, problem description, problem-solving attempt, and solving the problem, stories may differ more or less depending on how completely these problem-solving stages have been described in the plot of the story. In contrast to the two variables discussed in connection with the HST theory, the effects of the type of specifically mentioned problem-solving stages on text comprehension and reproduction are less well known.

The present study is an effort to learn more about the impact of children's knowledge about the qualitative structure of social action on the processing of complete and incomplete stories.

In a study of the processing of scripts in young children Wimmer (1979) gave 4- and 6-year-old children an incomplete shopping story which ended before the paying scene at the cashier. However, the girl who wanted to pay had lost her wallet with the money.One task of Wimmer's subjects was to complete the story fragment. Wimmer found that more than 60% of the 4-year-olds and all of the 6-year-olds completed the story by indicating the impossibility of the paying action which normally follows. These results indicate that the children's knowledge of relevant social actions in processing the fragment of the story which they heard was applied to a medium or high degree.

In completing fragments of a story the children have to draw certain inferences. Hildyard (1979) investigated children's prompted production of action-based inferences as for example the statement "The dog runs through the trees" which can be inferred from the sentences "The dog chases the cat. The cat runs through the trees" or the inference "Jose was injured and his arm was broken", following from the sentences "Jose ran into the road without looking. His arm was in a plaster cast for several weeks". When controlled for memory differences the inference achievement did not differ significantly between Grade 1, Grade 3, and Grade 5 children. According to this study Grade 1 children were able to draw as many action-based inferences as the older children. In addition, and highly relevant for the present study, Hildyard classified the inferences into several types, three of which referred to the presuppositions, the enabling events, and the consequences of the described actions. She did not analyse these different types of inferences statistically because of the small and unequal numbers of inferences involved. The distribution of the mean percent scores indicates only minimal differences between the three age groups in their handling of these inference types.

In the present study the stories were composed of three parts with different functions. The incomplete versions of the episodes consisted of two of these three parts, thus resulting, for each version, in qualitatively different information about the underlying social action system.

METHOD

Subjects

The 48 German speaking children belonged to three different age groups each of 16 children: a group of younger nursery school children (mean 4; 11, range 4;2 - 5;7), a group of older nursery school children (mean 6;6, range 6;2 - 6;10), and a group of Grade 5 school children (mean 11;4, range 10;6 - 12;4). There were eight boys and eight girls in both of the nursery school groups and ten girls and six boys in the Grade 5 group.

Texts

Each child was given four texts. The texts described fragments of episodes about well known events in a child's life: a birthday party, visiting a circus, shopping, and riding a bicycle. Each text consisted of six short sentences. The sentences were matched with respect to the function of the sentence content according to the co-operative problem-solving framework of the plot of the story. In particular, the first part of each episode, which consisted of three sentences, referred to the setting, the problem-causing action of person A, and the problem description. In the second part, which consisted of one sentence only, a problem-solving attempt of person A was described. The last part, which was two sentences in length, told about the successful problem-solving activity of person B and the consequences of the co-operation between person A und person B. The functional structure of the four episodes in combination with example sentences from the "Birthday Party" story is given in Table 1.

Table 1: The co-operative problem-solving structure of the four episodes with translated example sentences from the "Birthday Party" story.

Part A: Problem description

Sentence 1: Setting
          "Petra has invited Mark to her birthday party."

Sentence 2: Problem-causing action of person A
          "Mark wants to give Petra a present."

Sentence 3: Problem
          "But he doesn't know what to give."

Part B: Problem-solving attempt

Sentence 4: Problem-solving attempt of person A
          "Mark asks the sister of Petra what Petra would like
          to get for a birthday present."

Part C: Solving the problem

Sentence 5: Problem solving by person B in co-operation with person A
"The sister of Petra says that Petra would like to
have a kite."

Sentence 6: Consequence
"Mark gives Petra a kite."

Each child was given one complete story (text version ABC), another story
where part C was missing (text version AB), one story where part B was missing (text version AC), and one story where part A was missing (text version
BC). The incomplete versions were cut out from the complete version tape in
order to have prosodically identical parts in all text versions. After giving
each of the four texts to the children music was played for an interval of 20
sec.

Procedure

Each child was tested separately. The children were instructed to listen to
some stories recorded on tape and after hearing each story to retell the
same. No indication was given that some of the presented stories were incomplete.

The children listened to the episodes in one of four versions. These were
either complete or one of the three combinations of two parts of the story.
Four children of each age group were presented with the complete version of
one story, four children with version AB of the same story, four children
with version AC, and four children with version BC. Within these subgroups
of four children the version types of the other stories and the presentation order were systematically varied.

With both the complete and incomplete text versions the experimenter prompted the recall by asking questions if a text sentence was not recalled spontaneously by the child. In addition, with the incomplete text versions the
experimenter asked questions which aimed at the missing part of the episode. For example, in the case of the "Birthday party" story the questions
for the three missing parts A, B, and C were:

Part A: What do you think happened before Mark asked the sister of Petra?
Part B: What do you think happened before the sister of Petra said that
Petra would like to have a kite?
Part C: What do you think happened after Mark asked the sister of Petra?

The experimental session for one child took about 10 to 15 minutes.

Data Analysis

The recorded recall and inference responses of the children were grouped into the following categories:

Reproductions: A sentence was scored as a reproduction if it included
the essential information of the given sentence. This
category was further divided into spontaneous reproductions and prompted reproductions.

Completions: A sentence was scored as a completion if it included some
essential information of the part of the story which had
not been given or other possible inferences drawn from

the story. This category was also further divided into
spontaneous completions and prompted completions.

Elaborations: A sentence was scored as an elaboration if it could
not plausibly be integrated into the plot of the story.

The few cases in which scoring problems occured were resolved after discussion between the experimenters.

RESULTS

Comparability of the four stories

The most critical and sensible test for the comparability of the four stories seems to be the distribution of spontaneous reproductions across the
sentences of the stories. A chi-square test showed that according to this
distribution the stories did not differ significantly ($chi^2=5.57$; df=15;
n.s.). It can be concluded from this result that the subjects responded in
a similar way to all four stories. Consequently, in the following the
four episodes are not treated separately but are referred to as a common
abstract text base which is structured according to a co-operative problem
solving sequence.

Spontaneous reproduction

For each subject the percentage of spontaneous reproductions with respect
to the maximal reproduction score in each text version was computed. These
maximal reproduction scores were 6 in the complete text version, 4 in the
AB version, 5 in the AC version, and 3 in the BC version. These percentage
scores were subjected to an analysis of variance with subject groups as a
between factor and the four text versions as a within factor. This analysis
showed significant differences between subject groups (F=28.66; df=2, 45; p
<.001),but no effects for the text versions (F<1) or for the interaction
between subjects and text versions (F<1). According to Newman-Keuls tests
(p<.01) the younger nursery school children (mean 26.97%) recalled fewer
sentences spontaneously than the older nursery school children (mean
52.22%). Both groups of nursery school children recalled fewer than the
Grade 5 children (mean 84.94%).

We also looked for differences in the spontaneous reproductions of the single sentences in the complete text version. Although in all three age
groups sentence 1 (setting) was the least recalled sentence, and sentence
3 (problem) one of the best recalled sentences, the observed differences were
not large enough to yield significant values based on chi-square analyses
($chi^2 \leq 5.76$; df=5; n.s.).

Overall reproductions

An analysis of variance with subject groups as a between factor and text
version as a within factor of the percentage scores of the overall reproductions (spontaneous + prompted reproductions) showed a significant effect of
the subject groups (F=16.03; df=2, 45; p<.001), but neither an effect of
the text versions (F<1) nor an effect of the interaction between subject
groups and text versions (F<1). According to Newman-Keuls tests (p<.05)
the younger nursery school children (mean 55.72%) reproduced fewer sentences of the texts than the older nursery school children (mean 68.27%).

Both groups of nursery school children reproduced fewer than the Grade 5 school children (mean 88.75%). These results are quite similar to the results for the spontaneous reproductions which have been reported above.

The results for the distribution of the single sentences for the overall reproduction scores, however, differ from those for the spontaneous reproductions. Now the low level of performance in the case of the first sentence reaches such a discrepancy if compared with the performance of the other sentences that chi-square tests for the two nursery school groups yield significant values (for the younger group $chi^2=12.38$; df=5; p<.05; for the older group $chi^2=21.31$; df=5; p<.01). For the Grade 5 children there was a similar tendency to recall the setting sentence least but this tendency was not strong enough to give a significant difference ($chi^2=2.39$; df=5; n.s.). This may be due to a ceiling effect.

Spontaneous completions

A one-factorial analysis of variance on the spontaneous completion scores revealed no significant subject group effect (F=3.35; df=2, 45; p<.10) with group means of 1.19, 1.81, and 2.88. When an analysis of covariance was used to equate statistically the age groups according to the reproduction performance, again there was no significant difference (F=2,98; df=2, 12; p<.10).
However, specific chi-quare tests for the three incomplete text versions showed significant age groups differences. There were significant age differences for the text version AB ($chi^2=11.13$; df=2; p<.01), and for the text version AC ($chi^2=8.38$; df=2; p<.05), but not for BC ($chi^2=3.29$;df=2). Comparisons by means of chi-square tests between the three text versions and with respect to those completions which referred to information before the beginning of the text proper, after it, or between the text sentences were all non-significant.

Overall completions

A one-factorial analysis of variance on the overall completion scores (spontaneous + prompted completions) showed a significant effect of age groups (F=6.57; df=2,45; p<.05). According to Newman-Keuls tests (p<.05) the younger nursery school children (mean 3.25) produced less completions than the older nursery school children (mean 5.13) and the Grade 5 children (mean 5.50). The latter two groups did not differ. This was probably due to a ceiling effect in the school children. However, when the groups were equated statistically according to their reproduction performance by means of an analysis of covariance, the significant effect of age groups disappears (F=2.13; df=2, 12; n.s.).

Specific chi-square tests for the three incomplete text versions showed highly significant differences for both the text version AC and the version BC ($chi^2=9.47$ resp. 11.66; df=2; p<.01), but no significant age difference for the text version AB ($chi^2=5.74$; df=2; p<.10). There were no significant differences between the three text versions or with respect to those spontaneous completions which referred to information before the text proper, after it, or between the text sentences.

Elaborations

A chi-square test between the age groups on the number of elaborations showed that the nursery school children produced more elaborations (means 0,81) than the Grade 5 children (mean 0.38; chi^2=7.38; df=2; p<.05).

Correlations between the dependent measures

Pearson product-moment correlations between the spontaneous completion and the overall reproduction scores showed quite different values for the three age groups: for the younger nursery school group r=.55; p<.05, for the older nursery school group: r=.01; n.s., and for the Grade 5 group 5=-.67; p<.01.

Pearson product-moment correlations between overall completions and overall reproductions showed a highly similar pattern to the above listed correlations: for the younger nursery school group r=.61; p<.05, for the older nursery school group r=.35; n.s., for the Grade 5 group r=-.54; p<.05.

Pearson product-moment correlations between the spontaneous completion scores for the six sentences of the texts and their corresponding overall reproduction scores resulted in a medium but non-significant degree of relationship (r=.48; n.s.). The same correlation for the overall completion scores, however, was highly significant and positive (r=.94; p<.01).

Since elaborations occured only rarely, in this case phi coefficients were computed. These showed in all three age groups significant negative relationships between the occurrence of elaborations and the overall reproduction level of the children: for both nursery school groups phi=-.77; p<.01 and for the Grade 5 group phi=-.54; p<.05.

DISCUSSION

The most important results of the present study may be summarized as follows:
(1) Not very surprisingly there was a steady increase in both the spontaneous and the overall reproduction achievement across the three age groups. However, the versions of the text had no effect on reproduction achievement.
(2) When the completion scores were controlled for reproduction differences between the age groups there were no age differences with respect to either spontaneous or overall completion scores.
(3) However, for both the spontaneous and overall completions the children seemed to handle the three text versions differently. The text version BC in which the problem description part of the episode is missing prompted the young children most strongly to complete the missing part spontaneously. Therefore, for this version only no significant differences between the three age groups on the spontaneous completions were observed. In contrast to this pattern of results, in the overall completions there was no age difference only on the text version AB in which the final problem solution part of the episode is missing. This result is again due to a relatively good achievement of the younger children in this particular text version.
(4) The children tended to recall the setting sentence of the texts least of all and the sentence in which the problem of the episode is stated best of all.
(5) The correlations between both the spontaneous completions and the overall completions on the one hand and the overall reproduction on the other hand were positive for the younger nursery school children, non-significant for the older nursery school children, and negative for the Grade 5 children.

(6) Both nursery school groups produced more elaborations than the Grade 5 children. The correlations between the elaborations and the overall reproduction achievement were strongly negative in all three age groups.

In the following, each of these main issues of the study is discussed in turn.

The fact that we did not find any effect of text versions on the reproduction achievement of our subjects may partially be due to the shortness of our experimentally applied texts. In the complete version the texts consisted of six sentences and in the shortest version of three sentences. Another cause for this failure to find significant differences between the text versions might be that the qualitative differences between the text versions might not have been strong enough since all text versions focussed upon some well known actions in the daily life of the children.

In good conformity with the study of Hildyard (1979) we found that the age differences for the completion performance disappeared when differences in the reproduction performance were controlled. In contrast with these two studies, Omanson, Warren, and Trabasso (1978) reported that when their five and eight year old subjects were matched for retrieval of propositions, crucial to the observed inferences, the older children still made more inferences. It may be that the differences between the three studies are partially related to the types of inferences under investigation. Omanson et al. (1978) worked with several types of inferences. Some of these are much more specific regarding information which has to be inferred than in the study of Hildyard and the present study.

Those results of our study which are related to specific text version differences between the age groups must be interpreted with caution because in the chi-square tests the overall reproduction achievement could not be controlled for. What may be tentatively concluded in spite of this however, is that the missing first part of the texts in which the problem description is given, seemed to prompt also the younger children to infer the missing part spontaneously. In the case of the missing first part of the episode it is most obvious that something has been left out by the story teller.

The situation for the overall completions seems to be quite different from that for the spontaneous completions. With overall completions the text part completed most easily was the last part. This was also the case for the younger children. The first and middle parts seemed to be more difficult and thus resulted in significant age differences. This similarity in the results of the two first parts of the text for the overall completion performance may lead to the hypothesis that the difficulty of the young children to complete these story parts were caused by their failure to understand the word "before" in the questions for the two parts. If this were the case the older nursery school children should be better than the younger children in answering the questions, because their level of competence for the word "before" is higher than that of the younger children. Such a tendency was only observed for the first part but not for the second part of the text. Thus, we conclude that the problems the younger children seemed to have in inferring the first two parts of the texts are at least partially cognitive in nature.

This closely corresponds to the conclusion of Stein and Glenn (1979, p.118)

that "when the first category in an episode is deleted, young children may
have more difficulty adding information to the story than older children".

In the present study the least recalled and inferred sentence of the texts
was the first sentence in which the setting (e.g. "Petra has invited Mark
to her birthday party") is given. This result might be seen in contrast
to the well replicated result with longer stories namely, that the setting
is one of the best recalled story parts (e.g. Stein & Glenn, 1979). In
short and simple texts which refer to such well known events, as in the
present study, the setting information is much more superfluous than in
longer fictional stories about less well known situations, characters, and
events.

The positive correlations between completions and overall reproduction in
the younger nursery school children and the negative correlations between
these variables in the Grade 5 children point to the different problem-solving situation for these two age groups. For the nursery school children it
seems important to collect all available knowledge about the social actions,
occuring in the texts, in order to cope with the inferential demands of the
texts. Accordingly, those children who have a differentiated knowledge base
on the actions talked about also did well in completing the missing information. For most of the Grade 5 children the problem situation seemed to be
quite different. These children have already a well structured basic knowledge which makes it easy for them to understand and recall the texts. In
addition, they are familiar with the task of reproducing a text. Thus, they
concentrate particularly on the information they have heard and neglect all
other complementary information which results from their knowledge of the
actions. Only those Grade 5 children who still have difficulties with the
task react in a way similar to that of the nursery school children. This
hypothetical pattern of problem-solving strategies should result in the observed correlations between reproduction and completion performance (Fig.1).
The different correlations in the younger and older children are an
example of the interaction between the two levels of problem solving within
story comprehension. This we referred to in the introduction.

Fig.1:   Hypothetical relationship between reproduction and completion
         performance across different knowledge levels

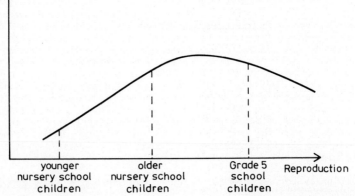

The relatively high frequencies of elaborations in the two nursery school groups and the negative correlations with the overall reproduction performance again confirm that for some of these children the texts, and the tasks of reproducing and answering questions, were difficult and sometimes resulted in unsuccessful search processes in the memory store. Another interpretation refers to the rather strange task for these subjects to reproduce a text which they had just heard in an artificial and non-functional experimental situation.

In conclusion, the present study shows a very differentiated and highly complex picture of the recall and text completion performance in nursery school and school children. We feel that it could be a promising way to handle these complicated data if text processing is modeled theoretically as a specific type of problem solving. The various stages, strategies, and interactions between the text and the listener or reader in this problem-solving process must be analysed carefully using different methods so as to get converging evidence about the functioning of the cognitive processes in these types of problem solving.

REFERENCES

Anderson, R.C. Schema-directed processes in language comprehension. In A.M. Lesgold, J.W. Pellegrino, S.D. Fokkema, & R. Glaser (Eds.), Cognitive psychology and instruction. New York: Plenum Press,1978

Black, J.B. Story memory structure. Unpublished doctoral dissertation. Stanford University, 1978.

Black, J.B. & Bower, G.H. Episodes as chunks in story memory. Journal of Verbal Learning and Verbal Behavior, 1979, 18, 309-318.

Black, J.B. & Bower, G.H. Story understanding as problem-solving. Poetics, 1980, 9, 223-250.

Black, J.B. & Bern, H. Causal coherence and memory for events in narratives. Journal of Verbal Learning and Verbal Behavior, 1981, 20, 267-275.

Bower, G.H. Experiments on story comprehension and recall. Discourse Processes, 1978, 1, 211-231.

Bower, G.H., Black, J.B., & T.J. Turner, Scripts in memory for text. Cognitive Psychology, 1979, 11, 177-220.

Bruce, B.C. Plans and social actions. In R.J. Spiro, B.C. Bruce, & W.F. Brewer (Eds.), Theoretical issues in reading comprehension. Hillsdale, N.J.: Erlbaum, 1980.

Clark, H.H. Inferring what is meant. In W.J.M. Levelt & G.B. Flores d'Arcais (Eds.), Studies in the perception of language. New York: Wiley, 1978.

De Beaugrande, R. Text, discourse, and process. London: Longman, 1980.

Graesser, A.C. How to catch a fish: The memory and representation of common procedures. Discourse Processes, 1978, 1, 72-89.

Graesser, A.C., Robertson, S.P., Lovelace, E.R., & Swinehart, D.M. Answers to why-questions expose the organization of story plot and predict recall of actions. Journal of Verbal Learning and Verbal Behavior, 1980, 19, 110-119.

Hildyard, A. Children's production of inferences from oral texts. Discourse Processes, 1979, 2, 33-56.

Kintsch, W., Mandel, T.S., & Kozminsky, E. Summarizing scrambled stories. Memory & Cognition, 1977, 5, 547-552.

Lichtenstein, E.H., & Brewer, W.F. Memory for goal-directed events. Cognitive Psychology, 1980, 12, 412-445.

Omanson, R.C., Warren, W.H., & Trabasso, T. Goals, inferential comprehension,
        and recall of stories by children. <u>Discourse Processes</u>, 1978,
        <u>1</u>, 337-354.
Schank, R.C. The structure of episodes in memory. In D.G. Bobrow & A. Collins
        (Eds.), <u>Representation and understanding</u>: <u>Studies in cognitive
        science</u>. New York: Academic Press, 1975.
Stein, N.L., & Glenn, C.G. An analysis of story comprehension in elementary
        school children. In R.O. Freedle (Ed.), <u>New directions in
        discourse processing</u>. Norwood, N.J.: Ablex, 1979.
Voss, J.F., Vesonder, G.T., & Spilich, G.J. Text generation and recall by
        high-knowledge and low-knowledge individuals. <u>Journal of Verbal
        Learning and Verbal Behavior</u>, 1980, <u>19</u>, 651-667.
Wimmer, H. Processing of script deviations by young children. <u>Discourse
        Processes</u>, 1979, <u>2</u>, 301-310.

DISCOURSE PROCESSING
A. Flammer and W. Kintsch (eds.)
© *North-Holland Publishing Company, 1982*

LEVELS OF FUNCTIONING IN SEMANTIC MEMORY
AND LEVELS OF COMPREHENSION OF TEXTS

Stéphane Ehrlich, Jean-Michel Passerault, and Georges Personnier

Laboratoire de Psychologie
(E.R.A. 797 du C.N.R.S.)
Université de Poitiers
Poitiers, FRANCE

We assume that a text representation can be defined as
an organized group of concepts. The different concepts
which form the representation are activated and their
informative content is determined. The concepts are coordinated by a set of relations which stabilize the representation into a definite organization. Our results
show that the activation of the first base concepts involves the activation of the superordinate concepts.
However, this vertical activation does not allow anticipation of further events. Yet the thematic concept,
when activated, does facilitate the integration of these events.

INTRODUCTION

To understand a text a subject must build a text representation, which requires that he specify the semantic content of one or several concepts and
of the semantic relations established between these concepts. To do so
the subject performs a mental rereading of his/her representation.

We must therefore distinguish two successive stages in the comprehension
process: (a) the building of the text representation which involves activation and coordination of a group of particular concepts that correspond
to the text; and (b) the explanation of the representation which involves
mental rereading and response to specific questions about the text.

We are primarily interested here in the first stage, i.e., the construction of the text representation. We will emphasize the concept activation
and coordination processes. Our hypothesis is that the construction of
the representation is made on the basis of concept activation with several
hierarchical levels. This activity uses text elements which are base
concepts (N level). Higher-level concepts reduce some base concepts (N +
1 concept activation), which are themselves reduced until the N+X thematic
concept that encompasses the whole text is reached. This view of text
representation is in large part similar to those developed by Schank and
Abelson (1977), Mandler (1978), Kintsch and van Dijk (1978), among others,
who assume text representation to be a hierarchical system. However, we
will dwell particularly on the representational content (macrostructure)
rather than on the rules (schemata) that are used for its construction.

Three questions will be of primary concern. First, at what moment in the reading of the text are N+1, N+2, N+X concepts likely to be activated? Is some anticipation possible? In other words, does activation of a N+1 concept, corresponding to the beginning of the text, involve anticipatory activation of a N+1 concept related to the middle or the end of the text? That will be the object of our first experiment.

Secondly, does activation of the N+X thematic concept facilitate activation of the N+1 lower concepts? Under what conditions?

The third question deals with the efficiency of the N+1 concepts when used as cues in recall. We should like to know if the N+1 concepts' efficiency as retrieval cues is proportional to their degree of activation. Our second experiment refers to the latter two points.

Generally speaking, these studies are relevant to a theory of how semantic memory functions during the construction of a text representation. We assume that the processes of activation and coordination take place in working memory. These processes affect concepts formed on the basis of past experience, concepts which constitute a person's permanent memory (Ehrlich, 1979). These determination-activation-construction processes involve changes in the state of concepts, in that concepts which were previously inactive are activated; concepts which were previously independent are coordinated; and concepts which were previously indefinite in their informative content are filled with a specific content (Ehrlich, in press). Here we are interested in this complex activity which depends at the same time on text information given to the subject, on his previous knowledge, and on a set of cognitive operations (analysis, and direct and inferential synthesis).

ACTIVATION OF CONCEPTS AT DIFFERENT LEVELS

Let us return to the first problem: at what moment in reading the text does concept activation occur at different levels of the hierarchy?

The first experiment uses a text about a sports competition; this text is divided into four paragraphs. Figure 1 shows its conceptual structure.

Three hundred subjects were used; half of them read the text and the others listened to it. For the purpose of our experiment, there was no difference between reading and listening. These two conditions have thus been grouped together in the description of the results.

Subjects were divided into four groups. Group I read (or listened to) the first paragraph only, Group II read (or listened to) paragraphs 1 and 2. Group III read (or listened to) paragraphs 1, 2, and 3, and Group IV dealt with the whole text. There was only one trial; after reading (or listening) the subjects had to write down the answers to two questions, each of which concerned one of the hierarchical concepts. The subjects were asked if a given concept (for instance, "preparation of the group") was directly or indirectly present in the text, or absent altogether. They were told, by means of an example, what was meant by "directly present" (including pragmatic evidence if a concept was not really explicit in the text), by "indirectly present" (probable pragmatic inference) and by "missing information" (that which cannot be decided either directly or indirectly).

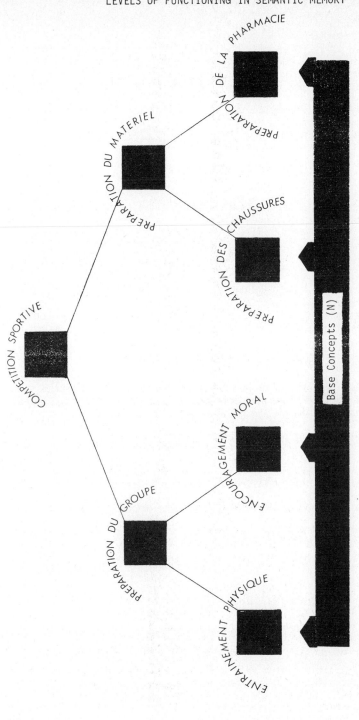
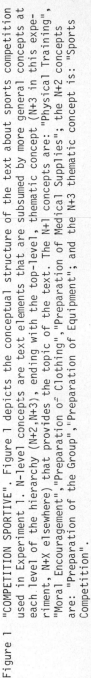

Figure 1   "COMPETITION SPORTIVE". Figure 1 depicts the conceptual structure of the text about sports competition used in Experiment 1. N-level concepts are text elements that are subsumed by more general concepts at each level of the hierarchy (N+2;N+3), ending with the top-level, thematic concept (N+3 in this experiment, N+X elsewhere) that provides the topic of the text. The N+1 concepts are: "Physical Training", "Moral Encouragement","Preparation o⁼ Clothing","Preparation of Medical Supplies"; the N+2 concepts are: "Preparation of the Group","Preparation of Equipment"; and the N+3 thematic concept is: "Sports Competition".

Thus, we obtained 15 to 20 answers for each of the seven concepts forming the conceptual hierarchy. For each of the seven concepts we noted the frequency of "positive" answers, i.e., the answers that indicated a direct or indirect presence of the concept in the part of the text dealt with. Figure 2 shows these frequencies. Two groups can be distinguished. The black squares are those for which the frequency of positive answers is significantly higher than chance (66%); the mean frequency varies from 91% to 93%. The white squares are those for which this frequency is less than chance (the mean frequency varies from 23% to 26%).

Two points may be made on the basis of these results:

(a) As soon as subjects became familiar with the first paragraph, all of the directly superordinate concepts were activated, and this is true for every level of the hierarchy, N+1, N+2, and N+3. In other words, subjects immediately accessed the more general concept (sports competition), i.e., the text topic.

(b) There was no anticipation: Access to the N+3 topic concept did not allow subjects to anticipate the N+2 and N+1 concepts corresponding to the text information of later paragraphs. Thus, knowledge of the topic, at least in such a text, does not in itself allow anticipation of further events described in the text. There remains a great deal of indeterminacy.

VERTICAL INTERACTIONS IN CONCEPT ACTIVATION AT SEVERAL LEVELS

Let us now try to answer the second question: when a representation of the entire text has been constructed, does activation of the N+X concept facilitate activation of the lower N+1 concepts? To answer this question a second experiment was conducted, using another text about a fishing trip. This text falls into six paragraphs; each paragraph contains several base concepts, each describing a specific action, such as, "The man was on his way towards the river...", or "...without breaking any twigs...." The base concepts of each paragraph could be reduced to a N+1-level concept, such as, "To tread softly". Since there are six paragraphs, there are six N+1-level concepts. Finally, the whole text can be summarized by a thematic concept (N+X level), "a fishing trip".

Four versions of this text were constructed. The first and last sentences (1 and 3) were the same for all versions, while four variants (A-D) were constructed for the middle sentence (2), as shown for the first paragraph, below:

1. The man was on his way towards the river
2. { A. He was very careful
     B. to go fishing; he was very careful
     C. His new boots hurt him
     D. to go fishing; his new boots hurt him
3. He tiptoed lightly on the ground, without breaking any twigs.

The first version, or "fishing version" (A), describes the successive stages of a fishing trip. The second version, or "fishing version with fishing theme" (B), includes the same information as in the fishing version, but in every other paragraph it is stated that the topic is a

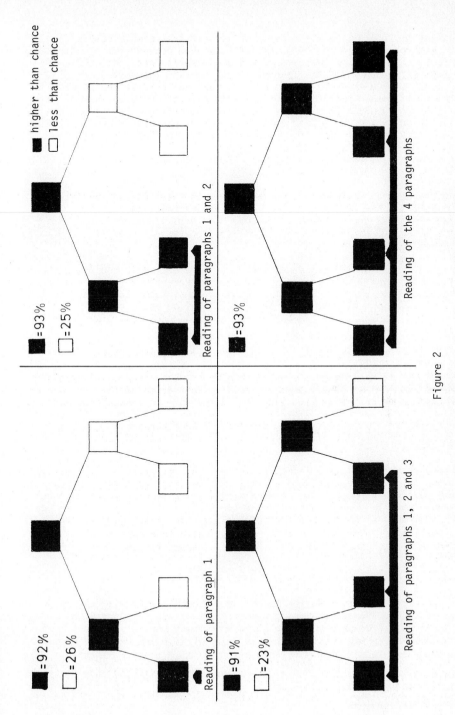

Figure 2

"COMPETITION SPORTIVE": Frequencies of positive answers

fishing trip. This is a reinforced fishing version that should facilitate
the activation of N+1 and N+X concepts. The third version, or "hiking
version" (C), includes the same textual information as the fishing version,
except for a substitution: in each one of the six paragraphs, one item of
fishing version information is replaced by another piece of information
that modifies the meaning and should make more difficult the activation
of the N+1 concepts and of the thematic N+X concept. The fourth version,
or "hiking version with fishing theme" (D), includes the same information
as the previous one, but in each of the three odd-numbered paragraphs it
is stated that a fishing trip is involved. It is an ill-knit version in
which there is internal incoherence between two possible interpretations,
"fishing" or "hiking".

Six groups of subjects, from 17 to 20 each, were used for this experiment.
The subjects had to read the text paragraph by paragraph. After each
paragraph they had to answer two questions. Two groups read the fishing
version (A) or hiking version (C), respectively. The questions were the
same for the two groups and for the six paragraphs, and are as follows:

    Q1: "Do you think that the text deals with a fishing trip?"
    Q2: "Do you think that the text deals with a hiking trip?"

Each of the four remaining groups read one of the four versions A, B,
C, or D. The two questions are the same for the four groups, but they
are different from one paragraph to another. They successively concern the six N+1 concepts related to the six paragraphs. For instance,
after they have read the first paragraph, subjects have to answer the
following questions:
Q1: Do you think that the man is treading softly? (fishing interpret.)
Q2: Do you think that the man is limping? (hiking interpretation)
Subjects have to answer "yes","no" or "I don't know" to each question.

For each question subjects had to answer with "yes", "no", or "I don't
know". Subjects were given 15 sec. to read and 20 sec. to answer each
paragraph.

A cued recall took place immediately after the presentation of the six
paragraphs; the cues were the six N+1 concepts. Three successive trials
were given: reading and question answering for each paragraph, followed
by cued recall. Our concern here is to consider the activation of the
N+1 concepts, given the N+X concept activation corresponding to the
"fishing trip", which is one of the two possible interpretations. For
each subject, on each trial and for the six paragraphs we counted the
number of affirmative answers only for the questions that concern the
fishing interpretation (Q1 in the previous example). This number varied
from 0 to 6 for each subject.

The results are presented in Figures 3a and 3b. Averages in Figure 3a
correspond to the activation of the N+1 concepts in the four A, B, C, and
D versions. Averages in Figure 3b correspond to the activation of the
N+X thematic concept in the A (fishing) and C (hiking) versions only.
As expected, the frequency of activation of the thematic N+X concept
varies as follows: fishing version > hiking version. However, for the
N+1 concept activation we obtained: fishing version with fishing theme
(B) > fishing version (A) > hiking version with fishing theme (D) >
hiking version (C).

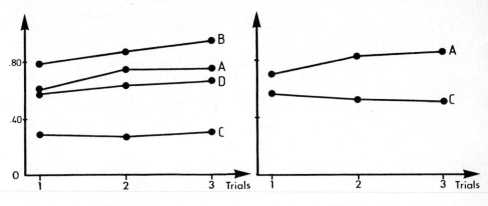

Figure 3a

Mean degree of activation
of the N+1 concepts

Figure 3 b

Mean degree of activation
of the N+X concept

An analysis of variance confirms that both effect of text version and
number of trials on the N+1 concept activation are significant (p < .001).
There was no version x trials interaction effect.

The N+1 concept activation is also better for the fishing version with
fishing theme (B) than for the fishing version (A) (p < .001), and for
the hiking version with fishing theme (D) than for the hiking version (C)
(p < .001).

As far as the previous comparisons are concerned, the versions differ only
on one point: whether or not the text contains information that insures
N+X concept activation. Moreover, we can see that thematic activation is
effectively realized if we examine the mean results reported in Figure 3b.
The increase in the N+1 concept activation from the fishing version to
the fishing version with fishing theme, on the one hand, and from the
hiking version to the hiking version with fishing theme, on the other,
thus can only be attributed to the increase in the N+X concept activation.
This is what we wanted to demonstrate, namely, that the N+1 concept activation, together with determining the informative content, both result
from the activation of the base concepts (N) and of the thematic concept
(N+X).

VERTICAL COORDINATION AT THE DIFFERENT LEVELS OF THE CONCEPTUAL HIERARCHY.
EFFICIENCY OF N+1 RETRIEVAL CUES

We can now attempt to answer the third question: Is there any relation
between the degree of activation of the N+1 concepts and their efficiency
as retrieval cues for the text?

After reading the text and answering the six questions corresponding to
the six paragraphs, each subject in each of the six experimental groups
was asked to recall the text. The six N+1-level concepts corresponding
to the fishing version were used as retrieval cues. Here, we shall only

consider the results of the four groups of subjects who encoded the N+1
cues, i.e., subjects who had to make a decision about the N+1 concepts
corresponding to each paragraph.

For each subject and for each of the three trials, we noted the items of
text information (base concepts) retrieved. We considered only text information common to the four versions A, B, C, and D of the text (12
information items). Two kinds of analysis were performed: first on the
cued recall of the first trial alone, then on all three trials together;
secondly, on the relations between the cued recall and the degree of
activation of the N+1 concepts estimated in the previous experiment.

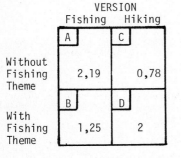

For the first trial
(Max. = 12)

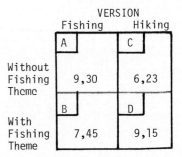

For all three trials
(Max. = 36)

Table 1

Mean number of base concepts recalled per subject

For the first trial, the only significant effect (p < .001) is the interaction between the two factors: in the case of the fishing version, the
text without the fishing theme provides the best results; in the case of
the hiking version, on the contrary, the text with the theme condition is
better retrieved.

The same interaction may be seen (p < .05) when we total the performance
on all three trials. Number of trials is also significant. We can see
here that the efficiency of the N+1 concept as retrieval cues appreciably
differs from one text condition to another.

For a better view of these variations we have shown in Figure 4, the mean
values of the cued recall on the first trial (Y axis) in terms of mean
values of the degree of activation of the N+1 concepts (X axis).

We find that the efficiency of the N+1 concepts as cues is highest for an
average degree of activation (about .50). This is true for both conditions,
the fishing version without fishing theme (A) and the hiking version with
fishing theme (D).

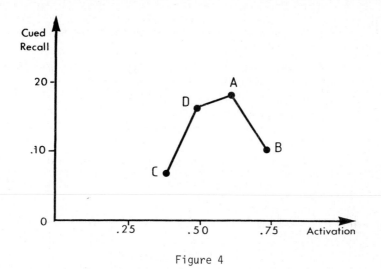

Figure 4

First trial: Mean proportion of base concepts recalled in terms of degree of activation of the N+1 concepts.

On the other hand, the efficiency of the N+1 concepts as cues is low when their degree of activation is also low -- the hiking version without fishing theme (C) -- or when their degree of activation is high -- the fishing version with fishing theme (B). The reason for this is that in the case of the hiking version without fishing theme (C) the text is barely understood, and the base concepts (N) are difficult to reduce into N+1 concepts corresponding to the fishing version. As a result, the degree of activation of the N+1 concepts is low as well as their efficiency as cues. In the case of the fishing version with fishing theme (B), the activation of the N+1 concepts is not problematic (high degree of activation). But this activation is produced more by the N+X thematic concept than by the base concepts (N) of the text.

In other words, the subject builds a text representation at a high hierarchical level by coordinating the N+1 and N+X concepts, which is certainly a good strategy for comprehension of the text. Yet at the same time, he does not take into account the base concepts. Hence, such a strategy prevents him from recovering them afterwards and therefore is bad for memorizing the text.

The efficiency, as retrieval cues, of the N+1 concepts is greatest when activation and coordination of the concepts occurs at the three hierarchical levels N, N+1, and N+2. The conditions which seem to be optimal are those of medium difficulty: the fishing version without fishing theme (A) and the hiking version with fishing theme (D). These are conditions in which the N+1 concepts cannot be activated without considering simultaneously the N and N+X concepts.

CONCLUSION

Briefly, as far as the texts in this study are concerned (whose semantic content consists of a group of hierarchical concepts), the building of a text representation shows the following characteristics:

1. While reading or listening, textual information activates both the base concepts (N) and the superordinate concepts (N+1, N+2,...N+X) as well. In the best case the subjects are able to grasp the highest thematic concept (N+X) as soon as they read the first paragraph. However, they are not able to anticipate the N+1 and N+2 concepts which refer to later paragraphs (Experiment I).

2. There are complex interactions between the concepts activated at different levels of the conceptual hierarchy. We have shown that the activation of a N+1 concept was highly dependent on the activation of the N base concepts of a paragraph as well as on the activation of the N+X thematic concept (Experiment II).

3. Generally speaking, text comprehension and recall require a vertical coordination of the N, N+1, and N+X concepts which are activated at different levels of the hierarchy of concepts. This coordination may be complete (comprising all three levels of the hierarchy) or partial. An N+1 concept is an efficient retrieval cue for a paragraph only if complete coordination can be achieved, especially, a coordination of the base concepts N and of the N+1 concept corresponding to each paragraph. This vertical coordination of the concepts causes difficulties with texts which are either too difficult or too easy to understand (Experiment II).

REFERENCES

Ehrlich, S.   Semantic memory: a free-elements system.   In C.R. Puff (Ed.), Memory, organization and structure.   New York: Academic Press, 1979.

Ehrlich, S.   Un aspect du fonctionnement de la mémoire sémantique: la construction d'une représentation de texte par niveaux hiérarchisés. Bulletin de Psychologie, Numéro spécial (in press).

Kintsch, W., & van Dijk, T.A.   Toward a model of text comprehension and production.   Psychological Review, 1978, 85, 363-394.

Mandler, J.M.   A code in the node: the use of a story schemata in retrieval.   Discourse Processes, 1978, 1, 14-35.

Schank, R. & Abelson, R.   Scripts, plans, goals and understanding: An inquiry in human knowledge and structures.   Hillsdale, N.J.: Lawrence Erlbaum Associates, 1977.

DISCOURSE PROCESSING
A. Flammer and W. Kintsch (eds.)
© *North-Holland Publishing Company, 1982*

THAT'S IMPORTANT BUT IS IT INTERESTING? TWO FACTORS
IN TEXT PROCESSING

Suzanne Hidi, William Baird and Angela Hildyard[1]
Ontario Institute for Studies in Education
Toronto, Canada

This paper examines the characteristics of different text
types used in natural school settings and relates some of
these characteristics to children's ability to recall the
texts. Our findings suggest that while interesting information in narratives also tends to be important, the same
is not true for expositions. For one type of exposition
(mixed texts) where narrative elements were included in the
expositions, interesting and important information was found
to be unrelated; in the other type of exposition, where no
intrusions occurred, the material was generally not considered very interesting. These differences in text types
were found to be related to differential recall by children.

INTRODUCTION

Recent research on how meaningful prose materials are remembered has focused
on narrative texts. Some of the narratives investigated have been stories
passed from one generation to the other in the oral tradition like Indian
folk stories or fairy-tales (Bartlett, 1932; Bower, 1976; Brown & Smiley,
1977; Kintsch, 1977; Mandler, Scribner, Cole & DeForest, 1980; Rumelhart,
1975). Others have been taken from well known literary sources like
Boccaccio's Decameron (Kintsch, 1977) or O'Flaherty's The Sniper (Johnson,
this volume). In addition, a great deal of research has been based on narratives which were constructed by researchers for experimental purposes
(Bower, this volume; Bower & Black, 1977; Stein & Glenn, 1979; Stein &
Nezworski, 1978).

It is easy to explain the over-representation of narratives as text materials in memory research. In contrast to other literary forms such as
expositions, opinion essays, descriptions, etc., narratives deal primarily
with living beings (humans or animals) and we seem to have special sets of
strategies to remember the temporally sequential goal-directed actions and
causal events that are normally associated with the lives of experiencing
and purposive subjects (Kintsch, 1980; Lichtenstein & Brewer, 1980). It
has also been amply demonstrated that good stories have well defined structures (episodes or plot units which can be further subdivided into structural categories) and that the representations of such structural units
guide the encoding and subsequent recall of the texts (Bower, 1976;
Haberlandt, Berian & Sandson, 1980; Kintsch, Mandel & Kozminisky, 1977;
Mandler & Johnson, 1977; Stein & Nezworski, 1978).

It is paradoxical that while memory research on meaningful materials has focused on narratives, from an educational point of view memory for genres other than stories is most crucial. Although children deal with narratives in school--usually in the language arts programs--the great majority of information that they are expected to acquire through their readings is presented to them in some form of expository prose.

In our study, we explicitly wanted to look at the types of texts that elementary school children naturally encounter in their classrooms and libraries. We had to find materials that were of comparable complexity because, in addition to examining some of the characteristics of the texts, we wanted to see how children recall these different types of texts. After a somewhat extensive but fruitless search we came across a recent study by Kirkwood and Wolfe (1980) who assessed through the Cloze procedure (Bormuth, 1967, 1968) the readability of text materials currently in use in the Ontario school system. This large-scale investigation (over 7,000 students were involved) evaluated grade 4, 7, and 10 materials found in language arts and social sciences. We were fortunate enough to gain access to the evaluated text materials and selected six passages from the grade 4 materials, each about 230 words in length.[2]

Aside from comparable scores on the readability measures our selection criterion was somewhat intuitive. Reading through the materials we noticed that there were some story-type narratives (usually in the language arts materials), some expositions that dealt primarily with facts, explanation and/or instructions and a third, "mixed" category which we perceived as expositions containing some narrative episodes or elements. These narrative elements frequently seemed intended by the curriculum writers not so much to convey essential information as to maintain children's attention and interest. For example, in one text that dealt with diving and the limitations of ancient and earlier divers who had to rely on their own lung powers, the following episode was included:

> There is a legend that, twenty-two centuries ago,
> Alexander the Great descended into the sea in an
> airtight box to observe the creatures there. This
> story may well be true, even if we doubt the rest
> of the tale--that he saw a fish so huge that it
> took three days to swim past although it was moving
> as swiftly as a flash of lightning. This sea mon-
> ster must have been a billion and a half miles long.
> Some fish!

Clearly, the function of this episode is to entertain more than to convey essential information about diving which is to be remembered. The important question about these types of texts is not so much whether children recall the interesting episodes, but how these non-essential episodes influence the retention of the other, essential information.

The six selected texts (two from each category) are listed in Table 1 together with a short summary description of each. To examine the validity of our three categories we asked five graduate students to rank the six texts from the most story-like to the least story-like. These rankings are also included in Table 1. No statistical analysis is needed to conclude that our categories are supported by the rankings. The narratives were

Table 1

Description of the Selected Six Texts

Narratives

Toad   Introduces Hector the dog and old Toad and narrates a fight between them and its aftermath.

Hobo   Introduces a hobo living in Paris and describes how one day he finds three little children hiding in his "hidey-hole".

Mixed Texts

Divers   Discusses diving and explains the limitations of ancient divers who had to rely on their own lung power rather than using some form of breathing-gear. Includes an anecdote about Alexander the Great's adventures in the sea.

Easter Island   Describes geographical and archaeological characteristics of an island in the Pacific. Includes some specific details of what the island's ancestors did, e.g. dragged some huge statues 13 kilometres and fought a war between slender and stout people.

Expositions

Orienting the Map   Explains and instructs the usage of maps.

Electricity   Explains the characteristics of good and bad conductors, the dangers of electricity and how to avoid being shocked or electrocuted.

Ranking of the Texts from Most Story-like to Least Story-like

---

	Rates				
	A	B	C	D	E
Old Toad	2	2	1	2	1
The Hobo	1	1	2	1	2
Divers	3	3	3	3	4
Easter Island	4	4	4	4	3
Orienting Map	5	5	5	5	5
Electricity	6	6	6	6	6

A - E are rankings of five graduate students.
1 - 6 goes from most story-like to least story-like.

considered most story-like and the expositions least story-like. Our contention that the mixed texts had some narrative components was further
supported by several raters who commented that the two mixed texts were
somehow between the stories and the "non-stories".[3]

Before we proceed to describe our study, we would like to discuss one more
point pertaining to the selected materials. The texts that we have been
working with, while ecologically valid, are not particularly well organized
or well formed, nor do they have distinguishing rhetorical styles. However,
it may be that the encoding and retrieval of these text types differ from
both qualitatively better literary texts or texts that are constructed by
researchers for laboratory investigations. Specifying the characteristics
of these text types and their effect on subjects' recall is essential if
we want to understand how children process school materials and to be able
to advise educators on how to write better curriculum materials (see also
Pearson, 1981).

The procedure of the study involves two distinct parts. First, the texts
were rated by adults and secondly, grade 5 and grade 7 children were asked
to recall the passages and the results were related to the adult ratings.
We will first discuss the text analyses resulting from the ratings and then
report on the memory experiment.

TEXT ANALYSES

We were primarily concerned with the relation between important and interesting information in the three text types.

First, groups of five adults (graduate students) for each text were asked
to evaluate how essential information was. They were given the original
texts and asked to underline the information they found "essential", that
is, information that was most important to understanding the text. They
were also asked to cross out "inessential", that is, unimportant information.

Secondly, the same raters were asked to rate the texts for saliency, in the
same manner. Each rater received a different text for each of two ratings.
They were asked to underline the most interesting segments of the text and
to cross out the most boring, least interesting segments. Thus, for both
sets of ratings, we had three types of evaluative segments: underlined,
unmarked and crossed out. For each rating the raters were encouraged to
first preread the texts.

To compare and relate the two sets of ratings we had to assign the evaluations to a common textual segmentation. Consequently, each text was parsed
into idea units following procedures used by Johnson, 1970; Brown & Smiley,
1977; Brown & Day, 1981. Operationally, an idea unit was defined as a main
clause plus any related subordinate clauses or phrases which expressed self-
contained ideas. A few adjustments were made to the initial idea unit
parsing to accommodate clear boundaries generated by the evaluation of
essential and salient information which had been missed. Most of these
adjustments required the breaking up of no more than two units in any text
into two more elementary units.

To derive the "essentiality" scores, each idea unit was given scores of
1, 2, 3 for underlined, unmarked and crossed out importance ratings respectively for each rater and then averaged over the five raters. (e.g. if all
five raters underlined an idea unit it received a score of 1.) In the
great majority of cases the evaluative rating-segments matched idea unit
boundaries, but in those cases where complex sentences received two
different ratings--the better essentiality rating (i.e., "lowest" score
1-3) was the one used to represent the entire idea unit.

To derive the "saliency" scores the same procedure was repeated as on the
essentiality ratings. Our rating procedures are somewhat similar to those
reported by Brown & Smiley, 1977, 1978; and Brown & Day, 1981. These
researchers parsed the texts so that each line included a single idea unit.
Raters repeatedly eliminated one quarter of the least important idea units
until the final remaining quartile, which was considered to be the most
important. Our method differed from Brown et al. in that we did not parse
the texts in advance and raters scored the texts on a single reading
following a preview.

Now, turning to our results, the correlations between the essentiality and
saliency scores of each idea unit are shown in Table 2 together with the
percentage of idea units considered really interesting and important
(idea units having average of 1-1.4 scores).

Table 2

Correlations of Essentiality and Salience Ratings of Different Text
Types and Percentage of Idea Units Rated Essential and Salient

	Correlation Between Essentiality and Salience Ratings	Percentage of Idea Units Judged*	
Narratives		Essential/ Important	Salient/ Interesting
A Toad	.638	39%	30%
B Hobo	.778	43%	43%
Mixed Texts			
C Divers	.153	50%	31%
D Easter Island	.005	25%	30%
Expositions			
E Orienting the Map	.643	33%	0%
F Electricity	.517	42%	5%

* Idea units which had an average score of 1-1.4 on the essentiality and
  the saliency ratings were included.

The high correlations (r = .64, .78) show that in the narratives the most interesting idea units tend to be also important. In the mixed texts, however, no relation seems to exist between saliency and essentiality (r = .15, .01). Finally, looking at the factual expositions, the reasonably high correlations (r = .64, .52) are misleading, since practically no ideas were found to be very interesting in this category by our raters (0 and 5%). Thus, the correlations only indicate that the moderately interesting ideas tend to be more important than the least interesting ones.

These data clearly show that there are significant differences between the relationship of importance and interestingness in the three text types. Two hypotheses, both warranting further investigation, may be put forth on the basis of these results. First, it may be an inherent characteristic of good stories that the most interesting information also tends to be important. This relation between essentiality and saliency may contribute, as do the structural features and temporal frames of stories, to our ability to recall narratives better than many other types of texts. Bower (this volume), reports that the more unusual or novel a particular text segment, the more likely people consider it important. He was reporting on narrative texts. These results seem to corroborate our findings that importance and saliency correlate highly in narratives. The same does not seem to be true for our other two text types. Second, perhaps one major problem with expository texts is that it is difficult to produce expositions in which the important/essential and interesting/salient information converge.

RECALL

Twenty-seven grade 5 and twenty-eight grade 7 children participated in this part of the study. Each subject received only one of the six texts; the texts were distributed randomly. The children were asked to read the passages until they would be able to recall them; the time spent reading the texts was self-controlled. As a child signalled that he was finished, the text was collected, the time was marked and the child was asked to recall the passage as close to its original form as possible in a written form (Immediate recall). Four days later we returned to the school and tested the children again. We reminded them of our previous encounter and asked them to write down everything that they recalled from the passage (Delayed recall). Each child was given a blank sheet to write on, which had the original title of their passage as a cue (e.g., Divers).

The data, in summary, includes immediate and delayed recall for two grades, 5 and 7, for six different texts in three categories.

The recall protocols were compared with the original texts. Two raters independently assessed whether or not an idea unit from the original text was present in the recall, either in a verbatim or paraphrase form (interrater reliability was 92%). Analyses were then conducted on proportional recall scores (number of idea units recalled divided by number of idea units in the original text) for both the Delayed and Immediate recall conditions.

The Immediate recall scores don't show any significant grade or text differences although, not surprisingly, narratives tend to be recalled best.

The Delayed recall scores show an interaction between age and text types. In grade 5 differences are small between text types--narratives tend to be recalled best--in Grade 7, however, differences are much larger, more than double essential idea units being recalled in narratives than in the mixed texts. Expositions place approximately half way between the other two categories. The slopes of lines in Figure 1 also illustrate that while the decay (differences between Immediate and Delayed recall) ranges between 40%-50% in grade 5 for all text types, in grade 7 there is no decay for narratives (actually recall slightly increases over time), 20% for expositions and over 50% for the mixed texts. These results suggest that grade 7 children concentrate on salient ideas in the mixed texts and they either don't store or cannot retrieve over delay the essential idea units the same way as when interesting ideas correlate with essentiality.

To further demonstrate the above point, Figure 2 compares the delayed recall of essential and non-essential idea units. This figure clearly illustrates the significant differences we found between text types. In the case of narratives and expositions, a greater proportion of essential idea units were recalled than non-essential idea units. In the case of the mixed texts there was no difference between the two categories in grade 5 and a reverse trend was found at grade 7, 50% more non-essential idea units being recalled than essential ones.

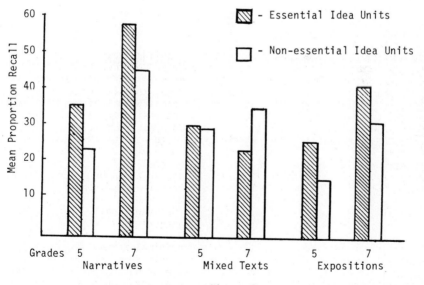

Figure 2
Comparison of Essential and Non-Essential Idea Units--Delayed Recall

Paradoxically, these findings indicate that if essential ideas are to be retained over a period of time it may be better to give children somewhat boring expositions rather than texts that mix interesting and important information in an unrelated manner.

Intrusions comprised less than 10% of total recall, and were equally distributed over different texts and groups, therefore not encouraging further
analysis. Also, reading time did not show group differences as a covariate.

In addition, we computed the number of words recalled over the number of
words in the original texts. The correlation between this proportion and
the proportion of idea units recalled was .93 for immediate and .94 for
delayed recall. This finding corroborates some of our previous results
(Hidi & Hildyard, 1980) showing extremely high correlations between word
counts and propositional counts in natural texts.

As our main interest focused on how well the most essential information of
the different text types was retained, we separated the proportional recall
score of each subject for the essential idea units (idea units which had
an average score of 1-1.4 on the essentiality ratings) and the non-essential
idea units (idea units which had an average score of 1.5-3 on the essentiality ratings). Figure 1 shows the mean proportion of the essential idea
units recalled of the three text types for the Immediate and Delayed recall
conditions.

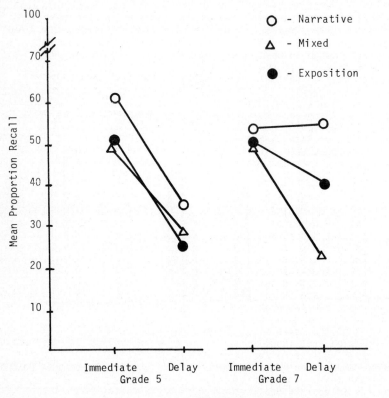

Figure 1
Mean Proportion Recall of Essential Idea Units

GENERAL DISCUSSION

The differential recall of the three text types by grade 5 and 7 students over a four day delay suggests differential processing of the texts. The important finding is that our subjects recalled essential information better than non-essential information only in narratives and expositions. With mixed texts there was no trend to recall the crucial information differentially from the rest of the text, suggesting that the children did not focus on the essential/important segments of the materials.

Why did our subjects do so poorly with the mixed texts? How did the narrative elements interfere with the comprehension and/or recall of the essential/important text segments?

If a series of propositions occur in a text that is not clearly related to previous and subsequent information, a distance is created between the two bordering essential propositions. This distance can only be bridged in memory storage by eliminating the trivial unrelated proposition. Brown, Campione & Day (1981), and Brown & Day (1981), claim even young children can delete trivial information. However, these researchers used expositions especially written by them for experimental purposes and thus it is unlikely that the trivial segments that had to be eliminated were highly salient. In our mixed texts, trivial information was sometimes very interesting and children had problems deleting these segments. Thus, it seems that it is not enough to have content knowledge to enable one to recognize and eliminate trivia. If the trivial information is highly salient it may interfere with the normal selection strategies of text processing.

Previous research has shown that if stories violate some of the structural expectations of the genre, then the texts are harder to comprehend and are more readily forgotten (Bower, 1976; Thorndyke, 1977). Analogously, it seems that if we violate some of the structural expectations of expositions-- at least at the ages when children are just getting acquainted with the expository genres, the same patterns of decreased comprehension and recall may emerge.

Given that the salient/interesting segments which violate the structure of an exposition are of another genre type than the rest of the text (e.g. narrative elements in an exposition), additional problems may arise. Kintsch (1980) argued that understanding text is an act of problem solving, (cf. Schank & Abelson, 1977 and Black & Bower, 1980) and that in this problem solving approach text-type specific structures and characteristics play a crucial role. Therefore, aiding our comprehension of stories, expositions, opinion essays, etc. is a set of genre-specific problem solving strategies which identify, locate and organize the incoming information in accordance with our general knowledge about the structure of the particular genre. For example, when something unexpected happens in a story, our story-specific problem solving strategies help us identify the curious event as the conflict or complication. Now, imagine that you are reading an exposition about scientific matter, like the breathing problems of ancient divers, and suddenly an unexpected, interesting anecdote about Alexander the Great appears in the text. The genre-specific problem solving strategies which have been set in gear to deal with expositions are looking for the traditional elements of scientific expositions such as causal and functional analyses, identifications, classifications and definitions, etc. (Kintsch, 1980) and may have to struggle to help comprehend such an unexpected and incongruous

input as a narrative anecdote. What may be required to guide and control
comprehension at this point are specific narrative problem solving strategies. Obviously, problems may be created either by having our young readers
switch back and forth between genre-specific strategies or by requiring
them to deal with unexpected information with inappropriate strategies.

According to the Kintsch and Van Dijk (1978) model, text comprehension is
an automatic cyclical process which has normally low resource requirements.
In each cycle certain propositions are retained in the short-term buffer
to be connected with the input of the next cycle. If sequential propositions are unrelated, no connections can be made and resource consuming
search or inference operations are required which result in noticeable
deterioration of performance.

In our mixed texts, where trivial information is not readily discardable,
serious interruptions may occur in the automatic process. The macro-
operators that transform the text base into a set of macropropositions
representing the gist of the text are seriously interfered with by the
highly salient, trivial information. The result of such interference seems
to be a shift between the macrostructure intended by the curriculum writer
(containing all of the important text segments) and those abstracted by
the readers (containing few of the important text segments). The conclusion that macrostructures are effected by the characteristics of mixed
text is also supported by the fact that while little effect of mixed text
is apparent on immediate recall, large differences appear after delay.
Macrostructures are presumed to be the structures responsible for long-term
memory while microstructures are presumed to have a central role in short-
term memory storage.

In the above discussion, we implied that the more salient the structurally
interfering information is, the more likely it is to disrupt normal processing. We seem to be dealing with an affective component of texts which can
be dealt with independently of structural considerations. This highly
neglected aspect of text processing is only now starting to emerge in the
memory research of meaningful prose.

Bower (this volume), for example, reports on the role of novel, interesting
information in narrative texts. Anderson (this volume) also looks at the
effect of saliency in sentence processing.

In a recent paper, Brewer (1981) presented a structural-affect theory which
relates certain discourse structures to particular affective states and
then related these two factors to story enjoyment. The affective component
is presumed to capture the fact that stories entertain through evoking
affects such as suspense, surprise and curiosity. While these categories
can be easily tied to structural properties of stories, relating affective
components to discourse structures in other genres is much more tentative.
For example, mixed texts of the kind we looked at have no clear cut structural relations that could be readily related to affective states and interesting information seems to compete with important information that is
structurally based.

Our results suggest that in addition to specifying the structure of text
(Meyer, 1981), we must also consider saliency relations, i.e. how saliency
interacts with structural considerations. These patterns may be crucial
to comprehension and subsequent recall of text.

Footnotes

[1]Partial support for this paper was provided by the Ontario Institute for Studies in Education.

[2]Kirkwood and Wolfe (1980) reported that in general the texts were too difficult at the grade levels they were used at. Since we wanted to test grade 5 and grade 7 children we felt comfortable using grade 4 materials.

[3]Our narrative and exposition categories bear a resemblance to Nancy Marshall's (this volume) distinction of temporal and topical categories and Brewer's (1981) distinction between the time series thrust of narration and the logical thrust of exposition.

References

Anderson, R.C. Allocation of attention during reading. This volume.

Bartlett, F.C. Remembering: A study in experimental and social psychology.
        Cambridge, England: Cambridge University Press, 1932.

Black, J.B. and Bower, G.H. Story understanding as problem solving.
        Poetics, 1980, 9, 223-250.

Bormuth, J.R. Comparable close and multiple-choice comprehension test
        scores. Journal of Reading, 1967, 10, 291-299.

Bormuth, J.R. Close test readability: Criterion reference score.
        Journal of Educational Measurement, 1968, 5(3), 189-196.

Bower, G.H. Experiments on story understanding and recall.
        Quarterly Journal of Experimental Psychology, 1976, 28, 511-534.

Bower, G.H. Plan-goal processes in narrative understanding. This volume.

Bower, G.H. and Black, J.B. Action schemata in story comprehension and
        memory. Paper presented at the American Psychological Associa-
        tion annual meeting, San Francisco, 1977.

Brewer, W.F. The structure of stories in western culture: Cross-
        cultural implications. Paper presented at the OISE conference
        on the nature and consequences of literacy, St. Mary, Canada,
        October, 1981.

Brown, A.L., Campione, J.C., and Day, J.D. Learning to learn: On training
        students to learn from texts. Educational Researcher, 1981,
        10(2).

Brown, A.L. and Day, J.D. Strategies and knowledge for summarizing texts:
        The development of expertise. Unpublished manuscript, 1981.

Brown, A.L. and Smiley, S.S. The development of strategies for studying
        texts. Child Development, 1978, 49, 1076-1088.

References (Cont'd)

Brown, A.L. and Smiley, S.S. Rating the importance of structural units of
    prose passages: A problem of metacognitive development.
    Child Development, 1977, 48, 1-8.

Haberlandt, K., Berian, C., and Sandson, F. The episode schema in store
    processing. Journal of Verbal Learning and Verbal Behavior,
    1980, 19, 635-650.

Hidi, S. and Hildyard, A. The comparison of oral and written productions
    of two discourse types. Paper presented at the annual meeting
    of the American Educational Research Association, Boston,
    April 1980.

Johnson, R.E. Prose learnings: How escapeth thee from the porous storage
    vault? This volume.

Johnson, R.E. Recall of prose as a function of the structural importance
    of the linguistic units. Journal of Verbal Behavior, 1970, 9,
    12-20.

Kintsch, W. On comprehending stories. In P. Carpenter & M. Just (Eds.),
    Cognitive processes in comprehension. Hillsdale, N.J.:
    Erlbaum, 1977.

Kintsch, W. Text representations. Paper presented at the conference on
    reading expository materials, Madison, Wisconsin, November 1980.

Kintsch, W., Mandel, T.S., and Kosminsky, E. Summarizing scrambled
    stories. Memory and Cognition, 1977, 5(5), 547-552.

Kintsch, W. and Van Dijk, T.A. Toward a model of text comprehension and
    production. Psychological Review, Sept. 1978, 85(5), 363-394.

Kirkwood, K.J. and Wolfe, R.G. Matching students and reading materials:
    A cloze-procedure method for assessing the reading ability of
    students and the readability of textual materials. Toronto:
    OISE Publications, 1980.

Lichtenstein, E.H. and Brewer, W.F. Memory for goal-directed events.
    Cognitive Psychology, 1980, 12, 412-445.

Mandler, J.M. and Johnson, N.S. Remembrance of things parsed: Story
    structure and recall. Cognitive Psychology, 1977, 9, 111-151.

Mandler, J.M., Scribner, S., Cole, M., and De Forest, M. Cross-
    cultural invariance in story recall. Child Development,
    1980, 51, 19-26.

Marshall, N. The effects of temporality upon recall of expository prose.
    This volume.

References (Cont'd)

Meyer, B.J.F. Prose analysis: Procedures, purposes and problems. Paper
        presented at the American Educational Research Association
        convention, Los Angeles, April 1981.

Pearson, P.D. Analysis of text-flow structure in children's content area
        materials. (Technical Report). University of Illinois,
        in press.

Rumelhart, D.E. Notes on a schema for stories. In D. Bobrow and A. Collins
        (Eds.), Studies in cognitive science. New York: Academic Press,
        1975.

Schank, R.C. and Abelson, R. Scripts, plans, goals and understanding.
        Hillsdale, N.J.: Erlbaum, 1977.

Stein, N.L. and Glenn, C.G. An analysis of story comprehension in
        elementary school children. In R.D. Freedle (Ed.),
        New directions in discourse processing (Volume 2).
        New Jersey: Ablex Publishing Corp., 1979.

Stein, N.L. and Nezworski, T. The effects of organization and instruc-
        tional set on story memory. Discourse Processes, 1978, 1,
        177-193.

Thorndyke, P.W. Cognitive structures in comprehension and memory of
        narrative discourse. Cognitive Psychology, 1977, 9, 77-110.

DISCOURSE PROCESSING
A. Flammer and W. Kintsch (eds.)
© *North-Holland Publishing Company, 1982*

EXPECTANCY STRUCTURES IN PROSE READING

Margret Rihs-Middel

Department of Psychology
University of Fribourg
Fribourg
Switzerland

Analysis of reading time for sentences of two subsequently presented stories led to proposing two
types of expectancy structures affecting story processing; an expectancy structure assumed to stem
from knowledge acquired in a long-term learning
process and an expectancy structure developed on
the basis of an experience immediately preceding
story reading. Thorndyke's story grammar served as
operational tool in defining story structure.
A conceptual framework is presented proposing the
comparison of perceptive and expectancy structures,
the fusion of which yields a knowledge structure
stored in memory.

INTRODUCTION

Recent advances in prose research have underscored an increasing concern
with the processing and representation of coherent prose passages. The central
topic of this paper is the question what types of anticipation play a role
in reader's processing. Text processing is generally viewed as the encoding
of a given text into already existing knowledge structures (Bock, 1978) a
process Norman (1978) labelled "acretion". The notion of preprocessed
knowledge structures has been an important issue in artificial intelligence
(Minsky, 1975; Schank and Abelson, 1977). Whereas Bock tends towards the
view that a given prose passage is reorganized by the reader around an
organizational node and subsequently stored in memory, the artificial
intelligence people seem to assume that each incoming bit of information is
directly incorporated into a heavily preprocessed structure such as a
frame or script. According to this point of view anticipation does not
seem to be an active ongoing process but rather a well-organized data
base.

Thorndyke (1975, 1977) seems to subscribe to the artificial intelligence
point of view by postulating a story grammar that may as well be written
as a frame structure (1975). The story grammar, in his view, serves as
an expectancy structure that equips the reader with a hierarchical
organization permitting a more efficient storage of the written material.
Thorndyke was able to support these notions using recall measures as the
dependant variable.

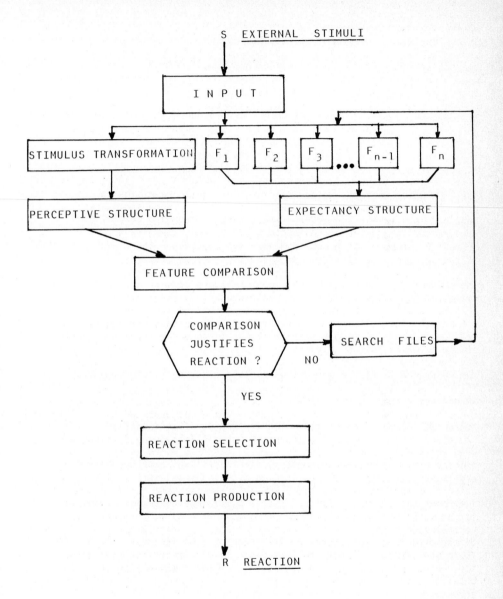

S   EXTERNAL STIMULI

I N P U T

STIMULUS TRANSFORMATION F_1 F_2 F_3 ... F_{n-1} F_n

PERCEPTIVE STRUCTURE   EXPECTANCY STRUCTURE

FEATURE COMPARISON

COMPARISON
JUSTIFIES
REACTION ?   SEARCH FILES

NO

YES

REACTION SELECTION

REACTION PRODUCTION

R   REACTION

$F_1 - F_n$: MEMORY FILES

Figure 1

Process model for the simultaneous build-up of perceptive structures and
expectancy structures.

Whether the focus of prose research should rather be on text paraphrasing
or on pre-established knowledge structures seems to depend on the type of
prose studied, on the previous knowledge of the reader, on the nature of the
reading assignment, and on the researcher's inclination towards linguistics,
memory research or artificial intelligence. It appears to me, however, that
both aspects deserve further consideration.

Giving each aspect its merit, I would like to present some suggestions about
what is going on during reading. I assume that the reader creates two types
of structures during reading, called perceptive structures and expectancy
structures. The perceptive structure is assumed to reflect the reading
process as it proceeds from left to right and from one proposition to the
next. Complementary to the perceptive structure, an expectancy structure is
built up which reflects which aspects of his prior knowledge the reader
brings into play to understand what he is reading. Both structures are
combined in a comparison process which is guided by the reader's
preferences, priorities, and mathemagenic options. The result of the
comparison process is stored in memory and contains the perceived deviations
of the perceptive structure from the expectancy structure.

The present work focusses on the role of expectancy structures in fairy
tales. It is assumed that a fairy-tale-specific expectancy structure is
created as soon as the reader perceives an opening line like "once upon
a time...". This element of the perceptive structure evokes well-ordered
sets of elements in memory that are combined according to the requirements
of the actual situation to form the expectancy structure. Ratcliff (1978)
has described a similar process for the retrieval of a probe item from a
memory set. Rihs (1982) has discussed this process in more detail.
Figure 1 illustrates the simultaneous build-up of perceptive and expectancy
structures.

It becomes clear from the flow-diagram that deviations of the perceptive
structure from the expectancy structure should lead to a slow-down of
reading, since a more exhaustive memory search is needed in order to
produce a better fitting expectancy structure. I do assume, however, that
expectancy structures for very common types of text, such as fairly tales,
are rather stereotyped and are commonly present as the first line of text
is processed. The story teller in this type of prose usually observes a
set of rules with respect to the setting, course of possible action,
general structure, outcome, and style. These rules are assumed to correspond
to the expectancy structures of the reader. Since the rules formulated by
Thorndyke (1975, 1977) proved to be effective in predicting retention,
the present work focusses on the question whether these same rules have
predictive value when they are used to represent the reader's expectancy
structures.

Another facet of an individual expectancy structure is assumed to stem from
those experiences that immediately precede the reading of a given text.
If the preceding situation has elements in common with the actual reading
situation the prior experience might have the same properties as an adaptation level and brings the reader into a state of mind against which the new
experience is contrasted. An experiment was designed to test separately
the influence of these two types of expectancy, namely:

- the influence of knowledge structures acquired in a long-term learning process; and
- the influence of an experience immediately preceding the reading of a given text.

METHOD

60 social science students participated in this study on a voluntary basis.

Materials
two fairy tales of the Grimm brothers were modified using Thorndyke's story grammar in order to provide an identical structure for both stories. The first story was either presented according to story grammar structure or in a scrambled version with the story sentences being randomly assigned to presentation position. The second story was either shown according to story grammar structure or with the concluding sentence being presented instead of sentence Nr. 18, low in the hierarchy, or instead of sentence Nr. 22, high in the hierarchy (see Figure 3). All of the presented sentences were made identical with respect to number of words (8) and number of syllables (12). In both stories, all versions contained the same 25 sentences with only presentation position altered.

Apparatus
A Kodak Carrousel Slide Projector served for stimulus presentation on a conventional projection screen. In front of the subjects there was a board with three response buttons. The pressing of any of these buttons resulted in the projection of the next sentence. Responses were measured by an electonic stop watch, scale 1/100 second.

Procedure
The students sat in a booth visually separated from the experimenter. There was only one reader at a time. The instructions were read aloud. The students were instructed to press the green button when they felt that they understood the projected sentence quite well, to press the yellow button when they felt something was not clear, and to press the read button when they had a question with respect to the projected sentence. They were asked to try out the mechanism first and to press any of the buttons. Then, the 25 sentences of the first story were presented without interruption. Afterwards, those sentences that had led to ambiguous responses were presented again and the students had to explain what bothered them. The procedure for the second story was the same. Presentation of the second story followed immediately after the questioning of the students. The interval between the slide change and subjects' button pressing was taken as the reaction time. The reciprocal reaction time (1 / reaction time in seconds) was defined as reaction speed.

RESULTS AND DISCUSSION

The sentences of the first story were taken together in order to form groups of five sentences according to presentation position. The means of the reciprocal reaction times for the coherent and the scrambled presentation group are shown in Figure 2. A split-plot design was used for

analysis of data. Examination of the simple main effects proved the
repetition factor to be significant with F= 3.75; P<.01 (df = 4) for the
well-ordered condition and F= 12.28; P<.01 (df = 4) for the scrambled
condition. The between subjects comparison of the well-ordered with the
scrambled condition yields an F= 4.33; P<.05 for the single comparison
(df = 1).

According to these results the students in the well-ordered condition read
the first five sentences rather slowly, then speeded up their reading time
and read the last five sentences slowly again. The comparison of the first
five and the last five sentences with the sentences 6 to 20 by the Scheffé
test is significant with an F= 22.9; $F_{critical}$= 17.37 (for the .05 level).

These reaction speed results fit quite well the structure of the story
grammar underlying the two stories, since the first five sentences and the
last five sentences correspond to levels 1 and 2 of the story grammar
hierarchy whereas the middle 15 sentences correspond to the levels 3 and 4
of the story grammar (see Figure 3).

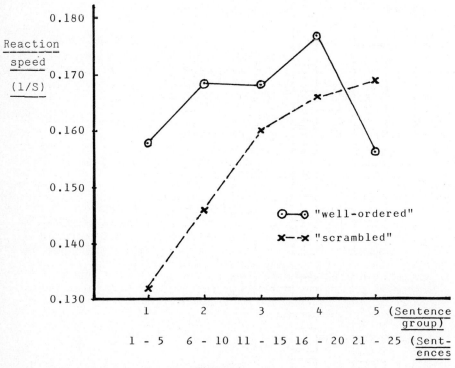

Figure 2

Means of reciprocal reaction times of first story as a function of
presentation order of the sentences.

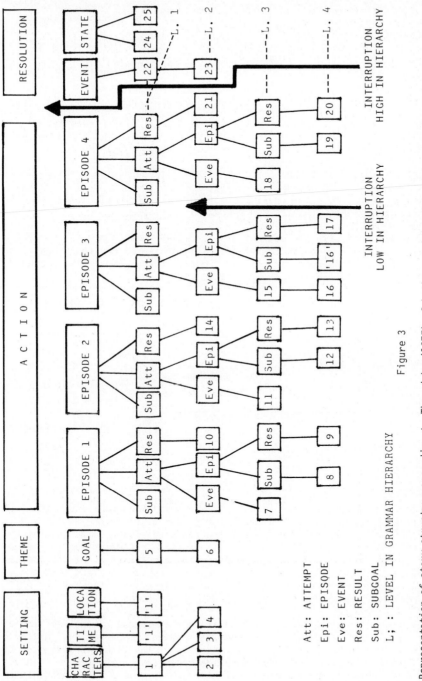

Figure 3

Att: ATTEMPT
Epi: EPISODE
Eve: EVENT
Res: RESULT
Sub: SUBGOAL
L; : LEVEL IN GRAMMAR HIERARCHY

Representation of story structure according to Thorndyke (1977) of both experimental stories; numbers refer to sentence numbers

In the scrambled condition, however, reaction speed is slowest during the first five sentences, then increases sharply over the sentences five to fifteen, whereas the increment is less for the last ten sentences. The comparison of sentences 1 - 5 with sentences 6 - 10, by the Tukey test, yields a significant q - value of 4.4; $q_{critical}$= 2.2 (for the .05 level). This is true also for the comparison of sentences 6 - 10 with sentences 11 - 15, with q = 4.3.

These findings support the notion that the students' reading of the well-ordered first story is guided by the expectancy structures constructed during the first sentences of the story which are combined during the last sentences to form the substrate of what might be stored in memory.

The interpretation of the data from the scrambled condition seems to imply the same process of constructing an expectancy structure which, in this particular case, amounts to making sense out of unconnected sentences and then trying to finish the task as quickly as possible.

In a further analysis, the data of the scrambled condition were rearranged in order to permit a comparison of identical sentences and 25 one-way analyses of variance were carried out. Four of these comparisons proved to be significant. They are shown in Table 1.

Table 1. Significant differences for sentences of the first story with
         identical content (wo = well-ordered, s = scrambled)

Sentence shown in position:		Mean Reaction Speed (1/S)		F - value	Error Probability
wo	s	wo	s		
8	5	0.179	0.128	15.5	0.01
14	22	0.183	0.146	5.1	0.05
16	3	0.184	0.143	8.7	0.01
20	2	0.176	0.134	9.7	0.01

The rather strinking general result that presentation order seems to affect the processing rate rather little for sentences with identical number of words and syllables, makes the few significant comparisons even more salient for theoretical considerations. As a matter of fact, three of the four significant differences refer to the first five sentences for the scrambled condition. This finding might be interpreted to mean that the first sentences of a text serve to set up an expectancy structure regardless of wether the text is coherent or scrambled.

It could also be suggested that the differential course of the reaction-speed curve for the scrambled and the well-ordered condition are just a matter of artefact. However, a close analysis of the first 17 sentences of the second story, where sentences and the presentation order were identical, would not support this argument, but rather point toward the hypothesis of

a build-up of two different types of expectancy structures during the
reading of the first story.

It becomes apparent from Figure 4 that subjects who first experienced a
well-structured story, read the subsequent story more slowly than those
subjects who first read a scrambled version of the same story. It looks as
if the faster processing of sentences, observed towards the end of the first
story under scrambled condition, carried over to the processing of the
second story. Students with a well-ordered first story, on the other hand,
seem to have processed the second story at just about the same pace as the
first story.

Considering the course of the two reaction speed curves shown in Figure 4,
one may conclude furthermore that the quality of processing does not seem
to be affected by diverse prior experience since ups and downs move along
similar lines for both conditions, with the basic difference in reaction
speed remaining rather constant. As for the analysis of variance, the first,
fifth, nineth and fifteenth sentence comparison are not significant, but
point in the same direction as the other 13 sentences. It might be argued
that the non-significant differences are due to a ceiling effect, since
reaction speeds of those four sentences are among the faster ones.

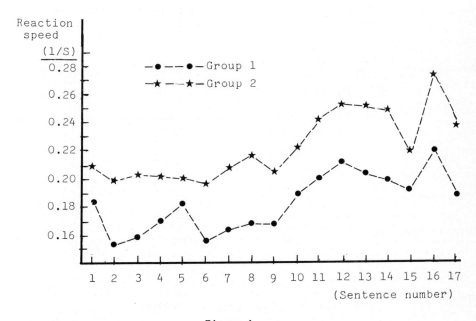

Figure 4

Means of the reaction speed measured during the presentation of the second
story for the sentences 1 - 17; the first story was either shown "well-
ordered" (Group 1) or "scrambled" (Group 2)

The impact on quality of processing by immediate and remote prior experience
was further studied in a two-way analysis of variance design. For this
purpose, the same concluding sentence had been presented either in terminal
position (TERMINAL), or instead of a sentence low in story grammar hierarchy
(LOW) or instead of a sentence high in story grammar hierarchy (HIGH). This
interruption factor together with the prior experience factor (well-ordered,
wo, and scrambled, sc) is depicted in Figure 5 with the mean reaction speeds
of the six groups as dependent measures.

Figure 5 shows that the group with a well-ordered story as prior experience
had - as already mentioned above - lower reaction speeds than the group
with a scrambled version as first story. Here, too, this type of effect
seems to be limited to the processing rate only, without affecting quality
of processing, since the interruption condition yields the same picture
for both prior experience conditions, i.e., reaction speed is highest in
terminal position, stays at rather fast levels for the "high in story
grammar condition", whereas it does decrease in the "low in story grammar"
condition.

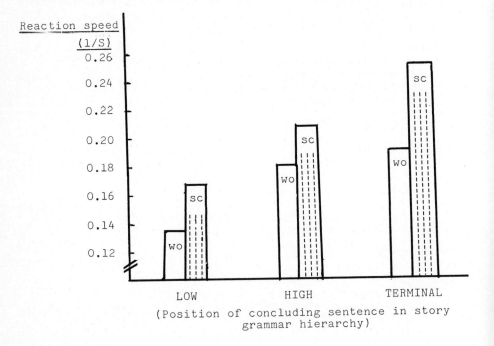

Figure 5

Mean reaction speed measured for terminal sentences placed at different
hierarchical positions in the second story; the first story was either shown
in a well-ordered (wo) or scrambled (sc) version

The prior experience factor proves to be significant in the two-way analysis of variance, with F= 6.1, and an error probabilty p= 0.017. The interruption factor is significant, too, with F= 6.2 and p= 0.004. There was no significant difference for the interaction between the two factors. Therefore, the comparison of means was analyzed for the interruption factor only. The difference found between terminal position and interruption low in story grammar hierarchy is significant. The interruption factor low versus high in story grammar hierarchy is not significant, but points to a trend in the opposite direction.

As illustrated in Figure 3, the interruption by the terminal sentence instead of a sentence high in story grammar hierarchy coincided with the end of the story. This might be the reason why reaction speed for the sentence in terminal position and high in story grammar hierarchy was rather similar.

The fact, however, that a terminal sentence of a rather unspecific nature "then finally the happy life began" seems to interfere with readers' expectancy for the next sentence in the middle part of the story, supports the notion of expectancy - guided reading in the middle part of the story. This type of expectancy is assumed to stem from knowledge structures acquired in a long-term learning process which, in this particular case, is not affected by an experience immediately preceding the reading of the story. Thus it is argued that two independent types of expectancy operated in the present case, an expectancy arising out of well established knowledge structures and an expectancy arising from an immediately preceding experience.

CONCLUDING REMARKS

Analysis of the data lend to support the following notions as far as story processing in this particular case is concerned.

1. During the first five sentences readers read the first story rather slowly, then speeded up during the middle section and read the last section more slowly again. This finding corresponds exactly to the hierarchical level of the story grammar shown in Figure 3 and is interpreted to imply the construction of a story-specific expectancy structure which subsequently is compared with the particular data read in and finally integrated to form a "ready-to-store" version of the story.

2. A scrambled version of the same text is read slowly in the beginning with a gradual speed-up for the rest of the story. This might be viewed as an expectancy structure building up during the first few sentences without a summing-up at the end of the story that represents a combination of expected and read material.

3. The response speed shown in the scranmbled version of the first story seems to carry over to the second story, since the second story is read consistently faster by the group that had a scrambled first story as compared to the group that had a well-ordered version of the first story. This illustrates one type of expectancy due to an immediately preceding experience. The first story is assumed to serve as a pace-setter for the

subsequent story.

4. Interruption of the course of the story as defined by the story grammar
led ot a significant decrease in reaction speed when the interruption occured
in a low hierarchical position according to the story grammar. This is
viewed as the influence of expectancy structures stemming from a
stereotyped knowledge about the course of fairy tales.

5. Taken together, the presented results seem to argue for viewing story
processing as a combined top-down and bottom-up process which is modified
by "mathemagenic" factors such as the carry-over of fast reactions from the
scrambled condition in the first story to the processing of the second
story.

ACKNOWLEDGEMENT

The research reported here was supported through a research grant to Prof.
Dr. A. Flammer, grant Nr. 1.181-0.75 and Nr. 1.714-0.78 from the Swiss
National Fund for Scientific Research. My particular thanks go to Professor
Flammer for his helpful encouragement and support of this work.

REFERENCES

Bock, M. Wort-, Satz-, Textverarbeitung. Stuttgart: Kohlhammer, 1978.
Minsky, M. A framework for representing knowledge. In P. Winston (Ed.),
      The psychology of computer vision. New York: McGraw-Hill, 1975.
Norman, D.A. Notes towards a theory of complex learning. In A.M. Lesgold,
      J.W. Pellegrino, S.D. Fokkema, and R. Glaser (Eds.), Cognitive
      psychology and instruction. New York: Plenum Press, 1978.
Ratcliff, R. A theory of memory retrieval. Psychological Review, 1978, 85,
      59 - 107.
Rihs-Middel, Margret. Erwartung, Wahrnehmung und Fragen. Doctoral thesis,
      University of Fribourg: Department of Psychology, 1982.
Schank, R.C. and Abelson, R.P. Scripts, plans, goals and understanding.
      New York: Wiley, 1977.
Thorndyke, P. Cognitive structures in comprehension and memory of narrative
      discourse. Cognitive Psychology, 1977, 9, 77 - 110.
Thorndyke, P. Cognitive structures in human story comprehension and memory.
      Doctoral dissertation, Stanford University, Stanford, Ca. 1975.

DISCOURSE PROCESSING
A. Flammer and W. Kintsch (eds.)
© North-Holland Publishing Company, 1982

HOW DO DIFFERENT READERS LEARN WITH DIFFERENT TEXT ORGANIZATIONS?

Wolfgang Schnotz

Deutsches Institut für Fernstudien
an der Universität Tübingen
Tübingen
Federal Republic of Germany

The interaction between different types of text organization and different learners was investigated for a more
complex instructional text. Two objects were described
according to various aspects, whereby the content was organized by object in the one case, and by aspect in the
other case. The two types of text organization confront
the learner with different processing demands, and interact differently with his/her individual learning characteristics: They accentuate different semantic relations
within the text content, the scope they provide for individual processing is different, and they vary in the degree of "sensibility" towards differences in prior knowledge. Practical conclusions on how to match learners
and text organizations are pointed out.

INTRODUCTION

With instructional texts the same content can often be presented in different ways. In this case the author has to ask himself which text organization would be most adequate. For one thing, a specific text organization
signals to the reader what is important and what is less important. Therefore, the author usually tries to organize the text in such a way, that the
information, which is most important according to his educational objectives, will be accentuated. On the other hand, a specific text organization
has specific processing requirements. The degree to which the learner will
be willing and able to meet these requirements depends on his/her individual
learning characteristics, i.e., prior knowledge, cognitive skills, expectations, goals, interests etc. (see McConkie, 1977; Anderson, 1977).

An increasing amount of research on prose learning is concerned with the
problem of learner-text interaction (e.g., Frederiksen, 1977; Kintsch and
van Dijk, 1978; Lesgold and Perfetti, 1978), but most studies carried out so
far were restricted to very short simple narrative passages. Research on the
effects of the types of text organization used in instructional and expository texts is just beginning (see Meyer, 1979, 1980; van Dijk, 1980). In
particular, there are nearly no investigations on the interaction of these
text organizations with specific individual learning characteristics. Such
an analysis would be of great practical use in helping to make better
founded decisions concerning the most adequate type of text organization
for specific learners in order to reach specific educational objectives.

The following study aimed at getting more information concerning this inter-action. Two types of text organization often used in instructional texts were selected: The author of instructional texts is often confronted with the problem of having to present various objects (events, facts, various opinions etc.) and to compare them with each other. Each object will usual-ly be presented from several different viewpoints. As an example let us assume that the objects to be presented are: psychoanalysis and behavior therapy. In this case, one could describe each kind of therapy according to the following aspects: Some statements concerning its theoretical foun-dations, its therapeutic principles, its assumptions on the nature of neu-rotic disorders and, finally, its position within the scientific tradition. A specific text organization (or "superstructure" according to van Dijk, 1980) can be characterized by a set of specific content categories subsuming the propositions of the text that follow each other in a specific order. One possible basic type of text organization in the example presented above would be to first describe psychoanalysis as a whole, i.e., according to all aspects presented above, and to proceed with behavior therapy in the same way. This type may be called "organization by object". Another basic type of organization would be to first describe psychoanalyses and behavior therapy from the first aspect, then to deal with both therapies from the next aspect etc. This type may be called "organization by aspect". Several years ago, some investigations were carried out to analyze the different effects of both types of organization on learning and recall (Frase, 1969, 1973; Schultz and DiVesta, 1972; Friedman and Greitzer, 1972; Perlmutter and Royer, 1973; Myers, Pezdek and Coulson, 1973; DiVesta, Schultz and Dangel, 1973). In these studies only simple name-attribute associations were used as learning content. Furthermore, prior knowledge was eliminated as much as possible by using fictitious subject matter. In the normal course of events, however, people read in order to increase knowledge they already possess and to elaborate it. The amount of prior knowledge affects the kind of pro-cessing they do. So it was precisely the interaction of text organization with prior knowledge that was eliminated in these investigations from the start.

For this reason, in the following study a learning situation was selected in which a learner, who already has some prior knowledge about the topic, is given a rather long instructional text with complex subject matter to read. In one case, the content was organized by object and in the other case by aspect. The following questions were to be answered:

- How do alterations in text organization correspond to changes in proces-sing demands?

- How do these processing demands interact with prior knowledge? In other words: Do specific differences in prior knowledge have different effects on processing, depending on the type of text organization?

COHERENCE AND PRIOR KNOWLEDGE

The knowledge conveyed by a text represents a coherent whole which can be imagined as a kind of network. During text processing the learner has to reconstruct this network by finding the appropriate place to connect each new piece of information with the knowledge structure acquired so far (see Frijda, 1978; Aebli, 1980). The difficulty of reconstructing a coherent knowledge structure differs depending on the kind of text organization. For example, organization by aspect (A-organization) contains several thematic ruptures where we switch from one object to the other, in the example presented above, from psychoanalysis to behavior therapy, and vice versa. At these points, the reader is forced to make a mental switch, i.e., he/she has to repeatedly turn to the other subject matter. The knowledge structure on this subject acquired so far has to be reactivated in memory in order to relate the following propositions to prior information in the text. If the text is organized by object (O-organization), however, it is not necessary to make such frequent mental switches to repeatedly reactivate knowledge structures, because each object is described as a whole before the next one is taken into consideration, and, thus, the text runs through more or less smoothly. Texts organized by aspect could be said to contain obstacles, which do not occur in texts organized by object. The rate at which an A-organized text can be processed depends among other factors on the speed with which these obstacles can be overcome.

Mental switches should be the easier for a reader, the better he/she is already acquainted with the topic area, i.e., the more prior knowledge he/she has about the text content. In general, one can expect a learner with greater prior knowledge to be able to perform more processing operations during a specific time period and so to have a higher rate of processing, than other learners with less prior knowledge. But, since the specific problem of mental switches mentioned above only occurs in the case of A-organization, the hypothesis can be formulated that the rate of processing will depend more strongly on prior knowledge in the case of A-organization than in the case of O-organization.

STAGING, READING PERSPECTIVE, AND PRIOR KNOWLEDGE

The structure of a text usually corresponds to a specific communicative function, i.e., in choosing a particular text organization the author presents the content from a particular point of view. By means of the text organization attention is focussed onto specific propositions and the semantic relations between them. Grimes (1975) refers to this as "staging". Texts describing two objects and comparing them with each other allow for a distinction between two main types of semantic relations: Relations within the objects refer to the coherence among the propositions describing each of the objects. Since in this case, the comprehension process consists in constructing an integrated mental representation of the object at hand, this may be called "integrative processing". Relations between the objects, on the other hand, refer to the similarities and differences between the objects, i.e., the comparison between them. Processing of these relations may be called "comparative processing"

In order to relate two propositions to each other both must be activated simultaneously, i.e., they have to be in working memory. Since processing capacity is limited, this is only possible for a small number of propositions. According to the model of text comprehension of Kintsch and van Dijk (1978), the processing of a new proposition whose referent is no longer available in working memory or in the short-term memory buffer requires the reader to engage in elaborate and time-consuming searches in episodic long-term memory to find this referent in order to connect the new proposition to it. In addition, one could hypothesize that the searches become harder, the further back the processing of these referents occurred. From this the following may be deduced: If a reader is processing the second of two semantically related propositions, this relation becomes more apparent and its processing easier, the smaller the distance between these two propositions (see Walker and Meyer, 1980).

Since alterations in text organization result in changes in the distance between propositions in the text with respect to the staging dimension, the following differences between the two types of text organization can be deduced: With O-organization propositions concerning the same object follow rather immediately upon each other, so the distances between them are relatively small. However, the distances between the corresponding propositions in the two object descriptions are rather great, since first one object is described as a whole before the next one is taken into consideration. The opposite is true in the case of A-organization. Here the distances between the corresponding propositions in the two object descriptions are relatively small. On the other hand, the distances between propositions referring to the same object are greater on the average because two paragraphs on the same object are always separated by one paragraph on the other object due to the alternating presentation. From this one can deduce that O-organization focusses attention above all on integrative processing and that under this condition this kind of processing is relatively easy. Here, comparative processing is not accentuated and doing it would be relatively difficult. A-organization, on the contrary, focusses attention on comparative processing, and it is this kind of processing which is facilitated in this case. But, since a comparison is only possible if the interrelations within the objects have been understood, A-organization not only calls for comparative processing, but for integrative processing, too. In a simplifying way, the difference between both types of text organization with respect to staging may be characterized as follows: With O-organization the reader is implicitly called upon to construct a consistent mental representation of each object. A-organization on the other hand demands that the reader construct not only a consistent mental representation of the objects, but also find out how much they have in common and how they differ.

It seems reasonable to assume that learners are to some extent guided by the staging of the text. Thus, disregarding individual differences, one can make the hypothesis that readers presented with a text organized by aspect do more comparative processing on the average than readers presented with O-organization. If one further assumes that the amount of integrative processing in both cases is about the same, it is also to be expected that the readers of a text organized by aspect will on the average do more processing altogether and therefore, take more reading time, than the readers of a text organized by object.

However, the learner is not compelled to join the perspective suggested by the staging of the text. He may choose his own personal reading perspective and process the text accordingly. Pichert and Anderson (1977) and Anderson, Reynolds, Schallert and Goetz (1977) found the learners' individual reading perspective to have a strong influence on learning and recall. Although in the case of O-organization attention is focussed only on integrative processing - according to the hypothesis mentioned above - the reader can of his/her own initiative choose a comparative reading perspective and, therefore not only do integrative processing but comparative processing as well. When reading a text organized by aspect, however, the learner has much less scope to choose his/her own perspective, as the staging of the text will induce him/her to do both types of processing anyway. This leads to the following hypothesis: When reading a text organized by aspect all learners will principally do comparative processing - within the limits of their individual capabilities (prior knowledge, skills etc.), of course. If the text is organized by object, the readers are free to choose whether they will do comparative processing. Hence, some readers will engage in this kind of processing, whereas others will not. Thus, greater individual differences in the amount of comparative processing are to be expected in the case of texts organized by object, than in the case of texts organized by aspect. Since comparative processing is relatively difficult with O-organization and, since this difficulty is less severe for readers with higher prior knowledge, it can also be expected that learners with more prior knowledge will be more likely to engage in additional comparative processing.

METHOD

Experimental text. The text used in this study was a description of psychoanalysis and behavior therapy as mentioned above. Text length was 1079 words. To describe each object one paragraph was used for each aspect. The paragraphs were ordered in such a way as to produce either a text organized by object or a text organized by aspect. For both types of organization there was a version starting with psychoanalysis and a version starting with behavior therapy, resulting in 4 text variants altogether.

Subjects. 20 students participated in the experiment. They were randomly assigned to the different text variants so that each of the 4 variants was given to 5 subjects. In order to assess prior knowledge on the text content, the subjects were first given a number of concepts about psychoanalysis and behavior therapy which they were asked to explain. They received knowledge scores for their answers.

Procedure. Subjects were asked to read the text in such a way as to be able to retell the content by free recall to another student later on. The content should be presented in such a way that the other student would be capable of answering comprehension questions on it. Task-oriented reading was supposed to be induced by this instruction. The introduction of a real addressee for communicating the text content to after the learning period was supposed to make the experimental situation more realistic. There was no limit to reading time. Reading time was recorded. After an interval of 15 minutes following the reading period, the subjects communicated the content to another student. Afterwards, they were presented with statements comparing psychoanalysis and behavior therapy. These statements were partly true and partly false. The subjects were asked to judge whether they were true or false with reference to the text and to give reasons for their answers. The aim of this comparison task was to find out how well the students had identified the similarities and differences between both types of therapy. For each subject, the number of errors which he/she had identified in these statements was scored. In sum, the following measures were available for each subject: Prior knowledge, reading time, recall performance (number of text propositions recalled correctly) and performance in the comparison task. Furthermore, the number of correctly recalled propositions per reading time was computed for each subject.

RESULTS

Table 1 shows the means and standard deviations of the measures mentioned above for the group who read a text organized by object (O-group) and for the group who read a text organized by aspect (A-group). As one can see, prior knowledge was nearly the same for both groups on the average ($\bar{x} = 14.4$, $\bar{x} = 14.2$ respectively). Table 2 contains these correlation coefficients which are relevant for testing the hypothesis mentioned above

Table 1. Means ($\bar{x}$) and standard deviations (s) in both groups

	object group	aspect group
Prior knowledge	$\bar{x}$ = 14.4	$\bar{x}$ = 14.2
	s = 7.99	s = 5.87
Reading time	$\bar{x}$ = 17.4	$\bar{x}$ = 18.7
	s = 5.9	s = 3.7
Recall performance	$\bar{x}$ = 51.4	$\bar{x}$ = 55.3
	s = 17.4	s = 15.2
Recall per reading time	$\bar{x}$ = 3.16	$\bar{x}$ = 3.03
	s = 1.23	s = 0.92
Comparison task performance	$\bar{x}$ = 3.70	$\bar{x}$ = 5.30
	s = 2.31	s = 1.06

and the corresponding coefficients of determination.

It may be assumed that an increase in the number of processing operations
leads to a better integrated memory structure with more interconnections
between the stored propositions. This results in an increase in retrievability of the learned information during recall. Thus, recall performance may
serve as an index of the amount of processing done by the learner. In addition, recall per reading time may therefore be used as an index of the rate
of processing. If, according to the hypothesis mentioned above, rate of
processing depends more strongly on prior knowledge with a text organized
by aspect than it does with a text organized by object, the correlation between prior knowledge and recall per reading time in the A-group should be
higher than in the O-group. As appears in Table 2, there is indeed a clear
difference: The coefficient of determination only amounts to r^2 = 7% in the
O-group, whereas in the A-group it amounts to r^2 = 56% which is significantly different from zero (p = .006). The difference between both groups is
especially remarkable considering the fact that the variance of prior knowledge in the A-group is even smaller than the variance in the O-group (see
Table 1). The difference between the two coefficients does not reach the
5% level of significance, since the number of degrees of freedom is rather
small, but the result clearly tends to support the hypothesis, that rate of
processing depends more strongly on prior knowledge in the case of a text
organized by aspect than in the case of a text organized by object.

The hypothesis that readers do more comparative processing on the average
when reading an A-organized text than when reading an O-organized text was
also clearly supported: mean performance in the comparison task amounted to
$\bar{x}$ = 5.3 in the A-group opposed to only $\bar{x}$ = 3.7 in the O-group. The difference was significant (t = 1.99, p = .03). The hypothesis that learners reading
a text organized by aspect will on the average do more processing altogether

Table 2. Correlation coefficients, partial correlation coefficients and corresponding coefficients of determination in both groups.

	r object	r aspect	r^2 object	r^2 aspect
Recall/Reading Time, Prior Knowledge	.27	.75**	7%	56%**
Comparison Task, Reading Time Prior Knowledge	.67*	.03	45%*	0%
Comparison Task, Prior Knowledge	.39	.42	15%	18%

* $p < 5\%$
** $p < 1\%$

and take more reading time than learners reading a text organized by object only receives weak support from the data. The means were $\bar{x}$ = 55.3 propositions recalled correctly and $\bar{x}$ = 18.7 minutes reading time for the A-group, versus $\bar{x}$ = 51.4 propositions and $\bar{x}$ = 17.4 minutes reading time for the O-Group. Both differences were not significant due to the high variance within both groups. One reason for the rather small differences could be that readers of a text organized by aspect, although they engage in more comparative processing, also compensate by doing less integrative processing, as compared to the readers of a text organized by object. The small average difference in reading time between the two groups may also be due to the fact that some learners in the O-group not only engage in integrative processing, but disregarde the staging of the text and engage in comparative processing as well, as will be shown later on. Since this kind of processing is relatively difficult and therefore rather time consuming with an O-organized text, this may lead to a strong increase in average reading time due to the additional processing.

If some of the learners in the group with O-organized texts engage into comparative processing, they need additional time which results in higher overall reading time. The rest of the group with no comparative processing should need comparatively less reading time. Of course, differences in reading time may also be due to differences in processing rate. But if processing rate were more or less equal for all learners, individual differences in reading time would reflect the amount of processing done by each individual. Hence, if comparative processing is only done by some of the learners of the group with texts organized by object, one would expect under a constant processing rate the amount of comparative processing to correlate with reading time because learners differ in how much they engage in this type of processing. As processing rate is influenced by the amount of prior knowledge, differences in processing rate may be partly eliminated by controlling for prior knowledge. Thus, if the assumption mentioned above proves true, a positive partial correlation is to be expected for the O-group between the amount of comparative processing and reading time when controlling for prior knowledge.

In the group with texts organized by aspect, on the other hand, comparative processing is assumed to be principally done by all learners. Individual differences in reading time in this case should be relatively small and should result merely from the individual differences in processing rate. It is no longer the occurrence of comparative processing as such that affects reading time, but rather, the speed with which it is done. If processing rates were equal, the correlation between the amount of comparative processing and reading time should disappear. Since processing rate depends on prior knowledge to some extent, this factor may again be partly controlled for to eliminate differences in processing rate. Accordingly, when controlling for prior knowledge the partial correlation between the amount of comparative processing and reading time should be minimal for the group reading texts organized by aspect.

According to Table 2 the two groups clearly differed: For the O-group the coefficient of determination amounted to $r^2 = 45\%$, which is significantly different from zero ($p = .02$), against $r^2 = 0\%$ for the A-group. This result supports the hypothesis that essentially all learners reading a text organized by aspect engage in comparative processing, whereas for learners with a text organized by object comparative processing is optional and, thus, some will do it and others will not. This assumption is also supported by the fact that both groups differ in their interindividual variance with respect to the degree of comparative processing: Standard deviation was $s = 2.31$ for the O-group, against only $s = 1.06$ for the A-group, the corresponding variances being significantly different ($F = 4.77$; $p = .03$). Table 2 shows a positive correlation between prior knowledge and the degree of comparative processing for the O-group ($r^2 = 15\%$). From this it may be assumed that learners with greater prior knowledge are more likely to engage in additional comparative processing. (Since with A-organization, too, higher prior knowledge is helpful for comparative processing, no specific difference should be expected between the two groups). But, since the amount of variance accounted for ($r^2 = 15\%$) is rather small, other factors (e.g., learning habits like carefulness, etc.) seem to be the main influence on whether or not a reader of a text organized by object is willing to do comparative processing.

Another question concerns the effectiveness of learning with both types of text organization for learners with different prior knowledge. Figure 1 shows the regression lines for predicting recall performance per reading time from the amount of prior knowledge. According to the different impact of prior knowledge on the rate of processing depending on the type of text organization, there is an interaction effect between prior knowledge and text organization with respect to recall performance per reading time. From these data it may be concluded that if prior knowledge is low, more effective processing is possible with O-organization with regard to time economy, whereas A-organization tends to benefit readers with high prior knowledge. The considerations above suggest the following interpretation for this result: The mental switches necessary when reading an A-organized text are so hard to perform for a learner with low prior knowledge that he/she will be strongly inhibited in his/her processing. Therefore, integrative as well as comparative processing will be impaired. The learner will do less processing per time unit than he/she would have been able to do if reading a text organized by object, at least as far as integrative processing is concerned, because this text runs through rather smoothly. Learners with high prior knowledge seem to have no serious difficulties with these mental switches with an A-organized text. They are able to do integrative processing with A-organization nearly as well as if they were reading a text

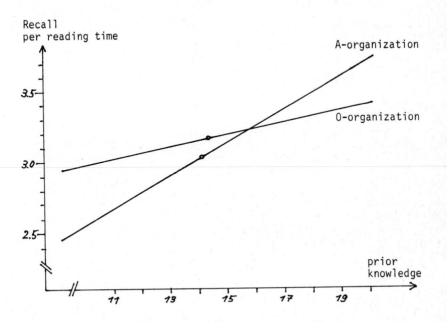

Figure 1

Regression lines for the prediction of recall
performance per reading time from prior knowledge

organized by object. At this point the fact that comparative processing is
relatively easy with an A-organized text appears as a special advantage. In
this case, the amount at processing that can be managed per reading time is
greater than for a text organized by object due to the difficulty of comparative processing, which takes more reading time for the same amount of
processing.

SUMMARY AND CONCLUSIONS

Taken altogether, the data yield to the following picture: With a text
organized by aspect essentially all learners do integrative as well as comparative processing. With a text organized by object only the integrative
processing is done by all learners. In the latter case, comparative processing is optional. Therefore, only some of the learners will engage in it,
needing relatively much time. Rate of processing depends on prior knowledge
more strongly in the case of organization by aspect than in the case of organization by object presumably because of the frequent mental switches.
Learners with higher prior knowledge seem to have less difficulty with these
switches, whereas with low prior knowledge this type of processing tends to
be a handicap. Hence, with organization by aspect learning results are affected more strongly by differences in prior knowledge, whereas organization
by object seems to be less sensitive in this respect. Organization by object

enables learners with low prior knowledge to use a higher rate of processing at least with respect to integrative processing. Hence, learning is more effective than it would be with organization by aspect because the problem of mental switches does not appear. For learners with high prior knowledge organization by aspect seems to be most conductive to efficient learning, since on the one hand, the frequent mental switches do not cause serious difficulties and, on the other hand, the facilitation of comparative processing becomes an advantage.

If one tries to draw practical conclusions from these results, the suggestions would be as follows: If the educational objective at hand only emphasizes integrative processing, organization by object would be appropriate. If comparative processing is required above all, organization by aspect should be chosen. But if there is no clear emphasis on integrative or comparative processing and if learning efficacy is the major goal, the interaction between text organization and prior knowledge must be taken into consideration: If all learners have high prior knowledge, organization by aspect would be adequate, because both integrative and comparative processing can be done effectively under these circumstances. If all learners have low prior knowledge, organization by object would be appropriate, since at least integrative processing can be carried out effectively. The decision becomes more difficult in the case of learners with heterogeneous prior knowledge. Organization by object probably would be the best choice here, because it is more flexible in its processing requirements: Learners with low prior knowledge may restrict themselves to integrative processing and would not have much difficulty. Learners with high prior knowledge are free to do comparative processing in addition on their own initiative.

It would be premature to consider such conclusions as definite on the basis of only one study. Further research is needed to test the hypothesis and support the results. In any case, the present study clearly indicates that different text organizations confront the learner with different processing demands and interact differently with his/her individual prior knowledge. The investigation of this interaction could provide a basis for making better decisions on how to match different text organizations and different groups of learners.

REFERENCES

Aebli, H. Denken: Das Ordnen des Tuns: Kognitive Aspekte der Handlungstheorie. Bd. 1. Stuttgart: Klett-Cotta, 1980.

Anderson, R.C. The notion of schemata and the educational enterprise. In R.C. Anderson, R.J. Spiro and W.E. Montague (Eds.), Schooling and the acquisition of knowledge. Hillsdale, N.J.: Lawrence Erlbaum Associates, 1977.

Anderson, R.C., Reynolds, R.E., Schallert, D.L. and Goetz, E.T. Frameworks for comprehending discourse. American Educational Research Journal, 1977, 14, 367-381.

DiVesta, F.J., Schultz, C.B. and Dangel, T.R. Passage organization and imposed learning strategies in comprehension and recall of connected discourse. Memory & Cognition, 1973, 1, 471-476.

Frase, L.T. Paragraph organization of written materials: The influence of conceptual clustering upon the level and organization of recall. Journal of Educational Psychology, 1969, 60, 394-401.

Frase, L.T. Integration of written text. Journal of Educational Psychology, 1973, 65, 252-261.

Frederiksen, C.H. Structure and process in discourse production and compre-
    hension. In M.A. Just and P.A. Carpenter (Eds.), Cognitive processes in
    comprehension. Hillsdale, N.J.: Lawrence Erlbaum Associates, 1977.
Friedman, M.P. and Greitzer, F.L. Organization and study time in learning
    from reading. Journal of Educational Psychology, 1972, 63, 609-616
Frijda, N.M. Memory processes and instruction. In A.M. Lesgold, J.W. Pelle-
    grino, S.D. Fokkema and R. Glaser (Eds.), Cognitive psychology and in-
    struction. New York: Plenum Press, 1978.
Grimes, J. The thread of discourse. The Hague: Mouton, 1975.
Kintsch, W. and van Dijk, T.A. Toward a model of text comprehension and
    production. Psychological Review, 1978, 85, 363-394.
Lesgold, A.M. and Perfetti, C.A. Interactive processes in reading compre-
    hension. Discourse Processes, 1978, 1, 323-336.
McConkie, G.W. Learning from text. In L.S. Shulman (Ed.), Review of research
    in education. Itasca, Illinois: Peacock, 1977.
Meyer, B.J.F. A selected review and discussion of basic research on prose
    comprehension. Prose learning series, research no. 4, Department of
    Educational Psychology, College of Education; Arizona State University,
    1979.
Meyer, B.J.F. Text structure and its use in the study of reading comprehen-
    sion across the adult life-span. Paper presented at American Educational
    Research Association Convention in Boston on April 1980.
Myers, J.L., Pezdek, K. and Coulson, D. Effect of prose organization upon
    free recall. Journal of Educational Psychology, 1973, 65, 313-320.
Perlmutter, J. and Royer, J.M. Organization of prose materials: Stimulus,
    storage, and retrieval. Canadian Journal of Psychology, 1973, 27, 200-
    209.
Pichert, J.W. and Anderson, R.C. Taking different perspectives on a story.
    Journal of Educational Psychology, 1977, 69, 309-315.
Schultz, C.B. and DiVesta, F.J. Effects of passage organization and note
    taking on the selection of clustering strategies and on recall of textual
    materials. Journal of Educational Psychology, 1972, 63, 244-252.
Van Dijk, T.A. Macrostructures. Hillsdale, N.J.: Lawrence Erlbaum Associates,
    1980.
Walker, C.H. and Meyer, B.J.F. Integrating information from text: An evalua-
    tion of current theories. Review of Educational Research, 1980, 50,
    421-437.

COHERENCE

DISCOURSE PROCESSING
A. Flammer and W. Kintsch (eds.)
© *North-Holland Publishing Company, 1982*

TOWARDS A PROCESSING ACCOUNT OF REFERENCE

Anthony J. Sanford and Simon C. Garrod

Department of Psychology
University of Glasgow
Glasgow
Scotland

This paper is a description of a theory of
text representation. In particular, the processing of referring expressions is considered.
Reference is construed as memory search, and
the paper contains discussions of both the
structure of memory (the search domains) and
the structure of the referring expressions.
Pronouns, definite noun-phrases, and restrictive relative clauses are seen as processing
directives to search different parts of memory,
the object of the search being to append new
information to existing memory structures.

INTRODUCTION

The process of reference resolution must be an important element in any
account of text comprehension. It is through reference that a reader knows
what a text is about, and it is central to the cohesiveness of a text. In
this paper we shall outline an account of some work which we have been
carrying out on this problem, and indicate some of the problems which require solutions.

For convenience, we shall broadly define reference as using some natural
language string to address some mental representation. Although broad,
such a definition is not loose: rather, it results from the view that much
of text comprehension depends upon the retrieval of the relevant information
from memory. In cases where a particular referent is to be found in recent
memory for text, then the reference will be anaphoric. If the referent is
to be found outside of memory for text, then the references are de novo,
linguistically speaking. While such a distinction is extremely important,
both types of reference are, in general, references to memory. The framework which we shall put forward is one in which referring expressions are
considered as instructions to a processor to execute a memory search on the
basis of the information in the expressions. We shall consider two main
aspects of this formulation: the structure of memory and the structure of
the referring expressions themselves.

TEXT MEMORY REFERENCES

Let us begin by contrasting what we shall term text anaphors with situational anaphors. A simple text anaphor is a referring expression which has as
referent something which has already been introduced in a text, as in

(1)   Muriel prepared a casserole for dinner.
(1')   It was appreciated by all the guests.

It is an anaphor for a casserole.   Such expressions are not restricted to
pronouns, but can of course include noun-phrases.   A situational anaphor
is something rather different, in that it refers to something the existence
of which must be inferred from the prior discourse, as in

(2)   Simon flew to the Kleves conference.
(2')   The plane was right on schedule.

Although strictly a de novo mention, The plane may be thought of as functioning like an anaphor, except that the referent entity is only implied,
rather than being explicitly stated.

De novo references are not always situational anaphors, of course.   In
(1), both Muriel and a casserole refer to new entities, and are in no
sense anaphoric.   Garrod and Sanford (1981a) contrasted texts in which
references were made de novo either after a preamble in which the entities
were a necessary (but implied) part, or after one in which they were not a
necessary part.   For instance, in a story about a court case, the presence of a "lawyer" is implied but in a story about being untruthful, it is
not, although the introduction of a lawyer could easily fit both preambles.
Using a self-paced passage reading paradigm (Garrod & Sanford, 1977;
Sanford & Garrod, 1981a), it was established that the subject's dwell
times for the sentences introducing the references of interest were shortest when the entity was implied.   Furthermore, these times were not
measurably longer than cases in which an explicit antecedent was introduced into the preamble.   It was concluded that a sentence is represented
in part as a mental model in which a whole scenario (e.g. "being at a
courtroom") is made available to a reader, such a scenario containing default information regarding the existence of entities which were not explicitly introduced.   (See also Garrod & Sanford, 1981b, and Sanford &
Garrod, 1981b for a fuller discussion.   The idea that the appropriate
mental representation of a discourse incorporates a mental model is also
put forward by Johnson-Laird, 1980).

There are two points to make here.   First, that the range of "anaphoric"
referents immediately available to a resolution mechanism is more than
those which have been explicitly introduced.   Rather, there is an extended domain of reference, which is implicit.   Secondly, if an entity is
resolved (mapped) through the implicit component of the domain, then it
will automatically be restricted as to its role.   This second point requires clarification.   Suppose that we are reading a passage about watching a football match.   A reference to the goalkeeper will not merely be
resolvable because one might expect to find a goalkeeper at a football
match, but it will be taken to mean "a goalkeeper at the match in question"
because it will be mapped into one of the goalkeeper roles in the scenario.
As such, it will be distinguished from any other goalkeeper and any other
kind of goalkeeper, such as one at an ice-hockey match, with all the atten-
dant differences in dress.   Subsequent definite references to the goalkeeper will map onto the appropriate role-defined individual, so that
essentially elliptical reference forms can be used.   Indeed, it would
seem strange to use a reference to the goalkeeper meaning some other goalkeeper.

In summary, we construe reference space as consisting of an explicit domain, with representations of entities actually mentioned, and an implicit domain, consisting of a scenario elicited by the text itself, but augmenting it.   The mental representation of a discourse at any point is then these two representations together with the role mappings of the explicit into the implicit.

We might represent this state of affairs, as shown below, for the sentence pair.

(3)   Harry's divorce case came up in court.
(3')   The solicitor outlined Harry's grounds.

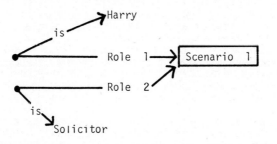

This representation simply consists of three nodes, one each for Harry and the solicitor, and one for the scenario.   The scenario 1 node is assumed to be a pointer to a currently active part of long-term memory - the implicit part of the reference space.   The scenario node can be thought of as a restriction on which parts of long term memory will be preferentially searched by new referring expressions.

While we believe the considerations above force upon us the need to consider an implicit component for the reference domain they do not make the distinctive characteristics of the two clear.   Because "Mary dressed the baby" necessarily involves Mary transferring clothes to the baby does not mean that it is equivalent to "Mary put the clothes on the baby" in a mental representation.   Indeed, the nonequivalence can be illustrated by noting admissable and inadmissable anaphoric references in the two cases.
It is reasonable to write

(4)   Mary put the clothes on the baby.
(4')   The material was pink wool.

But it is less acceptable to write

(5)   Mary dressed the baby.
(5')   The material was pink wool.

Indeed, reading time studies show that (5') is read more slowly than (4'), even though it is ultimately integrated with its antecedent (Garrod & Sanford, 1981a).   This suggests that while the conceptual dependents of entities represented in the explicit domain are readily accessible in the implicit domain, the conceptual dependents of entities in the implicit

domain are not so readily accessible.   Thus the actual asserted information determines the implicit referent structure.

Another distinction between the two concerns pronominal reference. While
explicit information can easily be accessed by a pronoun, it is unusual to
use a pronoun to access implicit information.

(6)   John was taking the boat to Cuba.
(6')   It sank without trace.
(7)   John was sailing to Cuba.
(7')   It sank without trace.

These two examples were chosen to make anaphoric resolution as easy as
possible in the first (difficult) case;   other examples where there is a
little possibility of an ambiguous reading makes the difficulty more
obvious:

(8)   Mary was dressing the baby.
(8')   They were made of pink wool.

Although this is ultimately intelligible, it is **inelegant** English, and
they seems to refer to Mary and the baby.

This observation has led us to suggest that the mental processor treats
pronouns as a directive to search the explicit reference domain. Only if
this fails will more complex inferences be made.

In summary, not only is an implicit reference domain necessary, but it also
appears to be preferentially addressed by different referring expressions.
Of necessity, the explicit domain will consist of a smaller amount of information than the implicit domain, and so will provide a very small search
set for referring expressions. The advantage of a small search set is that
the specifying information for a content address search can be very
limited.   In language, pronouns would seem to fit this bill very well,
being short character strings converying little information (gender, number,
etc.). On the other hand, noun-phrases convey much more information, and
can be used to address both explicit and implicit domains. This makes a
comparison of noun-phrase and pronoun anaphora interesting.   Normally,
instead of using a repeated noun-phrase to refer to things just mentioned,
a pronoun is used, thus the following sounds strange:

(9)   The truck roared through the village and the truck
        narrowly missed a pedestrian.

A pronoun would be more suitable.   Indeed, there is some evidence that
for fairly contiguous anaphora, a pronominal reference is resolved more
rapidly than a corresponding noun-phrase reference (Sanford & Garrod,
(1981a).

FOCAL REFERENCES

If the introduction of a background-knowledge mapping extends the domain
of reference, the introduction of focus will reduce it. Here we shall use
focus in the sense used by Grosz (1977) as the focus of "attention" when
understanding a discourse.   An example of what we mean by this is as
follows.   If one is reading about a boy in a cinema, then some entities

and events relevant to being at a cinema will be in focus.   If the narrative shifts to one where he is now at home and being admonished by his
mother for spending too much money, then unless detailed reference is made
to the earlier cinema situation, entities and events relevant to the
cinema will no longer be in focus.   This simple example corresponds to an
episode change, and is often cued in a text by expressions such as "After
that, . . . ", "when he got home, . . . ", "then he went home"
etc.

It would be consistent with the idea of focus if an anaphoric reference to
an entity in a previous episode were more difficult to resolve than one to
an entity in a current episode.   Sanford, Henderson & Garrod (1980)
report an experiment in which this was tested.   In this study, subjects
read passages which were of equivalent length and surface complexity,
half of which were made up of two clearly marked episodes, and half of
which consisted of a single episode.   The final sentence contained a
reference to an entity in the first (or only) episode.   Furthermore, such
a reference could be either a situational anaphor (e.g. Mary dressed the
baby . . . The clothes were too tight) or a text anaphor (e.g. Mary
put the clothes on the baby . . . The clothes were too tight).   Subjects read through the passages one sentence at a time, and the dwell
times for each sentence were measured.   The results showed that for both
text and situational anaphors, an episode shift resulted in a 200 msec
increase in reading time for the final sentences.   Thus an episode shift
appears to reduce the accessibility of the representation of a referent,
be it implicit or explicit.   Similar results have been obtained with less
direct ways of cueing a change of focus - most situations are characterised by being bounded in duration (Grimes, 1975) and by indicating that a
boundary duration has been exceeded, a previous episode can be put out of
focus (Sanford & Garrod, 1981a; Anderson, Garrod & Sanford, in preparation).

Such results may be viewed as a simple extension of the discussion of
reference domains.   If a scenario is used as a structure into which to
map a discourse, then a change of scene results in a change in scenario,
and provides a new mapping domain.   One way to realise this is as a
series of addressing restrictions to long term memory, such that all
references are resolved with respect to that part of memory pointed to by
the address of the "currently focussed" scenario.   A pronoun thus activates a procedure for search in explicit focus (of which we shall say more
shortly), and a noun-phrase activates one for searching the whole of focus.

Simple definite noun phrases (The + Noun) can be used to address both
focus partitions, but what of addressing entities outside of focus? Here
the principles of a tradeoff between search space and the information content of the description can be invoked again.   Consider the following
series of episodes:

(10)   Mary and her husband had a meal at Le Coq d'Or.   The
        waitress gave them prompt service.
        As a result, they had time to spare, so they went to
        the cinema afterwards.
        The film was a rather poor western.   Mary's only
        comment was that the saloon-girl looked just like
        the waitress.

Most readers find the definite anaphoric reference the waitress rather
strained.   Indeed, it should be in the light of the experiments described
earlier on reference resolution after a topic shift.   This and similar
passages were shown to a number of readers who were asked to choose between the waitress and the waitress from the restaurant as potential descriptions to keep the passage smooth-flowing.   The majority chose the
restrictive relative clause (RRC) over the definite noun-phrase.   This
is one line of evidence in favour of the claim that one function of an RRC
is to provide sufficient information in a description to enable a successful search to be carried out in the static partitions of memory, whether a
referent is found in long term memory or in general long-term memory. Of
course, with the example shown above, a noun-phrase will serve to enable
coreference to be established, but it is uncomfortable to use and the RRC,
providing a fuller description of the referent, is preferable.   Under
certain circumstances, simpler noun phrase will provide adequate information, however.   For instance, if we have been reading a piece about
"Chomsky's theory", then even after discussing something else, the phrase
"Chomsky's theory" should be sufficient to enable ready resolution.
Similarly, if we have been reading a story about a character "John", then
temporarily shifting the emphasis away from John to another character
should not invalidate the use of "John" as a satisfactory description, because "John" serves to point to a substantial package of information in
memory.   Finally, let us note that the RRC, while eminently suitable for
addressing outside of focus, is also sometimes necessary as a descriptor
for addressing focus, even explicit focus.   This occurs when there are
two or more entities in focus which would be addressed by the same simple
noun-phrase, but which have to be discriminated (e.g. two men, one with a
hat, where the expression "the man who was wearing the hat" might be
used.)   This observation raises the question of how an RRC is recognised
by the processor - obviously it cannot be assumed that the RRC is simply
recognised as a unit, and then activates an instruction to search outside
of focus.   This leads to the next section of the paper, which deals with
just three problem areas that have to be tackled within a psychological
theory of reference.

THREE PROBLEMS FOR REFERENCE THEORIES

Parsing and reference recognition

Any comprehension process has to start by obtaining a representation of the
input.   We cannot attempt to enter into a description of parsers here, but
shall point out that a good descriptive framework and mode of implementation for parsers appears to be the Augmented Transition Network (ATN)
(Woods, 1970; Johnson-Laird, 1977).   Such a system operates in a sequential way on an input, and has subnetworks for recognising noun-phrases,
etc.   Following Johnson-Laird (1977), it is possible that once a noun-
phrase (for instance) has been recognised, some general procedure called
"seek referent" is activated.   Obviously, such a procedure has to be activated at some point in order to attach any significance to a referring
expression, and to enable anaphora to be resolved; the question is at what
point in the process does this occur?   We shall suggest one possibility,
based on a primary processing principle.

According to this idea (Sanford & Garrod, 1981a), a processor attempts to
establish coherence (hence, by implication, referential mapping) on the
minimum of evidence.   Our predispositions sway in this direction because

in natural conversation one frequently finds extreme ellipsis and yet the
participants can understand one another.   So a simple definite noun
phrase should be sufficient to implement a "seek referent" procedure
(search focus).   If no suitable representation can be found, the processor
can do no more and has to store the noun phrase while taking in more input.
In the case of an RRC, the results of this will be to add specifying information to the stored noun-phrase, which is still in a seek-referent state.
The additional detailed description will provide sufficient information to
resolve the reference if the writer is sensitive enough to produce "considerate" discourse.   Such a characterisation implies that noun-phrases
actually serve as directives to search the whole of memory, but again
there will be a preference for focus, and a simple definite noun-phrase
will not serve to pick out any particular referent in the absence of more
information.   After all, the description "The man . . . " enables us to
map onto nothing more than (a singular, adult male human entity) and
carries no significance.

The primary processing principle will operate in different ways at different times.   Let us consider the opening sentence of a discourse:

(11)   The man delivered the carpets to our house today.

No significance could be attached to this until a whole event had been
parsed, and the "seek referent" flag would still be active.   There will
be nothing in focus for any part of the sentence to map into; but when
the whole event has been parsed, it should provide the basis for retrieving
a corresponding situation from long term memory, thus providing a mental
model.   In a considerate discourse the model will provide an appropriate
frame of reference: one seldom begins a discourse with an irrelevant orientation.

Explicit representation

Up to now the nature of focus representations has been left vague.   Yet
focus has to capture the essential differences between various descriptions.   We shall consider some aspects the definite/indefinite distinction
as an example.   Definite noun phrases are generally assumed to assert the
existence of a particular member of the class which the noun designates.
Used anaphorically, such a phrase serves to single out a particular exemplar, the one mentioned before.   Used de novo, it serves to assert parti-
cularity.   Thus it seems appropriate to view definite noun phrases as
being primarily search directives.   In the anaphoric case, the effect
should be to lead the processor to construct a network in explicit focus
in which the antecedent node simply has new information attached to it (a
subset of the Given-New principle - c.f. Halliday, 1967; Garrod & Sanford,
1981b).   In the de novo case, a mapping failure should result in a new
node being constructed in explicit focus.

Indefinite expressions are somewhat different.   They are generally used
to designate any single but unspecified member of a set.   Since they are
used to convey new information, it follows that they be characterised as
being primarily directives to set up a new node in explicit focus.   This
is easily illustrated by the oddness of examples of attempted anaphora
using the indefinite:

(12)   An American flew to New York.

An American got airsick.

This kind of example seems to produce a strange effect.   At once readers
seem to entertain the possibility that there are two Americans, yet that
they are probably one and the same person!   The point is that while an
indefinite is primarily used to set up a new node, it also serves as a
search directive.   Indeed, sometimes the search aspect can be undesirable.
The following two-line snippet exemplifies those used in a study by Garrod
& Sanford (1977; 1978):

(13)   The bus/tank came trundling down the hill.
        It almost hit a vehicle.

The second sentence here is one of those awkward truncated ones sometimes
met in psycholinguistic experiments.   But what is it that makes it awkward
and truncated?   Our experiments demonstrated that the time to match an
anaphoric reference to the vehicle to the antecedent bus was faster than
onto tank, because it is a poorer exemplar of the class (e.g. Rosch, 1973).
This difference, the conjoint frequency effect, is sensible when coreference is being established.   However, its presence with examples like (13)
suggests that coreference is being entertained between bus/tank and a
vehicle by the processor.   Finally, the reader is invited to consider
whether the second sentence of (13) would seem less "truncated" were it to
be

(14)   It almost hit another vehicle.

Although no formal experiment has been carried out to check preferences in
this case, it could be, and the use of another (x) would serve as a directive to set up a further node in explicit focus.

Indefinite expressions can, of course, be used for situational anaphora, as
can definites.   Thus, following on a text about a restaurant, we could
refer to "a waiter" or "the waiter".   With this example, the ultimate ex-
explicit focus representations would be the same, although the node should
be set up first with the indefinite, and the relevant implicit focus representation identified initially with the definite.   There are, of course,
situations where using the definite and indefinite like this would not be
interchangeable.   Thus it seems odd to say:

(15)   Jonathan was riding on a bus.
        A conductor took his fare.
        (There is only one conductor on a bus).

To tackle these instances, we have to consider the nature of the implicit
focus search set in a little more detail.   Although the term "seek antecedent" is generally useful, the basis of the primary processing principle
lies in the establishment of a mapping relationship between explicit and
implicit focus.   Now if the scenario is riding on a bus, the implicit
representation will have only one variable-slot for "conductor".   Yet the
logic of the indefinite suggests it names any one of a set.   It is quite
conceivable that a fuller description of the indefinite procedure would
include "seek a mapping of this node onto an arbitrary member of a set of
semantically-matching representations".   Such a procedure would enable
comprehension of somewhat rarer uses of the indefinite, such as

(16)   A Kripke would be aghast at all this.

There is no multiple-element set of Kripkes (the logician), so it is necessary to implement a search for a set, which turns out to be Kripke-like
entities (e.g. eminent logicians).   According to this argument, (15)
should sound odd because the processor attempts to find a set of conductors.

These examples are meant to illustrate some of our ideas concerning the
procedural definition of simple noun-phrases.   Definiteness and indefin-
iteness are viewed as triggers for procedures which are initial searches
and initial constructions respectively.   Although we have only covered a
few instances of usage for these expressions, our current research is extending the range of usages considered.   It would be true to say that
psychological studies of reference have been fairly restricted in the
usages considered, and have tended not to be rooted in a general theory of
comprehension.   A full account of reference must be able to accommodate
all usages and should capture or explain the different underlying logical
forms which logicians have used as representations (c.f. Stenning, 1975,
for an excellent discussion from a philosophico-linguistic standpoint).

Examples, counter examples and augmentations

The use of examples is a necessary part of theorising about language, and
yet for any example cited in support of a claim, it seems to be possible
to generate a counter example, or a further example which is so different
as to be difficult to accommodate.   Our third problem is what to do about
this.

In normal usage, some referring expressions seem more satisfactory than
others - better or less strange.   Strange usages may be considered as
breaking rules (e.g. Grice's conversational postulates; Grice, 1975) producing unusual effects, or discourse which is difficult to understand.
By definition, strange usages have a low frequency of occurrence in
natural language, and it would seem unreasonable to expect a processor to
be tailored to the analysis of such usages.   It is perhaps more profitable to suppose that a processor would falter on encountering them, and
that various types of problem-solving are indulged in to find an interpretation if possible.   For instance, in a full analysis of pronominal anaphora, one inevitably encounters examples such as Wilk's (1975):

(17)   Give the monkey's the bananas although they are not
        ripe because they are very hungry.

Such a sentence demonstrates that pronoun anaphora can be resolved on the
basis of general knowledge about bananas and monkeys.   Yet such a sentence is particularly strange, and it would be undesirable to assume that
all pronoun resolution utilises general knowledge (See Sanford & Garrod
(1981a) for a fuller discussion).   The same sort of argument can be
applied to all kinds of usages.   For instance, should we alter the defi-
nitional procedures for definite and indefinite descriptions to allow for
generic expressions?   This may not be necessary, since generic expressions are seldom used in isolation.   In general, it is clearly advisable
to consider the usual contexts of utterances before trying to model the
utterance itself.   Thus, sentences which sound strange may sometimes be
strange regardless of context, or may be quite acceptable within a particular, usually narrow, range of contexts.   We must be clear that such use

of context is not a way of offloading sentences which one does not wish to tackle, but provides a potential means for accommodating a wide range of strange examples within a simple focus framework.   Indeed, it is quite easy to present subjects with various sentences and ask them to provide contexts in which they would expect them to occur.   Only when this is impossible is it fair to consider a sentence as totally abnormal.

CONCLUSION

In this paper we have described part of an account of reference which is rooted in a more general theory of comprehension.   The guiding principle behind the theory is that of primary processing, embodying the assumption that the processor attempts to determine significance as early as possible in the processing sequence.   Reference is construed as a directive for memory search, and the discussion of such searches ranged from pronominal anaphora to event-scenario matching.   In our account, much has been left out.   However, within such a framework it is possible to interpret and examine many aspects of reference and anaphora.   The strength of the account does not simply come from the extension of the reference domain to include implicit information, but also from the mapping relations between explicit and implicit focus, and from treating forms of nominal and event references as processing directives rather than as problems for stative representation.

REFERENCES

Anderson, A., Garrod, S. C. & Sanford, A. J.   Effects of changes in narrative present on the availability of referents: implications for written discourse comprehension. (in prep.).

Garrod, S. C. & Sanford, A. J.   Interpreting anaphoric relations: the integration of semantic information while reading.   Journal of Verbal Learning and Verbal Behavior, 1977, 16, 77-90.

Garrod, S. C. & Sanford, A. J.   Anaphora: A problem in text comprehension. In R. N. Campbell & P. T. Smith (Fds.), Recent Advances in the Psychology of Language.   New York: Plenum Press, 1978.

Garrod, S. C. & Sanford, A. J.   Bridging inferences and the extended domain of reference.   To appear in J. Long & A. Baddeley, (Eds.), Attention and Performance IX, Hillsdale, N.J.: Lawrence Erlbaum, 1981 (a).

Garrod, S. C. & Sanford, A. J.   Topic dependent effects in language processing.   To appear in G. B. Flores d'Arcais & R. Jarvella (Eds.), The process of language understanding, Chichester: John Wiley & Sons, 1981 (b).

Grice, H. P.   Logic and conversation.   In P. Cole & J. L. Morgan (Eds.), Syntax and Semantics 3, Speech Acts.   New York: Seminar Press, 1975.

Grimes, J. E.   The Thread of Discourse, The Hague: Mouton, Janua Linguarum, 1975.

Grosz, B.   The representation of focus in dialogue understanding.
Technical Note 15, SRI Artificial Intelligence Center, 1975.

Halliday, M. A. K.   Notes on transitivity and theme in English, Parts 1
& 2, Journal of Linguistics, 1967, 3, 37-81, & 199-214.

Johnson-Laird, P. N.   Psycholinguistics without linguistics. In N. S.
Sutherland (Ed.), Tutorial Essays in Psychology, I, 1977, Hillsdale,
N.J.: Lawrence Erlbaum Associates.

Rosch, E.   On the internal structure of perceptual and semantic categories.   In T. E. Moore (Ed.), Cognitive development and the acquisition of language, New York: Academic Press, 1973.

Sanford, A. J. & Garrod, S. C.   Memory and attention in text comprehension: the problem of reference. In R. Nickerson (Ed.), Attention and
Performance VIII, Hillsdale, N.J.: Lawrence Erlbaum Associates, 1980.

Sanford, A. J. & Garrod, S. C.   Understanding Written Language, Chichester: John Wiley & Sons Ltd, 1981 (a).

Sanford, A. J. & Garrod, S. C.   The role of background knowledge in psychological models of text comprehension. To appear in J. Allwood & E.
Helmquist (Eds.): Foregrounding Background (1981 (b).

Sanford, A. J., Henderson, R. J. & Garrod, S. C.   Topic shift as variable
in text cohesion: experimental evidence from studies in reading time.
Pape- presented to a meeting of the Experimental Psychology Society,
Cambridge, July, 1980.

Stenning, K.   Understanding English Articles and Quantifiers, Ph.D.
Thesis, Rockefeller University, 1975.

Wilks, Y.   A preferential pattern-seeking semantics for natural language
inference.   Artificial Intelligence, 6, 1975, 53-74.

Woods, W. A.   Transition network grammars for natural language analysis.
Communcations of the A. C. M. 1970, 13, 591-606.

DISCOURSE PROCESSING
A. Flammer and W. Kintsch (eds.)
© *North-Holland Publishing Company, 1982*

TOWARD A MODEL OF MACROSTRUCTURE SEARCH

Ulrich Glowalla & Hans Colonius

Institut für Psychologie
Technische Universität Braunschweig
Federal Republic of Germany

It has been argued that the macrostructural
organization of a text is central to comprehension and retention of discourse. In a recognition experiment, some aspects of the macrostructural representation have been investigated.
The results give some preliminary support to
the Roter Faden model (Glowalla, 1981). In
addition, a quantitative model capturing some
features of macrostructure search is outlined.

INTRODUCTION

It has been stressed by a number of people that the process of condensing
the full meaning of a text into its gist is central to the comprehension
and retention of discourse (e.g., Kintsch and van Dijk, 1978). The main
goal of this paper is to investigate this process further. It has become
convenient to use the term macrostructure for such global descriptions of
the semantic structure of a text. In contrast, the term microstructure has
been introduced for the structure of individual text sentences and their
relations. To consider a piece of discourse coherent, two conditions must
hold: its respective sentences should be connected at the microstructure
level and these sentences should be organized in larger conceptual units
at the macrostructure level. Thus, as has been argued elsewhere (e.g.,
Sanford and Garrod, 1981), only models for text processing incorporating
both of these aspects may attain theoretical as well as empirical significance.

In fact, quite a few models for text processing incorporating micro- and
macro-level descriptions have already been proposed (Glowalla, 1981; Graesser, 1981; Kintsch and van Dijk, 1978; Schank and Abelson, 1977). However,
the models differ with respect to the format of the microstructure and/or
the macrostructure. As to the latter, several conceptions are under discussion. The existing alternatives may roughly be classified as follows:
The micropropositions of a text are transformed into a set of macropropositions by so-called macro-operators. Recursive application of these macro-
operators leads to macrostructural descriptions at different hierarchical
levels. The resulting macrostructure represents the gist of the text. This
concept of macrostructure has been developed by Kintsch and van Dijk (1978).
Alternatively, the macrostructure of a text may be conceived of as a
hierarchical tree structure consisting of nodes representing conceptual
units of a text and links representing the relations between conceptual
units. The microstructure units of a text, i.e., its micropropositions, are

represented by the terminal nodes of the tree structure. Internal nodes represent conceptual units of the macrostructure on different hierarchical levels. No specific assumptions are made about the contents represented by the node. Distances between microstructure units in the tree structure representing the macrostructure are viewed as a measure of their connectivity, i.e., whether they belong to the same or different macrostructural units. As a matter of fact, structure diagrams defining the constituent structure of a piece of discourse (e.g., Rumelhart, 1977) may be interpreted in this way. This view does not imply that people cannot construct macropropositions out of a set of connected micropropositions, i.e., that they are unable to produce a summary of the main contents of a text. Again, Rumelhart (1977) has been able to predict observed summaries quite nicely by postulating additional summarization rules. The only proposition made here is that we may know too little about the cognitive operations producing the theoretical macrostructure. We should therefore avoid making too many initial assumptions. Moreover, with respect to the memory representation of discourse, assumptions about the contents of macrostructure nodes may even prove to be unnecessary.

In the following we shall present some experimental results about search processes on macrostructures. The data originate from an experiment to test some predictions of a recently proposed model for text processing called the "Roter Faden" (main train of thought; Glowalla, 1981). In the subsequent section we shall give an outline of a quantitative model. As what follows will be presented in the theoretical framework of the Roter Faden model, we commence with a short survey of the main assumptions of this model.

THE ROTER FADEN MODEL

The Roter Faden model has been designed to capture comprehension and retention of discourse, in which purposive action sequences of human beings are described. The model consists of an interactive processing system based on specific assumptions about the processing devices involved in the comprehension of discourse, together with a set of knowledge structures necessary to fulfil the task. The model starts off with the question how incoming text information has to be processed to produce a memory representation of it. Clauses are taken as units in this analysis; a clause is defined here to be a proposition containing an active or stative verb. At each processing step, the model tries to find answers to the following questions:
1. What is the functional meaning of an incoming clause? (A functionally identified clause will be termed a microstructure unit.)
2. How may the present microstructure unit be connected to already encoded units?
3. Which inferences have to be generated, if no direct connection exists between two successive units?
4. Which expectations may be generated about the text information yet to come?
5. Is it possible to condense already encoded microstructure units into more global macrostructure units?
The interactive processing system produces answers to these questions utilizing the assumed knowledge structures. Both of these components of the Roter Faden model will be outlined in turn. The processing system consists of a central processor called CONSTRUCT and four subprocessors termed IDENT, INFER, MACRO, and ERWIN. The central processor executes the various

processing operations in actual fact, utilizing the information produced by
the subprocessors. It is assumed that these subprocessors work independently of each other and communicate exclusively via the central processor. All
processing devices differ with respect to two properties, namely their task
and their ability to access the assumed knowledge structures. The central
processor CONSTRUCT actually produces the memory representation of a text
by processing its information clause-by-clause. Subprocessor IDENT tries to
identify the functional meaning of each incoming clause. During this process expectations are utilized that have been derived from text information already encoded. If no match between the present clause and one of
these expectations is found, subprocessor INFER becomes activated. INFER,
then, generates chains consisting of one or more inferences in order to
connect the new piece of information to the structure already existing. At
each processing step, subprocessor MACRO checks for the possibility of condensing a set of coherent microstructural units into more global macrostructural units and ERWIN, finally, generates expectations about the text
information yet to come.

Up to now, all processing devices are realized by detailed flowcharts
modelling the comprehension of text information according to the Roter
Faden model. Moreover, the processing devices are purely functional in
nature. Thus, specific world knowledge is not considered, for example,
whether a specific method encountered by the main character of an action
sequence is suitable to reach a certain goal. In addition, no capacity
limitations of working memory are considered, as has recently been done by
Kintsch and van Dijk (1978). However, to implement the processing model as
a computer program, assumptions about both of these aspects would have to
be incorporated. Nevertheless, by giving a detailed account of the operations performed during the next comprehension process, the processing devices allow for successive experimental testing. In actual fact, one important feature of the model, namely the process of generating expectations
has already been investigated and led to supportive evidence for the Roter
Faden model (Pohl, this volume).

During the comprehension process the processing system is assumed to have
access to different knowledge structure. These knowledge structures consist of three action schemata and a set of ten configural rules. The former specify our abstract knowledge about the typical structure of action
sequences and the latter define our knowledge about permitted deviations
from the typical structure. To apply these knowledge structures to the
comprehension process, it must be shown which units of a text may be identified with units of the knowledge structures. In the Roter Faden model it
is assumed that clauses taken as units of text information belong to either
of three basic categories. These categories correspond to the different
functional meanings of certain clauses with respect to the structural properties of a text. The categories are termed Intention (goals, conceptions,
wishes), Action (state changes), and State (conditions of the world). It is
assumed that the functional meaning of a clause may be derived from the
semantic import of it unambiguosly and independently of surrounding clauses. Microstructural units belonging to the same category will be further
differentiated with respect to the action schema of which they are a constituent and with respect to whether the main character is involved. These
subcategories are detailed below:
    1. Intention
        1.1 Goal (desire for the occurrence of a certain event or state)
        1.2 Conception (formation of a PLAN)
        1.3 Select (selection of a certain method)

2. Action
    2.1 Do (application of a selected method)
    2.2 Event or Obstacle (an objective occurrence or an action by ano-
           ther character)
3. State
    3.1 positive or negative Outcome (of an ACTION)
    3.2 positive or negative Consequence (of a PLAN or an EPISODE)
    3.3 Setting or Obstacle (a condition of the world existing inde-
           pendently of a main character's ACTION)

All Intention-subcategories, the ACTION-subcategory Do, and the State-
subcategories Outcome and Consequence involve the main character. All these
subcategories form a constituent of one of the action schemata that will be
described in the next section. Whether an Outcome or a Consequence is positive or negative and whether an Event or a Setting is an Obstacle is determined relative to the current Intention of the main character.

The action schemata assumed by the Roter Faden model are termed EPISODE,
PLAN, and ACTION; they are given in the form of rewrite rules:

1. EPISODE = Goal + $\begin{pmatrix} \text{ACTION} \\ \text{or PLAN} \end{pmatrix}$ + Consequence

2. PLAN = Conception + $\begin{pmatrix} \text{p ACTIONS} \\ \text{and / or q PLANS} \end{pmatrix}$ + Consequence

      (with $(p+q) \geq 2$; $p, q \in |N_0^+$)

3. ACTION = Select + Do + Outcome

Note that these schemata allow for recursive application. The action schemata express our abstract knowledge about the purposive behavior of human
beings. They are assumed to guide behavior as well as the comprehension of
discourse that describes goal-directed human activities. Note that the constituents of these schemata cover most of the microstructural units introduced in the previous section; only Setting, Event, and Obstacle do not
occur and an evaluation of units Outcome and Consequence is missing. This
is motivated by the fact that these elements are not considered properties
of our abstract knowledge about the typical structure of action sequences.
Nevertheless, one can say that access to these schemata would greatly faciliate the text comprehension process: This would allow for generating
inferences about information not explicitly stated in a text as well as
expectations about text information yet to come. Moreover, single microstructural units may be conceived of as belonging to larger structural
units of a text and might therefore be summarized according to these action
schemata. Thus, the action schemata correspond to the macrostructural units
of the Roter Faden model.

There is a problem, however: The action sequences realized in many pieces
of discourse display considerable deviations from the typical form expressed by the schemata. Certain states of the world or events may detain
the main character from pursuing his goals. Moreover, the action schemata
do not contain any information about the possible connections between
successive microstructural units, for example, under which conditions it is

possible that the Outcome of a certain ACTION is succeeded by the Conception of a new PLAN. It is assumed that these conditions consist in configural restrictions based on surrounding microstructural units. In the Roter
Faden model the conditions for connecting successive microstructural units
are realized by configural rules. These rules define which two functional
units may follow one another in the microstructure of a text. A simplified
version of one of the rules will serve as an illustration. Note that the
microstructural units in question are underlined:

Obstacle p   (after the selection of a method to achieve goal r)

$$\rightarrow \left\{ \begin{array}{l} \underline{\text{Goal } r + 1}: \text{Remove obstacle p} \quad (+ 1) \\ \underline{\text{Select}} \text{ alternative method for goal r} \\ \underline{\text{Negative Consequence}} \text{ for goal r } (- 1) \end{array} \right.$$

This rule says that whenever an Obstacle blocks the application (Do) of a
selected method, the main character has exactly three strategies to choose
from: To set himself the Goal to remove the obstacle, or to Select an alternative method that will prevent him from encountering the experienced
obstacle, or finally to give up the intended goal (Negative Consequence).
The numbers in parantheses indicate that the course of action goes into
more detail or onto a more global level. This is indicated in the memory
representation by changes in the hierarchy level, i.e., one level down
(+ 1) or one level up (- 1).

Both of these knowledge structures, namely action schemata and configural
rules are utilized by the processing system of the Roter Faden model. As an
example, the final representation of one of the texts used in a recognition experiment to test the Roter Faden model is shown in Figure 1. The
symbol string connected by dotted lines and running across different hierarchical levels represents the Roter Faden, or main train of thought, of
that specific text interrupted by dead-end structures (unsuccessful action
sequences). Both consist of explicit, i.e., actually stated in the text, or
implicit, i.e., inferred, functional units, together with their respective
connections according to the configural rules defined in the knowledge
structure. This string of connected functional units is equivalent to the
microstructure of the text. The circled symbols E, P, and H represent the
three different types of macropropositions according to action schemata,
again defined in the knowledge structure. These macropropositions, together with their connecting continuous lines, represent the theoretical
macrostructure. This concept of a macrostructure represented by nodes and
extra connections between coherent functional units of the microstructure
will be further investigated later on. But first, we shall give an outline
of an experiment that was conducted to test some properties of the memory
representation produced by the Roter Faden model.

AN EXPERIMENTAL TEST OF THE ROTER FADEN MODEL

As has already been indicated, the model allows for discrimination of the
Roter Faden and dead-ends of a text on the one hand, and more or less complex units in the macrostructure on the other. These two are, to our knowledge, the only variables for which consistent empirical results have been
obtained in experiments designed to test structural properties of memory
representations for pieces of discourse. The first variable has proved to
be effective in studies conducted by Black (1978), Glowalla (1981a), and
Omanson (1979), the second variable in a study by Black and Bower (1979).

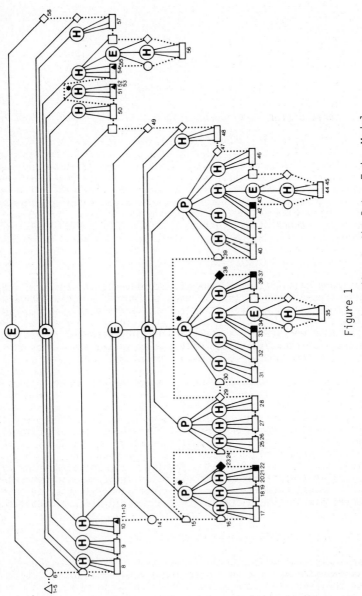

Figure 1

Representation Graph of a Text According to the Roter Faden Model
The Numbers Refer to the Micropropositions of the Text. Explanation of Symbols: E: EPISODE;
P: PLAN; H: ACTION; ▭ , ▬◀ : Action with Pos.Outcome, Neg.Outcome, or Obstacle;
▢ , ■ : Pos. or Neg.Outcome; ◇ , ◆ : Pos. or Neg.Consequence; △ , ▲ : Setting/Event or Ob-
stacle; ○ : Goal; D : Conception; ✳ : Dead-End Structures.

Comparable predictions are also made by Schank and Abelson's (1977) "Conceptual Dependency / Knowledge Structure" computer simulation model. Tests of other structural properties of memory representations of discourse - like membership of different episodic categories or position in the text structure hierarchy - have led to inconsistent results (Omanson, 1979; Trabasso, 1980).

Nevertheless, it is not clear which of the two variables is the more effective. The reason for this lies in the fact that in experiments investigating one of these variables, possible effects of the other variable have not been controlled for. In the following recognition experiment, these two variables have been varied independently. In this experiment subjects were tested in three different sessions with exactly the same procedure. Each session started with a study period in which two texts were presented acoustically to the subjects. During each session, a different pair of texts was used. After an intervening perception task, the subjects were tested on retention of the previously learned text pair in the following way: On each trial two sentences stemming from the text pair were presented visually. Subjects had to decide whether both sentences originated from the same or different texts. Percentages of correct answers and response latencies were measured. All probe sentences originated from three different types of macrostructural units, namely a PLAN dominating an EPISODE, a PLAN consisting of several ACTIONs, and finally a single ACTION. For each of these structure types there existed two comparable units, one belonging to the Roter Faden and the other being a dead-end. As an example, look at the text representation shown in Figure 1. The macrostructural units PLAN with embedded EPISODE consist of the microstructure units 30 to 38 and 39 to 47, respectively, the first being the dead-end structure and the second being the Roter Faden structure. Both sentences of a positive probe stemmed from the same macrostructural unit and both either belonged to the Roter Faden structure or to the corresponding dead-end structure. This is also true for negative probes with one important exception: One sentence originated from the first text and one from the second test.

The observed reaction times have been analysed by several ANOVAs; the main results are as follows: If a piece of information belongs to the Roter Faden, it receives some sort of structural benefit insofar as a strong decay in availability is compensated for when it originates from a less important macrostructural unit. If the piece of information stems from a dead-end structure, the decay in availability will be intensified. These results led to the conclusion that any model must account for the effects of both of these properties. The substantially stronger effects of membership in more or less complex macrostructure units led to the further conclusion that the macrostructural organization of texts should be investigated more thoroughly in the future. For details of this experiment see Glowalla (1981).

PRELIMINARY RESULTS ON MACROSTRUCTURAL ORGANIZATION

As a matter of fact, part of the data of the experiment just described allows for some preliminary insights into these phenomena. During the stepwise construction of the memory representation for a given text according to the Roter Faden model, macrostructural connections between coherent microstructural units (those belonging to the same macrostructural unit) are established via a node representing that piece of the macrostructure as a whole. Pairs of microstructural units differ with respect to their distance in the macrostructure. The distance is expressed by the number of links on the path between two respective units. If, for example, two microstructural units are dominated by the same macrostructure node H, their distance is 2, if they are dominated by the same node P but belong to different ACTIONs, their distance is 4. It may be asked whether different response latencies are to be observed for probes having different distances in the macrostructure. Assuming equal search rates for all links in the macrostructure, search times should increase with increasing distance.

This prediction can be tested by inspection of part of the data from the described recognition experiment. In structure type 1 (PLAN with an embedded EPISODE) there are probes with distances of 2, 4, or 6 links, respectively. If one takes the data of all six texts that originate from structure type 1 and computes mean reaction times for the three distinct categories separately, the results are as follows: 2443 ms, 2546 ms, and 2742 ms for probes with distances 2, 4, and 6 links. The observed differences of 103 ms and 196 ms are statistically reliable ($F_{2,88} = 68.28$; $p < .001$). Similar reaction time differences can be obtained if this analysis is performed for each text separately, but for two out of six texts these differences are not significant. This result may be taken as supporting evidence for the macrostructure assumptions of the Roter Faden model.

However, one can object that the variable distances in the macrostructure are confounded with another variable, namely the number of clauses between the two sentences of a probe in the surface structure of a given text. In fact, this variable should affect response latencies, since the mean number of coherence relations between two sentences is inversely related to the number of intervening sentences (Clark and Sengul, 1979; Lesgold, Roth and Curtis, 1979). Whether this property had any influence on the observed response times has been investigated by a separate analysis involving probes of structure type 2 (PLAN consisting of several ACTIONs). The sentences of these probes possess the same distance of 4 links in the macrostructure together with 0, 1, or 2 intervening sentences. Over all six texts used in the experiment, mean reaction times of 2716 ms, 2811 ms, and 2861 ms were observed for probes belonging to these different categories. The reaction time differences of 95 ms and 50 ms are statistically significant ($F_{2,88} = 7.99$; $p < .01$). With minor qualifications similar differences were observed for every single text.

As it stands, the distance effect might be explained by the number of intervening sentences as well. To clarify whether the observed differences in response latencies are affected by both of these variables or depend exclusively on the number of intervening sentences with respect to the sentences of a probe, a third analysis was conducted. A subset of probes belonging to structure type 1 proved to be suitable for such an analysis. The sentences of these probes are separated by two intervening sentences in the surface structure of the respective text and connected via 4 or 6 links in the macrostructure. Considering such probes of all six texts together, mean reaction times of 2606 ms and 2822 ms were observed. The difference of 216 ms is statistically significant ($F_{1,44} = 23.26$; $p < .001$). Again, similar results are obtained, if separate ANOVAs are conducted for single texts. A joint consideration of all three analyses led to the following conclusion: Both variables, namely the distance in the macrostructure as well as the number of intervening sentences as a measure of coreferentiality, affect the underlying response process.

A MODEL FOR MACROSTRUCTURE SEARCH

In this section, we give an outline of a quantitative model for the search processes hypothesized in the above experiment. Ideally, one would expect such a model to account for all main features of the data, that is, the dependence of reaction times and proportion of correct answers on the various probe types. It should be clear from the outset that what follows is only meant as a starting point toward such a model. Moreover, the model building here is a post-hoc enterprise and thus, no model testing is yet involved.

It is common in reaction time-studies of long-term memory search to conceive of total reaction time (RT) as an additive composition of two parts: a search time (S) depending on the experimental condition, and a residual time (R) consisting of encoding and motor components that are constant over experimental conditions (cf. Pachella, 1974):

$$RT = S + R$$

An important presupposition in the following argument is that the S component of the reaction time in the above experiment can be taken as generated by a search process of the macrostructure that resembles the spreading activation assumptions used in semantic network models (cf. King and Anderson, 1976). A finding supporting this view is the afore-mentioned increase in mean reaction time as a function of the number of links separating two probe sentences in the macrostructure graph representation. Before introducing some specific aspects of this search process, two remarks are apposite. Firstly, while our data analysis suggested an effect of the number of microstructure links between the probe sentences on RT, this has not yet been incorporated into the model assumptions, since the experiment was not especially designed to explore the nature of this effect. The obvious alternatives to handle this would be either to postulate appropriate search processes on the microstructure links or to let some parameters of the macrostructure search depend on the microstructure distance between the two probe sentences. Secondly, a similar point should be made for the effect of another variable, the macrostructure type which the probe sentences form part of. One way to take this effect into account would be to break down the search time (S) into another two additive subcomponents, one being the actual time to activate all necessary links, the other representing the time to gain access to the microstructure representation of the probes, where the latter time component may differ from one macrostructure type to the next. The following only refers to the activation search process itself:

(a) each node and link either is in the active state or not;
(b) if a link is in the active state, then the two nodes connected by the link are also active;
(c) the time for activation to spread from an active node to an incident link is an exponentially distributed random variable with a rate inversely related to the total number of links incident to that node;
(d) activation spreads independently from both probe nodes and the subject gives an answer whenever a path connecting both probe nodes is activated.

The exponential distribution is used mainly for mathematical tractability: 1) the minimum of a finite number of independent exponentially distributed random variables with rates r_j is again exponentially distributed with rate

$$\sum_j r_j \; ,$$

and 2) the probability of the i-th variable being the minimum is

$$r_i / \sum_j r_j \; .$$

The assumption that the rate of activation spreading from a node towards an incident link depends on the total number of links incident with that node is motivated by the so-called fan-effect in semantic network research (cf. King and Anderson, 1976).

Given (a) - (d) it is a routine matter to compute the expected search times for any macrostructure configuration. Let us illustrate this with an example of a macrostructure graph segment (vis. Figure 2). Suppose the microstructure nodes labeled 2 and 4 are activated by the probe sentences. In order to compute the expected time the path a-b-c-d from 2 to 4 needs to be activated, we have to consider all possible ways this activation may come about. Suppose the order of activation of the links is a, b, d, c. If r is the parameter of the exponential distribution, the expected time for a to be activated from 2 is $1/r$; for b , the time to be activated is $3/r$, since there are three links incident with H_2 not yet active; then for d , the time is again $1/r$, while for c , we have $1/2r$, since activation may spread from both E and H_4 . Thus the expected time for the order a,b,d,c is $5.5/r$. The probability of this order occurring is $1/2$ (a "winning" against d) times $1/4$ (b "winning" against d) times $1/2$ (d "winning" against c) = $1/16$.

In order to get the expected total activation time we have to sum over the expected activation times of all possible orders weighted by their respective probabilities of occurrence. It is not difficult to show that for a path of n links there are 2^{n-1} different possible activation orders. Thus, computation load increases quickly with n . However, in most cases n is only of moderate size and, in any event, the task should be amenable to programming.

In the above example, the expected total time to activate the 4 links connecting the test probes 2 and 4 can be shown to be about $5/r$ by evaluating all 8 different activation orders. The corresponding time for test probes 1 and 2 with only 2 connecting links is $1.75/r$. It can be shown more generally that, no matter what the specific configuration, the expected total time is an increasing function of the number of links constituting the path connecting the two test probes.

As it stands, the model allows some fairly definite predictions to be made. In addition to the monotonicity property just mentioned, one would expect equal total activation times - apart from statistical variability - for a number of test probe pairs due to an inherent symmetry in the macrostructure graph, for example for the pairs 1 - 3, 2 - 3, 1 - 4, and 2 - 4. It should be pointed out, however, that any conclusion drawn from a test of these predictions is only valid if the influence of the other factors on RT discussed above has been accounted for appropriately.

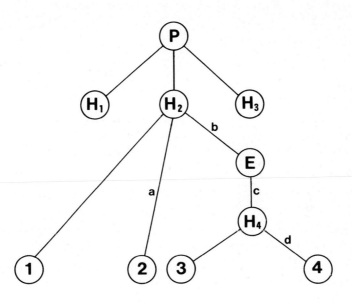

Figure 2

Segment of a Macrostructure Tree
The Numbers refer to Microstructure, the Capital
Letters to Macrostructure Nodes.

CONCLUSION

It has been argued that the macrostructure of a text can be represented by
a graph, dividing coherent microstructural units into clusters at different
hierarchical levels. The quantitative model outlined in the previous section makes some definite predictions about search processes on macrostructure graphs. Most importantly, the time to verify a probe should be an increasing function of the number of links constituting the path connecting
the two sentences of the probe in the macrostructure. The observed response
latencies in the reported recognition experiment are in accordance with
this prediction. However, as has already been pointed out, the experiment
was not especially designed to investigate search processes on macro-
structures. Thus, no reasonable test of the proposed model could be performed. We shall therefore conclude with some suggestions about the design
of such an experiment.

Retaining the recognition technique presented, one effective modification
could consist of the additional employment of probes with sentences
stemming from different structure types. In an experiment investigating
the joint representation of several partially coherent texts (Glowalla,
1980), reliable reaction-time differences between probes from the same or
different structure types have been observed. By altering the distance of

macrostructure units out of which the two sentences of a probe are taken
simultaneously, a strong test of the proposed quantitative model should be
possible. Another modification might consist in a variation of the presentation order of probe sentences. This variable has proven to be highly
effective in research on activation of semantic networks (Glowalla, Schulze
and Wender, 1980). We assume that an alteration of presentation order
should fundamentally influence the effects of the number of microstructure
links (as a measure of coreferentiality) on RT. In the experiment reported
here, the order of probe sentences corresponded to their appearance in the
surface structure of a text. The opposite order should result in a decrease of coreferentiality effects on RT. The use of these two and other
similar modifications in experiments on macrostructure search should lead
to a deeper understanding of the nature of macrostructures and their application during the processing of discourse.

REFERENCES

Black, J.B.   *Story memory structures*. PhD Thesis, Stanford University,
    1978.

Black, J.B., and Bower, G.H.   Episodes as chunks in narrative memory.
    Journal of Verbal Learning and Verbal Behavior, 1979, *18*, 309 - 318.

Clark, H.H., and Sengul, C.J.   In search of referents for nouns and pro-
    nouns. *Memory and Cognition*, 1979, *7*, 35 - 41.

Glowalla, U.   *Der Rote Faden - ein handlungstheoretisches Modell zur Text-
    verarbeitung*. Dissertation, Universität Braunschweig, 1981.

Glowalla, U.   Reproduzieren und Zusammenfassen von Texten. *Sprache und
    Kognition*, in press.

Glowalla, U.   *Probleme beim Enkodieren und Dekodieren mehrerer Problem-
    lösegeschichten*. Unpublished manuscript, Universität Braunschweig, 1980.

Glowalla, U., Schulze, H.H., and Wender, K.F.   The activation of senten-
    ces in semantic networks. In F. Klix and J. Hoffmann (Eds.), *Cognition
    and Memory*. Amsterdam: North Holland, 1980.

Graesser, A.C.   *Prose comprehension beyond the word*. New York: Springer,
    1981.

King, D., and Anderson, J.R.   Long-term memory retrieval: An intersecting
    activation process. *Journal of Verbal Learning and Verbal Behavior*,
    1976, *15*, 587 - 605.

Kintsch, W., and van Dijk, T.A.   Toward a model of discourse comprehens-
    ion and production. *Psychological Review*, 1978, *85*, 363 - 394.

Lesgold, A.M., Roth, S.F., and Curtis, M.E.   Foregrounding effects in
    discourse comprehension. *Journal of Verbal Learning and Verbal Behavior*,
    1979, *18*, 291 - 308.

Omanson, R.C.   *The narrative analysis*. PhD Thesis, University of Minne-
    sota, Minnesota, 1979.

Pohl, R.F.   Acceptability of story continuations. In A. Flammer, and W.
Kintsch (Eds.), *Text processing*. Amsterdam: North Holland, in press.

Pachella, R.G.   The interpretation of reaction time in information-processing research. In B.H. Kantowitz (Ed.), *Human information processing:
tutorials in performance and cognition*. Hillsdale, N.J.: Erlbaum, 1974.

Rumelhart, D.E.   Understanding and summarizing brief stories. In D. La-
Berge, and S.J. Samuels (Eds.), *Basic processes in reading*. Hillsdale,
N.J.: Erlbaum, 1977.

Sanford, A.J., and Garrod, S.C.   *Understanding written language*. New York:
Wiley, 1981.

Schank, R.C., and Abelson, R.P.   *Scipts, plans, goals, and understanding*.
Hillsdale, N.J.: Erlbaum, 1977.

Trabasso, T.   *Relevance perception in text comprehension*. Paper presented
at the Department of Psychology, Universität Braunschweig, 1980.

DISCOURSE PROCESSING
A. Flammer and W. Kintsch (eds.)
© *North-Holland Publishing Company, 1982*

ACCEPTABILITY OF STORY CONTINUATIONS

Rüdiger F. Pohl

Institut für Psychologie
Technische Universität Braunschweig

The Roter Faden model (Glowalla, 1981) has been developed to account for the processing of narrative
discourse. An important feature of the model, the generating of expectations, was examined in a story continuation task. Subjects had to decide whether or not a
given sentence appeared to be an understandable continuation of a previously read story fragment. As measures of acceptability percentage of yes-answers and response latencies were recorded. The results allowed for
specifying form and content of expectations leading to
the distinction of redundant, expected, and distant
story continuations. As a consequence, the importance
of the macrostructure of a story for the comprehension
process is emphasized.

INTRODUCTION

One of the most important features of story understanding is the ability to
draw inferences between different sentences of a story. Many studies have
stressed the importance of inferential processes (e.g., Clark, 1977;
Crothers, 1978, 1979). But trying to bridge a gap between two pieces of information involves at least one other process, namely generating expectations. These two processes, generating expectations and drawing inferences,
which are also called forward and backward inferencing, usually work hand
in hand and almost automatically. In general, expectations faciliate the
comprehension process by providing highly probable text continuations and
thereby help to encode incoming information: During and after reading one
sentence, expectations are built up about what comes next. Then, during and
after reading the next sentence, if it does not fit any of the generated
expectations, inferences are drawn backward in order to find the relationship between these two sentences. These processes, depending on how large a
gap has to be bridged, should need different amounts of time to be accomplished. And there should be two extreme cases: One occurs, if the second
sentence fits exactly the most prominent expectation of the first; comprehension time should be shortest. The other occurs, if the second sentence is just at the edge of being understood because it needs relatively
many inferences to be connected to the first; then comprehension time
should be very great. This leads to the two major questions that are investigated in the present study:
1. What does an expectation look like?
2. What is the extreme point up to which a gap can be bridged?

Forty-eight subjects were given several short text fragments with unlimited reading time. After a text fragment had been read, a single sentence was given, and the subjects had to decide whether or not this sentence appeared to be an understandable continuation of the previously read story fragment. Measures of acceptability were percentage of yes-answers and response latencies. Reaction time was limited to 10 seconds, after which the next text fragment was given.

Each of the 32 text fragments, that were arranged to form a coherent story about a troublesome day in the life of a psychology student, ended with a hindrance or an obstacle for the protagonist of the story. An example of such a text fragment is shown in Figure 1 (the original material is in German). What can the protagonist do after such an obstacle has been encountered? He must choose between three strategies, the first two of which consist of several different methods:

    1. Subgoal-action (i.e., remove the obstacle)
    2. Alternative-action (i.e., change the plan)
    3. Give up

In a pilot study 20 subjects rated the plausibility of 202 possible methods as continuations to 48 different obstacles, each of which was given in the same context as in the main study. 32 obstacles were chosen, 16 of which have a continuation method rated very plausible and 16 rated very implau-

---

Text :

(a) Peter wanted to buy an old frame at the flea market.

(b) But when he asked for the price of a beautiful one,

(c) the seller demanded a price Peter could not afford.

Near probes :

(1) Peter wanted to lower the price for the frame.

(2) Peter wanted to bargain with the seller.

(3) Peter bargained for the price with the seller.

(4) Peter's price offer was accepted by the seller.

Far probes :

(5) Peter now considered the price to be reasonable.

(6) Peter wanted to pay the new price for the frame.

(7) Peter paid the agreed upon price to the seller.

(8) Peter received the purchased frame from the seller.

Figure 1

Text and probe examples of a plausible subgoal method

sible. From each group 8 belonged to the subgoal-strategy and 8 to the al-
ternative-strategy (the third strategy was not investigated further). These
were taken to be the first two experimental variables. Hypotheses are (1)
that sentences containing a highly plausible method will be more often and
much more quickly accepted as a continuation than those with an implausible
method; and (2) that the strategy of the continuation will not produce any
effect as long as the plausibility is controlled.

The third experimental variable concerns the functions of the test sentences. The Roter Faden model (Glowalla, 1981; see also Glowalla and Colonius, this volume), which is based on the story theory of Rumelhart (1977),
but takes a completely different approach in form of a very detailed process model, is used for constructing the representation of the deep structure of the 32 text fragments and their continuations. The Roter Faden deep
structure of the given example is shown in Figure 2, wherein the meaning of
the symbols is as follows:

```
○ - Goal, Subgoal ...............................................
▷ - Conception .............................................. ⎫
▷ - Select ....................................... ⎬
◁ - Do                                        ⎬ ACT ⎬ PLAN ⎬ EPISODE
□ ■ - positive, negative Outcome ..... ⎭
◇ ◆ - positive, negative Consequence ........ ⎭ .......
△ ▲ - Setting, Obstacle
```

These are, according to the Roter Faden model, the micro- (in small letters) and macrofunctions (in capital letters) of the deep structure of a
problem-solving story. They are arranged according to a set of configural
rules that are part of the postulated knowledge structures of the model.
These rules specify which functional units may follow each other. An
example of such a rule will serve as an illustration (micro-units are underlined):

Obstacle p after Selecting a method for Goal r

$$\longrightarrow \begin{cases} \text{Goal r+1: Remove Obstacle p} \quad (+1) \\ \text{Select alternative method for Goal r} \\ \text{Negative Consequence for Goal r } (-1) \end{cases}$$

This rule says: Whenever an Obstacle blocks the application (Do) of the
selected method, the protagonist has exactly three strategies to choose
from, namely, to set himself the Goal of removing the Obstacle, or to
Select an alternative method that will prevent him from encountering the
experienced Obstacle, or to give up the intended Goal (Negative Consequence). The numbers in parentheses indicate changes in the hierarchy level
of the memory representation, that is whether the representation goes into
more detail, i.e., one hierarchy level down (+1), or onto a more global
level, i.e., one hierarchy level up (-1).

There are three abstract, macrostructural schemata (EPISODE, PLAN, and
ACTION) in the model. Of special interest here is the ACTION-schema (or
ACT) which consists of the micro-units Select, Do, and Outcome (cf. Figure
2).

From the structures in Figure 2 and the text example in Figure 1 it seems
obvious that telling something about the subgoal-ACT or alternative-ACT is
of major importance for understanding the story. So the hypothesis is that

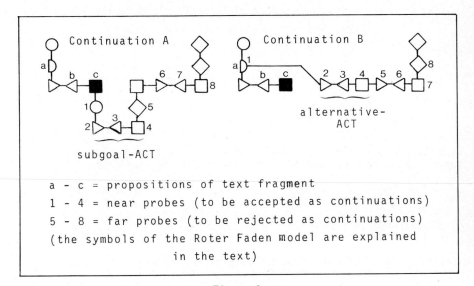

Figure 2

Locations of near and far probe sentences
in the deep structure of the continuations

all sentences representing any of the functions up to the Outcome of the
subgoal-ACT or alternative-ACT will be accepted as continuations, whereas
sentences representing functions following the Outcome of the subgoal-ACT
or alternative-ACT will be rejected, since the gap is too large to bridge.
According to this distance measure the first are called "near" probes, the
latter "far" probes. It can be expected that far probes will need longer
to be rejected than near probes will to be accepted.

As can be seen in Figure 2 the functions of near probes are Select, Do,
Outcome, and, in the subgoal-condition, Subgoal. In order to match this
latter function in the alternative-condition, the last Conception is also
treated as a near probe. Of course, there is one substantial difference
that should produce a significant effect: The Conception is completely
"old" to the subject, while the Subgoal is partially "new" (Clark and
Haviland, 1974). Therefore Conceptions should not be accepted as often as
Subgoals. Nevertheless both have in common that they do not specify the
method that is to be selected in the following ACT, so this fourth near
function will be labeled "without method".

Serving as far (i.e., to be rejected) probes are sentences representing
corresponding functions (Select, Do, Outcome, and without method). They are
located in the deep structure following the subgoal-ACT or alternative-ACT,
respectively (cf. Figure 2). Only Consequences function as "without method".
Hence, the third experimental variable (function) is used for matching
near and far probes (Table 1).

Table 1

Number and functions of near and far probes

		without method	Select	Do	Outcome
distance	near	32	32	32	32
	far	32	32	32	32

In order to avoid unwanted material effects (like different reading times) the following characteristics of test sentences are controlled:

1. The name of the protagonist always appears at the beginning of a test sentence.
2. The construction is very similar in all sentences.
3. The number of syllables is held constant.
4. No unfamiliar or foreign words are used.

Specific hypotheses concerning the response latencies to the different functions of near probes are guided by considering "the usual way of thinking", which is reflected in story telling and writing. This way of thinking (and writing) should be organized around the planning of hierarchical and/or sequential chains of actions that need to be performed in order to achieve a certain goal. The Select of a method and its Outcome are usually redundant and therefore seldom mentioned. When an obstacle has been encountered the Do of a possible continuation method should come very close to the actual expectation and thus be accepted faster than any other of the near functions. Since Select and Outcome also contain the continuation method, they should yield second shortest response latencies, but with Outcomes taking longer because they call for inferencing the Do of the ACT in order to be understood. The reaction time to the "without method" function should be longer than to the Select since no expected method is specified; therefore they might be equal or similar to those for Outcomes.

These hypotheses, if not contradicted, will extend and modify the assumptions of the Roter Faden model, which for theoretical reasons are formulated as simply as possible. In the model the processing of a text is provided by an interactive system consisting of a central processor and four subprocessors. The subprocessor ERWIN (generating expectations) is of special interest for this experiment. It utilizes the configural rules that have been exemplified above. The given rule specifies that the reader will expect either a Goal, a Select of an alternative method, or a Negative Consequence after having encountered an Obstacle. Thus ERWIN produces a set of functional meanings one of which may immediately follow in the deep structure of the text. Though no direct assumptions are made in the model about the comprehension time of certain sentences, it can be argued that the microfunction immediately following the obstacle in the deep structure should yield shortest reaction times for being accepted as a continuation. With an increasing number of microfunctions between obstacle and probe, response latencies should grow in a linear fashion until some subjective criterion is reached above which no more probes will be accepted as a continuation. Finding some references to the existence and the characteristics of this criterion and of the active expectation is the major goal of this study.

METHOD

Forty-eight high school students aged from 16 to 19 years (30 female and 18 male) took part in the experiment, which was run with one subject at a time on a Commodore PET 3001. Every subject was presented with one probe at a time after a text fragment had been read, i.e., 32 times. Sixteen of these probes represented near and 16 far functions. Each of the 16 near probes belonged to one of the 16 treatment combinations (strategy(2)x plausibility(2)xfunction(4)). While reading time for the text fragments was unlimited, probe presentation time was limited to 10 seconds. Subjects were asked to decide as fast as possible whether or not the given probe sentence appeared to be an understandable continuation of the previously read story fragment. Measures of acceptability were percentage of yes-answers and response latencies. For practice four additional text fragments (with an obstacle and a probe each) were given first.

RESULTS

The acceptance rate of the different probes is shown in Figure 3a-d. Percentage of yes-answers is assigned to the vertical axis and near and far functions are assigned to the horizontal axis. The following abbreviations of functions are used: wm = without method, Sel = Select, and Out = Outcome. While all of the far probes are rejected (with an average of only 15 % yes-responses), only 10 of the 16 near probe types can be regarded as accepted story continuations (with an average of 84 % yes-responses). The acceptability of 4 of the near probe types has to be considered random, and 2 are even rejected. Thus the hypothesis about the maximum size of an information gap was not rejected for far probes, but has to be modified for near probes. Of these the "old" Conceptions of alternative-strategies and the Outcomes of implausible methods receive an acceptance rate of less than 50 %.

"Old" Conceptions are presumably not accepted as continuations because they contain only information that the reader already knows. An interesting result is that acceptability is the same whether the Conception has actually been stated in the text or had to be inferred.

The Outcomes of implausible methods, which are the second group of unaccepted continuations, show two important features: First, they contain an implausible method which was not expected so that its adequacy has to be checked, and second, understanding them involves inferring that between the obstacle and the probe something must have been done by the protagonist. Presumably the cognitive effort for these two processes is too large in order to accept such probes as understandable continuations. This consideration is supported by the result that probes which need only one of the two processes in order to be understood are accepted as story continuations (with an average acceptance rate of 75 % and 63 % respectively), while probes which need neither one of them receive the largest acceptability (95 %, Table 2).

The two differences in acceptability due to these processes are both highly significant (p<.001). Moreover, these effects are very similar for both strategies. Generally, the acceptance of corresponding functions of the two strategies (with the exception of "without method" probes) does not

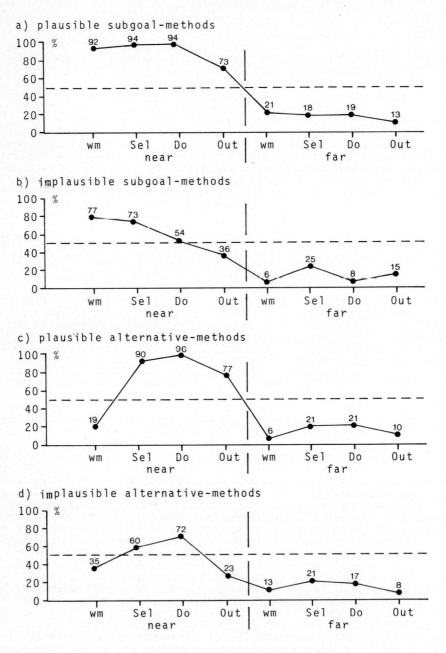

Figure 3
Acceptance rates

Table 2

Acceptance rates as a consequence of two different processes

		Inference needed ?		
		No	Yes	
Plausibility-check needed ?	No	95 %[a]	75 %[b]	85 %
	Yes	63 %[c]	30 %[d]	47 %
		79 %	53 %	

[a] Do of plausible methods
[b] Outcome of plausible methods
[c] Do of implausible methods
[d] Outcome of implausible methods

differ significantly (Figure 4a), whereas the plausibility causes large differences for all comparable functions ($p<.001$, Figure 4b). These results are in accordance with the above formulated hypotheses.

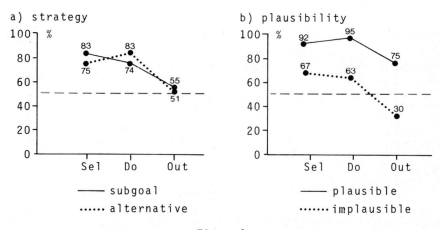

Figure 4

Acceptance rates for the two strategies
and the two levels of plausibility

The mean reaction times of yes-answers to probes that received an acceptance rate of more than 50 % are shown in Figure 5. On the vertical axis are mean reaction times in milliseconds, on the horizontal one the four functions of near probes. The number of observations for each treatment combination is given in parentheses. Rejected probes are not included in this analysis since their few yes-answers are probably based on different comprehension processes than those of accepted probes.

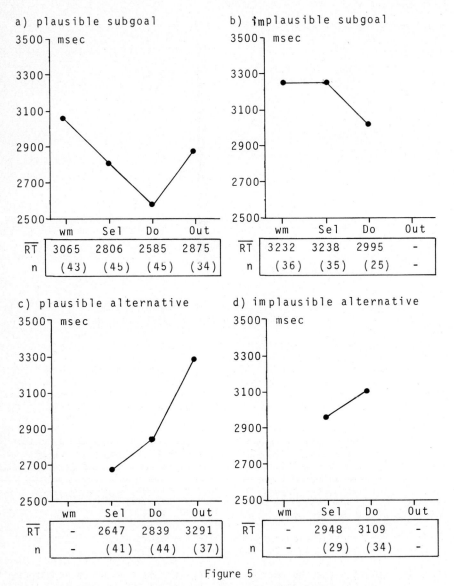

Figure 5

Mean reaction times of yes-answers

The question of major importance is whether or not the hypothesized processes that led to different acceptance rates will be confirmed by corresponding reaction times. Table 3 gives a clear answer: The difference between mean reaction times due to drawing an inference amounts to 536 msec
(p<.001), which is almost the same as the one due to an adequacy-check

(526 msec, p<.001). Despite necessary caution in interpreting these results, it seems clear that neither Outcomes nor implausible methods fit the active expectation after an obstacle has been encountered.

Table 3

Mean reaction time of yes-answers
as a consequence of two different processes

	$\overline{\text{RT}}$ n	Inference needed ? No	Yes	
No		2711 [a]	3092 [b]	2880
Plausibility-check needed ?		(89)	(71)	(160)
Yes		3061 [c]	4134 •[d]	3406
		(59)	(28)	(87)
		2851	3387	
		(148)	(99)	

    [a] Do of plausible methods
    [b] Outcome of plausible methods
    [c] Do of implausible methods
    [d] Outcome of implausible methods
    • not accepted as continuation

Across all of the four conditions only the functions Select and Do are comparable (cf. Figure 5). The difference in their mean reaction times due to a different strategy is not significant (Figure 6a), whereas the difference due to a different plausibility is significant (for both p<.05, Figure 6b). These results are in accordance with the observed percentage rates, which are equal for the two strategies, but are significantly different for the two levels of plausibility.

The mean reaction times for accepting sentences representing the functions Select and Do are very similar (2891 and 2851 msec, respectively). This unexpected result is presumably caused by the instruction to imagine the situation described in the text fragment and to think about possible continuations of the story, before the probe is presented. Thus focus of attention (and expectation) partially shifts away from the Do to the Select of a possible method.

Since all functions of plausible subgoal methods are accepted, this condition can be regarded as a somewhat "normal" continuation (cf. Figures 3 and 5). The mean reaction times to its functions, however, show clear differences: Accepting the Do needs significantly less time than accepting the Select (p<.10) and Outcome (p<.05), the reaction times of which are about equal, whereas accepting the Subgoal (i.e., "without method") yields the longest reaction times (p<.10). This supports the notion that the usual way of generating expectations is not in the small steps of microfunctions, as is assumed for the subprocessor ERWIN in the Roter Faden model, but rather in the larger steps of macrofunctions (here: ACTs) that are best reflected in the Do of the ACT's method. Similar considerations have been stressed elsewhere (Kintsch and vanDijk, 1975; vanDijk, 1977).

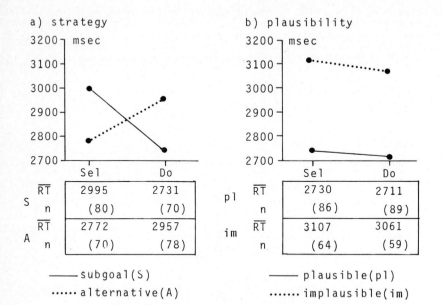

Figure 6

Mean reaction times of yes-answers for the two strategies
and the two levels of plausibility

The larger steps also are near to the medium redundancy level that is required for guaranteeing an optimal information exchange in a given amount
of time (Grice, 1975; Slobin, 1979).

The last result to be reported concerns the reaction times of no-answers
to far (rejected) probes compared to those of yes-answers to near (accepted) probes. The first have a mean of 3036 msec (640 answers), the latter
2951 msec (394 answers). This surprisingly small difference can be accounted for by considering the possible outcomes of a matching process
between expectation and probe:

1. Complete or large enough similarity so that the probe can be accepted immediately.
2. Only partial similarity, but enough to search for a reasonable connection between probe and text fragment (e.g., by drawing inferences
   or checking the plausibility).
3. No or not enough similarity so that the probe can be rejected immediately.

These assumptions which are necessary to explain the observed data make
the original hypothesis more specific.

DISCUSSION

The experimental technique of measuring the acceptability of story continuations has proved to be an interesting approach to the investigation

of comprehension processes. In particular the subjects' expectations that
are generated after an obstacle has been encountered were specified in several aspects. According to the observed data these expectations are highly plausible methods in the function of a Do or a Select. Secondly, the
extreme point up to which a gap can be bridged not only depends on the
number of intervening microfunctions which call for drawing inferences, but
also on other cognitive processes that are needed for comprehending a particular probe (e.g., checking the plausibility of a given method). Usually
all probes representing functions of the subgoal- or alternative-ACT are
accepted as continuations, whereas probes, from which nothing can be inferred about the subgoal-ACT or alternative-ACT that must have taken place,
are rejected by a vast majority of subjects. Exceptions among the near
probes are only those that are "old" to the subject or those that call for
an unreasonably large effort to comprehend them, which is the case for the
Outcomes of implausible methods.

For accepted probes it was shown that all deviations from the hypothetical
expectation cause less acceptability (i.e., larger response latencies and
fewer yes-answers), thus giving support to the hypothesis about form and
content of expectations. Besides, these results clearly indicate the great
importance of expectations in the course of story understanding.

Finally it should be noted that the Roter Faden model with its detailed
process assumptions has been a very helpful approach not only in constructing the deep structures of the used text material, but also in representing
and describing the complicated information processing through which the
understanding of a text is achieved. Only a small part of this process, the
generating of expectations, has been studied in this experiment. The results suggest some modifications and extensions of the expectation subprocessor ERWIN. Especially the typical redundancy level of stories should be
taken into account, in addition to their deep structures. This would probably lead to an increased interest in the macrostructure of a story, for
this structure seems to be the actual skeleton of the comprehension process.

REFERENCES

Clark, H.H.   Inferences in comprehension. In D. LaBerge and S.J. Samuels
    (Eds.), Basic processes in reading: Perception and comprehension.
    Hillsdale, N.J.: Erlbaum, 1977.

Clark, H.H. and Haviland, S.E.   Psychological processes as linguistic ex-
    planation. In D. Cohen (Ed.), Explaining linguistic phenomena. New York:
    Wiley, 1974.

Crothers, E.J.   Inference and coherence. Discourse Processes, 1978, 1,
    51-71.

Crothers, E.J.   Paragraph structure inference. Norwood, N.J.: Ablex, 1979.

vanDijk, T.A.   Semantic macro-structures and knowledge frames in discourse
    comprehension. In M.A. Just and P.A. Carpenter (Eds.), Cognitive proces-
    ses in comprehension. Hillsdale, N.J.: Erlbaum, 1977.

Glowalla, U.   Der Rote Faden - ein handlungstheoretisches Modell zur Text-
    verarbeitung. Dissertation, Universität Braunschweig, 1981.

Glowalla, U., and Colonius, H.   Toward a model of macrostructure search.
    In A. Flammer and W. Kintsch (Eds.), Text Processing. Amsterdam: North
    Holland, in press.

Grice, H.P.   Logic and conversation. In P. Cole and J.L. Morgan (Eds.),
    Syntax and semantics, Vol. 3: Speech acts. New York: Seminar Press, 1975.

Kintsch, W. and vanDijk, T.A.   Recalling and summarizing stories. Lang-
    ages, 1975, 40, 98-116.

Rumelhart, D.E.   Understanding and summarizing brief stories. In D.
    LaBerge and S.J. Samuels (Eds.), Basic processes in reading: Perception
    and comprehension. Hillsdale, N.J.: Erlbaum, 1977.

Slobin, D.I.   Psycholinguistics. Glenview, Ill.: Scott, Foresman & Co.,
    1979.

DISCOURSE PROCESSING
A. Flammer and W. Kintsch (eds.)
© *North-Holland Publishing Company, 1982*

SEMANTIC DISCONTINUITIES AS TEXT PRODUCTION
STRATEGIES

Vanda L. Zammuner
Institute of Psychology
University of Padova
35100 Padova
ITALY

Speech may be seen as a discourse action performed
in order to achieve contextually relevant goals by
the speaker S. To attain these goals, plans and
strategies are worked out. The recourse to semantic
discontinuities (d) is one such cognitive strategy.
Three aspects of it will be considered, to introduce
a d, to perpetuate or aggravate a d, and to resolve
a d. A theoretical discussion of recourse to d is
presented together with results obtained from
analysis of four texts, produced in a debate context.
It is shown that individual and context variables
affect the recourse to d and its role within the
entire linguistic interaction.

1. INTRODUCTION

Conversations, discussions, or any type of discourse/text production need
to be constructed in conventionally acceptable and understandable forms and
according to the speaker's goals. This is a complex task (e.g., de Beaugrande, 1979, 1980; van Dijk, 1977, 1979; Freedle, 1977; Reichman, 1978;
Schank, 1977). Among other things, a speaker S needs to take into account
the audience/hearer's (H) knowledge of the discussion topic (s), H's status
and sex, conversational rules of different types, relevant characteristics
of setting, and so forth.

Leaving aside the discussion of other decision processes not very relevant
to my purpose, at the long-term level S faces the task of selecting an
overall content area for a communication (C) congruently with predetermined
goals and with pertinent characteristics of H and of the specific situational context (CNT). At the short-term level, S has to make decisions which
are more relevant locally. These include how a certain propositional content
is verbalized (Chafe, 1977) according to intermediate level goals and plans
and to conversational rules and constraints due to the specific CNT in
which an interaction occurs. Within the short-term planning level, a most
important decision concerns the semantic relations to be assigned to a set
of propositions that S intends to express in a C; this amounts to the

selection of what relations will hold among discourse parts, be they single words, sentences or larger text units. This stage is hypothesized to be expressed, together with other processes, with recourse to a specific type of strategies dependent on short-term plans and goals. Their activation is based upon S's knowledge of the world and of how to be effective in communication. These strategies have been termed 'Cognitive Manoeuvres' (CM) (Zammuner, 1981; Zammuner and Job, 1979). Their function is to ensure that propositions and propositional chunks are oriented and commented on according to the "communicative action play" (Schmidt, 1973) in which S is engaged.

CM have been hypothesized to be organizing principles of language product-ion that intervene during the speech event to structure the C as it is produced. They are to be seen as structures that are responsible for the organization of information to be expressed in a C; therefore they deter-mine the C structure and form at different levels (e.g., from some prosodic features to the logical structure of a C). Being dependent on S's goals and plans -- tailored to CNT and H's relevant characteristics -- they reflect conditions of text production (Segre, 1979), help ensure that a C is coher-ent and cohesive, and adequate to S's aim to achieve a desired state (de Beaugrande, 1979). They are further hypothesized to be important in com-prehension (e.g., to help H understand S's frame of mind and goals).

It is beyond doubt that discourse is rule-governed and that speakers know these rules and resort to different kinds of plans and strategies to attain their goals. A communicative failure often results from S's inadequacy to structure a C in these terms. Since most linguistic interactions represent successful information exchanges and allow participants to achieve their goals, the important issue is to discover which rules and strategies people use and when and how they apply them.

Among the CM speakers are hypothesized to use there are strategies such as that of drawing a conclusion and stating a premise, as well as having recourse to criticism, irony and stress, and the use of summarizations (Zam-muner, 1981). In this paper one such kind of strategy will be discussed, namely, the recourse to semantic discontinuities (d).

Three aspects of this strategy are considered, (1) introducing a d, (2) per-petuating or aggravating a d, (3) resolving a d. In general, a d is set up whenever S structures his/her talk so that (a) there is a clue signalling that incoming information is going to modify the semantic world already established, (b) it is signalled that new information has to be sought with respect to that given, (c) the existence of alternatives is referred to or implied, and (d) it is signalled that a previously established context has to be reactivated since the incoming information is related to it. A d is perpetuated or aggravated whenever S has recourse to (a-d) in relation to the same item for which the d was introduced. A solution for a d is provid-ed when S or H asserts something that takes into account the d in the pro-

posed action or evaluation. Aggravation or solution of a d cannot be produced unless a d is introduced while, particularly in everyday interactions,
a d might not be explicitly solved, either because of S's or H's unwillingness to do so, or because it is obvious. Whether it will be S or H that
aggravates or solves a d seems to be related to the interactive CNT.

2. THE INTRODUCTION OF A DISCONTINUITY

A discontinuity is a lack of balance, a gap, a break in continuity. Certain
linguistic forms used to express one's own ideas, feelings, evaluations, or
wishes are assumed to introduce such a gap in the semantic world, so far
rendered contextually relevant by means of the previous linguistic context.
Normally, such a break needs repairing to ensure completeness and smooth-
ness in a C, or, better, to recompose a semantic world that in some way has
been disrupted. In other words, a d has to be solved, but, before this is
done, once clues have been given that a d exists, it has to be rendered
explicit. Thus it is hypothesized that, once S signals a d, H will have
expectations about the likely continuation of the C, that is, H will expect
that S will solve the introduced d or will make explicit what it is and
then proceed to solve it. In some circumstances H might do it, e.g., if H
has been assigned this task, implicitly or explicitly, or if H believes
that this should be his/her own task. In both cases, H will do so on the
basis of his/her hypotheses about the likely goals of S either concerning
the introduction or the solution of a d.

2.1   Let us analyze some examples of a d introduction.

S1	It's easy, but...	Sc1 It's going to take time
		$H1-2_1$ But what?
		$H1-2_2$ What's the problem?!
		$Hc1_1$ You don't want to do it?
		$Hc1_2$ I know, it'll take so much time!
S2	We could do it, but...	$Sc2$ I wonder if we should
		$Hc2_1$ It's too expensive, you think
		$Hc2_2$ Yes, perhaps we shouldn't
S3	Peter is nice but not stupid	
S4	Peter is nice but not always	
S5	Peter is nice but clever too	
S6	Peter is nice but stupid	

If a S had said either S1 or S2, H could expect that a coherent completion
of the unfinished utterance (UTT) would be something like Sc1 or Sc2 (Sc,
Hc: S's or H's completion of the UTT). In both cases, in fact, there is
opposition between the two assertions. This discrepancy is necessary once
S has pointed out its existence by means of the conjunction but. In Sc1, S
blocks the idea that "easy" things can be done in little time and the inference possibly associated with it that "it" should/it's going to be done. By
means of Sc2, S introduces the doubt that the action referred to in S2 is

advisable, thus signalling that H's possible inference is not correct. In
terms of Rieger's (1974) definition of inferences types, Sc1 and Sc2 block
an "action prediction inference". They both refer to a state of affairs
that deviates from the possible and likely expectations generated by the
previous UTT (see also Abraham, 1975; Wilson, 1976; Posner, 1977). That
is, depending upon the content of the UTT preceding the adversative conjunction, the use of but -- and similar conjunctions -- will limit the extent of
an inferred result, deny a motive, an enablement condition, a usual function
or a prediction. What is important is the fact that S implicitly instructs
H about the correct paths that exist according to S and in relation to S's
hypotheses about H's expectations (for example, S3-S6).

2.2   The remaining examples in 2.1 represent appropriate hypothetical
replies by H to S1 or S2. They show that H would have to take into account
the introduction of a d by the previous S in order to produce an UTT that
adequately commented on it. H1 and H2 represent requests to specify what
is the intended d; they could be uttered if H wanted to signal a disbelief
in its existence, thus implicitly telling S that he/she should not introduce
a d because it would disrupt the C. They could also be produced with a
cooperative aim if H could not predict the d on the basis of the available
(mostly contextual) information, or if H preferred S him/herself to complete
the C. H's actual reaction to UTTs like S1 and S2 would very much depend
upon CNT factors such as H's degree of acquaintance with S, nonverbal clues
concomitant with the UTT, and characteristics of the situational context.
The production itself of S1 or S2, as much as S's reception of H1 or H2,
would be based upon the same kind of variables.

$Hc1_1$ represents a tentative completion for S1. It shows H's selection of
one out of a set of possible d, S might have had in mind and it expresses
H's question about its correctness. $Hc1_2$ shows instead H's confidence in
the selected d and his/her agreement with S's doubts, thus with S's introduction of a d too. In $Hc2_1$, H's interpretation of S's intentions and preferred course of action is expressed in a form ("you think") that signals
H's wish to be corrected if wrong, while $Hc2_2$ is another instance of a confident interpretation both of the d and of its solution.

2.3   A hearer may of course disregard S's intention to set up a d in the
conversational domain with respect to an action or item referred to, as
the examples below show. $Hc1_3$ and $Hc2_3$ would not represent appropriate
reactions to the input UTT S1 or S2 since they violate a conversational con-
vention that requires adjacent UTTs -- both intra- and inter-turn -- to be
semantically congruent with the previous context.

$Hc1_3$ Allright, we shall do it! $Hc2_3$ Let's go!

However, speakers may change their intentions or goals even within a short
time. $Hc1_3$ could be uttered by S provided that there were a short pause
between the two UTTs or that S or H had indicated in some way that a d

should not be introduced (e.g., if S notices H's signs of impatience toward him/her). In the latter case H would be aware that S had changed his/her goals and would disregard S1 on the assumption that the last UTT expresses S's real intentions at that point in time. The difference between the S's and H's role is that S is free to introduce a d or signal that there is a d and then change his/her mind, while H has to take into account both the introduction and the signalling of a d, unless H wants to disrupt the C on purpose. Both S and H are free to aggravate/perpetuate a d or solve it, though they may not have to do it.

These hypothetical examples show that the introduction of a d is a psychologically and semantically relevant phenomenon. To disregard the introduction of a d, in fact, amounts to producing incoherent and pragmatically inappropriate communications that disrupt a linguistic interaction, unless there are concurrent factors that modify the import of the introduction of, or simply the hint of a d in the world considered by the linguistic C.

2.4   Discontinuities may be introduced and signalled by means of other linguistic forms. But is a very commonly used conjunction to signal that incoming information conflicts somewhat with that already given, i.e., it is used for type (a) of discontinuities. However, but is also used to give a clue that a previously established or known context has to be reactivated because the incoming information is related to, and has to be evaluated with respect to that context.

S7   But didn't you say that you were going to the movies?
S8   But you don't have that much money!
S9   But won't he be tired of just listening?!

Though they are not preceded by any UTT to which the adversative conjunction might be related, S7, S8, and S9 represent examples of UTTs that would be appropriate conversational openings under certain circumstances. This is due to the fact that the introduced d is related to a situational CNT that is known to both S and H and therefore needs not be expressed explicitly in the UTT. The use of but -- that can be dispensed with in all these examples without altering their meaning -- seems to have the function of signalling that there are conflicting elements in the present CNT in relation to the 'given' CNT. S assumes that this might have escaped H's attention and thus explicitly introduces a 'Stop!' signal. In S7 the conflict is related to S's knowledge of H's intentions and the unexpected showing up of H. In S8 the contrast is about H's present action and his/her financial state. In S9 the discrepancy is about the likely lack of interest by a third party toward a prolonged interaction between S and H. It should be noted that this particular use of but seems to be very frequent in daily interactions.

According to my own observations and partially on the basis of excerpts from tapes of daily conversations, but is also used as a means to justify a S's

interruption of another S or the beginning of a conversation after a silence
occurred. In these cases there is no real d introduced, except at a pragmatic level. We may thus extend our concept of introduction of a d to include
this particular use of but, that once more corresponds to giving H a signal
that there is change from the expected course of events.

Finally, but is used in normal conversations as a linguistic device to
reflect a "context space transition", as Reichman (1978) terms it. That is,
it signals a change from a topic under discussion to one that was previously discussed. Her data support this hypothesis. However, in this case too,
to see the use of but as a means to signal that there is a d adequately
captures both a S's purpose and the structural effect derived from it with
respect to a given discourse unit. Moreover, due consideration is thus
given to the H's need to be aware of the introduction of a d, since otherwise he/she would not understand properly what is the relationship between
the present and a preceding text unit; and so it takes into account both
the S's and the H's tasks and goals.

2.5   The second type of discontinuity is introduced whenever it is signalled that new information has (necessarily) to be sought with respect to
that known or given.

S10   This solution is the best one. Not only this...
S11   Not only this solution is the best one...
S12   This is the best solution. Why?...
S13   Why is this the best solution?...

S10 ans S11 contain the phrase not only as a means of signalling the introduction of a d. As with previous examples, a d may be introduced only after
a certain assertion has been made (S10) or right away (S11). A still
different means of introducing a d is provided by recourse to what normally
would be considered a rhetorical question, as in S12 and S13. In certain
circumstances it will be obvious that S is not really waiting for H to provide an answer (the solution of the d), though H might do it since, at least
superficially, the UTT might be interpreted as a normal question. Thus,
usually, after introducing a d by means of a question, S will proceed to
give the additional information thought to be necessary to support the
truth value of a previous assertion. Nonrhetorical questions might also
be hypothesized to introduce a d.

2.6   Discontinuities may be introduced by still other means which characterize the third type of d, namely referral to explicit or implicit existence of alternatives.

S14   Instead of going out... $Scl4_1$ we could watch television!
                                      $Scl4_2$ let's invite few friends!
S15   Peter eats much. Instead Silvia eats too little.
S16   Peter is playing, instead he should be studying.

S17   Instead of playing Peter should be studying
S18   He always looks very happy...
S19   It seems a good idea...   Hc19 But you don't want to!
S20   He thinks it's fine... It isn't!

Instead of signals a d in that it is obvious that S intends to point out
the existence or necessity of a different action or evaluation in relation
to that mentioned. Instead, and on the contrary and on the other hand, have
the same function. The effect obtained seems to be that of underlining the
difference or conflict between two alternatives, thus making it more
salient for H.

That a d has been set up can be seen in S14, for example, if we assume that
S does not complete the UTT with Sc14. H could then likely reply with
something like H1-2$_2$ or Hc1$_1$. These UTTs would be appropriate because they
would take into account the introduced d. For the same reason Hc2$_3$ would be
inappropriate.

In S18-S20 there is at least the possibility that a d is signalled
linguistically by means of verbs such as to seem, to think and to look (and
to believe, to appear, etc.). That is, it is possible that S intends to
signal that there is a discrepancy between the hypothesized or obvious
appearance/state of an actor/action/item and its real state. Often these
verbs are used in the past tense in conjunction with another verb in the
present tense (e.g., "I thought that... but now..."). Whether S intends to
actually introduce a d by these means can often be decided only by relying
on additional information such as prosodic features, nonverbal communication,
or contextually based knowledge. Of course the UTT -- if any -- that follows
one of these types may dispel all doubts. Hc19, thus, could be an appropriate reply to S19. The use of but would only reinforce or confirm the
introduction of a d by the previous S. S20 would be an example of S's
explicit mention that there is a d.

2.7   Another way to introduce a d is available to speakers. It still
expresses the introduction of a d of the third type, namely the referral to
alternatives. This is achieved by using any kind of conditional sentences.

S21   If one were to judge Peter on the basis of his theories, (a)
      everything would be fine! (b) Nevertheless he's not as bad as he
      seems to be.
S22   If I lived near my office I'd be in time for work.
S23   If I had worked harder, I could have managed.

Sentence (a) in S21 signals that the referred action (judging Peter on the
basis of his theories) is not thought to be the most appropriate one and
that a different perspective has to be applied in order to assess Peter's
qualities better. The d is about a possible and a necessary condition. The
main clause implicitly expresses the concept that Peter is "bad". The alternative path to be followed is not mentioned explicitly either, but it is

likely that it deals with Peter's behavior. In (b) there is another $\underline{d}$ introduced, related to the inference derived from the previous UTT. Sentence (b) limits the extent to which this inference is true. It should be noted that (b) is not an instance of aggravation of the previously introduced $\underline{d}$. On the other hand, it does not provide a solution for it either. The first $\underline{d}$ is of the third type, the second one, introduced by nevertheless, is of the first type. S21 can be compared, with respect to this, with S24 and S25-S26.

S24   Peter is nice but stupid. Nevertheless you can count on him.
S25   I didn't gain much from that transaction, nevertheless I managed to
       pay my debts.
S26   I managed to pay my debts though I didn't gain much...

In S24 the first $\underline{d}$ is similar to the second one, in that both limit the extent to which inferences derived from a previous assertion are valid. Thus two $\underline{d}$ of the first type are introduced, while S25 and S26 represent instances of introduction of one $\underline{d}$ only. It should be noted however that the blocked inference is different in the two UTTs, namely, "S did not manage to pay his debts" in S25, and "S got much money from somewhere" in S26. This fact is very relevant from a communicational standpoint and it is possibly related to S's knowledge of H's expectations. The following examples illustrate this point.

S27   Peter is nice but stupid   S28   Peter is stupid but nice
S29   Though stupid, Peter...   S30   Peter... though stupid

Different stress and different informational value are assigned to the characteristics "nice" and "stupid" depending upon what is presented first and what conjunction is used in which place.

2.8   Even incomplete conditional UTTs signal that a $\underline{d}$ of the third type is introduced. The main difference between S31 and the following examples is that the latter are based upon S's assumptions of shared knowledge or upon S's unwillingness to give the necessary information explicitly.

S31   If we were rich, I would immediately buy that house!
S32   I would immediately buy that house!
S33   If we were rich...

S31 is analogous to S21-S23 in terms of its introduction of a $\underline{d}$. That is, it signals that there is a discrepancy between the real state $\underline{x}$ in which S and Y are not rich and a desired state $\underline{z}$ in which they have much money and can afford to buy a house. Assuming that S32-S33 were uttered in a given context that enabled H to 'interpret' these UTTs, they would convey the same information as S31, as far as the introduction of a $\underline{d}$ is concerned. Depending upon this contextual information, H could in fact reply to S32 with $Hc32_1$ or $Hc32_2$, to S33 with $Hc32_1$ or $Hc33$.

Hc32$_1$ Why, don't you have enough money?!
Hc32$_2$ I know, Jane doesn't want to move...
Hc33   Yeah...if we were rich!

It can be hypothesized that d introduced by these means typicaly are not
solved, since their solution is obvious to both participants in the
interaction.

2.9   Speakers usually have a certain number (possibly infinite) of options
available to them to verbalize the experience or the conceptual reality they
want to talk about. Thus the S's choice to use constructions such as the
ones discussed here should be based on pragmatic goals that are relevant to
attaining hierarchically superior goals and should also be congruent with
the S's knowledge of communicational rules and constraints.

Assuming that Grice's maxims (1967) of quantity, quality, relation and
manner are valid and that speakers adhere to them, what is the purpose and
the effect of saying things that do not correspond to reality (e.g.,
conditional sentences), that give H redundant information (e.g., the 'known'
information usually preceding but and similar conjunctions, that mislead
him/her (by asking questions not meant to be answered), or that refer to
states or conditions not wanted or believed to be correct in the first place?

Despite the above negative summary, the contradiction is only apparent. The
main motive for introducing a discontinuity -- and therefore for doing all
the nasty actions mentioned -- seems to be a desire/need to set up an anchor
point in relation to which the message unfolds and has to be evaluated. The
setting up of a d can be seen as implicitly expressing a set of action/
comprehension instructions for the hearer or audience of a C.

(i1)   There is state/object/item X (in which we are interested)
(i2)   Assertion/predication Y (and W, Z, etc.) express properties of X
(i3)   From Y we (you) may derive Y_1 (and Y_2, Y_3, ...Y)
(i4)   STOP! Before we (you) do (i3) we (you) have to consider state/object/
        item K
(i5)   K is related to X
(i6)   K modifies Y
(i7)   K modifies Y_1 (and Y_2, ...Y)
(i8)   An adequate evaluation of X must take into account K

For UTTs like S1 and S2 only instructions (i1)-(i4) are given though even
(i4) is expressed only partially since it amounts to the Stop signal. In
S3-S6 all instructions are given -- here X would be "Peter" and Y "Peter's
niceness", while K would be "Peter's stupidity".

An UTT like S7 could be translated in the following terms. X is Peter, Y is
the non-expressed assertion "Peter has gone to see the movies", Y_1 is
something like "Peter will show up in two hours", K is "Peter enters the

house of S before the two hours have passed". K is in conflict with Y_1 and thus with Y. Y cannot be true. By means of S7 the speaker is making explicit this line of reasoning with the purpose of asking H whether Y is still true since it conflicts with K.

Whether all or only a subset of these or similar instructions are implicitly conveyed, and in what order, seems to be related to the communicative context, that is, to pertinent characteristics of S and H such as amount of shared knoweledge, goals of both participants, and information expressed by nonverbal clues. In written texts, in fact, it will rarely happen that a d is signalled but not made explicit, with perhaps the exception of short notes or letters to friends or colleagues who can supply the unexpressed information.

Further, while for most of the hypothetical examples used it could be assumed that part of the information related to a d was known to H, in longer linguistic interactions this assumption may not be valid. Every UTT may convey new information, but the introduction of a d signals to what information S is assigning more relevance or centrality (see S27-S30). Moreover, the introduction of a d may be seen as a means of substaining the H's attention, by arousing in him/her a state of expectancy; as a means of simply letting H be aware of the existence of a d in relation to a particular state/item S wants to focus on; as a means of satisfying interpersonal obligations without renouncing the expression of a certain evaluation (e.g., H: "What do you think of the new wall's color?", S: "It's very nice, but perhaps the next time you could be more daring and paint it red!").

A very important role of the strategy of introducing a d is in terms of the text structure and development, i.e., as a means of justifying the text production and/or as a clear clue of text unfolding and structure. For instance, in a recent article about psychological aspects of continuing adult education (Leon, 1978), the introduction ends with the sentence: "First of all, what image do we have about the adult student?" and, of course, the immediately following section is dedicated to the solution of this d, while, to readers, the use of first of all signals another d. It arouses the expectancy that the author thinks it necessary to consider other aspects of the topic "adult education" besides the image of adult students.

3. RECOURSE TO DISCONTINUITIES IN SPONTANEOUS CONVERSATIONS

Do people 'use' the strategy of introducing discontinuities in their speech? Are d aggravated and solved? Are there individual and context related differences? What role does the introduction of d play within the entire text structure? In order to start providing a plausible answer to these questions four talks were transcribed and analyzed (Zammuner, 1981). Speakers A and B talked about the abortion issue in a public debate; EL and UC talked about women's condition in a semi-public context. All talks were introductions to the debate itself; thus they are lenghty monologues. The abortion debate was characterized by a much higher degree of formality and by the speakers' attitude of opposition and non-cooperation towards most of their audience. Given these contextual characteristics it was hypothesized that speakers in the two debates would organize their talks differently, i.e., use different strategies and with different frequency. More specifically, speakers A and B were expected to introduce d more frequently, and to use more often type two of discontinuities.

3.1   To be able to compare the four talks, the total number of words (W) and the total number of Cognitive Manoeuvres produced by each speaker were used as parameters. The obtained results show that on the average speakers used content and function words with the same frequency. Roughly 45% of all words were content words. These results are similar to those obtained by Martin and Strange (1968) in their analysis of spontaneous speech; thus, our speakers behaved normally in this respect.

Since speakers talked for different amounts of time, the ratio between number of words and number of Cognitive Manoeuvres (CM) allows us to compare the complexity of the four talks in terms of the strategies speakers used to structure their speech. That is, we have an index that tells us how many words on the average were necessary for each speaker to express one strategy. Speaker B's talk has been found to be the most semantically complex, i.e., she produced the highest number of strategies in comparison to the number of words used to express them. In other words, she was semantically less redundant than the other speakers. On the other hand, speaker EL was the most redundant one, while A and UC were rather similar to each other and not very different from B. This first result is at least partially related to the fact that EL took great care to ensure that her talk was understandable and accepted -- she was the only speaker who produced dubitative forms with some frequency, talked in a very plain and quiet manner, used emphatic stress less often and set up many frames of reference for her subsequent speech. These results already point out the need to consider speakers' goals concerning the communication in order to understand individual differences.

Speakers	EL	UC	A	B
Content words (W)	47.1%	44.6%	46.2%	45.0%
Function words (W)	52.9%	55.4%	53.8%	55.0%
Number W per 1 CM	4.86	3.62	3.51	3.12
CM: Introduce a d	2.0%	4.4%	1.6%	4.8%
Aggravate a d	0.9%	0.4%	1.6%	1.8%
Resolve a d	1.5%	3.5%	1.6%	4.8%

Table 1

The introduction, aggravation or perpetuation, and solution of discontinuities (d) in relation to total number of Cognitive Manoeuvres (CM) and of words (W) produced by EL, UC, A, and B.

Both UC and B, it should be noted, talked as second speakers. This too
might partially help explain the greater similarity between them that also
is noticeable with respect to the introduction of a d. Both UC and B used
this strategy more than twice as often as EL and A, using as a parameter
the total number of strategies used by each speaker (table 1). If we look
only at the total number of times a d was introduced, results are even more
striking since EL, UC, A, and B produced this strategy 4, 9, 2, and 27
times, respectively. The aggravation of a previously introduced d is not
very common for any speaker, but A and B perpetuated a d twice as often as
EL and UC. This result seems to be related to the contextual differences.
A and B talked using rhetorical means more often.

The solution of a d should theoretically be as frequent as its introduction.
From these data it can be noted that this happens only for speakers B and A.
On the one hand, this result can be related to the stronger constraints
that a formal situation puts on speakers so that they exercise more control
over their talk. On the other hand, it was observed that a few times several d were introduced in succession and only one general solution was provided. Further, given the cooperative atmosphere of the debate on women's
condition, it happened that a solution was provided by someone from the
audience after EL or UC had introduced it. Solutions by speakers other than
the four mentioned were not computed. In the more formal debate on abortion
nobody from the audience would ever have thought of violating the implicit
rule of non-interruption of a speaker.

The use of rhetorical questions was very important in the structuring of
the analyzed talks. Speaker A, for instance, began her talk by formulating
two such questions and by organizing the remaining talk as a solution to
these d. However, this in turn was structured in terms of other strategies
(e.g., giving premises, drawing conclusions, stressing something, etc.).
Thus, at a local level, the effect of introducing a d might be very narrowly delimited, but, at a higher level, it makes it possible for speakers to
organize more or less large chunks of information. The same text structure
was even more pronounced in B's talk, in which d introduced by referral to
alternatives, by means of signalling the existence of discrepancies, and by
means of rhetorical questions, were very frequent and served as the 'back-
bone' of most of her talk. Discontinuities introduced by EL and UC generally had a locally relevant effect only, though UC at times showed a tendency
to behave as B did, particularly toward the end of her talk.

3.2   The above results -- though presented very briefly -- support the
claim that recourse to semantic discontinuities is a text production
strategy whose effects are evident both at a local and at a more general
level. From a communicative perspective the recourse to d is justified as
well as necessary in order to prevent one's audience from drawing conclusions that are thought to be inappropriate, to signal the 'direction' of a
communication, and to maintain the audience's attention. The recourse to
d, and more specifically the type of d introduced and the means used to
signal or set it up, as well as whether it is solved, show the speaker's

concern for his/her audience and the attempt to attain his/her goals taking into account conversational rules and contextual variables. These results tentatively indicate that there are both individual and contextual differences in the recourse to discontinuities. Experimental work and more data on spontaneous conversations are needed to judge what degree of interaction there is between individual tendencies and context related characteristics in the recourse to semantic discontinuities.

Though the analysis was carried out with Italian texts, it seems that a d is introduced in the same way in English and in French as well. Here, too, further studies are necessary. However, as far as the strategy per se is concerned, my opinion is that it is to be found in the cognitive repertoire of every person. Its linguistic means may vary from language to language, but its extension and nature should be very generalizable. Given this, a different problem remains to be examined, namely, the introduction of a d without recourse to explicit linguistic devices. This issue seems too complex to be approached at this stage of inquiry.

REFERENCES

Abraham, W.   Some semantic properties of some conjunctions. In S.P. Corder and E.Roulet (Eds.), Some Implications of Linguistic Theory for Applied Linguistics. Bruxelles: Aimav and Didier, 1975.

de Beaugrande, R.   Text, Discourse, and Process. London: Longman, 1980.

---- Text and sentence in discourse planning. In J.S.Petöfi (Ed.), Text vs Sentence. Basic Questions of Text Linguistics. Hamburg: Buske Verlag, 1979.

Chafe, W.L.   Creativity in verbalization and its implications for the nature of stored knowledge. In R.O.Freedle (Ed.), Discourse Production and Comprehension. Norwood: Ablex Publishing Company, 1977.

van Dijk, T.A.   Relevance assignment in discourse comprehension. Discourse Processes, 1979, 2, 113-126.

---- Text and Context. London: Longman, 1977.

Freedle, R.O.   Discourse Production and Comprehension. Norwood: Ablex Publishing Company, 1977.

Grice, H.P.   Logic and conversation. William James Lectures, Harvard University, 1967. In P.Cole and J.L.Morgan (Eds.), Syntax and Semantics. New York: Academic Press, 1975.

Leon, A.   Aspetti psicologici dell'educazione permanente. In M.Debesse and G.Mialaret (Eds.), Educazione Permanente e Formazione Continua. Rome: Armando Armando, 1980. Italian translation of Education Permanente et Animation Socioculturelle. Paris: PUF, 1978.

Martin, J.G., and Strange, W.   The perception of hesitations in spontaneous speech. Perception and Psychophysics, 1968, 3, 427-432.

Posner, R.   Problèmes fondamentaux de linguistique: Signification et usage des connecteurs propositionnels dans les langues naturelles. Mimeo, Technical University of Berlin, 1977.

Reichman, R.   Conversational coherency. Cognitive Science, 1978, 2,
     283-327.
Rieger, C.J.   Conceptual Memory: A Theory and Computer Program for Proces-
     sing the Meaning Content of Natural Language Utterances. PhD
     Dissertation, Stanford University, 1974.
Schank, R.   Rules and topics in conversation. Cognitive Science, 1977,
     1, 421-441.
Schmidt, S.J.   Texttheorie/pragmalinguistik. In H.P.Althaus, H.Henne,
     and H.E.Wiegand (Eds.), Lexicon der Germanistischen Linguistik.
     Tubingen: Niemeyer, 1973.
Segre, C.   The nature of text. In J.S.Petöfi (Ed.), Text vs Sentence.
     Basic Questions of Text Linguistics. Hamburg: Buske Verlag, 1979.
Wilson, D.   Presuppositions and Non-truth Conditional Semantics. New
     York: Academic Press, 1976.
Zammuner, V.L.   Speech Production. Strategies in Discourse Planning:
     A Theoretical and Empirical Inquiry. Hamburg: Buske Verlag, 1981.
Zammuner, V.L. and Job, R.   Analyzing conversations: The role of
     Cognitive Manoeuvres in linguistic planning. The Italian Journal
     of Psychology, 1979, 6, 81-98.

ACKNOWLEDGEMENTS

This research has been partially supported by a N.A.T.O. Study Visit
Award. The author whishes to thank the Department of Experimental Psychology of the University of Leiden for its hospitality and N.H.Frijda, of
the University of Amsterdam, for his helpful criticism and comments on
this research.

INFERENCE

DISCOURSE PROCESSING
A. Flammer and W. Kintsch (eds.)
© *North-Holland Publishing Company, 1982*

HOW DO YOU FILL IN THIS xxx?
ON SOME INTERPRETATION PROCESSES

Yvonne Waern

Department of Psychology
The University of Stockholm, Sweden

This report aims at describing how readers reason as
they search and interpret a missing word in a given
text. Each of thirty-seven psychology students were
instructed to think aloud while they attempted to interpret a missing word in short texts. The thinking-
aloud protocols indicated that the protocols differed,
depending upon how the text was encoded. The common
thought operations consisted in 1) locating schemata
from prior knowledge, 2) suggesting an interpretation,
within the restrictions of the schemata and encoding,
and 3) checking. Different strategies were used to
decide which operation to use and when.

There are two characteristics of texts, which make text processing interesting from a cognitive point of view: on the one hand texts are usually redundant with respect to the idea they convey, on the other they are incomplete in the same respect. When reading a text, the reader must adapt to
these text characteristics. A very redundant text can be quickly read,
once the reader detects the redundancies. A very incomplete text will have
to be carefully read and the gaps filled in with the help of other parts
of the text or the reader´s prior knowledge. Let me consider a special
kind of incompleteness, i.e. when certain words are left out from a connected text. In this case, the redundancy of the text as a whole may enable the reader to understand the meaning of the missing word. The so-
called "cloze" tests of reading comprehension are based on this situation.

The present study poses the question: What do people do when they encounter
an incompleteness in a text? What processes are involved, and what strategies do people use?

The task chosen to elucidate these questions is illustrated by the following example: "She was acapnotic. She simply did not want to smoke." What
does the word "acapnotic" mean?

This type of task, i.e. interpreting words from a context, was studied by
Werner & Kaplan (1952). It may now be possible to come up with some new
insights to Werner & Kaplan´s analysis by employing the tools of information processing psychology as well as making use of the modern developments in modeling text comprehension. In addition, the analysis of a word
interpretation task can complement the study of text comprehension.

The novelties in this investigation, as compared to Werner & Kaplan´s are three: Task requirements will be analyzed (based on Werner & Kaplan´s findings as well as our current knowledge of text-processing). Next, process tracing data in the form of thinking-aloud protocols will be collected. And finally, the protocols will be analyzed, taking the task analysis as the point of departure.

Task analysis

A task analysis aims at providing suggestions for the processes that are required to complete the task, as well as possible variations in these pro- cesses. There are two problems inherent in attempts to perform a task ana- lysis for the word interpretation task. The first has to do with the level of description: Complex processes can be regarded as being constructed from simpler processes, which in turn consist of even simpler processes and so on, until we reach the level of "elementary information processes". To date there is no consensus as to the level on which text comprehension processes should be described. This problem will be resolved by considering the type of data that it is possible to obtain. Here I will address thinking-aloud protocols. The second problem relates to the existence of differences in prior knowledge. Finding the meaning of an unfamiliar word from its context is a task that relies heavily upon prior knowledge. This means that the task performance will differ, depending upon the reader´s prior knowledge. It also means that the processes will differ. Therefore, the task analysis will have to take into account different possible effects of variations in prior knowledge.

The main requirements of the word interpretation task were formulated by Werner & Kaplan as follows: "Adequate signification is based on the compre- hension of a word as possessing a stable and relatively self-contained meaning; it also presupposes the perception and handling of a sentence as a semantically definite entity". (Werner & Kaplan, 1952, op.cit. p. 14.) It should be pointed out that Werner & Kaplan´s study dealt with children, whereas this investigation deals with adults. Considering the development found by Werner & Kaplan, adults should be able to meet these requirements. Thus, the task analysis will have to consider other aspects.

As mentioned above, it must be acknowledged that differences in prior know- ledge may lead to different processes. Prior knowledge may be conceptualized as the existence of "schemata", covering conceptual relationships at diffe- rent levels. I will use this concept to cover different suggestions, put forward by other researchers, such as the concept of "schema", used by Rumel- hart (cf. Rumelhart & Ortony, 1977), or "frame", used by Minsky (1975), or "script", used by Schank (cf. Schank & Abelson, 1977). In this report I will use the concept to cover the semantic aspect, i.e. most like the "script" notion and, for the moment, avoid considering the formal notion of text grammar, which is not relevant in the very short texts used. Schemata may lie on different conceptual levels, covering, for instance, on a low level single words or propositions, and on a high level whole situations.

During reading a text, schemata related to the text will be evoked. The level of these schemata will depend upon the unit of text considered and encoded at the moment of evoking the schema. The text offers different encoding possibilities. An overview of some of these is given in Figure 1.

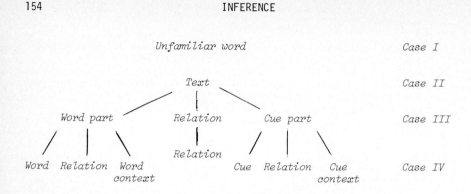

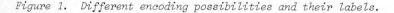

Figure 1. *Different encoding possibilities and their labels.*

<u>Case I</u> covers an encoding of the unfamiliar word. It will evoke phonetic
associations to the word, together with their semantic meanings.
<u>Case II</u> covers an encoding of the text as a whole (disregarding the unfami-
liar word). It will evoke prior knowledge consisting of similar situations
or events.
<u>Case III</u> covers an encoding of the text into three parts: one, where the
word is contained; one, containing a cue to the word; and one indicating
the relation between the word part and the cue part. It will evoke associations to the cue, and also conceptual relationships concerned with the cue
and the relation between cue part and word part.
<u>Case IV</u> covers an encoding of the text into still greater details as shown
in the figure. A prototypical example is an analogy, which will evoke
prior knowledge concerned with the cue and its context and with the different relations expressed in the text.

To continue the analysis, a second suggestion will be made. Within each
encoding case, the same principal operations will be required. They may
be described as follows: 1) identifying that a word is unfamiliar or
missing; 2) seeking prior knowledge schema (or schemata); 3) suggesting
a conceptual interpretation on the basis of this schema (these schemata)
and the restrictions imposed by the encodings; 4) suggesting a word, which
covers the interpretation. One of the operations 3 and 4 may be optional;
5) checking of intermediate and final results. When a check leads to an
unsatisfactory result, the process may repeat itself, with changes of encoding, schemata, or interpretations.

This analysis reveals that the interpretation process as a whole will be
longer and more complex from Case II through Case III to Case IV. More
schemata will be involved as well as more restrictions. This also means
that the more detailed the encoding, the greater the chance for unsatisfactory intermediate results.

This task analysis will now be used in the interpretation of comments,
given by subjects performing the task under a thinking-aloud instruction.

METHOD

Subjects

Thirty-seven undergraduate psychology students participated in the study.
Although participation was voluntary, it should be noted that participation
in psychological experiments is a course requirement.

Material

The texts consisted of two clauses (or sentences), one, where a word was
missing or unfamiliar, the other containing a cue for the word. The
clauses were related to each other in several different ways. The words
were taken from a dictionary of unusual words (Heifetz Byrne, 1974). In
Table 1 each word is presented in a sample sentence, together with the
intended relationship. The texts have been translated from Swedish, where
the unfamiliar words were spelled somewhat differently.

Table 1. Examples of text used.

Text	Intended relationship
She was acapnotic. She had never smoked and did not want to start either.	*Paraphrase*
He wanted to impress people. Therefore his jactancy was rather great.	*Cause*
The lift was full of chankings. In particular, she noted evidence of a zealous use of snuff.	*Subordination*
Hamartiology is as useful for a prospective sinner as psychology for a prospective psychologist.	*Metaphor or analogy*
Some people regarded him as an example of the exinanition of classical thought, but he was, in fact, a subtle and thoroughly philosophical thinker in the best classical tradition.	*Contrast*

The translations of the words according to the dictionary are given in
Table 2.

Table 2. Definitions of the unfamiliar words used.

Word	Definition
Acapnotic	*A non-smoker*
Exinanition	*Loss; destitution*
Chanking	*Spat-out food, such as rind or pits*
Hamartiology	*The study of sin*
Jactancy	*Boasting; bragging*

Each word was used once in each of the five different relations. Thus, 25 different texts were constructed. Each subject read five different texts, each containing one of the unfamiliar words and one of the relations.

PROCEDURE

The subjects were given the texts, one at a time, with the following instruction: "Read this aloud and say aloud all your thoughts while you read". After reading each text, the subjects were asked to 1) paraphrase the meaning of the text, and 2) try to define the meaning of the unfamiliar (or missing) word. The subjects were given some training on the thinking-aloud method before the actual experiment. Twenty subjects read the texts with the unfamiliar word inserted, the other seventeen read the texts with xxx inserted in the place of the unfamiliar word.

RESULTS

Protocol analysis

Each protocol was studied with respect to the following: 1) case analysis. Each protocol was judged as reflecting one or several of the cases, suggested by the task analysis; 2) process analysis. In each protocol, traces of the operations suggested by the task analysis were judged. Protocols indicating operations not contained in the task analysis were sorted into a residual category.

The results will be presented first by analyzing protocols representing "pure" cases and "simple" case combinations. The protocols containing comments which reveal operations not covered by the case analysis will be discussed. Finally, some strategies which can give rise to the thinking behind the protocols will be suggested.

Case I. Word schema.
As mentioned above, twenty subjects were given the unfamiliar word in the text. Thus, 100 protocols could reflect the use of a word schema. Only two protocols indicate that the word schema alone was used. One of these is presented in Table 3.

This protocol reflects all operations suggested by the task analysis: 1) identification of the foreign word (the interruption in reading); 2) the seeking (or here, direct finding) of a word schema (comment 1); 5) a result of a check (comment 4); and 4) a suggested interpretation of the word (comment 5). The proposed operation 3), containing a suggestion of a concept of the word, is not expressed in this protocol. As indicated in the task analysis, this operation is optional.

Table 3. An example of Case I, word schema alone.

Text: The engine worked like a child who doesn't like the food offered: it took in the material and spat out the chankings (Swedish: lankingar) at the same place.

Comment	*Interpretation*

---

1. Yes, this reminds me of "lanka" which you use when you play cards, they are these small cards (this comment occurs when the text has been read as far as "chankings")	*The subject associates directly to some word schema.*
2. "at the same place"	*Continued reading.*
3. Rereads the whole text	*Encoding text.*
4. Yes, I know that	*Check with positive result.*
5. I think "chankings" means small garbage.	*Word suggestion.*

The protocol in Table 3 is interesting, not only because it contains all the operations suggested, but also because it discloses how the context restriction (i.e. engine) changes the original schema (small cards) to a suggestion, which better fits the context (small garbage). This can be interpreted as an example of an assimilation-accommodation cycle, very similar to those described by Piaget (e.g. 1963). First the word is assimilated to the schema, then the schema accommodates to the context.

Case II. Text schema.
This case was defined as being based upon an encoding of the text as a whole, or an encoding of the word clause alone without any relation to the context clause.

Case II alone is reflected in 35 of the protocols. One example is given in Table 4.

Table 4. Example of a protocol, providing evidence for the use of Case II.

Text: The machine worked like a child who doesn't like the food offered: it took in the material and spat out the xxx at the same place. (xxx = chankings)

Comment	*Interpretation*

---

1. Products	*Suggestion of word*
2. at the same place (Experimenter: What did you think, then?)	*already during reading.*
3. Well, I saw some time ago some candy factory, where they did take in different things and there was a lot of that stuff which you usually question in other circumstances, which came out in the form of candy.	*Schema for the factory situation.*

The subject´s comment after the suggestion can either be a construction by afterthought or a real retrospection. Whatever the case, it is interesting to note the detail of the association, (candy factory). The suggested interpretation is much more general (products). Again, this can be regarded as a result of an assimilation-accommodation process. Here, the particular schema is replaced by a more general one, probably due to the lack of detail in the context.

For a comparison with the task analysis all protocols were interpreted and encoded as indicated in the example. Only one occurrence of a particular operation was counted in each protocol. Table 5 shows the number and proportion of protocols, where traces of the operations suggested were found.

Table 5.   Frequencies and proportions of comments, reflecting processes suggested in the task analysis for Case II.

Comment referring to	Unfamiliar word group		Missing word group	
	Frequency	Proportion	Frequency	Proportion
Identification of unfamiliar word	4	.50	--	--
Text schema	4	.50	9	.33
Conceptual interpretation	4	.50	12	.44
Word suggestion	6	.75	24	.89
Check	4	.50	20	.74
Total number of protocols	8		27	

It is evident that much of the processing suggested is not expressed. This is typical for the thinking aloud procedure. It is difficult to interpret the missing traces. They might indicate that the operations suggested are not performed at all, or are performed in an automated way, so that they will not be attended to, or that they are heeded but not mentioned. Here, there exists a possibility to compare the comments given with the actual occurrence of an operation. The identification of the unfamiliar word should have been performed by every subject who read the unfamiliar word and accepted the task. However, only 50 % of the protocols show any trace of this process. If we compare the rest of the comments with this figure, we find that all operations suggested by the task analysis are represented in the protocols to about the same extent or higher, with one exception. This exception concerns comments related to the text schema in the missing word group. In this group the task seems easier. More precise word suggestions rather than conceptual interpretations were given by these subjects. An easy task may be characterized as one, where the subjects process ready-made approaches to solve the task, and thus do not have to attend to the details of the processes. The subjects who are given the unfamiliar word can choose between different approaches, which might make them more attentive to detail.

Case III. Clause schema.
This case was identified in the protocols whenever the subjects mentioned a cue in some way, or attempted to map a cue against the unfamiliar or missing word.

Case III is the most common "pure" case, covering 63 protocols.   One example is given in Table 6.

Table 6.   Example of a protocol, providing evidence for the use of Case III.

Text: He started to study hamartiology.   His first book contained a description of different types of sin.

Comment	*Interpretation*
1. *Yes, I wonder of course what hamartiology means.*	*Identification of unfamiliar word.*
2. *It seems to be something philosophical.*	*Expression of schema.*
3. *Sins, that's so abstract.*	*Identification of cue.*
4. *Or could it be something to do with religion?*	*Search for alternative schema for the cue.*
5. *He studied the Bible in some way too, trying to find out different types of sin performed.*	*A further development of the context part schema; probably as a part of a check.*
6. *It must have something to do with religion.*	*A conceptual interpretation, which is accepted.*

We see in Table 6, how the subject is trying some different schemata on different levels of abstraction: philosophy, religion, Bible.   It is interesting to note how the subject shifts attention from the cue (comment 3) to the text as a whole (comment 5).   This is characteristic for the so-called hermeneutic circle, (cf Palmer, 1969).

All the protocols reflecting Case III were analyzed for comparison with the task analysis as exemplified in Table 6.   Counting only one occurrence of each operation trace per protocol, the figures presented in Table 7 are obtained.

Table 7.   Frequencies and proportions of comments, reflecting processes suggested in the task analysis for Case III.

Comment referring to	*Unfamiliar word group*		*Missing word group*	
	Frequency	*Proportion*	*Frequency*	*Proportion*
Identification of unfamiliar word	28	.78	--	--
Text schema	3	.08	0	0
Cue schema	29	.80	20	.54
Conceptual interpretation	29	.80	18	.49
Word suggestion	22	.60	37	1.00
Check	30	.80	29	.78
Total number of protocols	36		37	

The figures in Table 7 show that the comments correspond rather well to the task analysis. The few associations to the text as a whole may be regarded as a combination of schemata, but were placed here because these associations were so well integrated into the process as a whole.

If we compare the operation traces found in the different groups, it is evident that the subjects in the group given the unfamiliar word are much more explicit about the intermediate results of operations, leading to the suggestion. Further, the subjects in the unfamiliar word group do not always arrive at a specific word suggestion, which on the other hand, the subjects in the missing word group do. The explanation of these differences may be the same as was suggested for Case II above: the task gets "easier", when the word is not presented.

Case IV. Analogy schema.
This case was analyzed only for the texts, which contained an explicit analogy. Three texts, and a total of 21 protocols, were relevant for a Case IV analysis. Of these, only five protocols showed clear evidence of using analogical reasoning. An example of pure analogical reasoning is found in Table 8.

The comments are in agreement with the analysis of analogical reasoning suggested by Sternberg (1977).

Table 8. An example of analogical reasoning.

Text:	A prospective sinner can have as much use of the study of hamartiology as a psychologist has of the study of psychology.	
Comment	*Interpretation*
1. Well then hamartiology must be related to sinner as psychology to psychologist.	*Encoding into an analogy.*
2. Psychology for a psychologist that must be the most important.	*Schema for cue related to cue context.*
3. What can that mean, it must be ...	*Search for concept.*
4. Psychology, that is the science of the psyche.	*Schema for cue.*
5. Then hamartiology must mean the science of sin.	*Suggestion for word.*

Simple case combinations.
It was found that two of the cases suggested could easily be identified in one and the same protocol. These concern combinations with Case I, the word schema search. Other case combinations were more difficult to discern. Let me here give some examples of Case I, combined with some other cases. Such combinations are reflected by 32 protocols, belonging of course, to those 100 who were given texts containing the unfamiliar word.

In many of the combinations with Case I, this case was attempted first, and abandoned for some other case when no suggestion could be found. An example is shown in Table 9.

The protocol from subject 4 in Table 9 shows how the word schema search in comments 3-5 is abandoned and a context directed process is started by attending to the text as a whole. It is difficult to tell why the subject does not develop a clear suggestion from the general concept (something which is the opposite to ...). Maybe the word search operation is too disturbing, as indicated by the subject´s own comment 8.

Table 9.   Example of a protocol, providing evidence for a case shift
*   from Case I to Case III.*

Text: Many people considered him to be an example of the exinanition of
*   classical thought; but he was, in fact, a subtle and thoroughly*
*   philosophical thinker in the best classical tradition.*

Comment	Interpretation
1. *Exinanition? Queer word.*	*Identification of unfamiliar word.*
2. *Well, that exinanition, that is really disturbing.*	*Hung-up on unfamiliar word.*
3. *Ex, that means out or out of.*	*Attempt to use word schema (Case I).*
4. *Inan, I don´t know at all what that means.*	*Continued attempt with word schema.*
5. *It kind of destroys the whole text.*	*Indicates difficulties with encoding.*
6. *So, it must be something which is the opposite to being a thoroughly philosophical thinker, since it says:*	*Expresses the relation between word and cue, derived from*
7. *"He was, in fact, a thoroughly philosophical thinker."*	*Encoding the cue.*
8. *What you stumble on is the word kind of, and you want to get its meaning from the other things,*	*Comment related to the thought process.*
9. *but this is the only thing it is possible to get out of this, I think.*	*Abandoning the task.*

In other protocols, Case I is not abandoned but combined in some way with another case. This often requires an adaptation of either the word to the context interpretation or the context interpretation to the word schema. An example of an adaptation of the context interpretation to the word schema is found in Table 10.

Table 10.   An example of a protocol indicating an adaptation of the
*   text interpretation to a word schema.*

Text: His exinanition consisted in a decline in the value in the
*   bonds he owned.*

Comment	Interpretation

Comment	Interpretation
1. Existence?	Suggestion based upon word schema.
2. Yes, maybe. (Examiner: How do you mean?)	Check and (partial) acceptance.
3. That all his assets consisted in the bonds he owned, and if the value of the bonds declines, then his existence is at stake.	The suggestion of the word changes the interpretation of the text as a whole — an assimilation/distortion effect.
4. Yes.	Suggestion accepted.

An example of an adaptation of the word to the context interpretation is
given in Table 11.

Table 11.   An example of an adaptation of the word to the context
*   interpretation.*

Text: She did not show any great jactancy.   Rather, she was somewhat
*   reluctant to show her ability.*

Comment	Interpretation

Comment	Interpretation
1. She did not show any great jactancy ...	
2. Could it be something with estimation of herself.	Concept, based upon context.
3. "I" (Swedish: jag) and "jact" would be close enough.	Adaptation of word context.
4. Self-reliance or something (the continuation indicates how the cue is used).	Suggestion for word.

These examples from simple case combinations show, that the analysis in
terms of operations to be performed has to be supplemented with an analysis
of the strategy used with the subject. The strategy specifies, when a certain operation shall be used. It is evident that the reader has to decide
where to start, how to continue, if the first attempt fails, and when to
end the process. In the cases presented in Tables 9 and 10, a simple description of the strategy used may be made as follows:

1)   Start with Case I (search for word schema).
2)   If no word schema is found, try another case.
3)   If a word schema is found, seek a schema for the text within the confines of the word schema found.
4)   If a schema has been found for both text and word, insert the schema of the word in the schema for the context.
5)   If the word schema fits in the context schema, accept word schema as an interpretation of the word.
6)   If the word schema fits the context, use the word schema for the interpretation of the word, and end.
7)   If no word interpretation is found, and attempts have been made within some cases, end.

For the protocol exemplified in Table 11 a somewhat different strategy must be proposed. The following rules may be suggested:

1)   Start by considering the context (Case II or III).
2)   If a context schema is found, use the context schema to find a conceptual interpretation.
3)   If a conceptual interpretation has been found, check against word schema.
4)   If a schema has been found for both text and word, insert the schema of the word in the schema for the context.
5)   If the word schema fits in the context schema, use the conceptual interpretation as an interpretation for the word.

By combining different rules for how to start, proceed, and terminate, a very great variety of sequences of operations may be obtained, representing processes actually indicated in the protocols, as well as other possible processes.

Residual

So far, 142 or 75 % of the collected protocols have been described by referring to the task analysis. The remaining 47 protocols indicate operations, not covered by the task analysis. I will not go into the detail of these, but simply characterize the protocols roughly as containing the following: Difficulties in finding an adequate word suggestion, failure of preliminary encodings, encoding difficulties, and distortions of interpretation. Since the task analysis aimed at establishing requirements for a successful interpretation, possible operations behind unsuccessful interpretation processes were, of course, not analyzed. There may be several reasons for an interpretation to fail. The residual protocols obtained may represent some of the most common reasons.

DISCUSSION

It can now be asked how this investigation relates to and supplements current text processing models.

Most empirical research on comprehension processes during reading have used observations of reading times, using more or less fine-grained units of analysis, (e.g. eye fixations by Just & Carpenter, 1980, Carpenter & Just, 1977, or reading times for single phrases by Miller & Kintsch, 1980). The reading times can be used to check hypotheses about reading and comprehension processes, but they cannot themselves give rise to any ideas about text processing. Thinking-aloud protocols are rich enough in information to suggest unforeseen processes as well as to confirm the existence of hypotesized processes.

In the present data, the contents of the thinking-aloud protocols have con- firmed and supplemented the central suggestions found in recent text pro- cessing models.

First, the importance of the reader's prior knowledge has been confirmed. The present data revealed that a great deal of the processing consisted of evoking prior knowledge, here called schemata.

Second, the processing behind attempts to link new material to familiar ma- terial has been detailed. The possibility of finding or constructing such a link has been suggested to be an important determinant of the difficulty people have in processing texts, (cf Haviland & Clark, 1974, Kintsch & van Dijk, 1978, and Miller & Kintsch, 1980). The present data indicate that several operations are invoked in the linking: locating schemata, sug- gesting interpretations within the confines of schemata and encoding, and checking the part and end results.

One unforeseen process was found in some of the protocols, i.e. a process which adapted schemata to interpretations or interpretations to schemata. This process can be regarded as an extension of the linking process. In constructing a link between text as encoded and prior knowledge, encodings as well as schemata may have to be slightly changed. This change is super- vised by the checking operation, which indicates when a change is admissible and when a suggestion is too remote to be acceptable. The data give very few indications about how admissibility or acceptability is determined. The adaptation process and the checking operation may thus present two areas, where further insight is desirable.

A further insight gained by examining the protocols consists of the finding that text processing models must take account of the different possible strategies used by readers to process texts. The possibility that diffe- rent encodings exist means that a strategic decision of how to start is re- quired. Strategic decisions regarding how to proceed and terminate are re- quired when the search does not give any result, or when the checking reveals, that a proposed interpretation does not fit. Strategies have been given very little consideration in recent research into text processing, whereas strategies emerge as a most important concept in problem solving research, (cf Newell & Simon, 1972). Text processing may not always be likened to problem solving. However, when difficulties arise, such as when interpretations are not immediately found, a problem solving account of text processing may be fruitful.

FOOTNOTE

The investigation has been supported by a grant from the Swedish Council for Research in the Humanities and Social Sciences. Data have been collected by Susanne Askwall. I am greatly indebted to Janet Powell at Yale University for giving me the words and letting me use texts, written by her, in some preliminary thinking-aloud sessions.

REFERENCES

Carpenter, P.A. & Just, M.A.   Reading comprehension as eyes see it.   In
    M.A. Just & P.A. Carpenter (Eds.).   Cognitive processes in comprehen-
    sion, Hillsdale, New Jersey: Lawrence Erlbaum Ass., 1977.
Haviland, S.E. & Clark, H.H.   Acquiring new information as a process in
    comprehension.   Journal of Verbal Learning and Verbal Behavior, 1974,
    13, 512-521.
Heifetz Byrne, J.   Mrs. Byrne's dictionary of unusual, obscure, and pre-
    posterous words.   Secaucus, New Jersey: University Books, Citadel Press,
    1974.
Just, M.A. & Carpenter, P.A.   A theory of reading: From eye fixations to
    comprehension.   Psychological Review, 1980, 87, 329-354.
Kintsch, W. & van Dijk, T.A.   Toward a model of text comprehension and
    production.   Psychological Review, 1978, 85, 363-394.
Miller, J.R. & Kintsch, W.   Readability and recall of short prose passages:
    A theoretical analysis.   Journal of Experimental Psychology: Human
    Learning and Memory, 1980, 6, 335-354.
Minsky, M.   A framework for representing knowledge.   In P.H. Winston
    (Ed.).   The Psychology of Computer Vision.   New York: Mc Graw-Hill,
    1975.
Newell, A. & Simon, H.A.   Human problem solving.   Englewood Cliffs, New
    Jersey: Prentice-Hall, 1972.
Palmer, R.E.   Hermeneutics.   Interpretation theory in Schleiermacher,
    Dilthey, Heidegger and Gadamer.   Northwestern University Press,
    Evanston, 1969.
Piaget, J.   The origins of intelligence in children.   New York: W.W. Horton,
    1963.
Rumelhart, D.E. & Ortony, A.   The representation of knowledge in memory.
    In R.C. Anderson, R.J. Spiro & W.E. Montague (Eds.).   Schooling and
    the acquisition of knowledge.   Hillsdale, New Jersey: Lawrence Erlbaum
    Ass., 1977.
Schank, R. & Abelson, R.   Scripts, Plans, Goals and Understanding.   An
    inquiry into human knowledge structures.   New York, London: Lawrence
    Erlbaum Ass., 1977.
Sternberg, R.J.   Intelligence, information processing, and analogical
    reasoning: The componential analysis of human abilities.   Hillsdale,
    New Jersey: Lawrence Erlbaum Ass., 1977.
Werner, H. & Kaplan, E.   The acquisition of word meanings: A developmental
    study.   Monographs of the Society for Research in Child Development,
    1952, 15, No. 1. (Whole No. 51).

DISCOURSE PROCESSING
A. Flammer and W. Kintsch (eds.)
© North-Holland Publishing Company, 1982

INFERENCE PROCESSES IN DISCOURSE COMPREHENSION
MEASURED BY SENTENCE READING TIMES

Karl F. Wender

Institut für Psychologie
Technische Universität Braunschweig

When reading a text a person will sometimes have a choice
between several inferences to connect two events. In such
an ambiguous situation the reader will not always immediately draw one of the inferences. If an additional cue
points to one of the inferences then the reader will
establish this connection. Different stories were constructed corresponding to a consistent, an inconsistent,
and a without-antecedent condition. Sentence reading time
was measured. The results lie in the predicted direction
but do not reach statistical significance.

INTRODUCTION

Many authors have stressed the importance of inferencing during discourse
processing. Trabasso and Nicholas (1980), for example, follow John Dewey,
when they state that the process of inferencing is most central in
establishing the meaning of a text. Others argue that inferences and
elaborations are essential for remembering and recall (Anderson, 1980).
Modifying the title of a book about causality by Mackie (1974), one might
say that inferences are the cement of discourse. Although many studies
have investigated the role of inferences there still remain open questions.

When given a piece of a text it is obvious that numerous inferences and
elaborations can be drawn based upon it. This has been called the explosion
of inferences (Rieger, 1975). One question now is which of all possible
inferences are established at a given time.

In this paper we will examine cases in which several inferences are
possible to connect two pieces of information in a text. This may be
looked at as an ambiguous situation. We make the hypothesis that in such
a situation the reader will not always immediately choose one of the inferences. In our interpretation the reader will select an appropriate inference when he gets an additional piece of information that disambiguates
the situation.

This view is similar to that of Singer (1979) who found that the agent,
patient, and instrument cases where not inferred during sentence encoding
but rather at the time when the inference was required by a test sentence.

The text material we use in this experiment is similar to that of Thorndyke (1976). However, he used a recognition test whereas we employ a technique that was introduced in a similar context by Haviland and Clark

(1974). The procedure consists of presenting a text sentence by sentence and measuring the sentence reading time. This assumes that the time sub-jects need to read a sentence is related to the ongoing processes. The technique has the advantage that something about the time course of in-ferencing can be said.

In this experiment we consider sentences of the form "event A has as a possible consequence event B." For example "The hamburger chain owner was afraid that his love for French fries might ruin his marriage." The love for French fries is event A and the ruined marriage is event B. In general there may be many reasons why event A leads to event B. The question of interest here is which of the possible reasons does the reader infer and at which point in time does he draw the inference. This may depend on several conditions. In this experiment we try to investigate a few of them.

In general our hypothesis is that the reader will draw an inference only if in some sense he is invited to do so. More specifically, if a sentence states that "A possibly leads to B" and if in the preceding text nothing relevant has been said about this relationship, then the reader will not necessarily search for a possible inference. If, on the other hand, the preceding text contains a possible reason, then the reader will look for a connection between this information and the sentence that "A possibly leads to B".

Our experimental approach is to measure sentence reading times. Assuming that drawing an inference takes some measurable amount of time we predict that reading the sentence "A possibly leads to B" should take more time if the text has already given some relevant information.

To give an example, if the sentence about the hamburger chain owner's love for French fries is preceded by a sentence stating that his wife did not like fat men then the reader may draw the inference that the cause for ruined marriage is the hamburger chain owner's weight problem.

We consider one further case. In some of our stories the sentence "A leads to B" is followed by a statement that the protagonist decided to take some action to prevent B from occuring. This sentence will be easier to under-stand if the reader already has a hypothesis in mind about why A leads to B. Otherwise he will have to draw an appropriate inference. Hence we pre-dict a shorter reading time for the sentence about the protagonist's pre-ventive action if the sentence "A possibly leads to B" is preceded by a statement about a possible reason.

METHOD

Subjects.   So far 12 adult subjects have participated in the experiment. All of them were native speakers of German.

Materials.   The verbal materials consisted of three basic stories. From each basic story six different versions were derived. For each basic story there was a set of critical sentences which were either included or not included in a specific version of a story. The stories were between 13 and 18 sentences long.

The way in which the different versions were constructed may be illustrated

by the story about Johanna. Johanna is described as a coed living together
with other students in an apartment. Because she has had a disagreement
with her father he does not pay for her studies any more. Therefore she has
to work for her living and she takes a job at a nightclub.

The set of critical sentences was as follows. In the experiment the stories
were presented in German.

(1 A)   During the day she was often very tired and could not concentrate
        on her studies.

(1 B)   She was careful that her prudish professor did not hear about her
        job in the nightclub.

(2)   She was afraid that the job in the nightclub might ruin her
        academic career.

(3 A)   She decided to look for a daytime job.

(3 B)   She decided to look for a more respectable job.

Table 1 shows which of the critical sentences were included in each of the
versions of this story. It also indicates whether each specific story was
classified as consistent, inconsistent, or without antecedent. The logic
behind this classification was as follows.

Table 1: Critical sentences included in stories 1 to 6

No. of story	sentences included	condition
1, 7, 13	1 A, 2, 3 A	consistent
2, 8, 14	1 B, 2, 3 A	inconsistent
3, 9, 15	- , 2, 3 A	without antecedent
4, 10, 16	1 A, 2, 3 B	inconsistent
5, 11, 17	1 B, 2, 3 B	consistent
6, 12, 18	- , 2, 3 B	without antecedent

Sentence (2) states Johanna's fear that the job in the nightclub might
have a negative effect on her academic career. In order to find out why
one may draw one or more out of several possible inferences. Two possible
reasons are given in sentences (1 A) and (1 B). The reader may take these
as antecedents for an appropriate inference about the destructive effect of
nightclub jobs on academic life. Sentences (3 A) and (3 B) describe a
possible consequence Johanna may decide to take.

It is obvious that sentence (3 A) is directly related to sentence (1 A) and
also (3 B) is related to (1 B). Thus stories number 1 and 5 are called con-

sistent. On the other hand, if sentences (1 B) and (3 A) or sentences (1 A) and (3 B) appear together in one story we call this condition inconsistent. If neither sentence (1 A) nor sentence (1 B) is included we call this the condition without antecedent.

Procedure. The experimental design followed a 3 x 3 Latin-square with factors (A) condition (consistent, inconsistent, without antecedent), (B) stories, and (C) groups of subjects. Each group of subjects consisted of four members. Subjects were tested individually. Stories were presented sentence by sentence on an CRT screen. There was one additional first story that was used to familiarize subjects with the task and was not included in the analysis. Each sentence remained on the screen until the subject pressed a key. Then this sentence disappeared and was replaced the next sentence. Time was measured from the appearance of the sentence until the subject pressed the key. Subjects were instructed to read the sentences with normal speed and to treat them as a coherent story.

RESULTS AND DISCUSSION

Two dependent variables were analyzed. The first was the reading time for sentence 2. The second was the reading times for sentences 3 A and 3 B which were averaged. For sentence 2 the consistent and inconsistent conditions were combined since these make no difference before sentence 3 has occurred.

For sentence 2 we have two conditions to compare: With antecedent (stories 1, 2, 4, and 5) and without antecedent (stories 3 and 6). From our hypothesis we derive the prediction that under the condition with antecedent reading times should be longer than without antecedent.

In the data mean reading times were almost identical, 2532 msec. with antecedent and 2515 msec. without antecedent. Although in the predicted direction the difference is statistically nonsignificant.

The predictions for sentence 3 were as follows. When coming to sentence 3 in a consistent text the reader has already found a relationship between sentences 1 and 2. Since this relation is consistent with sentence 3 reading time for sentence 3 should be relatively short. Under the inconsistent condition, on the contrary, the reader detects a partial contradiction which should lead to an increased reading time.

For the condition without antecedent we also predict that reading sentence 3 should take longer than under the consistent condition. If sentence 1 is not contained in a text then no information about the connection between sentences 2 and 3 has been available before sentence 3 appears. Therefore combining sentences 2 and 3 should take longer, which means an increased reading time for sentence 3.

Whether reading time for sentence 3 under the inconsistent condition should be longer or shorter than under the condition without antecedent is not clear. At least we don't have a specific prediction.

Mean reading times for sentence 3 are given in Table 2. An analysis of variance following a 3 x 3 Latin-square had the following results. The factors (A) condition and (B) story were not significant. The factor (C)

group of subjects and the general interaction term reached significance at
the 1 % level.

Table 2: Mean reading times (msec.) for sentence 3
         G i is the group number

| stories | condition | | | mean |
	consistent	inconsistent	without antecedent	
1 - 6	G 1 2325	G 2 1825	G 3 2845	2332
7 - 12	G 3 3085	G 1 3010	G 2 2375	2823
13 - 18	G 2 1985	G 3 2945	G 1 2625	2518
mean	2465	2593	2615	2558

The mean reaction times for factor A show the predicted order. However, the
differences are not large enough to reach statistical significance. Therefore the conclusions have to be very cautious. The result that the observed
differences did not reach significance may be due to the small sample size.
Hence our next step is to include more subjects.

A strong effect in the data comes from the individual differences. As a
main effect this may not be so interesting. If, however, as our data
suggest, there is an interaction between individuals and conditions and/or
stories this may result from different strategies subjects employ. Further
research will have to look for means to handle them. As a further remark
we want to point to two directions for future research. One is to look for
a combination of the measurement of sentence reading times with a recognition or recall procedure. This would be desirable to validate the experimental approach. A second possibility would be to investigate in more
detail the conditions which lead to the selection of one inference in an
ambiguous situation. Memory load as well as real world knowledge may be
influential.

For the present study we come to the following conclusion. Although the
results were statistically not significant we have the impression that the
verbal material as well as the experimental procedure are well suited for
our purposes. Therefore, rather than giving up our hypothesis we will continue the investigation.

REFERENCES

Anderson, J.R. Cognitive psychology and its implications. San Francisco: Freeman, 1980.

Haviland, S., and Clark, H.   What's new? Acquiring information as a process in comprehension. Journal of Verbal Learning and Verbal Behavior, 1974, 13, 512-521.

Mackie, J.L.   The cement of the universe, a study of causation. Oxford: Oxford University Press, 1974.

Rieger, C.   Conceptual memory. In R. Schank (Ed.). Conceptual information processing. Amsterdam: North-Holland, 1975.

Singer, M.   Processes of inference during sentence encoding. Memory & Cognition, 1979, 7, 192-200.

Thorndyke, P.W.   The role of inferences in discourse comprehension. Journal of Verbal Learning and Verbal Behavior, 1976, 15, 437-466.

Trabasso, T., and Nicholas, D.W.   Memory and inferences in the comprehension of narratives. In F. Wilkening, J. Becker, and T. Trabasso (Eds.). Information integration by children. Hillsdale, N.J.: Erlbaum, 1980.

DISCOURSE PROCESSING
A. Flammer and W. Kintsch (eds.)
© *North-Holland Publishing Company, 1982*

ANSWERING QUESTIONS FROM TEXT: A PROCESS MODEL

Murray Singer

Department of Psychology
University of Manitoba
Winnipeg, Canada

Singer (1979, 1981) has presented data supporting a process
model that addresses sentence verification and question
answering in relation to antecedent sentences. The present
study asked whether the predictions of the model are
accurate when the antecedent messages are brief texts. In
Experiment 1, readers verified sentences that were true or
false, and explicit or implicit, in relation to antecedent
passages. In Experiment 2, readers used the responses YES,
NO, or DON'T KNOW to answer questions about brief passages.
The response latencies were generally consistent with the
predictions of the model. Neither the response latencies
nor the error rates were prohibitively inflated, relative
to those measured when single sentences were used as the
antecedent messages.

During the first half of the 1970's, proposals were made concerning a series of
sentence verification models (Carpenter & Just, 1975; Clark & Chase, 1972;
Glucksberg and Trabasso, 1973; Trabasso, Rollins, & Shaughnessy, 1971). These
models quite successfully specified the mental operations that are executed when
one has to decide if a sentence is true in the context of a picture, another
sentence, or long-term knowledge of the world. In two recent studies, these
methods have been applied to the verification of test sentences in relation to
realistic messages (Singer, 1979, 1981). Singer (1981) presented one model that
specified the processes that contribute to the verification of test sentences
that, in relation to their antecedents, are (1) either true or false, and (2)
either explicit or implicit. A second model included reference, for the first
time, to the reader's option of responding DON'T KNOW, in addition to TRUE and
FALSE. This model generated the accurate prediction that correct DON'T KNOW
responses would be faster than correct FALSE responses.

The data used to evaluate these models were derived from tasks such as the
following. Subject viewed an antecedent sentence like the aunt made the
purchase at the shop on a television screen for 3.0 seconds. Immediately after,
the antecedent was replaced by a corresponding test sentence, like the aunt
bought some flowers. The subjects had up to 4.0 seconds in which to judge the
test sentence TRUE, FALSE, or DON'T KNOW, responding by means of appropriately
labelled switches.

One limitation of these studies is that the messages that have served as the
antecedent materials have consisted of a single sentence. This approach made
the initial evaluation of these models easier in at least two ways. (1) Readers
can maintain the representation of a single sentence in a short-term working
memory (Kieras, 1981; Kintsch & van Dijk, 1978). With one-sentence messages,
subjects have not needed to execute searches of long-term memory (LTM) which are
more time consuming (Norman, 1976), and most likely more variable in duration.

(2) Longer texts would be expected to raise the readers' error rates for at least two reasons. First, there is a distinct possibility that each fact would not be stored in LTM. Second, readers might fail to retrieve a stored fact in the allotted time, because of the increased complexity of the message. If error rates were high, this would mean that a relatively large proportion of correct trials would be based on the reader's accurate guesses, rather than the operations specified by the proposed model. It would thus be misleading to interpret the response latencies as reflection of the model.

Despite these pitfalls, Singer's (1981) verification models need to be evaluated with reference to data based on more extensive tests. Otherwise, they will not serve as useful instruments for assessing what a reader has learned from a message. The present study was designed for this purpose.

The Model

The model is referred to as VAIL, an acronym for "Verifying the Assertions and Implications of Language." While different versions of VAIL comment upon different verification tasks, all versions are closely related in that they consist of component operations drawn from a very limited set. For this reasons, the essential principles of the model can be explained with reference to any version.

VAIL1 is the version that addresses the verification of test sentences that are explicit or implicit, and true or false, in relation to their antecedents. Consider sentence set (1). Sentences (1a) and (1b) are possible antecedents, and (1c) and (1d) are possible tests. For example, after reading (1b), the patient was examined at the hospital, one can judge sentence (1d), a principal examined the patient, to be false. The reason for this is that (1d) conflicts with the implication of (1b) that the relevant agent is a doctor. Sequences (1a-1c), (1a-1d), (1b-1c), and (1b-1d) exemplify the experimental conditions explicit true, explicit false, implicit true, and implicit false, respectively.

(1) a. The doctor examined the patient at the hospital.
     b. The patient was examined at the hospital.
     c. A doctor examined the patient.
     d. A principal examined the patient.

VAIL1, shown in Figure 1, comments upon the verification of the test sentence in this task. (Figure 1 also shows features of a second version of VAIL, discussed below). At stage 1, the test sentence is encoded to its propositional form. For example, the propositional notation for a doctor examined the patient is (EXAMINE, DOCTOR, PATIENT) (Kintsch, 1974). It is assumed that "given" and "new" information from the test sentence are distinguished in this representation (Haviland & Clark, 1974).

At stage 2, the reader matches the given information, patient (modified by the definite article, the), with the corresponding information in the representation of the antecedent. Stage 3 is a test that asks whether the antecedent representation includes any information for the case (Fillmore, 1968) of the new element of the test sentence. In the present example, the new element, doctor (modified by the indefinite article, a), fills the agent case. For the sequence (1b-1c), the output of stage 3 is "no", since (1b) does not mention an agent. In this event, the reader searches LTM at

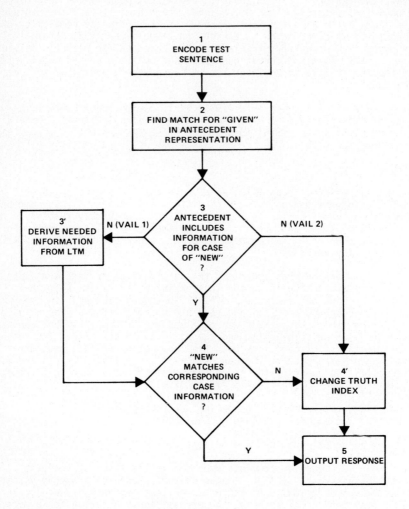

Figure 1
Combined Flowchart for Process Models VAIL1 and VAIL2

stage 3', to determine whether there is a concept that typically fills the "empty" case. For sequence (1b-1c), this search retrieves the fact that doctor is the agent that usually conducts medical examinations.

At stage 4, the new element of the test sentence is compared either with the concept filling the corresponding case in the antecedent representation, or with the concept retrieved from LTM. When a match is found, the subject can output a response index, initialized at TRUE (Clark & Chase, 1972), at stage 5. In the event of a mismatch, the response index must be changed from TRUE to FALSE at stage 4' before a response is made.

VAIL1 specifies that operations 1, 2, 3, 4, and 5 are common to all four experimental conditions, and that, in addition, 3' needs to be executed for the implicit conditions and 4' for the false conditions. Consistent with these predictions, Singer (1979, Experiment 4) measured mean correct latencies of 1926, 2167, 2302, and 2480 msec for the true explicit, false explicit, true implicit, and false implicit conditions, respectively.

Additional assumptions of the model are described by Singer (1981). Other versions of VAIL differ slightly from VAIL1, and one in particular will be discussed in the treatment of Experiment 2.

EXPERIMENT 1

The first experiment was designed to determine whether the predictions of VAIL1 are supported when the antecedent message consists of a brief text rather than a single sentence. In particular it was predicted that correct response latencies would be longer for test sentences expressing ideas implicit in the text than for explicit ones, and longer for false than true test sentences.

Method

Materials. The verbal materials consisted of 24 prose passages and corresponding test sentences. The passages were based upon sets of sentences like set 1, discussed earlier. Each passage consisted of three sentences, which described a simple situation or event.

The 24 sentence sets were drawn from the 36 inspected by Singer (1979, Experiment 4). Of the 24, 8 sets addressed each of the agent, patient, and instrument cases (Fillmore, 1968). The crucial sentence comprised either the first or second of its passage, but never the third.

Table 1 shows one sample set of materials. The subjects could view the passage either with or without the parenthetical phrase, followed by a test sentence that included the word either before or following the slash. The four passage-test combinations correspond to the four experimental conditions obtained by crossing explicit-implicit and true-false.

Table 1
Sample Materials for Experiment 1 (Instrument Case)

Antecendent or Test	Passage or Sentence
Antecendent	The hikers doused the bonfire (with the water)[a][b].
	The rising sun was the signal to move on. This had been the nicest of their campsites.
Test	The hikers used some water/shears[c].

[a]The critical antecedent sentence is underlined.
[b]The phrase in parentheses was included in the explicit antecedents, and excluded in the implicit antecedents.
[c]The true and false test sentences used the words before and after the slash, respectively.

From the 24 sets of material, four lists were created, each of which included 2 passage-tests sequences for each of the conditions obtained by crossing explicit-implicit, truth, and case. Across the lists, each set of materials appeared in each experimental condition exactly once.

The critical implications of the sentence sets are ones that most members of the subject population agree about, according to norms described by Singer (1977, 1979). Singer's subjects were asked to specify the three concepts most likely to fill a particular case in relation to some action. For the phrase, hit the nail, for example, 96% of subjects gave hammer as the first choice instrument. The 24 phrases examined here made implications that agreed with the first choices of 89.0% of subjects in the norming studies.

Four passage-test sequences were included at the beginning of each list for practice. Finally, the choice of the falsifying elements like shears in Table 1 has been described in detail by Singer (1979, p. 198).

Subjects. The subjects were 53 male and female students of Introductory Psychology at the University of Manitoba. All subjects were native speakers of English. They participated in partial fulfillment of a course requirement.

Procedure. The sessions were conducted with groups of one to four subjects. Each group was randomly assigned to view one of the four experimental lists. The passages and test sentences were displayed on television monitors controlled by a DEC PDP8/A computer. Subjects registered their responses by means of two switches labelled TRUE and FALSE.

The session consisted of 4 practice and 24 experimental trials. The subject held his/her index fingers on the response switches. On each trial, a fixation point appeared on the screen for 3 sec. Immediately afterwards, the subject viewed the three sentences comprising a passage, one sentence at a time. Each sentence appeared for 3 sec. After the removal of the third sentence, the screen remained black for 5 sec. The subject then had 4 sec to view the test sentence and register a response. Responses and response latencies were recorded automatically. The intertrial interval was 5 sec. The subject did not receive feedback after each trial. Practice trials were not explicitly distinguished for the subjects.

Results

In all analyses, the effects of concern were explicit-implicit, truth, and case. Whether these variables are "between-" or "within-" depends on whether subjects or materials is the random variable.

Errors. Subjects made errors by pressing the incorrect switch or by failing to respond within the 4 sec limit. A criterion of 14 correct reponses for the 24 experimental trials was adopted. On this basis, the data of one subject, who made 12 errors, were discarded.

The error rates for Experiment 1 are shown in parentheses in Table 2. The mean error rate was .125. Analysis of variance was applied to these values, alternately treating subjects and materials as the random variable. (An α level of .05 is adopted). There was a main effect of case only for the subjects-random analysis, $F_1(2,98)=4.31$, $MSe=.21$, with mean values of .164, .114, and .098 for the agent, patient, and instrument cases, respectively. The explicit-implicit and truth effects were not significant. Case interacted with truth, $F_1(2,98)=14.9$, $MSe=.19$, $F_2(2,21)=13.5$, $MSe=.007$, and marginally with explicit-implicit, $F_1(1,49)=4.10$, $MSe=.22$, $F_2(1,21)=3.87$, $MSe=.009$, $p=.07$. Finally, the subjects-random analysis revealed several significant interactions involving the subject group variable, although the group main effect was not itself significant, $F<1$.

Table 2
Response Latencies (msec) and Error Rates (in Parentheses) for Experiment 1

Case	True		False	
	Explicit	Implicit	Explicit	Implicit
Agent	1921 (.14)	2172 (.22)	2273 (.18)	2488 (.12)
Patient	1931 (.06)	2038 (.08)	2279 (.14)	2393 (.18)
Instrument	1896 (.10)	2028 (.22)	2183 (.03)	2066 (.05)

Response latencies. Of particular concern are the correct response latencies, also shown in Table 2. Analysis of variance applied to these scores revealed significant main effects both of explicit-implicit and truth. Subjects needed 2000 msec to repond on true trials, and 2280 msec on false trials, $F_1(1,49)=53.7$, $MSe=195704$, $F_2(1,21)=37.8$, $MSe=49801$. The mean correct latencies for explicit and implict items were 2082 and 2197 msec, respectively, $F_1(1,49)=14.4$, $MSe=154995$, $F_2(1,21)=7.7$, $MSe=40765$. The case main effect reached significance only for the subjects-random analysis, $F_1(2,98)=13.0$, $MSe=118958$, with values of 2218, 2160, and 2043 msec for the agent, patient, and instrument cases, respectively. As in the error analysis, several interactions involving the subject group factor emerged as significant in the subjects-random analysis, and the subject group main effect was not significant.

Inspection of Table 2 reveals that of the six comparisons of explicit versus implicit latencies, there was one reversal: For the false instrument condition, correct latencies of 2183 and 2066 msec were measured for the explicit and implicit tests items, respectively. The explicit-implicit by truth by case interaction, however, was not significant.

Discussion

The latency scores are in good agreement with those derived from the single sentence antecedent procedure (Singer, 1979): Analyses revealed main effects of the explicit-implicit factor and of truth, with no interaction between the two. The fact that implicit latencies exceed explicit laten- cies indicates that subjects do <u>not</u> reliably draw highly probably pragmatic inferences during reading. Singer (1979) attributed this to the very large number of implications of even simple messages. By now, several factors that guide inference processing in reading have been examined, including the preservation of text coherence (Hayes-Roth & Thorndyke, 1979; Singer, 1980), and thematic relatedness (Walker & Meyer, 1980).

One concern about extending these techniques to brief text antecedents was that it would result in higher error rates. The error analyses, however, revealed effects neither of explicit-implicit nor truth. More importantly, the overall error rate of .125 is comparable to that of .110 measured by Singer (1979, Experiment 4), whose antecedent messages were single sentences.

Given the nonsignificance of the explicit-implicit by truth by case intera- ction, it is difficult to assess the explicit-implicit reversal detected for the false instrument latencies. It should be noted that, though Singer (1979) did not obtain this reversal, his false instrument materials yielded the smallest of the six explicit-implicit differences. This suggests that, above and beyond the consistent patterns measured here, the idiosyncratic semantic features of experimental materials may have a discernable impact on the results. This issue will receive further attention later.

The overall mean correct latency of 2140 msec for Experiment 1 was actually lower than the value of 2219 msec measured using single sentences as the antecedents (Singer, 1979, Experiment 4). This is quite surprising, given that the present subjects needed to examine their memory for more detailed message than did Singer's. This result is, however, in good agreement with the similarity of error rates measured in the two studies. While it is possible that between-experiment subject differences contributed to this latency pattern, this does not seem very likely, since both experiments used data from more than 40 individuals drawn from the same pool. In conclusion, the results generally support VAIL1, and indicate that the verification technique may be fruitfully used with brief passages as the antecedent messages.

EXPERIMENT 2

The tasks that have been addressed by previous sentence verification models (Carpenter & Just, 1975; Clark & Chase, 1972; Trabasso et al., 1971) permitted subjects to respond only TRUE or FALSE. Singer (1981) has argued that, in relation to realistic messages, subjects should be given the option of saying that they do not know whether a test item is true or false. Consider sentence set (2). When sentence (2d) follows (2a), it is true; and when it follows (2b), it is false. Just as obviously, we can agree that the truth value of 2d is unknown when it follows (2c).

(2) a. The tourist ate the egg on the patio.
     b. The tourist ate the fish on the patio.
     c. The tourist ate on the patio.
     d. The tourist ate an egg.

Singer (1981) presented a model, VAIL2, which addresses this task. As shown in Figure 1, the only difference between VAIL2 and VAIL1 is as follows. For VAIL1, the failure of test 3 led to an attempt to retrieve the needed information from LTM at stage 3'. For the present task, test 3 fails only for the DON'T KNOW (DK) condition. Consider the sequence (2c-2d). Antecedent (2c) specifies no patient case, the case of the "new" test element, egg. This permits control to flow from stage 3 directly to stage 4', where the response index is changed from TRUE to DK. The subject may then respond at stage 5. For TRUE and FALSE items, the necessary mental operations are the same as those   described for VAIL1.

VAIL2 thus specifies the sequences 1-2-3-4-5, 1-2-3-4-4'-5, and 1-2-3-4'-5 for TRUE, FALSE, and DK items, respectively. Accordingly, it generates the prediction that FALSE latencies will exceed DK latencies by the duration of the matching test, stage 4. VAIL2 also predicts faster TRUE than FALSE latencies. The TRUE tests include one more content word in common with their antecedents than do the FALSE tests (i.e., the critical element, egg). Since this extra overlap might speed up the TRUE responses, the prediction of greatest interest concerns the FALSE-DK comparison. Finally, the truth index is again assumed to be initialized at TRUE, and it is further assumed that it takes the same amount of time to change the truth index to DK as to FALSE.

The purpose of Experiment 2 was thus twofold: to inspect the predictions of VAIL2, and to further consider the usefulness of the present paradigm for assessing knowledge acquisition from text.

Method

Materials. The experimental materials were 27 passages based upon sentence sets like (2) above. As in Experiment 1, each passage expanded upon its sentence set to describe a simple situation or event in three sentences. There were nine passages for each of the agent, patient, and instrument cases. Table 3 shows one sample passage and corresponding test items.

Table 3
Sample Materials for Experiment 2 (Patient Case)

Antecedent or Test	Passage or Question
Antecedent	The aunt purchased the flowers at the shop.[a]
	The aunt purchased the pen at the shop.[b]
	The aunt made the purchase at the shop.[c]
	Then she took a taxi to the station.
	The visit would be fun.
Question	Did the aunt purchase some flowers?

[a]Critical sentence for YES antecedent.
[b]Critical sentence for NO antecedent.
[c]Critical sentence for DON'T KNOW antecedent.

Table 3 shows that the test items were phrased as questions to be answered rather than sentences to be verified. Clark and Clark (1977, p. 111) have noted that, in the context of an antecedent like the aunt purchased the flowers at the shop, it does not make much difference whether we verify the test sentence, the aunt purchased some flowers, or answer the question, did

the aunt purchase some flowers. Because answering yes-no questions seems
somewhat more natural than verifying sentences, the subjects were instructed
to answer questions using the responses YES, NO, and DK. The VAIL2 analysis
and predictions, however, are not changed.

The questions for the agent case passages were phrased in the passive, as in
was the book read by a chemist? The reason for this is that it is more
usual for the new element of the question, which is the element being
interrogated, to appear at the end of the question (cf. Clark & Clark, 1977,
Chapter 3). In order to use agent questions with this "usual" given-new
order, it was necessary to phrase the agent questions in the passive voice.

Three test lists were contructed. Each list included 27 experimental
passage-question sequences: three for each of the nine conditions
obtained by crossing response (YES, NO, DK) with case. Across the lists,
each passage occurred once in each response condition. Four practice
passage-test sequences were included at the beginning of each list.

An examination of Table 3 shows that the crucial sentences in the YES and
NO conditions included three nouns, as compared with only two for the DK
condition. While the complexity of the passages would make it difficult
for subjects to use this information, six filler sequences were nevertheless
added to obscure this relationship. In the filler passages, the crucial
antecedent sentences included only two nouns, but the answer for the
corresponding test items were either YES or NO.

Subjects. The subjects were 31 individuals drawn from the same pool as that
used for Experiment 1.

Procedure. The procedure was identical to that described for Experiment 1.
The subjects registered their responses by means of three switches labelled
YES, NO, and DK. Since the crucial comparison was between the NO and DK
conditions, all subjects used their left index finger for the YES switch,
and the index and middle fingers of their right hand for the NO and DK
switches. The finger assignments for NO and DK were made in a random
fashion.

Results

Errors. A criterion of 17 correct responses in 27 experimental trials was
set. Of the 31 participants, 6 did not meet this standard, and their data
were discarded.

The proportion of errors for the different experimental conditions are
shown in parentheses in Table 4. Across all conditions, the error rate was
.229. The only effect to reach significance was the response by case
interaction, $F_1(4,88)=7.58$, $\underline{MS}_e=.59$, $F_2(4,48)=7.71$, $\underline{MS}_e=1.18$.

Table 4
Response Latencies (msec) and Error Rates (in Parentheses) for Experiment 2

Case	YES	NO	DON'T KNOW
Agent	2810 (.25)	2815 (.18)	2870 (.34)
Patient	2249 (.13)	2590 (.16)	2477 (.34)
Instrument	2188 (.16)	2632 (.41)	2390 (.09)

Response latencies. The mean correct response latencies are also shown in Table 4. Analyses of variance revealed a main effect of response, $F_1(2,44)$ =7.89, $\underline{MS}_e$=143124, $F_2(2,48)$=6.26, $\underline{MS}_e$=3654611, with means of 2416, 2679, and 2579 msec for YES, NO, and DK responses, respectively. The effect of case was also significant, $F_1(2,44)$=20.5, $\underline{MS}_e$=220897, F_2=(2,24)=6.92, $\underline{MS}_e$= 5279568 with means of 2831, 2439, and 2404 msec for the agent, patient, and instrument cases, respectively.

The NO latencies exceeded the DK values for the patient and instrument, but not the agent case. The corresponding response by case interaction was significant only for the subjects-random analysis, $F_1(4,88)$=4.26, $\underline{MS}_e$=117359. Finally, several interactions involving the subject group variable reached significance in the subjects-random analysis, but the group main effect was not significant.

Discussion

In contrast with Experiment 1, the error rate of .229 for this experiment was substantially higher than the value of .114 measured for the single-sentence procedure (Singer, 1981, Experiment 1). Even so, this rate was inflated by error rates of over .5 for 9 of the 81 sentence-set by response combinations. The mean error rate for these 9 items was .625 ($\underline{SD}$=.043). Without the influence of these outliers, the mean error rate is reduced to .180, which is not unusually high for studies of this sort (cf. Clark & Chase, 1972, Table 5).

Most of the item error rates of over .5 can be traced to some unanticipated but reasonable semantic interpretation on the part of the readers. For example, an intended NO sequence was the janitor cleaned the jar with the brush, did the janitor use a cloth? Most subjects responded DK, presumably because a cloth might have been used in addition to a brush. This example indicates that semantic factors not represented in VAIL can sometimes exert a large impact on question answering.

The data of six subjects had to be discarded due to failures to meet the adopted criterion for correct responses. Most of the errors made by these individuals involved the interchanging of the NO and DK responses. Many of the errors were likely due to confusions of the sort mentioned for the janitor example. The failure of large numbers of subjects to perform the task correctly would threaten the use of these techniques.

In general, however, the absence of error main effects of response and case in Experiment 2 is reassuring, in that it indicates that the response latency differences are not simply due to differences in difficulty across the conditions. The error-measure response by case interaction, furthermore, seems due to the fact that the three conditions with higher error rates (see Table 4) were those that included most of the items with error rates over .5, as follows: instrument-NO, $\underline{n}$=2; agent-DK, $\underline{n}$=3; patient-DK, $\underline{n}$=2.

Most important is the fact that DK latencies once again exceeded the NO latencies. This pattern was detected only for the patient and instrument cases, while the agent case showed little difference from one response condition to the other. It is quite likely that the use of the passive voice for the agent questions obscured the response effect for that case. One reason for this suggestion is that Singer's (1981) agent test items were presented in the active voice, and his NO latencies exceeded both the DK and YES values, as predicted. Certainly, the passive construction seems to have had an overall impact on the agent latencies: They exceeded the others by about 400 msec.

The mean correct latency for Experiment 2 was 2558 msec, which is 365 msec slower than the value measured by Singer (1981) using the single-sentence antecedent procedure. This is a difference that was anticipated, since readers in the present study needed to examine the internal representation of a more complex message.

GENERAL DISCUSSION

The present results are generally consistent with the single-sentence antecedent experiments of Singer (1979, 1981). They provide additional support for the VAIL model and indicate that the present procedures may provide a useful technique for examining the information that readers abstract from a message.

Care is necessary in the use of alternate response options like DK. Glucksberg and McCloskey (1978), for example, instructed subjects to respond DK rather than NO to <u>Bob had a pencil</u>, <u>did Bob have a book</u>. In their study, the logic was that Bob may have had a book as well as a pencil. Instructions to subjects must precisely convey the intended use of each option.

The VAIL model makes no reference to certain semantic factors that presumably do influence performance in these tasks. Rips, Shoben, and Smith (1973), for example, have shown that it takes longer to agree that "a bat is not a bird" than "an elephant is not a bird." Future elaborations of VAIL should address such effects.

The VAIL model promises to generate testable predictions for wh- questions: ones that ask who, what, or where about a situation. For the sequence <u>the aunt made the purchase at the store</u>, <u>what did the aunt buy</u>, VAIL states that a test like stage 3 (Figure 1) would establish that the antecedent included no information for the relevant case, the patient. The reader could then respond "don't know." The extension of VAIL to other question types carries the promise of further expanding our understanding of the representation of text and the processes of question answering.

REFERENCES

Carpenter, P. A., & Just, M. A. Sentence comprehension: A psycholinguistic model of verification. <u>Psychological Review</u>, 1975, <u>82</u>, 45-73.

Clark, H. H., & Chase, W. G. On the process of comparing sentences against pictures. <u>Cognitive Psychology</u>, 1972, <u>3</u>, 472-517.

Clark, H. H., & Clark, E. V. <u>Psychology and language</u>. New York: Harcourt Brace Jovanovich, Inc., 1977.

Fillmore, C. J. The case for case. In E. Bach and R. Harms (Eds.), <u>Universals in linguistic theory</u>. New York: Holt, Rinehart, & Winston, 1968.

Glucksberg, S., & McCloskey, M. <u>Knowing that you don't know: Rapid decisions about ignorance</u>. Paper presented at the annual meeting of the Psychonomic Society, San Antonio, November, 1978.

Glucksberg, S., Trabasso, T., & Wald, J. Linguistic structures and mental operations. <u>Cognitive Psychology</u>, 1973, <u>5</u>, 338-370.

Haviland, S. E., & Clark, H. H. What's new? Acquiring new information as a process in comprehension. <u>Journal of Verbal Learning and Verbal Behavior</u>, 1974, <u>13</u>, 512-521.

Hayes-Roth, B., & Thorndyke, P. W.   Integration of knowledge from text.
    Journal of Verbal Learning and Verbal Behavior, 1979, 18, 91-108.
Kieras, D. E.   Component processes in the comprehension of simple prose.
    Journal of Verbal Learning and Verbal Behavior, 1981, 20, 1-23.
Kintsch, W.   The representation of meaning in memory.   Hillsdale, New
    Jersey: Lawrence Erlbaum Associates, 1974.
Kintsch, W., & van Dijk, T. A.   Toward a model of text comprehension and
    production.   Psychological Review, 1978, 85, 363-394.
Norman, D. A.   Memory and attention: An introduction to human information
    processing (2nd ed.).   New York: Wiley, 1976.
Rips, L. J., Shoben, E. J., & Smith, E. E.   Semantic distance and the
    verification of semantic relations.   Journal of Verbal Learning and
    Verbal Behavior, 1973, 12, 1-20.
Singer, M.   Inferences about instruments: Response norms.   Manuscript,
    University of Manitoba, 1977.
Singer, M.   Processes of inference in sentence encoding.   Memory and
    Cognition, 1979, 7, 192-200.
Singer, M.   The role of case-filling inferences in the coherence of brief
    passages.   Discourse Processes, 1980, 3, 185-201.
Singer, M.   Verifying the assertions and implications of language.   Journal
    of Verbal Learning and Verbal Behavior, 1981, 20, 46-80.
Trabasso, T., Rollins, H., & Shaughnessy, E.   Storage and verification
    stages in processing concepts.   Cognitive Psychology, 1971, 2, 239-289.
Walker, C. H., and Meyer, B. J. F.   Integrating different types of informa-
    tion in text.   Journal of Verbal Learning and Verbal Behavior, 1980,
    19, 263-275.

FOOTNOTE

Identification footnote.   This research was supported by grant A9800 from
the Natural Sciences and Engineering Research Council of Canada, and a
grant from the University of Manitoba and SSHRC Fund Committee of the
University of Manitoba.   I would like to thank Adrian Kuryliw, who
conducted the sessions of Experiment 2.

MEMORY

DISCOURSE PROCESSING
A. Flammer and W. Kintsch (eds.)
© *North-Holland Publishing Company, 1982*

MEMORY FOR TEXT

Walter Kintsch

Department of Psychology
University of Colorado
Boulder, Colorado
U.S.A.

The experimental study of memory is now about 100 years old, and we have learned a great deal from it. The associationistic concepts and the experimental designs introduced by Ebbinghaus have dominated the first 80 years of memory research. In the last two decades the information processing approach has taken a hold in the field of memory and greatly expanded and complemented the earlier results. Indeed, in the short years between about 1959 (the date of the publication of a new method for assessing short-term memory by Peterson & Peterson) and 1972 (the date of Craik & Lockhart's article on levels of processing) we have seen a veritable information explosion in memory research.

We have learned much about memory, but of course we don't know everything. Indeed, the problems about which we have adequate knowledge today are quite restricted in scope. First of all, the bulk of our experiments and theories concerns episodic memory, as distinguished from general knowledge.[1] Secondly, memory research has been concerned with lists of items (words, nonsense syllables, even sentences), but not with texts. Thus, we know quite well how people remember a list of words in the laboratory, but very little about how they learn physics in school from listening to a lecture, reading a textbook, or doing problems.

The temptation at that point is to say that we know the wrong things, or that what we know is not worth knowing. It gets strengthened by some simple observations. It is well known that if subjects in the laboratory are presented a list of 40 common words at a rate of one word every 2 seconds, they will be able to recall immediately afterwards about 6-7 words, mostly from the very end of the list (e.g., Murdock, 1962). On the other hand, if subjects read a simple story for the same amount of time, they may read about 200 words and then recall 80-100 of these words, though for the most part not verbatim. What is the relevance of the laboratory work, if people recall more than 10 times as much from a text than from a list? The comparison can easily be pushed to greater extremes: suppose someone spends hours to read a novel; he or she could then reproduce and reconstruct major portions of that novel. Ebbinghaus himself was about the only one to devote hours to learning nonsense lists - only to succumb to a variety of interference effects.

Text memory is so superior to performance in the usual laboratory list-learning paradigms that it is easy to doubt the relevance of the latter. As Jenkins asked in 1974: "Do you remember that old theory of memory? Well, forget it!". Nevertheless, we believe that that old theory holds the key to understanding text memory, and that if we want to explain the phenomena of text memory, we need the concepts and models of the traditional memory literature, for all their limitations. Episodic text memory is best understood within the framework of current memory theory.

To make this argument, we begin this chapter with a brief synopsis of current memory theory. We shall then make explicit the way in which episodic text memory is related to list learning results, and finally discuss in detail the memorial implications of a model of text comprehension that several colleagues and I have been developing over the past few years (van Dijk & Kintsch, Forthcoming; Miller, 1981).

1. Some Principles of Memory Derived From List Learning Experiments.

A review of the memory literature would be quite beyond the scope of this paper. Instead, I assume at least a superficial similarity with that literature, and merely cite some of the relevant principles of memory as we know them from list learning experiments. These same principles will later be applied to an analysis of text memory.

First, there is the notion of short-term memory. Of primary concern is its limited capacity. The capacity restriction is in terms of chunks. Acoustic rehearsal is a preferred way of maintaining information in short-term memory.

Memory is a byproduct of processing - one remembers what one does. The level of processing is, however, decisive, because deeper, more elaborate processing results in better memory codes. Imagery supports memory especially well.

Retrieval is just as important as encoding. The retrieval cue must be appropriate to the encoded memory episode. The nature of the encoding-retrieval interaction determines the efficiency of memory.

Retrieval structures are systems in which each retrieval cue not only retrieves a memory, but also produces the appropriate retrieval cue for the next episode. Existing knowledge structures form the basis of retrieval structures. New information becomes associated with old structures which are often hierarchical in nature.

These familiar principles of laboratory memory hold the key to an explanation of text memory.

2. Episodic Text Memory.

If a person reads a text, what he or she remembers about this text is called episodic text memory, in extension of the common use of the term episodic memory. The question I raised at the beginning of this paper is why episodic text memory (ETM) is so much better than episodic memory for a list of random words. In a general sense, the answer is of course obvious: texts are so much better organized, they are meaningful, they often interest us, we have much more experience with texts than with random word lists or nonsense syllables - therefore texts can be remembered so much better. Such an answer is correct, but not very helpful. What we need to know in detail are the mechanisms that are responsible for text memory.

The hypothesis made here is that memory for text is closely associated with text comprehension.[2] To understand ETM we must, therefore, start with comprehension models. The first version of our model for text comprehension (Kintsch & van Dijk, 1978) was already concerned with this problem. Indeed, successful prediction of text recall was one of the main achievements of that model (Kintsch & van Dijk, 1978; Miller & Kintsch, 1980; Vipond, 1980; Spilich, Vesonder, Chiesi & Voss, 1979). However, in spite of its predictive adequacy, the model is clearly oversimplified in its treatment of memory, and needs to be revised. Since our present model is a direct descendant of that earlier work, we shall first recapitulate the principal memory assumptions of the Kintsch & van Dijk model, and then point out in which ways these are deficient.

Short-term memory plays a crucial role in the Kintsch & van Dijk model. Text is being processed in cycles (corresponding, say, to sentences). In order to relate information from one text cycle to the next, some propositions from that cycle have to be retained in a short-term memory buffer while the input from the next cycle is being processed. Formal statistical rules (the "leading edge strategy") are used to decide which propositions are to be retained in each cycle. The capacity of the buffer is strictly limited, the actual number of propositions that it contains being a free parameter to be estimated from the data. These estimates were either one or two in the Miller & Kintsch data, while slightly higher estimates were obtained elsewhere.

The long-term memory assumptions of the Kintsch & van Dijk model are very simple: each time a proposition is processed, it is stored in long-term memory with some probability, which again has to be estimated from the data. Interesting recall predictions result from this model, nevertheless, because some propositions are processed more than others, and the nature of processing is not the same for all propositions. The reason why some propositions are processed repeatedly is that some propositions have to be held in the short-term memory buffer between cycles to assure the continuity of the text base. Thus, each text proposition has either 1, 2, ..., chances of being stored in long-term memory, depending on whether and how often it was selected for retention in the short-term memory buffer.[3] Since the leading edge strategy tends to pick out important propositions for the buffer, which are therefore more likely to be stored, the model makes the correct prediction that certain important propositions are recalled best. Thus, structurally important, salient propositions are more likely to be stored in memory, not because of their structural role per se, but because the comprehension processes tend to be more concerned with them than with structurally unimportant propositions: they are processed in several different contexts, and hence more likely to be stored. Structure is, of course, important in text memory, but it is the structure-process interaction that must be considered, not just structure per se.

However, not only the quantity but also the quality of processing can vary: most text propositions play a role only in the microstructure of the text. In the model, these propositions are assigned a storage probability p. Some propositions, however, are globally significant and used for the derivation of the macrostructure, too, or are themselves designated as macropropositions. Thus, these propositions receive a different kind of processing, reflected in the model by a storage probability m, $m>p$. The model, thus, makes some quite simple and sensible assumptions: everything is processed for the microstructure, with some memorial consequence measured by the parameter $\underline{p}$, while some propositions are also processed at the macrolevel, resulting in the parameter $\underline{m}$. Furthermore, some propositions may participate in more than one processing cycle and therefore have repeated chances of being stored in memory.

Note that this memory mechanism concerns storage only. The Kintsch & van Dijk model does not have a retrieval component: everything is retrieved with probabilities proportional to the probability of storage.

There are a number of reasons why we think that this model of text memory is too simple. First, some experimental findings have been reported recently that indicate some additional complexities. More important, however, is a second reason: the model explains too little, it makes too little contact with what we know about memory, particularly about the importance of retrieval processes. There is, for instance, nothing in this model that might tell us why people find it so much easier to remember a text than a word list. This seems to us the most salient phenomenon about text memory, badly in need of explanation.

In the Kintsch & van Dijk model, when propositions are first processed at the microlevel, all are treated alike except that at the end of each processing cycle some are selected for reprocessing in the next cycle and therefore are recalled better. Such a model suggests that during initial encoding, that is on first reading, all portions of the text should be read at about the same rate. The differences between well recalled and poorly recalled propositions comes about because of reprocessing in later cycles. In terms of eye movements, one would therefore expect that those portions of the text that correspond to important, frequently recalled propositions show a greater incidence of regressive fixations, because the reader has to return to them in constructing a coherent text base. Frequently, this would be a purely mental process, but readers might also support reinstatement searches in memory with regressive eyemovements to the appropriate portions of the text. That is exactly what Mandel (1980; also 1979) found in an M.A. thesis done at the University of Colorado. Phrases that correspond to important, frequently recalled propositions were between 2.7 and 5.6 times more likely to be the target of a regressive eyemovement than phrases dealing with unimportant detail. (The larger ratios were observed for the more difficult texts). On the other hand, Mandel also observed something that suggests that regressive eyemovements do not give us the whole story behind the recall superiority of important propositions: there was also a small but statistically significant tendency to fixate more often words belonging to high-level, important propositions than low-level propositions, irrespective of regressions. High level propositions received between 1.3 and 1.2 times as many fixations as low-level propositions. It is as if the reader selected the important portions of the text right away for special processing. Mandel's conclusions are supported by the results of an experiment reported by Cirilo & Foss (1980). Cirilo and Foss embedded a short sentence into different story contexts in such a way that in one case it played a superordinate role in the text-base hierarchy, and in the other a low-level role. When the sentence was high in the story structure, reading times averaged 1954 msec, but when it was low in the hierarchy, the same sentence was read only for 1672 msec (data for their Experiment I). Thus, there may be cues in the text itself that signal to the reader the importance of a sentence or phrase when it is first encountered, and make them read it more carefully.

Before we abandon the attractively simple explanation for the recall
superiority effect offered by the Kintsch & van Dijk model in the face of
these data, we should consider some alternative explanations within the
framework of the model. We have so far considered only the microprocessing
component of the model. It would seem quite possible that the reading
time effects obtained by Cirilo & Foss and Mandel have to do with macro-
processing: the well-recalled propositions which received extra reading
time might have been propositions that were macrorelevant, which for that
reason were processed longer and recalled better. Mandel worked with very
short paragraphs out of context for which the macrostructure was quite
ambiguous. Macroprocesses might have been more important in the Cirilo &
Foss experiment, where the strongest reading time effects were observed.
Of course, there is no way to be sure that this explanation of the reading
time data in the Cirilo and Foss experiment is correct, without a complete
re-analysis of their texts and data within the framework of the Kintsch &
van Dijk model. But the explanation is plausible enough, so that we are
tempted to accept it at least provisionally.

The absence of a retrieval component is a more serious problem for the
Kintsch & van Dijk model. Indeed, retrieval processes in general have
received relatively little attention by students of text memory. This is
quite surprising, since retrieval plays such a central role in classical
memory theory. A study that suggests that it might play an equal role with
respect to text memory is one by Anderson & Pichert (1978), in which encoding perspectives and retrieval cues were varied systematically.
Anderson & Pichert had their subjects read a description of a house either
from the perspective of a house buyer or a burglar. Subjects first recalled the text with the same perspective as they used in reading, and
then attempted a second recall with instructions to change their perspective. The results showed that the change in the retrieval cue produced
more recall of the previously unimportant information, but less of the
previously relevant information. For instance, in their Experiment 1,
subjects recalled 7.1% of the newly relevant information, in addition to
what they had recalled before, but at the same time missed 7.2% of the information that had become irrelevant.

While the whole area of retrieval effects in text memory deserves a great
deal more investigation than it has received so far, it is clear that a
theory like Kintsch & van Dijk which lacks a retrieval component altogether is inadequate in this respect. We also suggest that the lack of a
retrieval model in Kintsch & van Dijk prevented it from dealing with the
main problem of text memory: why it is so much better than list memory.

3. Text memory is expert memory

Memory for text is hard to compare directly with memory for lists, because
it is generally not verbatim. It is clear, nevertheless, that people can
remember texts much better than word lists, whatever the exact numbers
might be. We must, however, qualify this statement in an important way:
it is true only if we compare text memory with the usual laboratory performance of inexperienced subjects. If we take expert memorizers, performance levels that compare very well with the text memory of average
subjects are not rare at all. There is a long line of reports of truly
fabulous feats of memory (Chase & Ericsson, 1981): the discussion of the

"art of memory" as it was practiced in classical antiquity by Yates (1966), the memory of experienced telegraphers (Bryan & Harter, 1899), the skills of experts in mental calculation (Müller, 1911; Hunter, 1962), the memory performance of chess players (de Groot, 1966; Chase & Simon, 1973), laboratory subjects who were trained in the use of mnemonic devices (Bower, 1972), or who invented their own ideosyncratic strategies for remembering (Chase & Ericsson, 1981). In comparison with these studies, text memory does not appear extraordinary at all. These mnemonists, however, were experts in the use of particular menomonic techniques, and it might seem unfair to compare what they do with the text memory of ordinary people, who as we know do quite poorly in list-learning, laboratory experiments. We argue that they do so badly in these laboratory tasks because they are put into a situation for which they have no well-developed mnemonic strategies. When the same people are asked to remember texts, however, they behave like experts (given texts about suitably familiar subjects). As we have tried to show in van Dijk & Kintsch (forthcoming), people have very well practiced, highly over-learned comprehension strategies - they are true experts when it comes to comprehend ordinary texts. We shall show that these same comprehension strategies also serve as mnemonic strategies and support a level of text memory that is quite comparable to expert memory in other areas. In order to make this argument, we shall first have to consider in some detail the characteristic features of expert, skilled memory.

A recent paper by Chase and Ericsson (1981) provides an excellent account of these features, and we shall do no more here than summarize their main conclusions. Chase and Ericsson discuss a case study of one SF who learned to memorize sequences of over 80 random digits in a memory span task. The memory span test is often considered primarily a short-term memory task, and since we have some rather solid evidence about the capacity limitations of short-term memory, it seems puzzling how SF was able to expand this capacity to that extent. He did not; SF's short-term memory capacity was completely normal and unchanged. Chase & Ericsson have excellent evidence for this claim. The chunks that SF formed always consisted of 3-4 digits. The phonemically coded rehearsal groups in short-term memory were similarly limited, and always less than 5 or 6. SF could never keep the order straight for more than 3 or 4 groups (which eventually forced him into inventing a hierarchical organization scheme to overcome this problem). Thus, the working capacity of SF short-term memory was no different from that of ordinary subjects who can remember only 7 or 9 items on a digit span test.

If it wasn't short-term memory, how, then, did SF do it? The trick involves efficient use of long-term memory, almost making it into a functional equivalent of short-term memory. First of all, there is a chunking mechanism that binds stimulus traces to a hierarchical semantic structure. SF invented a complex set of strategies to encode digit sequences in terms of running times, something he was both interested and familiar with. He became expert at generating encoding features for digit strings in terms of running times which then served as unique retrieval cues for that string. Not unlike the orator in Cicero's Rome, he deposited the to-be-remembered numbers in particular places in his semantic structure about running times (e.g., under 1-mile-times, near-world-record). This binding process takes place in working memory, and is a form of chunking: a rich, well-organized knowledge base about running times permits the immediate recognition of relevant patterns which are bound to semantic features in the running-time structure. Retrieval is achieved because the current location in that retrieval structure activates the long-term memory traces that have been associated with it. In this way SF could directly access a large amount of information, almost as if it all were still held in short-term memory, but without overburdening his short-term memory. In short-term memory a small set of information can be accessed without search, while in skilled memory a much larger information set can be accessed almost equally well, because future information requirements had been anticipated and associations were formed within a semantic system that serves as a retrieval structure.

There are two characteristic features of this process. First, that it involves the use of a rich knowledge base. None of this would be possible without SF's elaborate network of running times. This is also the case for all the other cases of skilled memory that have been studied. The second concerns the rapidity with which these storage and retrieval operations occur. The relevant patterns from semantic memory are retrieved quickly and efficiently, while retrieval from episodic memory (that is, the memorized string itself) is somewhat slower. Speed in all these cases is crucial, because otherwise too much information would have to be held in short-term memory for ready access. A very large amount of practice is required before this can be achieved.

The analogy with text memory is striking. Text memory is very good, if readers have the elaborate knowledge base to support it. Comprehension strategies have received an enormous amount of practice in the course of a person's life, and they are fast and automatic. More than that, the model outlined in the previous chapters describes exactly the kind of binding of new, textual information to existing knowledge sources that we have found to be characteristic of expert memory. Knowledge frames with their slots filled with text propositions form effective retrieval structures for text memory.

Only a few unusual people can learn to remember 80-item strings of random numbers; only very few people are real mnemonic experts when it comes to dealing with such materials. When it comes to dealing with everyday texts, everybody is an expert. Thus, the use of the term "expert" might strike one as inappropriate here, but it merely reflects the obvious fact that when it comes to everyday life, all people are indeed experts. As soon as more specialized knowledge is required to understand a text, differences arise among people in relation to their expertise: chemists can remember chemistry papers, and psychologists psychology papers, but not the layman. Text memory is expert only so long as the reader has available a well established knowledge base to organize the content of the text. Indeed, it is instructive to consider cases of text memory where it is clearly not expert. A simple way to destroy a reader's expertise at comprehension is to give him something to read for which he or she does not have the necessary knowledge background. Although anecdotal evidence comes readily to mind suggesting that performance breaks down in such cases, experimental demonstrations do not exist, perhaps because they are all too obvious. However, in several experiments it has been shown that more familiar texts are recalled better than less familiar ones. Thus, Kintsch, Kozminsky, McKoon, Streby, & Keenan (1975) found better memory for history paragraphs which were of narrative form than for more descriptive and unfamiliar science paragraphs. Graesser, Hoffman & Clark (1980) found that narrativity was the most important text characteristic that predicted ease of comprehension - presumably because narratives are concerned with human actions, a topic for which every reader is a true expert, having built up a relevant knowledge base not only while reading innumerable stories, but above all in interpersonal interactions every day of his or her life. Another way to study text comprehension and memory without knowledge is to make the knowledge sources which would be appropriate for a text unavailable to the reader. Bransford & Johnson (1972), in a well-known experiment, have done that. They wrote a paragraph (e.g., about washing clothes) in such a way that the reader never could figure out what the text was about, could not activate his or her knowledge to interpret the paragraph, and remembered only a few disjoint bits of it (3.6 out of 14 idea units). However, the same paragraph with a title that identified the knowledge sources relevant to the understanding of this text was understood and remembered quite well (8 out of 14 idea units). When subjects were allowed to use their expertise on the topic, comprehension and memory were assured; but when they were prevented from doing so, their memory for the uncomprehended text was no better than for a list of random words. Expert and non-expert memory are directly contrasted here.[4]

4. Retrieval in episodic text memory.

Within the limits of this presentation, it is not possible to describe in detail the general model of text comprehension which we have been developing (van Dijk & Kintsch, forthcoming). Instead, I shall merely sketch the rough outlines of the model - describing approximately what is happening, now how - and then show how this model of comprehension serves as a natural base for a model of text memory.

Figure 1 shows the basic components of the model. Comprehension is treated as a process that occurs in parallel at several levels, with a special kind of representation of the text being associated with each level. Processing at each level is autonomous, but the outputs of the various levels interact in important ways. Starting with the text itself, we have a verbal representation, that is, strings of words organized into phrases, sentences and paragraphs that serve as the input to the system. A parsing process (which is circumvented in this model) derives from the verbal input a sequence of semantic units (atomic propositions) which represent the meaning elements of the text. The focus of the model is on the further processing that these semantic text units undergo. Specifically, we deal explicitly with the organization of semantic units into chunks called text propositions. The basic process here is that the model makes some strategic decisions to focus on a particular semantic unit, retrieves from its knowledge base a knowledge structure (frame) that corresponds to that semantic unit and uses that knowledge structure to organize the other semantic text units. As far as possible, new text units will be fitted into the slots of the chosen frame or appended to it as modifiers. When the character of the input changes so that the semantic units can no longer be related to the presently activated frame, it will be replaced in working memory by a new one that is more suitable, while the old frame which is by now filled with textual information is stored in episodic text memory (ETM). Thus, reading a text in this model results in the storage of a sequence of interrelated chunks of textual information. Formally, each such chunk has the structure of a (text) proposition.[5]

When people read a text they not only form a representation for that text (the episodic text memory) but they also use the information from that text

to form (or update) their model of the world. Thus, in addition to the
episodic text memory (the memory for the text proper) we have, in general,
another level of episodic memory for the information itself, distinct from
the way in which it was presented in the particular text. Thus, if one
reads an article in the newspaper about the decision to build neutron bombs,
one not only constructs a memory representation for that article, but the
memory about neutron bombs itself may be modified, and the latter modification may still be effective long after the article per se is forgotten.

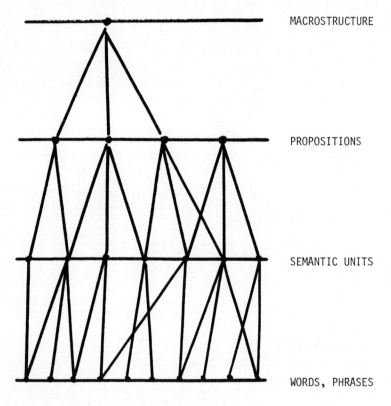

Figure 1

The structure of the van Dijk & Kintsch
model of comprehension

Finally, memory for a text is not only memory for all the detail in the
text, but also for its gist. That is, a representation of the macrostructure of the text is generated along with the propositional text base.
Indeed, as we show elsewhere, the macrostructure is often necessary for
the successful construction of the propositional representation itself.
This macrostructure is hierarchical and fulfills a very important function
in a retrieval system: by hierarchically subordinating the text proposi-

tions under various levels of macropropositions an efficient retrieval structure is obtained. It is of course true that text propositions are interrelated (frequently, one text proposition refers to another, or to elements of another proposition), but it is the hierarchical organization provided by the macrostructure that makes efficient retrieval possible in recall.

A concrete example as in Figure 2, might help to clarify the interrelated processing levels described above. Figure 2 shows a sentence at the bottom which is to be taken as an excerpt from a longer text. The sentence is then broken down into semantic units - the result of the parsing process. A syntactic strategy is used to pick the sentence predicate as the basis for the propositional organization. Thus, a "nailing" frame is

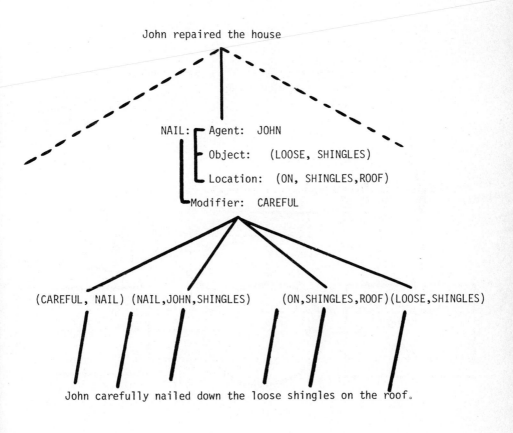

Figure 2

An example of the kind of analysis provided
by the van Dijk & Kintsch model of comprehension

retrieved from long-term memory and those slots of the frame that are referred to in the text are connected with the appropriate textual information. We know that nailing needs an agent, and "John" is specified as
agent; we know that nailing requires a certain kind of object, a board,
plank, etc., and "shingles" is specified by the text; furthermore, both
"shingle" and "nailing" are modified; finally, a location slot is
specified. Note that other possible slots of the nailing frame are not
activated. For instance, no instrument (such as a hammer) is mentioned in
the text and the instrument slot is therefore not activated. On the basis
of the proposition shown in Figure 2 and others like it not shown, a
macroproposition "John repairs the house" is generated, which dominates a
whole set of propositions, and may in turn be dominated by other, higher
order macropropositions. Note that the macroproposition may never have
been stated directly in the text, but may be inferred.

A processing model has to show how all this is produced in real time.
Again, I can not go into any details, but the basic ideas are sketched in
Figure 3. A sequence of words is the input to a working register, where
the multi-level analyses described above are performed. Processing in the
working register is governed by a control schema, which represents the
reader's goals, interests, and other high-level information, e.g., that
one is reading a newspaper story, etc. The working register has direct
access to a limited capacity short-term memory buffer. This buffer holds
the current text proposition, so that new semantic units can be added to
it as they are formed. When a new proposition is generated, the old one
is transferred to episodic text memory. Reading, thus, generates a string
of interrelated propositions in episodic memory. At certain points in

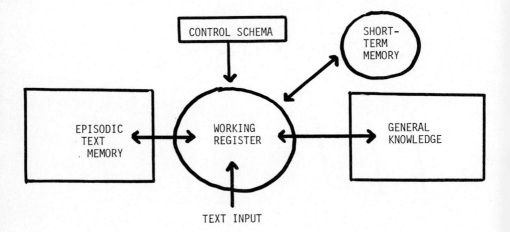

Figure 3

The processing characteristics of the
van Dijk & Kintsch model of comprehension

this process macropropositions are formed which are also stored in episodic
text memory. Thus, the result of reading is not merely a string of propositions, but a string with a hierarchical superstructure. This superstructure
is generated rapidly, unconsciously, and with little effort during normal
reading. It guarantees efficient retrieval from episodic memory (we shall
neglect here episodic memory proper). Note that efficient retrieval is
often required during reading, not just at recall: situations will arise
when previous textual information will have to be brought back from ETM into
the working register for one reason or another (see, for example, the reinstatement searches of Kintsch & van Dijk, 1978). Depending on the level
of integration achieved during reading and the extent to which a suitable
macrostructure had been formed, such reinstatements of earlier information
may be more or less successful and more or less resource consuming. In the
ideal case of real "expert" reading, when a person has available rich knowledge sources to build complex but well structured propositions, and has
formed an elaborate macrostructure, retrieving information from ETM might
relatively fast and almost as easy as retrieving information from STM. At
the other extreme, when no organization of the semantic text units is
achieved (as in the experiment by Bransford & Johnsons, 1972, referred to
earlier), retrieval from ETM can break down entirely.

Our present model makes the same assumption about memory storage that was
made in the Kintsch & van Dijk model: memory is regarded as a consequence
of processing; what is remembered is what has been processed. Propositions
processed more than others (e.g., because they are structurally central, or
because they are particularly salient and macrorelevant) are remembered
better, in proportion to the amount of processing they have received.
These assumptions were elaborated into a quantitative model in the Kintsch
& van Dijk theory, and while I can not do this here, it is clear that the
same assumptions can serve once more as the basis of a model for memory
storage.

Unlike in the Kintsch & van Dijk theory, however, the present model also
contains an explicit retrieval component. The retrieval of a proposition
depends on the strength of the connections between it and its macroproposition. Strength is a matter of processing: those propositions that were
used in inferring a macroproposition are assumed to be more strongly related to it than others that were irrelevant to the inference.

Retrieval differences also occur within propositions: we make the assumption that semantic units that fill frame slots are more retrievable than
semantic units that are merely appended to the proposition as modifiers.

Furthermore, if the macropropositions are themselves organized in some
schematic way (e.g., corresponding to a story schema), then those macropropositions that fill the slots of the schema become more easily retrievable.

Recall in this model is a joint function of storage and retrieval. The
more processing a proposition (or macroproposition) has received, the
greater its storage probability. On top of that, however, there are retrieval differences at the various processing levels: macropropositions
that are schema conforming, propositions that were macrorelevant and hence
are directly connected to macropropositions, and finally semantic elements
for which there are pre-existing slots in a proposition are more readily
retrieved than their less advantaged co-elements.

5. The mnemonic properties of episodic text memory.

Let us now look at the properties of such a system as a retrieval structure. In a recent review of mnemonic devices Bellezza (1981) discusses
four properties of mnemonic systems. Belezza was concerned with traditional mnemonics, such as the method of loci or chained pairs. However,
the argument made here is that readers construct a retrieval system with
similar properties as an integral part of the process of text comprehension. If one reads as an expert, in the sense noted above, then episodic
text memory will be an efficient retrieval system, not because one has
performed any special mnemonic coding operations, but because of the very
nature of comprehension.

Bellezza (1981) notes four important characteristics of efficient retrieval structures. First, there is the constructibility of the retrieval
cue: at each point in the process, it must be possible to construct the
next retrieval cue reliably and rapidly. (For instance, in the method of
loci, constructibility is achieved by the prememorized system of places,
in the method of linked chains by the overlap among the elements of the
chain). In order to be effective, retrieval cues must also have high
discriminability, to avoid confusion between them. (Once again, in the
method of loci we have the requirement to make the various places as
different from each other as possible). The next requirement is that of
associability. The to be remembered material can easily be associated
with good retrieval cues. Rich, elaborate cues that provide many potential links, and high imagery, concrete cues are indicated by this requirement. Finally, retrieval structures must have the property of invertibility, because the to be remembered material is often not associated
directly with the retrieval cue but via some mediator (e.g., a phonetic
one, as when one is trying to remember "origin" as "orange"). It is not
enough to retrieve the mediator in this case, but one must also be able to
invert it to the original item that was to be remembered.

The structures that are generated by our model during text comprehension
have precisely these properties - and that is why text memory is so good
under normal conditions. Constructibility is guaranteed by the hierarchical macrostructure. A good macrostructure provides reliable guidance
through a text, one proposition serving as the cue for the next one, via
their association to their superordinate node. These associations are
strong because the superordinates were constructed from the subordinate
propositions. This processing, we assume, leaves its trace in memory in
the form of an association. Thus, retrieval of a story, for instance, is
assumed to be top down, from the most superordinate macroproposition (perhaps the title) to the macroproposition dominating the first episode of
the story, from which one after the other of the lower level macropropositions are retrieved, plus their associated micropropositions. Note that
the ordering of propositions at a given level must be determined by other
factors than their association to a common superordinate: at lower levels
in a story these might be temporal and especially causal relations, while
at the top level of the structure schemata may play a very important role
in the ordering of macropropositions. If one reads a story which has certain conventional components (such as exposition, complication, resolution),
the ordering of the macropropositions is in part determined by the fixed
slots of the story schema. Hence, conventionally organized texts (like
stories, arguments, procedural descriptions) should give rise to especially
stable and well differentiated retrieval structures. Indeed, there are

reports in the literature that schematically well organized texts are recalled better than texts without a schematic organization (Meyer, Brandt, &
Bluth, 1980) and that the differences between such texts is indeed in the
macrostructure, as claimed here (Kintsch & Yarbrough, 1981).

How discriminable the macropropositions of a text are from each other is,
in general, not under the control of the reader but is determined by the
nature of the text itself. In stories, discriminability is usually no
problem because authors are trying to make the different episodes novel and
interesting, and hence distinct. However, if stories are written in such a
way that they contain many similar episodes, confusions occur in recall, as
was observed by Bower, Black & Turner (1979). Hence, discriminability
among the macropropositions of a text appears to play a role analogous to
discriminability among the retrieval cues in a mnemonic system.

Associability, too, is only indirectly under the control of the comprehender and is in part determined by the nature of the to be comprehended
material. Associability depends on rich and elaborate knowledge sources
which can serve as a basis for the propositional organization of a text.
Imagery certainly also plays a role at this point: concrete, easily imaged
materials may not be any easier to comprehend than abstract materials, but
if the proposition construction is accompanied by the generation of imagery
in one case but not in the other, his differences in recall can be expected.
No systematic study of imagery effects in text memory as yet exist, but
anecdotal evidence tends to support the conjectures made here.

Something corresponding to the invertibility of mnemonics may also play a
role in text memory. We have assumed that the text is organized in terms
of propositions, which are retrieved via the hierarchical macrostructure.
Now consider what happens when a proposition is retrieved. The information
associated with the various slots of that proposition is an integral part
of the proposition and is therefore highly available. However, semantic
units that did not fit into any pre-existing slot but were merely appended
to the proposition in the form of modifiers may be much less readily available. Hence we predict that even if a particular chunk of text (a proposition) is retrieved, those portions of it that are structurally important
are recalled better than the portions which play no structural role.
Whether or not the analogy with the invertibility of mnemonic devices is a
compelling one, the retrieval disadvantage of modifier elements appears to
be a real one, as suggested by the common observation that adjectives and
adverbs, which tend to end up in the modifier slots of propositions, are
among the most poorly recalled parts of a text.

5. Some preliminary experimental results.

Under ideal conditions, text memory has all the properties of a highly
sophisticated retrieval system, because comprehension by its very nature
results in structures that function that way. In van Dijk & Kintsch
(forthcoming) a number of experimental results are described that tend to
support empirically one or the other aspect of this claim. The ability to
predict prose recall data even the earlier version of our model possessed
to a quite satisfactory degree (Kintsch & van Dijk, 1978), but more
analytic experiments are required to assess our model than over-all free
recall data. I shall describe here some preliminary results from a pilot
study that bear more directly on some of the crucial assumptions about
memory and propositional chunking that we have made. The study is modelled

closely after one by Ericsson & Chase (1981). These authors investigated the chunking that their memory expert was employing for remembering strings of random numbers. They knew through protocol analyses and from other experimental results pretty well what numbers were being chunked together and where the chunk boundaries were. Thus, they could select small groups of digits from the to be remembered strings in such a way that they did or did not coincide with a chunk boundary. These digit groups were used as recall cues: the subject was instructed to recall the digits following or preceding them in the original string. The results were quite interesting and strongly supported the chunking hypothesis. Whenever the recall cue formed only part of a chunk, the rest of the chunk was recalled very well; however, if the recall cue coincided with a chunk boundary so that the digits following it belonged to a different chunk, recall was more difficult. The chunks as determined from the protocol analysis thus appeared to be functional units in recall.

Much the same procedure can be used with text. Again, our theory tells us where the chunk boundaries are supposed to be, so that if we cue recall with a group of words that is or is not a chunk boundary, we would expect similar performance differences as in the case of Ericsson & Chase's mnemonist. We have used a non-technical psychological research report as our stimulus material. Subjects listened to it in 250-word fragments. After each fragment a phrase 6-10 words long from the passage just read was repeated, and the subject had to try to recall the words immediately following that phrase in the original text. Subjects were instructed to recall verbatim if possible, or whatever they could remember. Our preliminary results are quite interesting. Consider an example of a recall cue that ends abruptly in the middle of a chunk:

(1) CUE: This discrepancy reflects not only our

     CONTINUATION: society's concentration of formal educational effort..

Three illustrative responses from subjects are the following:

(2a) RESPONSE: society's concentration of effort...

(2b) RESPONSE: society's focus on formal education...

(2c) RESPONSE: the shift in concentration of educational research...

What we see from these examples is first of all that subjects are able to respond with a good continuation that more or less completes the chunk correctly. Secondly, the subjects' response is largely verbatim: in (2a) there are some omissions, in (2b) there is both an omission and the use of a synonym, but otherwise the responses stick quite close to the text; (2c) is less precise, but two of the principal content words are still reproduced. That is not a bad feat, considering that the subjects heard the text only once, and that another 150 words followed the particular text passage illustrated here. Clearly, subjects were not recalling from short-term memory, by any reasonable definition of this term.

Now let us consider an example where the recall cue completes a chunk and hence forces the subject to retrieve the next one:

(3) CUE: As shown primarily by the work of Schaie,

     CONTINUATION: a peak in intellectual performance occurs later for current adult cohorts than indicated by cross-sectional research.

The subjects' responses appear to be quite different now. First of all, we can draw a complete blank in about a third of all cases, where the subject simply can not remember anything (This has never happened, so far, when the cue and the response were part of the same organizational text unit). If there is a response, it tends to be more of a paraphrase of the original text than a verbatim reproduction, such as

(4a) RESPONSE: <u>some abilities don't reach their peak until sometime later</u>.

(4b) RESPONSE: <u>the peak occurs much later than previously believed and no decline in intelligence</u>.

Particularly interesting is a response like (4c).

(4c) RESPONSE: (after a long latency): <u>He was finding results that differed from the previously held ideas</u>.

This response suggests that the subject was not able to retrieve the successor proposition in response to the recall cue, but instead managed a partial reconstruction of its gist by accessing the appropriate macroproposition. (For this part of the text that macropropositions probably were something like <u>Old research shows X - in contrast - Schaie shows Y</u>).

Given that we have only unsystematic pilot data of unproven reliability and representativeness, the conclusions drawn from these data must remain tentative. However, several features of our model for text memory appear to be reflected in these results. It seems that if subjects are given a (sufficiently discriminable) portion of text as a retrieval cue, they are able to complete the text unit of which that retrieval cue is a part under the conditions of our experiment. Though never perfect, their completions tend to be partly verbatim, or fairly close paraphrases of the original text. We have tapped directly into the text representation, and are getting back a low-level, incomplete but fairly accurate record. If, on the other hand, the cue is such that a continuation response involves retrieving the chunk (text proposition) next in line, this is not always possible. The subject may be unable to remember anything at all, or generates a reconstructive response on the basis of a macroproposition. Even if the correct text proposition is retrieved, the response now tends to be less verbatim (if we can trust our sketchy data that far). Presumably, retrieval has occurred top down, via the macroproposition, and what is retrieved is a conceptual, propositional representation, with less of a chance of retrieving the actual words and phrases from which this propositional representation had been generated. With cues like (1) we tap directly in both the propositional level and the linguistic level; cues like (3), on the other hand, are farther removed from their successor words in the original text - they have to get to them via a superordinate macroproposition and the micropropositional representation.

If these data hold up, they might help us to understand better the nature of text memory and its relationship to "expert" memory and conventional laboratory phenomena. Clearly, I am unable as yet to substantiate empirically the speculations I have offered here in this respect. At best, perhaps, I can claim to have made a plausible story. But it is, I think, a story worth investigating, because if it is true, at least in its general outlines, it can account for text memory in a very natural way: no special theory of text memory is needed at all, the existing theory of comprehension plus some rather well-known general principles of memory suffice for the understanding of episodic text memory.

Footnotes:

1. The traditional term in psychology is "semantic memory," but "knowledge" more clearly indicates the intended meaning. Tulving (1972) distinguished between episodic and semantic memory: episodic memory is the memory for having something personally experienced in a particular context; semantic memory corresponds to general, context-independent, impersonal knowledge. Intermediate, partly decontextualized memory episodes are also possible.

2. This claim does not mean that memory and comprehension are one and the same, or even that memory is directly proportional to comprehension.

3. In principle the model could be easily extended to account for the possibility that some text propositions are not encoded at all. Indeed, Miller & Kintsch (1980) make use of this feature for redundant information in the text, which subjects frequently do not reproduce on a recall test, either because they failed to encode it, or because of output restrictions that prevent redundancies, even in those cases where the redundancies were present in the original text.

4. A recent study by Alba, Alexander, Hasher, & Caniglia (1981) supports the contention that we are dealing here with a retrieval problem. No differences were found between the title and no-title conditions when a recognition test was used instead of a recall test. Apparently, subjects were able to comprehend the texts without titles at a surface level and store information about that level in memory, but they were unable to build the propositional structures that people ordinarily construct during reading, with the result that whatever memory traces were formed remained inaccessible on a recall test.

5. We apologize for a shift in terminology: what is here called "semantic unit" (or "atomic proposition") corresponds to the "proposition" of Kintsch & van Dijk (1978); what we now call "proposition" was discussed earlier as "fact".

REFERENCES

Alba, J.W., Alexander, S.G., Hasher, L. and Caniglia, K. The role of context in the encoding of information. Journal of Experimental Psychology: Human Learning and Memory, 1981, 7, 283-292.

Anderson, R.C. and Pichert, J.W. Recall of previously unrecallable information following a shift in perspective. Journal of Verbal Learning and Verbal Behavior, 1978, 17, 1-12.

Belletta, F.S.   Mnemonic devices: Classification, characteristics, and criteria. Review of Educational Research, 1981, 51, 247-275.

Bower, G.H.   Mental imagery and associative learning.   In L.W. Gregg (Ed.) Cognition in learning and memory.   New York: Wiley, 1972.

Bower, G.H., Black, J.B. and Turner, T.J.   Scripts in memory for text. Cognitive Psychology, 1979, 11, 177-220.

Bransford, J. and Johnson, M.K.   Contextual prerequisites for understanding: Some investigations of comprehension and recall. Journal of Verbal Learning and Verbal Behavior, 1972, 11, 717-726.

Bryan, W.L. and Harter, N.   Studies on the telegraphic language: The acquisition of a hierarchy of habits.   Psychological Review, 1899, 6, 346-375.

Chase, W.G. and Ericsson, K.A.   Skilled memory.   In J.R. Anderson (Ed.) Cognitive skills and their acquisition.   Hillsdale, N.J.: Erlbaum, 1981.

Chase, W.G. and Simon, H.A.   Perception in chess.   Cognitive Psychology, 1973, 4, 55-81.

Cirilo, R.K. and Foss, D.J.   Text structure and reading time for sentences. Journal of Verbal Learning and Verbal Behavior, 1980, 19, 96-109.

Craik, F.I.M. and Lockhart, R.S.   Levels of processing: A framework for memory research.   Journal of Verbal Learning and Verbal Behavior, 1972, 11, 671-684.

van Dijk, T.A. and Kintsch, W.   Strategies of comprehension.   New York: Academic Press, forthcoming.

Graesser, A.C., Hoffman, N.L. and Clark, L.F.   Structural components of reading time.   Journal of Verbal Learning and Verbal Behavior, 1980, 19, 135-151.

de Groot, A.D.   Perception and memory versus thought: Some old ideas and recent findings.   In B. Kleinmuntz (Ed.) Problem solving: Research, Method, and Theory. New York: Wiley, 1966.

Hunter, I.M.L.   An exceptional talent for calculative thinking.   British Journal of Psychology, 1962, 53, 243-258.

Jenkins, J.J.   Remember that old theory of memory? Well, forget it! American Psychologist, 1974, 29, 785-795.

Kintsch, W. and van Dijk, T.A.   Toward a model of text comprehension and production.   Psychological Review, 1978, 85, 363-394.

Kintsch, W., Kozminsky, E., Streby, W.J., McKoon, F. and Keenan, J.M. Comprehension and recall of text as a function of content variables. Journal of Verbal Learning and Verbal Behavior, 1975, 14, 196-214.

Kintsch, W. and Yarbrough, J.C. The role of rhetorical structure in text comprehension. Journal of Educational Psychology, in press.

Mandel, T.S. Eye movement research on the propositional structure of short texts. Behavior Research Methods and Instrumentation, 1979, 11, 180-187.

Mandel, T.S. The relationship between eye movements and propositional text structure. Unpublished M.A. thesis, University of Colorado, 1980.

Meyer, B.J.F., Brand, D.M. and Bluth, G.J. Use of top level structure in text: Key for reading comprehension of ninth-grade students. Reading Research Quarterly, 1980, 16, 72-103.

Miller, J.R. A computer simulation model of text comprehension. (Forthcoming)

Miller, J.R. and Kintsch, W. Readability and recall of short prose passages: A theoretical analysis. Journal of Experimental Psychology: Human Learning and Memory, 1980, 6, 335-354.

Murdock, B.B., Jr. The serial position effect in free recall. Journal of Experimental Psychology, 1962, 64, 482-488.

Müller, G.E. Zur Analyse der Gedächtnistätigkeit und des Vorstellungsverlaufes. Zeitschrift für Psychologie, Ergänzungsband 5, 1911.

Peterson, L.R. and Peterson, M.J. Short-term retention of individual items. Journal of Experimental Psychology, 1959, 58, 193-198.

Spilich, G.J., Vesonder, G.T., Chiesi, H.L. and Voss, J.F. Text processing of domain-related information for individuals with high and low domain knowledge. Journal of Verbal Learning and Verbal Behavior, 1979, 18, 275-290.

Tulving, E. Episodic and semantic memory. In E. Tulving and W. Donaldson (Eds.) Organization of memory. New York: Academic Press, 1972.

Vipond, D. Micro- and macroprocesses in text comprehension. Journal of Verbal Learning and Verbal Behavior, 1980, 19, 276-296.

Yates, F.A. The art of memory. London: Rutledge and Kegan, 1966.

DISCOURSE PROCESSING
A. Flammer and W. Kintsch (eds.)
© *North-Holland Publishing Company, 1982*

KNOWLEDGE UPDATING IN TEXT PROCESSING

Steen F. Larsen

Institute of Psychology
University of Aarhus
8240 Risskov
Denmark

Updating one's knowledge is necessary to keep it current
despite continuous changes in the world. Updating is
argued to be basic to survival and to developing a knowledge of historical events, including one's personal
history. Texts particularly contribute to update knowledge of the world beyond personal experience, e.g., in
the case of news reports. A distinction between corrective updating (maintaining the currency of knowledge)
and progressive updating (maintaining out-of-date knowledge) is proposed and several subtypes are outlined.
In discussing the cognitive process of updating, a number of empirical problems are pointed out.

INTRODUCTION

When we read or listen to a text for the first time, we usually encounter
much information that is new to us. But it is seldom totally new in the
sense that we cannot relate it in any way to our previous knowledge. A
particular kind of relation to previous knowledge which occurs quite frequently is that the new information may serve to update our prior knowledge. That is, we register the new piece of information as representing a
more current situation in the world than the situation we already know.
The present paper is concerned with such knowledge updating.

The cognitive process of knowledge updating owes its existence to the fact
that a vast number of phenomena in the world are not static but rather
change over time. The study of learning and memory has focused almost
exclusively on the acquisition of knowledge about the invariant properties
of the world, or, at the most, knowledge about events that have already
been concluded so that no further changes will take place. In contrast,
updating is concerned with knowledge about ongoing events in real time
where it is a basic problem that one's knowledge may at any moment be
rendered out-of-date by subsequent events. It is my claim that knowledge
updating provides a perspective on knowledge acquisition in general that
differs from the ones that are established within either the verbal learning tradition or the discourse processing tradition. This has only been
partly recognized by the small handful of investigators who have dealt with
different aspects of the concept of updating.

By way of introduction, updating may be defined as a kind of knowledge
acquisition that serves the function of keeping the individual's knowledge
current despite continuous changes in the world which is the object of

knowledge. This implies four characteristics of the updating process.
First, the person must receive information that he believes to reflect the
current state of affairs in the world in some respect. Second, he must
relate this information to his knowledge of a previous state of affairs
which he recognizes as a precursor of the new one. Third, he must correct
his knowledge for the changes in the world that are indicated by the new
information. Fourth, he must deal with the pieces of knowledge that are no
longer considered to represent the current situation (outdated knowledge):
Should they be retained -- thus running the risk that they may be confused
with current knowledge; or should they be disposed of -- with the risk that
they might become useful on a later occasion?

With this abstract task analysis in mind the role of updating in everyday
life, in previous research, and in an ecological perspective shall now be
considered. In later sections, the problems of correcting previous knowledge and of retaining out-of-date knowledge will be discussed in more
detail, and finally an account of the process of updating will be proposed.

CONTEXTS OF UPDATING

Everyday knowledge updating

The everyday importance of knowledge updating has been pointed out only a
couple of times before. Thus, Rand Spiro (1977) claimed that updating of
one's knowledge is "one of the main reasons in everyday life for relating
new information to old" (p. 140), but he did not develop this line of
thought. Robert Bjork and his associates (Bjork, 1978; Bjork & Landauer,
1978) have done the most extensive studies of updating. They have given
several examples to demonstrate that updating is a common memory task;
e.g., "we need to remember where we left the car today, we need to remember
our current phone number, and we need to remember what the trump suit is on
this hand" (Bjork, 1978, p. 237). Bjork also called attention to the
decisive role of updating in many job environments, from air-traffic con-
trollers to short-order cooks, where permanent storage of information would
not only be useless but also risk the danger of interfering with information about the current situation.

Finally, I have argued that updating is prominent in some areas where
information is primarily acquired from texts (Larsen, Note 1). For instance, all researchers are familiar with the problem of keeping their
knowledge of new empirical studies and theoretical developments current.
A more commonly known example, at least to people in the industrialized
countries, is the daily updating of knowledge of world events by means of
the news services provided by papers, radio, television, and so on. A
demonstration of this is available in a study of memory for real-life news
(Larsen, Note 2). Among information in a radio news bulletin, news about
current events were significantly better recalled than new facts about past
events (new "background information"). Thus, a strategy that favored
updating seemed to be spontaneously employed by the subjects.

Research on knowledge updating

These examples suggest the broad scope of updating processes in everyday
life. Nevertheless, investigations of updating are very few, as are stud-

ies of many other mundane memory tasks (Neisser, 1978). In the chapter by
Rand Spiro mentioned above (Spiro, 1977), he asserted that discourse memory
studies had ignored updating by using fictional materials so that the
subjects had no previous knowledge available to update. This criticism is
undoubtedly correct. But from a theoretical point of view, the reason that
updating has been ignored by discourse processing research is rather that
interest has been focused on previous knowledge of a general nature, vari-
ously called schemata, frames, scripts, story grammars, etc. (Johnson and
Mandler, 1980). Since such knowledge structures are not specific to any
particular episode, they cannot be updated by information about specific
events (Larsen, in press). This does not exclude the possibility of updating specific information assigned to a schema or script, a problem that
Schank and Abelson (1977) have treated briefly as will be shown later.

In contrast to the discourse processing approach, the verbal learning
tradition has for a century been concerned with specific knowledge (accompanied by a total neglect of general knowledge). But the notion of updating appears foreign to verbal learning theory. First, because all
knowledge acquisition is conceived as the strengthening of associations so
that out-of-date knowledge cannot be corrected, it can only be overwhelmed
by stronger associations or laboriously unlearned. Second, because associations are assumed to be content-free, the temporal or causal relations
between successive events cannot be distinguished theoretically from any
other associations. Moreover, the verbal learning tradition has employed
artificial experimental materials to a far greater extent than the discourse studies crititicized by Spiro (1977). In spite of these facts, the
experiments by Bjork's group, which will be considered later, have fed on
inspiration from the verbal learning approach and its interference theory
of forgetting. Particularly, the theory has drawn attention to the possibility that outdated knowledge may interfere with memory for current information.

Ecology of updating: Correction and progression

The main reason for the neglect of updating presumably goes deeper, namely,
the fundamental status of this concept in knowledge acquisition has
not been realized. As indicated above, the need for knowledge updating
arises from the continuous stream of changes in the world around us that is
a basic condition of existence. The ontological thesis that the material
world is in continuous movement goes back at least to the Greek philosopher
Heraclitus about 500 B.C., and it is a cornerstone of dialectic materialist
philosophy (Kröber, 1974). As a consequence, any organism that in some way
stores knowledge of the world must face the fundamental task of keeping its
knowledge in accord with the current situation. If this task is ignored or
fails, the knowledge will after a period be inadequate for supporting
action and the preparation of action. We may say that updating is the
ecologically primary form of knowledge acquisition, in the sense that the
survival value of knowledge depends decisively upon keeping it maximally
current.

Corrective updating. The task of updating described so far may be carried
out simply by correcting pieces of knowledge that are recognized as being
out of date. That is, current information replaces outdated knowledge,
which is completely lost or deleted in the process. An organism that has
only this corrective updating at its disposal will know the current state

of the world and nothing else. Perhaps the most primitive case of corrective updating is seen in the orienting reflex and its habituation that
occurs even in very primitive animals as a reaction to changes of stimulus
details within an otherwise constant situation (Sokolov, 1977). Corrective
updating may be sufficient for survival in many cases, not only in primitive animals but also in some human tasks where it would be useless to
carry around a burden of past knowledge. Recall, for instance, Bjork's
example of remembering where one has left the car. As Bjork noted, out-of-
date information might even cause confusion, or, in other words, it requires mental capacities for handling it and keeping it from interfering
with ongoing behavior.

Progressive updating. Nevertheless, it has obvious advantages for survival
to know more than just the present state of the environment. In the midst
of continual change, some aspects of the world are relatively stable, other
aspects vary in a lawful way, whereas still others vary randomly (at least
as far as the conditions of a given organism will allow it to perceive).
If an organism shall be able to appreciate such differences and eventually
to detect the laws of change, it must to some extent retain information
that is out of date so that past events can be compared with current and
future observations. When a more or less complete chain of outdated information is retained as antecedents of the current situation, it constitutes
a chart of the progression of events that has resulted in the present
state. Therefore, I propose the term progressive updating for cases where
correction of changes is supplemented by some retention of outdated pieces
of knowledge.

Progressive updating is different from the kind of knowledge acquisition
that results in habits and skills. In such cumulative learning, individual
events blend together and become indistinguishable contributors to the
final disposition or aptitude of the organism. In Jerome Bruner's (1969)
words, this is "memory without record", whereas the past events in progressive updating preserve at least some of their individuality -- it is
"memory with record" of its circumstances of acquisition, although many of
the details of the original record may well be lost.

Because progressive updating involves retention of specific information
about the progress of events in time, it is a necessary precondition for
attaining a "historical consciousness" in relation to current events --
that is, an understanding of how the present state of the world has developed. But progressive updating does not automatically provide that understanding which involves more than just a knowledge of historical facts.
Although a discussion of this problem is beyond the present paper, it will
be argued later that an important beginning is to consider how the outdated
information -- the historical knowledge -- is organized.

Episodic and factual updating

So far, it has been tacitly assumed that the knowledge to be updated concerns the world outside and is independent of the person. But the knowledge
people have also includes themselves and the things that they have personally experienced in the past. Because new experiences are continuously
made and the situation of the person undergoes continuous change, updating
of this knowledge must be very important. Consider a situation where new
information is acquired by direct experience, with the subject as an eye-

witness or participant. This new information will by necessity reflect a
more recent situation than any other known by the person. It may then be
used for updating in two respects, depending upon which kind of previous
knowledge it is related to. On the one hand, it may update the person's
knowledge of what he has himself experienced, his autobiographical or
episodic knowledge. This episodic updating will keep the person's knowledge of his own doings current, and it may add one more bit to his personal history, which is presumably a condition for an individual's sense of
continuity in his life. It will result in knowledge like, for instance,
"The last novel I read was Doris Lessing's Memoirs of a Survivor".

On the other hand, the newly experienced situation may also be related to
the subject's knowledge of events in the world independent of his experience, to his factual and historical knowledge (which should not be confused with his generalized and conceptual knowledge, often called semantic
knowledge (see Larsen, in press)). This factual updating is illustrated in
pure form by cases where we know the current state and background of our
immediate surroundings without remembering the experience of acquiring that
knowledge. However, knowledge acquired by direct experience most often
appears to be coded both episodically and factually. But factors like
personal interest, active participation in the events, and functional
importance of the environmental changes probably influence both coding and
retention.

Of course, we also acquire knowledge that represents permanent qualities of
the world, or is mistakenly thought to do so. Such knowledge cannot be used
for factual updating, although the experience of acquiring it may update
one's episodic knowledge. Hence, you do not update your knowledge of French
each time you learn a new word (unless you specifically note that the word
has come in use recently); rather your knowledge of French is increased. In
other words, becoming wiser is not necessarily an instance of updating.

The problems of acquiring a personal history have almost never been studied
(but see Linton, 1978); but it is suggested that the concept of episodic
updating will be a useful point of departure in this endeavour. Presently,
we shall focus on factual updating, however.

Updating in text processing

In some respects, updating from texts presents more complicated problems
than updating from direct experience. The general issue of learning by
experience versus learning at second hand has a long history in philosophy,
but it has rarely been considered in cognitive psychology as Neisser noted
in the last paragraph of his 1976 book.

In the context of knowledge updating, there are two fundamental problems.
First, knowledge obtained from a text is never current in a strict sense.
Even in the news media the text has to be prepared some time after the
events described and some time before publication. The concept of updating
would lose its precision, if the currency criterion was given up so that
any acquisition of time-referenced information was counted as updating
(e.g., learning new details about Napoleon's death does not update your
knowledge). To solve this currency problem, the subject's conditions of
knowing must be taken into account, requiring only that the new information
should represent the nearest approximation to the current situation which

is available to him. Thus, even though the subject may be aware that the
situation has probably changed already, he may consider the new information
to provide the best picture of the current state of affairs that he can get
with the effort he is willing to spend.

The second problem with updating from texts concerns which area of knowledge is to be updated. A text not only provides information concerning
the situation it describes (its reference), but also more or less explicitly bears evidence of the situation in which it was produced (e.g., who
authored it, under what conditions, for what reasons). This is clearly
seen in news and scientific reports. For instance, a treatise on Napoleon
in 1814 may have been produced in 1980, and a news story written in New
York yesterday may describe events in Iran the day before. Therefore, the
subject may update either his knowledge of the situation of reference or
his knowledge of the situation of production (or both), depending upon what
previous knowledge he has accessible and takes an interest in keeping up-
to-date.

In the case of a scientific text, the situation of reference is the object
that is studied. This is usually not time-dependent. Consequently, the
information acquired does not update the subject's knowledge, but rather
increases or revises it. The situation of production, on the other hand, is
an event in the development of the scientific discipline concerned. Hence,
if the subject views the text as representing current thinking in the field
more accurately than his previous knowledge, information from the text may
be used to update his knowledge of the historical progress and present
state of science. Note that this updating does not necessarily imply a
belief in the veridicality of the information, which is an issue belonging
to the sphere of reference of the text. The subject may well believe the
new "facts" or theories to be wrong; only the most naïve or optimistic
researcher will regard the latest in science as being ipso facto the best.
It is precisely to distinguish scientific truth from scientific news that
the reference and production aspects of a text should be kept apart.

News reports in some way illustrate the opposite of scientific reports.
News is consumed to update knowledge of the world, not to increase it in
any substantive sense. (Sometimes the purpose is only to ensure that
nothing important has happened, but even then, so-called background materials may impart an increased knowledge to the public). Thus, although the
referents of the news stories usually dominate in people's minds, the
production aspect of the text may occasionally attract attention. If we
assume the attitude of a news editor, we relate the report to previous
knowledge about journalists, news agencies, possible purposes of manipulation, the debate on "freedom of information", etc. This knowledge may
then be updated instead of (or simultaneously with) knowledge concerning
the referents. For instance, your reaction to a telegram from the French
press agency AFP in Teheran might be, "Well, I thought that the French had
left Iran several months ago, but that is apparently not so".

Finally, it should be noted that the personal experience of reading or
listening to a text may update the subject's episodic knowledge, his auto-
biography, just like any other experience may do. This is particularly
likely to happen if the text refers to events to which the subject attaches
deep personal significance. A famous example is that many people seem to
remember their reaction and what they were doing when they received news of
President Kennedy's assassination (Greenberg, 1964). Also, it is a common

and frustrating experience to recall when and where one has read a paper at
the expense of recalling its contents.

VARIETIES OF UPDATING

Corrective updating

The updating process will now be discussed in detail, beginning with an
attempt to explicate the two aspects of updating that were introduced
above, correction and progression. Some notions to this end may be derived
from previous studies.

One of the programs that Schank and Abelson (1977) wrote to illustrate their
theory of scripts incorporated facilities for corrective updating. This
program -- called FRUMP for Fast Reading Understanding and Memory Program
-- was designed for skimming newspaper articles dealing with certain types
of news events for which the program was equipped with schematic knowledge,
so-called "sketchy scripts". The scripts had open slots for some of the
variables of the news stories. For example, the script for vehicle acci-
dents had six slots: type of vehicle, object of collision, geographical
location, number of deaths, number injured, and allocation of fault. When
FRUMP encounters a newspaper article that is identified as describing a
vehicle accident, this script is instantiated and FRUMP then searches for
and retains information that fits into the slots, whereas everything else is
ignored.

The decisive point is that FRUMP is also able to update the information it
has gathered if it is later presented with another news story about the
same event. Two types of updating corrections are possible. First, if a
slot had not been filled because of missing information in the first story,
appropriate information in the second story is simply inserted into the
slot. Second, if the more recent information in the second story differs
from the previous knowledge obtained from the first one, the new information is substituted into the slot, thus erasing the old slot value.

FRUMP illustrates the approach of schematic discourse theories very clearly, including the fact that the general knowledge of the script is not
affected, only the specific knowledge assigned to the variables in the
script is updated. To what extent FRUMP simulates human performance has
not been investigated.But from the present perspective, several limitations
are obvious. Since the open script variables have to be determined in
advance, FRUMP cannot retain anything unusual as humans are apt to do.
This drawback might be overcome by providing for a third type of corrections, namely addition of new variables required by the received information. On the other hand, such a mechanism would create further problems
concerning procedures for limiting the number of variables, and so on.

Furthermore, the kind of stories that FRUMP can process are descriptions of
events that are instantaneous, so to speak -- they happen in a moment and
are finished when the story is received. Therefore, no subsequent events
have to be accomodated later. Only corrections or completions of the
original information are possible. It is not clear how FRUMP should be
modified to deal with the long chains of events that are frequently in the
news -- sometimes very long ones indeed, like the Middle East peace nego-
tiations. A third limitation is closely related, namely that FRUMP automatically deletes outdated slot values, just like ordinary computer memo-

ries do. This is a most serious shortcoming, as the next section will
confirm; although people often seem to have short memories, total erasure
of knowledge of the past is too radical.

On the assumption that scripts (or similar structures) are adequate for
describing knowledge of events, the following types of updating corrections
have thus far emerged:
(1) No change of old slot value.
(2) Insertion of value in empty slot.
(3) Substitution of new value for old value.
(4) Addition of new variable to accept unexpected value.

It is entirely possible that more extensive transformations of previous
knowledge are sometimes necessary. Imagine, for instance, your reaction to
the news that Ayatollah Khomeini had declared himself a Soviet agent. Such
changes may involve corrections of knowledge stretching far into the past
and thus overlap with the notion of progressive updating. This concept
will be discussed in the next section, before speculating on the processing
characteristics of the different types of corrections.

Progressive updating

The problems of progression in updating have been explored by Robert Bjork
and his collaborators. Starting from the perspective of the verbal learning tradition, their methodology was a variant of the standard paired-
associate paradigm. In one experiment (Bjork & Landauer, 1978) the materials were lists of paired names, one male and one female. The pairs were
presented to the subjects as the names of persons who were married to each
other (A + B), divorced (A - B), perhaps remarried (A + C), and so on.
Through different sequences of shifting partnerships, it was the subjects'
task to remember the final marital status and the name of the spouse of
each "stimulus person" involved (i.e., the A names). The results showed
that the name of a former spouse was very often given instead of the correct, "current" one. Thus, outdated information was not erased as implied
by the FRUMP model of corrective updating. Rather, it competed with the
current information and seemed to win the battle as often as not. In both
cases, the likelihood of recall was low, however.

Another experiment (Bjork and McClure, cited in Bjork, 1978) was concerned
with the organization of outdated information. The materials were pairs of
unrelated nouns with constantly changing response terms (the A-B, A-C, A-D,
... paradigm). Organization was manipulated by instructing the subjects to
use three different encoding strategies. Bjork & McClure found that the
encoding strategies differed in the degree to which they favored recall of
the last response terms (i.e., the current information) as well as recall
of earlier (outdated) responses. However, one strategy yielded better
recall of both current and outdated responses than any other, namely, a so-
called structural updating strategy where the subjects were asked to construct a simple story, starting with the stimulus word and including each
new response word in a continuation of the story line. Bjork assumed that
the encoding of successive new words with the story as an organizing
structure had preserved information about the order of the words, thus
specifying which word was the most recent one. However, he did not attempt
to propose a theory of the phenomena of updating, but rather viewed the
results as a challenge to interference theory.

Conclusions from these studies must be cautious since the materials and procedures were very far from everyday updating. In particular, the use of unrelated words and names facilitated confusions; the story lines were totally uncontrolled, subjective constructions instead of being based in the objective structure of the materials; and the information could not be related to other events experienced concurrently in the subjects' normal course of life. Nevertheless, it is apparent that the way out-of-date knowledge is organized has a great impact on memory and may differentially affect retention of current and past information. From other research, it is not surprising that the construction of a coherent story is an especially powerful tool for remembering. Several other ways of organizing temporally specified information are suggested by common experience, however. I propose that three principal types be distinguished:

(1) Unordered: The knowledge items that have been replaced by more recent
ones are retained as a mere collection without internal ordering. An
everyday example is when people talk about "the good old days" and mix
together happy memories from any period in their past.

(2) Successive: The outdated pieces of knowledge are ordered in a fixed
sequence but are otherwise not connected. The sequence may or may not
be specified in relation to calendar time. Historical events that are
remembered merely by the year they happened may serve as an example.

(3) Structural: The outdated knowledge is incorporated into a structure
of relations, a causal or intentional chain of antecedent and consequent events, e.g., a coherent story. The structure may be hierarchical to a greater or lesser extent, involving higher-order relations.

I should be evident that these types of organization cannot be equally effective in terms of either retention of past knowledge or differentiation from current information. Consider, for instance, knowledge of the exchange rate of the US dollar. If past rates were totally unordered, one could perhaps remember the top and bottom rates from recent years, but not the movements of the rate; still, the magnitude of the current rate might be reasonably well recalled. In case of successive organization, the patterns of movement should be known, like in a graph, perhaps even specified in time; most of us presumably have a rough picture of this kind covering the last 5-10 years. A structural organization might in addition include principles or reasons to account for the movements, for example, that a drop in the rate resulted when the USA left the gold standard about 1970, and that the present, high exchange rate is caused by a high rate of interest in the States. Again, many people may have such isolated structural organizers, whereas only bankers and businessmen are likely to possess a tighter structure, a hierarchical script.

This example illustrates a number of issues raised by the concept of progressive updating. How selective is retention? What is selected? How is a relation to calendar time established? What is the relation between such factual knowledge of the past and the person's autobiographical knowledge? What means may be used for structural organization and how are they acquired? Instead of pursuing these questions, the next section will give a general outline of the process of updating and suggest some possibilities for empirical research.

THE PROCESS OF UPDATING

Automatic and controlled updating

The preceding discussion implies that the occurrence of updating is to a significant extent dependent upon the subject's processing of the information obtained. This was so both in regard to how the new information was related to prior knowledge and with regard to the subject's perception of the currency of the information. The question then arises whether updating is carried out automatically as a primitive routine of the cognitive system, or whether it is a special strategy controlled by higher-order, executive processes (Shiffrin and Schneider, 1977). The studies by Schank and Abelson (1977) and by Bjork (1978) appear to imply that updating is relatively automatic, although Bjork acknowledges that it may be influenced by rehearsal and encoding strategies. On the other hand, in a conference discussion Spiro and Meyer (1977; see also Meyer, 1977) agreed that updating was a specific reading strategy, in contrast to reading for complete comprehension and memory; but they disagreed concerning the extension of the strategies in everyday life. Whereas Meyer claimed that updating was restricted to situations when a reader skims a text, Spiro maintained that the updating strategy is typical of everyday reading.

In the more precise sense of updating that is used here, the issue is less clearcut. Episodic updating would seem to be ordinarily an automatic process. We seldom turn the acquisition of our personal history into an intentional project, thinking something like, "This is an important event in my life, I must remember it by any means"; but in situations of major decisions or crises it may, of course, happen. Similarly, much of our factual updating appears to be automatic, perhaps on a very low level of control as suggested by the mechanism of habituation and by the evolutionary value of keeping track of environmental changes (cf. above). Since progressive updating is considered less primitive than pure correction, this argument also implies that the former is more accessible to, and more dependent on, intentional control than the latter.

In text processing the case may be somewhat different. Text processing is an activity that is purely concerned with the manipulation of knowledge, and therefore the person's purposes in relation to knowledge acquisition are not obscured by the practical goals that usually control our dealings with the non-textual environment. News, scientific reports, and other kinds of documentary texts present clear examples of text processing that are often controlled by an intentional updating strategy -- a wish to know what is new. Of course, even such texts may be processed differently, for instance to entertain, in which case updating is relegated to an incidental result of the main acitivity. Fictional texts read primarily for entertainment may be characterized in a similar way; but the entire problem of fictional versus non-fictional text processing is largely unexplored.

Three components of the updating process

It would be premature to propose a theory of updating. However, updating must be considered just one of the many tasks the human cognitive system is able to perform. Therefore, the general principles of such a theory should be compatible with established cognitive theories. With this constraint in mind, the main components of the updating process may be outlined as three phases that are cyclically related:

(1) Recognition of relations between the new information and relevant
     previous knowledge.
(2) Coding of appropriate corrections and organization of knowledge of the
     progression of events.
(3) Retention of current as well as past knowledge.
The second phase comprises updating proper and is assumed to be the heart
of the process, in accordance with the principle of encoding specificity
(Tulving and Thomson, 1973).

Recognition. In the context of updating, recognition concerns how the
subject evokes those parts of his previous knowledge which may be updated
by the new information. This is a problem of accessing and retrieving
knowledge, where questions may be asked about the conditions determining
the accessibility of different areas of a subject's knowledge (e.g., recency, organization, functional value). Also, certain variables in the new
message are presumably used as index variables to gain access to the pertinent knowledge, thus posing the question whether different variables are
equally efficient. It may be, for instance, that geographical locations
and prominent persons are good cues because they are familiar ones; on
the other hand, they may be bad cues because the familiarity means that
they are associated with many diverse knowledge items. A similar problem
has been investigated by Reder and Anderson (1980).

So far, recognition has been described as a bottom-up, data-driven process
(Norman and Bobrow,1975). This may cover incidental updating. But in cases
of intentional updating, expectations derived from prior knowledge must be
assumed to direct an active search for missing information, consequences of
events, etc., to satisfy open variables in the previous knowledge structure. A top-down or conceptually driven model will fit this process more
closely, thus turning the problem of accessing previous knowledge into one
of tuning the cognitive system to be sensitive to updating information.

Coding. The two aspects of updating which were distinguished earlier,
correction and progression, may be viewed as processes of coding the new
information. Correction consists in coding the changes that have occurred,
progression in coding relations with the subject's prior body of knowledge
about the event.

Three types of corrections were noted in the discussion of Schank and Abelson's (1977) FRUMP program, substitution and insertion of new values, and
addition of new variables required by the input. Besides, a possibility of
coding "no change" was included, e.g., to account for the frequent experience that there was "nothing new" in the news (i.e., at least nothing
worth noting). Among the questions raised by this classification, it would
be interesting to study whether the different corrections are made equally
readily. For instance, addition of new variables would seem to require
more processing resources than the other three because it involves changes
in the general framework (script) applied to the event. Again, substitution
should require more extensive processing than the remaining two because the
outdated slot value must be dealt with.

Progression -- the coding and organization of prior knowledge and its
relation to new information -- was classified into unordered, successive,
and structural progression. Studies of news memory (e.g., Findahl and Höijer,
1975) have suggested that unordered progression is very common, but the
exact conditions promoting the use of different types of organization are
poorly understood. On the assumption that people always attempt to per-

ceive some meaning in events in terms of previously known scripts, it may
be profitable to investigate the kinds of scripts people apply -- and what
scripts are available at all. As an example, people often seem to interpret social and political events in terms of the whims and motives of the
individual actors. If such scripts derived from personal interaction are
applied, the person will presumably miss the higher-order, political and
economic reasons that constitute the long-range significance of the events;
the succession of related episodes will tend to be reduced to unordered
curiosities characterizing the VIP's who are involved. To study these
problems, one might examine the expectations of the subjects concerning
succeeding information, either by a procedure of generation or by reaction
time measures.

Retention. Of course, retention of both current and outdated knowledge must
depend upon the coding and organization of knowledge. According to common
sense as well as   the extensive empirical evidence from research on
memory, unordered, successive, and structural progression may be assumed to
enhance retention with increasing probabilities. When errors of retention
occur we may gain some insight into the nature of the progressive organization. For instance, if the current value of some variable is forgotten
without any awareness on the part of the subject, this will suggest an
unordered progression that cannot specify the point where a piece of knowledge is missing. Intrusions of outdated knowledge should be particularly
revealing of the organization employed.

One of the most important questions raised by the concept of updating
concerns how the concrete details of day-to-day updating become integrated
to form a more general view of what has happened during a considerable
period of time. In theory, scripts of a very high order may be invoked to
account for this development of a knowledge of contemporary history. The
process appears very difficult to investigate because of its long range and
the multitude of impressions that may contribute to it. Neisser's (1981)
ingenious study of John Dean's memory may be seen as an example of a viable
approach, but such cases are very uncommon. An intriguing problem in this
context is the revisions of knowledge that may occur when a course of
events is later reflected upon. Such reflection is probably done by most
people now and then, and it is very common around the turn of a year or a
decade, when numerous comments in the media offer views that may serve the
individual as models for interpreting his own experience.

A final note about methods

Many of the questions for research that have been suggested in the present
paper should be quite straightforward to study by adapting established
methodology. It is an easy step to devise materials that are sufficiently
realistic, and to present it successively so that the gradual process of
building a representation of the events described can be examined. Inter-
mittent tests of the state of knowledge attained by the subject (free
recall, forced choice, reaction time) and concurrent measurement of reading
time will be useful methods in this effort.

REFERENCE NOTES

1. Larsen, S.F. Memory for radio news: Discourse structure and knowledge
    updating (Psychological Reports Aarhus, Vol. 5, No. 1). Aarhus:
    University of Aarhus, Institute of Psychology, 1980.
2. Larsen, S.F. Text processing and knowledge updating in memory for
    radio news. Manuscript submitted for publication, 1981.

REFERENCES

Bjork, R.A. The updating of human memory. In G.H. Bower (Ed.), The
    psychology of learning and motivation (Vol. 12). New York: Academic
    Press, 1978.
Bjork, R.A. and Landauer, T.K. On keeping track of the present status of
    people and things. In M.M. Gruneberg, P.E. Morris and R.N. Sykes (Eds.).
    Practical aspects of memory. New York: Academic Press, 1978.
Bruner, J.S. Modalities of memory. In G.A. Talland and N. Waugh (Eds.). The
    pathology of memory. New York: Academic Press, 1969.
Findahl, O. and Höijer, B. Effect of additional verbal information on re-
    tention of a radio news program. Journalism Quarterly, 1975, 52, 493-
    498.
Greenberg, B.S. Diffusion of news of the Kennedy assassination. Public
    Opinion Quarterly, 1964, 28, 225-232.
Johnson, N.S. and Mandler, J.M. A tale of two structures: Underlying and
    surface forms in stories. Poetics, 1980, 9, 51-86.
Kröber, G. Bewegung. In G. Klaus and M. Buhr (Eds.). Philosophisches Wör-
    terbuch (Vol. 1, 10th ed.). Leipzig: VEB Bibliographisches Institut,
    1974.
Larsen, S.F. Specific background knowledge and knowledge updating. In J.
    Allwood and E. Hjelmqvist (Eds.). Foregrounding background. Stockholm:
    Doxa, in press.
Linton, M. Real world memory after six years: An in vivo study of very
    long term memory. In M.M. Gruneberg, P.E. Morris and R.N. Sykes (Eds.).
    Practical aspects of memory. New York: Academic Press, 1978.
Meyer, B.J.F. What is remembered from prose: A function of passage
    structure. In R.O. Freedle (Ed.). Discourse production and compre-
    hension. Norwood, N.J.: Ablex, 1977.
Neisser, U. Cognition and reality. San Francisco: Freeman, 1976.
Neisser, U. Memory: What are the important questions? In M.M. Gruneberg,
    P.E. Morris and R.N. Sykes (Eds.). Practical aspects of memory. New
    York: Academic Press, 1978.
Neisser, U. John Dean's memory: A case study. Cognition, 1981, 9, 1-22.
Norman, D.A. and Bobrow, D.G. On data-limited and resource-limited proces-
    ses. Cognitive Psychology, 1975, 7, 44-64.
Reder, L.M. and Anderson, J.R. A partial resolution of the paradox of inter-
    ference: The role of integrating knowledge. Cognitive Psychology,
    1980, 12, 447-472.
Schank, R.C. and Abelson, R.P. Scripts, plans, goals, and understanding.
    Hillsdale, N.J.: Erlbaum, 1977.
Shiffrin, R.M. and Schneider, W. Controlled and automatic human information
    processing: II. Perceptual learning, automatic attending, and a
    general theory. Psychological Review, 1977, 84, 127-190.

Sokolov, E.N. Brain functions: Neuronal mechanisms of learning and memory. Annual Review of Psychology, 1977, 28, 85-112.

Spiro, R.J. Remembering information from text: The "state-of-schema" approach. In R.C. Anderson, R.J. Spiro and W.E. Montague (Eds.). Schooling and the acquisition of knowledge. Hillsdale, N.J.: Erlbaum, 1977.

Spiro, R.J. and Meyer, B.J.F. Open discussion on the contributions of Meyer and Carter. In R.C. Anderson, R.J. Spiro and W.E. Montague (Eds.). Schooling and the acquisition of knowledge. Hillsdale, N.J.: Erlbaum, 1977.

Tulving, E. and Thomson, D.M. Encoding specificity and retrieval processes in episodic memory. Psychological Review, 1973, 80, 352-373.

DISCOURSE PROCESSING
A. Flammer and W. Kintsch (eds.)
© *North-Holland Publishing Company, 1982*

RETRIEVAL CUES AND THE REMEMBERING OF
PROSE: A REVIEW

Ronald E. Johnson

Purdue University
W. Lafayette, Indiana
U.S.A.

A widespread assumption is that the inducement of
remembering is largely a matter of finding appropriate retrieval cues. In the present paper the
literature is reviewed to ascertain the conditions
under which retrieval cues assist in the remembering
of prose. Special attention is given to comparisons
in which cues are given prior to attempts at remembering as opposed to cues that are provided after
learners have attempted recall on their own. Attention also is directed to the relative effectiveness of different types of retrieval cues.

Based upon the review of the literature, it may
be concluded that we know surprisingly little
about the types of cues that can be used to facilitate (or hinder) the remembering of intact prose
passages. Retrieval cues have been found which
markedly influence the remembering of sentences
presented in isolation, but efforts to induce the
remembering of intact prose passages generally
have not been successful. The remembering of intact
prose appears to be surprisingly impervious to the
availability or nonavailability of formal retrieval cues.

What determines the amount of remembering that learners show? Perhaps the
most important determinant is the degree of original learning. Typically,
the higher the degree of original learning, the better is remembering.
Another determinant of remembering is the extent to which other learnings
interfere with the remembering of the target content. Although interference clearly is an important determinant of the remembering of nonsense
syllables and lists of words, the evidence is much less convincing for the
remembering of prose. Evidence can be found for interference in remembering prose (e.g., Anderson & Myrow, 1971; Bower, 1974), but such
interference becomes evident only under a limited set of circumstances.

Yet, forgetting takes place - even for content that has been learned well.
If such forgetting cannot be attributed to interference, then what is
responsible? One possibility is that the learner lacks appropriate
retrieval cues for remembering. In a sense this interpretation simply
shifts the problem of explaining why the content is forgotten to the
problem of explaining why retrieval cues become increasingly unavailable
or else ineffective. However, before taking the cuing explanation

seriously, it would appear appropriate to examine the empirical evidence
to determine the extent to which textual remembering is influenced by the
availability of potential retrieval cues. In the present paper the
literature is reviewed to ascertain the conditions under which retrieval
cues affect the remembering of prose.

The scope of the review is limited to those studies in which the prose
unit that was learned was as large or larger than an intact sentence.
Excluded from this review then are studies in which the content to be
learned was phrase units such as adjective-noun combinations (e.g.,
Anisfeld, 1970; Cofer, Segal, Stein, & Walker, 1969; Horowitz & Prytulak,
1969). However, the review includes those studies in which the presentation of intact sentences then was followed by retrieval cues probing the
remembering of individual words.

A further limitation was to include only those studies in which a
retrieval cue was presented at the time of attempted retrieval. Excluded,
therefore, are studies in which cues were provided at the time of
learning. Although such cues may continue to exist in memory, and
thereby influence retrieval, the possibility exists that the major effect
of such cues is to direct learning rather than to influence retrieval.
The review, however, does include such studies when the experimenter also
included other groups that received explicit retrieval cues at the time
of remembering and not at the time of learning.

The availability of retrieval cues at memory, however, did not automatically warrant the inclusion of the study in the review. Many studies,
for example, were found in which the experimenter provided all groups
with the same set of retrieval cues at the time of remembering. Such
studies, alas, do not provide information on the effectiveness of
retrieval cues. The review, however, does include those studies in which
free or noncued recall was followed by cued remembering. From a methodological viewpoint, there is need to alert ourselves to the possibility
that an earlier unaided test of retention may influence the outcomes
of later tests with cues. An advantage of such studies, though, is to
provide information on the extent to which retrieval cues allow the
learner to dredge up information that otherwise would not be remembered.

Another potential pitfall is the possibility that the differential
effectiveness of a prompt in retrieving different types of prose content
may not be an accurate reflection of the differential effectiveness of
the prompt per se. Instead, the differing amounts of remembering may stem
from the fact that the various types of prose were not learned equally
well. For example, if learners encounter both normal sentences and sentences that violate normal expectations (e.g., "the tray loved the house"),
and a subsequent cue results in better retrieval of the normal sentence
(Graesser, 1978), it does not necessarily mean that the cue works better
with normal sentences. The outcome may simply reflect superior learning
of the normal sentences.

Finally, the review does not include those studies in which the primary
dependent variable was a measure of reaction time. There are many
experiments in the literature in which a contextual phrase or a semantic
probe was used either as a priming stimulus or as a retrieval cue.
Learners were requested to respond as quickly as possible to whether the
probe was somehow related to a target sentence (e.g., Green, 1975). Such

studies were excluded from the review since their interpretation is not obvious. For example, if one type of probe bears greater similarity to the target sentence than another probe, would reaction times be faster or slower? An examination of the literature reveals that some experimenters interpret a faster response as evidence of closer semantic similarity, while other experimenters assume a slower response is evidence of similarity.

EFFECTS OF CUING - QUANTITATIVE OUTCOMES

Facilitation of Remembering. The literature provides convincing evidence that cuing can result in the retrieval of content that normally would not have been retrieved without the cues. As compared with noncued groups, most of the cued groups showed higher levels of recall (e.g., Chiesi, Spilich & Voss, 1979, 29% to 54% advantage over noncued recalls; Sehulster & Crouse, 1972, approximately 100% advantage for cued group on content drawn from the later portions of the passage).

Null Outcomes. Although cuing typically facilitates remembering, some studies have been reported in which the presence of cues had negligible effects. Summers & Fleming (1971), for example, found that reinstating all sentences of a passage except for the target sentence had no influence on the remembering of the target sentence. Other experimenters reporting meager or no facilitation from cues include Barclay, Bransford, Franks, McCarrell, & Nitsch, 1974, Exp. 4; Bransford, Nitsch & Franks, 1977; Rubin, 1977, free recall vs. context group in Exp. 3; Till & Walsh, 1980, Exp. 1 & 2; Johnson, Notes 2, 3, & 4).

Interference from Cuing. A few experimenters also have reported comparisons in which retrieval cues interfered with retrieval (Barclay et al., 1974, Exp. 4; Britton, Meyer, Hodge, & Glynn, 1980, Exp. 2; Kolina, 1972; Johnson, Note 2). In a similar vein, Schustack & Anderson (1979) reported an experiment in which some learners were informed at the time of testing that the biographies they had previously studied paralleled the biographies of famous people. As compared with learners who were not told of the parallel, the learners who received the cue more often erroneously endorsed thematically related statements as having been in the original biographies.

Delayed Retention. With longer retention intervals learners might be expected to forget not only the semantic content of the text, but also their self-generated retrieval cues. Therefore, it might be predicted that the influence of retrieval cues would be relatively greater at longer retention intervals. Unfortunately, few experimenters have examined the effects of retrieval cues at different retention intervals. Rubin (1978) found that the relative advantage of cuing groups over a no-cues group increased across retention intervals ranging up to one month. With retention intervals of 2, 7, or 28 days, however, Summers & Fleming (1971) reported no advantage for cued groups at any retention interval.

Recognitive Performances. Though most investigators of retrieval cues have used only measures of recall, several experimenters have demonstrated that retrieval cues also can influence recognition (Baker & Santa, 1977; Morris, 1978; Schustack & Anderson, 1979). In the Morris study, for example, capitalized target words were presented in sentence contexts that either were congruent with normal usage (e.g., "The PICKLE was served

with slaw") or else were incongruent (e.g., "The PICKLE jammed the
saxophone"). At recognition the target nouns were embedded either in
their original contextual frame, in new congruous contexts (e.g., "The
PICKLE was on top of the sandwich") or in new incongruous contexts (e.g.,
"The PICKLE was cut by the chain saw"). Overall, recognition of the
target nouns was best in the old sentence context. Nouns presented
originally in a congruous context, however, were better recognized when
embedded in a new congruous context then in a new incongruous context.
The nouns originally presented in an incongruous context, in contrast,
were better recognized in a new incongruous context than in a new
congruous context. Recognition thus was better when the cuing context
was more similar to the original encoding context.

EFFECTS OF CUING - QUALITATIVE INFLUENCES

Retrieval cues can influence the type of error made in remembering.
In the Turner & Rommetveit (1968) study, for example, the nature of the
retrieval cue influenced the extent to which the original sentences were
transformed to the active or passive voice in recall. Likewise, though
Schustack & Anderson's (1979) learners showed higher accuracy levels when
reminded that the previously studied content had parallels with famous
characters, the learners also were more likely to falsely recognize
thematically related foil statements.

Primacy Effects. Aside from influencing the quality of the remembered
responses, cuing also can influence the type of content that is remembered. In a study by Sehulster & Crouse (1972), comparison was made
of the effectiveness of cuing as a function of the serial location of the
information within a passage. The advantages of cuing were much more
evident for information occurring later in the passage. When questions
were used as probes for knowledge of content within the passage, there
were no serial position effects. Without the cuing questions, however,
strong primacy effects were evident in recall. Similarly, Rubin (1977)
reported that primacy effects were less when prompts were given for the
long-term recall of previously memorized passages. A seemingly related
outcome also has been reported for the recall of information taken from
a sequence of four biographies (Sehulster, McLaughlin, & Crouse, 1974).
Under free recall, remembering was better for information in earlier
presented stories than in later stories. When recall was cued, improvements in performance were evident primarily for content located in the
later stories.

Existing Knowledge and Cue Effectiveness. The influence of cues in
determining the type of content that is remembered is illustrated further
by the work of Meyer (1975) and her colleagues (Britton et al., 1980).
Under conditions of free recall, a paragraph ranked high in the logical
structure of a passage was remembered better than when that same paragraph was ranked low. When learners were provided with a random
assemblage of all the content words of the target paragraph, however,
and asked to reproduce the target paragraph as exactly as possible, the
differences in performance were virtually eliminated.

Owens, Bower, & Black's (1979) work also suggests that the availability
of cues can mitigate the disadvantages of learners with lower levels of
knowledge. Their learners read a story containing five event sequences
detailing the making of a cup of coffee, going to a doctor, shopping for

groceries, attending a lecture, and attending a play. Prior to reading
the story, some learners were given information suggesting that the main
character in the story was an unmarried coed who had become pregnant
from an affair with her college professor. These learners were able to
recall more of the story than those who were not given the preliminary
information. After the test for unaided recall, learners in both groups
were given the episode titles as potential retrieval cues for recalling
additional content from the story. The learners who had not been
exposed to the motive description recalled nearly four times as many new
units as did those who had received the motive description. In effect,
the provision of the episode titles as retrieval cues essentially
eradicated the overall difference in recall that existed between the two
groups on the original test of free recall.

Other data from the Owens et al. (1979) study suggest that the effects
of a retrieval cue might depend upon the organizational status of the
learners' knowledge. When aided by the motive description, learners
apparently were able to develop an organizational structure that unified
the incoming information from the five episodes. Without the motivational
description, learners apparently organized the different episodes into
separate chunks or entities. Consistent with this interpretation,
during free recall the motive-description group retrieved information
from more of the five episodes ($\overline{M}=3.67$) than did the no-description
group ($\overline{M}=2.50$). When the episode titles were used as retrieval cues,
however, the no-description group was able to retrieve information from
as many episodes ($\overline{M}=4.75$) as the motive-description group ($\overline{M}=4.56$). This
outcome suggests one possible explanation for the effects of cuing. Cues
may provide learners opportunity to tap previously unrecalled clusters
or chunks of related information.

Before detailing additional support for this generalization, it is worth
noting that the Owens et al. (1979) study is one of the few in the literature in which the experimenter was successful in stimulating substantial
additional retrieval from a lengthy intact prose passage. Note too that
each of their five retrieval cues was directed toward a rather large
target cluster of 10 to 13 sentences. Most experimenters, in contrast,
have restricted their cuing efforts toward single target sentences or
toward individual words or phrases within a single sentence.

The hypothesis that retrieval cues open new semantic chunks also allows
an interpretation of Anderson & Pichert's (1978) data. Learners in that
study were given an encoding perspective (e.g., homebuyer) while reading
a passage that included a description of a home. After recalling as much
as they could, learners were told to adopt a new perspective (e.g., a
burglar) and to recall the story again from the new perspective. Although
the second rendering of the story resulted in a loss of 2.9% to 21% of
the information that was relevant to the first perspective, there was a
gain of 7 to 10% for the information that was related to the retrieval
cues provided by the new perspective.

Extending Anderson & Pichert's (1978) work, Flammer & Tauber (Note 1)
induced a shift in recall perspective either prior to immediate recall
or else immediately prior to delayed recall. As compared with learners
whose perspective did not change, the learners who had a new perspective
showed less remembering of content related to that new perspective.
Further, in a final recall in which learners were asked to recall all

content from the story, regardless of the content's relevance to a particular perspective, learners with a changed perspective were neither better nor worse than those having no change in perspective. Clearly, any retrieval gains that were induced by a change in perspective were offset by losses in information relevant to the initial perspective.

In an apparent contradiction to the Owens et al. (1979) finding that cues facilitated performance more for learners with lesser knowledge, Chiesi, Spilich, & Voss (1979) report data suggesting that retrieval cues provided more assistance for learners having higher levels of knowledge of a content domain. Chiesi et al. first identified learners having high knowledge or low knowledge of baseball. The two groups of learners then read 24 three-sentence passages on baseball. Following attempts at free recall, learners received a cued recall task in which the retrieval cues were the first two sentences or else just the second sentence. The target sentences were the final sentence in each triad. As might be expected, the high knowledge learners performed better in free recall. In contrast with the Owens et al. (1979) finding, however, the high knowledge learners showed a larger increase in recall (54%) than did the low knowledge learners (29.4%). Moreover, when there had been no prior recall of a part of the target sentence during free recall, facilitation from cuing was greater for the high knowledge group (80%) than for the low knowledge group (46%). In additional comparisons, Spilich, Vesonder, Chiesi, & Voss (1979) also have reported evidence consistent with the interpretation that retrieval cues benefit high knowledge learners more than low knowledge learners.

To resolve the apparent contradictions among studies as to whether cuing is most beneficial to the high knowledge learners or the low knowledge learners, it may be helpful to think of retrieval cues as being potentially facilitative whenever the cues allow learners to tap previously unrecalled chunks of the target content. In addition, cues may remind learners of potential retrieval routes that can be used to find missing target content. The Owens et al. (1979) learners presumably had untapped target knowledge that was associatively related to the episode label. Further, the episode label presumably was sufficiently similar to the learner's own organizational representation so that there could be a match between the external retrieval cue and the learners' own organizational representation. Why wasn't such knowledge equally helpful to those who had been given the motive description? One likely explanation is that the advantage of these learners was evaporated by giving the no-description learners access to the episode labels. By this maneuver, both groups had equal access to the five episodes.

The Anderson & Pichert (1978) learners, though, probably were able to use their existing schematic knowledge about the second perspective to form a retrieval search in which matches might be made with previously unrecalled information. For example, with a burglar perspective, the learner could raise the question of whether the story mentioned valuables such as money, gold, or diamonds. The retrieval search might raise similar questions regarding the suitability of the house for an undetected burglary, the features that might enhance easy entry into the house, etc. In the Chiesi et al. (1979) study, learners with high knowledge may have used their superior knowledges of sequential events in baseball to remember or to construct the probable third sentence in the sequence. For the learners with low knowledge about baseball, providing them with the earlier sentences may not have helped because their existing knowledges were not sufficient to allow them to bridge the gap between the first two sentences and the target sentence. Here, as in the other studies, the effectiveness of a cue presumably is related to the extent to which the cue allows learners the opportunity to open up a related body of target information that has not been previously tapped.

CHARACTERISTICS OF CUES

Nonverbal Cues. Although most experimenters have used verbal retrieval cues, several investigators have provided nonverbal cues to stimulate remembering. Rubin (1977), for one, tested learners' remembering of the words of their national anthem. When provided with an instrumental rendition of the melody, learners recalled 65% of the words. A noncued group, in contrast, recalled 40% of the words, while learners cued with an inappropriate march melody recalled only 35% of the words.

During learners' attempts at the oral recall of a textual passage, Van Dam & Brinkerink-Carlier (Note 5) sounded a buzzer whenever they felt that learners might "know more than was just stated." The learner then was to attempt additional recall of content being recalled prior to the sounding of the buzzer. Although one might expect that such interruptions would interfere with remembering, the signaled learners recalled more detail than learners who were not interrupted. Moreover, the interruptions did not hinder learners' remembering of the main ideas. The buzzer thus served as a generalized retrieval cue for remembering detail that otherwise would have been omitted during recall. An unanswered question, however, is the extent to which the results are dependent upon experimenters' intuitions as to when additional recall is possible.

In another successful instance of nonverbal cuing, Turner & Rommetveit (1968) tested children's memory for auditorily presented sentences such as "The bunny was eating the carrot" or "The carrot was eaten by the bunny." At the time or presentation, the sentence was accompanied either by a picture of the actor, a picture of the acted-upon element, a total picture with both elements, or no picture. At the time of retrieval, learners were cued with one of the three types of pictures. The presence or absence of a picture at the time of learning had little effect on retention. Recall, however, was consistently better when learners were cued with the total picture than with the other two types of pictorial cues. When the original sentence was in the active voice, the best partial cue was the actor picture. For passive-voice sentences, however, the best partial cue was the acted-upon picture. Moreover, the nature of the partial cue also influenced the type of error made in recall. When the original sentence was in the active voice, the acted-upon cue at retrieval resulted in more recall transformations to the passive voice. When the original sentence was in the passive voice, recall trans-formations to the active voice were more likely with the actor picture or the total picture. Finally, in an apparent contradiction to the notion of encoding specificity, learners who received a partial picture at encoding and a partial picture at retrieval performed better if the retrieval cue was a different picture than the picture shown at learning.

Only one other study was found in which pictures were used as retrieval cues for prose. Johnson (Note 4) presented Bartlett's "War of the Ghosts" on slides one phrase at a time, with each of the 66 phrases ac-companied by a picture depicting the content of the slide. After a five-day retention interval, one-third of the learners received a retrieval

packet containing 22 of the 66 pictures prior to a 15-min recall period.
Others did not receive the retrieval cues until after 10 min of unaided
recall. Some learners received pictures depicting the 22 units judged
to be highest in structural importance, while other learners received
pictures depicting the 22 units judged lowest in importance. A control
group received no retrieval cues. Regardless of which pictures were
received, and regardless of when learners received their pictures, the
pictorial cues had no influence on remembering.

Literal Prompts. Many studies have examined the effectiveness of different
types of prompts in cuing the retrieval of individual sentences. Often
the prompt has been a word or a phrase taken from the target sentence
itself, and the learners' task was to recall the remaining portion of the
sentence. The research literature provides abundant evidence that literal
cues can facilitate retrieval (e.g., Anderson, 1972; Anderson & Bower,
1973). Even after retention intervals of years, literal cues still
possess the potential for stimulating remembering (Rubin, 1977).

If learners are given access again to one or two sentences preceding a
target sentence, remembering can be increased (Chiesi et al., 1979;
Mistler-Lachman, 1973). The literal context thus can have influence that
crosses sentence boundaries.

Although there are interesting exceptions, a usual outcome is that
literal cues result in more remembering than paraphrased cues (e.g.,
Anderson, 1972; Gibbs, 1980). Surprisingly, even for idiomatic sentences,
literal prompts were found to be more effective than prompts that
preserved the idiomatic meaning (Gibbs, 1980). Thus, for the expression
"You can let the cat out of the bag," the literal cue "cat" was more
effective than the phrase "reveal secret."

As the retention interval lengthens, however, the relative advantage
of a literal cue over a paraphrase or gist cue may diminish (Carter &
Van Matre, 1975; Mistler-Lachman, 1973). Such an outcome is consistent
with knowledge that learners' memory for syntactic-lexical information
declines faster than semantic knowledge (Begg & Wickelgren, 1974; Sachs,
1967).

Grammatical Role. The effectiveness of a word prompt is related to
the grammatical role served by the prompt in the original sentence.
Subject nouns, for example, result in more retrieval than object nouns
(Horowitz & Prytulak, 1969; Perfetti & Goldman, 1974). Blumenthal &
Boakes (1967) also report noun prompts to be more effective than
adjectival prompts in sentences such as "John is eager to please" and
"John is easy to please," but the authors note that such a comparison is
confounded with the original serial positions of the prompts. More
interesting, perhaps, was the finding of a significant interaction between
type of prompt and type of sentence. When the prompt noun ("John") had
been the logical subject of the sentence, the increment in performance
over free recall was larger than when the prompt noun was the logical
object of the sentence. For the adjectival prompts, however, the
increase in retrieval was greater when the adjective ("easy") modified
the whole sentence ("John is easy to please") than when the adjective
("eager") modified the noun ("John is eager to please").

A frequently replicated outcome is that verbs are less effective prompts than subject or object nouns (Anderson & Bower, 1972, 1973; Horowitz & Prytulak, 1969; Thios, 1975; Thorndyke, 1975). An acknowledged complication in such comparisons, however, is that the various grammatical components themselves also differ in retrievability (Anderson, 1976; Anderson & Bower, 1973). Either in the absence of retrieval cues (Clark, 1966), or in response to retrieval cues (Anderson & Bower, 1972, 1973; Jones, 1979), verbs are not remembered as well as nouns. This outcome perhaps is a consequence of verbs being lower in concreteness than nouns (Paivio, 1971, p. 80; Raeburn, 1979). Salient to this issue, Horowitz & Prytulak (1969) have marshalled broad support for the conclusion that the more easily retrieved components of associations also tend to be the most effective as retrieval cues. Given such relationships, the question arises as to whether the lesser cuing power of verbs is due to their grammatical role or to their semantic characteristics as words.

To unravel this question, Raeburn (1979) examined the cuing effectiveness of verbs which were equated with nouns on concreteness and word frequency. In one experiment, for example, the same root word was used as the subject of the sentence (as in "His design completed the project"), as a verb (as in "His architect designed the project"), or as a direct object (as in "His architect completed the design"). When the verbs were equivalent to the nouns in imagery, the verbs were remembered as well as subject nouns and object nouns. Moreover, the verbs were equivalent to nouns in their cuing effectiveness.

Concreteness of Retrieval Cues. Raeburn's (1979) outcome thus implies that the concreteness of the verb is a determinant of its cuing effectiveness. However, in a direct manipulation of the imagery level of the verb, Thorndyke (1975) found no cuing advantage for high imagery verbs. This null outcome held whether the verb was the only retrieval cue or whether the verb was used in combination with subject or object nouns. Comparable to Raeburn's finding, however, the imagery level of the verb was positively related to its retrievability as a target.

Anderson, Goetz, Pichert, & Halff (1977) also used cuing phrases that differed in concreteness. Their sentences had subject nouns with concrete modifiers (e.g., "The parking regulations annoyed the salesman") or else redundant modifiers (e.g., "The official regulations annoyed the salesman"). Prior to attempting recall, learners were tested on a recognition task containing the originally presented subject phrases intermixed with distractor phrases constructed from the alternate version of the sentences. When the original noun phrase was used as a retrieval cue for recalling the rest of the sentence, the concrete noun phrases were more effective as retrieval cues. The superiority as a retrieval cue, however, was evident only when learners had correctly identified the cuing phrase during the recognition task. Though not the interpretation offered by the authors, an alternative explanation might be that the nonredundant modifier simply adds a second cue that the learner can use in retrieving the sentence. The redundant modifier, in contrast, merely duplicates the existing cue. If this explanation of the Anderson et al. outcome is valid, there is no convincing evidence that the concreteness of a cue is a determinant of retrieval effectiveness.

This conclusion, it may be noted, undermines the generality of Paivio's (1965, 1971) "conceptual-peg" hypothesis. According to the conceptual-peg hypothesis, a stimulus word (or subject noun) serves as a "peg" to

which the response word (or object noun) is hooked during learning. As
quoted from Paivio (1971, p. 248), "the more concrete the stimulus, the
more 'solid' it is as a conceptual peg and the better the recall." A
bit later, Paivio (p. 248) states that "the conceptual-peg hypothesis
is essentially a retrieval theory - a high-imagery item is especially
effective as a retrieval cue for the to-be-recalled associate." Though
there is much supporting evidence for the conceptual-peg hypothesis
in the remembering of paired associates, there is virtually no supporting
evidence for the hypothesis in the retrieval of prose.

Complexity of Verb Cues. Verbs also differ in conceptual complexity
and may be decomposed into differing numbers of "primitive actions"
(Schank, 1972). As analyzed by Thorndyke (1975), the verb in the
sentence "The doctor watched the lawyer" contains only one underlying
conceptualization, namely, "doctor look-at lawyer." For the verb in
the sentence "The spy obeyed the barber," the representation requires
conceptualizations related to (1) message transmitted from barber to
spy, (2) message included a request from barber to spy, (3) the spy
performed the requested action, and (4) the spy's performance took place
at a later time. Since a complex sentence presumably requires the
formation of more associative links during encoding, it may be hypothesized
that the complexity of the conceptual representation would influence
the effectiveness of the verb as a retrieval cue. In a test of this
hypothesis, Thorndyke (1975) found that the underlying conceptual
complexity of the verb was not a determinant of its effectiveness in
inducing retrieval of the remaining sentence elements.

Nonliteral Cues. Some experimenters have reported comparisons in which
gist cues have been more effective than literal cues. Alternately
stated, retrieval probes sometimes can be found which are more effective
in inducing remembering than cues that were actually part of the target
sentence (Anderson & Ortony, 1975; Barclay et al., 1974; Corbett & Dosher,
1978; Gumenik, 1979; Marschark & Paivio, 1977).

Anderson & Ortony (1975), for example, tested the remembering of sentences
such as "The fish attacked the swimmer" with the subject noun as a cue
("fish") or an exemplar of the noun that fit the context of the sentence
("shark"). The originally presented noun was a less effective retrieval
cue than the specific exemplar. As interpreted by Anderson & Ortony
(1975), the learners had constructed an elaborative representation that
was particularized in the form of an exemplar that fit the meaning of
the sentence. To use their term, the general noun of fish had become
"instantiated" into the specific exemplar of shark. Consistent with this
interpretation, exemplars were effective cues only in those sentences in
which the overall meaning was a match for the relevant characteristics of
the exemplar. Thus, for a sentence such as "The fish avoided the swimmer,"
the word "shark" was not a better retrieval cue than "fish." Similar
findings were reported by Anderson, Pichert, Goetz, Schallert, Stevens,
and Trollip (1976).

Pursuing this same issue, Gumenik (1979) suggested that the effectiveness
of the specific cues might not be due to instantiation. Instead, he
hypothesized that the advantage occurred because the semantic features of
the specific cue overlapped more with the target content than did the
associative characteristics of the general cue. In a test of this interpretation, learners were presented either the original sentences or else

just the predicates of the sentences. Since there was no subject noun in the latter case, there presumably was little or no likelihood that the unpresented general noun would become instantiated. The exemplar, nevertheless, cued the remembering of the phrase almost as well as when the general noun had been part of the sentence. Moreover, in a second study, retrieval cues that were closely related to the overall meaning of the sentence were just as effective cues as the presumed instantiations. In the sentence "The weapon was protruding from the corpse," for example, "knife" was a better cue than "weapon," but the related cue "murder" was just as effective as "knife."

To summarize, the evidence is not sufficient to support the interpretation that learners routinely represent general nouns by specific exemplars. Probably such instantiation occurs only when the overall meaning of the sentence points to an exemplar that is a better match than the original noun. Both studies, however, provide evidence that literal cues sometimes are not as effective retrieval cues as are those cues that represent the gist of the sentence.

Number of Retrieval Cues. Various types of evidence support the conclusion that the greater the number of available retrieval cues, the better is remembering. Some experimenters have directly varied the number of literal cues provided to the learner. When a sentence is cued with two word prompts, remembering of the uncued portion is better than when only one prompt is available (Anderson, J.R., 1976; Anderson & Bower, 1973; Anderson, R.C., 1974; Corbett & Dosher, 1978; Foss & Harwood, 1975). Moreover, after learners have attempted recall aided by a single prompt, the provision of a second cue typically results in additional remembering (Anderson & Bower, 1973).

Additional illustrations of this principle may be found in studies in which free recall is followed by cued recall. Almost always, cuing results in additional remembering. Geiselman (1974), for example, presented sentences one by one, and then informed the learner as to whether the just presented sentence was to be remembered or forgotten. Following an unexpected final free recall for both types of sentences, learners were provided a completion test in which the most important target word or phrase was missing. With the additional cuing context provided by the completion format, memory for the "remember" sentences improved from 74% in free recall to 87% on the completion task. Improvement for the "forget" sentences went from 40% in free recall to 75% on the completions.

Going one step beyond the skeletonized completion format used by many investigators, Rubin (1977) tested learners' remembering of Lincoln's "Gettysberg Address" when cued with varying amounts of the verbatim transcript. Learners could remember 7.5% of the content words on their own, 10.9% of the content words when all content words were replaced with blanks, and 26.4% of the content words when each of the blanks also was accompanied by the correct initial letter of each missing word.

As the retrieval context becomes more complete, one might expect that guessing would play a larger role in determining performance. Lending credence to this supposition, Hall & Geis (1980) reported that the percentage of correct words attained by guessing ranged from 7 to 50%. The longer the sentence in which the target word was embedded, the greater was the success rate in guessing the missing word.

An improvement in performance, however, is not an inevitable outcome when additional context is provided. Summers & Fleming (1971), for example, presented 16 paragraphs and then tested remembering with 48 factual multiple-choice questions. At retention intervals of 2, 7, or 28 days, learners attempted to answer the questions either unaided by retrieval cues or else with the assistance of all the original sentences except those sentences containing the exact content that was tested. Despite the large amount of context provided, the presence of the contextual sentences did not facilitate performance at any retention interval. Learners in another study (Johnson, Note 3) were provided the entire first half of a story as a potential retrieval cue for remembering the second half. Remembering of the final portion of the story was not facilitated by the presence of the initial portion. This null outcome occurred regardless of whether the context was provided prior to a recall attempt or else provided after learners had attempted 10 minutes of recall on their own.

In another study in this same series (Johnson, Note 2), learners were provided either with no retrieval cues, a listing of the 22 most important subunits of a 66-unit story, or else a listing of the 22 least important subunits. The cues were arranged either in their original temporal order or else randomly. As in the previous study, some learners received their cues prior to attempting recall, while others were not provided cues until they had attempted recall on their own. The importance level of the cues did not influence recall, and neither did the sequencing variable. Contrary to expectations, the presence of the cues hindered recall. When cues were provided prior to attempts at remembering, recall was worse during the initial recall period. When cues were provided immediately prior to the final recall period, recall was worse in the final period. Clearly there are some instances in which a more complete retrieval context does not facilitate remembering.

Configural Properties of Multiple Cues. An interesting question is whether there are configural properties that emerge from a combination of two or more retrieval cues (Anderson & Bower, 1972). If so, the combination of two cues into a unified gestalt might induce greater remembering than would be expected on the basis of the cuing power of each of the two cues taken separately. The encoding specificity hypothesis, as well as the configural or Gestalt viewpoint, would predict an advantage for a retrieval environment that most closely represented the original encoding. An associationist, however, might assume that the only effective routes for retrieval come from individual word probes. This interpretative viewpoint thus would deny the existence of an additional retrieval route from the configural combination of a two-word probe.

To test this, Anderson & Bower (1972) presented pairs of sentences such as:
    (1) The child hit the landlord.
    (2) The minister praised the landlord.
Learners then were tested for their recall of the direct object either with single word cues or else two cues. For the present example, the testing frames were:
    (3) The child.....the _____. S
    (4) The.....hit the _____. V
    (5) The minister praised the _____. S_1V_1
    (6) The child praised the _____. S_1V_2

According to the gestalt viewpoint, the configural cue of the original subject and verb in sentence (5) should be a more effective cue than crossover frames such as sentence (6) in which the subject and verb are taken from separate sentences.

The results of Anderson & Bower's (1972) experiments showed that the crossover cues were as effective as the configural cues. Moreover, the amount of retrieval to the configural cue did not exceed the amount of recall that had been predicted from the probabilistic combination of recall attributable to the noun cue alone and the verb cue alone.

Since then, however, a number of experimenters have reported evidence showing that the configural cue sometimes is more effective than would be predicted from the recall induced by the separate cues (Anderson, J. R., 1976, Chap. 10; Foss & Harwood, 1975; Marschark & Paivio, 1977; Till, 1977). Whether configural effects become evident appear related to a number of factors. The configural effect is more likely to occur when learners have been induced to encode the sentences meaningfully (Anderson, J. R., 1976). Configural effects also are more evident when a gist scoring procedure is used (Anderson, J. R., 1976, pp. 411-412). Foss & Harwood (1975) have suggested that the effect can be demonstrated only when the amount of recall to individual cues is low. John Anderson's (1976, pp. 416-417) comparison of experiments, however, indicates that configural effects can occur even when recall is relatively high to the single cues. Configural effects in recall also may be dependent upon whether the learners can recognize the cues as having come from the studied sentence (Anderson, J. R., 1976, pp. 418-420; Anderson, R. C. et al., 1977).

Although no empirical comparisons have been reported, configural effects presumably would be more evident in some sentences than others. Maximal effects might be predicted for sentences in which the object noun is difficult to recall from either the subject cue alone or the verb cue alone, but which could be remembered from a combination of the two cues. Possible examples of such sentences might be "The minister hit the booze," and "The miser filled his pillow."

Finally, the possibility exists that all of the published experiments actually provide evidence of configural properties in cuing. The judgment of whether configural effects are in evidence depends upon the amount of recall that is expected. With the Anderson & Bower (1972) formula that has been adopted by all experimenters, the subject probe and the verb probe are assumed to account for separate portions of the recall variance. When both cues are presented, some of the recall is attributed only to the power of the noun cue, and the remaining recall is attributed exclusively to the verb cue. On many occasions, however, recall of a particular target word can be induced either by the subject prompt alone or else by the verb prompt alone. The two cues thus are not always independent in their capacities as inducers of recall. When such nonindependence occurs, the present configural formula leads to inflated predictions for expected recall.

A further complication is that the subject cue and the verb cue also possess some capability of reintegrating each other. On a certain portion of the retrieval trials, then, what appears to be a single prompt is actually two retrieval cues. For the crossover combination, in contrast,

the presentation of one of the two cues probably is less likely to induce
the remembering of the cue from the other sentence. Further, in comparison with the two configural cues, the two crossover cues would appear
to be more independent of each other in their capacities to induce
retrieval of the object noun. In sum, if prediction formulas were developed
that took into account the differing degrees of independence of the
predictor cues, the data might show convincing evidence of configural
properties in cuing.

RELATIONSHIP BETWEEN CUE AND TARGET

Semantic Similarity. Cues vary in the extent to which they are similar
to the content to be remembered. At the theoretical level it is not
easy to provide a satisfactory definition of what constitutes semantic
similarity. A judgment that two cues differ in their similarity to
target content may be based upon one or a variety of judgmental dimensions.
Further, there is always the temptation to engage in the circular
reasoning that one retrieval cue must have been more similar than another
cue because the cue stimulated more recall.

Nevertheless, at the empirical level, the data virtually force the
conclusion that retrieval cues that are more similar to the target
content are more effective in stimulating remembering (Anderson, 1972;
Anderson & McGaw, 1973; Anderson & Ortony, 1975; Barclay et al., 1974;
Blumenthal & Boakes, 1967; Gumenik, 1979; Lesgold, 1972; Marschark &
Paivio, 1977; Morris, 1978; Till, 1977).

As one example of a study supporting this conclusion, Anderson (1972)
presented sentences such as "The canary escaped from its cage." The
most effective cues were the original nouns (90% recall). Closely
related superordinate cues (e.g., "bird") were more effective (81% recall)
than remote superordinates (e.g., "animal", 72% recall). Closely related
exemplars of the remote superordinate (e.g., "duck") were more effective
as cues (73% recall) than were distantly related exemplars (e.g., "tiger";
44% recall).

A final example may be found in the study by Barclay et al. (1974). When
learners received the sentence "The man lifted the piano," the cue
"something heavy" was effective whereas the cue "something cuddly" was
not effective. When the sentence was "The man lifted the infant,"
however, "something cuddly" was effective whereas "something heavy" was
ineffective.

Associative Integration Between Cue and Target. Formal similarity between
the cue and the target may not be sufficient to induce retrieval. Instead,
the formal similarity must be translated into psychological similarity
as perceived by the learner. A cue which is not meaningful in the
context of the target content is not likely to be effective as a retrieval
aid. Hall & Geis (1980), for example, presented some target words (e.g.,
"hog") in sentence contexts that either were sensible ("The hog is fat")
or not sensible ("I made my hog"). When learners were cued with the
contextual frame of all words except the target word, only the sensible
contexts facilitated retrieval beyond the levels evidenced in free recall.

Even a sensible context may not be sufficient unless the learner actually
has established an association between the cue and the target during

encoding. Masson (1979), for example, presented sentences such as "The container held the apples." At the time of presentation, the sentence either was or was not preceded by a cue (e.g., "basket"). Learners who received such a cue were told the cue might help them in comprehending the sentence. Afterwards, half the learners were given a free recall test, while the other learners received the cues as a possible aid in retrieval. For those who received the cues at recall, half had not seen the cues previously. The retrieval cues were effective only when the cues also had been seen during the original presentation of the sentences.

Retrieval cues also may be more effective when the prior content of a passage focuses on the topic designated by the prompt word. Perfetti & Goldman (1974) presented paragraphs in which the last sentence was the target sentence for recall. For a target sentence such as "The serfs rebelled against the baron," serfs was a more effective cue for recalling the sentence than was baron (65 vs. 48% recall, respectively) when the preceding content of the paragraph focused on the serfs. When the preceding content focused on the baron, the cue baron was almost as effective as serfs (61 vs. 65% recall, respectively). As interpreted by Perfetti & Goldman, "a probe which has been thematized by its occurrence in a meaningful passage acquires a retrieval power that it otherwise lacks."

Perfetti & Goldman's (1974) conclusion may be valid only when the word used as a probe has been repeatedly referenced within the text. Even at the initial presentation of a sentence, the sentence structure normally allows a division of content into that which presumably has been referenced before ("old or given") and that which is now being asserted ("new" information). Following a single presentation of a list of unrelated sentences, Singer (1976) found that the "new" noun of a given-new sentence served as a slightly better prompt than the "old" noun (36.5% vs. 30.6% recall, respectively).

Encoding Specificity. Under most circumstances, if a cue is to acquire the potential to induce remembering, the linkage between the cue and the target must be established at the time of learning. A substantial number of experimenters have presented ambiguous passages that are difficult to understand unless learners are provided a clue to the main topic of the passage. Examples of such passages include Bransford & Johnson's (1972) "Washing Clothes" and Dooling & Lachman's (1971) "Christopher Columbus Discovers America." When such titles are provided only at the time of retrieval, i.e., as potential retrieval cues, remembering is no better than if the learner had not received the retrieval cue (Bransford & Johnson, 1972; Dooling & Mullet; 1973).

On the surface, this outcome appears to contradict the earlier generalization that gist cues can enhance remembering. Indeed, the title would appear to be the best cue of all for representing the gist of a passage. When gist cues have been effective, however, the target sentences have been comprehensible. The content of each sentence can be easily related to known referents, and the sentences are obviously interrelated via common referents. Further, those nonliteral cues that are effective ostensively represent the essence of the interpretative encoding established at learning.

For ambiguous passages, however, the content as a whole cannot be easily related to learners' existing knowledges. From a psychological viewpoint, it is not reasonable to expect that a title presented at retrieval would result in the simultaneous transformation of all input sentences into a new interpretative format. Moreover, it is not reasonable to assume that such sentences are even represented in memory at the time the title is presented.

If this analysis is valid, then both types of studies may be interpreted as providing support for Tulving's encoding specificity hypothesis. As documented by Tulving and Thompson (1973), the effectiveness of a retrieval cue in facilitating remembering appears dependent upon the extent to which the retrieval cue was associated with the target at the time of encoding. Within the prose literature, additional supporting evidence for the encoding specificity hypothesis may be found in experimental outcomes reported by Anderson (1972, 1974), Masson (1979), Morris (1978), Schustack & Anderson (1977), and Sefkow & Myers (1980). The encoding specificity hypothesis also receives support from previously discussed studies showing that the more closely the retrieval context matches the original learning context, the better the remembering.

SUMMARY

Perhaps the most interesting characteristic of the retrieval literature is the virtual absence of studies in which retrieval cues induced additional remembering of intact prose passages. A notable exception was the success of Owens et al. (1979) in stimulating additional retrieval of a story by providing episode labels. Three additional studies provided evidence of facilitation from other types of retrieval cues, but these cues resulted either in countervailing losses of other information (perspective change, Anderson & Pichert, 1978), were applicable only to the remembering of words in musical scores (melody, Rubin, 1977), or were dependent upon experimenters' intuitions as to when cuing might be effective (buzzer, Van Dam & Brinkerink-Carlier, Note 5).

Researchers, however, have been successful in assessing the influence of retrieval cues on the remembering of unrelated sentences and words within such sentences. Based upon this literature, a number of generalizations may be drawn. First, retrieval cues typically facilitate remembering. Studies have been reported, however, in which cues had no influence or even negative effects on remembering. Though the data are sparse, some evidence suggests that retrieval cues exert a proportionately greater influence at longer retention intervals.

Retrieval cues can influence the types of errors that learners make in recall or recognition. Cuing also can influence the type of content that is remembered. Thus, in some experiments, the presence of retrieval cues eliminated the occurrence of primacy effects. As to whether retrieval cues provide more assistance to learners with higher levels or lower levels of knowledge related to the target passage, experiments can be found that support either outcome. The particular outcome that occurs appears dependent upon the organizational status of learners' existing knowledges, the extent to which the cues provide relevant knowledges that would otherwise be unavailable, and the extent to which learners can use the cues to build new retrieval routes to knowledges that are otherwise inaccessible.

Both nonverbal and verbal cues can stimulate additional remembering. For verbal cues, a typical outcome is that verbatim cues are more effective than cues that represent the gist. Some experimenters, however, have reported studies in which the gist cues were more effective. Such an outcome occurs primarily when the gist cue represents the overall meaning of the sentence better than the verbatim cue. As time passes, and surface memory fades, the relative advantage of literal cues also fades.

The effectiveness of a word cue also is related to its grammatical role. Subject nouns are more effective than object nouns; noun prompts are more effective than adjective prompts; and verbs are less effective than nouns. The relative advantage of one type of grammatical cue over another appears dependent upon the extent to which such cues are equated on other dimensions such as meaningfulness and word frequency. The size of the advantage also depends on the differential availabilities of the sentence components that are the retrieval targets. Though a number of experimenters have assumed that the concreteness of retrieval cues is a determinant of effectiveness, the empirical evidence so far is not convincing. Similarly, the complexity of the verb appears unrelated to cuing effectiveness.

Typically, the greater the number of retrieval cues available to the learner, the greater the amount that was recalled. Under certain conditions, in fact, the presence of multiple cues resulted in configural increments in recall. Configural increments were evident primarily when sentences were encoded meaningfully, when gist representations were credited, and when recall to single cues was sufficiently low to allow incremental gains from multiple cues. Gains were not evident, however, when learners received access again to large portions of the original text and then attempted to remember the remaining target sentences.

The similarity of the cue to the target is another important determinant of cuing effectiveness. Moreover, consistent with the encoding specificity hypothesis, the effectiveness of retrieval cues appears directly related to the extent to which the meanings aroused by the cue overlap with the meanings established during the encoding of the target sentences.

REFERENCE NOTES

1. Flammer, A., & Tauber, M. Where in time do organizational aids help? Paper presented at the International Symposium on Text Processing, Fribourg, Switzerland, September 1981.
2. Johnson, R. E. Schemas, cuing, and the remembering of prose. Paper presented at the meeting of the American Psychological Association, New Orleans, September 1974.
3. Johnson, R. E. Contextual redintegration and the remembering of prose. Paper presented at the meeting of the American Educational Research Association, Washington, D.C., March 1975.

4. Johnson, R. E. Retrieval cues in the remembering of prose. Paper
    presented at the International Congress of Applied Psychology,
    Munich, W. Germany, August 1978.
5. Van Dam, G., & Brinkerink-Carlier, M. The reproduction of forward
    and downward knowledge during text recall. Report No. 26,
    Psychological Laboratory, University of Utrecht, Netherlands,
    April 1981.

REFERENCES

Anderson, J. R. Language, memory, and thought. New York: Wiley, 1976.
Anderson, J. R., & Bower, G. H. Configural properties in sentence memory.
    Journal of Verbal Learning and Verbal Behavior, 1972, 11, 594-605.
Anderson, J. R., & Bower, G. H. Human associative memory. New York:
    V. H. Winston, 1973.
Anderson, R. C. Semantic organization and retrieval of information from
    sentences. Journal of Verbal Learning and Verbal Behavior, 1972,
    11, 794-800.
Anderson, R. C. Concretization and sentence learning. Journal of
    Educational Psychology, 1974, 66, 179-183.
Anderson, R. C., Goetz, E. T., Pichert, J. W., & Halff, H. M. Two faces
    of the conceptual peg hypothesis. Journal of Experimental
    Psychology: Human Learning and Memory, 1977, 3, 142-149.
Anderson, R. C., & McGaw, B. On the representation of meanings of general
    terms. Journal of Experimental Psychology, 1973, 101, 301-306.
Anderson, R. C., & Myrow, D. L. Retroactive inhibition of meaningful
    discourse. Journal of Educational Psychology, 1971, 62, 81-94.
Anderson, R. C., & Ortony, A. On putting apples into bottles-A problem
    of polysemy. Cognitive Psychology, 1975, 7, 167-180.
Anderson, R. C., & Pichert, J. W. Recall of previously unrecallable
    information following a shift in perspective. Journal of Verbal
    Learning and Verbal Behavior, 1978, 17, 1-12.
Anderson, R. C., Pichert, J. W., Goetz, E. T., Schallert, D. L., Stevens,
    K. V., & Trollip, S. R. Instantiation of general terms. Journal
    of Verbal Learning and Verbal Behavior, 1976, 15, 667-679.
Anisfeld, M. False recognition of adjective-noun phrases. Journal of
    Experimental Psychology, 1970, 86, 120-122.
Baker, L., & Santa, J. L. Semantic integration and context. Memory &
    Cognition, 1977, 5, 151-154.
Barclay, J. R., Bransford, J. D., Franks, J. J., McCarrell, N. S., & Nitsch,
    K. Comprehension and semantic flexibility. Journal of Verbal
    Learning and Verbal Behavior, 1974, 13, 471-481.
Begg, I., & Wickelgren, W. A. Retention functions for syntactic and
    lexical vs. semantic information in sentence recognition memory.
    Memory & Cognition, 1974, 2, 353-359.
Blumenthal, A. L., & Boakes, R. Prompted recall of sentences. Journal
    of Verbal Learning and Verbal Behavior, 1967, 6, 674-676.
Bower, G. H. Selective facilitation and interference in retention of
    prose. Journal of Educational Psychology, 1974, 66, 1-8.
Bransford, J. D. & Johnson, M. K. Contextual prerequisites for understanding:
    Some investigations of comprehension and recall. Journal of
    Verbal Learning and Verbal Behavior, 1972, 11, 717-726.
Bransford, J. D., Nitsch, K. E., & Franks, J. J. Schooling and the
    facilitation of knowing. In R. C. Anderson, R. J. Spiro, & W. E.
    Montague (Eds.), Schooling and the acquisition of knowledge.
    Hillsdale, N. J.: Erlbaum, 1977, 31-55.

Britton, B. K., Meyer, B. J., Hodge, M. H. & Glynn, S. M. Effects of the organization of text on memory: Tests of retrieval and response criterion hypotheses. Journal of Experimental Psychology: Human Learning and Memory, 1980, 6, 620-629.

Carter, J. F., & Van Matre, N. H. Note taking versus note having. Journal of Educational Psychology, 1975, 67, 900-904.

Chiesi, H. L., Spilich, G. J., & Voss, J. F. Acquisition of domain-related information in relation to high and low domain knowledge. Journal of Verbal Learning and Verbal Behavior, 1979, 18, 257-273.

Clark, H. H. The prediction of recall patterns in simple active sentences. Journal of Verbal Learning and Verbal Behavior, 1966, 5, 99-106.

Cofer, C. N., Segal, E., Stein, J., & Walker, H. Studies on free recall of nouns following presentation under adjectival modification. Journal of Experimental Psychology, 1969, 79, 254-264.

Corbett, A. T., & Dosher, B. A. Instrument inferences in sentence encoding. Journal of Verbal Learning and Verbal Behavior, 1978, 17, 479-491.

Dooling, D. J., & Lachman, R. Effects of comprehension on retention of prose. Journal of Experimental Psychology, 1971, 88, 216-222.

Dooling, D. J., & Mullet, R. L. Locus of thematic effects in retention of prose. Journal of Experimental Psychology, 1973, 97, 404-406.

Foss, D. J., & Harwood, D. A. Memory for sentences: Implications for human associative memory. Journal of Verbal Learning and Verbal Behavior, 1975, 14, 1-16.

Geiselman, R. E. Positive forgetting of sentence material. Memory & Cognition, 1974, 2, 677-682.

Gibbs, R. W., Jr. Spilling the beans on understanding and memory for idioms in conversation. Memory & Cognition, 1980, 8, 149-156.

Graesser, A. C. Tests of a holistic chunking model of sentence memory through analyses of noun intrusions. Memory & Cognition, 1978, 6, 527-536.

Green, D. W. The effects of task on the representation of sentences. Journal of Verbal Learning and Verbal Behavior, 1975, 14, 275-283.

Gumenik, W. E. The advantage of specific terms over general terms as cues for sentence recall: Instantiation or retrieval? Memory & Cognition, 1979, 7, 240-244.

Hall, D. M., & Geis, M. F. Congruity and elaboration in free and cued recall. Journal of Experimental Psychology: Human Learning and Memory, 1980, 6, 778-784.

Horowitz, L. M., & Prytulak, L. S. Redintegrative memory. Psychological Review, 1969, 76, 519-531.

Jones, G. V. Multirate forgetting. Journal of Experimental Psychology: Human Learning and Memory, 1979, 5, 98-114.

Kolina, J. G., III. Cued recall of prose as a function of the structural importance of the linguistic units. Unpublished Master's thesis, California State College, Long Beach, 1972.

Lesgold, A. M. Pronominalization: A device for unifying sentences in memory. Journal of Verbal Learning and Verbal Behavior, 1972, 11, 316-323.

Marschark, M., & Paivio, A. Integrative processing of concrete and abstract sentences. Journal of Verbal Learning and Verbal Behavior, 1977, 16, 217-231.

Masson, M. E. J. Context and inferential cuing of sentence recall. Journal of Verbal Learning and Verbal Behavior, 1979, 18, 173-185.

Meyer, B. J. F. The organization of prose and its effects on memory. Amsterdam: North-Holland, 1975.

Mistler-Lachman, J. L.   Depth of comprehension and sentence memory.
    Journal of Verbal Learning and Verbal Behavior, 1974, 13, 98-106.
Morris, C. D.   Acquisition-test interactions between different dimensions
    of encoding. Memory & Cognition, 1978, 6, 354-363.
Owens, J., Bower, G. H., & Black, J. B.   The "soap opera" effect in
    story recall. Memory & Cognition, 1979, 7, 185-191.
Paivio, A.   Abstractness, imagery, and meaningfulness in paired-
    associate learning. Journal of Verbal Learning and Verbal
    Behavior, 1965, 4, 32-38.
Paivio, A.   Imagery and verbal processes. New York: Holt, Rinehart &
    Winston, 1971.
Perfetti, C. A., & Goldman, S. R.   Thematization and sentence retrieval.
    Journal of Verbal Learning and Verbal Behavior, 1974, 13, 70-79.
Raeburn, V. P.   The role of the verb in sentence memory. Memory &
    Cognition, 1979, 7, 133-140.
Rubin, D. C.   Very long-term memory for prose and verse. Journal of
    Verbal Learning and Verbal Behavior, 1977, 16, 611-621.
Sachs, J. S.   Recognition memory for syntactic and semantic aspects of
    connected discourse. Perception & Psychophysics, 1967, 2, 437-442.
Schank, R.   Conceptual dependency: A theory of natural language under-
    standing. Cognitive Psychology, 1972, 3, 552-631.
Schustack, M. W., & Anderson, J. R.   Effects of analogy to prior knowledge
    on memory for new information. Journal of Verbal Learning and
    Verbal Behavior, 1979, 18, 565-583.
Sefkow, S. B., & Myers, J. L.   Review effects of inserted questions on
    learning from prose. American Educational Research Journal, 1980,
    17, 435-447.
Sehulster, J. R., & Crouse, J. H.   Storage and retrieval of prose material.
    Psychological Reports, 1972, 30, 435-439.
Sehulster, J. R., McLaughlin, J. P., & Crouse, J. H.   Separation of
    storage and retrieval processes in recall of prose. Journal of
    Experimental Psychology, 1974, 103, 583-586.
Singer, M.   Thematic structure and the integration of linguistic information.
    Journal of Verbal Learning and Verbal Behavior, 1976, 15, 549-558.
Spilich, G. J., Vesonder, G. T., Chiesi, H. L., & Voss, J. F.   Text processing
    of domain-related information for individuals with high and low
    domain knowledge. Journal of Verbal Learning and Verbal Behavior,
    1979, 18, 275-290.
Summers, S. A., & Fleming, J. S.   Construction and reconstruction in
    memory. American Journal of Psychology, 1971, 84, 513-520.
Thios, S. J.   Memory for general and specific sentences. Memory &
    Cognition, 1975, 3, 75-77.
Thorndyke, P. W.   Conceptual complexity and imagery in comprehension and
    memory. Journal of Verbal Learning and Verbal Behavior, 1975, 14,
    359-369.
Till, R. E.   Sentence memory prompted with inferential recall cues. Journal
    of Experimental Psychology: Human Learning and Memory, 1977, 3,
    129-141.
Till, R. E., & Walsh, D. A.   Encoding and retrieval factors in adult memory
    for implicational sentences. Journal of Verbal Learning and Verbal
    Behavior, 1980, 19, 1-16.
Tulving, E., & Thompson, D. M.   Encoding specificity and retrieval processes
    in episodic memory. Psychological Review, 1973, 80, 352-373.
Turner, E. A., & Rommetveit, R.   Focus of attention in recall of active
    and passive sentences. Journal of Verbal Learning and Verbal Behavior,
    1968, 7, 543-548.

DISCOURSE PROCESSING
A. Flammer and W. Kintsch (eds.)
© *North-Holland Publishing Company, 1982*

WORKING MEMORY AND CONTEXTUAL PROCESSING IN READING

Maryanne Martin

Department of Experimental Psychology
University of Oxford
Oxford
England

The role of working memory in mediating contextual
influences upon reading is investigated. Efficiency
of contextual processing is assessed by the accuracy
and latency with which people read heteronyms
embedded in disambiguating text. Working memory is
manipulated by preloading readers with varying numbers of digits to be subsequently recalled. It is
concluded that it is the central executive rather
than the articulatory loop component of working
memory that is crucial for contextual processing.

INTRODUCTION

It has been proposed by several theorists that language comprehension
requires the utilisation of a working-memory space in which linguistic or
linguistic-based segments may be temporarily both stored and processed
(e.g., Baddeley & Hitch, 1974; Bower, 1975; Just & Carpenter, 1980;
LaBerge & Samuels, 1974). The present paper focusses upon one particular
role that working memory is hypothesised to perform in text processing.
This is its role in mediating contextual influences upon the reading process. It is assumed that these contextual influences are of several
different forms, ranging from syntactic expectations on the one hand to
script-based implicit knowledge of the world (e.g., Bower, Black & Turner,
1979; Schank & Abelson, 1977) on the other, but that it may nevertheless be
possible to observe systematic constraints imposed by working memory upon
their operation as a whole.

According to Baddeley and Hitch (e.g., Baddeley, 1977; Baddeley & Hitch,
1974; Hitch & Baddeley, 1976), two important components of working memory
consist of a central executive system and an articulatory loop. The
central executive system is involved in information processing and decision
taking as well as storage, while it is the articulatory storage loop that
endows short-term memory with its speech-dependent characteristics. The
articulatory loop functions like an audio tape loop of limited duration
(Baddeley, 1977), liberating an equivalent space in the central executive
component for processing purposes. It is capable of storing a limited
amount, about three items, of speech or speech-recoded material in its
order of input; if this capacity is not exceeded, little storage demand on
the central processing component of the system will occur (Baddeley, 1976).
On the other hand, the storage of six items, for example, will require the
use of both the articulatory loop and the central executive (Baddeley, 1977).

From the Baddeley and Hitch model it is possible to derive some relatively straightforward predictions. If the articulatory loop is a necessary component of the processing or storage of sentential context, then holding three digits in memory while reading a sentence should be damaging to performance. If on the other hand the articulatory loop is not normally involved in contextual facilitation then there should be no difference between reading performance with and without concurrent retention of three digits. Similarly, if the central executive is a necessary component of the processing or storage of sentential context, then holding six digits in memory should be damaging compared to holding only three digits or none at all. Further, if the central executive is viewed as a pool of general processing capacity (Baddeley & Hitch, 1974) then if the number of temporarily stored digits is increased beyond six, for example to ten, then increased demands on the central executive should lead to a further deterioration in context-dependent performance.

In order to investigate the role of context in reading it is important to be able to assess empirically the extent of processing of the contextual text. Possible methods include requiring subsequent recall of the text or asking questions concerning its content. Though useful, these methods do perhaps introduce atypical task demands into the reading process. Thus for the experiment to be reported a new task was devised.

In the task used here, subjects were asked to read silently all but the last word of a sentence, which was read aloud. Usually, it would not be possible to tell whether the context had been read, or just the last word. To overcome this difficulty, the last word in this experiment was chosen to be a heteronym, that is, a word which is pronounced in different ways depending on the meaning which it carries. For example, the word "sow" is pronounced /səʊ/ in the sentence "The seed packet had instructions on how to SOW", but pronounced /saʊ/ in the sentence "The piglets followed after the SOW". Monitoring the accuracy of pronunciation of the heteronyms allows a check on the processing of context in each condition.

It is perhaps of interest that homographs, words such as "bank" with two different meanings (money, river), have been used extensively to investigate lexical coding (e.g., Conrad, 1974; Hogaboam & Perfetti, 1975; Holmes, 1979; Marcel, 1980; Simpson, 1981; Tanenhaus, Leiman & Seidenberg, 1979). On the other hand, heteronyms have been little used, though with some recent notable exceptions (e.g., Carpenter & Daneman, 1981; Warren, Warren, Green, & Bresnick, 1978).

METHOD

SUBJECTS

Thirty-two women from the Oxford subject panel participated in this experiment. They were aged between 18 and 46 years. All had normal or fully corrected vision. They were each tested individually in a session lasting about one hour and fifteen minutes.

STIMULI AND APPARATUS

Forty relatively frequent heteronyms were selected from a list compiled by Martin, Jones, Nelson and Nelson (1981). For each heteronym two different sentences were constructed, both containing the heteronym as last word.

The two different sentences unambiguously determined the two different
senses (and hence the two different pronunciations) of the heteronym.
Examples of two such sentences are
The Sahara and Kalahari are large DESERTS
and
In the end the villain got his just DESERTS.
In the first sentence "deserts" is standardly pronounced /'dezəts/, and in
the second /'dɪ-zɜːts/. The complete set of eighty sentences used in the
experiment, together with the correct pronunciations for the heteronyms
(given in international phonetic symbols) is shown in Table 1.

In addition, there was for each heteronym a control word that did not fit
either sentential context. The control word was matched with the heteronym
in three ways. First, it had the same number of syllables; second, it had
the same initial phoneme as the heteronym; third, its frequency was matched.
The frequency of the heteronym was assessed from the Kučera and Francis
(1967) norms. The distinct meanings of a heteronym are not listed individually in the frequency norms, so it was not possible to match a control
word to each meaning of the heteronym separately. Instead, the best
estimate for each meaning was taken to be half the overall frequency of the
heteronym. Thus control words were chosen such that they occurred half as
frequently as the corresponding heteronyms. As an example, the control
word for the heteronym "deserts" was "dullest".

Each sentence frame (i.e., sentence without its heteronym) was typed in
black (12 characters to the inch) on a 15.2 x 10.1cm blank white card.
The sentence started 2.0cm from the left edge of the card and 5.2cm from
the top. It began with a capital letter, with the remainder (except
initial letters of proper nouns) in lower case. The heteronym (or control
word) was typed in capitals on a separate card, in a central position
7.5cm from the top of the card. The cards were presented in a Cambridge
three-field tachistoscope linked to an Electronic Development voice key
and Advance Instrument TC11 Timer Counter.

The concurrent memory load lists were prepared using digram-balanced Latin
squares (Wagenaar, 1969) so that each digit occurred equally often in each
serial position and equally often next to every other digit. The digits
used were nought to ten, excluding seven (because of its bisyllabic rather
than monosyllabic nature).

DESIGN

There were two sets of sentences with heteronyms, each set containing one
member of the pair of sentences appropriate to each heteronym. The control
sentences for the first set consisted of the sentence frames from the
second set together with the appropriate control words instead of the
heteronyms, and similarly the control sentences for the second set used
the sentence frames of the first set. The two sets of stimuli were each
viewed by half the subjects.

Each sentence was accompanied by a memory load of either zero, three, six,
or ten digits. Each subject was tested ten times using each combination
of the four memory loads and the two types of sentential context, appropriate and inappropriate. In addition, each subject first received eight
practice trials. The 80 experimental trials were made up of eight blocks
of five trials each in each of two halves of the session. Within each

Table 1

The Heteronyms (in CAPITALS), their Context,
and their Pronunciation

People between forty and fifty are middle-AGED /eɪdʒd/
The charity was called Help the AGED /'eɪdʒɪd/

In the string quartet he played the double BASS /beɪs/
A common British fish is the BASS /bæs /

The crowds in St Peters Square knelt to be BLESSED /blest/
The Beatitudes all begin with the word BLESSED /'blesɪd/

She was dressed up in buttons and BOWS /bəʊz/
The ship's cannon was fired across the BOWS /baʊz/

The Sahara and Kalahari are large DESERTS /'dezəts/
In the end the villain got his just DESERTS /'dɪ'zɜ:ts/

He said: Thank you, I don't mind if I DO /dʊ/
She finished singing the scale: la, te, DO /dəʊ /

It now matters little whatever she says or DOES /dʌz /
Female deer are known as DOES /dəʊz/

To loud applause she made her ENTRANCE /'entrəns/
Her superb performance never failed to ENTRANCE /ɪn'trɑ:ns/

The seasick girl looked green about the GILLS /gɪlz/
In a pint measure there are four GILLS /dʒɪlz/

In the cemetery he dug a GRAVE /'greɪv/
Two types of accent in French are acute and GRAVE /grɑ:v/

His elderly mother was an INVALID /'ɪnvəlɪd/
Until it was stamped the passport was INVALID /ɪn'vælɪd /

The employment exchange offered him a JOB /dʒɑb/
Despite misfortune he was as patient as JOB /'dʒəʊb/

At the finish the champion was in the LEAD /li:d/
The old waterpipes were made of LEAD /led/

The child's multiplication tables had been well LEARNED /lɜ:nt/
The mediaeval scholars were most LEARNED /'lɜ:nɪd/

This is the house where he LIVES /lɪvz/
It is said that a cat has nine LIVES /laɪvz/

There are sixty seconds in a MINUTE /'mɪnɪt/
Compared with an elephant a mouse is MINUTE /maɪ'nju:t/

The pregnant woman visited the clinic marked Ante-NATAL /'neɪtl/
A province of South Africa is NATAL /nə'tæl /

The teacher said: Poking out your tongue is not very NICE /naɪs /
Her favourite resort on the French Riviera is NICE /ni:s /

For lunch he ate a Cornish PASTY /'pæstɪ /
Lack of fresh air made his face look PASTY /'peɪstɪ /

The old man could afford few luxuries on his PENSION /'penʃn/
A cheap French hotel is called a PENSION /'pɑ̃:ŋsɪɔ:ŋ/

The mahogany shone with French POLISH /ˈpɑlɪʃ/
The nationality of the people in Warsaw is POLISH /ˈpəʊlɪʃ/

The scarecrow's clothes were old and RAGGED /ˈrægɪd/
At school, the fat child was unmercifully RAGGED /rægd/

Illiterate people cannot write or READ /riːd/
His encyclopaedic knowledge of books showed that he was well READ /red/

In the library he spent all his time READING /ˈriːdɪŋ/
Trains from Oxford to London stop at READING /ˈredɪŋ/

The athlete broke the world RECORD /ˈrekɔːd/
In the studio the orchestra had just started to RECORD /rɪˈkɔːd/

He disliked the request but he was too polite to REFUSE /rɪˈfjuːz/
The dustbin men collected all the REFUSE /ˈrefjuːs/

After a delay the referee ordered play to RESUME /rɪˈzjuːm/
The main findings were summarised in a brief RESUME /ˈrezjuːmeɪ/

She planted the seeds in a straight ROW /rəʊ/
The argument developed into a terrible ROW /raʊ/

The Cambridge boat sank but Oxford continued ROWING /rəʊɪŋ/
The argumentative couple were always publicly ROWING /raʊɪŋ/

The drains flowed into the main SEWER /sjʊə/
She was a better knitter than SEWER /ˈsəʊə/

When a snake sheds old skin it is said to SLOUGH /slʌf/
He worked in a chocolate factory in SLOUGH /slaʊ/

The seed packet had instructions on how to SOW /səʊ/
The piglets followed after the SOW /saʊ/

During the drought water was in short SUPPLY /səˈplaɪ/
The old man did his exercises surprisingly SUPPLY /ˈsʌplɪ/

A leading port in Morocco is called TANGIER /tænˈdʒɪə/
The latest batch of lemons tasted even TANGIER /tæŋɪə/

He was already late but continued to TARRY /ˈtærɪ/
In the sun the road surface melted and became TARRY /ˈtɑːrɪ/

On hearing the story she wept bitter TEARS /tɪəz/
The old clothes had many patches and TEARS /teəz/

Paris is famous for the Eiffel TOWER /ˈtaʊə/
The broken-down car was pulled away by the TOWER /ˈtəʊə/

The cinema was showing Gone With The WIND /wɪnd/
The clock's stiff spring was difficult to WIND /waɪnd/

On the top of the cliffs it was very WINDY /ˈwɪndɪ/
The sheltered path was meandering and WINDY /ˈwaɪndɪ/

The swordsman inflicted a grievous WOUND /wuːnd/
Each day the clock had to be WOUND /waʊnd/

block, the load and context conditions were constant (of course, the digits of the load differed on each trial). Each combination of load and context occurred once in each half of the session. The order in which the conditions were carried out was counterbalanced across subjects using a digram-balanced Latin square, and each sentence occurred equally often with each digit load.

PROCEDURE

Typed instructions explaining the task were given to each subject at the start of the experiment. Subjects had to memorize the identity and order of a set of digits and to read aloud as fast as possible the word in capitals that followed the sentence frame. At the start of each trial the experimenter told the subject whether or not the sentence frame was helpful, and the size of the memory load. Subjects looked at the screen of the tachistoscope while the experimenter read aloud the digits at an even rate of one digit per second. Immediately after the last digit the subject silently read the sentence frame which was displayed for 4 sec. This was immediately followed by a capitalized word for another 4 sec. The subject read this word aloud as fast as possible into a microphone. The time elapsed between the onset of the single word and the subject's response was noted by the experimenter, together with the pronunciation of the word. Next, on trials with a memory load the word "Recall" was displayed. Subjects wrote down the digits they could remember from left to right in boxes in response booklets, in the order the digits had been presented (guessing if necessary). On trials without a memory load the word "Wait" was displayed instead.

RESULTS

This section reports the reading latencies and errors, and the digit recall data.

READING LATENCIES

Figure 1 shows the effect of varying concurrent memory load on the latency of correctly pronounced words preceded by either appropriate or inappropriate context. When an error was made in pronouncing either one or both of a matched pair of words, the reaction times for both words were removed from consideration.

The data were subjected to a three-way analysis of variance (context type by size of memory load by subjects). Words with appropriate contexts were read significantly faster (720.1 msec) than words with inappropriate contexts (786.3 msec), $F(1,31) = 68.74$, $p < 0.001$. There was also a significant effect of size of concurrent memory load (means were 778.3, 779.7, 800.7, and 807.2 msec for memory loads of zero, three, six, and ten items, respectively), $F(3,93) = 4.00$, $p < 0.01$. The appropriate-context data were further examined using a Scheffé S test. Reading times were significantly longer for concurrent memory loads of six and ten items (744.0 msec) than for zero and three items (696.2 msec), $p < 0.05$, while there were no significant differences within these two pairs.

Further interest relates to the influence on these data of the frequency of occurrence in English of the words that were read. Because of the ambiguousness of frequencies for different senses of heteronyms, only the inappropriate-context data were analysed. The words were divided into two equal halves on the basis of their Kučera and Francis (1967) frequencies. The twenty words in the high frequency group had a mean frequency of 87.2, and the twenty in the low frequency group one of 3.65. Figure 2 shows the effects of word frequency and of memory load. Slightly more data were

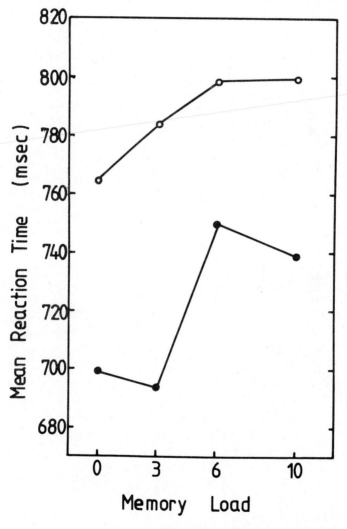

Figure 1

Reading Latencies for Different Memory Loads, with Filled and Unfilled Circles referring respectively to Appropriate and Inappropriate Context

used in this analysis than the previous one since only inappropriate-context pronunciation errors were excluded, and not also data yoked to appropriate-context pronunciation errors. A three-way analysis of variance (word frequency by size of memory load by subjects) showed that high frequency words were read significantly faster (766.9 msec) than low frequency words (816.1 msec), $F(1,31) = 23.88$, $p < 0.001$. There was no significant main effect of memory load, $F(3,93) = 1.10$, or of an interaction between word frequency and memory load, $F(3,93) = 1.77$.

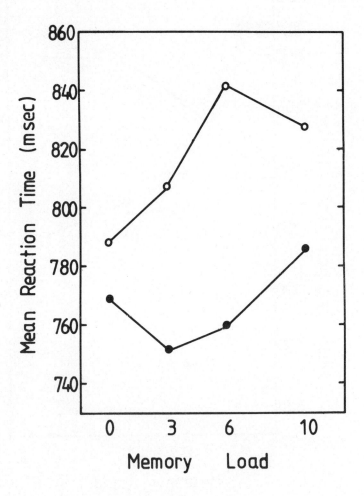

Figure 2

Reading Latencies for Different Memory Loads, with Filled and Unfilled Circles referring respectively to High and Low Word Frequency.

READING ERRORS

The level of accuracy of pronunciation was high throughout. Those errors that did occur can be categorized into two types. The first consists of completely mistaken readings, for example "bass" read as "brace" (appropriate context), and "impromptu" read as "important" (inappropriate context"). These errors occurred at an extremely low and approximately constant rate throughout the experiment: for appropriate context, rates were 0.6%, 0%, 0% and 0.3% (for memory loads of zero, three, six, and ten, respectively), while corresponding rates for inappropriate context were 0.6%, 0%, 0.3% and 0.9%.

The second type of error consists of pronouncing a heteronym in one legal manner when the context prescribes the other, for example reading /'ɪnvəlɪd/ rather than /ɪnvælɪd/ in the sentence "Until it was stamped the passport was INVALID". This type of error (which can occur only in the appropriate context condition) was submitted to a two way analysis of variance (size of memory load by subjects). Mean rates for loads of zero, three, six, and ten were 8.4%, 9.4%, 11.3%, and 10.6%, and did not differ significantly, $F(3,93) = 0.48$. Analysis of the summation of both types of error revealed that memory load was not significant either as a main effect, $F(3,93) = 0.45$, or in interaction with type of context, $F(3,93) = 0.35$.

ACCURACY OF RECALL

Figure 3 shows the percentage recall of the digit lists used as memory loads (three, six, or ten items), as a function of serial position of

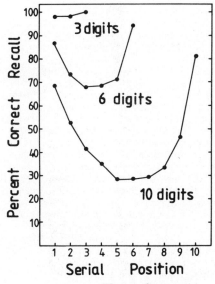

Figure 3

Percentage Recall of Memory Loads of Different Lengths
as a Function of Presentation Serial Position

presentation. An item was only scored as correct if its serial position
as well as its identity was correctly remembered.

The total number of items recalled from each list was submitted to a two-
way analysis of variance (length of memory load list by subjects). There
was a significant main effect of the length of the list, $F(2,62) = 63.76$,
$p < 0.001$; on average, subjects correctly recalled 2.96, 4.61, and 4.44
items from lists of lengths three, six, and ten, respectively. These mean
recall levels were further examined using a Scheffé S test, which revealed
that with three-item lists subjects recalled significantly fewer items than
with either six-item lists, $p < 0.001$, or ten-item lists, $p < 0.001$, but
that there was no significant difference between six-item and ten-item
lists.

DISCUSSION

Clear evidence that contextual processing was greatly used in the reported
experiment, as anticipated, is provided by the high level of correct dis-
ambiguation of heteronym pronunciation (e.g. pronouncing "wound" as /waund/
rather than /wu:nd/ when the context implies an injury). In the absence of
contextual processing, pronunciation would on average have been expected to
be correct on 50% of occasions, but the actual value was approximately 90%
in all conditions. It was indeed somewhat surprising that the percentage
of correct pronunciation did not differ significantly among different
memory load conditions. Latency of correct pronunciation did on the other
hand vary systematically as a function of memory load.

It was found that the imposition of a memory load of three digits did not
impair the latency of contextually-based pronunciation relative to that
when reading normally. A load of six digits, on the other hand, produced
a large decrement in performance, which remained at approximately the same
level when the load was increased still further to ten digits.

The absence of an effect of a three-item memory load suggests that
Baddeley and Hitch's articulatory loop component of working memory is not
utilized in mediating the effects upon reading of linguistic contextual
information. This finding is consistent with those of Baddeley and Hitch
(1974) themselves that the articulatory loop is not utilized in verbal
reasoning or the comprehension of visually presented materials, which are
similarly unaffected by the retention of three items. The impairment
observed here with a concurrent load of six items, on the other hand,
implicates the central executive of working memory in contextual mediation.
Again, similar results have been obtained by Baddeley and Hitch (1974) and
Hitch and Baddeley (1976) when investigating verbal reasoning and comprehension. The present result suggests that the underlying reason for these
results may have been that in both cases heavy demands were placed upon the
processing and storage of information of use in promoting top-down influences upon text processing. Finally, although individual differences were
not studied in the present work, the results are consistent also with the
recent finding by Daneman and Carpenter (1980) of a positive correlation
between individuals' working memory and reading abilities.

It was expected that the reading of relatively low-frequency words might
place greater demands upon linguistic processing (Just & Carpenter, 1980),
but a significant interaction between word frequency and size of memory

load was not in fact observed. However, high-frequency words were overall
read faster than low-frequency ones, in accord with previous findings
(Berry, 1971; Forster & Chambers, 1973).

An alternative account of these results may be offered within the terms of
the recent Maltese cross model of Broadbent (1980, in press-a, in press-b).
According to this model, the cognitive system is conceptualised as a Maltese
cross. The end of each arm holds a different type of memory store: an input
buffer, an output buffer, a long-term associative memory, and a work space.
Information flow is both centripetal, from the end of each arm to the centre
of the cross, and centrifugal, from the centre to the ends of the arms. At
the centre of the cross is a processor whose function is simply to direct
the flow of information between the stores. It is the workspace arm that
Broadbent proposes holds the context of a sentence while it is being read.
The absence of a decrement in reading performance upon the addition of a
small memory load of three digits suggests that these are stored in an arm
other than that of the workspace. The considerable decline in reading
performance that occurs when three further digits are imposed implies that
this second arm has only a small capacity. Furthermore, considerable forgetting of the stored digits seems to have occurred during the short
forgetting interval between their presentation and recall. From lists of
both six and ten items only about four and a half were recalled on average,
well below the usual immediate digit span of approximately seven (see
Cavanagh, 1972; Martin, 1978). Thus these data suggest that while contextual processing is mediated by the workspace arm of the model, a concurrently
processed digit list is held in a store of small capacity and rapid forgetting. The output buffer should be occupied by the process of reading
aloud, and hence the likely candidate for this digit store would, according
to this model, appear to be the input buffer arm.

ACKNOWLEDGEMENTS

The author wishes to thank Sara Dickson for testing the subjects, Donald
Broadbent and David Clark for valuable discussion, and the Medical Research
Council for their support.

REFERENCES

Baddeley, A.D. The psychology of memory. New York: Harper & Row, 1976.
Baddeley, A.D. Working memory and reading. Paper presented at the
     International Symposium on Processing of Visible Language, Geldrop, The
     Netherlands, September 1977.
Baddeley, A.D. & Hitch, G. Working memory. In G.H. Bower (Ed.), The psych-
     ology of learning and motivation. New York: Academic Press, 1974.
Berry, C. Advanced frequency information and verbal response times.
     Psychonomic Science, 1971, 23, 151-152.
Bower, G.H. Cognitive Psychology: An introduction. In W.K. Estes (Ed.),
     Handbook of learning and cognitive processes. Hillsdale, NJ: Erlbaum,
     1975.
Bower, G.H., Black, J.B., & Turner, T.J. Scripts in memory for text.
     Cognitive Psychology, 1979, 11, 177-220.
Broadbent, D.E. The minimization of models. In A.J. Chapman & D.M. Jones
     (Eds.), Models of man. Leicester: The British Psychological Society,
     1980.

Broadbent, D.E. From the percept to the cognitive structure. In
   A.D. Baddeley & J. Long (Eds.), Attention and performance IX. Hillsdale,
   NJ: Erlbaum, in press. (a)
Broadbent, D.E. Perceptual experiments and language theories. Proceedings
   of the Royal Society of London, in press. (b)
Carpenter, P.A., & Daneman, M. Lexical retrieval and error recovery:
   A model based on eye fixations. Journal of Verbal Learning and Verbal
   Behavior, 1981, 20, 137-160.
Cavanagh, J.P. Relation between the immediate memory span and the memory
   search rate. Psychological Review, 1972, 79, 525-530.
Conrad, C. Context effects in sentence comprehension: A study of the
   subjective lexicon. Memory & Cognition, 1974, 2, 130-138.
Daneman, M., & Carpenter, P.A. Individual differences in working memory
   and reading. Journal of Verbal Learning and Verbal Behavior, 1980, 19,
   450-466.
Forster, K.I., & Chambers, S.M. Lexical access and naming time. Journal
   of Verbal Learning and Verbal Behavior, 1973, 12, 627-635.
Hitch, G.J., & Baddeley, A.D. Verbal reasoning and working memory.
   Quarterly Journal of Experimental Psychology, 1976, 28, 603-621.
Hogaboam, T.W., & Perfetti, C.A. Lexical ambiguity and sentence compre-
   hension. Journal of Verbal Learning and Verbal Behavior, 1975, 14,
   265-274.
Holmes, V.M. Accessing ambiguous words during sentence comprehension.
   Quarterly Journal of Experimental Psychology, 1979, 31, 569-589.
Just, M.A., & Carpenter, P.A. A theory of reading: From eye fixations to
   comprehension. Psychological Review, 1980, 87, 329-354.
Kučera, H., & Francis, W.N. Computational analysis of present-day American
   English. Providence, RI: Brown University Press, 1967.
LaBerge, D., & Samuels, S.J. Toward a theory of automatic information
   processing in reading. Cognitive Psychology, 1974, 6, 293-323.
Marcel, T. Conscious and preconscious recognition of polysemous words:
   Locating the selective effects of prior verbal context. In
   R. S. Nickerson (Ed.), Attention and performance VIII. Hillsdale, NJ:
   Erlbaum, 1980.
Martin, M. Memory span as a measure of individual differences in memory
   capacity. Memory & Cognition, 1978, 6, 194-198.
Martin, M., Jones, G.V., Nelson, D.L., & Nelson, L. Heteronyms and
   polyphones: Categories of words with multiple phonemic representations.
   Behavior Research Methods & Instrumentation, 1981, 13, 299-307.
Schank, R.C. & Abelson, R.P. Scripts, plans, goals and understanding:
   An inquiry into human knowledge structures. Hillsdale, NJ: Erlbaum,
   1977.
Simpson, G.B. Meaning dominance and semantic context in the processing of
   lexical ambiguity. Journal of Verbal Learning and Verbal Behavior,
   1981, 20, 120-136.
Tanenhaus, M.K., Leiman, J.M., & Seidenberg, M.S. Evidence for multiple
   stages in the processing of ambiguous words in syntactic contexts.
   Journal of Verbal Learning and Verbal Behavior, 1979, 18, 427-440.
Wagenaar, W.A. Note on the construction of digram-balanced Latin squares.
   Psychological Bulletin, 1969, 72, 384-386.
Warren, R.E., Warren, N.T., Green, J.P., & Bresnick, J.H. Multiple semantic
   encoding of homophones and homographs in contexts biasing dominant or
   subordinate meanings. Memory & Cognition, 1978, 6, 364-371.

DISCOURSE PROCESSING
A. Flammer and W. Kintsch (eds.)
© North-Holland Publishing Company, 1982

AGE, READING ABILITY, AND SEMANTIC INTEGRATION:
AN INFORMATION PROCESSING MODEL

John R. Kirby

University of Newcastle
New South Wales, Australia, 2308

This paper examines the relationship between reading
comprehension and semantic integration (as measured by
inferencing in a recall task) in various age groups. Results
are discussed in terms of a model in which inferencing
occurs in response to two individual difference variables:
the ability to recode or integrate information (which
increases with developmental level), and the need to recode
or integrate (which decreases with developmental level).
It is concluded that the relationship between reading
ability and semantic integration will depend upon task
demands and subjects' perceptions of task demands, in
addition to developmental level.

One of the fundamental issues in text processing concerns how information
is integrated in the brain. Because cognition is limited in the number of
chunks of information which can be maintained, incoming information must be
rapidly and, hopefully, efficiently recoded into larger chunks of information. Thus a great amount of information can be stored in a relatively
small number of chunks. The importance of this recoding is particularly
apparent in an activity such as reading, in which the flow of new information is quite fast.

Three factors can be seen to influence what recoding is performed. The
first two of these are perceived relations among the units of the input or
new information, and perceived relations between input information and
already-known or old information. These two factors clearly interact, as
relations among new information units will almost always be perceived with
reference to existing knowledge schemes. It can also be seen that this
relating of information to other new or old information captures what is
usually meant by reading comprehension.

The third factor influencing recoding is more strategic in nature, and
represents choices (conscious or unconscious) made by the individual reader
about how to process the reading material. These choices are made on the
basis of habitual response patterns, or in response to perceived task
demands.

Current theories of semantic integration (e. g. Bransford & Franks, 1971;
Hayes-Roth & Thorndyke, 1979; Kintsch, 1974; see Walker & Meyer, 1980, for
a review) agree that inferences, in the form of relations among units of

new material, are formed at input. There is disagreement, however, concerning the nature of the stored information (abstract-propositional vs. verbal), whether or not the original information is encoded as well as the inference, and what task factors influence the drawing of inferences.

One obvious area of application for this research is the teaching of reading comprehension. When we teach reading, other than at a very basic word-recognition level, we are trying to teach the child to extract meaning from the text, and in particular to construct meanings which aren't explicitly present in the text. Most measures of reading comprehension attempt to assess these skills by the inclusion of questions of both "literal" and "inferential" comprehension. Inferential comprehension, if not reading comprehension in general, should be a function of semantic integration.

Blachowicz (1977-78) has begun the study of semantic integration in the context of children's reading. She presented subjects, who ranged in age from 7 years to adult, with 10 short 3-sentence paragraphs like the following:
> The birds sat on the branch.
> A hawk flew over it.
> The birds were robins.

Subjects were instructed to " understand and remember" the paragraphs, and were given 5 minutes to do so. Then, following a 3-minute filler task, they were given a set of recognition sentences, and asked to select which sentences they had seen previously in exactly the same form. Four recognition sentences were constructed for each paragraph: one sentence that had appeared (True Statement), one sentence that was an acceptable inference from two or more of the actual sentences (True Inference), one sentence that contradicted one that was given (False Statement), and one which contradicted an acceptable inference (False Inference). The recognition sentences were presented in random order.

Blachowicz' results were quite clear: younger subjects recognized (correctly or incorrectly) more sentences than older subjects, and all subject groups showed a similar pattern of response, in which True Inferences were selected far more often than all other types of sentences, including True Statements. While reading comprehension ability could be presumed to increase across age groups, Blachowicz made no use of comprehension scores within age groups.

The purpose of the present study was to replicate Blachowicz' experiment for 7, 9, and 11 year olds, with two modifications and the inclusion of reading comprehension scores. One modification was to shorten the study time to 3 minutes from 5 as this provided all subjects ample time to read all paragraphs several times. The second modification was more major, the elimination of the filler task. This was done so that the task more resembled the normal reading comprehension task, in which questions immediately follow reading. Reading comprehension were used to investigate whether readers of the same age but of different levels of reading ability would perform differently on the inferencing task.

Four predictions were formed, on the basis of Blachowicz' results and the suggested relationship between reading and inferencing. These predictions also assume that the experimental modifications and the different experimental materials would not have any effect. The predictions were: (1) young subjects would select more sentences than older subjects, (2) the response pattern would be similar across age groups, (3) all groups would show a preference for True Inferences, and (4) that reading comprehension scores would be positively related to selection of True Inferences, though this relationship might only emerge after a certain age was attained. As will be seen below, the failure of the fourth prediction necessitated further data collection and a more comprehensive theoretical framework. These will be described below.

METHOD

SUBJECTS

The subjects were 29 age 7, 29 age 9, and 30 age 11 children. Each age group was further divided into two on the basis of reading comprehension scores, which were from the A. C. E. R. Silent Reading Test for age 7 and from the N. Z. C. E. R. Progressive achievement Test for ages 9 and 11. These are standard reading comprehension measures, requiring subjects to answer multiple choice questions after reading short passages. Comprehension scores were in stanines, so for the present purposes subjects in each age group with stanine scores of 4 or less were placed in the low comprehension group, and those with 5 or more in the high comprehension group. In this way, there were 20 children in the age 7 high comprehension group, 9 in the low; 14 in the age 9 high comprehension group, 15 in the low; and 11 in the age 11 high comprehension group, 19 in the low.

MATERIALS AND PROCEDURES

Children were tested in class-sized groups. Each was given 3 minutes to read 10 short paragraphs, each of which concerned a spatial/locational relation of the type used by Blachowicz (1977-78). All paragraphs were composed of words used in grade two reading materials, and should have been understandable by all subjects. Subjects were instructed that they should study the paragraphs carefully, in order to "understand and remember" them, as they would later "be asked questions about them." (Instructions were deliberately made similar to those of Blachowicz.)

After the 3-minute study period, the paragraphs were collected and the answer sheets distributed. The answer sheet contained 40 sentences, 4 for each paragraph. As in Blachowicz' study, one of these 4 was a sentence that had appeared in the paragraphs (a True Sentence), one was an inference combining 2 sentences that had been given (True Inference), one was a contradiction of a paragraph sentence (False Sentence), and one a False Inference. The 40 test sentences appeared on the answer sheet in random order, with the constraint that no two sentences about the same paragraph appeared consecutively. Subjects were instructed to indicate which of the sentences had been seen, in _exactly_ the same way, in the paragraphs.

For each subject, the number of True Sentences, True Inferences, False Sentences, and False Inferences chosen were counted.

RESULTS AND DISCUSSION

The data were analyzed by means of a 3 (Age) x 2 (Comprehension group) x 4 (Response type: True Sentence or Inference, False Sentence or Inference) analysis of variance, with repeated measures on the last factor. Only 4 effects are significant at the .05 level. The most powerful of these is the main effect for Response, $\underline{F}(3,246) = 311.60$, p < .0001. This indicates that more True Sentences and Inferences are selected in general; this implies little more than that subjects do remember the paragraphs.

The Age x Comprehension effect, $F(2,82) = 5.49$, $p < .01$, is graphed in Figure 1, and demonstrates that more test sentences are selected by 7 year old high comprehenders than by 7 year old low comprehenders, regardless of correctness.

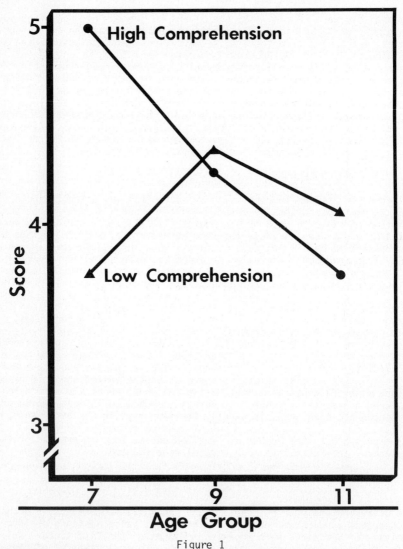

Figure 1
Age x Comprehension effect (score = number of items selected)

The Response x Age effect, $\underline{F}(6,246) = 17.32$, p$<$.0001, is presented in Figure 2. In general, there is a trend for True Sentences and Inferences to be selected often, False Sentences and Inferences infrequently. Only the 7 year olds deviate from this pattern, selecting fewer True Inferences, and more False Sentences and Inferences. The 7 year old children do not appear to be any less accurate with respect to True Sentences, but make fewer True Inferences and select more incorrect sentences. Although the Response x Age

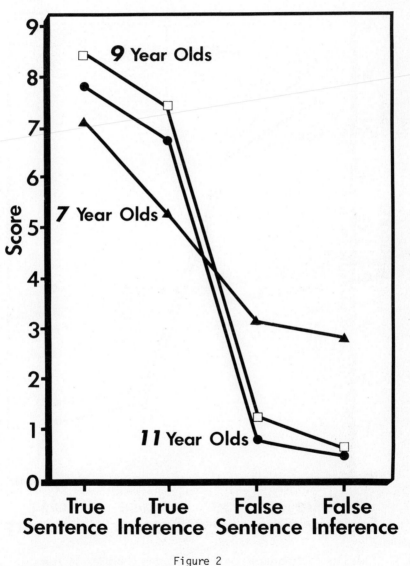

Figure 2
Response x Age effect (score = number of items selected)

x Comprehension effect was not significant, there was a trend for the 7 year old low comprehenders to select fewer True Inferences than did the high comprehenders. Both high and low comprehenders at age 7 selected a large number of False Sentences and Inferences.

The Response x Comprehension effect, $\underline{F}(3,246) = 2.72$, $p < .05$, is shown in Figure 3, and indicates that the high comprehenders select somewhat more

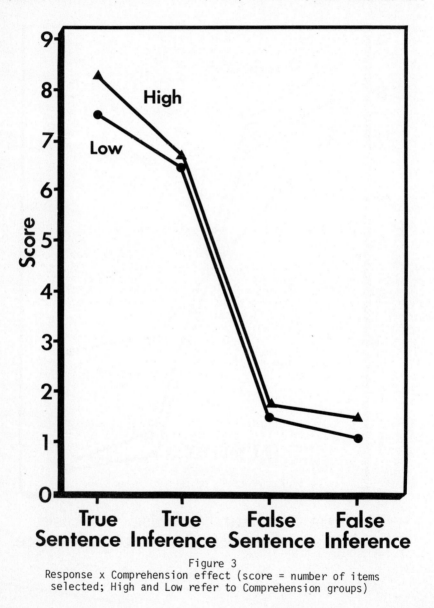

Figure 3
Response x Comprehension effect (score = number of items
selected; High and Low refer to Comprehension groups)

True Sentences and False Inferences than do low comprehenders. The True
Sentence difference suggests that the most important difference across
comprehension groups is one of absolute accuracy and not one of inferencing.
The greater number of False Inferences is more difficult to explain, and
may be due to chance.

What does this experiment have to say about the predictions raised previously? The first prediction, it will be remembered, was that there would
be an overall age effect, with younger subjects selecting more sentences in
general. While this did not occur, 7 year old high comprehenders did
select more sentences than their low comprehending counterparts (see the
Age x Comprehension effect, illustrated in Figure 1). Thus it was only the
7 year old low comprehenders that varied from Blachowicz' pattern. It is
possible that Blachowicz' 7 year olds were of a higher, and more uniform
level of reading competence than those employed in the present study.

The second and third predictions were that the pattern of sentence selection would be similar across age groups, and that all groups would select
more True Inferences. These predictions are clearly disconfirmed: 7 year
olds showed a distinctly different pattern of response, and no age group
showed a preference for True Inferences. At all age levels more True
Sentences were selected than True Inferences: this is most likely to be due
to the design of the present study, in which subjects did not perform a
filler task between reading the paragraphs and recognizing the sentences.
It is less likely that the shorter reading time could have this effect.

The final prediction was that reading comprehension would be related,
perhaps developmentally, to inferencing, as represented by selection of
True Inferences. While 9 and 11 year olds did select more True Inferences
than did 7 year olds (Figure 2), high comprehenders did not select them
more often than low comprehenders (Figure 3). Although the Response x Age
x Comprehension effect was not significant, there was a trend for 7 year
old low comprehenders to select fewer True Inferences than all other
subjects.

Most of these results are intuitively quite acceptable. It is not surprising, for instance, that less inferencing is done in the absence of a
filler task. This would support the contention that the "raw data" are
preserved following encoding, at least for a while (Hayes-Roth & Thorndyke,
1979). What is surprising and disappointing is the lack of relation between
inferencing and reading comprehension.

One possibility is that the inferencing-comprehension relationship develops
subsequent to the ages included in this study. (This could arise because
the nature of skilled reading changes with age, or because the nature of
reading comprehension tests changes with age.) In order to examine this
possibility, two further sets of data were collected, one from a group of
13 year olds, and one from a group of University students (mean age = 22
years). The former group was divided into high and low comprehension groups
on the same basis as the younger subjects had been, and the latter group
was assumed to consist of only high comprehenders.

The 13 year olds showed much the same pattern as the younger subjects, with
the exception that the high comprehenders selected almost as few True Inferences as did the 7 year old low comprehenders. Even greater doubt is
cast upon the proposed relationship between comprehension and inferencing

by the University results: these subjects selected even <u>fewer</u> True Inferences than did the 7 year old low comprehenders.

The True Inferences results for all subjects are presented in Figure 4,
together with those for True Sentences. It should be noted that the horizontal scale is at best an ordinal one, as no attempt has been made to
equalize the intervals between groups. Here the pattern of results becomes
more apparent: while selection of True Sentences increases only slightly
within the 7 year old group and remains constant thereafter, selection of
True Inferences increases to age 9 and then decreases sharply. These

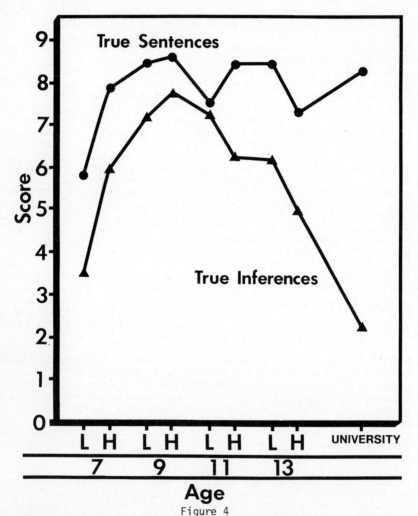

Figure 4
Developmental trends for True Sentences and Inferences (score = number
of items selected; H and L refer to high and low reading ability)

results suggest modification of semantic integration theory, especially with regard to task demands and reading competence.

A PROPOSED MODEL

The minimum that these results suggest is that the task demands of the present experiment, or at least the perceived task demands, differed importantly from those of Blachowicz' study. As has been said above, the absence of a filler task probably allowed subjects to retain more detailed encodings of the original paragraphs. In addition, it could also be suspected that the present subjects took their instruction to "remember" the paragraphs more literally than did Blachowicz' subjects. While both of these factors explain the increase in True Sentence scores, and could explain an equivalent decrease in True Inference scores, they are insufficient to explain the observed curvilinear pattern of True Inference scores.

A model that would predict these results is illustrated in Figure 5. In this model, semantic integration or inferencing is seen to occur or to not occur in response to two types of processing resources, both of which are conceived of in terms of individual difference variables, and both of which change with developmental level. The first of these resources is the ability to integrate or to recode information, on the basis of relationships either within the current material or between the current material and stored information. This relating ability is the basis of much mental ability and clearly increases with developmental level. If only this factor were operating, True Inferences would increase monotonically with age, and little could be predicted concerning True Sentences.

The second factor operating is the need to recode or integrate incoming information. This need is inversely related to the availability of working memory space and the efficiency of information transfer from working memory to long term memory. As both of these increase, the processing system becomes more and more able to retain information in its veridical form, if that is the goal of the operating information processing plan.

Thus integration or recoding occurs to allow economical use of scarce working memory space. The ability to retain information in veridical form can also be seen to increase developmentally, thus the need to recode decreases with developmental level. If only this factor were operating, True Sentences would increase with age while True Inferences would decrease, if accuracy of recognition were seen as the goal.

If both factors are operating, in the presence of a goal of accurate recognition, the pattern seen in Figure 5 would be predicted, which is essentially that which was observed in the present study. Younger or less able children do not integrate because they can not; older children (age 9 in the present study) do integrate information, because they can and they have to, given their restricted working memory; and still older subjects do not integrate information, even though they could, because they are not forced to do so by limited working memory.

It is important to note that task demands and subjects' goals will alter this pattern radically: for example, interpolation of a filler task between reading and recognition will place more strain upon working memory resources and increase the liklihood of semantic integration (given adequate relating ability). Similarly, longer or more difficult texts will increase the need to recode. Subjects' goals can be manipulated by varying the

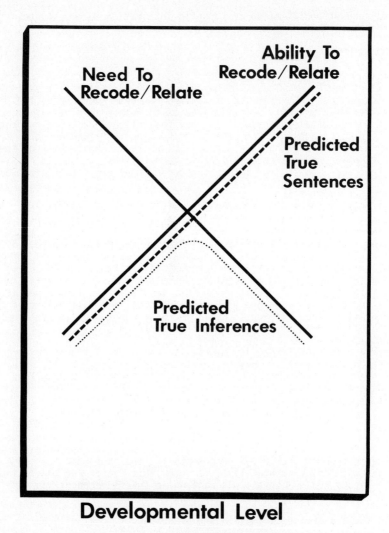

Developmental Level

Figure 5
Proposed developmental model

perceived task: in the place of "understand and remember" as in the present study, the task of "drawing a picture to represent each paragraph" would increase recoding, while the task of "memorizing each word" would decrease recoding.

The present context allows space for only two further observations. The first of these is that the two abilities referred to above, relating ability and working memory efficiency, figure prominently in individual differences models of information processing. Relating ability recalls

Jensen's (1970) Level II ability, and Das, Kirby and Jarman's (1979) simultaneous processing.It also seems relevant to the concept of "chunk size" (Simon, 1974), in that essentially it describes how large or complex an information integration unit will be formed.

If relating ability determines chunk size, working memory efficiency determines how many chunks will be stored. This is clearly related to Jensen's Level I ability, and can be argued to be Das et al.'s successive processing (see Kirby & Biggs, 1981, for this argument). In fact the two information processing abilities suggested in the present paper could form the basis for a rapprochement between the theories of Jensen and Das et al.

The second observation is that the relationship between inferencing, represented by selection of True Inferences in paradigms such as the present one, and reading comprehension is likely to be complex. That relationship will certainly depend upon the task requirements and the subjects' own goals in performing the task. From the point of view of semantic integration theory, it would seem useful to explore the variety of task parameters and subject abilities that influence whether and how much inferencing will occur. Once this has been done, it should become possible to design reading instruction to encourage students to inference or not to inference, or more importantly to know when inferencing is appropriate. In this way, the instructional goal becomes one of processing flexibility, rather than of one type of processing.

ACKNOWLEDGMENTS

This research was supported by an Education Research and Development Committee grant to the author and P. J. Moore. The author would like to acknowledge the contributions of P. J. Moore to the project, and the assistance of R. Cantwell, D. Porter and K. Russell in data collection. This paper was written while the author was on leave at the University of Alberta.

REFERENCES

Blachowicz, C. L. Z. Semantic constructivity in children's comprehension. Reading Research Quarterly, 1977-78, 13, 188-199.
Bransford, J. D. & Franks, J. J. The abstraction of linguistic ideas. Cognitive Psychology, 1971, 2, 331-350.
Das, J. P., Kirby, J. R.& Jarman, R. F. Simultaneous and successive cognitive processes. New York: Academic, 1979.
Hayes-Roth, B. & Thorndyke, P. W. Integration of knowledge from text. Journal of Verbal Learning and Verbal Behavior, 1979, 18, 91-108.
Jensen, A. R. Hierarchical theories of mental ability. In W. B. Dockrell (Ed.), On Intelligence. Toronto: Methuen, 1970.
Kintsch, W. The representation of meaning in memory. Hillsdale, N. J.: Erlbaum, 1974.
Kirby, J. R. & Biggs, J. B. Learning styles, information processing abilities, and academic performance. Final report to the Australian Research Grants Committee, Canberra, Australia, 1981.
Simon, H. A. How big is a chunk? Science, 1974, 183, 482-488.

Walker, C. H. & Meyer, B. J. F. Integrating information from text: An
    evaluation of current theories. <u>Review</u> <u>of</u> <u>Educational</u> <u>Research</u>, 1980,
    <u>50</u>, 421-437.

DISCOURSE PROCESSING
A. Flammer and W. Kintsch (eds.)
© North-Holland Publishing Company, 1982

THE MODALITY EFFECT ON TEXT PROCESSING
AS A FUNCTION OF ORGANIZATION

Machiko Sannomiya[1]

Faculty of Human Sciences
Osaka University
Suita, Osaka, Japan

The effect of presentation modality on text memory
was reexamined. It was different from that on memory
for semantically unrelated materials: (1) The effect
was obtained only for material difficult to comprehend. (2) Audiovisual presentation was not superior
to visual presentation. (3) The effect was not restricted to the recency part of the material. The
findings can be accounted for by the assumption of
capacity shortage due to automatic translation of
visually presented verbal stimuli into an auditory
form. They would not be predicted from the assumption
of separate precategorical stores with different
retention times for auditory and visual input.

INTRODUCTION

The term "modality effect" refers to the effect of presentation modality on
memory for verbal materials. For semantically unrelated materials, e.g.,
letter-, digit-, nonsense syllable-, or word-lists, the superiority of auditory and audiovisual presentation over visual presentation is well established.
The effect is, however, restricted to recency items of a list (Penny, 1975).

Two main explanations have been advanced for this effect: (1) The "precategorical store hypothesis" is based on the assumption of separate precategorical stores, PAS and PVS, for auditory and visual stimuli. It postulates that
information in PAS is retained longer than in PVS and therefore is more likely
to facilitate recall for recency items (Crowder and Morton, 1969). (2) The
"translation hypothesis" is based on the assumption of a translation of visually presented verbal stimuli into an auditory form. It postulates that the
additional process of translation requires cognitive capacity, and therefore
less capacity remains for further processing in the case of visual presentation (Laughery and Pinkus, 1966).

Kintsch et al. (1975) compared recall of simple stories after listening and
after unpaced reading. They failed to obtain the modality effect. Sannomiya
(1980) studied the modality effect on immediate free recall of two texts which
differed in judged difficulty level but were almost equal in judged interest
level and length (number of words, noun concepts, and idea units). Visual presentation was unpaced, but subjects were instructed to read at a constant
pace and not to return to earlier parts of the text. The results showed a
significant superiority of auditory presentation over audiovisual as well as

visual presentation for the difficult but not for the easy text. The difference was not restricted to the recency part of the text.

The above findings suggest that the modality effect on text memory is different from that on the memory for semantically unrelated materials: First, the modality difference in recall holds only for material difficult to comprehend. Secondly, audiovisual presentation is inferior to auditory and not superior to visual presentation. Thirdly, auditory superiority is not restricted to the recency part of the material.

In order to establish this effect more thoroughly and to specify the difficulty-variable, at least two kinds of difficulty have to be separately investigated, (1) semantic difficulty or difficulty of content and (2) syntactic difficulty or difficulty of structure. The influence of the former difficulty has been examined with mixed lists of concrete and abstract sentences (subject + verb + object) and word-pairs (subject + object) (Sannomiya, 1980). A modality effect was found for abstract but not for concrete word-pairs, i.e., visual presentation was inferior to auditory and audiovisual presentation. The effect was not restricted to recency items. The results from sentence lists were similar but lacked significance.

In the present experiment, the influence of syntactic difficulty on the modality effect was examined by manipulating the organization of texts. If syntactic difficulty has the same influence on the modality effect as unspecified judged difficulty or semantic difficulty, the effect is to be expected only for the difficult (disorganized) text.

METHOD

Subjects. Subjects were sixty undergraduate students at Shitennoji University, Japan.

Design. A 3 x 2 between-subject factorial design with 10 subjects per cell was used, the factors being presentation modality (auditory, visual, and audiovisual) and organization level of texts (organized vs. disorganized).

Materials. A portion of a Japanese essay entitled "Literature and Adolescence" was used as the organized text. The disorganized text was constructed by altering the sequence of propositions (see Appendix). In order not to make the disorganized text meaningless, some connective phrases had to be introduced. They did not carry any additional information but resulted in a somewhat longer length of the disorganized text (526 vs. 489 Japanese letters). For auditory presentation the texts were recorded on tape with a female voice at a rate of 6.5 letters/sec in terms of Japanese Kana letters. Care was taken not to make strong intonations or long pauses which could become recall   cues. For visual presentation each sentence was typewritten on a 6.5 x 18.0 cm white card and all cards were made up into a booklet.

Procedure. Subjects got accustomed to the prescribed pace of presentation during a training session. Those of the visual group learned to read through a sentence exactly once in the given time. After the training session, the text was presented three times in succession. Overt vocalization was not permitted. Visual presentation was paced by the sound of a whistle which indicated that the page should be turned. All subjects were informed about the title of the essay. Immediately after the third presentation, subjects were asked to write down what they remembered, if possible in its original form. Recall time was unlimited.

RESULTS

30 propositions, common to both texts, were to be recalled. Recall protocols
were rated by two judges, who showed 95% agreement. The propositions disagreed upon were rated by a third rater. A proposition was regarded as correctly recalled if its gist was contained in the protocol. Fig.1 shows mean
correct recall for the 6 conditions. A 3 x 2 (modality x organization level)
analysis of variance yielded significant main effects for modality ($F(2,54)$
= 4.67, $p < .05$) and organization level ($F(1,54) = 21.7$, $p < .01$), and a
significant interaction ($F(2,54) = 3.43$, $p < .05$). No modality effect was
observed for the organized text, whereas the disorganized text was significantly better recalled after auditory than after visual presentation
($t = 3.59$, $p < .01$). The apparent superiority of auditory over audiovisual
presentation lacked significance ($t = 1.90$, $.05 < p < .10$). Impairment of
performance due to disorganization was significant in the visual ($t = 4.97$,
$p < .01$) and audiovisual ($t = 2.66$, $p < .05$) conditions.

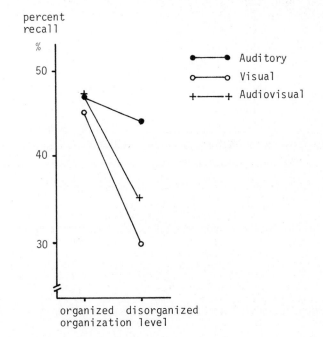

Figure 1
Recall as a Function of Presentation Modality
and Organization Level of the Text

No indication of a modality x serial position interaction was found, i.e.,
the observed modality effect was not restricted to the recency part of the
disorganized text (see Fig. 2). In order to ascertain the absence of the
interaction more strictly, the modality difference for the last three propositions of the disorganized text was examined: The average difference of

recall between the auditory and visual condition was slightly larger for the
last three than for all propositions (1.66 vs. 1.50) of the disorganized text.
However, also in the case of the organized text, the average difference for
the same three propositions, which occupied middle positions here, exceeded
that for all propositions (1.33 vs. 0.14). Therefore the slightly larger
modality effect at the end of the disorganized text must be due to chance
or other factors than serial position.

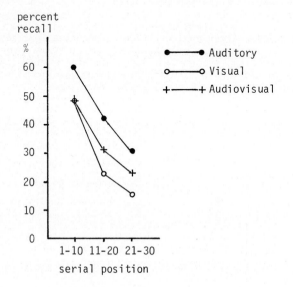

Figure 2
Recall of Disorganized Text as a Function of Presentation Modality and Serial Position of Propositions

DISCUSSION

The results of the present experiment confirm the points of difference between the modality effect on text memory and on memory for semantically unrelated materials, which were found by Sannomiya (1980):

(1) Presentation modality interacts with difficulty of comprehension. The
    modality effect is obtained only for difficult texts.

(2) Audiovisual presentation is not superior to visual, but is probably
    inferior to auditory presentation.

(3) The modality effect on text memory is not restricted to the recency part
    of the material.

Obviously the precategorical store hypothesis cannot account for the modality
effect on text memory. Its predictions are at variance with the last two findings and it cannot predict the first. The organized and disorganized texts

seem to be alike in their demand on perceptual processing but differ in demand on further processing. Therefore we should attend to the process of comprehension rather than to that of perception when searching for an explanation of the modality x difficulty interaction. In that respect the translation hypothesis can be of help. It suggests the following speculation: The processing of a difficult text needs more cognitive capacity than that of an easy text. Therefore the processing of a difficult text is more liable to be impaired by the shortage of cognitive capacity due to the translation of visual stimuli into an auditory form. The modality effect on text memory thus reflects a modality difference in text comprehension. If we assume the translation process to occur automatically, as in the interpretation of the Stroop-effect, we can also explain the inferiority of audiovisual to auditory presentation: Because of its automaticity, the translation process cannot be dispensed with even if it is unnecessary.

REFERENCES

Crowder, R.C., and Morton, J. Precategorical acoustic storage (PAS). Perception and Psychophysics, 1969, 5, 365-373.

Kintsch, W., Kozminsky, E., Streby, W.J., McKoon, G., and Keenan, J.M. Comprehension and recall of text as a function of content variables. Journal of Verbal Learning and Verbal Behavior, 1975, 14, 196-214.

Laughery, K.R., and Pinkus, A.L. Short-term memory: Effects of acoustic similarity, presentation rate, and presentation mode. Psychonomic Science, 1966, 6, 285-286.

Penny, C.G. Modality effects on short-term verbal memory. Psychological Bulletin, 1975, 82, 68-84.

Sannomiya, M. Bunsho-kioku ni okeru teiji-yoshiki no koka (The modality effect on text memory). Master's thesis, Faculty of Human Sciences, Osaka University, 1980.

APPENDIX

1. Organized Text:

I shall describe literature. It is during adolescence that we first encounter literature. In adolescence, one of the motivations for studing literature is to examine the fundamental questions of life. Since literature is closely related to life, I will describe in the following my ideas about the stages of life. There seem to be four birthdays during life. The first one is the real birthday, when we emerge from our mother's womb. The second birthday is adolescence, when we become aware of our own selves and begin to function independently as a human being. The third birthday is the prime of life, when we experience the pain of life. It is the stage when we try to live once again with a fresh outlook. This might be called a religious birthday when we aim at spiritual rebirth. The fourth birthday is the stage of death, when we are reborn as God or Buddha. Here I will especially deal with adolescence. Since adolescence is the stage when we begin to think independently, we can gain a lot from good literature. This can be explained as follows: In order to improve our minds it is necessary to grapple with the fundamental

questions of life which cannot be easily answered. Good literature raises
such questions. For example, there are questions such as "What is life?",
"What is love?", and "Does God exist?". These questions might not ever be
answered during our lives.We should not overlook such questions. In dealing
with literature it is important not to forget our original outlook throughout life.

2. Disorganized Text:

I think there are some stages of life which are like birthdays.For example,
there is the prime of life when we experience the pain of life. During this
stage we try to live once again with a fresh outlook and aim at spiritual rebirth. This can be called a religious birthday. Obviously there is the real
birthday when we emerge from our mother's womb. There is also the stage when
we become aware of our own selves and begin to function independently as a
human being. This is also one of the birthdays. It is during adolescence
when we first encounter literature. During adolescence, one of the motivations for studing literature is to examine the fundamental questions of life.
Finally we die and are reborn as God or Buddha, and we can also call this
stage a birthday. Since literature is closely related to life, I have described the stages of life, the four birthdays of life. In dealing with
literature, it is necessary not to forget our original outlook throughout
life. We should not overlook questions such as "What is life?", "What is
love?", and "Does God exist?" which good literature raises. Such questions
are fundamental ones which cannot be easily answered, and might not ever be
answered during our lives.We can gain a lot from good literature during
adolescence. This can be explained as follows: During this stage we begin to
think independently, good literature raises such fundamental questions as
mentioned above, and in order to improve our minds it is important to
grapple with such questions.

FOOTNOTE

I wish to thank Miss Yoshiko Harakawa for her cooperation in the collection
of data.

DISCOURSE PROCESSING
A. Flammer and W. Kintsch (eds.)
© North-Holland Publishing Company, 1982

REMEMBERING WHAT YOU SAID VERSUS REMEMBERING WHAT YOU WROTE:
CHILDRENS' RECALL OF THEIR OWN ORAL AND WRITTEN NARRATIVES

Angela Hildyard and Suzanne Hidi

Ontario Institute for Studies in Education
Toronto, Ontario

The study described in this paper looks at the effect of
modality upon Grade 6 students' initial production of
narratives and then upon the students' recall of their productions. Contrary to earlier findings, the written original
narratives were found to be qualitatively superior to the
oral narratives, leading us to suggest that the act of writing
permits more careful analysis of structure and content. In
terms of recall, those students who recalled their original
written narratives in a written form were able to retain substantially more of the surface features of that original
narrative. It seems, then, that writing promotes differential
encoding both at production, and at recall.

An interesting aspect of discourse processing, and one which is of prime importance to educators, is the extent to which written and oral discourse processes
differ. Researchers across Europe and North America have looked at the relationship between oral and written language in terms of structure (Chafe, in press;
Olson and Hildyard, 1981; Tannen, in press; Vachek, 1979), recall and recognition
(Hildyard and Olson, in press; Horowitz, 1968; Sachs, 1974), production (Bereiter
and Scardamalia, 1980; Shuy, 1981; Hidi and Hildyard, 1980), and in terms of the
acquisition of literate competencies (Hildyard and Olson, in press; Ehri, in
press; Wells, in press).

In recent papers, Chafe (1981, in press) has argued that there are two basic
structural differences between written and oral language: written language has
an integrated quality while spoken language has a fragmentary quality; and,
written language is detached while spoken language assumes a social involvement.
Tannen (in press) expands these distinctions by adding that, in written language
cohesion is signalled through lexicalization (for example, conjunctions), while
in oral language such ties are signalled through paralinguistic or nonverbal
means.

With these and other distinctions in mind, Hildyard and Olson (in press) and
Sachs (1974) have looked at the recall of spoken and written language. Hildyard
and Olson, for example, had children in Grades 3 and 5 either read or listen to
a short narrative and then answer a series of questions. They found that the
readers were more accurate than the listeners, firstly, in terms of the recall of
non essential story information, and secondly, in terms of tne differentiation of
what was given in the narrative from what was inferred. These data led Hildyard
and Olson to argue that reading permits one to capitalize upon one component of
written language, namely its permanence, such that readers pay more attention to
the surface form of the sentences. Kintsch and Van Dijk (1978) have similarly
argued that reading/listening differences occur with respect to surface form,
although they further argue that modality differences do not occur at the semantion
level.

These suggested differences, in terms of recall and structure, are somewhat at variance with the results of studies aimed at the comparison of written and oral production. Gould (1980), for example, reports no differences between adults' written versus dictated business letters. Bereiter, Scardamalia and Goelman (in press) report similar findings for children, namely, that few qualitative differences exist between children's dictated versus written productions. These findings were essentially corroborated by Hidi and Hildyard (1980) who, in a study of Grade 3 and Grade 5 children's production of narratives and arguments, reported that although the oral protocols were significantly longer, both forms were equivalent in terms of semantic well-formedness. There was a tendency, however, for the written protocols to be more cohesive.

Why these discrepant findings? Why do differences emerge with respect to the recall and structure of spoken and written language, but not with respect to production? The purpose of the present study was to investigate further the relationship between the production and subsequent recall of narratives by children.

A basic assumption underlying this study is that the processes involved in the production of discourse are guided or determined by discourse schemata (cf. Kintsch, in press; Schallert, in press). It is also assumed that the schemata are genre specific, that is, that we have a production schema for informal conversations which is qualitatively different from the schema which guides the production of expository prose, (cf. Bereiter, et al, in press; Hidi and Hildyard, 1980). Hidi and Hildyard (1980) for example, found evidence of significant differences between the schema guiding the production of narratives and that guiding the production of arguments for children in Grades 3 and 5.

If it is the case, as suggested by Shuy (1980) that the production of a discourse type is not affected by modality, then we might assume that the schemata which guide that discourse production are modality general. On the other hand, since the recall of spoken language appears to be qualitatively different from the recall of written language, then it would appear that the schema for the recall of spoken language is different from that for written recall. We might question, therefore, what happens if one is required to recall one's own production. Do modality differences in recall still emerge even though the retrieval mechanisms are being applied to productions guided by modality general schemata?

To assess these questions, children in Grade 6 (12 years of age) were asked to produce a narrative, either in written or spoken form. Four days later the children were asked to recall their narratives, half of them in the same modality and half in the alternative modality. Being able to compare the structure of the discourse originally produced in one modality with the recall of the discourse in the same or alternative modalities, permits a closer examination of the effect of modality upon the instantiation and subsequent recall of a schema.

METHOD

Subjects: Thirty-six Grade 6 children were selected randomly from two Grade 6 classrooms.

Materials: In order to provide some control over the content and structure of the individual protocols, five narrative introductions were prepared

and each child was given one of these. The introductions (see Table 1)
contained information which served to introduce a main character and set
up an initiating event.

```
+-------------------------------------------------------------------------+
|                             Table 1                                     |
|                      The Story Introductions                           |
|                                                                         |
|   Once upon a time there was a king who was so greedy that no one really|
|   liked him.  Very early one morning the king heard someone knocking at |
|   his door.                                                             |
|                                                                         |
|   A long time ago there was a boy who was very selfish.  One morning    |
|   while he was out for a walk he saw something lying by the side of     |
|   the road.                                                             |
|                                                                         |
|   Once upon a time there was a fox who was so bad-tempered that he had  |
|   no friends.  One sunny morning the fox heard something tapping on his |
|   window.                                                               |
|                                                                         |
|   There was once a boy who was so friendly that he always had lots of   |
|   friends coming to visit him.  One day the boy opened his door and found|
|   someone there crying.                                                 |
|                                                                         |
|   Many years ago there lived a princess who was so shy that she never   |
|   spoke to anyone.  One day while out in the forest she heard someone   |
|   making a strange sound.                                               |
+-------------------------------------------------------------------------+
```

Procedure: The children were assigned to either the oral or the written
production groups. Those children in the oral group were seen individually. They were given a sheet on which was typed one of the five introductions. The child was asked to read the introduction and then to carry on
with the story. The child held the microphone and continued speaking until
he/she had indicated that the story was complete.

The children in the written group were seen in groups of nine. Each child
received a sheet with one of the five introductions and was asked to continue the story. The children wrote for as long as they wished.

Four days later the children were seen again. Half of the written group
were asked to rewrite their stories in exactly the same form as the
originals. They were given the appropriate introductions. The remaining
half of the written group were seen individually and asked to recall, into
a tape recorder, their original production. Again each child was given the
appropriate introduction.

Those children who had originally produced their narratives in an oral form
were also divided into two groups. Half of them were asked to recall their
original productions orally and the other half were asked to write the
recall. Both sets of children were provided with the appropriate introductions. The oral protocols, for both the original and the recall productions, were carefully transcribed.

Comparison of Original Protocols: The protocols from the original oral and
written productions were subjected to a series of analyses. These analyses
were directed towards both qualitative and quantitative dimensions, as
follows:

(i) Number of words: The number of words in each protocol were counted excluding exact repetitions and conversational "floor-holders", such as "um" from the oral protocols. The average length of the 18 written origin- als was 149 words. The average length of the 18 oral originals was 151 words. Clearly, there were no significant differences between the two sets of protocols.

(ii) <u>Number of idea units</u>: The number of idea units in each protocol were counted by two independent raters (86% agreement between raters). In general an idea unit consists of a clause (verb, subject, object, etc.) which contains one main verb. The written protocols were found to contain an average of 18 idea units and the oral protocols 19 units. Again, such differences are clearly not significant.

(iii) <u>Structure</u>: It has been argued by several researchers (e.g. Kintsch, 1977; Propp, 1968) that every story contains certain key elements including a setting with characters, a conflict and a resolution of that conflict. The protocols were rated with respect to the extent to which they contained these elements. Up to two points were awarded for an elaborated setting, up to two points for the introduction of the conflict and up to two points for the satisfactory resolution of that conflict. In addition, up to two further points were awarded to those students whose narratives served to tie together the structural components, for example, taking account of the fact that the king was greedy, the princess was shy, etc. The written protocols were awarded an average of 6.8 points (out of a maximum of eight points). While the oral protocols were awarded an average of 5.1 points. This difference was found to be highly significant ($p < 0.001$).

(iv) <u>Semantic well formedness</u>: Simply including the essential components of a story does not necessarily imply that the story will be interesting. Therefore, all protocols were rated on a five point scale for their semantic well formedness, taking into account the content of the story, how interesting/unique, etc. it was. The average score for the written protocols was 3.2 and that for the oral protocols 2.75. These differences were also highly significant ($p < 0.001$).

A summary of these measures is found in Table 2.

Table 2
Comparison of The Original Written
and the Original Oral Stories

	Written (N=18)	Oral (N=18)
Average Number of Words Produced	149	151
Average Number of Idea Units	18	19
Structure (Max. = 8)	6.8	5.1 **$p < 0.001$
Semantic Well Formedness (Max. = 5)	3.2	2.75 **$p < 0.001$

Contrary to earlier findings (Hidi and Hildyard, 1980), the oral and the written protocols were found to be equivalent in terms of the number of words and the number of idea units. This is surprising in the light of Chafe's most recent paper (in press) in which he argues that idea units in written language are longer than those in spoken language with the result that we would expect longer written protocols. Of course, Chafe conducted his research with adults and it may be that these Grade 6 students have not yet mastered the strategies of nominalizations, attributive adjectives and restricted relative clauses, etc. which Chafe suggests, are used to increase the informational content of the written idea units. In fact, the equivalence in length of the oral and written protocols might indicate that these children had a sense of the amount of information to be included in a story and that this was independent of modality (Frank Smith personal communication.)

With respect to the qualitative measures, these new data are quite differ-ent from those collected previously by Bereiter et al, Gould and Hidi and Hildyard. These new written protocols were not found to be qualitatively similar to the oral protocals but, rather, to be qualitatively superior. Several explanations may account for these data. Firstly, these children were older than those used in Hidi and Hildyard's previous study. Perhaps, as children get older, writing becomes a more automated process thereby encouraging productions which are both semantically and structurally better formed. That Gould found no qualitative differences between oral and written business letters may indicate that modality interacts with only some genres: that is, the constraints or parameters of some genres may override modality differences. Of course, it is also possible that schemata are modality specific, thus we have both an oral narrative schema and a written narrative schema. We prefer, however, to argue that the same discourse schema controls both oral and written productions, but that the process of writing, with its less time-constrained and slower rate of production, allows more precise, conscious decisions and repeated scanning which thereby facilitates the initiation and efficient performance of the controlling schema.

Comparison of the Originals with the Recall Protocols: Several analyses were conducted to compare the original productions with the recall pro-ductions, which were either in the same mode or the alternative mode.

The first analyses looked at the relationship between the idea units in the original and the idea units in the recall. Using the analysis of the original protocals into idea units as the basis, two independent raters looked for the occurrence of these idea units in the recall. The nature of the relationship was categorized as Verbatim (the surface form of the idea unit was retained), Partial Verbatim (some minor, non-semantic, differences occurred between the original and the recall), Paraphrase (the gist of the idea unit was retained but its surface form was altered), Omission (an idea unit in the original was not retained in the recall), Intrusion (an idea unit in the recall did not occur in the original).

Table 3 shows the percentage of occurrence of each of these categories across the four conditions (written original, written recall; written original, oral recall; oral original, written recall; oral original, oral recall).

Table 3
Percent* of Idea Units Recalled in Verbatim Form,
Paraphrase Form or Omitted together with percent of Intrusions
(*The percentages sum to more than 100% due to the Intrusions)

	** W.O./W.R. (N=9)	W.O./O.R. (N=9)	O.O./W.R. (N=9)	O.O./O.R. (N=9)
Verbatim	36%	18%	21%	14%
Partial Verbatim	28	28	20	28
Paraphrase	16	20	22	20
Omissions	21	32	42	39
Intrusions	6	11	5	19

** W.O. - Written Original   ** O.O. - Oral Original
   W.R. - Written Recall   O.R. - Oral Recall

These figures indicate that, first of all, the children did surprisingly
well in recalling the story content four days after the original productions: over 60% of the idea units originally produced were recalled. This,
of course, is in marked contrast to children's recall of school-type texts
(Hidi, Baird and Hildyard, this volume). Table 3 further shows that the
children who both produced and recalled in a written form recalled substantially more than the other three groups. It is, moreover, especially
interesting to note that the differences seem to occur at the verbatim and
partially verbatim levels, indicating that the writing process not only
enhances recall, but also enables students to pay closer attention to the
surface form.

Any idea unit not recalled in some verbatim form was classified as an
omission. The data shows that the number of idea units omitted depended
upon the modality of the original production: those children whose
original productions were oral, omitted significantly more of the idea
units than did those children whose original productions were written. An
analysis of the nature of these omissions showed that the majority were
elaborative omissions - that is, an idea unit which contained elaborative
detail would be omitted from the recall. To illustrate, one child's
original oral production contained the following: "The King got some gold
things. He got a pin, a bowl, a dish, and some jewellery. Later he ....".
The recall was as follows: "The king got some gold things. Later he ...".
In other words, the child left out the list of items, which, for this story,
simply provided non essential detail.

Approximately one third to one quarter of the omissions were classed as
central omissions, that is, the idea unit left from the recall was considered to be essential to the coherence of the story (cf. Hildyard and
Olson, 1978). As with the elaborative omissions, there were fewer central
omissions from the written originals than from the oral originals.

That the written original productions resulted in significantly fewer
elaborative and central omissions supports the suggestion that writing

permits one to focus more carefully upon the content and form of the narrative. Not only are the written originals structurally and semantically better formed, but the children are better able to recall the idea units contained therein. It would appear, then, that the effect of modality upon initial production and subsequent recall is additive: not only are the written originals superior, but recall in the same modality is more accurate.

A final analysis of the original and recall protocols concerned those idea units which were included in the recall but not the originals. Here we found the modality of recall to be important: significantly more intrusions occur for the oral recall than for the written recall. Thus, those children required to recall in a spoken form, tended to include more new information within their stories. It is interesting, however, to note that the number of intrusions was greater when the original had also been in the oral form, again suggesting that the act of writing that initial narrative focussed students' attention upon the specific content and not simply the gist of the story.

The protocols from two Grade 6 students - one in the written original and written recall group, and one from the oral original and oral recall group - are included to illustrate some of the issues presented above. Table 4 shows the written protocols. It is apparent that very little is modified over the four day period.

Table 4
An example of a written original and the child's
written recall of that narrative.

Original

Once upon a time there was a fox who was so bad-tempered that he had no friends. One sunny morning the fox heard something tapping on his window. He went to see what it was and no one was there. So he opened the door and saw that there was some bushes rustling. He went over to the bushes parted them and pssst he was got. He stank. He parted the bushes again and saw a skunk with glasses and a briefcase. He said "I am very sorry every time I bend down that happens and I had dropped my pen in the bushes". "Okay". "Now by the way I am an air freshener salesman, would you like to buy some"? Sorry I already have some". "Well I think you should use it because it smells pretty bad around here. Goodbye sir".

Recall

Once upon a time there was a fox who was so bad-tempered that he had no friends. One sunny morning the fox heard something tapping on his window. He looked out the window and didn't see anything so he opened the door and saw the bushes rustling. He went and parted the bushes and pssst he was got. He ducked then came and parted the bushes again and saw a skunk with glasses and a briefcase and he said, "I am very sorry that always happens when I bend and I had dropped my eraser in the bushes". Fox, "It's all right". "Oh by the way I am a salesman and I am selling air freshener would you like to buy some"? "No I already have some". "That's good because you really need it"!

The oral protocols in Table 5, on the other hand, do show substantial modifications.

Table 5
An example of an oral original and the child's oral recall of that narrative

Original

Once upon a time there was a fox who was so bad-tempered that he had no friends. One sunny morning the fox heard something tapping on his window. He jumped up from bed, all of a sudden when he heard, this fox because he was very hungry. He had had a restless night and was eager for something to eat. When he got to the window he found that it was a hare. So he went to the door and invited the hare in for some tea. As soon as the hare reached the door he grabbed it and held it with all his might. He put it in the box and kept it there and put some water on to boil. He skinned the hare and then put it in the pot and cut up some vegetables and put them in with the hare and set it into the oven. He let it cook for about half an hour, pulled it out, checked it and it still wasn't done so he put it in again. Finally when he thought it was done he took it out and realized then, (um) that it was a fake, it was a decoy.

So by that time he was very mad and ran out of the house and into the woods quickly killed a nearby owl and gobbled it up.

Recall

Once upon a time there was a fox who was so bad-tempered that he had no friends. One sunny morning the fox heard something tapping on his window. The fox was hungry after a good night's sleep and he jumped up from his bed to see who was at the door. He found a hare at the door and thinking very smart he invited the hare in for some tea. The hare got in the house (pause) and was invited to sit down, and instead of getting the fox some tea, he prepared a pot with potatoes and vegetables and then when he went to give him the tea, he grabbed at the fox - grabbed at the hare, and put him in the oven. And he let it cook for about an hour and took it out and checked it, and then put it back in - it wasn't cooked. After two more hours, he took it out and found no hare. The fox was very angry by this time and he had been deceived. And it was just a decoy. And he ran outside and seeing yet another hare and quickly killed it and ate it.

Note, for example, that the child confuses the role of the central character. In the original, the fox is always assumed to be the central character - the one doing the cooking and eating. In the recall the child first starts by having the fox as the central character, then changes to the hare and halfway through the narrative realizes that it was the fox who cooked the hare and not vice versa.

Summary

The intent of this paper was to look at the relationship between production and recall as they relate to modality, or, more precisely, to determine the effect of modality upon recall schemata which operate upon production schemata.

Contrary to earlier findings, it was found that Grade 6 students' written narrative productions were superior to oral narrative productions, leading to the suggestion that in writing one is able to capitalize upon the relative lack of time constraints by scanning and rereading, in order to produce a structurally more complete narrative. If later asked to recall that narrative, then more accurate recall results when the original production is written and the recall is written. This again suggests the notion that the writer is able to pay closer attention to both the structure and the form of the production than is the speaker, or, in Olson's (1977) terms, writing permits closer attention to what was explicitly mentioned.

These data, then do suggest that writing promotes differential encoding both at the production and at the retrieval stages. The extent to which such findings are age or genre specific remains to be seen.

References

Bereiter, C., Scardamalia, M., & Goelman, H. The role of production factors in writing. In M. Nystrand (Ed.) What Writers Know: The Language and Structure of Written Discourse. New York: Academic Press, (in press).

Bereiter, C., & Scardamalia, M. From conversation to composition: The role of instruction in a developmental process. In R. Glaser (Ed.) Advances in Instructional Psychology, (Vol. 2) Hillsdale, N.J.: Erlbaum Assoc., 1980.

Chafe, W. Integration and involvement in speaking. In D. Tannen (Ed.) Cohesion in Spoken and Written Language, Norwood, N.J.: Ablex, (in press).

Chafe, W. Linguistic differences produced by differences between speaking and writing. Paper presented at the Conference on the Consequences of Literacy, Stratford, Ontario, 1981.

Ehri, L. The effects of printed language acquisition on speech. In D.R. Olson, N. Tarrance, & A. Hildyard (Eds.) The Cognitive Consequences of Literacy, (in press).

Hidi, S., Baird, W., & Hildyard, A. That's important but is it interesting? Two factors in text processing (this volume).

Hidi, S., & Hildyard, A. The comparison of oral and written productions of two discourse types. Paper presented at the annual meeting of the American Educational Research Association, Boston, 1980.

Hildyard, A., & Olson, D.R. Forms of comprehension in texts. In W. Otto (Ed.) Reading Expository Material. New York: Academic Press, (in press).

Hildyard, A., & Olson, D.R. On the comprehension and memory of oral vs. written discourse. In D. Tannen (Ed.) Cohesion in Spoken and Written Language, Norwood, N.J.: Ablex, (in press).

Hildyard, A., & Olson, D.R. Memory and inference in the comprehension of oral and written discourse. Discourse Processes. 1978, 1, 91-117.

Gould, J.P. Experiments on composing letters: Some facts, some myths and some observations. In L.W. Gregg & E.R. Steinberg (Eds.) Cognitive Processes in Writing. Hillsdale, N.J.: Erlbaum Assoc., 1980.

Howowitz, M.W. Organizational processes underlying differences between listening and reading as a function of complexity of material. Journal of Communication, 1968, 18, 37-46.

Kintsch, W. Text representations. In W. Otto (Ed.) Reading Expository Material. New York: Academic Press, (in press).

Kintsch, W. On comprehending stories. In P. Carpenter & M. Just (Eds.) Cognitive Processes in Comprehension, Hillsdale, N.J.: Erlbaum Assoc., 1977.

Kintsch, W., & Van Dijk, T.A. Toward a model of text comprehension and production. Psychological Review, 1978, 85, 363-394.

Olson, D.R., & Hildyard, A. Literacy and the comprehension of literal meaning. In F. Coulmas (Ed.) Writing in Focus. Bielefeld: Universitat Dusseldorf, 1981.

Propp. V. Morphology of the Folktale. Austin: University of Texas Press, 1968.

Sachs, J. Memory in reading and listening to discourse. Memory and Cognition, 1974, 2, 95-100.

Schallert, D.L. Synthesis of research related to schema theory. In W. Otto (Ed.) Reading Expository Material, New York: Academic Press, (in press).

Shuy, R. Relating research on oral language function to research in written discourse. Paper presented at the annual meeting of AERA, Los Angeles, 1981.

Shuy, R. Question-asking strategies: Styles in the classroom. Paper presented at the annual meeting of AERA, Boston, 1980.

Tannen, D. Spoken and written narrative in English and Greek. In D. Tannen (Ed.) Cohesion in Spoken and Written Discourse. Norwood, N.J.: Ablex, (in press).

Vachek, J. Selected Writings in English and General Linguistics by Joseph Vachek. The Hague: Mouton, 1976.

Wells, G. Preschool literacy-related activities and success in reading. In D.R. Olson, N. Torrance, & A. Hildyard (Eds.) The Cognitive Consequences of Literacy, (in press).

DISCOURSE PROCESSING
A. Flammer and W. Kintsch (eds.)
© North-Holland Publishing Company, 1982

EFFECTS OF VERBAL AND PICTORIAL CONTEXT CUES
ON FREE RECALL AND CLUSTERING OF TEXT THEMES

Eugen Hinder

Department of Pedagogy
University of Fribourg
Switzerland

A total of 163 seventh-grade students read 16 prose passages
about types of sport which could be grouped according to two
alternative category systems of four categories each. Passages
were accompanied by either verbal or pictorial illustrations
representing the categorically related instances. Pictorial
illustrations improved free recall and free recall clustering.
The results indicated that picture adjuncts affected not only
the amount of retention but also its organization. It was suggested that pictorial illustrations provided a context within
which the prose passages could be more deeply processed.

INTRODUCTION

The present study deals with the examination of quantitative effects of picture adjuncts. Its main emphasis, however, is on the investigation of qualitative effects of pictorial illustrations. The question of interest is
whether illustrations affect not only the amount of retention but also its
organization. Dealing with qualitative effects may help increase our theo-
retical-psychological understanding of the efficacy of picture adjuncts.

A number of studies have demonstrated that appropriate visual illustrations
increase the amount of prose-learning; that is, pictures as prose-learning
adjuncts have a quantitative facilitative effect (for reviews, see e.g.,
Levin, 1976; Levin & Lesgold, 1977). A possible interpretation of this effect is that pictorial illustrations provide a context within which the verbal information can be more deeply processed, thus augmenting both comprehension and retention (e.g., Bransford & Johnson, 1972; Craik & Lockhart,
1972).
Some investigations have shown that providing contextual information such as
different titles (e.g., Schallert, 1976), learning goals (e.g., Gagné, Bing,
& Bing, 1977), or perspectives (e.g., Anderson & Pichert, 1978; Pichert &
Anderson, 1976) affected not only the amount of retention but also its organization: students who were given different contexts to the same content
organized their recall differently, always according to the provided
context. The crucial role of semantic context and its underlying processes
have been discussed by many investigators (e.g., Ausubel, 1960; Craik & Tulving, 1975; Frederiksen, 1975; Kozminsky, 1977; Paris & Lindauer, 1977; Van
Dijk, 1977) from various angles (advance organizer, schema, frame, macrostructure, schema-evoking context, ...). Contexts are assumed to activate
the relevant higher-level knowledge structure and to make the relations between the concrete text elements more intelligible. Thus a context enables
the learner to organize more effectively the passage information at the

moment of encoding and/or to reproduce the information in an organized manner during reconstructive recall.

Yet not only (contextual) information presented in addition to the text material (prior to or accompanying the text) were used as organizational cues
at encoding and/or recall, but also structural properties of the material.
Studies using conceptually organized material, especially learning elements
from "name x attribute" word matrices, consistently showed a recall advantage for both name and attribute organization over the randomly organized
passages; moreover, when measures of output organization were calculated,
clustering was higher for the conceptually organized passages than for the
random condition (for reviews, see e.g., Kulhavy, Schmid, & Walker, 1977;
Yekovich & Kulhavy, 1976). These results may be considered part of the
welldocumented effect which Bousfield (1953) called "categorical clustering". Presenting category instances in blocks, i.e., first presenting
all members of one category, then all members of another, and so on, augmented both categorical clustering and recall (e.g., Cofer, Bruce, &
Reicher, 1966). Obviously the learner was able to organize the information
according to the dimensions inherent in the passages; that is, the blocked
presentation of categorically related passages served as an organizational
cue by providing for the learner the superordinate category which in turn
was used as organizer and thus facilitated the acquisition and the clustering of the passages.

From these two lines of research one can conclude that what people remember
from a text and how they recall (group) its elements is influenced by both
the structure of the content (text organization) and the additional information (context organization). One purpose of the present study was to
show how learners can use such organizational cues to activate processes
that promote the recalling and clustering of prose material; furthermore
to investigate whether one of the two forms of organizational cues (text
organization or context organization) is more effective than the other.
Nevertheless the main purpose of this study was to ascertain whether pictorial context cues do have greater quantitative and qualitative effects than
verbal supplements.

METHOD

Subjects

The subjects were 170 male and female seventh-grade students (13 to 15
years) of the district schools of Duedingen and Wuennewil, State of Fribourg. Seven subjects were dropped from the analysis because they did not
complete all parts of the experimental task. The remaining 163 students
(92 males and 71 females; 46 secondary school, 55 intermediate school, and
62 senior elementary school) were randomly assigned to one of the eight
conditions.

Materials

(a) Text materials: The text material consisted of 16 short passages (approximately 55 words), each describing a type of sport. The name of each
sport was set as title. The 16 types of sport could be grouped into two
alternative category systems (Table 1).
The columns of the matrix represent the A-categories, the rows specify the
B-categories. Thus each type of sport could be exactly assigned to two categories (to one A-category and to one B-category), and each category con-

tained exactly four types of sport (category instances). Both category
names defining a particular type of sport appeared in the actual passage.

Table 1
Matrix of the types of sport

B \ A	WATER	LAWN/SOFT FIELD	HARD GROUND	ICE/SNOW
TEAM	Water polo	Rugby	Volleyball	Ice hockey
SHOOT	Gun/harpoon	Archery	Rifle shooting	Biathlon
JUMP	High diving	Horse jump	High jump	Ski jump
MOTOR	Motorboat	Motocross	Car racing	Snow mobiling

The main difficulty in constructing the matrix was to find eight categories
which were clearly distinguishable on the one hand and not too small (too
subtle) on the other and which could only contain four category instances.
(The choice of the category "TEAM sports" for instance meant that except
for the four team sports all the other types of sport had to be single
sports. The same thing applied to all the other categories.) Therefore the
chosen categories are rather heterogeneous. The homogeneity may be seen in
the sense that all A-categories refer to locations (place, ground, terrain)
on or in which the types of sport are practised, whereas the B-categories
are related instead to an activity (shoot, jump, drive).

The 16 passages resulting from Table 1 were grouped in two ways yielding
the Text Organizations A and B:
The sequence of the passages in Text Organization A corresponded to reading
down the first column of Table 1, then the second column, etc. The sequence
of the passages in Text Organization B corresponded to reading across the
top row of Table 1, then across the second row, etc.

(b) Context cues: Contextual cues were either pictures or words. The
pictures were 16 black-and-white line-drawings (6 x 8 cm), each illustrating a type of sport.
According to Table 1 four pictures were always combined to form a context
cue for that category. For instance, the pictures "High diving", "Horse
jump", "High jump", and "Ski jump" formed the pictorial context cue "JUMP
sports" (Figure 1); the pictures "Water polo", "Gun/harpoon", "High diving",
and "Motorboat" defined the context cue "WATER sports".

The 16 names of the types of sport, which were written in rectangles of the
same format of a picture, served as verbal adjuncts. Analogous to the pictorial context cues the names were combined to form verbal context cues.

Corresponding to the two-by-four categories of Table 1, eight pictorial and
eight verbal context cues were constructed which were grouped into two
Context Organizations: Context Organization A consisted of the context cues
"WATER", "LAWN/SOFT FIELD", "HARD GROUND", and "ICE/SNOW"; Context Organization B included the context cues "TEAM", "SHOOT", "JUMP", and "MOTOR".

(c) Presentation of the text passages and context cues: Each
type of sport was presented on one page (DIN A4); the context cue was displayed in the upper half, the text passage in the lower part. This is how

an experimental book of 16 pages was formed. White blank sheets (DIN A5) were put between the experimental pages to cover the passages. Thus at first only the context cue could be seen (as advance organizer) then, after turning the interleaved blank sheet, both context cue and text passage were presented together.

The type of sport described in the passage appeared in the context cue always in the upper left position; the other three types of sport were arranged counter-clockwise according to their appearance in the sequence of the passages.

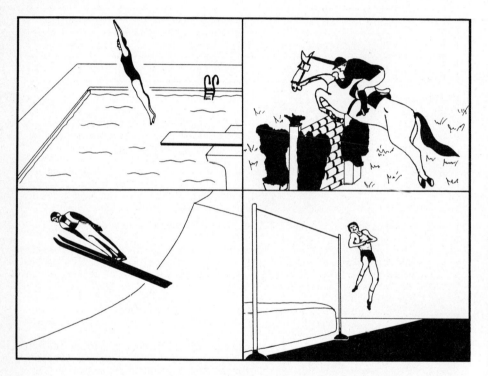

Figure 1
Example of a pictorial context cue, "JUMP sports"

Design

A 2 x 2 x 2 factorial design was used to get eight experimental conditions.

Factor 1: Context (pictorial vs. verbal); pictorial or verbal context cues were used.

Factor 2: Context Organization (A vs. B); the context cues illustrated the A- or B-categories.

Factor 3: Text Organization (A vs. B); the sequence of passages corresponded to reading down the columns (A) or across the rows (B) of Table 1.

The eight experimental conditions are represented by Figure 2: Each rectangle stands for one page of the experimental materials.

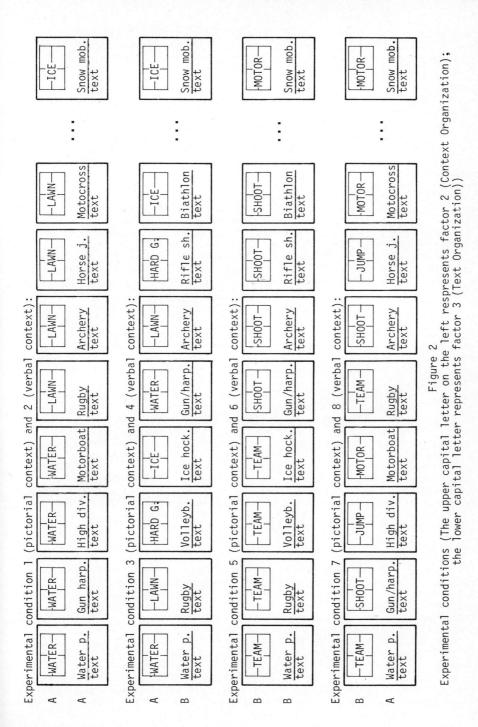

Figure 2

Experimental conditions (The upper capital letter on the left respresents factor 2 (Context Organization); the lower capital letter represents factor 3 (Text Organization))

Looking at the relation "Context Organization" and "Text Organization", we see that on the one side the experimental conditions 1, 2, 5, 6 are to be considered equivalent with each other as are on the other side the conditions 3, 4, 7, 8:

In the first case, the identical categorical organization is provided twice: once by the Context Organization and secondly by the Text Organization. Since merely presenting categorically similar passages in blocks has been shown to result in clustered recall, it was expected that the types of sport would be processed and recalled according to this twofold organization; that is, grouping by A for conditions 1 and 2, and grouping by B for conditions 5 and 6. Therefore context cues should at least contribute towards providing an organizational context.
In the second case (conditions 3, 4, 7, 8), the Text Organization provided one category system, while the alternative category system was illustrated by the Context Organization. Basically this combination permits processing by Text Organization or by Context Organization. Because of the prior presentation of the context cues, Context Organization was assumed to function as advance organizer, and therefore recall was expected to be clustered predominantly according to Context Organization. Hence, context cues were supposed to play the leading role in organizational processing in the sense that they require the reorganization of the alternatively presented passages.

Procedure and Instructions

The students participated in a single session held in a large regular classroom. The students were seated far apart from each other. Questions concerning procedures to be followed were answered. The experimental booklets were distributed randomly, envelopes containing the interpolated task and sheets of paper for free recall were placed on the chair next to each subject's chair. In addition to the 16 experimental pages, the booklet of material included an introduction telling the students that they would be reading 16 passages about types of sport. (Thus subjects were not told to expect a subsequent recall.) Following the study interval, learners were required to solve 20 arithmetic problems (complete numerical series) to preclude recall from short-term memory. The interpolated task was followed by the first free recall of types of sport. For the second free recall, immediately afterwards, subjects were informed of the probability of remembering more types of sport by writing down related types of sport in groups or category clusters. Neither of these tasks was subject to time constraints. Finally students were asked about their age, sex, type of school, participation and interest in sports.

Scoring

The dependent variables were free recall scores and free recall clustering. Free recall was considered to be the most appropriate measure to use in studying organizational processes in memory.
The free recall scores (T) were simply the total number of types of sports recalled. To measure categorical clustering in the subjects' free-recall protocols, the Frase (1969) clustering index was used as follows:
Index A measures the degree to which types of sport were remembered in their A-categories, i.e., on how often types of sport refering to the same A-category were recalled in order. Alternatively, index B indicates the percentage to which the recall was clustered by the B-categories. To compute index A, first of all the recalled types of sport were labelled with the A-categories they belonged to corresponding to Table 1. Then the amount

of clustering by A was expressed by counting the number of times an A-category was repeated consecutively (R_A) and dividing by the total number of
recalled types of sport (T) minus the number of A-categories used (K_A). For
example:

Water polo — Motorboat — High diving — Motocross — Rugby — Hockey — Ski jump
≙ WATER   ≙ WATER   ≙ WATER   ≙ LAWN   ≙LAWN   ≙ ICE   ≙ ICE

This example includes two repetitions of WATER, one repetition of LAWN, and
one repetition of ICE. There are three A-categories, therefore index A =
(R_A/(T-K_A)) x 100 = (4/(7-3)) x 100 = 100%. A similar index can be computed
for clustering by B. For all protocols, index A and B were computed.

The indices are also useful for determining the clustering of the presented
material. The percentages of Text Organization by A and by B were:
For the experimental conditions 1, 2, 7, 8: index A = 100%, index B =   0%
For the experimental conditions 3, 4, 5, 6: index A =   0%, Index B = 100%

RESULTS AND DISCUSSION

For the statistical computations, only the second free-recall protocols
were used. Statistical procedures were a three-factorial analysis of variance (BMDP 2V) and Scheffé's (1953) S method.

Recall

A three-factor (Context x Context Organization x Text Organization) analysis
of variance was performed on total types of sport recalled. The analysis
was significant only for the Context main effect, $F(1, 155) = 29.58$,
$p < .0001$. The mean number of types of sport recalled was 10.95 for the verbal context and 13.19 for the pictorial context.

Once again the quantitative (facilitative) effect of picture adjuncts was
confirmed. This result is unique on the one hand because the text material
contained (possibly familiar) factual information (most research has used
passages consisting of fictional narratives, i.e., unfamiliar information)
and on the other hand because retention was measured by free recall. Thus
this study tends to support the notion of the universal efficacy of pictorial illustration, in contradiction to Levin and Lesgold's (1977) statement
that "Our own problems with free-recall measures, for example, have shown
us that the efficacy of a picture adjunct is not universal".

Additional analyses (Table 2) showed that pictorial illustrations as compared with verbal illustrations enhanced recall for both females and males.
The amount of retention was consistently higher for males than females, by
about two types of sport. Neither type of school nor interest in sports account for this difference. Nevertheless this difference could be explained
by the actual familiarity with sports (knowledge about sports) of the females vs. males, in the sense that females estimate themselves to be more
interested in sports than they actually are in comparison with males.
Furthermore secondary school students, intermediate school students as well
as seniors of the elementary school profitted from pictorial illustrations
(Table 2). The three types of school represent different intellectual levels.
The students had been assigned to their type of school according to their
proven intellectual performance (marks in the preceding year and final test
results in German and Mathematics at the end of the same year), and according to their estimated intellectual potential (teacher's judgment, IQ-test).

The best students had been assigned to the secondary school (8%), the intermediate to the intermediate school (49.5%), and the intellectually poor students to the senior elementary school (42.5%). With this background, the study shows the generality of the efficacy of picture adjuncts across sex and intellectual ability.

In the same way, students with no, moderate, and great interest in sports (as measured by an attitude scale) used the facilitative effect of pictorial illustrations (Table 2).

Table 2

Mean number of types of sport recalled for sex, type of school (ELEM = senior elementary school, INT = intermediate school, SEC = secondary school), and interest in sports as a function of Context (V = verbal context cues, P = pictorial context cues)

	SEX girls		boys		TYPE OF SCHOOL ELEM		INT		SEC		INTEREST IN SPORTS no		moderate		great	
	n	$\bar{x}$	n	$\bar{x}$	n	$\bar{x}$	n	$\bar{x}$	n	$\bar{x}$	n	$\bar{x}$	n	$\bar{x}$	n	$\bar{x}$
V	38	9.84	42	11.95	33	9.87	26	11.03	21	12.52	6	9.50	41	10.56	33	11.69
P	33	11.69	50	14.18	29	13.03	29	13.13	25	13.44	2	15.50	38	12.84	43	13.39
F	10.98**		20.48**		24.17**		9.50**		1.50^{ns}		8.15**		15.54**		8.18*	

** = p < .01;   * = p < .05;   ns = non significant

The interpretation of the reported results is that pictorial illustrations provide a more effective organization, a more useful context within which the text material could be more appropriately structured than verbal illustrations. The resulting organization induced then, according to Craik & Lockhart (1972), a more deeper processing of the material.

Clustering

A Context x Context Organization x Text Organization analysis of variance on total clustering (index A plus index B) again showed significance only for the Context variable, $F(1, 155) = 6.94$, p<.001. The means for the verbal and pictorial context cues were 77.15% and 84.17%, respectively.

The essential outcome of this study is that pictorial context cues not only have quantitative but also qualitative effects: students reading categorically related passages which were accompanied by pictorial illustrations clustered their recall more than students whose passages were illustrated by verbal context cues. The qualitative effect of picture adjuncts is explained as a context effect: pictorial illustrations afforded an organizational context which enabled the learner to process the textual information semantically, i.e., to organize effectively the text information at encoding and/or to reproduce the information in an organized manner at reconstructive recall.

An identical analysis of clustering by A and clustering by B yielded significance for the Context Organization ($F(1, 155) = 13.71$, p < .0003 for index A, and $F(1, 155) = 23.03$, p < .0001 for index B) and for the Context x Context Organization interaction ($F(1, 155) = 12.69$, p < .0005 for index A, and $F(1, 155) = 17.52$, p < .0001 for index B). The means were 34.84% and 45.90% for index A and B, respectively.

With verbal context cues the difference between the two organizations was not significant, with a mean index A = 35.90% and a mean index B = 41.25%. For the pictorial context cues clustering by B was significantly higher (50.97%) than clustering by A (33.32%), $F(1, 150) = 16.45$, $p < .01$.

Thus both category systems were used as organizational cues; they can be designated alternative category systems. Indeed the category systems were not equivalent. The superiority of the B-categories is text-specific (content-dependent) in that they are more unequivocal, apparently.

A second series of analyses was aimed at determining the degree to which context cues are used (a) when Context Organization and Text Organization are identical, (b) when Context Organization and Text Organization are alternative, and (c) when (a) and (b) are contrasted.

(a) To answer this question, those experimental conditions were put together in which Context Organization and Text Organization provided the same category system: these are conditions 1 and 2 in which the A-categories were provided and conditions 5 and 6 in which the B-categories were provided. Clustering by Context Organization and Text Organization is compared with clustering by the alternative (neither provided by Context Organization nor by Text Organization) category system. The upper part of Table 3 presents the means.

Table 3
Mean values (clustering indices) for the Context x Context Organization x Text Organization interaction

	Context	n	clustering by Context Org.	alternative clustering
Context Organization and Text Organization are identical	pictorial	41	60.58	23.38
	verbal	39	44.67	35.49
Context Organization and Text Organization are alternative	pictorial	42	59.32	25.31
	verbal	41	34.48	40.12

When Context Organization and Text Organization provided the identical categories, the types of sport were more often recalled according to these categories than according to the alternative categories. This was true for the pictorial context cues: $F (1, 66) = 36.16$, $p < .01$. Surprisingly enough for the verbal context cues the difference was not significant: $F (1, 62) = 2.09$. Apparently, the students who had been given verbal context cues were not able to recognize and use the twice provided categories as organizational cues. From this one can conclude that these learners were in a situation comparable to a random presentation of the passages without accompanying context cues. Hence the learners were forced to search for appropriate categories. They then used categories they knew from previous experience or the other categories, i.e., categories from both systems. (This assumption may be tested with a randomized presentation of the passages.) From these results, it was not surprising that the difference in clustering between pictorial and verbal context cues was significant too: $F(1, 64) = 6.44$, $p < .05$.
(b) With the experimental conditions 3, 4, 7, 8 the question was investigated whether the Context Organization is also used as organizational cue

when it provided the alternative category system to the Text Organization.
The means are also shown in Table 3, lower part. As expected, clustering by
Context Organization was higher than clustering by Text Organization when
pictorial context cues were presented: $F(1, 68) = 30.95$, $p < .01$. Contrary
to expectation, students supplied with verbal context cues grouped a little
more by Text Organization than by Context Organization: $F(1, 66) = .83$.

This result suggests that pictorial context cues apparently have a leading
function in organizational processing: passages corresponding to the Text
Organization were not recalled by this category system but were reorganized
and grouped according to the organization provided by the pictorial context
cues.
The difference of clustering by Context Organization between verbal and pictorial illustrations was also significant: $F(1, 67) = 16.31$, $p < .01$.

(c) The comparison of conditions 1, 2, 5, 6 and conditions 3, 4, 7, 8 allows
one to determine whether the Context Organization is equally effective regardless of whether the identical or the alternative categories were provided by the Text Organization. The results (Table 3) indicate that with
pictorial illustrations clustering by Context Organization is just as high
regardless of whether the Text Organization afforded the identical categories (60.58%) or the alternative categories (59.32%), $F(1, 67) = .04$.
For the verbal illustrations, the difference was not significant ($F(1, 64)$
$= 2.64$); the means were 44.67% and 34.48% when Context Organization and
Text Organization were identical and alternative, respectively.

Thus pictorial context cues are used as organizational cues regardless of
the organization of the passages they accompany. The Text Organization seems
not to influence the organizational efficacy of pictorial context cues.
(This assumption may also be tested with a randomized presentation of the
passages.)
As a matter of fact, when verbal context cues were provided neither Context
Organization nor Text Organization were used as organizational cues. It is
possible that presenting the category names instead of presenting the related category instances would produce better results.

REFERENCES

Anderson, R. C., & Pichert, J. W. Recall of previously unrecallable informa-
    tion following a shift in perspective. Journal of Verbal Learning and
    Verbal Behavior, 1978, 17, 1-12.

Ausubel, D. P. The use of advance organizers in the learning and retention
    of meaningful verbal material. Journal of Educational Psychology, 1960,
    51, 267-272.

Bousfield, W. A. The occurence of clustering in the recall of randomly ar-
    ranged associates. Journal of General Psychology, 1953, 49, 229-240.

Bransford, J. D., & Johnson, M. K. Contextual prerequisites for understan-
    ding: Some investigations of comprehension and recall. Journal of Verbal
    Learning and Verbal Behavior, 1972, 11, 717-726.

Cofer, C. N., Bruce, D. R., & Reicher, G. M. Clustering in free recall as a
    function of certain methodological variations. Journal of Experimental
    Psychology, 1966, 71, 858-866.

Craik, F. I. M., & Lockhart, R. S. Levels of processing: A framework for memory research. Journal of Verbal Learning and Verbal Behavior, 1972, 11, 671-684.

Craik, F. I. M., & Tulving, E. Depth of processing and the retention of words in episodic memory. Journal of Experimental Psychology: General, 1975, 104, 268-294.

Frase, L. T. Paragraph organization of written materials: The influence of conceptual clustering upon the level and organization of recall. Journal of Educational Psychology, 1969, 60, 394-401.

Frederiksen, C. H. Effects of context-induced processing operations on semantic information acquired from discourse. Cognitive Psychology, 1975, 7, 139-166.

Gagné, E. D., Bing, S. B., & Bing, J. R. Combined effect of goal organization and test expectations on organization in free recall following learning from text. Journal of Educational Psychology, 1977, 69, 428-431.

Kozminsky, E. Altering comprehension: The effect of biasing titles on text comprehension. Memory and Cognition, 1977, 5, 482-490.

Kulhavy, R. W., Schmid, R. F., & Walker, C. H. Temporal organization in prose. American Educational Research Journal, 1977, 14, 115-123.

Levin, J. R. What have we learned about maximizing what children learn? In J. R. Levin & V. L. Allen (Eds.), Cognitive learning in children: Theories and strategies. New York: Academic Press, 1976.

Levin, J. R., & Lesgold, A. M. On pictures in prose. Theoretical Paper No. 69. Madison, Wisc.: Wisconsin Research and Development Center of Cognitive Learning, 1977.

Paris, S. G., & Lindauer, B. K. Constructive aspects of children's comprehension and memory. In R. V. Kail, Jr. & J. W. Hagen (Eds.), Perspectives on the development of memory and cognition. Hillsdale, N.J.: Lawrence Erlbaum Associates, 1977.

Pichert, J. W., & Anderson, R. C. Taking different perspectives on a story. Journal of Educational Psychology, 1977, 69, 309-315.

Schallert, D. L. Improving memory for prose: The relationship between depth of processing and context. Journal of Verbal Learning and Verbal Behavior, 1976, 15, 621-632.

Van Dijk, T. A. Semantic macro-structures and knowledge frames in discourse comprehension. In M. A. Just & P. A. Carpenter (Eds.), Cognitive processes in comprehension. Hillsdale, N.J.: Lawrence Erlbaum Associates, 1977.

Yekovich, F. R., & Kulhavy, R. W. Structural and contextual effects in the organization of prose. Journal of Educational Psychology, 1976, 68, 626-635.

ATTENTION AND CONTROL

DISCOURSE PROCESSING
A. Flammer and W. Kintsch (eds.)
© *North-Holland Publishing Company, 1982*

ALLOCATION OF ATTENTION DURING READING

Richard C. Anderson

Center for the Study of Reading
University of Illinois
Urbana-Champaign, Illinois
U.S.A.

This paper examines the theory that important text
information is better learned than less important
information because readers devote more attention to
important information. Previous research showing that
more attention is paid to important information is
inconclusive because the extra attention could be an
epiphenomenon. New research indicates that attention
is on the causal path between adjunct questions and
learning, but is not on the causal path between the
interestingness of the material and learning.

Perhaps the most consistent finding of research on discourse is that any
factor which would be said to make a text element "important" leads to better learning and recall of that element. An attractive theory to explain
this fact is that readers selectively attend to important elements. The
following is a simple version of this theory.
  (1) Text elements are processed to some minimal level and graded
       for importance.
  (2) Extra attention is devoted to elements in proportion to their
       importance.
  (3) Because of the extra attention, or a process supported by the
       extra attention, important text elements are learned better
       than other elements.
For shorthand reference, I will call this Theory I. The essential point of
Theory I is that the importance of a text element influences learning
because it influences attention. Evaluating Theory I is the major purpose
of this paper.

Before proceding I wish to acknowledge that my thinking about attention has
been influenced by the work of many other scientists, notably Daniel
Kahneman, Bruce Britton, Ernst Rothkopf, and David Navon, who was a visitor
in my laboratory last year. I particularly wish to acknowledge the important role played by my collaborators, Larry Shirey, Paul Wilson, and--
especially--Ralph Reynolds.

RIVALS TO A THEORY OF SELECTIVE ATTENTION

The first thing to recognize is that the importance of a text element may
affect other processes instead of, or in addition to, influencing attention.
Specifically, important text elements may be more retrievable than less
important text elements. This possibility is especially plausible when a
segment of text is "important" because of its role in a story schema

(Yekovich & Thorndyke, 1981), an author's high level organization of a text (Britton, Meyer, Simpson, Holdredge, & Curry, 1979), or any other schema that a reader has somehow been induced to bring to bear on a text (Anderson & Pichert, 1978). There is now considerable support for a theory which says that readers use their schemas for top-down searches of memory. In this theory, the typical schema is assumed to be a hierarchical structure. Important text information is represented at high level nodes in the structure and is, therefore, very likely to be retrieved in a top-down search. Less important information is represented at lower nodes, the search path is longer, and the information is less likely to be turned up.

Thus, one rival to Theory I is that the importance of a text element affects retrieval. In addition, Theory I has at least one plausible rival with respect to learning. I have previously called this rival "ideational scaffolding" theory in deference to David P. Ausubel (1963, 1968), one of the pioneers in theorizing about cognitive structures. The essential idea in this theory is that the schema to which a text is being assimilated contains slots, or niches, for certain kinds of information. What a reader tries to do is find the information in the text that fills the slots or fits into the niches. Ordinarily, the theory further supposes, to identify that a text element goes in a slot is tantamount to learning this information. In other words, whereas Theory I supposes that learning is a capacity-intensive process, the ideational scaffolding idea, as I have elaborated it, is one realization of the position that salient or distinctive information can come to be stored in long-term memory with little expenditure of cognitive resources.

Consider an illustration of how ideational scaffolding might work. To assimilate the following vignette, it may be supposed that readers would employ a Who Done It schema.

> Detective Lieutenant Bill Roberts bent over the corpse. It was apparent the victim had been stabbed. Roberts searched the room looking for evidence. There, near the foot of the bed, partly covered by a newspaper, he discovered the butcher knife.

The question is whether extra cognitive capacity will be devoted to processing the important information expressed by "the butcher knife." Presumably the Murder Weapon occupies an important slot in the Who Done It schema. Furthermore, the second sentence of the text constrains the murder weapon to a sharp instrument and a knife is a good example of a sharp instrument. The fact that the definite article in the phrase, "the butcher knife," strikes most readers as acceptable usage is an additional indication that a knife can be presupposed as given information. Thus, there is a slot established in the schema for which a knife is a leading candidate by the time the butcher knife is mentioned. As a consequence, it does seem as though the information about the knife ought to be readily assimilated. In accord with ideational scaffolding theory, there does not appear to be any good reason why the information ought to require, or will receive, extra attention.

Another alternative to Theory I has been formulated by Kintsch and van Dijk, (1978). They have theorized that important propositions are maintained in working memory throughout more processing "cycles" than less important ones. This is a kind of selective attention theory, since Kintsch and van Dijk hypothesize that important propositions are more memorable because of the greater amount of processing they receive. However, the extra attention is not given when the proposition is initially encountered, but rather is said to come later when subsidiary propositions are being processed.

RELATED RESEARCH

Attention during reading is currently a very active area of inquiry. I will
not attempt an exhaustive review. Instead I will discuss only a few
studies, ones that bear on Theory I and the more general issue of whether
both encoding and retrieval processes need to be postulated to explain the
effects of importance on recall.

Rothkopf and Billington (1979) conducted three experiments that clearly
invite interpretation in terms of a simple selective attention theory such
as Theory I. They asked high school students to memorize highly specific
learning objectives before studying a 1,500 word passage on oceanography.
Readers got either five or ten objectives, each relevant to a single readily
identifiable sentence in the passage. For instance, one of the learning
objectives was, *What is the name of the scale used by oceanographers when
recording the color of water?* The sentence in the text that satisfied the
objective was, *Oceanographers record the color of the ocean by comparison
with a series of bottles of colored water known as the Forel scale.* The
data confirmed that students who read with objectives in mind spent more
time on sentences relevant to these objectives and less time on ones not
relevant to the objectives than did students who read without objectives.
In the third experiment, patterns of eye movements were found to be consistent with the reading time results. In each study subjects learned and
remembered substantially more information relevant to assigned objectives.
These experiments produced exactly the results that would be expected on
the basis of Theory I.

Cirilo and Foss (1980) have reported two experiments that are also consistent with a selective attention theory. Time to read sentences was assessed
when the sentences were of high importance in one story and low importance
in another. The sentence, *He could no longer talk at all*, was highly important in a story in which it described the effect of a witch's curse on a
wise king. The same sentence was of low importance in a story in which it
described the momentary reaction of a simple soldier upon hearing that he
would receive a large reward for finding a precious ring. In both experiments Cirilo and Foss found that readers spent more time on a sentence when
it played an important role in a story.

Other investigators have collected data which suggests that readers selectively invest cognitive capacity to integrate the information in higher-order
units of text. Haberlandt, Berian, and Sandson (1980) found that, after
discounting variations in wording and syntax, readers spend extra time at
the beginning and the end of story episodes. These results imply that
readers have tacit knowledge of an episode schema, and that they use the
schema as a guide for allocating attention. In a parallel vein, Just and
Carpenter (1980) studied the eye movements of people reading expository
texts. Gaze durations were longer on sections marked as important in a
simple text grammar. For instance, the eyes rested longer on phrases
expressing a Definition, Cause, or Consequence than on phrases expressing
Details. Again, the implication is that readers possess textual schemata
that assist them in determining where to pay close attention.

One study that has yielded results inconsistent with Theory I was completed
by Britton, Meyer, Simpson, Holdredge, and Curry (1979). They used two
versions of a text on the energy crisis. In one, according to Meyer's
(1975) analysis, a paragraph on the breeder reactor was high in the content

structure; the passage said the fast breeder reactor is the solution to energy problems. In the context of the other passage, the paragraph was low in the content structure; the breeder reactor is only one of five possible solutions to the energy crisis. Subjects recalled more information from the critical paragraph when it was of high importance. However, they took the same amount of time to read the critical paragraph and the same amount of time to react to secondary task probes regardless of the paragraph's importance. Hence, the selective attention hypothesis was not supported.

Britton and his collaborators theorized that the superior recall of the critical paragraph when it was of higher importance was due to a memory process. However, this negative inference is sound only if it is assumed that the process of selectively encoding text information is necessarily capacity-intensive, and this assumption must be rejected if possibilities such as the ideational scaffolding hypothesis are entertained.

In summary, most of the available evidence is consistent with a simple selective attention theory such as Theory I.

DOES ATTENTION CAUSE LEARNING?

Causal arguments have a nasty tendency to crumble in your hands when you examine them closely. Even the strongest evidence in support of Theory I, say the Rothkopf and Billington (1979) data on learning objectives, falls short of being decisive. Objectives did influence measures of attention and objectives did influence learning, but this does not prove that attention was on the causal path between objectives and learning. The causal theory can be diagramed as follows:

Objectives⟶Attention⟶Learning.

The problem is, as Rothkopf and Billington carefully noted, that the evidence is also consistent with the interpretation that the effect of objectives on the measures of attention is an epiphenomenon. The rival interpretation can be diagramed in the following manner:

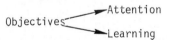

Neither the Rothkopf and Billington studies, nor any of the other studies reviewed in the preceding section, permits a data-driven choice between the interpretations of the type represented in the two diagrams.

There is widespread slackness in evaluating causal arguments in psychological and educational research. The general case is the claim that an independent variable, x, causes changes in dependent variable, y, because of an influence on a mediating variable, m. There are at least four entailments of a causal argument of this form. Other things being equal the causal argument implies:
(1) x is related to y
(2) x is related to m
(3) m is related to y
(4) when the relations of x to m and m to y are discounted, x is no longer related to y.
Customarily only entailments (1) and (2) are evaluated. Then a conclusion is reached, almost always in favor of the causal argument, based on the "weight of the evidence" and the failure to take seriously the possibility that the relation of x to m could be an epiphenomenon. In the research

summarized in the next sections of this paper my collaborators and I attempted to evaluate Theory I in terms of all four of the entailments on a causal theory listed above.

THE CONCEPT OF A VOLUME OF ATTENTION

Kahneman (1973, p. 25) has remarked that "... much of our mental life appears to be carried out at the pace of a sedate walk." One advantage of a "sedate walk" is that it requires less effort at any moment in time than a brisker pace. One disadvantage is that it takes longer to reach a destination if you walk than if you jog or sprint. Extending this analogy, no doubt people sometimes are willing to race their minds in order to save time or complete mental work within available time. Indeed, for just this reason it is commonplace in research on attention to place subjects under time pressure. Reading, however, is naturally a self-paced activity and placing readers under time pressure may fundamentally alter the phenomenon. A better policy is to directly face the fact that a reader may be able to maintain the volume of attention needed to comprehend a text by varying either amount of cognitive effort or the duration of processing.

One purpose of the research summarized in the following sections was to examine the utility of the concept of a "volume" of attention. The crux of this idea is that the total amount of attention a reader brings to bear is a joint function of duration, reflected in reading time, and level of cognitive effort, reflected in time to perform a secondary task. A minimum first requirement, if the approach is to have any value, is for the two measures to be at least somewhat independent. It is not obvious that they will be since both are measures of time.

An implication of the volume concept is that there can be trade-offs between duration and effort paralleling those between speed and accuracy. A reader who extends the duration of processing can keep the level of cognitive effort low. Conversely, a reader who invests a great deal of effort can reduce duration.

OVERVIEW OF METHOD

Three lines of research will be summarized in the following sections. Each investigated whether the effects of a factor which made certain text elements important could be explained in terms of selective attention. The three factors for inducing importance were adjunct questions, the interestingness of the reading material, and the assignment of perspectives prior to reading. The definition of importance was deliberately broad in order to provide a quick route for establishing, or rejecting, a parsimonious general theory.

It is a safe bet that many levels of linguistic analysis make demands on cognitive capacity (Graesser, Hoffman, & Clark, 1980; Just & Carpenter, 1980). Thus, in a program of research such as the present one, it is essential to control for such factors as lexical difficulty, syntactic complexity, and text cohesion. In the adjunct question and perspectives studies, this was done by counterbalancing; what was an important text element under one condition was unimportant under another. Counterbalancing was not possible in the interest study; in this case, variables affecting language difficulty were factored out using regression techniques.

In the present studies, subjects read from the screen of a computer terminal. The first measure was reading time, which is assumed to reflect duration of attention other things being equal. The computer made possible accurate measurement of time to read text segments. The second measure was time to perform a secondary task. Subjects were told that comprehending the text was their primary task. They were also told to depress a key as quickly as they could whenever a tone sounded through earphones they were wearing. We made the conventional assumption that variations in time to respond to the secondary task probes reflected the extent to which the mind was occupied with the primary task. In other words, probe time was taken to be a reflection of the proportion of cognitive capacity being devoted to reading.

Secondary task probes appeared during the reading of about 50% of the text segments. Placement of the probes was a problem since subjects read at their own rate (except in two conditions in the adjunct questions experiment). It is well-known that there are large individual differences in reading rate as well as systematic and not so systematic changes in rate throughout a text. Getting a secondary task probe to occur in a certain place during the processing of a certain text segment can be likened to throwing a dart at a moving target. Our solution was to program the computer to present the probes on the basis of a continuously updated calculation of each subject's reading rate. This works fairly well if the criterion is simply to get a probe to occur within the boundaries of a reader's processing of a given text segment.

ADJUNCT QUESTIONS AND ATTENTION

It is well-established that occasionally asking people questions while they are reading has both a strong "direct" effect and a small but reliable "indirect" effect on the learning of text information. The direct effect is simply the improvement in performance observed when the questions are repeated on the posttest. The indirect effect is so called because readers do better on new posttest items even when the answers cannot be deduced from the adjunct questions. For instance, knowing that a *bathescape* is a special type of submarine used in oceanographic research cannot directly help in determining that a *thermister chain* is an instrument which records water temperature at all depths while being towed behind a vessel. Nonetheless, Rothkopf and Bisbicos (1967), and a number of subsequent investigators, have shown that when questions of a readily identifiable type are asked during reading, performance improves on test items that are of the same type but which do not overlap in specific content.

The leading explanation for the indirect effect of questions is that readers pay more attention to segments of the text that contain information of the type addressed by the questions. The best available explanation of the direct effects of questions is that the questions permit mental review and further rehearsal. Presumably some of the direct effect is also attributable to increased attention to sections of the text containing question-relevant information.

There is experimental evidence consistent with a selective attention interpretation of the effects of adjunct questions. Reynolds, Standiford, and Anderson (1979) showed that subjects who received questions of a certain type spent more time on parts of the text containing information of this type than subjects who received questions of other types or subjects who read without questions. Britton, Piha, Davis, and Wehauson (1978) found that people who received questions took longer to respond to secondary task probes as well as taking longer to read.

While the results of two studies just reviewed are consistent with Theory I, neither provides decisive evidence. Reynolds and Anderson (in press) sought to provide a stronger test, one that could distinguish between the theory that attention is on the causal path between questions and learning and the possibility that deflection in measures of attention is an epiphenomenon. Seventy-seven college students were asked either questions that could be answered with a technical item, questions that could be answered with proper names, or no questions after every four pages of a 48 page oceanography text. Students who received questions did significantly better when the same questions were repeated on the posttest, and also did significantly better on new posttest items that tested information from the same category as the adjunct questions but which were otherwise unrelated. Thus, the study replicated the direct and indirect effects of questions observed in many previous studies. Furthermore, subjects who received questions had significantly longer reading times and significantly longer probe reaction times on a secondary task when processing segments of the text containing question--tion-relevant information.

Most important, Anderson and Reynolds squeezed their data to provide an answer to the question of whether selective attention to question-relevant text segments caused differential learning of question-relevant information. Two variables which exhausted the information in the probe time measure were included in analyses of posttest performance.[1] These were total probe time and the difference in probe time between question-relevant and question-irrelevant text segments. The differential probe time variable had a substantial effect, as Theory I predicts. It accounted for 7.7% of the variance of new posttest scores and 23.8% of the variance of repeated posttest scores, both significant effects. These analyses satisfy the third entailment of a causal theory set forth earlier.

Examined next, in order to evaluate the fourth entailment of a causal theory, was what happened to the differential effect of questions on learning when the differential probe time variable was entered into the analysis. In the case of the new posttest items, the variance explained by the question factor dropped from a significant 8.3% to a nonsignificant 2.4%. In the case of the repeated posttest items, when the differential probe time measured was entered first, the amount of variance attributable to the effect of questions fell from 63.6% to a still large and significant 39.9%. These analyses rule out the interpretation that the change in attention was an epiphenomenon. The conclusion is that a model that puts selective attention on the causal path between questions and learning can account for all, or most, of the indirect effect of questions and some, but not all, of the direct effect.

With respect to the volume-of-attention concept, a major worry is that reading time and probe time might tap essentially the same underlying factor. That is, it could be that summing the increments in time on the many small intervals sampled occasionally by the secondary task would yield total reading time over a broad interval. However, the data from the Reynolds and Anderson study suggest that probe time and reading time are independent. The average intercorrelation between the two measures within four-page sections of text was only .04, whereas the average intercorrelations of the same measure recorded from adjacent four-page sections were .46 and .64 for probe time and reading time, respectively. Moreover, there were striking differences in the behavior of the two measures from the beginning to the end of the text. The best fitting functions are plotted in Figure 1.

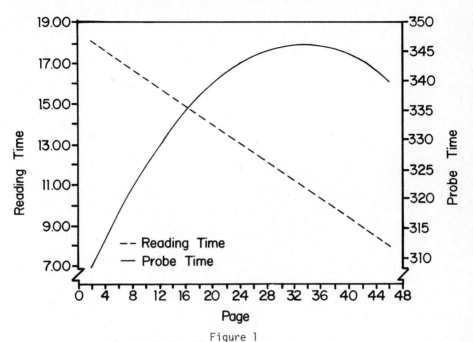

Figure 1
Reading Time (in Sec per four line segment)
and Probe Time (Msec) as a Function of Page in the Text

There was no change in the proportion of text information learned over the course of the text, a fact that is readily understandable in terms of a two-facet theory of attention: The increase in probe time over the course of the text, reflecting an increase in cognitive effort, compensated for the drop in reading time. Therefore, the total volume of attention devoted to the text can be construed to have remained approximately constant, and no change in the probability of learning text information was to be expected.

The strongest and most interesting form of the volume-of-attention concept requires cognitive effort and duration to have joint effects on learning as well as separate effects. Evidence corroborating this strong prediction was found in an analysis of the repeated posttest scores. When entered into a regression analysis successively, differential probe time, differential reading time, and the product of these two measures all accounted for significant variance in learning. However, a comparable analysis of new posttest scores was inconclusive, perhaps because the indirect effects of questions on learning are not very strong.

In order to test the idea that there can be trade-offs between level of cognitive effort and duration, Reynolds and Anderson placed two groups of subjects under time pressure, allowing them either about 70% or about 40% of the time that an average subject would take to read a typical text segment. The expectation was that readers under time pressure would increase cognitive effort in order to maintain comprehension, and that this would be reflected in an increase in probe reaction time. This expectation was not fulfilled; there were absolutely no differences in probe time among the self-paced group

and the two externally paced groups. Maybe level of cognitive effort during
reading is not easily brought under executive control, or perhaps there was
not an adequate incentive for working hard in this experiment. The hypothesis
that attention comes in volumes is not mortally embarrassed by this outcome,
since there were decreases in learning corresponding to the decreases in time
to read; still, it is not the outcome that an advocate of the hypothesis would
like to see.

INTEREST AND ATTENTION

If you were to ask school teachers why they prefer to use reading material
that children find interesting, they would tell you "because the children
will pay more attention and learn more." Thus, this is a case in which the
common sense view is identical with Theory I. While the results may not
surprise a school teacher, Larry Shirey, Jana Mason, and I were surprised
to discover in two studies involving 350 third graders the very strong effect
that interestingness has on children's learning. It accounted for over four
times as much variance as several measures of difficulty included in "readability" formulas used for grading children's texts and stories.

Briefly summarized here is an additional experiment that sought to determine
whether attention is on the causal path between interest and learning. The
subjects were 30 fourth graders who read 36 sentences. Reading times and
probe times were collected. The measure of learning was the percentage of
content words in the sentences that could be recalled to a gist criterion
immediately after reading, given the subject noun phrases as cues.

Interest value was operationalized as the mean rating of interest assigned
by a group of third graders. The mean rating on an arbitrary six point scale
was 3.7 and the standard deviation was .9. Two and one half units on this
scale encompassed the observed range of ratings. Below are two examples of
sentences that children find very interesting followed by two they find
uninteresting:

> *The hungry children were in the kitchen helping Mother make donuts.*
> *The huge gorilla smashed the bus with its fist.*
> *The old chair sat in the corner near the wall.*
> *The fat waitress stirred the coffee with a spoon.*

While I do not know for sure, because I have not done the research, I am
willing to take bets right now that these sentences vary primarily in their
capacity to arouse interest in a nine- or ten-year-old child, and not with
respect to some other property, say, image-evoking value. Even though the
children were reading from a computer terminal, wearing earphones, under the
supervision of a strange adult we frequently heard oohs, ahs, giggles, and
chortles as the children read sentences they found funny, scary, or impressive.

Interest value had significant relationships to percentage recall, reading
time, and probe time. For each unit increase in interest value, recall
increased 5.3%, reading time increased 12 msec per syllable (or 180 msec per
sentence), and probe time increased 44 msec. These results satisfy the first
two entailments of a causal theory.

The third entailment proved impossible to satisfy in the case of the probe
time measure. It accounted for nil variance in recall and, in fact, the
sign of the regression coefficient was negative. However, reading time did
have a significant positive relation to recall. Each 100 msec per syllable

increase in reading time was associated with a 4.3% increase in recall (which needs to be interpreted in light of the fact that the standard deviation of reading time was 118 msec per syllable, after an adjustment to remove between-subjects variance).

Finally, we asked whether the effect of interest value on recall would vanish when reading time was entered into the analysis. It did not. Reading time captured only a small, nonsignificant amount of the variance otherwise explained by interest value and the effect of interest value was still highly significant. Each unit increment on the interest scale is worth 4.8% in recall when reading time is in the equation as compared to 5.3% when it is not in the equation. The conclusion is that attention plays a negligible causal role in the effects of interest on learning.

It is important to emphasize that the analyses that have just been reported were completed with the entire matrix of 30 subjects x 36 sentences minus 19 missing cases = 1061 observations. If the data had been aggregated by sentence as, for instance, Just and Carpenter (1980) have done, it would have been impossible to reject Theory I. What the results show is that, while children pay more attention to interesting sentences and also learn more interesting sentences, for most children the set of interesting sentences to which attention is paid and the set of interesting sentences which are learned do not overlap very much. Thus, the pause to savor an interesting sentence is not the pause that supports the process that gives birth to learning.

With respect to the concept of a volume of attention, it was again found that reading time and probe time are independent. The correlation between reading time and probe time computed from the sentences in the odd and the even serial positions averaged .32 while the correlations of the measures with themselves were .87 for reading time and .62 for probe time. It was also found again that there were sharp differences in behavior of the two measures over the course of the task. The best fitting functions are plotted in Figure 2. In this study, unlike the adjunct question study, recall was an increasing linear function of serial position. Each advance in position was associated with a .5% increase in recall.

There are several possible explanations for the changes in reading time and probe time from the beginning to the end of the task that have now been observed in both the question study and the interest study. A plausible one is that subjects changed their priorities from an initial emphasis on the secondary task to a later emphasis on reading.

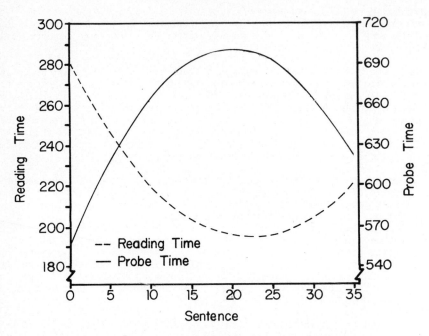

Figure 2
Reading Time (Msec per syllable) and Probe Time (Msec)
as a Function of Serial Position of the Sentence

PERSPECTIVE AND ATTENTION

A number of studies in my laboratory have examined the effects of the
reader's perspective on comprehension, learning, and recall (Pichert &
Anderson, 1977; Anderson & Pichert, 1978; Anderson, Pichert, & Shirey, 1979).
A story that has figured prominently in our research is about two boys at
home. Before reading the story, subjects are directed to take either the
perspective of a burglar or someone interested in buying a home. Our research has consistently shown that subjects recall more of the information
that is important in the light of their perspective. Furthermore, we have
found that when subjects shift perspectives and recall the story a second
time, they recall new previously unrecalled information important to the new
perspective but unimportant to the perspective operative when the passage
was read. For instance, subjects who shift to a burglar perspective become
more likely to recall information such as that the side door was always un-
locked, whereas subjects who shift to the homebuyer perspective are likely
at that point to remember that the roof leaked or that the place had attractive grounds. In several experiments employing this paradigm, from 65% to
more than 80% of the subjects have recalled at least one additional piece of
information important to their new perspective.

These results strongly implicate a retrieval process; however, our results
to date are equivocal about whether the schema operative when a passage is
read also influences encoding. The purpose of the first experiment I shall
describe here was to determine whether a reader's schema has both encoding

and retrieval effects. Two hundred and fifteen high school students were instructed to take one of two perspectives before reading a passage. After reading, half of the subjects shifted to the other perspective and then all subjects recalled the passage. Table 1 presents mean proportion recalled as a function of the importance of the information to the two perspectives. A significant effect was obtained for the importance of information to first perspective, operative when the passage was read, which suggests an encoding benefit. Also significant was the importance of information to the second perspective, operative during recall, which indicates a retrieval benefit.

Table 1

Mean Proportions of Text Elements Recalled

Importance to Recall Perspective	Importance to Reading Perspective	
	Low	High
High	.41	.51
Low	.32	.43

The conclusion that a schema induced after reading affects retrieval is irresistable. However, the explanation for the effect of a perspective assigned prior to reading may appear to be less certain. One would suppose that ordinarily people maintain the same schema when recalling a passage as when reading it. Thus, the influence of a schema induced beforehand might also be attributable to a retrieval process instead of an encoding process. A close look at the data, however, suggests that the reading perspective does affect encoding. Presumably a perspective shift disables the schema operative during reading, thereby preventing this schema from influencing retrieval. Consistent with this assumption is the fact that there was a sharp drop in recall of information that had been important to the reading schema but became unimportant when the perspective shifted. On the other hand, recall of this information was still superior to the recall of information unimportant to both the reading and the recall perspectives, a superiority which can be most plausibly accounted for in terms of an encoding process.

In three further experiments, we have sought to determine whether the possible encoding benefits of a perspective could be explained in terms of selective attention to perspective-relevant information. In all three experiments there was a trend toward longer reading times when subjects were processing text elements that contained information important to their perspective, a trend that was significant in two of the three cases. It should be noted in passing, though, that Grabe (1981) has failed to find longer reading times on perspective-relevant material. We assessed probe time in two of the experiments. In one, there was a marginally significant trend for longer probe times when subjects were processing perspective-relevant text elements; in the other, the data were completely flat. This research has been plagued by procedural problems. We are not yet confident of our results so we have not attempted a deep analysis of the possible causal role of attention.

SUMMARY

The purpose of the research described in this paper was to evaluate the simple theory that important information is better learned than less important information because readers pay more attention to important information. This theory was confirmed in an experiment on adjunct questions. There is now very good reason to believe that (a) questions cause readers to selectively attend to question-relevant information, and that (b) a process supported by the extra attention causes more of the question-relevant information to be learned. However, despite superficial appearances, it does not appear that attention lies on the causal path between the interest value of a sentence and the learning of this sentence. Children do pay more attention to interesting sentences and they do learn more interesting sentences. However, a deep analysis suggests that the extra attention is an epiphenomenon. So far research on whether attention plays a part in the learning of information important in the light of a reader's perspective has been inconclusive. The final conclusion is that Theory I fails as a general explanation of the effects of importance on learning.

Reading time and probe time proved to be independent measures in this research, which satisfies a first requirement of the concept of a volume of attention. Otherwise, except in the adjunct question study, the concept didn't prove very valuable. However, the problem may not be so much with the concept as with the method of assessing level of cognitive effort using discrete secondary task probes.

FOOTNOTE

[1]Reading time measures were included in subsidiary analysis only, because reading was self-paced for only a third of the subjects in this experiment.

REFERENCES

Anderson, R. C., & Pichert, J. W. Recall of previously unrecallable information following a shift in perspective. Journal of Verbal Learning and Verbal Behavior, 1978, 17, 1-12.

Anderson, R. C., Pichert, J. W., & Shirey, L. L. Effects of the reader's schema at different points in time (Tech. Rep. No. 119). Urbana: University of Illinois, Center for the Study of Reading, April 1979.

Ausubel, D. P. The psychology of meaningful verbal behavior. New York: Grune & Stratton, 1963.

Ausubel, D. P. Educational psychology: A cognitive view. New York: Holt, Rinehart, & Winston, 1968.

Britton, B., Meyer, B., Simpson, R., Holdredge, T., & Curry, C. Effects of the organization of text on memory: Tests of two implications of a selective attention hypothesis. Journal of Experimental Psychology: Human Learning and Memory, 1979, 5, 496-506.

Britton, B. K., Piha, A., Davis, J., & Wehausen, E. Reading and cognitive capacity usage: Adjunct question effects. Memory and Cognition, 1978, 6, 266-273.

Cirilo, R. K., & Foss, D. J. Text structure and reading time for sentences. Journal of Verbal Learning and Verbal Behavior, 1980, 19, 96-109.

Grabe, M. Variable inspection time as an indicator of cognitive reading behavior. Contemporary Educational Psychology, 1981, 6(4), 334-343.

Graesser, A. C., Hoffman, N. L., & Clark, L. F. Structural components of reading time. Journal of Verbal Learning and Verbal Behavior, 1980, 19, 135-151.

Haberlandt, K., Berian, C., & Sandson, J. The episode schema in story processing. Journal of Verbal Learning and Verbal Behavior, 1980, 19, 635-650.

Just, M. A., & Carpenter, P. A. A theory of reading: From eye fixations to comprehension. Psychological Review, 1980, 87(4), 329-354.

Kahneman, D. Attention and effort. Englewood Cliffs, N.J.: Prentice-Hall, 1973.

Kintsch, W., & van Dijk, T. A. Toward a model of text comprehension and production. Psychological Review, 1978, 85, 363-394.

Meyer, B. The organization of prose and its effect on recall. Amsterdam: North-Holland, 1975.

Pichert, J. W., & Anderson, R. C. Taking different perspectives on a story. Journal of Educational Psychology, 1977, 69, 309-315.

Reynolds, R. E., & Anderson, R. C. Influence of questions on the allocation of attention during reading. Journal of Educational Psychology, in press.

Reynolds, R. E., Standiford, S. N., & Anderson, R. C. Distribution of reading time when questions are asked about a restricted category of text information. Journal of Educational Psychology, 1979, 71, 183-190.

Rothkopf, E. Z., & Billington, M. J. Goal guided learning from text: Inferring a descriptive processing model from inspection times and eye movements. Journal of Educational Psychology, 1979, 71(3), 310-327.

Rothkopf, E. Z., & Bisbicos, E. E. Selective facilitative effects of interspersed questions on learning from written materials. Journal of Educational Psychology, 1967, 58, 56-61.

Yekovich, F. R., & Thorndyke, P. W. An evaluation of alternative functional models of narrative schemata. Journal of Verbal Learning and Verbal Behavior, 1981, 20, 454-469.

DISCOURSE PROCESSING
A. Flammer and W. Kintsch (eds.)
© *North-Holland Publishing Company, 1982*

INTENTIONAL LEARNING IN TEXT PROCESSING

Gery d'Ydewalle, Eddy M. Degryse, and An Swerts

Department of Psychology
University of Leuven
B-3000 Leuven
Belgium

Intentional learning of prose materials is investigated in
two different ways, looking either at the performance of
groups with and without intentional learning instructions,
or looking at the performance of two groups expecting a
different type of test (either a reproduction test or a
multiple-choice test). Idea units which are important for
understanding the story are well remembered by all subjects.
The intentional learning groups outperform the incidental
learning group on the reproduction of details from the first
part of the story. As the gist of the story has an intrinsic
saliency, the extra effort of the intentional learners is
reflected in remembering the unimportant events. Expecting
either a reproduction test or a multiple-choice test does
not produce any significant performance difference.

INTRODUCTION

Two decades ago, a considerable number of studies appeared on incidental
versus intentional learning of either unrelated items or paired associates.
The topic lost its research interest in contemporary studies on learning
and memory for a number of reasons, one being the increasing use of more
complex learning materials. Several attempts were made to develop structures
representing the interrelated idea units and sentences from paragraphs,
stories and other text materials. In the experiments, the subject was
assumed to be trying either to understand or to learn the content of the
passages, and no attention was given to the subject's own activities in
mastering the learning task. Although it was sometimes acknowledged that
the subject has at his/her disposal various learning strategies (McConkie,
1977), one did not look seriously at his/her activities of deploying these
strategies in an intelligent fashion by checking and monitoring their
suitability and efficacy for the task at hand.

One straightforward design used in text-processing experiments consists of
comparing two groups of subjects, one with intentional learning instructions
and the other with incidental learning, with an appropriate orienting task.
However, we believe that a different approach to the study of learning
intentions is also possible. Learning intention has been considered as a
single intervening process, implying that, regardless of what the learner
does, the fact remains that he/she has the intention to learn. A comparison
between different learning intentions could, perhaps, throw light on the
multiplicity of intervening processes involved in intentionally encoding
and retaining knowledge. By "learning intention" we do not mean only the

general intention to learn presented information but also the different possible strategies involved in encoding this information as a function of various intentions. Learning intentions are assumed to be affected mainly by the expectations of the persons undertaking the task. We could thus have two groups, both intentionally directed to encode and retain information as a function of an anticipated test. Differential learning intentions are developed by both groups as a function of different expected memory tests. Thus, although both groups have an intention to learn, they differ in the type of intentions. In the experiment reported here, there were three groups of subjects, one with incidental learning and two with intentional learning expecting either to reproduce the whole story or to answer a multiple-choice test on facts from the story.

For our purpose, it is important to know what aspects of the story structure are encoded by the subjects with different learning intentions. When looking at the representation of a story structure, different authors propose different solutions (see, for example, Anderson and Bower, 1973; Kintsch and Van Dijk, 1978; Meyer, 1975; Rumelhart, Lindsay and Norman, 1972). Therefore, we propose a rather empirical approach for distinguishing important and unimportant parts of the story.

Two quite general but contrasting hypotheses can be formulated. The first hypothesis leads us to predict a large difference in memory performance on parts that are important for mastering the whole story. An effective learner would not direct much attention to trivial units. Concentrating the focus of his/her efforts on the important elements of the story, the efficient student would enhance his/her recall of essential material, especially when the study time is restricted. The difference should be apparent between the incidental group and the two groups with intentional learning. Even among the two groups with intentional learning, some recall difference with respect to the structurally important elements may occur. Rickards and Friedman (1978), for example, found that subjects expecting an essay test chose, for note taking, sentences of greater importance to the overall meaning of the passage than those expecting a multiple-choice test. The essay test expectancy also yielded a higher recall level of the structurally important notes, while the total number of recalled notes was not different in the two groups. In d'Ydewalle, Swerts, and De Corte (1980), subjects expecting open questions used more study time and performed better on various memory tests than subjects expecting a multiple-choice test. This again leads us to predict a recall difference between the two intentional groups.

On the other hand, one could also predict an absence of recall difference with respect to the structurally important elements of the test. The gist of the story may have some intrinsic saliency and is, perhaps, well remembered independently of subject's intention to learn. The extra effort supposedly performed by intentional learners to master the learning task would then be reflected in trying to remember details and unimportant events. Britton (1978) reported that the level of recall in incidental prose learning was superior or equivalent to the recall level of intentional learning, but he did not make any distinction between structurally important and unimportant elements in the text. While the recall level correlated quite reliably with the importance level in Brown and Smiley (1978), these authors did not find any difference at each level of structural importance between incidental and intentional learning on an immediate test (on a delayed test, intentional learning was superior at all levels of importance).

In order to enhance the chances of being able to unravel the learning activities more precisely, we divided the stories into parts. Primacy effects, i.e., the superiority in recalling the first few sentences, have been reported but not always observed (for a review, see Meyer, 1975). Meyer and McConkie (1973) carefully scrutinized the data of their experiment and concluded that a primacy effect may be observed when the important ideas are located in the first paragraph. Kintsch et al. (1975) also showed that information at the beginning of a text improves recall only if it is important for the text as a whole. Following our first hypothesis, the largest difference between incidental and intentional learning should emerge from the important information elements at the beginning of the text. Accordingly, our experiment was set up with three basic conditions (an incidental learning group, and two intentional learning groups), and we organized the stories so as to have about an equal number of important and less important pieces of information in the different parts of the stories. One additional feature of the experiment has to be emphasized. From d'Ydewalle, Swerts, and De Corte (1980), we know that the learning differences between several intentional learning conditions only occur when the subjects are thoroughly acquainted with the processing requirements of the learning material. Accordingly, all the subjects received two successive texts. Those expecting to reproduce the text had to reproduce the first text, and those expecting a multiple-choice test received a multiple-choice test after the first text. All the analyses, however, were made on the recall performance from the second text.

MATERIAL, PROCEDURE, AND SUBJECTS

Kintsch (Kintsch and Kozminsky, 1977; Kintsch and Greene, 1978) used stories from Boccaccio's *Decameron*, and, because these texts meet the requirements of the present experiment, we also chose four texts from this book. The Dutch translations of the stories were adapted slightly to obtain more readable texts. To draw up questions for the multiple-choice test, we divided the texts into six equal parts and five questions were formulated for each part. Accordingly, there were thirty questions for each text. Two preliminary experiments were carried out. The incorrect responses on the open questions in the first experiment provided the material for choosing three distractor responses in the multiple-choice questions of the second preliminary experiment. After data analyses of the second experiment, two texts out of the four were chosen: "Story 4-Sixth Day" and "Story 1-Tenth Day". The results on the multiple-choice test indicated that both texts were approximately of the same difficulty and that the distractors and the imposed study time of eight minutes were appropriate. Some less suitable questions were omitted so that twenty-six questions remained for each text. The lengths of these stories were approximately 870 and 780 words, respectively.

To draw the attention of the subjects in the incidental learning condition to the text without evoking an intentional learning attitude, an orienting task was necessary. In both texts, thirteen verbs were put in the wrong tense. The task consisted in correcting these tenses to obtain a coherent and grammatically correct text. The same texts with the modification of the thirteen verbs were used for the other conditions so that no condition would benefit from a more coherent text. Therefore, the verbs for which the tenses were altered were chosen so that they were inconspicuous, and no changes were made in the first paragraph of the text. The errors were neither too disturbing nor too obvious.

The two texts were used in counterbalanced order in all conditions. The design consisted of three condition by two text orders. Accordingly, six different booklets were made up. The first page of each booklet contained either a presentation of the test type to be expected (multiple-choice test or reproduction) or instructions about the orienting task. Then followed one of the two texts. The subjects worked on the text for eight minutes before proceeding to the following page. Time signals were given by the experimenter. On the following page, the expected multiple-choice test or reproduction task was given. To keep the subjects of the incidental learning condition busy, a questionnaire on principles of verb tenses was given. The questionnaire was followed by some additional exercises on verb tenses. After this came an instruction for all conditions emphasizing that the same kind of task (test) as on Text 1 would follow after Text 2. Again eight minutes were available for Text 2, which was followed by a reproduction test for all conditions. Response time was unlimited for the reproduction test.

The experiment took place in a large classroom during a regular class period for first-year students in psychology at the University of Leuven, Belgium. The group consisted of 79 male and 57 female students. They all could be considered naive with regard to the subject matter of learning and memory in psychology. Paper of different colors was used for the pages on instructions, texts, and answers to the tests, which allowed three research collaborators to check whether all subjects were on the appropriate pages at a given time. To prevent cheating, the booklets were mixed so that neighboring students never had the same text and test.

RESULTS

The two texts were reduced to a number of very short sentences each describing one idea unit. The texts contained 97 and 89 idea units, respectively. Three judges were asked to rate on a five-points scale each idea unit on its importance for the structural development of the story. The intercorrelations between the three raters on "Story 4-Sixth Day" were +.60, +.65 and +.72, while on "Story 1-Tenth Day" the following values were obtained: +.55, +.69 and +.74. For every idea unit, the score of the three judges was added together. These sums ranged from zero (the three judges scoring zero) to twelve (the three judges scoring 4). Those idea units which every judge scored high, were considered as essential to the structure of the story. A frequency distribution was drafted, and the idea units were divided into three groups: low, medium, and high importance. The division was based on two criteria: The number of idea units were to be as equal as possible for the three groups and the number of idea units in each group should be equally distributed over the whole text. Therefore, the two stories were divided into three parts, and we obtained on each part about an equal number of idea units with low, medium, and high importance.

The reproduction of Text 2 was scored separately for each subject. The three judges were instructed to assess (again on a five-points scale) the extent to which each idea unit was present in the reproductions. It was emphasized that content was important, not a literal reproduction. For each judge, the ratings on the three groups of idea units (low, medium, and

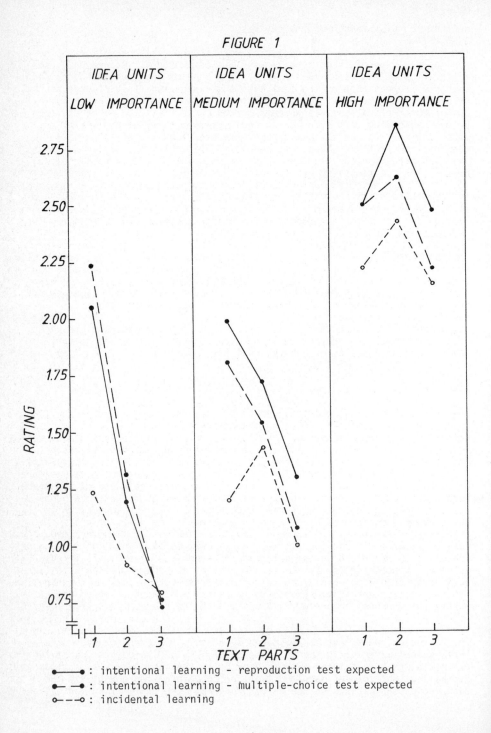

FIGURE 1

high importance) in each part were added together, and two kinds of analysis were performed. First, we carried out a multivariate analysis of variance with sex of subjects, text order, and learning conditions as between-subjects variables. The combined scores of the three raters (appropriately weighted for the number of rated idea units) were used as the three dependent variables. The second analysis of variance (univariate) was performed with the same independent variables but considered the scores of the three raters as another within-subjects variable (any interaction of this variable with another would cast some doubts on the validity of our scoring system). As both analyses provided basically the same pattern of results, we present here only the significant main values of the second analysis.

Three main effects emerged that were all involved in several higher-order interactions. The learning conditions were significant, $F(2, 112) = 7.37$, $MS_e = 500.631$, $p < .001$, with subjects expecting a test (either a multiple-choice test or a reproduction task) performing better than subjects without any learning instructions. The parts were significant, Part 1 being the best and Part 3 being the least well reproduced, $F(2, 224) = 65.80$, $MS_e = 119.352$, $p < .001$ (the linear trend component accounts for 97 % of the variance). There was also a significant effect of the importance of the idea units, with the most important idea units best reproduced, $F(2, 224) = 429.29$, $MS_e = 86.179$, $p < .001$ (here again the linear trend component accounts for 87 % of the variance).

Learning conditions were involved in an interaction with the importance of the idea units, $F(4, 224) = 2.46$, $MS_e = 86.179$, $p < .001$, and with parts, $F(4.224) = 6.21$, $MS_e = 119.352$, $p < .001$, producing finally an interaction between learning conditions, the importance of the idea units, and parts, $F(8, 448) = 3.00$, $MS_e = 63.269$, $p < .003$. This second-order interaction is conveniently arranged in three graphs in Figure 1. It is immediately apparent that the interaction was due to a large difference between the incidental learning group and the two intentional learning groups on Part 1 of the texts. This difference occurred especially with idea units of low or medium importance. A posteriori Tukey tests confirmed the reliability of the above described differences. With idea units of low importance, there was a significant difference in reproduction on Part 1 of the text between the incidental learning condition and the multiple-choice condition, $t(3, 448) = 8.643$, $p < .01$, and between the incidental learning condition and the reproduction condition, $t(3, 448) = 7.037$, $p < .01$. No significant differences occurred on Parts 2 and 3. With idea units of medium importance, there was again a significant reproduction difference on Part 1 between the incidental learning condition and the multiple-choice condition, $t(3, 448) = 5.243$, $p < .01$, and between the incidental learning condition and the reproduction condition, $t(3, 448) = 5.939$, $p < .01$; no other differences were significant. No significant differences were obtained when comparing the three learning conditions on the reproduction of highly important idea units.

DISCUSSION

From the data, it is clear that idea units are better recalled when they are important for comprehending the story. Also, all idea units (either details or important elements) are better remembered if they occur at the beginning of the text. These two facts are obtained independently from the presence of intentional learning. This may indicate that even with incidental learning, the subjects attempt to understand the course of the story, and this cognitive effort produces a better (incidental) recall of the important idea units. The decreasing recall level from Part 1 to Part 3 (especially with idea units of low importance) is probably due to higher demands on the working memory to understand the text as more information is being processed.

The major difference between the learning groups is on the less important idea units from Part 1 of the story. The better recall of less important idea units by the two intentional learning groups agrees with the prediction of our second hypothesis. The subject's attention is focused on the important idea units, regardless of the task instructions. Remembering less important idea units requires a deliberate effort from the subject to process the details. The incidental learning group does not pay attention to the details. The recall difference for less important idea units emerges mainly on Part 1 of the text. This is in agreement with many free recall studies of unrelated items (for a review, see d'Ydewalle, 1981): Subjects who are given intentional learning instructions show greater primacy effects than incidental learners, and this has been interpreted as suggesting a difference in subjects' effective attempts to store the information in the long-term store. As processing load increases from Part 1 to Part 3, the difference between intentional and incidental learning disappears on Parts 2 and 3.

There is no reliable difference between the reproduction performance of the two intentional learning groups although subjects expecting the reproduction test perform somewhat better. In d'Ydewalle and Rosselle (1978), subjects also received restricted study time on an one-page history text. Expecting open questions produced a better performance on the open questions than expecting a multiple-choice test. When study time was self-paced, subjects expecting open questions used more study time and recalled more than subjects anticipating a multiple-choice test (d'Ydewalle, Swerts, and De Corte, 1980). We favored the idea that the expectation of a test requiring more than simple recognition of correct answers (e.g., a reproduction test) enhances subjects' active involvement in mastering the learning material. In the present experiment, the performance difference between the two intentional learning groups is in the right direction although quite small and not significant.

The present study was also part of an initial attempt to relate research on cognitive style to study-technique effectiveness with prose materials. The Group Embedded Figures Test (Oltman, Raskin, and Witkin, 1971) was administered to all students to assess their cognitive style. We carried out a number of analyses, from simple correlations to stepwise regression analyses with the scores on the Group Embedded Figures Test and the experimental manipulations as predictors. Subjects with high scores on the Group Embedded Figures Test could be expected to distinguish more efficiently the high important idea units from the less important ones. However, nothing particularly revealing emerged. Another experiment using the same learning material and a similar design (but without an incidental learning group) provided strong correlations with some aspects of the reproduction performance (d'Ydewalle, Van Houtven, Degryse, and Swerts, in preparation). The difference between the results from the two studies appears to be due to the higher reproduction performance and the selective nature of the university subjects in the present study as compared with the much younger subjects in d'Ydewalle, Van Houtven, Degryse, and Swerts (in preparation).

REFERENCES

Anderson, J. R., & Bower, G. H. Human associative memory. Washington, D.C.: V. H. Winston, 1973.

Britton, B. K. Incidental prose learning. Journal of Reading Behavior, 1978, 10, 299-303.

Brown, A. L., & Smiley, S. S. The development of strategies for studying texts. Child Development, 1978, 49, 1076-1088.

d'Ydewalle, G. Test expectancy effects in free recall and recognition. Journal of General Psychology, 1981, 105, 173-195.

d'Ydewalle, G., & Rosselle, H. Test expectations in text learning. In M. M. Gruneberg, P. E. Morris, & R. N. Sykes (Eds.), Practical aspects of memory. New York: Academic Press, 1978.

d'Ydewalle, G., Swerts, A., & De Corte, E. Study time and test performance as a function of test expectations (Report No. 24). University of Leuven, Psychological Reports, September 1980.

d'Ydewalle, G., Van Houtven, A. M., Degryse, M., & Swerts, A. Cognitive style and test expectation in text processing. Manuscript in preparation.

Kintsch, W., & Greene, E. The role of culture-specific schemata in the comprehension and recall of stories. Discourse Processes, 1978, 1, 1-13.

Kintsch, W., & Kozminsky, E. Summarizing stories after reading and listening. Journal of Educational Psychology, 1977, 69, 491-499.

Kintsch, W., Kozminsky, E., Streby, W. J., McKoon, G., & Keenan, J. M. Comprehension and recall of text as a function of content variables. Journal of Verbal Learning and Verbal Behavior, 1975, 14, 196-214.

Kintsch, W., & Van Dijk, T. A. Toward a model of text comprehension and production. Psychological Review, 1978, 85, 363-394.

McConkie, G. W. Learning from text. In Review of research in education (Vol. 5). Itasca, Ill.: Peacock, 1977.

Meyer, B. J. F. The organization of prose and its effects on memory. Amsterdam: North-Holland, 1975.

Meyer, B. J. F., & McConkie, G. W. What is recalled after hearing a passage? Journal of Educational Psychology, 1973, 65, 109-117.

Oltman, P. K., Raskin, E., & Witkin, H. A. Group embedded-figures test. Palo Alto, Calif.: Consulting Psychologists Press, 1971.

Rickards, J. P., & Friedman, F. The encoding versus the external storage hypothesis in note taking. Contemporary Educational Psychology, 1978, 3, 136-143.

Rumelhart, D. E., Lindsay, P., & Norman, D. A. A process model for long-term memory. In E. Tulving & W. Donaldson (Eds.), Organization of memory. New York: Academic Press, 1972.

DISCOURSE PROCESSING
A. Flammer and W. Kintsch (eds.)
© *North-Holland Publishing Company, 1982*

RECALL AND THE FLEXIBILITY OF LINGUISTIC PROCESSING

Gregory V. Jones and Martin S. Payne

Department of Psychology
University of Bristol
Bristol
England

It is well established that those parts of a text that are of subjectively greater importance than other parts are retained better in memory. This type of phenomenon may be investigated with the aim of establishing either appropriate structural linguistic descriptions or, alternatively, general processing constraints. The latter course is adopted here in an experiment in which people's attention is directed towards differing components of linguistic material. The results are analysed in terms of the fragmentation model of recall, and shown to be consistent with the existence of limitations imposed by finite reserves of nonspecific linguistic processing resources.

INTRODUCTION

The purpose of this paper is to enquire into the nature of the processing constraints involved in the retention of linguistic information. This is a topic that few studies of linguistic processing have addressed directly. Rather, emphasis has been placed upon linguistic variables such as the particular location of information within some form of hypothesised symbolic representation of text.

A useful illustration of the complementariness of the two perspectives is provided by the finding that those parts of a narrative rated as being of high importance are better recalled than those rated of lower importance (Johnson, 1970). Two possible approaches to the further investigation of this phenomenon may be adopted. First, people may be asked to deliberately re-allocate the subjective importances of the different segments of text: In effect, to change their pattern of attention to the passage. An interesting question which arises then is whether or not such an alteration in the pattern of attention is injurious to the person's retention of the information conveyed by the passage. Here two positions may be distinguished. An ecological position would hold that the normal pattern of attention is optimally adapted to the particular passage structure. A nonspecific capacity position, on the other hand, would hold that attention can be freely redistributed without consequent deleterious effects upon the retention of linguistic material.

The second, more explored, line of research has been to seek linguistic correlates of the differing importances attached to different text segments, as has been performed by Mandler and Johnson (1977) and Thorndyke (1977) using story grammars similar to that of Rumelhart (1975). It was shown by Thorndyke (1977), for example, that propositions at the top of the hierarchical framework that symbolically represented one passage were recalled approximately twice as well as those at the bottom.

It should be noted that in addition to pursuing these two approaches separately, it is possible also to attempt the difficult task of combining them. Perhaps the best such attempt has been that of Kintsch and van Dijk (1978) and their colleagues. Their model has incorporated processing factors which are directed by the products of the model's linguistic analysis. For example, Miller and Kintsch (1980) applied the model to people's recall of a set of paragraphs. The model posits a short-term buffer in which at any time it is estimated that one or two of the (model-specific) propositions of a paragraph may be held. Entry of a processed proposition into the buffer is hypothesised to provide it with a second, independent chance of being subsequently recalled from long-term memory, the magnitude of which is equal to that provided by its initial processing. Selection of a proposition into the buffer is favoured by several factors, including its existence as the argument of another proposition already in the buffer, its recency, and its proximity (in terms of argument overlap) to the intuitively selected superordinate proposition. Miller and Kintsch found that the model was moderately successful, in that for 15 out of 20 texts it predicted recall better than did the null hypothesis that all propositions are equally well remembered. Nevertheless, in spite of this valuable work it still seems worthwhile to attempt also to investigate directly the effects of language processing constraints upon subsequent recall, independently of hypothesised linguistic structure.

A promising area in which to investigate directly the effects of processing constraints on language materials is that of the cued recall of individual sentences. This is because there exists a model of such performance whose validity is not dependent upon the making of structural linguistic assumptions. Rather, the fragmentation model (Jones, 1978b) acts more passively like a prism through which a set of recall data are refracted so as to display an orderly spectrum of those different fragments of the original material whose representations have been mentally retained. Although the model is thus limited in some respects (see also the Discussion), it has the advantage for the present purpose that its failure to carry any structural linguistic supercargo reduces potential ambiguity in the interpretation of observed effects of processing manipulations.

A previous investigation has failed to find reliable evidence that an attended element acts as a better cue for the recall of an unattended element than the reverse (Jones & Martin, 1980). Thus the present study is concerned instead with the effect that manipulation of processing priority has upon the distribution of encoded fragments of an utterance. Previous research provides surprisingly few guidelines as to what the constraints upon any distributional changes might be. Two general questions were pursued in the experiment to be reported next. First, are overall levels of recall dependent upon attentional instructions? Second, can a pattern of recall in one attentional condition be predicted from that in another? If attention is focussed on either one or other of two nonoverlapping parts of an utterance, how do the resulting effects compare with the effect of focussing on both parts?

METHOD

The subjects of this experiment were 40 students of Bristol University who
volunteered their services.

Each subject was presented with a set of 24 different sentences to
remember. Each sentence was of the form Location-Subject-Verb-Object
(L-S-V-O), with independently selected components. Examples are "In the
park the monkey found the cabbage" and "In the car the writer touched the
rabbit".

Equal numbers of subjects were assigned to four different attentional
conditions. Subjects were instructed to concentrate their attention either
equally upon all four content words (Control condition), on the first two
content words (First-half condition), on the last two content words
(Second-half condition), or on the combinations of the first two words
together and of the last two words together (Both-halves condition), and
were each given a relevant example.

Presentation of the sentences was followed by a delay, after which the
subject was provided with three incremental cues for each sentence. These
took the form of sentence frames from which three words, two words, and
finally one word were missing and had to be supplied by the subject, for
example "In the ---- the monkey ---- the ----", "In the ---- the monkey
---- the cabbage", and "In the park the monkey ---- the cabbage". Four
types of first cue may each be followed by three types of second cue and
two types of third cue. Each of these 24 possible sequences of cue was
used once for each set of sentences.

Subjects were presented with the sentences to be remembered at a rate of 10
sec per sentence. Presentation was followed by a mental arithmetic task of
duration 45 sec, after which recall commenced. Subjects were allowed 30
sec, 20 sec, and 10 sec for recall cued by one word, two words, and three
words, respectively.

RESULTS

The data were tabulated in a manner which assumes that each sentence gives
rise to a representation in memory of some or all of its components, and
that upon re-presentation each of these components is equally effective as
a cue in inducing recall of the other components stored within that memory
trace or fragment. Evidence that supports the making of this assumption in
the present experiment is described in this section, together with the
results of its application.

In the present experiment, 15 different types of memory fragment may be
distinguished. All four of the Location, Subject, Verb, and Object
components may be encoded (an LSVO fragment), or just three (LSV; LSO;
LVO; SVO) or two (LS; LV; LO; SV; SO; VO) of them, or all four as two
independent pairs (LS,VO; LV,SO; LO,SV), or just one or none of the
components (Null fragment). The reason why single-component fragments
cannot be separately distinguished here is that the experiment requires the
existence of a two-component fragment for recall to be possible (one
component corresponding to the cue and the other to what is recalled).

For each of the possible sequences of cues for an individual sentence, 15 possible patterns of recall corresponding to the 15 possible fragment types can occur. To provide some examples, consider the use as cues of first S, then S plus O, and finally S and O plus L. The recall in response to the first cue of all three components L, V, and O indicates the occurrence of an LSVO fragment; initial recall of nothing, followed by recall of L alone to the second cue, and by no further recall to the third cue, indicates an LO fragment; recall to the first cue of O alone, followed by no recall to the second cue, and by recall to the third cue of V, indicates an LV,SO fragment; and the recall of nothing to any of the three cues indicates a Null fragment.

Each pattern of data for each sequence of cuing was tabulated in accordance with the preceding scheme as corresponding to a particular type of fragment. If the assumptions underlying this procedure were correct, then for each subject the inferred distribution of the 15 different types of fragment over the 24 different types of cue sequence should be the same. This would not be true, on the other hand, if for example the different cues differed in their efficacies: If L were a better cue than S, say, then more examples of complete recall to the first cue (i.e., inferred LSVO fragments) should be apparent for cue sequences commencing with L than with S, for example.

In order to obtain adequate cell sizes for a statistical test of its assumptions, the tabulation was collapsed within the five major categories of memory fragment and the four types of first cue, and also over the subjects within a condition. The resulting table for each of the four attentional conditions is shown in Table 1. If the assumptions underlying the table are appropriate, the number of observations within each cell of a row should be approximately equal. Empirically, for each of the four conditions a chi-square test did not indicate a significant deviation from the predicted equalities: $\chi^2(12)$ was 19.09, 18.24, 7.33, and 20.56 for the Control, First-half, Second-half, and Both-halves conditions, respectively.

Following this positive result, estimates of the occurrence of each of the 15 types of fragment, summed over all cue sequences, were obtained for each attentional condition. Figure 1 shows the distribution of different types of memory fragment in the Control condition. It can be seen that the most frequent type of memory is the full LSVO fragment, and that the LSV, LSO, LS, and Null fragments are next most frequent (occurring roughly half as often as the LSVO fragment), indicating preferential retention of the first half of the sentence under normal conditions.

Interest in this experiment centres on the question of the effect upon recall patterns of attentional instructions. Figures 2, 3, and 4 show the differences in the shape of the fragment distributions (relative to that of the Control condition) that result from instructions focussing attention upon Location and Subject, Verb and Object, and the two pairs Location-Subject and Verb-Object, respectively.

An important result was that the probability of each cue sequence producing some correct recall was not significantly affected by attentional condition. This is shown by the lack of variation in the complementary measure, the observed frequency of the Null fragment, $F(3,36) = 0.15$. Nevertheless, the precise nature of the observed recall differed substantially among the four conditions.

Table 1
Recall Patterns for Different Cues, in Four Conditions

Fragment category	First cue			
	L	S	V	O
Control condition				
Quadruple component	17	22	7	15
Triple component	20	20	31	17
Double component	15	15	12	18
Two double components	2	0	2	3
Null	6	3	8	7
First-half condition				
Quadruple component	5	12	10	17
Triple component	17	19	21	16
Double component	32	20	18	15
Two double components	2	3	3	5
Null	4	6	8	7
Second-half condition				
Quadruple component	8	12	7	11
Triple component	15	17	17	18
Double component	25	19	19	23
Two double components	6	7	9	3
Null	6	5	8	5
Both-halves condition				
Quadruple component	16	13	10	17
Triple component	20	15	19	12
Double component	13	16	26	19
Two double components	4	12	3	6
Null	7	4	2	6

Note: L = location, S = subject, V = verb, O = object

The observed frequency of the LSVO fragment was substantially smaller in each of the focussed attention conditions than in the control condition, while that of the LS,VO twin fragment was substantially greater in each. Parenthetically, it may be noted that the SO fragment was also consistently smaller and the LV fragment consistently larger in the focussed conditions; the differences are small, however, and do not appear of importance (formal statistical analysis is rendered difficult by the covariation of the 15 fragment frequencies). The increase in frequency of the LS,VO fragment was indeed almost as great when attention was focussed only on the second half of the sentence as when it was focussed on the two separate halves. This is perhaps because the Control condition data discussed earlier showed that the first half of the sentence is retained well in any case.

In all three focussed attention conditions, recall of those parts of the sentence identified by the instructions was increased. However, the focussing of attention on the two halves of a sentence separately produced an increase in the frequency of the LS,VO fragment that was only approximately half that of the increases in the LS and VO fragments that were produced by instructions to focus on either the first or the second halves, respectively. Since an LS,VO fragment conveys as much information as an LS and a VO fragment together, it follows that the increases in the designated patterns of recall that were consequent upon three different forms of linguistic focussing were in informational terms approximately equal.

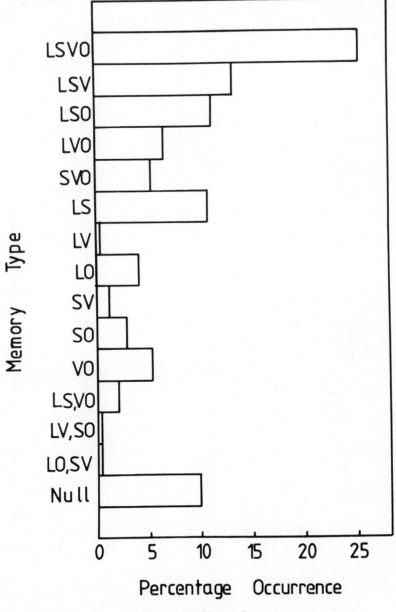

Figure 1
Distribution of Memory Fragments in Control Condition

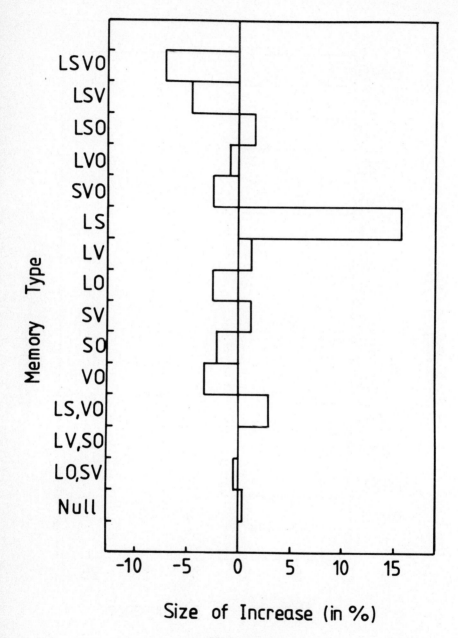

Figure 2
Change in Distribution of Memory Fragments in First-half Condition

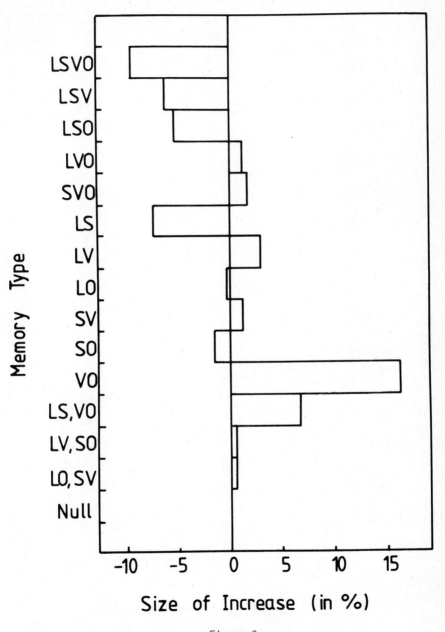

Figure 3
Change in Distribution of Memory Fragments in Second-half Condition

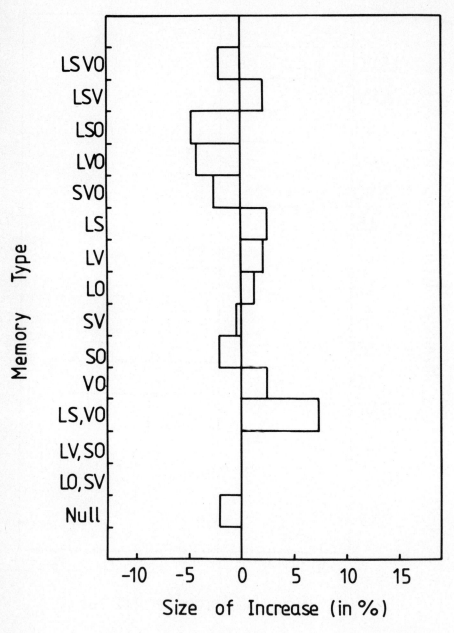

Figure 4
Change in Distribution of Memory Fragments in Both-halves Condition

DISCUSSION

The results of the experiment reported here are of interest from two principal points of view. Primarily, they provide evidence concerning the effects upon retention of manipulating processing priorities of different components of language material. They also, secondarily, relate to accounts of recall in general.

A model to account fully for the detailed changes in the distributions of different types of clusters of information retained in memory as a consequence of changes in attentional strategy has not been formulated here, though such a model is a suitable target for future research. Instead, two qualitative phenomena were observed. First, the overall level of perform- ance, as assessed by the probability of occurrence of partial or complete recall, did not differ significantly as a function of processing condition; there was no evidence that the normal attentional pattern of the control condition was an ecologically optimal one. Second, in three different focussed-attention conditions the improvements in retention of the specifically attended components of the utterance were in each case approximately equivalent. These results are accounted for most simply by positing the existence, within the domain of language processing studied here, of finite reserves of nonspecific linguistic processing resources which may be allocated freely so as best to allow task demands to be satisfied (cf. Martin, 1977; Shiffrin, 1975).

The experiment also provided information about the recall process itself. The control condition here was similar in nature to an experiment reported by Anderson and Bower (1973), whose results were also shown to be well represented by a distribution of memory fragments by Jones (1978b). Comparison of the two sets of results shows that the overall level of recall was considerably higher in the present experiment, perhaps because each person was shown only one set of material to remember, instead of three as previously. Nevertheless, four out of the five most frequent types of memory fragment were the same in the two experiments: the LSVO fragment (producing complete recall), the Null fragment (producing no recall at all), and the LS and LSO fragments (producing preferential recall of the first half of a sentence). In spite of the success of the fragment theory in these experiments, however, the existence of limitations upon its generality of application should be noted. For example, it requires augmentation by other, generative mechanisms if the different components of material to be remembered activate pre-existing specific relations that they bear to each another (Jones, 1978a, 1980; see also Ross and Bower, 1981, Expts. 1 & 2). Further, in common with other comparable models (in particular, the HAM model of Anderson and Bower, and the multicomponent model of Wender and Glowalla, 1979) it does not provide a direct account of the phenomenon (noted by Anderson and Bower, 1980, pp. 237-238) that, perhaps for motivational reasons, people are less likely to recall a particular part of a sentence if the appropriate cue has been preceded by an unsuccessful cue than if the appropriate cue occurs first; the magnitude of the effect, however, is not large.

REFERENCES

Anderson, J. R., & Bower, G. H. Human associative memory. Washington, DC: Winston, 1973.

Anderson, J. R., & Bower, G. H. Human associative memory: A brief
     edition. Hillsdale, NJ: Erlbaum, 1980.
Johnson, R. E. Recall of prose as a function of the structural importance
     of the linguistic units. Journal of Verbal Learning and Verbal
     Behavior, 1970, 9, 12-20.
Jones, G. V. Recognition failure and dual mechanisms in recall.
     Psychological Review, 1978, 85, 464-469. (a)
Jones, G. V. Tests of a structural theory of the memory trace. British
     Journal of Psychology, 1978, 69, 351-367. (b)
Jones, G. V. Interaction of intrinsic and extrinsic knowledge in sentence
     recall. In R. S. Nickerson (Ed.), Attention and Performance VIII.
     Hillsdale, NJ: Erlbaum, 1980.
Jones, G. V., & Martin, M. Recall cued by selectively attended and
     unattended attributes. Memory & Cognition, 1980, 8, 94-98.
Kintsch, W., & van Dijk, T. A. Toward a model of text comprehension and
     production. Psychological Review, 1978, 85, 363-394.
Mandler, J. M., & Johnson, N. S. Remembrance of things parsed: Story
     structure and recall. Cognitive Psychology, 1977, 9, 111-151.
Martin, M. Reading while listening: A linear model of selective attention.
     Journal of Verbal Learning and Verbal Behavior, 1977, 16, 453-463.
Miller, J. R., & Kintsch, W. Readability and recall of short prose
     passages: A theoretical analysis. Journal of Experimental
     Psychology: Human Learning and Memory, 1980, 6, 335-354.
Ross, B. H., & Bower, G. H. Comparison of models of associative recall.
     Memory & Cognition, 1981, 9, 1-16.
Rumelhart, D. E. Notes on a schema for stories. In D. G. Bobrow &
     A. Collins (Eds.), Representation and understanding: Studies in
     cognitive science. New York: Academic Press, 1975.
Shiffrin, R. M. The locus and role of attention in memory systems. In
     P. M. A. Rabbitt & S. Dornic (Eds.), Attention and performance V.
     New York: Academic Press, 1975.
Thorndyke, P. W. Cognitive structures in comprehension and memory of
     narrative discourse. Cognitive Psychology, 1977, 9, 77-110.
Wender, K. F., & Glowalla, U. Models for within-proposition representation
     tested by cued recall. Memory & Cognition, 1979, 7, 401-409.

DISCOURSE PROCESSING
A. Flammer and W. Kintsch (eds.)
© *North-Holland Publishing Company, 1982*

ACTIVATION AND RESTRUCTURING OF PRIOR KNOWLEDGE
AND THEIR EFFECTS ON TEXT PROCESSING

Henk G. Schmidt

Capacity Group of Educational Development and Research
Rijksuniversiteit Limburg
Maastricht
The Netherlands

In two experiments effects of a group problem-solving
procedure were assessed.
In Experiment 1 small groups of subjects were presented
with a problem they had to discuss. Compared with a
control condition the experimental subjects showed
superior reproduction and transfer of information
relevant to the problem. These effects were attributed
to the activating and restructuring properties of the
problem-solving procedure.
In Experiment 2 effects of activation and restructuring
of prior knowledge on subsequent text processing were
examined. A general facilitative effect was found. This
result cannot be explained in terms of selective attention
induced by prior problem analysis.

INTRODUCTION

Learning by discovery has been considered a useful addition and perhaps
even an alternative to existing educational procedures for some time.
Jerome Bruner for instance, the first who applied this method on a somewhat broader scale, was of the opinion that discovery learning more than
conventional education increases students' intellectual capacities. The
method was said to promote the learning of meaningful information, which
in turn would have positive effects on long-term retention and transfer. It
was also thought to stimulate a student's intrinsic motivation (Bruner,
1961). Bruner's ideas have given impetus to a lot of empirical research,
but the yield has not been very significant (Shulman and Keislar, 1966).
Learning by discovery does not seem capable of producing the predicted
extra learning results.

One may wonder why this should be so. After all, the learners in the
situations described by Bruner are cognitively active to a high degree and
this condition is generally recognized as favoring the learning process.
According to Mayer (1975) the disappointing outcome is probably accounted
for by the fact that discovery learning only leads to activation of
existing knowledge. If no confrontation with new knowledge takes place,
learning does not occur (Mayer, 1975, p. 539). Mayer derives this
hypothesis from his own assimilation theory, which states that new information is absorbed only if three conditions are fulfilled:
1. a certain amount of prior knowledge about the subject to be studied
should be present. This is referred to by Mayer as the *assimilative set*:
the body of knowledge into which the information newly to be acquired

325

should be assimilated;
2. the assimilative set should be actually *activated* by the education;
3. during the learning process, knowledge should *interact with new informat-ion* to allow development of new knowledge structures (Mayer, 1975; 1979a; 1979b).
As a rule, the third condition is not satisfied by discovery learning. While working on a problem, the student is expected to produce the required additional information *himself*. It does not seem reasonable however to assume that he is able to do so without external assistance.

But what would happen if we let students work on a problem first (as is usual for discovery learning) and *subsequently* confront them with new in-formation relevant to the problem? By modifying the discovery learning approach in this direction all three conditions for learning set by Mayer would be fulfilled in principle. In fact, experience with such a modi-fication is being obtained for a few years, notably in medical education (Neufeld and Barrows, 1974; Schmidt and Bouhuijs, 1980; Neame, 1981). A small group of students under the guidance of a tutor is offered a problem description. The problem usually includes a number of phenomena or events which can be observed in reality. Students are asked to *explain* these phenomena in terms of underlying processes, principles or mechanisms (Schmidt, 1979). They do so by utilizing prior knowledge to formulate hypotheses regarding the process or principle that might underlie the phenomena outlined. They are trying, as it were, to give a tentative description of this process. Subsequently, they collect or receive new information relevant to the problem, by which any ambiguities uncovered during the initial analysis of the problem can be clarified. This variant to learning by discovery is called problem-based learning (Barrows and Tamblyn, 1980).
To be able to make predictions about possible effects of problem analysis on the acquisition of additional information, we refer to schema theory, a much used description of human information processing (Bartlett, 1932; Ausubel, 1968; Minsky, 1975; Rumelhart and Ortony, 1977). This theory states that in the encoding of new information existing knowledge schemata are activated that regulate the process of comprehension (Dooling and Lachman, 1971; Bransford and Johnson, 1972; Anderson and Pichert, 1978). A decisive role in understanding new information is probably played by *inferences* generated by an activated schema (Schank and Abelson, 1977). Inferences may be regarded as hypotheses about information still to be stored that are tested against such information. The outcome of these tests decides on a possible change of existing schemata, which are then said to *accomodate* to the new information (Anderson, 1977). From this perspective learning can be considered a process of differentiation and reconstruction of existing cognitive structures.

Now, if we try with the aid of these notions to describe the cognitive pro-cesses taking place in students engaged in problem analysis, the following suppositions might be made. Thinking about the presented problem and dis-cussing it with others activates existing schemata more or less relevant to that problem. These schemata may derive from factual knowledge of the underlying principle or process, from knowledge of analogous processes, or from general world knowledge. The schemata will produce inferences with the aid of which students will try to develop their own cognitive repre-sentation of the processes that may be considered responsible for the phenomena contained in the problem description. If the problem cannot be satisfactorily solved with the help of knowledge that students already

Results

Items t
terion
the rep
coeffic
and for
those g
are con
measure
correla
in comm
small d
of the
fer tes
ed to a

Table 1:

Experime
Control

Total

Table 2:

Experime
Control

Total

The analy
experimer
level. Th
$F(1,37)=4$
introduct
seems tha
problem-c
restructu
experimen
compared

The chose
activatio
group act
subjects
items act
blem and

---

have available prior to the discussion, the cognitive representation of the processes underlying the problem will take the form of a *new*, more differentiated construction of the prior knowledge of each contributing individual. The tutor stimulates this process of activation and restructuring of prior knowledge by inducing students to explicate their inferences. He will do so by means of Socratic questioning (Collins, 1977).

In summary we may say that analysis of a problem leads to activation and 'recontextualization' of prior knowledge (Anderson, 1977) and, as a result of the production of inferences, to its restructuring. The availability of more differentiated schemata resulting from the problem analysis should in turn facilitate the processing of new information relevant to the problem.

In two experiments we have investigated a number of the hypotheses expressed here. The first was conducted to find out to what extent problem analysis leads to activation and restructuring of people's prior knowledge with respect to the problem and its underlying process. In the second experiment we examined the effect of problem analysis on the processing of new information. In each experiment we investigated effects on two dimensions customary in this kind of research, the degree to which subjects are capable of *reproducing* problem-relevant knowledge and the degree to which they are able to use this knowledge in new situations: the degree of *transfer* of knowledge.

EXPERIMENT 1

In Experiment 1 the effect of problem analysis on existing cognitive structures was investigated. The question to be answered was whether analysis of a problem according to the method described in the introduction leads to activation and restructuring of schemata.

Method

Subjects.
39 students (8 males, 31 females) of an institute for higher education participated in the experiment. All subjects had previously attended the same type of secondary education (in Dutch: HAVO), with their final examination including biology. They were paid for participation.

Materials.
The materials included a problem description, two multiple-choice tests, and a questionnaire. The *problem* was described as follows:
    A red blood cell (a red blood corpuscle) is transferred to pure water under a microscope. The blood cell swells rapidly and eventually bursts. Another red blood cell is added to an aqueous salt solution and is observed to shrink.
    How can these phenomena be explained?
Subjects were to account for the described phenomena in terms of an underlying process, mechanism, or principle. The problem refers to osmosis. This had been selected because inspection of four biology text books much in use at HAVO schools had shown that this subject was treated in a more or less identical fashion. Homogeneity of the subjects with respect to prior knowledge of biology of course reduces chance variation in the results of the experiment.
Dependent variables consisted of two tests: a reproduction and a transfer test. In the construction of the test items use was made of a text about osmosis and related subjects such as diffusion, turgor, and plasmolysis.

This f
is giv
The re
agreem
This n
variou
of the
answer
The tr
extent
items
aid of
i.e.,
formed
false
items
that t
The qu
examin

Proced
Subjec
group (
random
in pri
The mea
deviat
.69). 1
The exp
(N = 7,
these g
convers
Tutor a
she exp
and had
1. Refl
Elabora
Before
blem an
was iss
the dis
had bee
blem an
informa
the pro
verific
agreed
instruc
complet
control
questio
that th
good or
answer k
the iter
by count

relevant parts of the text. Given an equal amount of study time for both groups, the experimental group will perform better on items concerned with topics relevant to the problem, whereas the control group will do better with non-relevant items. Hence, no overall difference between the two groups is going to be observed in either test. The differential predictions discussed above are summarized in Table 3. The plus-sign means the problem analysis group will perform better on this test (or part of the test) than the control group. A minus-sign means that the control group performance will be better.

Table 3: Differential predictions about the influence of problem analysis on text processing

	reproduction	transfer
Schema theory (Rumelhart and Ortony, 1977)	+	+
Mayer and Greeno's (1972) specification	-	+
Selective attention theory (Rothkopf and Billington, 1979) items concerned with text relevant to problem	+	+
Selective attention theory (Rothkopf and Billington, 1979) items concerned with text not relevant to problem	-	-

Methods

Subjects.
48 students (42 females, 6 males) of an institute for higher education participated in the experiment. All subjects had attended the same type of secondary education (in Dutch: HAVO), with their final examinations including biology. They were paid for participating.

Materials.
The materials used in Experiment 2 were identical to those of Experiment 1. In addition, however, a written text was used.
The 2,220-word text was entitled 'Osmosis and Diffusion'. It had been designed to adapt as well as possible to subjects' prior knowledge. The description of the osmosis process was more detailed and precise than is customary for HAVO schools. The text dealt with the following topics: diffusion, diffusion rate, (semi-)permeability of cell membrane, osmosis, osmotic pressure, osmotic value, plant cell structure, turgor, and plasmolysis. Not all of these were directly relevant to the problem. In order to be able to test selective attention theory the two multiple-choice tests were subdivided by two independent judges, including the investigator, into items of immediate importance to the problem and those of lesser relevance. Agreement between judges was 76%. The items about which consensus had not been reached were classified in one of the two categories by mutual agreement. (Removal from the analysis would have left too few items.)

Results and discussion

Items that proved to be too easy were removed from the analysis. As a criterion a p-value ⩾.90 was used. It proved necessary to remove 10 items from the reproduction test and 5 from the transfer test. The alpha reliability coefficient for the resulting 23-item reproduction test was equal to .73 and for the 32-item transfer test to .69. These reliabilities compare with those generally obtained in examinations (Wijnen, 1971). The two instruments are considered different on a priori grounds. They were each supposed to measure a different aspect of the subjects' knowledge. Their product-moment correlation was equal to .41. Consequently they have about 16% of variance in common. This means that they each measure the same characteristic to a small degree and a different characteristic to a larger degree. The results of the reproduction test are summarized in Table 1 and those for the transfer test are summarized in Table 2. The results on both tests were subjected to a one-way analysis of variance.

Table 1: Means and standard deviations of reproduction scores for Experiment 1

	M	SD	N
Experimental group	10.90	4.17	20
Control group	8.63	3.00	19
Total	9.79	3.65	39

Table 2: Means and standard deviations of transfer scores for Experiment 1

	M	SD	N
Experimental group	16.55	5.08	20
Control group	13.26	4.40	19
Total	14.95	4.84	39

The analyses of variance show that the actual difference found between the experimental and control conditions are statistically significant at the 10% level. This applies to both reproduction, $F(1,37)=3.77$, $p<.06$, and transfer, $F(1,37)=4.96$, $p<.04$. These results support the theory advanced in the introduction with respect to cognitive effects of problem analysis. It seems that written problems indeed activate existing schemata and that the problem-connected inferences based on these schemata lead to their restructuring. Apparently, the restructured schemata enable subjects in the experimental condition to give better answers to the items of the tests, as compared with the control subjects.

The chosen experimental design does not allow us to separate the effects of activation from those of restructuring of schemata. For in the control group activation of prior knowledge also takes place, notably at the moment subjects in that condition answer the tests. Of course, reading the test items activates prior knowledge as well. Whether the combination of problem and test items activates prior knowledge to the same degree as answering the test items only - and whether the established effects should solely be ascribed to restructuring - remains unclear for the time being.

EXPERIMENT 2

What happens if you ask students who have just tackled the blood-cell problem to study a text about osmosis? What will be the effect of recontextualized and restructured prior knowledge on the processing of text relevant to the problem?

According to the position defended here, problem analysis functions as a bridge between prior knowledge and knowledge still to be acquired. Elaboration of prior knowledge by means of discussion of a problem causes existing cognitive structures to change in the direction of further differentiation and restructuring. Compared with the situation that exists before problem analysis the subjects' schemata will contain concepts that are clearer and have more and closer mutual relationships. In this way it provides a better ideational scaffolding for new information contained in a problem-relevant text (Anderson, et al., 1978). Information from the text will be processed more easily and, consequently, faster. In terms of the second experiment this means that given a standard amount of study time, persons who have first worked on a problem will process a problem-relevant text deeper than others who have only processed the text (Craik and Lockhart, 1972).

If this is the sole effect to be expected from problem analysis, one might just simply extend study time for subjects' text processing (Peeck, 1970) instead of presenting them with a problem-plus-text. However, subjects who have analyzed a problem beforehand will not only process new information faster but also *in a different way*. As a result of the structural changes to which existing schemata have been subjected new information will be comprehended in another, more differentiated manner. This subtler interpretation of the subject-matter will lead to a deeper understanding and consequently to improved application of knowledge in transfer tasks. In other words: schema theory predicts better retention as well as greater transfer. Mayer (1974, 1975) slightly modifies this prediction. He states that different educational procedures often do not lead to an *increase* (or decrease) in learning, but to learning results that are *structurally different*. For instance, education may emphasize the internal structure of information to be acquired, or it may stress relationships with other, already available, knowledge. In the former case, according to Mayer, a cognitive structure develops whose constituent concepts are strongly linked with each other but have few relationships with knowledge elements beyond the domain studied. Mayer refers to this as the 'internal connectedness' of that cognitive structure. In the latter case a cognitive structure develops which has strong connections with knowledge elements outside the specific domain ('external connectedness'). He predicts that educational procedures stressing the internal connections between new concepts lead to improved reproduction of such concepts, and that educational procedures emphasizing relationships between new concepts and other already available knowledge lead to better transfer but poorer reproduction. Research conducted by Mayer and Greeno (1972) demonstrated that these 'treatment post-test' interactions do occur. They gave instruction to subjects on binomial probability by means of two procedures. In one of these the relations between the variables of the binomial formula were emphasized and subjects learned to calculate by using the formula. In the other procedure they tried to establish connections between the variables of the formula on the one hand, and the prior knowledge and experience of subjects with chance,

trial, and outcome on the other. The results did not yield an overall
difference between procedures on a post test, but did show qualitative
differences in the answering of the items. As predicted, the 'internal
connectedness' group proved superior in answering items about the relations between variables of the formula, which means that they were better
in reproduction tasks. The 'external connectedness' group proved more apt
in recognizing unsolvable problems and in solving problems whose variables
were concealed in a story. This group, therefore, excelled in items involving transfer. It looks as if emphasis on external relationships of
concepts to be learned (the relationship between concepts and learners'
prior knowledge) is at the expense of the internal connectedness of concepts to be learned (the mutual relationship between the concepts). Assuming that the reproduction test applied in the present experiment aims exclusively at concepts from the text proper and at their mutual relationships, one would have to predict on the basis of Mayer's considerations
that the control group (text-only) will perform better on the reproduction
test, whereas the experimental group (problem-plus-text: emphasizing
relationships with prior knowledge) will demonstrate a better performance
on the transfer test.

The predictions expressed above have all been derived from schema-
theoretical notions with respect to how a text is processed. However, there
is also another theory about text processing that may be relevant within
the scope of this research. This theory is *selective attention theory*
(Rothkopf, 1970; Duchastel, 1979; Glynn and Di Vesta, 1979; Reynolds et
al., 1979). This theory simply postulates that whatever people learn from
a text is a function of the amount of attention paid to various test
passages. The amount of attention paid to various passages is in turn a
function of the *objectives* of the persons processing the text. Typical for
this approach is the following experiment: Two groups of subjects study
the same text. One group has been previously given a list of learning
objectives or questions relating to the text. Measurement of what has been
processed then shows that subjects who have studied the text guided by
learning objectives recall goal-relevant information better than the
control group. This is achieved however *at the expense* of the storage of
information not directly related to the learning objectives.

In an investigation into eye-movements during reading, Rothkopf and
Billington (1979) discovered that subjects fixated twice as much on
sentences relevant to a learning objective than on sentences which are not.
From this they drew the conclusion that what people learn is determined
by the amount of selective attention - expressed in amount of inspection
time - paid to the text passages to be learned.
The materials used in our experiment were constructed in such a manner
that a selective-attention explanation of possible effects could also be
tested. We started from the assumption that the blood cell problem (which
was worked on by the subjects of our experiment) might play the same role
as the learning objectives in the selective-attention experiments. This
means that working on problems would induce subjects to pay more attention
to problem-relevant passages of the text at the expense of those passages
that are less meaningful in the light of the problem. The text about
osmosis was edited to include information of lesser relevance to the
blood-cell problem. The selective attention theory predicts that subjects
of the experimental group (problem-plus-text) will pay greater attention
to problem-relevant text passages compared with the control group (text-
only), but also that such attention will reduce the attention paid to less

relevant parts of the text. Given an equal amount of study time for both groups, the experimental group will perform better on items concerned with topics relevant to the problem, whereas the control group will do better with non-relevant items. Hence, no overall difference between the two groups is going to be observed in either test. The differential predictions discussed above are summarized in Table 3. The plus-sign means the problem analysis group will perform better on this test (or part of the test) than the control group. A minus-sign means that the control group performance will be better.

Table 3: Differential predictions about the influence of problem analysis on text processing

		reproduction	transfer
Schema theory (Rumelhart and Ortony, 1977)		+	+
Mayer and Greeno's (1972) specification		-	+
Selective attention theory (Rothkopf and Billington, 1979)	items concerned with text relevant to problem	+	+
	items concerned with text not relevant to problem	-	-

Methods

Subjects.
48 students (42 females, 6 males) of an institute for higher education participated in the experiment. All subjects had attended the same type of secondary education (in Dutch: HAVO), with their final examinations including biology. They were paid for participating.

Materials.
The materials used in Experiment 2 were identical to those of Experiment 1. In addition, however, a written text was used.
The 2,220-word *text* was entitled 'Osmosis and Diffusion'. It had been designed to adapt as well as possible to subjects' prior knowledge. The description of the osmosis process was more detailed and precise than is customary for HAVO schools. The text dealt with the following topics: diffusion, diffusion rate, (semi-)permeability of cell membrane, osmosis, osmotic pressure, osmotic value, plant cell structure, turgor, and plasmolysis. Not all of these were directly relevant to the problem. In order to be able to test selective attention theory the two multiple-choice tests were subdivided by two independent judges, including the investigator, into items of immediate importance to the problem and those of lesser relevance. Agreement between judges was 76%. The items about which consensus had not been reached were classified in one of the two categories by mutual agreement. (Removal from the analysis would have left too few items.)

Procedure.
The procedure was largely identical to that of Experiment 1. In the experimental condition 23 subjects were tested and in the control condition 25. Following randomization it was established to what extent the two groups were comparable in prior knowledge of biology (expressed by the final examination grade). The average grade for biology in the control group was 6.36 (standard deviation .81) and 6.39 in the experimental group (standard deviation .94). The experimental group was subdivided into three smaller groups (N=8, 8 and 7). Each of them was randomly assigned an experienced female tutor. The tutor and her group proceeded in the way described for the first experiment. All groups needed less than 10 minutes for analysis. After that the experimental group answered the questionnaire. It was next given the text and instructed to study this. The control group answered the questionnaire and studied the text. Each group was allowed 15 minutes for study.
Finally, subjects took the reproduction and the transfer tests.

Results and discussion

Items having a p-value equal to or larger than .90 were removed from the analyses as being too easy.
The results for reproduction are given in Table 4 and those for transfer in Table 5.

Table 4: Means and standard deviations of reproduction scores for Experiment 2

	M	SD	N
Experimental group	16.17	2.46	23
Control group	14.48	2.63	25
Total	15.29	2.55	48

Table 5: Means and standard deviations of transfer scores for Experiment 2

	M	SD	N
Experimental group	20.04	3.01	23
Control group	17.56	3.45	25
Total	18.75	3.25	48

One-way analyses of variance on these results yield the following picture. Reproduction: $F(1,46)=5.26$, $p<.03$. Transfer: $F(1,46)=7.01$, $p<.02$. These results support the assertion expressed before that analysis of a problem in the way this is prescribed in problem-based learning causes new information to be better understood and remembered. Recontextualization of the assimilative set by means of problem analysis promotes interaction between prior knowledge and new information, which in turn is responsible for the observed gains in the reproduction of such information and its application.

The results do not however support the view of Mayer and Greeno (1972) that intensive interaction between prior knowledge and new information should lead to poorer performance on a test measuring knowledge of the 'autonomous' text (Anderson, 1977), whereas transfer should be promoted. The experimental subjects were also better in reproducing the text. There is a possibility that the reproduction test used in this experiment does not really measure Mayer and Greeno's 'internal connectedness' of the cognitive structure resulting from text processing. Mayer and Greeno do not indicate clearly what exactly they have in mind when using this term, so that our interpretation of the concept - that internal connectedness can be measured by text reproduction - was perhaps not quite correct.

However this may be, schema theory appears to allow correct predictions with regard to the influence activation and restructuring of existing schemata have on the processing of new information.

What about the support for selective attention theory? The answer to this question has not been made superfluous by the previous argumentation because, theoretically, it is possible that problem analysis has a schema-restructuring *as well as* a guiding function. In order to investigate this hypothesis we divided as mentioned the items of the tests into a set directly relevant to the osmotic process and a set of indirect relevance. Items relating to diffusion rate, osmotic value, plant cell structure, turgor, and plasmolysis were regarded as indirectly relevant to the problem. Each of the four subtests resulting from this subdivision has been subjected to an analysis of variance. In addition *all* items of direct relevance from the tests have been combined into a new test and subjected to an analysis of variance. The same was done with *all* indirectly relevant items. The results are given in Tables 6 and 7. These only show mean values and chance probabilities resulting from the analyses.

Table 6: Means and chance probabilities of subtests consisting of items directly relevant to the problem

	reproduction	transfer	total
Experimental group	7.43	11.13	18.57
Control group	6.80	10.16	16.96
Chance probability	<.14	<.13	<.08

Table 7: Means and chance probabilities of subtests consisting of indirectly relevant items

	reproduction	transfer	total
Experimental group	8.74	8.91	17.65
Control group	7.68	7.40	15.08
Chance probability	<.04	<.02	<.01

In the light of selective attention theory these results can hardly be interpreted. Selective attention theory predicted effects favoring the treatment group with respect to subtests consisting of items directly relevant to the problem, whereas the control group would demonstrate better performance on indirectly relevant items. This was not the case. Statistically significant differences were not found in the case of problem-relevant items, whereas the differences established for indirectly relevant items did favoring the treatment group.

If we should nevertheless want to maintain (a combination of schema theory and) selective attention theory in explaining these results, only the following line of thought seems plausible: the way in which the problem analysis group prepares for text study induces this group to pay less attention to problem-relevant information than the control group. Which means that this group has more time available for studying information which is relatively new in the light of the problem. As a result experimental subjects do better on indirectly relevant items and, while study time and type of preparation counterbalance each other on directly relevant information, they do not show poorer performance on directly relevant items. This explanation should be called a boredom-hypothesis, because it suggests that subjects in the treatment condition become bored earlier with the osmosis topic than the control subjects.

GENERAL DISCUSSION

The two experiments discussed here show that analysis of a problem in the way described in this contribution and elsewhere (Schmidt, 1979; Schmidt and Bouhuijs, 1980) causes existing knowledge schemata to be activated and restructured, and that this effect facilitates subsequent processing of a text relevant to that problem. With reference to the introduction of this contribution we may say that Mayer's (1975) diagnosis regarding the effects of discovery learning appears to be correct. Learning by discovery indeed leads to activation of the assimilative set and, as we have demonstrated, to its restructuring. This effect, however, is insufficient to produce the extra learning effects predicted by Bruner, for that calls for actual confrontation with new information.

Of course, the results of the present experiments should to a certain degree be regarded as isolated phenomena. Naturally, it is too early to conclude that elaboration of prior knowledge by means of problem analysis has, in general, a facilitating effect on text processing. We have shown, however, that conditions can be created under which problem analysis effects are demonstrable. Finding out how representative these conditions are and how general the effects certainly requires further research.

Moreover there are some other possible explanations for the results found, interpretations that could not be ruled out by the chosen experimental design. The first is that the established results could be generated by a *Hawthorne effect*. It is possible that the subjects experienced problem analysis as being so new and interesting that it increased their motivation. This alternative explanation might well hold true for Experiment 1. Not so for the second however. The subjects participating in the latter had, some time beforehand, gained an extensive three-months experience with this type of education, so the method was not really new to them. A second alternative derives from motivational descriptions of the learning process (Faw and Waller, 1976; Mayer, 1980). It is not impossible that working on an interesting problem has such a *motivating effect* on subjects that those who have carried out a problem analysis are more interested in a text relevant

to that problem than people who have not. There are indications that problem analysis indeed induces a slightly greater motivation. The latter
would in turn increase a subject's efforts, so that he/she learns more in
less time. However, research on motivation has only rarely established such
direct effects on learning. It has been found, though, that motivation
influences the *amount of time* students are prepared to spend on material
to be studied. We did keep study time constant in our research, so this
alternative is not a very likely one.

For that matter, it would be interesting to examine the influence problem
analysis has on study time. Would subjects be inclined to spend more time
on studying material relevant to a certain problem? Another question
concerns the influence of problem analysis on subsequent retrieval of knowledge stored in long-term memory. One could imagine that storage of
information, along with the cues provided by problem analysis, facilitates
subsequent retrieval (Tulving and Thompson, 1973).
Finally, interactions between subjects' prior knowledge and the structure
and difficulty of the text (Mayer, 1980; Kintsch and Van Dijk, 1978), as
well as variations in the nature of the problems presented should be studied.

REFERENCES

Anderson, R.C. How to construct achievement tests to assess comprehension.
  Review of Educational Research, 1972, 49, 145-170.
Anderson, R.C. The notion of schemata and the educational enterprise:
  general discussion of the conference. In R.C. Anderson, R.J. Spiro and
  W.E. Montague (Eds.). *Schooling and the acquisition of knowledge*.
  Hillsdale: Lawrence Erlbaum Associates, 1977.
Anderson, R.C. and Pichert, J.W. Recall of previously unrecallable infor-
  mation following a shift in perspective. *Journal of Verbal Learning and
  Verbal Behavior*, 1978, 17, 1-12.
Anderson, R.C., Spiro, R.J. and Anderson, M.C. Schemata as scaffolding for
  the representation of information in connected discourse. *American
  Educational Research Journal*, 1978, 15, 433-440.
Ausubel, D.P. *Educational Psychology, a cognitive view*. New York: Holt,
  Rinehart and Winston, 1968.
Barrows, H.S. and Tamblyn, R.M. *Problem-based learning*. New York: Springer,
  1980.
Bartlett, F.C. *Remembering*. Cambridge: Cambridge University Press, 1932.
Bormuth, J.R. *On the theory of achievement test items*. Chicago: University
  of Chicago Press, 1970.
Bransford, J.D. and Johnson, M.K. Contextual prerequisites for understanding:
  some investigations of comprehension and recall. *Journal of Verbal
  Learning and Verbal Behavior*, 1972, 11, 717-726.
Bruner, J.S. The act of discovery. *Harvard Educational Review*, 1961, 31,
  21-32.
Collins, A. Processes in acquiring knowledge. In R.C. Anderson, R.J. Spiro
  and W.E. Montague (Eds.). *Schooling and the acquisition of knowledge*.
  Hillsdale: Lawrence Erlbaum Associates, 1977.
Craik, F.I. and Lockhart, R.S. Levels of processing: a framework for memory
  research. *Journal of Verbal Learning and Verbal Behavior*, 1972, 11, 671-
  684.
Dooling, D.J. and Lachman, R. Effects of comprehension on retention of
  prose. *Journal of Experimental Psychology*, 1971, 88, 216-222.

Duchastel, P. Learning objectives and the organization of prose. *Journal of Educational Psychology*, 1971, <u>71</u>, 100-106.

Faw, H.W. and Waller, T.G. Mathemagenic behaviors and efficiency in learning from prose. *Review of Educational Research*, 1976, <u>46</u>, 691-722.

Glynn, S.M. and Di Vesta, F.J. Control of prose processing via instructional and typographical cues. *Journal of Educational Psychology*, 1979, <u>71</u>, 595-603.

Kintsch, W. and Van Dijk, T.A. Toward a model of text comprehension and production. *Psychological Review*, 1978, <u>85</u>, 363-394.

Mayer, R.E. Acquisition processes and resilience under varying testing conditions of structurally different problem solving procedures. *Journal of Educational Psychology*, 1974, <u>66</u>, 644-656.

Mayer, R.E. Information processing variables in learning to solve problems. *Review of Educational Research*, 1975, <u>45</u>, 525-541.

Mayer, R.E. Can advance organizers influence meaningful learning? *Review of Educational Research*, 1979a, <u>49</u>, 371-383.

Mayer, R.E. Twenty years of research on advance organizers: assimilation theory is still the best predictor of results. *Instructional Science*, 1979b, <u>8</u>, 133-167.

Mayer, R.E. Elaboration techniques that increase the meaningfulness of technical text: an experimental test of the learning strategy hypothesis. *Journal of Educational Psychology*, 1980, <u>72</u>, 770-784.

Mayer, R.E. and Greeno, J.G. Structural differences between learning outcomes produced by different instructional methods. *Journal of Educational Psychology*, 1972, <u>63</u>, 165-173.

Minsky, M. A framework for representing knowledge. In P.H. Winston (Ed.). *The psychology of computer vision*. New York: McGraw-Hill, 1975.

Neame, R.L.B. How to construct a problem-based course. *Medical Teacher*, 1981, <u>3</u>, 94-99.

Neufeld, V.R. and Barrows, H.S. The McMaster Philosophy: an approach to medical education. *Journal of Medical Education*, 1974, <u>49</u>, 1040-1050.

Peeck, J. Effects of prequestions on delayed retention of prose material. *Journal of Educational Psychology*, 1970, <u>61</u>, 241-246.

Reynolds, R.E., Standiford, S.N. and Anderson, R.C. Distribution of reading time when questions are asked about a restricted category of text information. *Journal of Educational Psychology*, 1979, <u>71</u>, 183-190.

Rothkopf, E.Z. The concept of mathemagenic activities. *Review of Educational Research*, 1970, <u>40</u>, 325-336.

Rothkopf, E.Z. and Billington, M.J. Goal-guided learning from text: inferring a descriptive processing model from inspection times and eye movements. *Journal of Educational Psychology*, 1979, <u>71</u>, 310-327.

Rumelhart, D.E. and Ortony, E. The representation of knowledge in memory. In:R.C. Anderson, R.J. Spiro and W.E. Montague (Eds.). *Schooling and the acquisition of knowledge*. Hillsdale: Lawrence Erlbaum, 1977.

Schank, R.C. and Abelson, R.P. *Scripts, plans, goals and understanding*. Hillsdale: Lawrence Erlbaum Associates, 1977.

Schmidt, H.G. Leren met problemen, een inleiding in probleemgestuurd onderwijs. In A.G. Vroon (Ed.). *Handboek voor de onderwijspraktijk*. Deventer: Van Loghum Slaterus, 1979.

Schmidt, H.G. and Bouhuijs, P.A.J. *Onderwijs in taakgerichte groepen*. Utrecht: Het Spectrum, 1980.

Shulman, L.S. and Keislar, E.R. (Eds.). *Learning by discovery, a critical appraisal*. Chicago: Rand McNally, 1966.

Tulving, E. and Thomson, D.M. Encoding specificity and retrieval processes in episodic memory. *Psychological Review*, 1973, <u>80</u>, 352-373.

Wijnen, W.H.F.W. *Onder of boven de maat.* Amsterdam: Swetz en Zeitlinger, 1971.

DISCOURSE PROCESSING
A. Flammer and W. Kintsch (eds.)
© *North-Holland Publishing Company, 1982*

METACOGNITIVE REGULATION OF TEXT PROCESSING:
ASPECTS AND PROBLEMS CONCERNING THE RELATION
BETWEEN SELF-STATEMENTS AND ACTUAL PERFORMANCE

Peter M. Fischer and Heinz Mandl

Deutsches Institut für Fernstudien
an der Universität Tübingen
Tübingen
Federal Republic of Germany

Current models of metacognitive or executive action regulation are based upon the assumption of the psychological
reality of some central processing unit controlling cognitive 'routines'. The current approach questions the homogeneity and consistency of this notion by showing that
there are at least two concepts of executive regulation,
a competence and a performance centered paradigm, which
largely differ with regard to the predictions they allow.
The theoretical inconsistencies are further emphasized in
light of empirical data.

THEORETICAL BACKGROUND

Two models of metacognitive regulation. The label "metacognitive" refers
to all those reflective processes, and the results of such processes, as
they serve an individual's own thinking or problem-solving processes, the
way they operate and their effectiveness. From the beginning of metacognitive theorizing, attempts have been made to subdivide metacognitions into
smaller, more differentiated categories. The first taxonomy of metacognitive
skills was proposed by FLAVELL and WELLMAN (1977). FLAVELL and WELLMAN
distinguish four categories of metacognitive skills:
- sensitivity to tasks and task demands as well to possible steps to solving
  it;
- personal-knowledge concerning the cognitive apparatus and its functioning;
- task variable/task category knowledge concerning possible types and
  characteristics of problems; and
- strategy variable/strategy category knowledge with regard to a learner's
  strategic repertoire for coping with tasks.

These four types of knowledge to a certain extent represent the data base
on which the metacognitive regulation processes operate. What remains largely undetermined, however, is the way "metacognitive knowledge" and "general
knowledge about the world" interact, as well as some disparities within the
data base of metacognitive knowledge: Should what has been subsumed under
the heading "strategy variable" be considered knowledge or data, or are we
really concerned with processes, routines for problem solving? Is the
distinction between world knowledge and metacognitive knowledge necessary
at all, and what are the critical features for such a differentiation? Are
both kinds of information stored in the same format and what does this imply
for the underlying network assumptions?

While earlier studies (e.g. KREUTZER, LEONARD and FLAVELL, 1975; FLAVELL, 1970; FLAVELL, FRIEDRICHS and HOYT, 1970; FLAVELL, 1976 a,b) were concerned with proving the psychological reality (and impact) of metacognitive knowledge primarily by investigating the developmental differences of memory functions at various ages. They assumed the level of metacognitive knowledge to be positively correlated with the performance level of intellectual functioning. The critical discussion concerning the relationship between self-statements and actual performance which has come into focus recently (NISBETT and WILSON, 1977) has forced reconsideration of the notion of meta-cognitive processes. Hence, FLAVELL (1978) added three new dimensions to the knowledge component to his process model of metacognitive functioning:
- cognitive goals
- metacognitive awareness
- cognitive actions, and
- metacognitive knowledge
which are assumed to be interrelated through complex interactions. Thus extended, the model now provides for functional subdivisions into process-related executive components (monitoring of one's actual state as metacognitive awareness and knowledge about one's cognitive endowment) and less process-like components (knowledge-based data or set points in the service of action regulation). It should be noted, however, that this does not so much represent a process model, as a heuristic device allowing for the integration of single observations into some general interpretative framework. A model of a less static nature and less centered on knowledge or data has been proposed by BROWN (1975, 1977, 1978). Her model of executive regulation refers to the paradigm of the "central processing unit" within the artificial intelligence approach, whose "executive" plans a sequence of solution steps, schedules the individual program-steps and monitors their execution and success, checks on the outcomes and evaluates them, controls for corresponding regulatory action, and thus exerts full control on the subroutines until the job is done. Correspondingly, the human problem-solver is seen to make use of two kinds of executive functions, data collection and process regulation, in order to organize his own cognitive functioning in a most economical and efficient way. BROWN's model, too, is based on developmental differences between younger and older children and between retarded and normal children. The question of the psychological reality of the model and its components, on the other hand, has been replaced by the issue of whether training may help to develop executive procedures able to compensate for shortcomings in the skills of planning, monitoring, checking, evaluation, and regulation as shown in the performance of the younger, retarded or novice as compared with the performance of the older, normal, or expert subject. According to BROWN, if it is possible to bring up to the performance deficits of the novice up to the level of the expert, we then have implicit proof that the previous differences in performance were due to differences in metacognitive or executive skills. This proof, on the other hand, is implicitly assumed to guarantee the psychological reality of the executive by means of an empirical test.
For BROWN there is no need to speculate about the nature of the data base or some metacognitive knowledge, which is needed to serve as markers for prospective (planning) or on-line (monitoring,testing,checking) or off-line (evaluation) control. All that is needed is some rule equipment, the rules being strategic in nature. And, since the rules are acquired through strategic training, all one has to do to get the adequate rules for (meta)-cognitive control of intellectual tasks is to engage in extensive training in a variety of cognitive tasks.
BROWN makes no further mention of the access of strategic skills or executive action to consciousness. So one can only speculate about the format

of the strategic rules or skills. However, there is some mention of normal, auto-pilot-regulation of thinking which is contrasted with conscious control of thinking in the "debugging-state" (BROWN, 1980). In normal reading, continuous regulation of information intake takes place without notice. Only when normal flow of processing is interrupted or distorted by some barrier of bottleneck, does a more conscious type of regulation come into action; the reader enters a debugging state of consciousness. Then, information processing is slowed down on the whole and becomes de-automatized. "We enter a reflective, planful and strategic state the instruments of which are metacognitive skills (which refer to) any reflected, planful control of activities leading to understanding". (BROWN, 1980).

It remains unspecified however, whether metacognitive skills merely represent the instruments for debugging - and what distinguishes them from auto-pilot-state-activities - or, whether the dependence of the debugging state results from a specific state of consciousness means that metacognitive activities should only refer to a (very small) subcategory of regulatory, trouble-shooting activities. Finally, the way in which "a reflective, planful and strategic state" leads to the use of metacognitive instruments remains unclear.

Particularly, the more recent work of BROWN and her coworkers (e.g.,BROWN and DAY, 1981) stresses that experts do not know what makes them expert, nor do they know what they are doing when their executive becomes active. From the methodological point of view, BROWN's inferences from actual academic performance to the psychological processes involved at its origin are retrodictions of the form: "It is possible that it was p that led to q". Or: "Since after some training I have observed q, it must have been p which I have trained. So some deficit in p earlier has caused a smaller grade of q". In other words, BROWN explains differences in performance between high and low performers by assuming a different level of efficiency in their executive skills. BROWN is not concerned with the question of whether differences in the activation of metacognitive skills also correspond to differences in the amount of the knowledge of strategic rules, or metacognitive knowledge, for she avoids drawing conclusions from actual cognitive performance to some kind of competence. The speechlessness of the experts who are incapable of telling what they do and how (cf. BROWN and DAY, 1981) suggests that BROWN is not primarily interested in finding a psychological or conscious counterpart for metacognitive skills. So BROWN's conception is seemingly not free of contradictions: while some of the assumptions about the debugging state almost necessarily imply that metacognitive processes are to be considered as a special subcategory of consciousness in the service of trouble-shooting when one is faced with a problem, the ordinary case of metacognitive activity seems to be that of an unconscious automatic pilot state. But then what calls the executive into service?

To summarize, FLAVELL's concept of metacognitive knowledge is explicitly based on the assumption of awareness, if not to say that metacognitive processes are due to consciousness if they are to work at all. The more elaborate and differantiated the metacognitive map of one's cognitive endowment, the more likely it would seem that this elaborate grade of reflection (about reflections) would also have a corresponding counterpart at the level of cognitive performance. Thus, FLAVELL predicts performance on the basis of competence which is reflected in the self-statements of the subject. In BROWN's earlier work (until about 1978) executive components of skilled behavior are isolated, and differences in executive skills are inferred from differences in actual performance. Training of executive skills leads to improved competence, for example flexible use of (strategic) rules or spontaneous transfer or generalization of a rule to new kinds of tasks, but what constitutes competence is not mentioned at all. BROWN's later work,

particularly the "tetrahedral model" in BROWN, CAMPIONE and DAY (1981), does
take into account differences in competence between good and bad learners to
the extent that domain-specific prior knowledge, knowledge concerning the
state of one's own cognitive apparatus, as well as knowledge about one's own
strategy repertoire is given a role for the explanation of differences in
performance, although, naturally, no competence data are being collected.

Metacognitive regulation of text processing. Text processing involves general knowledge about the world as well as domain-specific knowledge which
describes some special detail of world knowledge in a more differentiated
way. In determining the goals of a learning task (metacomprehension), in
evaluating the outcome of one's learning in the light of task-specific
goals or goal criteria, or in checking the plausibility of one's comprehension against common sense criteria, both kinds of knowledge are necessary.
In addition, learning from texts requires further knowledge: to be able to
plan one's studying adequately, one must also know how much time one has to
spend on the task of reading, how important it is to reach some goal, and
how much effort one has to invest to reach it, all of which call for further
information regarding the difficulty of the text or one's individual
strengths or weaknesses in reading skill or domain-specific prior knowledge.
Thus, to a certain extent, FLAVELL's metacognitive (competence) knowledge
might fit the requirement of the markers implied by BROWN's model of metacognitive regulation. With respect to "competence knowledge", as we term the
metacognitive knowledge of one's own cognitive peculiarities, KLUWE has
tried (most recently in 1981) to dispense with the unnecessary differentiation between knowledge and metacognitive knowledge (which has not yet been
precisely defined by FLAVELL). To do this, he subsumes world and domain-
specific knowledge as well as (metacognitive) knowledge about one's own
cognitive functioning under the one heading "declarative knowledge". Problem-
solving processes or routines for problemsolving, are considered part of the
data base which consists of stored problemsolving routines or solution
paths ("knowledge of transformations"), whereas the actual metacognitive
aspect is reserved for executive monitoring and control. While executive regulation refers to both the task of planning and scheduling the job of
reading, and the control and correction of comprehension, executive monitoring refers to the on-line sampling of ongoing processing. Declarative cognitive knowledge installs the markers or standards for planning and scheduling,
the allocation of attention to special parts of the text, and some overall
calculation of effort. It also serves as a criterion for the ongoing
matching processes, when monitoring data are checked and tested against task-
specific or learning goals. One might speculate about the degree of automa-
tion (and unconsciousness) of these processes in the mature reader, since it
is by no means neccessary to reserve deliberate control just for the debugging state, as BROWN does.

Specific predictions derived from the models proposed by FLAVELL and BROWN.
Following FLAVELL, differences between good and poor readers should appear
precisely in the fact that poor readers show less, or less differentiated,
knowledge in every relevant respect in the context of the reading task. Deficits in metacognitive knowledge or cognitive competence should lead to
deficits in 'knowing how to know' and deficits in the realm of set-points
or standards. According to BROWN differences between good and poor readers
should be reflected particularly in a smaller degree of executive regulation in the activity of the poor readers and in a blind application of rules
without checking on their adequacy, as inferred from their actual academic
performance in a specific task. Deficits in domain-specific knowledge should

lead to some inability to identify and locate important (or difficult) aspects of the text, thus making the poorer reader's enterprise rather diffuse and less efficient.

To test FLAVELL's approach empirically, one would have to collect self-statements from the learners, to classify them according to FLAVELL and WELLMAN's (1977) taxonomy and, if possible, to relate these data to performance data. To test BROWN's model empirically, one would have to find differences between good and poor readers at the performance level, to look at the product of their reading and to explain differences in the level of learning outcomes by different degrees of expertise. BROWN's expertise notion is largely based upon retrodictive statements about some hypothesized expert knowledge on how to proceed with text processing and on the experts' hypothetically different monitoring and control processes involved in the genesis of the observed outcome. Relevant data in BROWN's sense then, are the different learning outcomes, whose qualitative differences are traced back to underlying processes in the monitoring and executive processes of the good vs. the bad reader.

While FLAVELL's "competence" assumption says nothing about the psychological impact of competence on process regulation, BROWN's "expertise" assumption does not say a word about the psychological reality of expertise in terms of different competence endowments among experts.

BROWN is not interested in describing precisely or mapping the kind of competence leading to expertise, especially not in the sense of identifying knowledge elements of the expert's superiority. On the contrary, BROWN's interest is focussed nearly exclusively on the trainability of expertise in a variety of school-relevant tasks. Interestingly enough she does not even specify exactly the nature of what is to be trained. But what actually happens if a subject is first exposed to a summarization task that requires him to focus his attention on the most important parts of a message and, consequently, to neglect or delete less important information, after which he is given the task of rehearsing and selectively memorizing the same information? The latter task clearly calls for the opposite: Depending upon the outcome of earlier recall attempts the subject now has to focus on the less well recalled text units, and consequently, to memorize selectively only the less important aspects of the information. Does the subject know anything about the different task demands? And how does he use that knowledge? Or does he implicitly establish a rule for handling the task the way he performs it? What makes the subject build up rules,and what is the nature of these rules? What must the subject know about the conditions of application of some special rule? Is this kind of knowledge trained too? And what kind and degree of consciousness is required to solve the task of intelligent use of strategies? Finally, what makes the poor reader debug his processing in the training situation? Is consciousness an obligatory prerequisite of intelligent use of strategies?

And if so: why not specifically train the onset of deliberate control of one's activities in processing text?

There are many questions which remain unanswered: Are there valid differences between the kind of knowledge experts rely on and knowledge used by novices or poor readers? How do experts make use of their knowledge in the course of processing? What does in fact guide their different processing? To answer at least some of these questions, two experiments were conducted, the first aimed at adult learners' knowledge of how to proceed when processing a text for understanding and recall, the second aimed at the nature of existing differences between good and poor readers' processing.

TWO EXPERIMENTS ON THE PSYCHOLOGICAL REALITY OF LEARNING COMPETENCE AND
LEARNING CONTROL

EXPERIMENT 1: LEARNING COMPETENCE OF ADULT READERS - A TEST OF FLAVELL'S
'KNOWLEDGE' ASSUMPTION

If the psychological basis of efficient learning and control of learning
consists in the knowledge base of the mature reader, which in turn makes up
his competence, an exploration of the knowledge components that guide the
reader's actual activities should help to depict the cognitive map readers
possess about their reading endeavour. This first preliminary study was
therefore aimed at the full spectrum of readers' self-reflective thinking
during a reading task.
Sampling self-reflective data on psychological components of ongoing thought
has several methodological restrictions. Normal reading, in so far as the
reader is not faced with specific problems the text or with his/her own
comprehension of the text, is a smooth, continual process. Self-reports on
own cognitive processes are available during the course of thinking ("periactional"), before the onset of the thinking process ("pre-actional) of
following it ("postactional"). Since the latter two are subject to a temporal
lag between the real object of investigation, they may yield just a rough
copy of what the reader had planned to do, or, in the light of the outcome,
thinks he must have done. Periactional self-reports may interfere with the
task of reading or break the process down into unrepresentative, meaningless
fragments. Since our first preliminary study was aimed at the whole spectrum
of metacognitive reflection about the subject's knowledge about reading, at
an overall rather than at a fine-grained level of analysis, we decided to
restrict ourselves to postactional data about self-reflective components of
the reading process as the reader depicts it.

Procedure. Two or three days before the experiment started, the subjects
were invited to a preliminary interview in which they were told to choose
one text from their regular study material and to work it through. Three
days later the interviews were conducted, starting with the subject's report
on his actual text processing. Care was taken not to influence the statements of the subject in any way. All interviews were taped, transcribed,
and subjected to a content analysis based on a taxonomy scheme along the
lines of the theoretical concepts developed by FLAVELL and BROWN. The taxonomy consisted of two main parts. Part A referred to operational aspects,
such as learning tactics and learning strategies as well as to state-related
variables of the learner. Part B specifically focussed on statements concerning meta-operational components of learning regulation.
The absolute frequencies of utterances per category were transformed
into relative frequencies (percent of total utterances of an interviewee);
the data reported in Table 1 are the arithmetic means of these percentages
on the basis of all interviews (n = 12). In spite of the focus on a rather
narrow area of the actual learning process, a surprisingly large number of
statements referred to evaluative and/or affective attitudes towards learning
as a whole (as indicated in category B 6). To reduce the strong impact of
this category on the distribution of statements in the rest of the categories, a second analysis was done solely on the basis of categories A 1 to
B 5 (numbers in parentheses).

Table 1. Distribution of self-statements about operational (A) and meta-
operational (B) aspects of learning

	Category	mean percentage of statements	
A	Operational Level/Cognitive Knowledge (Competence)	35.43	(46.72)
A 1	information processing and information extraction	23.19	(24.90)
A 1.1	prereading activities	5.36	(7.07)
	orientation, categorization of task, text, topic and localization of difficulties		
	clarification of learning goals or criteria		
	calculation of effort; planning and scheduling with regard to the learner's specific or more general competence and previous knowledge; the learner's time budget, concrete learning conditions and personal learning habits or style		
A 1.2	surface structure techniques/strategies	8.78	(11.58)
	underlining, highlighting, ordering of information (outlining), note-taking, summarizing or questioning		
A 1.3	comprehension of the deep structure of the text	9.05	(11.93)
	knowledge about the different levels of processing, reconstructive, interpretative, inferential, elaborative, imaginative, or reductive processes		
A 2	memorizing and retrieval strategies	6.93	(9.14)
	knowledge about different modes of memory, encoding specificity, the learner's implicit memory theory, mnemonics or memorizing strategies, knowledge about primacy of recency effects, knowledge about effects and effort in memorizing		
A 3	criterional learning, implicit performance criteria	5.31	(7.00)
	knowledge about self-testing strategies or means, self-evaluation techniques and knowledge about how to diagnose performance		
B	Meta-operational Level/Executive Functions	64.57	(53.28)
B 1	on-line monitoring of ongoing activities	9.20	(12.13)
B 2	self-testing/checking of learning states, of learning outcome and effectiveness	2.13	(2.81)
B 3	evaluation of the results of self-testing	5.84	(7.70)
B 4	attributive behavior	12.35	(16.28)

(Table 1 cont.)

B 5	execution of regulatory or adaptive steps to bridge goal-state discrepancies	10.89	(14.36)
B 6	life goals, motivational and affective impact of values on learning	24.16	(-)

Results. The content analysis of the interview-data (cf. Table 1) shows that there are a considerable number of statements referring to knowledge based assumptions of the readers, especially related to knowledge about the reading task, steps to transform goals into action and measures about how to evalua- te reading outcomes. 23.19 % (24.90 %) of the utterances are focussed on the task of information processing and extraction of meaning from text. While the reported monitoring and state diagnosing activities are substantial (9.20 or 12.13 % respectively), the statements must aim at some rudimentary, rough or arbitrary diagnosis of the state of learning, since only 2.13 % (2.81 %) of the utterances refer to objective testing or checking of results. Interestingly enough, a large proportion of utterances apply to the emotio- nal affective processing of the results of learning state diagnosis: 42.35 % (23.98 %) of the statements are concerned with affective regulation of learning states. Evidently, there is some discrepancy between on-line data sampling of one's learning state and its affective results on the one hand, and objective learning data, which are obviously lacking, on the other hand. But how is one able to regulate one's learning efficiently if the data needed to guide learning regulation are lacking? Is it the low self-esteem on the part of at least some of our subjects which results in the predominan- ce of affective data? Since we did not collect data about the actual learning efficiency of our subjects in this study, we cannot rule out the possibility that the self-reflective data actually reflect the subject's failure/success orientation in general.

Conclusions. Mature readers actually possess substantial knowledge about concrete learning activities in the domain of reading, on the one hand, as is implied by the competence notion of FLAVELL, as well as about monitoring and regulatory steps in the sense of BROWN, on the other hand. Following FLAVELL, differences between efficient and less efficient readers should mainly consist of differences in the knowledge base of reading competence: following BROWN, these differences should mainly consist of differences in executive monitoring and regulation. To test these at least partly alterna- tive notions empirically, a second study was designed to relate learning outcome and efficiency more narrowly to concomitant thinking about learning.

EXPERIMENT 2: THE QUESTION OF A POSSIBLE RELATIONSHIP BETWEEN (METACOGNITIVE)
            SELF-STATEMENTS AND ACTUAL PERFORMANCE OF GOOD AND POOR READERS

Aims of investigation. Our next objective was to check whether the learning outcome could provide differential cues concerning the relationship between competence and performance on the one hand, and learning skill level of the subject on the other hand. 24 students from the department of biology were given an introductory text of about 2,600 words on ethical development in early childhood. They had to process the text in such a way as to understand its content and to be capable of using it later on (for instance in a group discussion). Preparation time was unlimited. After reading, the subjects either immediately had to recall the main ideas of the text, then to answer multiple-choice questions and to participate in a standardized interview, or had the interview first and then a delayed recall and comprehension test afterwards.

Scoring procedure. The free-recall protocols were parsed into macropropositions according to a modified procedure of analysis in the KINTSCH and VAN DIJK or MEYER approach. Each topic unit was scored according to its position in the text hierarchy. Additional marks were given for precision of recall. The total score of free recall (hierarchy and precision points) and comprehension (correct answers to the multiple-choice questions) were combined and transformed into percentile ranks. Processing time (i.e., duration of the text preparation) was also taken into consideration as a measure of economy. Hence, each subject received two percentile ranks, one referring to performance level regardless of processing time, the other referring to processing achievement per unit of processing time. On the basis of overall performance level, the subjects were subdivided into two groups: "good" vs. "poor readers". A content analysis was performed on the interview protocols in which a modified version of the taxonomy of the former study was used.

Results. Table 2 shows the proportions of utterances for the main categories of the content analized interview data, separately for the two groups of good (GR), and poor (PR) readers. The distribution of utterances, regardless of the groups, replicates the results of the first study: The depicted spectrum of statements refers to operational as well as meta-operational and strategic activities of the readers as the universe of their reading competence. Contrary to FLAVELLIAN expectations, a comparison between the groups does not yield significant differences with regard to the range, precision or intensity of statements about their learning competence. Good readers do not show a particularly superior degree of knowledge or reflection as compared with average or poor readers. Thus, differences in learning efficiency cannot be reduced to differences in the knowledge base. There is no such thing as "high-metacognitioners" (and good performers) in contrast to "low-metacognitioners" (and poor performers). Poor performers do not perform badly because they lack the metacognitive knowledge or awareness needed to regulate learning. But contrary to BROWN's assumptions, there also is no evidence for corresponding differences in executive monitoring and control, at least with regard to the amount and intensity of executive activities. But there are obvious differences in the focus and directionality of self-reflection during reading: While the good readers score below the poor readers with regard to those variables which refer to the reader's time-invariant traits (cf. the proportions of utterances between the two groups for A 2.1 - 2.15, i.e., references to the learner's self-concept as a learner, and for categories A 2.4 - 2.45 referring to the task-learner interaction, as well as for categories A 1.22 - 1.2232, the learner's specific orientation towards the content area), they score higher in those domains which relate to actual, on-line processing demands (cf. proportions of utterances to categories A 2.6 - 2.62, B 2.2 - 2.55, B 2.41 - 2.416, B 2.42 - 2.4292, and B 2.45 - 2.45252). The poor readers apparently behave like a rabbit facing a snake: They are so heavily concentrating on their own invariable state and the pending task, that their regulatory capacity is almost completely absorbed. The good readers, on the contrary, are not concerned as much with their status as a learner, and, hence, are able to focus on processing relevant information economically. To explain learner differences with respect to executive monitoring and regulation in the BROWN's sense, it is therefore not enough to train for quantitative intensification of self-reflection during learning, but rather subjects should be taught where to concentrate their attention. Thus, poor readers are characterized mainly by

Table 2. Self-statements about cognitive activities in different stages of the reading process (PR = poor readers; GR = good readers)

Category		Mean percentage of statements	
		PR	GR
A	Pre-reading Activities:		
A 1.1 - 1.1433	general orientation towards the task; definition of task specific goals	4.02	5.00
A 1.21 - 1.2116	specific orientation: formal aspects of the text	2.92	2.55
A 1.22 - 1.2232	specific orientation: content and domain specific variables	3.43	1.46
A 2.1 - 2.15	learner characteristics: interindividual metacognitive variables	8.11	5.60
A 2.2 - 2.222	definition of learner internal and external goals	2.21	2.92
A 2.3 - 2.33	references to situational variables and learning context	1.25	1.19
A 2.4 - 2.45	references to interactions of learner and text variables	3.13	2.84
A 2.5 - 2.55	consequences for planning/scheduling/ programming	4.20	5.10
A 2.6 - 2.62	consequences for executive regulation: monitoring and control agenda	.06	.18
B	During Reading Activities:		
B 1.1 - 1.144	operational activities and strategies of text processing	10.67	11.20
B 1.2 - 1.243	processes and strategies of comprehension	7.57	7.87
B 2.1 - 2.14	monitoring of comprehension state	7.30	6.59
B 2.2 - 2.55	testing/checking of comprehension	7.72	8.49
B 2.31 - 2.33	evaluation of testing outcomes	9.54	9.25
B 2.41 - 2.416	regulatory consequences	8.19	9.71
B 2.42 - 2.4292	single variables relevant for regulation	10.31	13.54
B 2.43 - 2.4325	task importance and number of processing cycles	5.12	3.62
B 2.44 - 2.443	goal achievement, certainty about goal achievement, stop decisions	1.09	.43
B 2.45 - 2.45252	checking of criteria fullfillment and criterion levelling/sharpening	1.21	1.60
B 2.46 - 2.463	flexibility of learning style	.51	.51
B 2.47 - 2.475	learning efficiency	.30	.37

(Table 2 cont.)

		PR	GR
C	Post-reading Activities:		
C 1.1 - 1.3	operational consequences of failure/ success for future learning activities	.63	.63
C 2.1 - 2.12	impact of failure/success on learner's self-concept	.18	.08
C 2.2 - 2.242	impact of failure/success on motivation and attributional style	.86	.44

their obvious tendency, especially in the pre-reading and post-reading phase, to focus on personal information, and to process this information mainly affectively and attributively. If one compares the proportion of utterances to the categories C 2.1 - 2.12, and C 2.2 - 2.242 which refer to the impact of learning outcome upon the learner's self-efficacy, poor readers seem to be much more concerned with their status than with regulatory consequences, than the good readers are.

Interpretation. The comparison of self-reflective statements on learning between high and low performers yields evidence that the latter do not perform worse because they are engaged in less executive monitoring than the former.They actually do more but at the wrong place. Since their status-orientation may impede or interfere with actual action-orientation, which is neccessary for efficient data-gathering with respect to the course and efficiency of one's learning progress, training measures should be aimed at breaking up the vicious circle of the poor learner's focussing on his own state. KUHL (1980, 1981) recently has reformulated SELIGMAN's theory of learned helplessness (1975) in terms of a dispositional orientation towards state- vs. action-orientation in the helpless as compared with the coping subject. If this analogy holds we have to train our failure-oriented subjects to change their orientation towards task-relevant features. But to do this we need some further information about the processing of self-reflective data directly stemming from or following learning situations. What use does the mature reader make of those data? What about rule-formation processes within and between tasks? How can we conceive of the trade-off between know- ledge and the use of knowledge in the course of learning with regard to task-relevant variables as well as to personal or learner variables? Learning from prose for understanding as well as for recall imposes complex constraints upon the reader's (meta)cognitive knowledge as well as upon the reader's skill in making use of his/her own learning experience in building up task- related processing rules! As yet, differences between good and poor readers are not conceptually understood precisely enough to lead to valid conclu- sions. The same holds true for the notion of the executive: It is by no means clear as yet what the term denotes. Is the executive an agent besides the thinking person, some homunculus within his/her head, or does the term actually refer to some way of controlling thinking, especially in the debugging state? But if so, why not abandon it? According to HERRMANN (1980) surplus meaning in psychological theories is not apt to make them more easi- ly testable or to make possible the derivation of clearly testable hypo- theses.

GENERAL DISCUSSION

Differences in the self-reflective monitoring and regulation of text learning
between high and low performers are mainly differences in terms of directionality and focus of self-reflectivity. In the light of our data, one cannot
rule out any of the alternative notions proposed by FLAVELL or BROWN. But
so far, neither FLAVELL's competence model nor BROWN's executive monitoring
and regulation model has been stated clearly enough to allow for a clear-
cut decision. Our data are inconsistent with solely competence-based learner
differences, as is implied by FLAVELL, as well as with monitoring differences as implied by BROWN. While FLAVELL's executive does know a lot but does
not do much, BROWN's executive does not know much - at least with regard to
the learner differences, as revealed by BROWN's empirical work - but it does
a lot.

Weaknesses and theoretical gaps in current theorization are particularly related to knowledge formation and resulting knowledge use in the course of
learning. (No kind of metacognitive learning theory is yet capable of
accounting for complex learning processes). This is not to deny that there
exist some promising fragments of such a theory, related to special learning
problems, such as the summarization of text content, cumulative rehearsal
or importance ratings for text segments, etc. But the yield of these studies
has not been integrated into one consistent theoretical framework. Current
heuristics allow, indeed, for some promising training work especially with
retarded learners. The state of the art in metacognitive research can be
described as one of successful implementation of heuristics into practice
without consistent theorization. But the search for task-related processing
rules and ways to train them does not tell the whole story: Questions about
how the mature reader actually integrates his/her learning experience into
some self-efficacy concept which for his/her part does exert some influence
on his/her future learning, or questions about the impact of attributions
on learning course and efficiency, and their processing by the subject in
the service of subsequent learning regulation, and the like, are still unanswered.

REFERENCES

Brown, A. L. The development of memory: Knowing,knowing about knowing, and
    knowing how to know. In H. W. Reese (Ed.), Advances in child development
    and behavior (Vol.10). New York: Academic Press, 1975.

Brown, A. L. Development, schooling and the acquisition of knowledge about
    knowledge. In R. C. Anderson, R. J. Spiro & W. E. Montague (Eds.), Schoo-
    ling and the acquisition of knowledge. Hillsdale, N.J.: Erlbaum, 1977.

Brown, A. L. Knowing when, where, and how to remember: A problem of meta-
    cognition. In R. Glaser (Ed.), Advances in instructional psychology (Vol.
    1). Hillsdale,N.J.: Erlbaum, 1978.

Brown, A. L. Metacognitive development and reading. In R. J. Spiro, B. Bruce
    & W. F. Brewer (Eds.), Theoretical issues in reading comprehension. Hills-
    dale,N.J.: Erlbaum, 1980.

Brown, A. L., Campione, J. C. & Day, J. D. Learning to learn: On training students to learn from texts. Educational Researcher, 1981, 10, 14-21.

Flavell, J. H. Developmental studies of mediated memory. In H. W. Reese & L. P. Lipsitt (Eds.), Advances in child development and behavior (Vol. 5). New York: Academic Press, 1970.

Flavell, J. H. Metacognitive aspects of problem solving. In L. B. Resnick (Ed.), The nature of intelligence. Hillsdale,N.J.: Erlbaum, 1976. (a)

Flavell, J. H. The development of metacommunication. Paper given at the 21st International Congress of Psychology, Paris, 1976. (b)

Flavell, J. H. Metacognition. In E. Langer (Ed.), Current perspectives on awareness and cognitive processes. Paper presented at the meeting of the American Psychological Association, Toronto, Canada, August 1978.

Flavell, J. H., Friedrichs, A. G. & Hoyt, J. D. Developmental changes in memorization processes. Cognitive Psychology, 1970, 1, 324-340.

Flavell, J.H. & Wellman, H. M. Metamemory. In R. V. Kail & J. W. Hagen (Eds.), Perspectives on the development of memory and cognition. Hillsdale,N.J.: Erlbaum, 1977.

Herrmann, T. Über begriffliche Schwächen kognitivistischer Kognitionstheorien: Begriffsinflation und Akteur-System-Kontamination. Bericht No. 15, Arbeiten der Forschungsgruppe Sprache und Kognition am Lehrstuhl Psychologie III der Universität Mannheim, September 1980.

Kluwe, R. Metacognition: To be the agent of one's own thinking. Invited Paper for the Dahlem-Conference on ' Human mind - animal mind',Berlin,1981.

Kreutzer, M. A., Leonard, C. & Flavell, J. H. An interview study of children's knowledge about memory. Monographs of the Society for Research in Child Development, 1975, 40, Ser. No. 159, 1-60.

Miller, G. A., Galanter, E. & Pribram, K. H. Plans and the structure of behavior. London: Holt, 1960.

Nisbett, R. E. & Wilson, T. D. Telling more than we know: Verbal reports on mental processes. Psychological Review, 1977, 84, 231-259.

Norman, D. A. & Shallice, T. Attention to action: Willed and automatic control of behavior. Center for Human Information Processing, Chip No. 99, University of California San Diego,La Jolla,Ca., December 1980.

Pylyshyn, Z. W. Complexitiy and the study of artificial and human intelligence. In M. Ringle (Ed.), Philosophical aspects in artificial intelligence. New York: The Humanities Press, 1979.

Reitman, W. Problem solving, comprehension and memory. In G. J. Dalenoórt (Ed.), Process models for psychology. Rotterdam: University Press, 1973.

DISCOURSE PROCESSING
A. Flammer and W. Kintsch (eds.)
© *North-Holland Publishing Company, 1982*

METACOGNITIVE VARIABLES IN THE LEARNING
OF WRITTEN TEXT[1]

Fredi P. Büchel

University of Basel
Basel, Switzerland

A preliminary version of a metacognitive model of self-directed learning is presented with the main components: metaknowledge, program and response generator, overt and covert strategies and world knowledge. Metacognition is defined as control of activity in human information processing. The model has been empirically evaluated with the help of thinking-aloud protocols. For the analysis of these protocols a category system has been developed. The categories are presented together with a set of rules for the definition of the units of analysis. Data from different learning tasks and different students are discussed.

THE CONCEPT OF METACOGNITION

The subject of metacognitive research is "the control of activity in information processing systems" (Kluwe (1980a)). The theory starts out from the idea that the human information processing system contains not only a world knowledge base and processes, but also, on a higher level, knowledge about the knowledge base and the processing system. The theory of metacognition included from the beginning the following two aspects of processing control: first the metaknowledge, that is, knowledge about the person as a learner, about the processing aspects of the task, and about possible strategies (Flavell and Wellman, 1977), and secondly executive control, that is, directing and evaluating the information processing. The understanding of executive control in the context of metacognitive theory was mainly advanced through research conducted by A.L. Brown and J. Campione, and by J. Belmont and E. Butterfield. Brown (1977) argues that "the particular forms of metamemory selected for study have encouraged an underestimation of the complexity of the operations involved". What she misses most is some kind of "central processor, interpreter, or executive, introduced as the overseer in many current models of memory" (p.7). Such an executive system would have to include "the ability to (a) predict the system's capacity limitations, (b) be aware of its repertoire of heuristic routines and their appropriate domain of utility, (c) identify and characterize the problem at hand, (d) plan and schedule appropriate problem solving strategies, (e) monitor and supervise the effectiveness of those routines it calls into service, and (f) dynamically evaluate operations."

The above mentioned bipolarity between metaknowledge and executive control may be one reason why, after ten years of extensive research, a commonly accepted definition of metacognition exists less than ever. Kluwe (1980a, 1980b, 1980c) suggests a functional model showing how these two groups of metacognitive variables could be interrelated and what kind of variables should be contained in each of these groups (Figure 1).

Our own research focusses the understanding of self-directed learning in complex learning tasks. This is conceptualized as metacognitive activity in a learning setting. The three main questions that should be the object of such research are planning, supervising, and learning strategies. As for the first question, Flavell proposes variables of planning knowledge, whereas Brown suggests the variables for the second question. But no activity is sufficiently described by planning and supervising variables, the plans have to be executed, too. For that aspect of the learning activity Kluwe's model proposes solution processes. In our model (Figure 2) solution processes are replaced by learning strategies. The model contains as its main components: Metaknowledge about tasks, about the learner and about strategies, a program and response generator to compile and supervise the plans, as well as strategies to execute the learning tasks, thus illustrating the process of self-directed learning. The model has been constructed in order to guide a series of training studies to be conducted over the next two years. The components of the model have already been discussed under different aspects in the current cognitive literature. But for some parts, e.g. metaknowledge, the empirical evidence is modest, and we do not have any experimental support for the assumption that all parts are necessary to understand self-directed learning. In this situation we are interested in finding out if a learner in a complex learning task uses all the instances proposed by the model. We presented subjects with instructional texts and invited them to read aloud, and in addition to speak out everything that went through their heads during reading and learning. All sessions were tape-recorded and we are trying to identify within these protocols verbal indicators of the theoretically postulated activities.

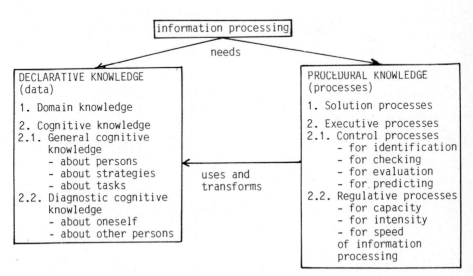

Figure 1
Types of knowledge involved in information processing
(from: Kluwe (1980b))

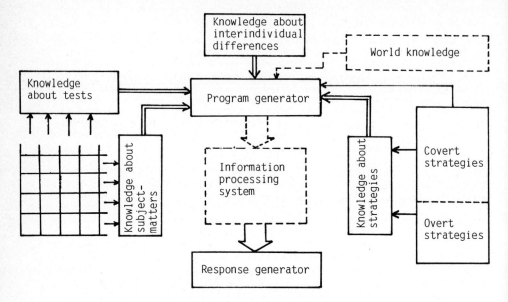

Figure 2
A model of self-directed learning

A CATEGORY SYSTEM OF METACOGNITION

In order to test our model with the help of thinking-aloud protocols every part has been defined by one or more categories to which verbal statements can be assigned. The following groups of categories will be discussed below.

I. Metacognitive knowledge consists of 4 categories containing subjects' statements which indicate awareness of the knowledge involved in self-regulated learning.

II. The program generator describes 5 categories of self-instruction which help the subject to define a learning goal, to regulate the information processing and to monitor it.

III. The response generator contains one category which indicates that a subject would evaluate his learning progress before communicating a solution or terminating a learning session.

IV. Covert strategies imply the use of cognitive operations with the help of which a learning task is performed.

V. Overt strategies contain operations which can be observed.

VI. Method-specific categories contain 3 categories of statements which are not metacognitive, but interactional and provoked by the test situation.

VII. World knowledge. This category, since it is not a metacognitive one, has been included for reasons of completeness in coding.

The definition of a unit of analysis proved to be a difficult problem, because in these protocols we seldom have grammatically complete sentences. We tried to use propositions (Kintsch, 1974), but this method turned out to be too costly for our purposes. To find a middle course between full sentences and propositions, we created the following rules:

1. Every grammatically complete sentence is a unit.

2. Subordinate clauses are treated as complete sentences.

3. If a complete sentence is linked with another sentence by a conjunction, it is treated as an independent unit.

4. Incomplete sentences are treated as a unit if they are isolated from the context by at least a pause (The transcription system contains special pause symbols).

5. Chains of the same word are treated as one unit.

6. Chains of different words, isolated or embedded in a sentence, are treated as different units.

The next three points are not unit rules, but general coding rules:

7. If the content of the main clause is a mental activity and the content of the subordinate clause is semantically related to the mental activity, then the subordinate clause is assigned to the same category as the main clause. For example, "I ask myself if I should it read once again" would be coded as (2 x checking), because "ask myself" is a checking routine.

8. The first reading of the learning text is not coded. If the text is read a second or a further time, this is coded as "re-reading".

9. Every statement can be assigned to only one category.

After a protocol is divided into units, every unit is assigned to one of the following categories:

I. M e t a c o g n i t i v e   k n o w l e d g e

1.1. <u>Knowledge about test situations and methods</u>. This is knowledge of possible ways of reproducing the learned content.

1.2. <u>Knowledge about the learner's relation to subject matter</u>. Flavell and Wellman (1977) have proposed the two variables knowledge about task features and knowledge about retrieval demands. But these two variables are overlapping categories. A learning task as presented in a learning experiment can be conceived as the intersection of two dimensions, subject matter and test (see Figure 2).

1.4. <u>Knowledge about interindividual differences in learning ability</u>. In addition to interindividual differences Flavell and Wellman (1977) propose a variable "intraindividual differences", but since intraindividual differences in ability are always related to different subject matters or test situations they are included in 1.1. and 1.2.

1.5. <u>Knowledge about strategies</u>. This is the feeling that a given strategy would be appropriate to a given task.

II. P r o g r a m   g e n e r a t o r

2.1. <u>Checking</u>. Continual control of one's own understanding.

2.2. <u>Instruction identification</u>.

2.3. <u>Transfer</u>. Detection of similarities and their application to examples.

2.4. <u>Intensity regulation</u>. Accuracy and investment are tuned.

2.5. <u>Time regulation</u>.

III. R e s p o n s e   g e n e r a t o r

3.1. Evaluation. Last checking of the whole task before final formulation.

IV. C o v e r t   s t r a t e g i e s

4.1. Paraphrasing.

4.2. Information supplement. In order to make the facts less arbitrary
     (Bransford et al., 1980), additional world knowledge is evoked.

4.3. Hypothesis generation.

4.4. Hypothesis evaluation.

4.5. Comments. Dissatisfaction or doubt or explicit confirmation of the
     given information.

4.6. Re-reading.

V. O v e r t   s t r a t e g i e s

5.1. Underlining.

5.2. Summarizing. Can also be realized as covert strategy, but is always
     coded as 5.2.

5.3. Literal extract.

5.4. Schema drawing.

VI. M e t h o d - s p e c i f i c   c a t e g o r i e s

6.2. Giving reasons about planning and strategies.

6.3. Emotional comments on the experimental situation.

6.4. Confirmation of a given instruction or explication.

VII. W o r l d   k n o w l e d g e

7.1. World knowledge. Knowledge of facts and the relations between facts.

FINDINGS

The category system is the result of repeated empirical testing and revision.
A first version was evaluated with 10 protocols from 5 adult subjects of a
technical high school. They read two rather difficult texts. The first dealt
with cybernetics and the second with human information processing. The subjects were instructed to read the text aloud and learn it afterwards. If
something was not understood and subjects would have consulted a dictionary
at home they could ask the experimenter for a short explanation. Additionally
subjects were told to speak out everything that went through their heads.
For each text the learning session lasted 10 minutes. All sessions were
tape-recorded.

A second evaluation was made with 4 protocols from two commercial school
students. The subjects were presented with a French text, with applied mathematics problems, with a list of words in French and German, and with a list
of nonsense-syllables paired with meaningful words.

A revised version of the system was tested with a different sample as represented in Table 1. We analyzed the protocols of 13 different tasks from 6
different students from different schools. It was possible to code all verbal
statements without problems. Figure 3 shows the distribution of the categories.

Title of the learning task	Subject 1	S2	S3	S4	S5	S6	Total
Dog story (Mandler and Johnson, 1977)	48	53					101
Stone soup (Brown et al., 1978)	54	53					107
A micro-computer (schema)	156	132					288
Human information processing	73	94					167
Cybernetics			172				172
Evolution theory		117	80				197
Anxiety			74	27			101
Complète avec le présent du verbe					39	34	73
Accorder des verbes					19	42	61
Avoir ou être?					29	70	99
Un peu de tout (phrases à compléter)					15		15
Vocabulaire						96	96
French-German-translation						57	57
Total of statements (units) analyzed							1534

Table 1
Analyzed texts in the last evaluation.

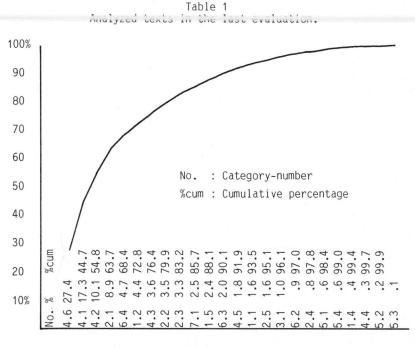

No.   : Category-number

%cum : Cumulative percentage

Figure 3
Distribution of 1534 verbal statements (Cumulative frequencies).

In order to obtain information about the objectivity of the coding, three
different protocol samples were coded by two raters separately. The raters
separated the protocols into units of analysis and then assigned the statements to the categories. As a rule, the chosen categories could only be identical if the two raters had created the same units. We calculated point-by-
point correspondence (Mees, 1977) and obtained the following precentages
(f(agreement)/(f(disagreement + agreement)):

Raters	A-B	A-B	A-C	A-C	A-C
Analyzed units	19	34	17	13	20
Correspondence (%)	79	62	77	92	70

Table 2
Point-by-point correspondences with two raters.

DISCUSSION

A model of self-directed learning was tested with the help of thinking-aloud learning protocols. It could be shown that all instances of the model were used by the subjects as predicted. However not all categories were used in every task, and not all categories were used by every subject. This is not surprising since previous data have also shown a strong task and subject dependency. One result in Figure 3 is particularly noteworthy: 54.8% of all analyzed units are part of the three categories re-reading, paraphrasing and information-completion, all of them are covert strategies. The categories from the group of metacognitive knowledge (1.1; 1.2; 1.4; 1.5) account for only 8.8%. These percentages are in contrast to the metacognitive literature in which most attention is given to categories of metacognitive knowledge. The presumption that the importance of metaknowledge in human information processing might be overestimated is supported by these data.

FOOTNOTE

1 The reported research is supported by the Swiss National Science Foundation (Grant No. 4.323.0.79.10).- The author acknowledge the valuable editorial support by Germaine Springinsfeld, University of Basel, Pasqualina Perrig-Chiello, and Margret Rihs-Middel, both University of Fribourg, and Klaus Bischof, University of Stirling, GB. Comments on an earlier version by Thomas Wehrmüller, University of Basel, and a last editing by Eileen Kintsch are acknowledged.

REFERENCES

Bransford, J.D., Stein, B.S., Shelton, T.S., and Owings, R.A. Cognition and adaptation: The importance of learning to learn. In J. Harvey (Ed.) Cognition, social behavior and the environment. Hillsdale: Erlbaum, 1980.

Brown, A.L. Knowing when, where, and how to remember: A problem of metacognition. Technical report No 47, Center for the Study of Reading, University of Illinois, Urbana, Champaign, 1977.

Brown, J.S., Collins, A., and Harris, G. Artificial intelligence and learning strategies. In H.F. O'Neil (Ed.). Learning strategies. New York: Academic Press, 1978.

Flavell, J.H. and Wellman, H.M. Metamemory. In R. Kail and J. Hagen (Eds.). Perspectives on the development of memory and cognition. Hillsdale: Erlbaum, 1977.

Kintsch, W. The representation of meaning in memory. Hillsdale: Erlbaum, 1974.

Kluwe, R.H. The development of metacognitive processes and performance. University of Munich, unpublished paper, 1980a.

Kluwe, R.H. Metakognition. Paper presented at the 32. Kongress der Deutschen Gesellschaft für Psychologie. Zürich, 1980b.

Kluwe, R.H. Metakognition: Komponenten einer Theorie zur Kontrolle und Steuerung eigenen Denkens. München, 1980c.

Mandler, J.M. and Johnson, N.S. Remembrance of things parsed: Story structure and recall. Cognitive Psychology, 1977, 9, 111-151.

Mees, U. Methodologische Probleme der Verhaltensbeobachtung in der natürlichen Umgebung: I. Zuverlässigkeit und Generalisierbarkeit von Beobachtungsdaten. In U. Mees and H. Selg (Eds.). Verhaltensbeobachtung und Verhaltensmodifikation. Stuttgart: Klett, 1977.

GOAL PERSPECTIVES

DISCOURSE PROCESSING
A. Flammer and W. Kintsch (eds.)
© *North-Holland Publishing Company, 1982*

THE ROLE OF PROBLEM ORIENTATIONS AND GOALS
IN TEXT COMPREHENSION AND RECALL

Norbert A. Streitz

Institut für Psychologie
RWTH Aachen
Aachen
Federal Republic of Germany

Based on a discussion of deficiencies of text-based models,
an extension is proposed which postulates an encoding and
a retrieval strategy. An experiment is reported which provides evidence for the existence of the two strategies by
inducing different problem orientations and goals in subjects for the same text. A story was constructed consisting
of elements to which different amounts of relevancy can be
assigned according to current orientations. An on-line registration of information during encoding was used. The results confirm the predictions of the extended model.

INTRODUCTION

Usually people do not read a text (or listen to discourse) in order to recall it either immediately, or after a boring and distractive intervening
activity to someone they are not interested in. On the contrary, they have
a specific intention when reading a text (which most of the time has been
chosen by themselves!). They might be interested in specific information
on a subject they believe to be covered by the text and intend to use the
extracted information in some subsequent behaviour. Or they may just be
interested in improving their knowledge in a given domain in a general
fashion in order to be up to date. It is also possible that someone might
be engaged in a problem-solving activity without making any progress. In
order to solve the problem it might prove useful to turn to a book or some
other source of information and look up additional advice. The newly acquired information is then used in the problem solving process.

In addition to the above mentioned factors controlling the acquisition of
information, it is necessary to point out that people have control over the
format and content of the information they reproduce, i.e., they decide
what they recall and what they do not recall. Of course, this decision depends on situational and personal factors. We shall deal with these
aspects of text comprehension and recall in more detail as we go along.

The research reported here is part of an attempt to develop a general framework for studying comprehension and problem solving in semantically rich
domains. Since the emphasis of this symposium is on text processing we will
mainly deal with the text comprehension aspect of our research. Nevertheless, in order to provide an appropriate perspective we will outline the
general framework and motivation which guided us in carrying out our re-

search.

1. TEXT COMPREHENSION

Over the last 10 years there has been considerable increase in research on text processing. This shows a growing interest in using more complex materials in verbal learning experiments. The focus is now more on encoding, retention, and retrieval of meaningful text, such as stories, fairytales, coherent discourse, written letters, paragraphs from textbooks, and other expository texts. However, although one uses different material today the methods of investigation are still the same. Two points, in particular, need to be reconsidered. First, most of the models proposed are mainly text-based and do not give enough attention to the active role of the reader in his/her interaction with the text. This can be seen not only in the models themselves but also in the paradigms used to evaluate these models. Second, in the real world learning from text is not an isolated situation; processing of text by the reader always depends on context which includes preceding and subsequent behavior.

Structure inherent in the text vs. structure imposed on the text

A great number of variables have been investigated in order to establish empirical evidence for their influence on the processing of such materials. The majority of these experiments, however, emphasized only those variables which reflect the structural and/or semantic properties of the text itself.

A case in point is the widely accepted procedure to capture the meaning of a text by means of a structured list of propositions. This text base as used by Kintsch (1974) serves as a reference list when scoring recall protocols for their match with the original text. This decomposition makes it possible to account for people's memory even for parts of a sentence, or paraphrases of utterances, or for their idea of the gist of the text. The propositional analysis implemented by LNR (Norman and Rumelhart, 1975) closely resembles that used by Kintsch. Other models following a similar approach to text analysis were proposed by Meyer (1975) and Frederiksen (1975 a).

Whereas models of this kind emphasize bottom-up, or data-driven processing, others favor a more top-down, or conceptually-driven approach. Looking for commonalities among texts led to models of comprehension for a certain text class, story, and to the development of story grammars (Rumelhart, 1975; Mandler and Johnson, 1977; Thorndyke, 1977). Of course, there are no pure representatives of either approach: Kintsch and van Dijk's model (1978), for example, stresses the importance of macropropositions and makes use of a controlling schema, although their model is mainly based on the propositional analysis of the text.

The common claim of these models is that it is possible to make valid predictions about the amount and type of information recalled on the basis of their position in the theoretically derived hierarchical structure. Accordingly, the predominant factor is the underlying hierarchy, either in terms of the coherence - dependency of the propositions (Kintsch, 1976; Meyer, 1975), or as a result of the recursive application of rewrite rules in the story grammars. Basically, this line of thought asserts that the objective structure of a text is <u>the</u> determining factor. In addition, one has to bear in mind that this structure results from a set of conventions agreed on by a linguistic community.

But how about a subjective structure imposed on the text by a reader? Does this subjective structure necessarily coincide with the objective structure and this again with the author's structure? There are reasons to doubt that.

There is a substantial body of research on factors affecting encoding, retention, recognition of word lists, and other materials of limited complexity (for example, Melton and Martin, 1972). This research has demonstrated that the information presented to subjects does not necessarily coincide with the information perceived and encoded by the subject. In order to account for this, the distinction between nominal (objective) and functional (subjective) stimuli has been proposed. Consequently, different encodings of information will result in different memory traces for the same information, which, in turn, serve as the basis for subsequent recall or recognition tasks. It seems reasonable to relate the idea of a subjective structure of text to differences in perception and encoding as has been demonstrated for word lists and similar material. This leads to the conclusion that each reader encodes the same text in a different way according to his/her present problem orientation or goal structure.

But how do these differences in problem orientation lead to different encodings and thus to different internal representations? To answer this question, we refer to schema theory (for example, Rumelhart and Ortony, 1977). The notion of a "schema" has been proposed in various disguises: as "frames" (Minsky, 1975), "scripts" (Schank and Abelson, 1977), and "macrostructures" (van Dijk, 1977). Most of the time, the use of schemata was restricted to structures which are present <u>in</u> the text which evoke a homomorphic structure in the reader controlling the way this text is processed. Well known examples are story grammars. Their proponents claim that the inherent structure which is common to most stories or certain classes of stories guides the processing and the recall of a particular story in a systematic way.

What is often ignored is that there are also well-defined schemata on the part of the reader which result from a specific purpose or goal, problem orientation, or instruction. Especially the context of preceding and subsequent behavior will determine the focus of these schemata. Consequently, the emphasis of this paper is on the interaction of the objective structure inherent in the text and the subjective structure imposed by the reader. This interaction does not cause any problems in cases where the two structures coincide, i.e., when the reader has the same intention in reading the text as the text suggests by its objective structure. Problems may, however, arise if the two structures are different from each other. This can result in a conflict in the reader in case he/she does not adopt one reading orientation or integrate both. A completely different situation arises when the reader's goals or problem orientations are so dominant that he/she does not even detect the inherent structure. In this case, one would predict that the subjective structure overrides the objective structure. Previous research provides support for this point of view. In a well-known study, Pichert and Anderson (1977) emphasized the influence of different perspectives of the reader on significance ratings and on the recall performance of ideas presented in a story. Effects of context were studied, for example, by Frederiksen (1975 b). Using a natural reading situation Graesser, Higgenbotham, Robertson and Smith (1978) studied the differences between self-induced and task-induced reading comprehension. Flammer, Schläfli and Keller (1978) demonstrated the influence of different personal interests on recall performance for a given text.

Stored representations vs. generated representations

Just as there is a need to reconsider the set of variables presumably affecting a person's perception and encoding of text, there is also a need to take a closer look at the processes controlling retrieval and subsequent organization of the recall. This is especially important because the dependent variable (comprehension) is based on the recall protocols.

It is claimed that the models presented above do not only provide a structural and/or semantic analysis of text but, at the same time, are a theory of people's memory representation of text (stored representation).

But there is good reason to assume that the recalled information (generated representation) is not isomorphic with the stored representation. At the time of retrieval and externalization, the product of recall is subject to processes controlling what and how much is recalled and how it is organized and (re)presented. Factors which might have an effect on the content and structure of the reproduction are manifold. Among them are, for example, type of recall instruction, its interpretation by the subject, type and content of questions asked in probing experiments, self-imposed restrictions induced by the situation or future context ("What kind of information is relevant for the current task and what do I need later on?"). In addition, one has to account for the fact that the probing process not only affects the generated representation, but at the same time changes the stored representation itself.

We can conclude, therefore, that the method utilized to probe the stored representation determines to a substantial extent whether the model's predictions are confirmed or disconfirmed. The reason why models may become sensitive to the choice of methods is mainly due to the fact that they do not include specific assumptions about the retrieval phase and possible factors affecting it. This is especially true for those models that are solely based on the structural and semantic analysis of text.
At the same time, this reflects the state of the art in research on text comprehension: so far, there exists no comprehensive and generally accepted operational definition of comprehension or understanding.

2. PROBLEM SOLVING

In problem solving, the concept of knowledge representation is central. In Streitz (1981), we have argued that different problem solvers will construct different representations of the same content domain presented to them. This will result in different problem representations and differences in the way the problem is tackled. In complex problem solving, for example, it is possible to identify successful problem solvers already in the first third of the problem solving situation, as they show significantly more problem relevant features in their behavior (Putz-Osterloh, 1981; Putz-Osterloh and Lüer, 1981).

One possible interpretation is that successful problem solvers build up an adequate problem representation right at the beginning. In order to establish direct evidence for this hypothesis it is necessary to induce different problem representations in different subjects for the same domain. These representations should be graded in terms of adequacy for the problem in question. In doing so, one is confronted with the difficulty of assessing the induced problem representation, i.e., of checking whether the design used for induction leads to different internal representations. In cases where the information relevant for solving a problem is represented by means of a text, results obtained in text comprehension research seemed to provide a useful aid. Unfortunately, we discovered that most of the models proposed could not solve our problem. In general, they do not deal with the stored representations' dependency on the problem orientation a subject might have during processing. In addition, the models were deficient in their treatment of the retrieval phase for situations when the stored knowledge is used in subsequent behavior.

We define the term "problem solving in text comprehension" as behavior which makes relevant use of the knowledge acquired, updated, or learned during a preceding text comprehension process. It is possible, that there is problem solving in the beginning which requires information not present in the person's mind. In order to find this information he or she might turn to a text and look for the missing information. Then, the integrated knowledge consisting of old and new information is applied in the attempt to solve the problem.
Thus, we use the term problem solving in text comprehension differently than in, for example, comprehension of problem-solving stories (for example, Thorndyke, 1977; Mandler and Johnson, 1977; Rumelhart, 1977); story understanding as problem solving (Black and Bower, 1980); reading and listening as problem solving (for example, Bock, 1978). Although it might be useful to integrate these notions within a comprehensive framework, we will not follow up this line of thought at this point.

3. AN EXTENDED MODEL OF TEXT COMPREHENSION

In the preceding sections, we pointed out some deficiencies of current text comprehension models, especially those which are mainly text-based. We argue for a revision of these models by extending them in such a way that they reflect not only the content and structure of the text but at the same time incorporate factors of the situation and the reader.
The main features which play a part in such a model are represented in Figure 1 which shows the flow of information and the way it is processed at different stages across time.

We start out by assuming that the reader is set to solve a certain text-related problem. This affects him/her in several ways. On the one hand, a corresponding problem orientation or perspective is induced which controls the subsequent processing. On the other hand, prior knowledge associated with or relevant to the indicated content domain is activated. This prior knowledge consists of factual information and of schemata structuring the domain indicated. In addition, the problem situation induces a goal structure which determines when and how the information acquired is used in subsequent behavior. Then, the material is presented. One has to bear in mind that the presented text is also only a representation (R_0) of the underlying structure and content, i.e., the meaning is expressed in a certain

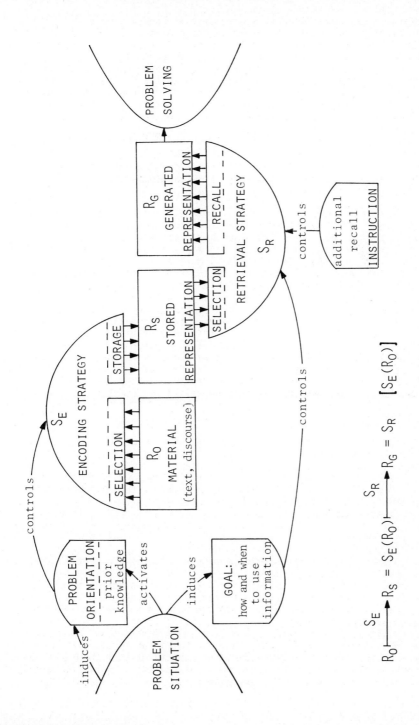

$$R_O \xrightarrow{S_E} R_S = S_E(R_O) \xrightarrow{S_R} R_G = S_R \left[S_E(R_O)\right]$$

Fig. 1. Main features of an extended model of text comprehension

format reflecting the structure in some way. Of course, there are different possible representations R_0 of the idea an author/speaker intends to put across.

During the presentation of the text, problem orientation and prior knowledge control the perception and encoding of the material. This <u>encoding strategy</u> S_E consists of two components. The first component scans the material, evaluates the information in terms of the problem orientation by assigning values of relevance to the problem, and selects the relevant information for subsequent storing. The second component supervises the storage of the selected information. Storing the information involves identifying the structure of the material, comparing this structure with existing structures of prior knowledge, restructuring the information in accordance with the given problem orientation, and finally constructing the stored representation R_S which serves as the basis of the retrieval phase.

After the presentation and storage of the text, there will be a time when the subject wants to access this stored representation. This is either a consequence of the goal or instruction that was part of the initial problem situation; in a second condition, an additional recall instruction is given to the subject after the presentation. The preceding goal and the subsequent instruction control the retrieval of the stored information. This <u>retrieval strategy</u> S_R consists also of two components. The first component searches the stored representation R_S in order to find the information asked for under the present circumstances of retrieval. It selects the information marked by a tag stating its relevance to a certain purpose. The information thus selected is organized into a format which seems to be highly appropriate to the goal that determines how this information is to be used in subsequent behavior. Finally, an external representation R_G is generated. It can consist of a written reproduction, an oral recall, or the answer to a question.
There is also the possibility that the generated representation is immediately used as new input for the same processor (reader, listener) in subsequent problem solving behavior.

The focus of the encoding and the retrieval strategy may not be the same depending on the controlling orientations and goals. It is important to keep this in mind when evaluating methods used to test models of text comprehension. Whereas text-based models predict that a proposition high in the theoretically derived hierarchy will be recalled with higher probability, our model predicts that this depends much more on the problem orientation during encoding and on the goal during retrieval. Thus, although the content structure is still assumed to be relevant, the original representation of the presented text has been subjected to two transformations (S_R, S_E) by the time the final recall is generated.
Obviously, specific predictions of the model, i.e., how these two transformations affect a given text, depend on the actual implementation of material and instructions. Therefore, we will deal with them in detail after the conditions of our experiment have been specified in the next section.

4. EXPERIMENT

In order to test the model, we designed an experiment that should be able to demonstrate the effect of the two proposed strategies during encoding and retrieval. Therefore, it is necessary to monitor both the perception and the recall phase independently. This was achieved by using a method of on-line registration of the information considered relevant by the subject at the time of perception. By placing subjects into different problem situations before listening to the same text we tried to induce different encoding strategies and, thereby, different representations stored by the subject.

At the same time, the experiment attempted to investigate how different representations of the same problem domain affect problem-solving processes and success. This way, it would be possible to assess the model's potential of becoming a component of a comprehensive model describing comprehension and problem solving in an integrated framework. Therefore, two "who-done-it" type deductive reasoning problems were embedded in the text which had to be solved by the subjects.

METHOD

Subjects. 96 students of the Technical University Aachen served as subjects in the experiment. Students majoring in psychology were not allowed to participate. All subjects were paid for their services.

Material. A 883-word story was written, consisting entirely of declarative sentences. A tape recording was made of the passage for presentation to the subjects. The passage was read at moderate rate by an experienced male reader. Reading time was five minutes.

The story is entitled "A concert by request in the hospital". It describes a sequence of events and episodes taking place in a hospital before, during, and after a concert given by a group of musicians in order to entertain the patients. For more details on the text refer to Appendix A.

The story's construction is based on the script (Schank and Abelson, 1977) of a concert but takes place in a hospital setting. This makes it possible to introduce in a natural way two groups of characters (patients and musicians) which are the respective carriers of relevant information for two problems P_1 and P_2. They constitute the premises for the independent but completely isomorphic deductive reasoning problems embedded in the story. Each problem involves four dimensions with five values on each dimension, i.e., names, diseases, room numbers, clothes for the five patients and names, instruments, positions on the stage, clothes for the five musicians. (This problem relevant information can be organized into two 4 x 5 matrices.) Three types of relations connect these information units with the text: affirmative, negative, and "in between" relations, thus constituting a network which represents the logical structure of the problem. There is a total of $2 \cdot 20 = 40$ problem relevant information units and $2 \cdot 13 = 26$ relations connecting them. The problems were constructed in a special way. In order to solve, for example, problem P_1: "What is the name of the patient who has the concussion?", it is necessary to integrate all 20 elements via at least 13 relations in a systematic way. (Of course, it is possible to establish additional relations between the elements by inference during listening or in the problem solving part of the experiment.)

Although these elements are necessary to solve the problems, they do not aid in grasping the gist of the story's plot. Therefore, they are not relevant for a general comprehension of what the story is all about. Since they state minor details about the characters they would be classified as being atypical or irrelevant for the underlying script and setting. On the other hand, story elements stating only the hospital setting and representing the characteristic features of the concert script are irrelevant for solving the problems. The distribution of the 41 story elements and the 40 problem

relevant elements including their relations in the story was organized in
such a way that there would be no position effect.

Design and Procedure. Subjects were randomly assigned to three experimental
conditions and run in individual sessions. Before listening to the story
they were given a written instruction which, in addition, was read to them
by the experimenter.

Common to all subjects was the instruction in Condition C(0).
It stated that they would hear a story from a tape twice. The first time
would serve the purpose of providing an overview. During the second time,
they would be allowed to take written notes (paper and pencil were provided)
while simultaneously listening to the tape. After the second time of listening they would be expected to recall the story orally. While recalling they
would be allowed to use their written notes.

In Condition C(1), the instruction contained an additional direction stating that they would have to solve a problem after having recalled the story.
The problem would be based on the presented story and would consist in answering the question: "What is the name of the patient who has a concussion?".
In Condition C(2), subjects received the same instructions as in C(1) except that they would have to solve two problems, i.e., the problem (P_1) we
mentioned before and an additional problem (P_2): "What is the name of the
musician who plays the guitar?" The instructions subjects were presented
with can be found in Appendix B. It should be noted that C(0) - subjects
did not know about any problem before listening to the story. Thus, the independent variable was the number of problems specified before listening
which had three values: 0, 1, and 2. There were 48 subjects in Condition
C(0) and 24 each in Conditions C(1) and C(2).

After having read the instructions, subjects listened to the tape twice,
took notes during the second time, and gave an oral recall of the story.
This recall was recorded on tape.

Since the experiment was designed not only to study text comprehension but
at the same time to investigate problem-solving behavior (all subjects had
to solve the problems afterwards), the subsequent problem solving was monitored. Since we will not report data on that part of the experiment in this
paper, we shall not describe the details of the further procedure at this
point. They can be found in Streitz (1981). In a final interview, we checked
whether some of the subjects in Condition C(0) had any speculations with
regard to the problems during listening. Twelve subjects out of forty-eight
reported they suspected that they would have to solve a problem based on the
story after having listened to the story for the first time. The reason was
that they were reminded by the story of similar problem-solving puzzles
they had experienced in newspapers or magazines. Since these subjects neither met the C(0)-Condition nor one of the other two conditions in the full
sense they were not included in the final data analysis. In addition, one
C(2)-subject did not meet the condition for other reasons. This left 36
C(0)-subjects, 24 C(1)-subjects, and 23 C(2)-subjects.

Scoring procedure. Written notes and oral recall protocols were scored for
their match with the original text. Story elements were defined by idea
units representing information on the setting (location, time, general
aspects of characters), actions,events, and episodes described in the story.
Protocols were scored for the gist of these idea units (identical, reduced,
or new) and for presence of the problem-relevant elements.

The model's predictions. Applying the model to this experiment, differential
predictions can be made for the dependent variables in terms of the three
categories described before. First, we will concentrate on the effects of
the proposed encoding strategy. During encoding, subjects in Condition C(0)

will be guided by the objective structure as suggested by the hospital
setting and the concert script. In contrast, $C(1)$- and $C(2)$-subjects will
predominantly focus on the problem-relevant elements in the text. The latter
two conditions should only show a difference in encoded P_2-relevant problem
elements. This should be the case because $C(1)$-subjects do not know about
P_2 and therefore are not expected to pay attention to it, whereas, there
should be no difference with regard to P_1-relevant elements. In addition,
one has to take into consideration that certain capacity limitations are
very likely. This should result in a trade-off between the different categories. In the case of story elements, for example, the increase in the
number of problems known before (the independent variable) should result in
a corresponding decrease in encoded story elements. Following this line of
reasoning, we present a summary of the predictions in Table 1.

Table 1. Predicted rank order of the three conditions
          according to the number of different text
          elements encoded during listening.

Type of text elements	rank order of conditions
story elements	$C(0) > C(1) > C(2)$
P_1-relevant elements	$C(1) = C(2) > C(0)$
P_2-relevant elements	$C(2) > C(0) > C(1)$

Second, we will consider the effects of the proposed retrieval strategy. In
the retrieval phase the induced goal of how and when to use information will
be decisive. Of course, the retrieval strategy can only operate on what is
available, i.e., the stored representation. Subjects in Condition $C(0)$
should only have the goal of recalling the story because they think that
this will be the end of the experiment. Therefore, there should not be a
great difference between the stored representation and the generated recall
except for some elaborations or omissions due to inaccuracy. In contrast,
$C(1)$- and $C(2)$-subjects know that the actual problem-solving part will
start subsequently to the recall task. They interpret the request to recall
the story as not being related to problem solving which is their ultimate
goal. Therefore, they are likely to suppress the respective problem-relevant information although it is present in the stored representation. Consequently, one would predict differences between stored and generated representations for P_1-relevant elements in both conditions. A substantial decrease in P_2-relevant information should only be expected in Condition $C(2)$.

5. RESULTS AND DISCUSSION

The experiment provides two sets of data. The first set results from the
written notes the subjects took while simultaneously listening to the tape.
We consider this note-taking as an on-line registration of that information
rated relevant by the subjects at the time of encoding in accordance with
their current problem orientation. It can be assumed that subjects participating in the experiment are very familiar with this kind of situation because they are used to taking notes while attending lectures and seminars.
Although the written notes are, of course, not the stored representation
itself they do reflect especially those features that will be affected

during encoding. The second set consists of data obtained from the tran-
scriptions of the oral recall protocols and is considered to reflect the
impact of the retrieval strategy.

The findings of greatest interest are shown in Figures 2, 3, and 4 which
present the data on both encoding and retrieval at the same time. The differences between the dashed and the solid lines demonstrate the effect of
the retrieval strategy operating on the stored representation R_S. Figure 2
presents the data for the story elements.

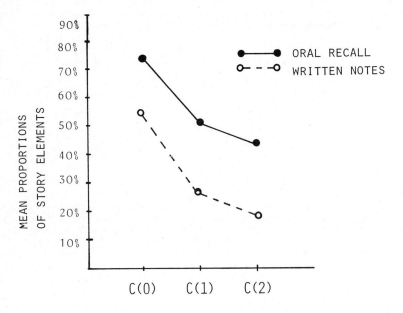

Fig.2. Number of story elements encoded and recalled.

Considering first the mean proportion of story elements in the written
notes, one finds a highly significant decrease as the number of problems
increases; $F(2,80) = 23.6$, $F_{crit}(2,80) = 4.85$ for $p < 0.01$. This indicates
that subjects were very sensitive to the induced problem orientation. The
same finding still holds for the oral recall, $F(2,80) = 20.2$, but there is
an interesting increase relative to the information present in the written
notes. Subjects in all conditions recall orally more than their written
notes on the story elements show. This is not surprising because the setting and script information provided by the text can be easily reconstructed
from just a few notes by means of inferences. Furthermore, one has to bear
in mind that subjects have additional information in their memory and thus
generate a more comprehensive picture of the story by filling in script-
based information. In summary, it should be noted that the more subjects
were oriented to a specific problem-solving task, the fewer story elements

were recalled. These story elements, however, would be high in a text base
hierarchy as proposed by the conventional text-based models reviewed in
Section 1. Therefore, they should be encoded and recalled to a high degree
which is not the case here. In contrast, their recall depends on the problem
orientation as predicted by our model and thus confirms our hypotheses as
stated in Table 1.

The following two figures show the recall pattern for problem-relevant information which consists of minor details in the description of the patients
(P_1) and musicians (P_2). According to a propositional analysis as, for
example, proposed by Kintsch (1974) and described in detail in Turner and
Greene (1977), this information would be represented by modifier propositions and therefore low in the hierarchy.

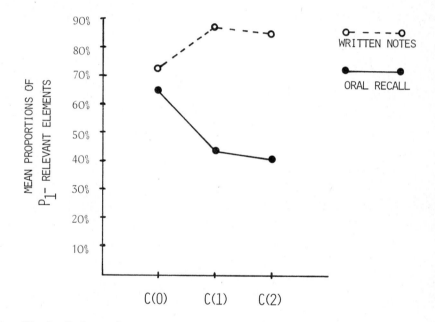

Fig.3. Number of P_1- relevant problem elements encoded
       and recalled.

As the dashed line in Figure 3 indicates, subjects in Conditions C(1) and
C(2) encode more P_1-relevant problem elements than group C(0); F(2,80)=6.2.
Computing contrasts, one finds two subsets: C(0) vs. C(1) and C(2). This
confirms again our prediction in Table 1 based on the proposed encoding
specificity according to a P1-problem orientation. On the other hand, subjects in C(1) and C(2) reproduce this information only to a small degree in
oral recall. This can be interpreted in terms of our proposed retrieval
strategy. The controlling goal at this point in time determines that the
problem-relevant information is not relevant for recalling the story because it is only needed in the subsequent problem-solving phase. There are

even a number of subjects in these conditions who stated this goal explicitly while generating their oral recall. This strategy is not followed by the
C(0)-subjects. They reproduce all they know about problem P_1, because they
do not have a further goal. (They did not know that there was a problem-
solving part to the experiment.) This difference in retrieval strategy is
reflected by the number of recalled P_1-elements, $F(2,80) = 6.5$, again resulting in two subsets C(0) vs. C(1) and C(2).

Finally, we will turn to P_2-relevant problem information. Only subjects in
the C(2)-condition did know about P_2 before listening to the story.

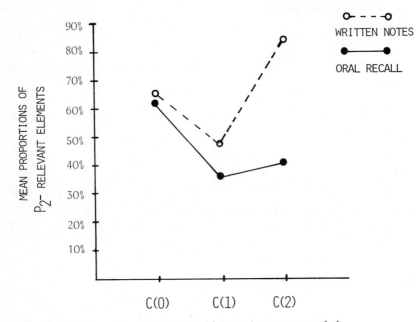

Fig.4. Number of P_2-relevant problem elements encoded
          and recalled.

Again, the results support our thesis. Figure 4 shows that C(2)-subjects
are superior to the other two groups with respect to the encoding of P_2-in-
formation; $F(2,80) = 12.3$. In this case, three subsets could be identified.
C(1)-subjects are worse than C(0)-subjects, because by knowing only about
P_1 before, they are set to deal with it exclusively. Although C(0)-subjects
did not know about P_2, they will write down some of this information as
they take notes on the whole story. Considering the recall data, the effect
of the retrieval strategy is quite noticeable. C(0)-subjects recalled almost everything they wrote down for P_2, whereas C(2)-subjects, having the
most information available, recalled very little of it. C(1)-subjects, having minimal information on P_2, consequently recalled the least of all three
groups; $F(2,80) = 6.8$.

In summary, we may conclude that the data of the experiment provided evidence for the existence of the postulated strategies of encoding and retrieval. Moreover, it has been demonstrated that the induced problem orientations and goals controlled these strategies in the predicted way. Although in this experiment different problem orientations and goals were only simulated, it seems to be necessary to extend text-based models in the proposed way if they are to deal with the real world.

ACKNOWLEDGMENTS

This research was supported in part by a grant from the Deutsche Forschungsgemeinschaft (Do 200/4) to Gerd Lüer. The author wishes to thank Hans-Willi Schroiff for useful ideas and his assistance at many stages of the research. Helmut Buchner, Monika Krummbach, and Jürgen Heck helped to collect the data. Wilfried Holtum and Thomas Staufenbiel are thanked for their help with scoring the protocols. Walter Huber provided helpful suggestions. The readability of the English version was improved by Ingwer Borg, Rüdiger Schreyer, and - during the final editing - by Eileen Kintsch. Finally, thanks are due to Gerd Lüer who made it all possible and provided guidance throughout the research.

REFERENCES

Black, J.B. and Bower, G.H. Story understanding as problem solving. Poetics, 1980, 9, 223 - 250.
Bock, M. Wort-, Satz-, Textverarbeitung. Stuttgart: Kohlhammer, 1978.
Flammer, A., Schläfli, A., and Keller, B. Meeting the reader's interests - Who should care? In M.M. Gruneberg, G.E. Morris, and R.N. Sykes (Eds.). Practical aspects of memory. London: Academic Press, 1978, 679 - 686.
Frederiksen, C.H. Representing logical and semantic structure of knowledge acquired from discourse. Cognitive Psychology, 1975 a, 7, 371 - 458.
Frederiksen, C.H. Effects of context-induced processing operations on semantic information acquired from discourse. Cognitive Psychology, 1975 b, 7, 139 - 166.
Graesser, A.C., Higgenbotham, M.W., Robertson, S.P., and Smith, W.R. A natural inquiry into the National Enquirer: Self-induced versus task-induced reading comprehension. Discourse Processes, 1978, 1, 355 - 372.
Kintsch, W. The representation of meaning in memory. Hillsdale, N.J.: Erlbaum, 1974.
Kintsch, W. Memory for Prose. In Cofer, C.N. (Ed.). The structure of human memory. San Francisco: Freeman, 1976.
Kintsch, W. and van Dijk, T.A. Toward a model of text comprehension and production. Psychological Review, 1978, 85, 363 - 394.
Mandler, J.M. and Johnson, N.S. Remembrance of things parsed: Story structure and recall. Cognitive Psychology, 1977, 9, 111 - 151.
Melton, A.W. and Martin, E. (Eds.). Coding processes in human memory. Washington, D.C.: Winston, 1972.
Meyer, B.J.F. The organization of prose and its effects on memory. Amsterdam: North-Holland, 1975.
Minsky, M.A. A framework for representing knowledge. In P.H. Winston (Ed.). The psychology of computer vision. New York: McGraw-Hill, 1975.

Norman, D.A. and Rumelhart, D.E. Explorations in cognition. San Francisco: Freeman, 1975.

Pichert, J.W. and Anderson, R.C. Taking different perspectives on a story. Journal of Educational Psychology, 1977, 69, 309 - 315.

Putz-Osterloh, W. Über die Beziehung zwischen Testintelligenz und Problemlöseerfolg. Zeitschrift für Psychologie, 1981, 189, 79 - 100.

Putz-Osterloh, W. und Lüer, G. Über die Vorhersagbarkeit komplexer Problemlöseleistungen durch Ergebnisse in einem Intelligenztest. Zeitschrift für Experimentelle und Angewandte Psychologie, 1981, 28, 309 - 334.

Rumelhart, D.E. Understanding and summarizing brief stories. In D. LaBerge and J. Samuels (Eds.). Basic processes in reading: Perception and comprehension. Hillsdale, N.J.: Erlbaum, 1977.

Rumelhart, D.E. and Ortony, E. The representation of knowledge in memory. In R.C. Anderson, R.J. Spiro, and W.E. Montague (Eds.). Schooling and the acquisition of knowledge. Hillsdale, N.J.: Erlbaum, 1977.

Rumelhart, D.E. Notes on a schema for stories. In D.G. Bobrow and A. Collins (Eds.). Representation and understanding. New York: Academic Press, 1975.

Schank, R.C. and Abelson, R.P. Scripts, plans, goals, and understanding. Hillsdale, N.J.: Erlbaum, 1977.

Streitz, N.A. Die Bedeutung der Repräsentation von Wissen beim Problemlösen. Aachen, 1981 (unpublished manuscript).

Thorndyke, P.W. Cognitive structures in comprehension and memory of narrative ciscourse. Cognitive Psychology, 1977, 9, 77 - 110.

Turner, A. and Greene, E. The construction and use of a propositional text base. Institute for the Study of Intellectual Behavior. Techn. Report No. 63, University of Colorado, Boulder, 1977.

van Dijk, T.A. Semantic macro-structures and knowledge frames in discourse comprehension. In M.A. Just and P. Carpenter (Eds.). Cognitive Processes in comprehension. Hillsdale, N.J.: Erlbaum, 1977.

APPENDIX A

This appendix is meant to provide a better idea of the content and the structure of the text used in the experiment. Due to limitations of space it is not possible to reprint the text. For the complete German version refer to Streitz (1981)

The text starts out with the introduction of the theme (concert by request) and of two groups of characters (patients and musicians). In addition, there is a general description of the setting (hospital, pediatrics ward, nurse, ward physician). Then the story continues as a sequence of the following episodes and events.

- conversation between a nurse and the ward physician about the announced concert
- request for permission by a patient to attend the concert
- arrival of the musicians in the hall
- setting up the equipment
- conversation between the musicians and the ward physician
- arrival of the audience (the patients) in the hall
- formation of the band on stage
- announcement of the band by the ward physician who organized the concert
- first part of the performance of the band interrupted by reactions and applause of the audience
- announcement of an intermission
- conversations and actions during the intermission
- second part of the performance of the band including enthusiastic reactions of the audience
- request for an encore
- encore
- end of the performance
- musicians are packing up their instruments
- audience leaves

Within these episodes information describing specific features of the five patients (P_1-relevant elements) and of the five musicians (P_2-relevant elements) is provided as demonstrated in the following examples (translated from the German version).

"In the meantime, the patients of Ward III assemble in the hall. First, a patient in a white night-gown enters the hall. Because he suffers from asthma he walks very slowly." ...
... "Bernd who wears a black leather vest asks his colleague to help him with setting up the equipment." ...

In the first example, "white night-gown" and "asthma" establish an affirmative relation between two P_1-relevant elements. The same is true for "Bernd" and "black leather vest" for problem P_2. Pairs (or triples) of this kind of problem-relevant elements establish the affirmative and negative (or "in between") relations. They are distributed over the text in such a way that there is no advantage for any of the two problem domains as might be possible by a primacy and/or recency effect. This is accomplished by inserting the problem relevant elements which are of no relevance for the story's plot in an alternating way in the above mentioned episodes.

APPENDIX B

INSTRUCTIONS subjects were presented with before listening to the tape.

Condition C(0):

You will now hear a story which has been tape recorded before. This story
will be the basis for the rest of the experiment.
You will hear the story twice.
During the first time, you will have the opportunity to obtain a general
impression of the story. Please, listen carefully.
During the second time, you will have the chance to take notes while listening. After having heard the story twice, you are to give an oral recall of
the story. You will be allowed to make use of your written notes and everything else that you still remember of the story.

Conditions C(1) and C(2):

(In these conditions subjects got the same instructions as the C(0)-subjects
and in addition the following problem orientations.)

The written notes and everything else that is still in your memory is supposed to be the basis for the following part of the experiment, namely, to
solve a problem. The problem is related to the story you will hear.

Condition C(1)	Condition C(2)
It consists in answering the following question: "What is the name of the patient who has the concussion?" You will have a sufficient amount of time to solve this problem.	It consists in answering the following two questions: "What is the name of the patient who has the concussion?" and "What is the name of the musician who plays the guitar?" You will have a sufficient amount of time to solve these two problems.

In all conditions, after having listened to the tape twice, subjects were
presented with the following recall instruction:

Now, please give an oral recall of the story you just heard. You are allowed to make use of your written notes and of everything else you still remember.

DISCOURSE PROCESSING
A. Flammer and W. Kintsch (eds.)
© North-Holland Publishing Company, 1982

CHANGING THE READER'S PERSPECTIVE[1]

August Flammer and Marianne Tauber

Department of Psychology
University of Fribourg
Switzerland

College students read a 748 word text either from the perspective
of a potential homebuyer or from the perspective of a potential
burglar. The text was an enlarged version of the one used in the
Anderson and Pichert (1978) experiment. A free recall test was
given either immediately or after a 20 minute delay, either from
the original reading perspective or from the later introduced
alternative perspective.

Recall from the shifted perspective was significantly lower than
from the reading perspective. Yet, contrary to the hypothesis,
which was based on the assumption of differential forgetting, this
recall difference was not bigger in the delay condition than in the
immediate condition. In comparing several interpretations most
additional evidence was found in favor of the interpretation that
suggests that the text's own perspective overrode the special
perspectives as instructed.

A schema may be defined as a mental device to organize a set of ideas.
Such an organization implies, among other things, the distinction between
important ideas and unimportant ideas. What an important idea is, has been
defined in different ways, i.e., in terms of a high position in the
proposition hierarchy of the text base according to Kintsch (1974), or of a
high position in the hierarchy of rewrite-rules in the story grammar
according to Thorndyke (1977) or simply by means of subjective ratings
(Johnson, 1970).   It has been repeatedly shown that the
importance/unimportance distinction has strong implications for the memory
processes (for a recent investigation see Yekovich and Thorndyke, 1981).

Most sets of ideas can be alternatively organized by several different
schemata. Pichert and Anderson (1977) had subjects read a 373 word passage
either with the perspective of a potential homebuyer or with the
perspective of a potential burglar. It had been determined beforehand by
subjective ratings, that under the different perspectives different ideas
were identified as important ones. Under both conditions, the subjects'
free recall data showed clear superiority of the ideas that were important
to their perspective over the ideas that were exclusively important to the
alternative perspective. This was not only true for the immediate recall
but also for the delayed recall of those ideas which already had been

---

[1] The contribution to the coding of data by Usula Waser is acknowledged.

recalled immediately. Thus, the superiority in recall of the important
ideas over the unimportant ones, as defined with respect to the actual
perspective, increased over time.

What happens if the reading perspective is changed before recall? Anderson
and Pichert (1978) used the same text and procedure as Pichert and Anderson
(1977), yet introduced a shift in perspective between the immediate and the
delayed recall. Subjects had to work on a distractor task for five minutes
between the immediate free recall and the delayed free recall. In one
experiment subjects with perspective shift produced on the second recall
clearly more ideas important to the second perspective that had been
unimportant to the first perspective and fewer ideas unimportant to the
second perspective that had been important to the first. Subjects
therefore did remember ideas in the second recall which they had not
remembered in the first recall. According to self-reports by the subjects
this was not to be attributed to an output editing selection process, but
rather to the perspective dependent retrieval of certain ideas.

In the Anderson and Pichert experiment the distinction between important
and unimportant ideas was therefore operative in the retrieval processes,
independent of whether or not it had already been operative in the storage
processes. Does this mean that any new perspective would be equally
operative after any retention interval? That schemata are able to determine
the result of the retrieval processes independently of their influence on
the storage processes does not imply that the schemata governing the
storage and retention processes are without influence on the result of the
retrieval processes. As Moscovitch and Craik (1976, p. 455) stated it,
"encoding operations establish a ceiling on potential memory performance,
and retrieval cues determine the extent to which that potential is
utilized." And depending on the time that follows storage this ceiling
might well change in different ways, both quantitatively and qualitatively.

The central question of the following experiment was whether the Anderson
and Pichert (1978) result was generalizable over any length of retention
interval. Or more precisely, does free recall from a new perspective
favor the newly important ideas over the formerly important ones
independent of the retention interval? According to the Moscovitch and
Craik (1976) ceiling concept, the answer depends on the fate of the memory
traces over time. If what is unimportant to the encoding schema is
unretrievable after a certain time, then certain kinds of new perspectives
might be quite inappropriate reproduction cues. New perspectives could
therefore yield qualitatively different recall protocols depending on the
length of retention interval.

In fact, it is widely held that less important ideas are typically
forgotten within a shorter time interval than the more important ideas.
This is most clearly demonstrated experimentally for the surface - non-
surface distinction, that is, arbitrary surface structure realizations are
more easily replaceable without being noticed (i.e., forgotten) than the
corresponding meaning or deep structure content (Sachs 1967; 1974; Begg,
1971; Bransford and Franks, 1971; Franks and Bransford, 1972; Anderson,
1974; Plas et al., 1977). These results are especially convincing because
they were gathered with a recognition procedure; differential forgetting as
demonstrated in free recall could just as well be attributed to a
production mechanism instead of a retention mechanism.

How about differential forgetting among semantic items? This has often been studied with the free-recall procedure (Johnson, 1970; Kintsch, 1974; Kintsch and van Dijk, 1975; Kintsch et al., 1975; Meyer, 1975; Pichert and Anderson, 1977). There are a few experiments done with the recognition procedure; the results partially point in the same direction.

McKoon (1977) had subjects verify sentences related to important vs. unimportant sets of ideas, either immediately after reading or 25 minutes later. In two experiments, importance did not affect the errors in immediate recognition but did affect the number of errors in delayed recognition, that is, important ideas were verified more accurately and faster than unimportant ideas.

Caccamise and Kintsch (1978) were able to show that correct paraphrases of topic ideas were more often correctly distinguished from false ones than correct paraphrases of detail ideas from false ones. This was true both in the immediate and in the delayed condition. The differential forgetting hypothesis has not been statistically tested, but the figures clearly show a greater superiority of the important ideas over the unimportant ones in delayed recognition as compared to immediate recognition.

There are also two studies that fail to support the differential forgetting hypothesis: Miller et al. (1977) could not find a significant difference at all in recognition of superordinate vs. subordinate ideas, neither immediately nor after a two day interval; and Yekovich and Thorndyke (1981) found neither a difference in recognition accuracy with respect to importance nor an interaction with the retention interval (0 vs. 60 minutes).

If it is the case that less important ideas are forgotten earlier than more important ideas we conclude that the way in that the retrieval result depends on the encoding schema would also change over the length of the encoding-retrieval interval. And building on this, we expect recall performance from a shifted perspective to depend on the time interval between the time that the information was stored and the point at which the perspective shift occurred. More precisely, we expect the retrieval of ideas that were unimportant at the time of encoding but are important to the retrieval perspective to be harder to recall after a certain retention interval than immediately after the storage phase.

While little work has been done on perspective shift, there exists an interesting body of knowledge on a comparable experimental variable, i.e., presence vs. absence of an appropriate text title. A title may be taken as clue to a certain organization both for the acquisition/encoding processes and for the retrieval/reconstruction processes; its absence might prevent subjects from achieving a convincing and thorough organization, leaving the content mentally unorganized or partially and inconsistently organized. Providing the title after the reading may introduce important/unimportant distinctions among sets of ideas insofar as they are still retrievable, in a way quite similar to the working of a new perspective.

It has been shown repeatedly that titles given at the beginning of texts do have a facilitating effect on free recall (e.g., most recently Bock, 1978, 1981; Schwarz and Flammer, 1979, 1981). Yet in several experiments the presentation of a title was not effective if given after reading the text instead of before (Bransford and Johnson, 1972; Dooling and Lachman, 1971;

Dooling and Mullet, 1973). This can indeed be taken as evidence for the
hypothesis that the traces of formerly unimportant and later important
ideas were no longer retrievable at the time of the title presentation. It
might seem surprising that forgetting was so fast; but one has to consider
that most of the title experiment texts were several pages long, while the
recognition experiments reported above used texts of some 200 to 400 words.
Furthermore, the title experiment texts were deliberately chosen to be
difficult to understand without titles so that -- unlike Anderson's
perspective experiments -- there simply was no appropriate and
comprehensive encoding schema available Hence much of the information
might never have been allocated the necessary encoding resources.

To remedy this, Schwarz (1980), in our laboratory had subjects read a
literary text that seemed quite easy to understand, although the main
message was somewhat unusual. Between the reading and the free recall all
subjects had to work on a ten-minute distractor task. There were four
conditions, three with an appropriate title and one without title
(control). The title was presented either before reading or immediately
after reading (with instructions to rehearse the text's content) or after
the distractor task, i.e., immediately before free recall (again with the
rehearsal instructions). Total processing time was held constant in all
conditions. Free recall was highest when the title was read first, second
highest when the title was given immediately after reading, and worst when
the title was either not given or given immediately before free recall but
after the intervening distractor task. Thus, although recall was boosted
most by processing the title before the text passage, the title was still
of significant help when given after the text, provided the time interval
between the original encoding and the title presentation was not as long as
the interval between encoding and recall.

As a parallel to the Schwarz design we adopted the following conditions in
this experiment: (1) no perspective shift (cf. title before reading), (2)
perspective shift introduced after reading and before immediate free recall
(cf. title immediately after reading), (3) perspective shift introduced
after the retention interval and before delayed free recall (cf. title
after retention interval). There was no parallel to the no-title
condition. The central dependent variable was the number of ideas recalled
which were important to the new perspective but not to the old one. The
hypothesis was that condition 1 would be superior to condition 2 and that
the latter would be superior to condition 3.

As a general model we assumed that given the instruction to recall from a
new perspective a subject would search through the set of encoded ideas --
as far as they were still retrievable -- and try to construct a meaningful
organization from the new perspective. The expected results would then
support the hypothesis that an encoding schema would already distinguish
between important and unimportant ideas in a way that would cause the
unimportant ideas to survive less long than the important ideas. If,
however, the survival probability were the same for important and
unimportant ideas and both would decrease equally over time, there should
be no difference between the shift and the no-shift condition, but an
overall recall difference between immediate and delayed recall. This
second result is not very likely given the finding by Pichert and Anderson
(1977) that under the same perspective condition the proportion of less
important ideas decreased from the immediate to the delayed recall.

METHOD

Subjects. Seventy-two University of Fribourg first and second year students
in psychology or in education volunteered as subjects. They were randomly
assigned to one of eight conditions, nine in each. All were native German
speakers; sex was disregarded.

Material. The 373-word Pichert and Anderson (1977) text was translated into
German, slightly adapted to Swiss conditions, and extended by adding new
information to double its length (748 words). The text described a boy
introducing his friend to his parents' house while nobody else was at home.
The description contained a set of items which would be of interest to a
potential homebuyer and an equivalent set of items which would be of
interest to a potential burglar.

The text was deliberately made longer than both the Anderson text and the
texts used in the differential recognizability experiments reported above;
this was in order to enhance the likelihood that there would be at least
some forgetting, which was a technical condition for the test to be
performed in the experiment.

Design. A completely randomized 2 x 2 x 2 between subjects design was used
with the factors: recall perspective (homebuyer vs. burglar), perspective
shift (no-shift vs. shift, i.e., same perspective in reading as in recall
vs. two different perspectives), and time interval between the end of
reading and the beginning of free recall (one vs. 20 minutes).

Procedure. The experiment was conducted with groups of 8 to 20 subjects
each. In each group all eight conditions were employed. The subjects
worked independently; the experimenter's role was to give a general
introduction and to pace the timing. The instructions were given in each
subject's booklet. First the subjects were asked to read the text for
which ample time was alloted, namely six minutes. Subjects were told to
read the text in order to be optimally prepared to reproduce relevant
information to a potential homebuyer/burglar afterwards. The one-minute
interval after reading was filled in all conditions with a
comprehensibility rating of the text's vocabulary and syntax. During the
following five minutes half of the subjects had to provide a written free
recall of important items from a given perspective (shift/no-shift), while
the others received a verbal comprehension test (Riegel, 1967)
(immediate/delayed recall). The next 20 minutes were filled with other
unrelated tasks out from the same test battery. When this 20-minute
interval was over, either the delayed recall (shift/no-shift) or the verbal
comprehension test was administered. Finally, all subjects were asked to
give a complete written free recall of each and every bit of information
they were still able to remember. Fifteen minutes were allowed for this
second recall.

RESULTS

A set of 90 ideas from the content of the whole text was selected and used
for the scoring of the recall protocols. In a preliminary experiment, four
psychologists from the Department's research staff had given independent
five-point scale ratings about how important each of the selected 90 ideas
were to the homebuyer perspective; four different psychologists had done

the ratings for the burglar perspective. Their agreement seemed to be
acceptable (average inter-rater correlation of .88 for the burglar
perspective and .81 for the homebuyer perspective). A set of fourteen
"important ideas" was chosen for each perspective, correspondig to the
criterion that the median rating was equal to or below 2 for one
perspective and equal to or above 4 for the other perspective, and vice
versa.

Data analysis was conducted with and without holding constant the
covariance between the dependent variables and the verbal comprehension
test as covariate. Since the analysis of covariance added nothing to the
power of the analyses, only the analysis of variance results are reported
here.

First recall

The first analysis was performed on the number of "important" ideas from
the respective recall perspective. Exact numbers are given in Table 1.
Two factors, recall perspective and perspective shift, produced significant
main differences; time of recall was not significant, nor were any of the
interactions.

Table 1

Average number of freely recalled ideas important
to the recall perspective

===

| | Recall perspective | |
	Burglar	Homebuyer
Without perpective shift		
Immediate recall	7.89	5.11
Delayed recall	7.67	4.00
With shifted perspective		
Immediate recall	5.44	4.44
Delayed recall	5.44	3.78

===

The perspective shift produced a generally lower recall score than the no-
shift condition: 4.78 vs. 6.18; $F(1,64) = 6.1$; $p = 0.016$. This result was
predicted. Also as predicted, the average immediate recall score was
higher (5.72) than the delayed recall score (5.22), but the difference did
not reach statistical significance. And it was also predicted that in the
delayed recall condition the shift would be relatively more detrimental
than in the immediate recall condition for the recall of the newly
important ideas; yet, the data did not show this interaction.

The remaining main effect concerns the recall perspective. There was an average of 6.61 important ideas for the burglar recall perspective and 4.33 for the homebuyer perspective; $F(1,64) = 16.3$; $p < .01$. This difference may be taken as a Swiss corroboration of the Pichert and Anderson (1977) result that American college students identified more leadily with the burglar perspective than with the homebuyer perspective. Another explanation is simply that the scoring procedure adopted here favored the burglar perspective. A later check of the scoring objectivity by rescoring a sample of the answer sheets by another person indicated that the first person often did not 'give' the score on a homebuyer idea where the second person judged the 'gist' of the idea to be sufficiently indicated. This was rarely the case for the burglar ideas. Thus, the number of agreed upon scores was a portion of .93 for the important burglar ideas, but .47 for the homebuyer ideas. In any case the data analysis was done with the scoring of the first scoring person.

The number of "important" ideas recalled from the 14 predefined ones might not have permitted a very powerful test of our hypotheses: there was some unreliability in the definition of these ideas, some unreliability in the scoring procedure (see above), and in any case a rather small number of countable ideas at all. We therefore decided to do two further analyses in order to handle more adequately the problem of the a priori definition of an idea's importance or unimportance.

The second analysis took into account that each subject could have had (and did employ) a different concept of what an important idea was for a given perspective. Thus, for each subject all ideas were counted as important for a given perspective if the subject had written it down on his/her free recall protocol, provided they belonged to the total set of the 90 predefined ideas.

This second analysis yielded one significant main effect, namely, perspective shift, and one significant interaction, namely, perspective shift x recall perspective. The analysis of the interaction ($F(1,64) = 4.9$, $p < .05$) led to the conclusion that the no-shift advantage was really due to a single perspective shift main effect in the burglar perspective condition (11.78 vs. 7.95 ideas, as opposed to 9.56 vs. 9.34 in the homebuyer perspective). Although there was no perspective main effect in this analysis, the interaction indicates that the two perspectives are not fully interchangeable.

The most important result of the second analysis was again the absence of a significant perspective shift x time of recall interaction.

A third analysis was done with each subject's recalled ideas weighed against the average importance rating that had resulted from the preliminary experiment, again, provided the recalled ideas belonged to the total set of the 90 predefined ideas.

The results did not lead to new insights. The analysis of the data weighed according to the burglar importance ratings yielded two significant main effects, recall perspective and perspective shift, and one significant interaction, recall perspective x perspective shift. This is what we had obtained in the earlier analyses.

The analysis of the data as weighed according to the homebuyer importance ratings yielded the same two significant main effects, recall perspective and perspective shift, and no other significant effect. Most importantly, the time of recall x perspective shift interaction again was not there, nor was there a significant time of recall main effect. Nevertheless, immediate recall was always better than delayed recall and the error probability of the difference smaller than .20 in each case.

Second recall

In the second free-recall attempt subjects were simply asked to reproduce everything they could remember. The protocols were scored with the number of reproduced ideas intersecting with the set of the 90 a priori defined admissable ideas. Neither of the three factors nor any interaction produced a significant effect on the total number of edited ideas.

An additional analysis was done on the second free-recall data but weighed for importance either to the one or to the other perspective. Again, neither of the three factors nor any interaction between them produced a significant effect.

DISCUSSION

When the reading perspective was not the same as the recall perspective, recall was worse than in the identical perspective (no-shift) condition. This means that ideas unimportant to the reading perspective had a smaller probability to be recalled, even if they had become important from the recall perspective. This can be taken as a consequence of the encoding ceiling which was biased by the encoding perspective. Some of the formerly unimportant material just might not have been encoded in some permanent way.

Indeed, the two perspectives adopted in this experiment were quite different and there were many ideas completely unimportant to one perspective and very important to the other. Examples are: the jewelry in the mother's closet, the father's coin collection, the newly painted living room, the leak in the old roof. Thus, many ideas may have been filtered out early in the reading process; they were therefore just not available for recall from whatever perspective. It might have been possible to infer them. Yet, with this material there was little chance from the outset to fill in correct ideas by mere inference because these ideas tapped very concrete facts and formed a small selection of the possible universe of such items.

A different interpretation, however, is not to be excluded, namely, that the perspective shift forced the subjects to retrieve and to edit to according a schema whose familiarity at the moment was less advanced than the retrieval/editing schema in the no-shift condition which had already been thoroughly activated in the reading phase.

It had been expected that the disadvantage of the shift condition as compared to the no-shift condition would have been stronger in the delayed recall as compared with the immediate recall. The assumption was that the less important ideas relative to the encoding schema would be forgotten faster than the more important ideas (differential forgetting hypothesis).

However, the experimental results did not support this kind of reasoning, since there was no significant interaction between the recall shift factor and the duration of retention interval factor. The results did not even indicate a trend in the expected direction, i.e., it was not the case that the inferiority of the shift condition to the no-shift condition was greater in delayed recall than in immediate recall. The results even pointed slightly in the opposite direction.

One possible explanation of this result could be that in so far as unimportant ideas are even encoded in some long-term store they are forgotten at the same rate as the important ideas. This explanation is not testable by our data, not even indirectly, since the time of recall factor did not produce any significant main effect, i.e., there was hardly any forgetting during the retention interval.

Although in our experiment there was no significant forgetting during the 20-minute interval, there was forgetting on the whole, since already in the immediate recall and no-shift condition only an average of about six of the 14 'important' ideas were reproduced. It seems as if there was a huge amount of forgetting during reading (e.g., by selection for permanent encoding) or instantly after reading. In designing the experiment two precautions were made in order to give to the unimportant ideas a real chance to become lost from the retrievable memory, i.e., by extending the retention interval (20 minutes, as opposed to 10 minutes in the Schwarz study and 5 minutes in the Anderson and Pichert study) and by lenghtening the Anderson and Pichert experimental text. The second interpretation that we offer is, then, that the last mentioned precaution led the subjects to a quite radical foregrounding of the important ideas and to a ready suppression, or filtering out, of the umimportant ideas. This means that the critical point in time where a great many of the unimportant ideas had already fallen below the retrieval threshold while significantly more important ideas were still above this threshold occurred even before the immediate recall, and that during the following 20 minutes forgetting was a minor event. This explanation fits both the absence of the shift x time of recall interaction and the significant shift main effect as discussed above.

We would like to offer some speculation concerning a third interpretation, based on the (not significant) result, that the perspective shift disadvantage tended to decrease (instead of increase) over the 20-minute retention interval: Perhaps storage in long-term memory was not so much organized according to the prescribed encoding schema, i.e., the proposed perspective, but according to some third perspective. This could have been either a very personal and idiosyncratic one or one that was more text-inherent than both the others, perhaps the text author's own. In an earlier experiment on question asking we were led to the comparable conclusion that subjects adopted more than one organizing schema while acquiring information (Flammer et al., 1981).

Assume that the alternative and nonprescribed perspective was more comprehensive and produced less bias in storage; the consequence would be that any prescribed recall perspective would offer a retrieval schema that is more or less different from the storage organization, and that after a certain retention interval even the perspective that was also prescribed in the reading phase would be a strange perspective with respect to the storage organization, thus reducing the superiority of the no-shift

condition over the shift condition during the retention interval as our
data suggest. The results of the second recall also favor the third
interpretation, though not strongly: The second recall (comprehensive,
without prescribed perspective) did not show any perspective-shift main
effect.

The third interpretation has a less demanding variant, one that does not
invoke the omnipresent idiosyncrasy of information processing to argue for
the interpretation that the mere prescribing of a reading perspective might
only have a minor effect on storage in long-term memory. In this
experiment a text was used which apparently was quite interesting to read.
Maybe it is just very difficult to adopt a suggested perspective while
reading a fascinating text with its own perspective. And there is even
more to this: going through the text again we realized not only that the
text did have its own schema, or perspective, i.e., the one of the two
boys' discovery adventure, but that its own perspective was not that
neutral with regard to the two experimental perspectives as Pichert and
Anderson and the authors of the present experiment had supposed it to be.
Although the two boys were not burglars, what they did was much nearer to
this than to homebuying: the boys stayed away from school, thus doing
something rather illegal; they intruded into a house whose owners were not
at home; they inspected each and every room, had a look at the father's
coin collection, his famous painting collection and the mother's jewelry,
certainly something they would not have done had the parents been at home.

If we adopt the idea that the perspective which is inherent in the text
itself overrides the suggested perspective in the long run and if we also
assume that the text's own perspective was much nearer to the burglar
perspective than to the homebuyer perspective, then another result is also
easy to understand, namely, that the scores on important ideas were higer
according to the burglar perspective than to the homebuyer perspective.
This is a finding that occurred throughout the first recall (immediate and
delayed). We also found it in the second or comprehensive recall, in
comparing the scores that were weighed according to importance for the
burglar perspective as opposed to the homebuyer perspective. However,
these are two different scales, and although intuitively comparable, they
are not necessarily equally demanding. Note finally that according to
Table 1 forgetting was much smaller from the burglar perspective than from
the homebuyer perspective, i.e., the between-subjects differences from the
burglar perspective were 0.22 (no-shift condition) and 0.00 (shift
condition) and the corresponding differences from the homebuyer perspective
were 1.11 and 0.68. This interaction is admittedly not significant
statistically but it fits the third interpretion.

Given the two variants of the third interpretation (idiosyncratic
organization on which the prescribed perspective would have had only a
short-term influence vs. text-inherent perspective which was much nearer to
the burglar perspective than to the homebuyer perspective) it is hard to
decide on the basis of these data which one to favor. The first variant
would have very strong educational implications in that orienting
instructions would not be very powerful in reading. This is not what much
of the research to date suggests (cf. Mayer, this volume), it is not what
faith in humanistic education would lead one to believe, nor is it what
earlier results from our laboratory on the effects of the reader
"focussing" suggested (Flammer et al., 1978). Thus, so far these authors
favor the second variant of the the third interpretation.

From this standpoint there are also two ways to interpret the corroboration of the Pichert and Anderson (1977) result that the recall of important ideas according to the prescribed burglar perspective was higher than the recall of important ideas according to the prescribed homebuyer perspective. One is that both American and Swiss college students would be more familiar with the burglar perspective than with the homebuyer perspective (Pichert and Anderson, 1977, p. 133). The other one, which we obviously prefer, is that the text itself suggested a perspective that was more of a burglar perspective than of a homebuyer perspective.

After completing this report, two recent papers came to our attention. The first is an unpublished study by Anderson, Pichert, and Shirey (1979). They reported two experiments which demonstrated that the perspective affected both encoding while reading, and retrieval. As in our data, shift of perspective yielded poorer free recall than the no-shift condition, even though the subjects were asked to recall "every bit of the story" -- unlike our subjects who were instructed to simply recall from the given perspective. Furthermore, the relative disadvantage of the shift condition increased slightly, although not significantly over a two-week interval.

The second study (Fass and Schumacher, 1981) used the Pichert and Anderson (1977) text; it demonstrated that "the retrieval perspective influenced the recall of additional important information when recall was immediate but not at delayed recall." Indeed, according to Fass and Schumacher's Table 1, the loss over time -- based on a between-subject comparison -- was clearly bigger in the shift condition than in the no-shift condition, both in absolute and in relative terms. This is what we had predicted but not obtained in our study.

This difference could be attributed to several factors: (i) the difference in the length of the interval between reading and the the delayed recall, which was 24 hours in the Fass and Schumacher (1981) study as opposed to 20 minutes in ours; (ii) Fass and Schumacher used the original text, while ours was doubled in length; (iii) the Fass and Schumacher asked their subjects to recall "as much of the exact passage as they could remember", while our subjects just had to recall from a specific perspective. Thus, both Anderson and Fass and Schumacher employed the same type of instructions as were used in all of Anderson's studies, while our instructions were different. It seems plausible that the retrieval and recall processes are quite different under the two different conditions. Recalling from a given perspective stresses more that perspective, i.e., having to restrict themselves to one perspective only may have led our subjects to try harder while recalling, in order to write a reasonable amount of text. Whether the use of this procedure in our study explains the non-occurrence of the predicted increase over time of the relative disadvantage of the shift condition remains to be studied under a strictly comparable experimental design.

REFERENCES

Anderson, J. (1974) Verbatim and propositional representation of sentences in immediate and long-term memory. Journal of Verbal Learning and Verbal Behavior, 13, 149-162.
Anderson, R.C. and Pichert, J.W. (1978) Recall of previously unrecallable information following a shift in perspective. Journal of Verbal Learning

and Verbal Behavior, 17, 1-12.

Anderson, R.C., Pichert, J.W., and Shirey, L.L. (1979) Effects of the
  reader's schema at different points in time. Technical Report No. 119.
  University of Illinois at Urbana Champaign: Center for the Study of
  Reading.

Begg, I. (1971) Recognition memory for sentences meaning and wording.
  Journal of Verbal Learning and Verbal Behavior, 10, 176-181.

Bock, M. (1978) Ueberschriftsspezifische Selektionsprozesse bei der
  Textverarbeitung. Archiv für Psychologie, 131, 77-93.

Bock, M. (1981) Eine aufmerksamkeitstheoretische Interpretation
  sprachlicher Selektionsprozesse. In Mandl, H. (Ed.) Zur Psychologie der
  Textverarbeitung. Muenchen: Urban and Schwarzenberg, 63-107.

Bock, M. (1981) Some effects of titles on building and recalling text
  structures. Discourse Processes, 3, 301-311.

Bransford, J.D. and Johnson, M.K. (1972) Contextual prerequisites for
  understanding. Journal of Verbal Learning and Verbal Behavior, 11, 717-
  726.

Bransford, J. and Franks, J. (1971) The abstraction of linguistic ideas.
  Cognitive Psychology, 2, 231-350.

Caccamise, D.J. and Kintsch, W. (1978) Recognition of important and
  unimportant statements from stories. American Journal of Psychology, 91,
  651-657.

Dooling, D.J. and Lachman, R. (1971) Effects of comprehension on the
  retention of prose. Journal of Experimental Psychology, 88, 216-222.

Dooling, D.J. and Mullet, R. (1973) Locus of thematic effects in retention
  of prose. Journal of Experimental Psychology, 97, 404-406.

Fass,W. and Schumacher, G.M. (1981) Schma theory and prose retention:
  boundary conditions for encoding and retrieval effects. Discourse
  Processes, 4, 17-26.

Flammer, A., Schlaefli, A., and Keller, B. (1978) Meeting the reader's
  interests -- who should care? In Gruneberg, M.M., Morris, P.E., Sykes,
  R.N., Eds., Practical aspects of memory. London: Academic Press.

Flammer, A., Kaiser, H., and Mueller-Bouquet, P. (1981) Predicting what
  questions people ask. Psychological Research, 34, 421-429.

Franks, J.J. and Bransford, J.D. (1972) The acquisition of abstract ideas.
  Journal of Verbal Learning and Verbal Behavior, 11,311-315.

Johnson, R.E. (1970) Recall of prose as a function of structural importance
  of the linguistic units. Journal of Verbal Learning and Verbal Behavior,
  9, 12-20.

Kintsch, W., Kozminsky, E., Streby, W.J., McKoon, G., and Keenan, J.M.
  (1975) Comprehension and recall of texts as a function of conctent
  variables. Journal of Verbal Learning and Verbal Behavior, 14, 196-214.

Kintsch, W. and van Dijk, T.A. (1975) Comment on se rappelle et on resume
  des histoires. Langages, 40, 98-116.

Kintsch, W. (1974) The representation of meaning in memory. Hillsdale,
  N.J.: Erlbaum.

Mayer, R.E. (1982) Instructional variables in text processing. In Flammer,
  A. and Kintsch, W. (eds.) Discourse Processing. Amsterdam: North-
  Holland.

McKoon, G. (1977) Organization of information in text memory. Journal of
  Verbal Learning and Verbal Behavior, 16, 247-260.

Meyer, B. (1975) The organization of prose and its effect on memory.
  Amsterdam: North-Holland.

Miller, R.B., Perry, F.L., and Cunningham, D.J. (1977) Differential
  forgetting of superordinate and subordinate information acquired from
  prose material. Journal of Educational Psychology, 69, 730-735.

Moscovitch, M. and Craik, F.I.M. (1976) Depth of processing, retrieval
    cues, and uiqueness of encoding as factors in recall. Journal of Verbal
    Learning and Verbal Behavior, 15, 447-458.
Pichert, J.W. and Anderson, R.C. (1977) Taking different perspectives on a
    story. Journal of Educational Psychology, 69, 309-315.
Plas, R., Segui, J., and Kail, M. (1977) Reconnaissance de phrases
    appartenant a un texte: aspects formels et semantiques. Psychologie
    experimentale et comparée. Hommage à Paul Fraisse. Paris: Presses
    universitaires de France.
Riegel, K.F. (1967) Der sprachliche Leistungstest SASKA. Goettingen:
    Hogrefe.
Sachs, J.S. (1967) Recognition memory for syntactic and semantic aspects of
    connected discourse. Perception and Psychophysics, 2, 437-442.
Sachs, J.S. (1974) Memory in reading and listening to discourse. Memory and
    Cognition, 2, 95-100.
Schwarz, M.N.K. and Flammer, A. (1979) Erstinformation einer Geschichte:
    Ihr Behalten und ihre Wirkung auf das Behalten der nachfolgenden
    Information. Zeitschrift fuer Entwicklungspsychologie und Paedagogische
    Psychologie, 11, 347-358.
Schwarz, M.N.K. and Flammer, A. (1981) Text Structure and Title - Effects
    on Comprehending and Recall. Journal of Verbal Learning and Verbal
    Behavior, 20, 61-66.
Schwarz, M.N.K. (1980) Struktur, Instruktion und Titel -- Ihre Effekte auf
    das Erinnern, Erfragen und Verstehen eines Prosatextes. Dissertation.
    Universitaet Freiburg/Schweiz.
Thorndyke, P.W. (1977) Cognitive structures in comprehension and memory of
    narrative discourse. Cognitive Psychology, 9, 77-110.
Yekovich, F.R. and Thorndyke, P.W. (1981) An evaluation of alternative
    functional models of narrative schemata. Journal of Verbal Learning and
    Verbal Behavior, 20, 454-469.

DISCOURSE PROCESSING
A. Flammer and W. Kintsch (eds.)
© *North-Holland Publishing Company, 1982*

INFLUENCES OF TITLES ON THE RECALL OF INSTRUCTIONAL TEXTS

Helmut M. Niegemann

Fachrichtung Allgemeine Erziehungswissenschaft
Universität des Saarlandes
Saarbrücken
Federal Republic of Germany

This study examines the hypothesis that titles influence
the quality of the recall of instructional texts in a
selective way. In three experiments one instructional
text at a time was provided with two different titles,
each referring to one of two aspects of the text. Subjects
read their text and recalled it in writing. Results
supported the hypothesis in each case. Subjects recalled
relatively more propositions related to the respective title.

There is only little experimental research explicitly concerning the
effects of titles on the comprehension and recall of instructional texts.
On the other hand, during the last ten years there have been some experiments published that study the effects of context in processing of text-
information using titles as specific context. Although one may conclude
from the results of these studies that titles may influence comprehension
and recall of texts, it seems rather difficult to deduce clear prescrip-
tions for the design of instructional texts because the studies mentioned
vary considerably in research intentions as well as in ways to operatio-
nalize relevant variables.

Among others, such differences concern

- the comprehension or interpretability of a text with or without
  a title (texts not understandable without title because of incomplete
  information about important referents; ambiguity of texts resulting
  from two possible interpretations; easily understandable texts, even
  without any title);
- type of titles (full thematic; perspective);
- type of texts (stories, narratives, descriptions, reports);
- tests of comprehension and recall (free recall, scoring words,
  sentences, ideas or propositions; questionnaires; rating of
  comprehensibility);
- underlying hypothesis (assuming mainly quantitative and/or
  qualitative effects).

An overview of some of these differences among experimental studies on
title effects is shown in Table 1.

In designing an instructional text there is normally no question whether
there should be a title, but rather what kind of title would potentially
lead to an increase in comprehension and recall. Instructional texts
themselves are (or should be) almost unambiguous and understood even
even without any title.

Table 1   Overview of relevant differences between experimental studies concerning title effects.

Study	Comprehensibility of texts used without any title	type of title	type of text	Test	Type of effects
DOOLING and LACHMAN (1971)	difficult to comprehend theme	thematic	story (?)	free recall (words)/ recognition (words)	quantitative
BRANSFORD and JOHNSON (1972)	difficult to comprehend theme	perspective	descriptive	free recall/comprehension rating	quantitative
DOOLING and MULLET (1973)	difficult to comprehend theme	thematic	story (?)	free recall (words, sentences, errors)/ questionnaire	quantitative
SCHALLERT (1976)	ambiguous	perspective	narrative	cued recall/recognition	quantitative/ qualitative
KOZMINSKY (1977)	comprehensible	perspective	descriptive/ narrative/ report	free recall (propositions)	quantitative/ qualitatitve
BOCK (1978)	comprehensible	thematic	report	free recall	qualitative
SCHWARZ and FLAMMER (1979, 1981)	comprehensible	full thematic	story	free recall/comprehension rating	quantitative
HARTLEY et al. (1980)	comprehensible	thematic	biograph. report	questions	quantitative

As the studies of Kozminsky (1977) and Bock (1978) demonstrate, titles
may bias the recall of texts in a selective manner. Therefore it can be
assumed, memory for the relevant ideas, according to some specific
instructional objectives, could be supported through the choice of
appropriate titles.

In three experiments one instructional text at a time was presented with
two different titles, each referring to one of two aspects of the text.
Propositions related to the one or the other aspect had been specified
previously based on an analysis of the texts' microstructures.

The experiments should investigate, whether the titles would bias the
recall of the texts differentially. The comprehensibility of the texts
should not be altered by titles in any way.

METHOD

Subjects. Forty-eight students from three colleges (last two years of
"Gymnasium") in the Saarland and fifty-seven first- and second-year
University of the Saarland students volunteered as subjects.

Materials. The three texts, with about 550 - 750 words each had not been
constructed, but were actual instructional texts. One was taken from the
study-material of a correspondence course in History, the others stemmed
from a German popular-science periodical (Bild der Wissenschaft):

> (1)   Title A: "The disintegration of Germanic family bonds by
>   Christianity",
>
>   B: "The reign of terror of King Chlodwig"
>   (The part of the text that title B refers to
>   functions as an exemplification of the parts
>   represented by title A);
>
> (2)   Title A: "Phosphates pollute waters",
>
>   B: "Zeolith A - a new substitute for phosphate";
>
> (3)   Title A: "Beryllium - seldom and desired",
>
>   B: "Beryllium - chemical inflammation of the lungs",
>   N(neutral): "Beryllium"

The analysis of the propositional microstructures and the decision to
assign a certain proposition as relevant to the one or the other title
followed essentially the procedures and rules described by Kozminsky
(1977). Nevertheless there were difficulties in assigning some propositions
definitely, especially with the first text. In these (few) cases the
respective proposition was eliminated from further analysis and scoring.

Design. The experimental design was a simple 2 x 3 factorial. The independent variables were the relevant propositions, each assigned to one
of the aspects of the respective text and titles (two titles concerning
one particular aspect of a text in each case and no title or a neutral
one for control). The dependent variable was the percentage of relevant
propositions recalled.

Procedure. Experiments were executed in groups of fifteen to thirty subjects. Subjects were told that they were participating in a study on the
comprehensibility of texts. They were asked to read their text carefully.
There was no time limit.

Each subject in the experimental groups received a type-written copy of
one of the texts, in which the first sheet contained merely one of the
titles. The control groups also received a copy of the text, however the
cover sheet was blank.

After having read the passage, subjects were given a comprehension rating
scale to answer. Having done this, they were asked to recall the text in
writing as closely as possible to the original text.

Experimenters were second-year University of the Saarland students ful-
filling a study requirement under the guidance and supervision of the
author.

Scoring. Each recall protocol was scored against its appropriate text
base: Propositions from the recall protocols were compared with those of
the text base, and in case of matching, a proposition was assigned to the
same category as the respective text-base proposition.

RESULTS

As expected, there were no differences in comprehensibility with or without
titles. Figures 1 - 3 show for each experiment the proportion of recalled
propositions according to their relationship to one of the two aspects of
the text, as a function of the title version given in each case.

To test the significance of the differences, a chi-square test for 2 x 3
contingency-tables was used. To localize effects, each contingency table
was partitioned into two specific components (cf. Sachs, 1974, p. 370 ff),
one concerning the interaction between the two titles and the relevant
propositions, the other concerning the differences between thematic titles
and none or a neutral title.

To assess the degree of contingency, the contingency-coefficient CC_{korr}
was computed (cf. Sachs 1974) in each case (see Figures 1-3).

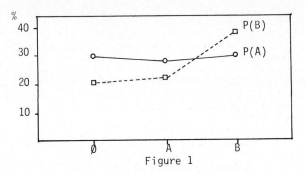

Figure 1

Experiment I. Proportion of recalled propositions as a function
of the title version. (Title A: "The disintegration of family
bonds..."; title B: "The reign of terror..."; $\emptyset$: no title.
P(A): Propositions related to title A; P(B): Propositions
related to title B.)

Overall differences were significant ($\chi^2(2) = 9.61$, $p < .01$, $CC_{korr} =$
.18), as was the interaction between titles and relevant propositions
($\chi^2(1) = 4.52$, $p < .05$, $CC_{korr} = .15$) and the differences between titles
and no title with regard to relevant propositions ($\chi^2(1) = 5.05$, $p < .05$,
$CC_{korr} = .14$).

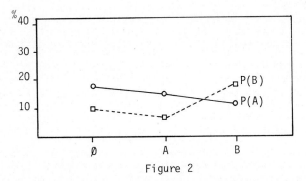

Figure 2

Experiment II. Proportion of recalled propositions as a function
of the title version. (Title A: "Phosphates pollute waters";
title B: "Zeolith A..."; $\emptyset$: no title. P(A): Propositions related
to title A, P(B): Propositions related to title B.)

Both overall differences and the interactions between titles and relevant
propositions were significant at the .001 level ($\chi^2(2) = 14.98$, $CC_{korr} =$
.31, and ($\chi^2(1) = 11.22$, $CC_{korr} = 34$, respectively). However, the difference between the title and no-title conditions was not significant with
regard to relevant propositions ($\chi^2(1) = 3,56$, $p > .05$).

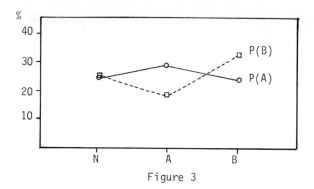

Figure 3

Experiment III. Proportion of recalled propositions as a function of the title version. (Title A: "Beryllium - rare and desired"; title B: "Beryllium - chemical inflammation of the lungs"; N (neutral title): "Beryllium".)

Similiar results were obtained in Experiment III, in which overall differences and the interaction between titles and relevant propositions likewise obtained significance at the .001 level ($\chi^2(2)$ = 17.04, CC_{korr} = 21; and ($\chi^2(1)$ = 16.77, CC_{korr} = 24.81, respectively). Differences between titles A and B and the neutral title with regard to the relevant propositions were not significant ($\chi^2(1)$ = .30, p > .05).

DISCUSSION

Consistent with Kozminsky's (1977) and Bock's (1978) findings, the results this study support the hypothesis that titles may influence recall of texts in a qualitative manner. This effect occured in three independent experiments with different texts and different subjects.

The fact that the degree of contingency between specific titles and recall of relevant propositions is merely moderate is not surprising: It seems clear that recall of texts is widely influenced by much more important variables, such as, among others, macro- and superstructures (cf. Van Dijk 1977, 1980; Kintsch and Van Dijk, 1978), prior knowledge, and degree and specifity of individual interest in the content area of the text. According to the work of Schwarz and Flammer (1979, 1981), primacy effects may also bias what is remembered from a text.

Thus, text-structure variables and/or primacy effects could have caused the differences in the proportion of propositions recalled in the no-title versions in Experiment I and II.
Similarly, the fact that only in Experiment I were the differences between the title and no-title versions significant, could possibly be explained by the specific structure of the History text:
One part (the first) describes historical events, the other part is a generalization and explanation on a higher level.

Insofar as a text-grammar or super-structure model (cf. Rumelhart, 1975; Thorndyke, 1977; van Dijk, 1978, 1980) has not yet been developed, neither for history nor for science/technology texts, there are mere speculations. Thus, it seems reasonable to base further investigation of the biasing effects upon analyses of the underlying text schemata.

With regard to the practical purpose of designing instructional texts, one may cautiously conclude that there is some evidence that:

   (1) according to the findings of Kozminsky (1977) and Bock (1978) and the results of this study, titles related to a specific part or aspect of the text in question may bias memory in a selective way; and

   (2) according to the findings of Schwarz and Flammer (1979, 1981) full-thematic titles may have quantitative effects on rerembering text propositions.

Thus, it seems reasonable to recommend that designers of instructional texts try to use these effects by deliberately selecting titles that would enhance the quantity as well as the quality of propositions remembered by readers in accordance with the desired instructional objectives.

REFERENCES

Bransford, J.D. and Johnson, M.K. Contextual prerequisites for under standing: Some investigations of comprehension and recall. Journal of Verbal Learning and Verbal Behavior, 1972, 11, 717 - 726.

Bock, M. Der Einfluß von Kontextfaktoren auf die Sprachverarbeitung. Sprachpsychologische Überlegungen zu einer Theorie der Mediengestaltung. Psychologische Rundschau, 1978, 29, 183 - 194.

Bock, M. Wort-, Satz-, Textverarbeitung. Stuttgart: Kohlhammer, 1978.

Dooling, D.J. and Lachman, R. Effects of comprehension on retention of prose. Journal of Experimental Psychology, 1971, 88, 216 - 222.

Dooling, D.J. and Mullet, R.L. Locus of thematic effects in retention of prose. Journal of Experimental Psychology, 1973, 97, 404 - 406.

Hartley, J., Kenely, J., Owen, G. and Trueman, M. The effect of headings on children's recall from prose text. British Journal of Educational Psychology, 1980, 50, 304 - 307.

Kintsch, W. and Van Dijk, T.A. Toward a model of text comprehension and production. Psychological Review, 1978, 85, 363 - 394.

Kozminsky, E. Altering comprehension: The effect of basing titles on text comprehension. Memory and Cognition, 1977, 5, 482 - 490.

Rumelhart, D.E. Notes on a schema for stories. In D. Bobrow and A. Collins (Eds.). Representation and understanding: Studies in cognitive science. New York: Academic Press, 1975.

Sachs, L. Angewandte Statistik. Berlin: Springer, 1974.

Schallert, D.L. Improving memory for prose: The relationship between depth of processing and context. Journal of Verbal Learning and Verbal Behavior, 1976, 15, 621 - 632.

Schwarz, M. and Flammer, A. Erstinformation einer Geschichte: Ihr Behalten und ihre Wirkung auf das Behalten der nachfolgenden Information. Zeitschrift für Entwicklungspsychologie und Pädagogische Psychologie, 1979, 11. 347 - 358.

Schwarz, M.N.K. and Flammer, A. Text structure and title - Effects on comprehension and recall. Journal of Verbal Learning and Verbal Behavior, 1981, 20, 61 - 66.

Thorndyke, P.W. Cognitive structures in comprehension and memory of narrative discourse. Cognitive Psychology, 1977, 9, 77 - 110.

Van Dijk, T.A. Semantic macro-structures and knowledge frames in discourse comprehension. In M.A. Just and P.A. Carpenter (Eds.). Cognitive processes in comprehension. Hillsdale, N.J.: Erlbaum, 1977.

Van Dijk, T.A. Textwissenschaft. München: dtv, 1980.

DISCOURSE PROCESSING
A. Flammer and W. Kintsch (eds.)
© *North-Holland Publishing Company, 1982*

THE IMPACT OF PRIOR KNOWLEDGE ON ACCESSIBILITY
AND AVAILABILITY OF INFORMATION FROM PROSE

Samuel R. Mathews II

Educational Research and Development Center
The University of West Florida
Pensacola, Florida
U.S.A.

The effects of prior knowledge on accessibility and
availability are examined in this work. The impact of
prior knowledge on accessibility was primarily qualitative while the effect on availability was quantitative.
Evidence for the effect was observed at both encoding
and retrieval. Further, the hierarchical structure of
text was shown to be particularly vulnerable to prior
knowledge while the logical relations among concepts in
the text was not.

Anytime a reader interacts with a text, that reader's knowledge about the
content of that text affects the nature of the information stored and retrieved. For example, Anderson and Pichert (1978) demonstrated that when
different bodies of prior knowledge were accessed, different parts of a
given text were retrieved. They demonstrated this by asking subjects to
read a text from one of two perspectives. Following the reading task,
subjects were asked to recall the text from the original presentation. A
second recall task was then attempted. This time the subjects were provided with an alternative perspective and asked to recall the text a second
time. Anderson and Pichert (1978) found that different information was
accessed when different knowledge bases were instantiated with the different
perspectives on the text. They suggest that the knowledge base determines
which information is accessible at retrieval for a free recall task.

Other researchers assume a somewhat different perspective and suggest that
text structure determines to a great extent which information is accessible. For example, Meyer (1975) analyzed texts into a content structure
(Grimes, 1975) which yielded a hierarchy of information contained within
the text. This hierarchy is made up of concepts from the text which are
interconnected with relational terms. Some of these terms according to
Grimes (1975) connect two concepts in such a manner that one is superordinate to the other which yields the hierarchy of concepts in the text.

Meyer (1975) had adults read the passages and freely recall them. She
found that information which occurred at a point high in the hierarchy was
more likely to be recalled than information lower in the hierarchy of that
text. Meyer (1975) concluded that the structure of a text (the hierarchy
of information) was the major source of variation in memory for text.

There are three issues addressed in this study. They are: (1) the apparent discrepancy between the conclusions drawn by Anderson and Pichert (1978) and Meyer (1975) regarding accessibility; (2) the effect of prior knowledge on availability; and (3) the parameters of the locus and nature of the effects of prior knowledge.

There is a manner in which the discrepancy between the Anderson and Pichert (1978) findings and the findings observed by Meyer (1975) can be resolved. For Meyer's subjects, prior knowledge about the passages used in her exper- iment was not controlled nor explicitly called into play. One might con- clude then, that when prior knowledge is called into play as in the Anderson and Pichert (1978) study, that accessibility of information is predictably affected by that prior knowledge. For readers who are either naive with regard to the topic of a text or whose prior knowledge is not directly addressed when reading or retrieving information, accessibility of informa- tion can be predicted by the characteristics of a text.

The other issue of interest in the present study is the availability of in- formation in memory for texts. While accessibility refers to that informa- tion that can be retrieved from memory with little or no cueing (e.g., as in a free recall task), availability refers to that information which is present in memory but only retrievable when the subject is provided with some greater degree of cueing (e.g., as in a probed recall task).

One study which addressed the issue of the impact of prior knowledge on the availability of information in prose was conducted by Pace (1978). In this study, Pace identified topics so that they ranged from very familiar to her sample of kindergarteners, second, fourth, and sixth graders to topics which were totally unfamiliar to even the oldest children. Using the "knowledge bases" provided by her subjects, Pace constructed stories ap- propriate for each topic. Each subject listened to each story and answered probe questions. This provided a measure of availability of textual infor- mation in memory.

Basically, Pace found that at all ages, the greater the level of prior knowledge, the greater the number of questions accurately answered. Thus, if one possesses an appropriate knowledge base, more information will be retained for a given text than if that knowledge base is missing.

One controversy which has seen discussion as of late is that of the locus of the effect of prior knowledge on text memory. There seems to be a division of conclusions between those which favor the locus of effect at encoding and those who believe that the major impact is at retrieval. As with most dichotomies we construct in behavioral sciences, it is probably not an "either-or" case. It is more likely that prior knowledge impacts on memory for text at both points--encoding and retrieval (e.g., Pace, 1978 and Anderson & Pichert, 1978 respectively). Further, for readers who have no specific prior knowledge about a text the hierarchical structure of the text will probably have a marked effect on accessibility of information from that text (Meyer, 1975) with this effect occurring at encoding.

One assumption made in this study is that while the particular information accessed or available in memory may be affected by prior knowledge, there are aspects of a text which must remain intact in order to assert that memory for a text is present. That aspect is analogous to what Kintsch has described as the cohesion graph (Kintsch & van Dijk, 1978). If we examine the model proposed by Kintsch and van Dijk (1978), we find two levels of text structure which might be differentially affected by prior knowledge. One is the schematic structure (Kintsch & van Dijk, 1978). This describes the overall organization of the text and provides a guide for determining the "gist" of a passage. The other level is the micro-structure. The micro-structure allows us to recognize a text as distinct from a series of randomly selected words in that it explicates the interrelationships between the words (concepts) in the text.

Three predictions evolved from the results of earlier studies. First, subjects with different knowledge about a text should form different "macro-structures" and access different information during recall. The second prediction is that although different parts of a text may be accessed during recall, that information recalled should maintain certain structural characteristics of the text even for subjects with different levels of prior knowledge. Finally, prior knowledge will provide a conceptual-peg-like construct, thus increasing the amount of information available in memory.

The prime objective of this study is to describe the impact of prior knowledge on that information which is accessible (in both quantitative and qualitative terms), compare this impact with that of text structure, and determine the impact of prior knowledge on availability of information in memory for text.

Method

Subjects

Thirty fourth-graders were selected to participate in the study. Their average age was 9.5 years (S.D. = 5 months), and there were 14 males and 16 females. School-aged children were selected since their day-to-day activities in school involve applying information acquired on one day to a subsequent day's learning demands, usually through some form of text processing.

Design

A two-group between subjects design was used. Each child heard and recalled a passage following one of two kinds of experiences. The subjects heard either a passage related to the target passage (prior knowledge) or an unrelated passage (unrelated knowledge). An equal number (n = 15) of subjects was asssigned to each group.

Treatments

In the prior knowledge treatment, the subjects heard a passage which provided prior knowledge related to a target passage. In the unrelated knowledge treatment, the subjects heard a passage unrelated to the target passage. Subjects in the two knowledge treatment conditions heard the target passage and completed memory tasks 24 hours after being exposed to the respective knowledge passages.

Assessment of Memory for Information from the Target Passage

Two memory tasks were used to assess recollection of information from memory for text. The measures were free recall and probed recall. The first, free recall, was used to assess two aspects of accessibility. One was the amount of information accessed and the other was the content and structure of the recall.

The amount recalled was measured by simply counting the number of correctly recalled micropropositions in each protocol. The content and structure of recall was determined by using Meyer's (1975) level-in-the-hierarchy analysis and a procedure for comparing matrix structures respectively.

The second task used to assess recollection of information from the text was probed recall. It was anticipated that this measure would provide an index of that information available in memory but not accessible to free recall. A total of eight probe questions was asked of each subject.

Materials

The stimulus materials used in the present study consisted of: (1) the target passage; (2) the prior knowledge passage; and (3) another passage which was unrelated to the target passage. The target passage appears in Figure 1.

---

*

[1]The small towns in Wisconsin in the 1800's did not provide jobs for the youngsters growing up in them. [2]One town like this was Pleasant Ridge. [3]Although it was different from many other towns, [4]all the people who lived there were farmers and there were no stores or factories in the town. [5]For a long time, the small town had only one building. [6]All the town's meetings and parties were held in that building.

[7]When the youngsters from the small town grew up, they moved away. [8]They left to find better jobs. [9]The reason that the youngsters wanted better jobs was that the town's school gave them a good education. [10]The log schoolhouse had been built by the farmers and it was the only one of its kind in the nation. [11]The teachers were very good and the students liked their school. [12]When they finished school, they wanted to move away and see other places.

[13]Once the youngsters moved away from the small town, they never returned. [14]Soon, the town was deserted. [15]The only part of the town left is a cemetary where the settlers of the town are buried.

Figure 1
Target Passage

* The numbers in text refer to the numbers in Figure 2.

The target passage and corresponding knowledge base were written so that they were related in the following manner. The knowledge base described

the growth of a small midwestern American town and included information
about its school. The target passage described that town's demise. The
unrelated knowledge base was about a desert region and had no connection to
either of the other two texts. All texts were selected to assure that they
would interest the children to be tested.

The passage was written so that it was comprehensible by fourth-graders.
This was confirmed by a pilot study. The passage is approximately 160
words long. When analyzed, the passage contained 82 micropropositions and
15 higher level units. The micropropositions were analyzed according to
Kintsch's (1974) text base. The higher level organization of the passage
was determined by Grimes (1975) rhetorical predicates as used in Meyer's
work (Meyer, 1975). Figure 2 illustrates the network of the higher level
organization of the target passage. This level of structure is analagous
to the rhetorical structure of Grimes' (1975) system and the schematic
structure of Kintsch and van Dijk's (1978) model. If one uses a levels in
the hierarchy approach such as that used by Meyer (1975), unit 1 is located
at the highest level, units 2 and 7 at the next lowest level and so on.
If, one considers the structure as a series of interrelated concepts, with
no regard for hierarchical structure, then, a series of simple relationships (e.g., 2-3, 3-4) and complex relationships (e.g., 1-2 and 1-7 simultaneously; 7-8, 12, and 13) can be represented. Thus, both the hierarchical and logical structure may be represented using such a system.

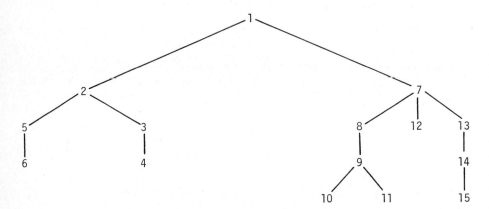

Figure 2
The Network of Interrelations of the 15 Rhetorical
Propositions in the Target Passage

Procedure

There were two groups. One received the prior knowledge passage prior to
the target passage and the other an unrelated knowledge passage. The procedure was the same for both groups except for the nature of the initial
passage. On the first day, each subject listened to the knowledge base
appropriate to the group. The tape was stopped at various intervals and
mastery questions asked of the subjects to determine whether or not the

material in the particular knowledge base was being mastered. This continued until the passage was completed. At the end of the tape, each subject was asked to answer all of the mastery questions. The tape was replayed until all questions were answered correctly. All subjects except two reached the criterion of 100% mastery by the third repitition of the tape.

On the second day, each subject listened to a recording of the target passage. Following this, each subject was instructed to "Tell as much as possible as you remember from the tape you just heard. Try to remember exactly, but if you can't remember exactly use your own words." The recall of each subject was recorded. When the subject hesitated, a prompt "Can you remember any more?" was given. This continued until the subject said no more information could be remembered. Following recall, the probe questions for the target passage were asked and responses recorded.

Protocol Analysis

The responses of each subject were transcribed and the free recall analyzed in the same manner as the text of the target passage. The micropropositions which appeared in each protocol were compared to those in the text analysis. A scoring criterion which allowed a recalled proposition to be scored as correct if it was semantically equivalent was adopted. The level of the text structure in which a correctly recalled microproposition appeared and its relationship(s) with other propositions was noted.

Interrater agreement for the protocol analysis was obtained by having an independent rater analyze randomly selected protocols from each group. The analysis of each protocol scored by the independent rater was compared to the analysis of that protocol done by the author. Propositions which occurred in both scoring protocols were scored as an agreement. Using this method, an interrater agreement of 93% was obtained. All disagreements were resolved by discussion.

Results

Accessibility

The accessibility of information was measured by free recall. There are three comparisons of interest to be made between the two groups. One is a simple comparison of the number of propositions recalled. A t test for independent means indicated no difference between the two groups in terms of the overall amount of recall ($t<1$). The more interesting comparison of what was recalled by the different groups did yield significant results.

Levels in the hierarchy. Meyer (1975) provided data which supported the idea that information high in the structure of a text (Grimes, 1975) is more accessible than information lower in that structure (unit 1 vs. unit 15 in Figure 2 respectively). Anderson and Pichert (1978) have suggested, however, that prior knowledge mediates this effect and is responsible for a deviation from the "structural" prediction.

A comparison of the number of propositions recalled by each group at the highest and lowest level of the hierarchy provided results which support the text structure approach for the unrelated knowledge group and the prior

knowledge mediation prediction for the prior knowledge group. That is, at
the highest level in the hierarchy, the unrelated knowledge group recalled
significantly more than did the prior knowledge group [t(28) = 2.37 MSe =
1.228, p<.05 following Dunn's procedure]. At the lowest level in the hierarchy the opposite results were obtained. That is, the prior knowledge
group recalled significantly more than did the unrelated knowledge group
[t(28) = 2.37, MSe = 6.25, p<.05].

Logical relations in the text. A majority of the research reported on the
impact of prior knowledge on accessibility of information from text has
dealt with only one aspect of a text--the proposed hierarchy of information
within a text. The present study provides information regarding the impact
of prior knowledge on another characteristic of texts--logical relations
among concepts. These relations are described in the present study by
Grimes' (1975) rhetorical predicates and make up a structure analogous to
Kintsch and van Dijk's (1978) schematic structure.

The Quadratic Assignment Procedure (QAP) described by Hubert and Schultz
(1976) was used to examine the structural similarity of the recalls in this
study. Basically, QAP is a procedure in which the similarity of two matrices is determined. In this case, the matrices are dimensioned by the
number of rhetorical propositions in the target passage (15 total). Thus a
15-by-15 matrix is produced. One matrix is designated as the structure
matrix. This is constructed by assigning a value of 1 to those cells which
represent an existing relation between two rhetorical propositions in the
text and a value of Ø to those cells not representing existing relationships in the text. So, based on the network in Figure 2, the cell indexed
by 1, 7 would be assigned a value of 1 and the cell indexed by 2, 9 a value
of Ø. Thus a 15-by-15 matrix with values of 1's and Ø's is constructed.

The second matrix is the data matrix. This matrix is the same dimension as
the structure matrix. The difference is that the values for the cells are
determined by the relationships observed in the subjects' protocols. That
is, the number of subjects recalling a particular relationship between two
propositions in the text becomes the value for that particular cell. Those
cells representing relationships not present in recall are valued at Ø.

The analysis proceeds as follows. First the sum of the cross products of
the structure and data matrix is computed. Then a random juxtaposition of
a row and corresponding columns in the data matrix occurs followed by a
second computation of the sum of the cross products. A predetermined
number of these juxtapositions occurs and a distribution of the sums of the
cross products constructed. An exact test comparing the original sum of
the cross products of the data and structure matrices is then conducted.
The higher the value of the sum of the cross products, the more similar the
matrices. The QAP tests the hypothesis that the two matrices are randomly
related. A rejection of this hypothesis implies that there is a systematic
relationship between the matrices.

Three comparisons were conducted using QAP. First, a data matrix was constructed for both the prior knowledge and unrelated knowledge groups.
These were compared individually with the structure matrix of the target
passage. Both comparisons between the data matrix and the structure matrix
reached significance (p<.001). That is, for both groups, prior knowledge
and unrelated knowledge, the relationships present in the text were present
in recall.

Of particular interest is the comparison between the two groups. The data matrix for the unrelated knowledge group was arbitrarily defined as the structure matrix and another QAP was conducted. Based on this comparison, the hypothesis of random relations between the matrices was not rejected. That is, the two matrices reflected different structures--the subjects in the different groups recalled different relationships from the text.

Availability

In order to assess whether or not prior knowledge affected the amount of information retrievable beyond free recall, each subject answered eight probe questions. Two comparisons are of interest here. One is simply an assessment of the average number of questions answered correctly by each group. A t-test for independent means yielded a significant difference, in favor of the prior knowledge group ($t(28)$ = 3.72, p<.05).

A second comparison of interest involves whether the responses to the probe questions included information not contained in the subjects' recalls and whether the two groups differed on this measure. If the responses were merely restatements of information included in recall then there would be no need for the constructs of accessibility and availability. If there is a difference then the two constructs might prove useful. In order to pursue this notion, the contents of each subject's protocol was compared with the responses to the probe questions and the number of responses containing information beyond that in the recall was computed. A comparison between the groups yielded a significant difference in favor of the prior knowledge group ($t(28)$ = 2.26, p<.05). Thus, the prior knowledge group had more information available beyond that contained in free recall than did the unrelated knowledge group.

Discussion

This study was based on the assumption that prior knowledge affects what is learned from texts. The results support this notion and suggest some specific ways in which the effect manifests itself.

Accessibility

First, the group who received relevant prior knowledge accessed different information during recall from the group who received prior knowledge irrelevant to the target passage. While this finding in and of itself replicates those of other studies (e.g., Anderson & Pichert, 1978), certain parameters of the effect have been provided. The impact of prior knowledge relative to two components of text structure was examined. One component is a hierarchical structure (Meyer, 1975) and the other a logical cohesion of concepts.

When text structure is defined in terms of a hierarchy of information as in Meyer's studies (Meyer, 1975) we find that different levels of prior knowledge elicit results different from those predicted by a hierarchical structure approach. This finding is consistent with other studies which considered prior knowledge (Anderson & Pichert, 1978). It appears then that the only time accessibility is determined predominantly by a hierarchical structure of text is when the reader is of average ability and is relatively naive to the topic of the given text (the unrelated knowledge group in the present study).

When the logical cohesion of text is considered, as in the Quadratic Assignment Procedure used in the present study, a slightly different interpretation can be made concerning the effect of prior knowledge. In this case, both groups--prior knowledge and unrelated knowledge--produced recalls which were faithful to the logical organization of the text. They merely accessed different parts of the text. This type of analysis is less frequently encountered in the literature, but does provide insight into the nature of the impact of prior knowledge as well as an appropriate interpretation of which aspects of text structure might have a consistent impact across groups.

It seems that the effect of the hierarchical structure of a text is quite fragile, only occurring in certain conditions and not in others. The relationship between the logical structure of a text and subjects' recalls is isomorphic--the relationships observed in a text occur in recall regardless of prior knowledge condition. Again, however, groups receiving different levels of prior knowledge accessed different parts of the text.

One conclusion to be drawn from these results addresses the issue of text structure. The case can be made that since the impact of the hierarchical structure of text is so fragile, it may be advisable not to classify it as a text variable, but rather a cognitive construct susceptible to prior knowledge and other individual differences. On the other hand, the logical relations expressed in text by linguistic conventions seems to be more robust in terms of their impact on recall. That is, although different levels of the text were recalled by different groups, the relationships among those parts were isomorphic to those in the text. Prior knowledge affected what was accessible, but not the relationship between the structure of the protocols and the structure of the text. Thus, the relationship between concepts in a text--the logical structure--may be appropriately considered a text variable.

Availability

The impact of prior knowledge on the availability of information was also examined in the present study. Recent studies have attempted to demonstrate that one locus of the effect of prior knowledge is at retrieval (e.g., Anderson & Pichert, 1978). The present study provides support for an impact of prior knowledge at encoding. That is, the prior knowledge group answered significantly more probe questions correctly than did the unrelated prior knowledge group. The only difference between the group was the prior knowledge treatment before encoding. This is consistent with Pace's (1978) findings that a higher level of prior knowledge was associated with a higher level of performance on probe questions.

Others have reported an advantage for prior knowledge groups in the amount of accessible information as well (Royer & Cable, 1975). Although different information was accessible to the groups in the present study, no quantitative advantage was evidenced for either group. One possible explanation is that for young children, search strategies are limited and any impact prior knowledge might have would be evidenced only in a qualitative assessment of free recall. When additional aids in memory search are provided (probe questions in this case), the advantage falls to the group having more information available in memory, the prior knowledge group. Thus, both search and retrieval are aided by the cues.

Conclusions

What was observed in the present study were basically two effects of prior knowledge. On the one hand, different (not merely more) information was accessible to the two groups examined, and on the other, more information was available to the prior knowledge group than the unrelated knowledge group. When novel information is to be learned, the impact of prior knowledge is observed at both encoding and retrieval and makes a difference for both quantitative and qualitative variables.

Finally, the issue of whether or not prior knowledge influences the relationship between the structure of free recall and the structure of text was addressed. When the hierarchical structure of information in the text was considered, prior knowledge was associated with a drastic departure from results predicted by such a text structure. When logical relationships among concepts in the text were considered, prior knowledge was not associated with a distortion of those relationships. Based on the present study as well as others (Anderson & Pichert, 1978), the classification of hierarchical structure as a text characteristic can be called into question. It is perhaps more appropriately classified as a cognitive construct (as in Kintsch & van Dijk's, 1978 model) influencing accessibility only for naive readers. The logical relations among concepts in a text were faithfully maintained in recall regardless of the prior knowledge condition and in this case are appropriately classified as a text variable.

References

Anderson, R. C., & Pichert, J. W. Recall of previously unrecallable infor mation following a shift in perspective. Journal of Verbal Learning and Verbal Behavior, 1978, 17, 1-12.

Grimes, J. The thread of discourse. The Hague: Mouton, 1975.

Hubert, L. J., & Schultz, J. V. Quadratic assignment as a general data analysis strategy. The British Journal of Mathematical and Statistical Psychology, 1976, 29, 190-241.

Kintsch, W. Representation of meaning in memory. Hillsdale, N. J.: Lawrence Erlbaum Assoc., 1974.

Kintsch, W., & van Dijk, T. A. Toward a model of text comprehension and production. Psychological Review, 1978, 85, 363-394.

Meyer, B. J. F. The organization of prose and its effects on recall. Amsterdam: North-Holland Publishers, 1975.

Pace, A. J. The influences of world knowledge on children's comprehension of short narrative passages. Paper presented at the Annual Meeting of the American Educational Research Association, Toronto, Canada, 1978.

Royer, J. M., & Cable, G. W. Facilitated learning in connected discourse. Journal of Educational Psychology, 1975, 67, 116-123.

INSTRUCTIONAL IMPLICATIONS

DISCOURSE PROCESSING
A. Flammer and W. Kintsch (eds.)
© *North-Holland Publishing Company, 1982*

PICTURES AS PROSE-LEARNING DEVICES

Joel R. Levin

Department of Educational Psychology
University of Wisconsin
Madison, Wisconsin
U.S.A.

Popular strategies for improving prose processing
consist of procedures that force attention either
to the text's macrostructure or to the organization
and interconnections of the text's propositions.
These strategies are assumed to enhance students'
comprehension of the text as encoded, as well as to
afford students with an efficient storage and
retrieval scheme for long-term recall of text
information. However, with expository or instructional
texts containing factual information that is
unfamiliar, complex, abstract, or--for whatever
reason--simply difficult to remember, comprehension
strategies of the kind just described may not be optimally
suited for enhancing long-term recall. Rather,
mnemonic strategies that are designed expressly for
storage and retrieval of difficult-to-remember
information would seem to be preferable. Several
recent experiments are reported, to provide
preliminary support for this view. It is proposed
that prose-learning strategies that combine the
critical components of comprehension-directed
techniques with those of memory-directed techniques
will ultimately prove to be the most successful.

The focus of this paper is on pictures as devices for making prose content
more memorable. The term "device" was selected to emphasize the bridges
that can be built from the basic learning-and-memory literature to the
prose-learning domain. I refer, in particular, to mnemonic devices, which
have been scrutinized heartily in the context of unconnected word lists,
yet hardly in the context of connected discourse (see, Bellezza, 1981;
Bower, 1970; Higbee, 1979; and Levin, 1981a). The argument advanced here
is that the same kind of mnemonic devices that have brought about dramatic
recall increases in simple list-learning experiments can be adapted to
yield comparable benefits with respect to information contained in more
complex prose passages.

The argument depends critically on the acceptance of certain definitions
of and premises about prose-learning strategies, where the term "strategy"
refers to any auxiliary materials or learner activities designed to
enhance processing of a text. In the first section of the paper, I
distinguish between two general classes of prose-learning strategy:

412

(<u>a</u>) strategies directed primarily at the <u>main ideas</u> of a passage; and (<u>b</u>) strategies directed primarily at a passage's <u>factual details</u>. Given these two kinds of general strategy, a further distinction is made between strategies whose primary job is to enhance students' <u>understanding</u> of text information and strategies whose primary job is to enhance a text's <u>memorability</u>. In the next two sections of the paper, pictures are introduced into the prose-learning scenario, along with their presumed functions and consequences. Included here are several recent investigations in which pictorial mnemonic devices have played a central role. Although to date, prose-learning applications of mnemonic devices have been confined mainly to the processing of factual details, the potential of mnemonics for main idea processing is explored in the paper's final section. Of special significance is the question of the comparative effectiveness of compound mnemonic strategies, alternative nonmnemonic strategies, and mnemonic/nonmnemonic strategy combinations for enhancing students' comprehension and recall of both passage main ideas and details.[1]

PROSE-LEARNING STRATEGIES: DEFINITIONS AND PREMISES

Macrostructure Versus Microstructure Strategies

As was just indicated, in this paper a variety of prose-learning strategies are conceptualized in terms of the type of text information for which they appear to be intended. By <u>type</u> of text information, I mean the general <u>level</u> of information within a text hierarchy (i.e., higher-level main ideas on the one hand versus lower-level factual details on the other). In recognition of Kintsch's (e.g., Kintsch & van Dijk, 1978) pioneering work in the area of text analysis, I will refer to those prose-learning strategies that seem to be well suited to the processing of main ideas as <u>macrostructure strategies</u>. As will become apparent, macrostructure strategies are those that are directed toward identifying, analyzing, or integrating information within the text's macrostructure. Of course, the complementary strategies--those that seemingly are intended for the processing of details--will be termed <u>microstructure strategies</u>. This is the general framework that will be adopted throughout the paper, as well as in our discussion of Figure 1, which follows.

Comprehension-Directed Versus Memory-Directed Strategies[2]

As may be seen from Figure 1, within the two general classes of strategy just discussed (macro- and microstructure strategies), a distinction can be made with respect to the primary cognitive function presumably served by that strategy. That is, is the strategy one that is intended primarily to enhance the student's <u>comprehension</u> of text that is being, or that is about to be, processed? Or is the strategy one that is intended primarily to improve the student's <u>memory</u> for text that is being, or that has just been, processed? Levin and Pressley's (1981) recent discussion of <u>stage-setting</u> strategies (where the emphasis is on comprehension) and <u>storage/retrieval</u> strategies (where the emphasis is on retention) captures some of the flavor of the present distinction.

At the same time--and as was noted by Levin and Pressley--comprehension- and memory-directed activities are certainly not mutually exclusive. For instance, it is well known that the meaningfulness and comprehensibility of information processed are directly related to the amount of that information later remembered. Yet, even though it may be assumed that enhanced comprehension leads to enhanced memory, the present comprehension/ memory distinction appears to be worth making when classifying existing

MACROSTRUCTURE STRATEGIES

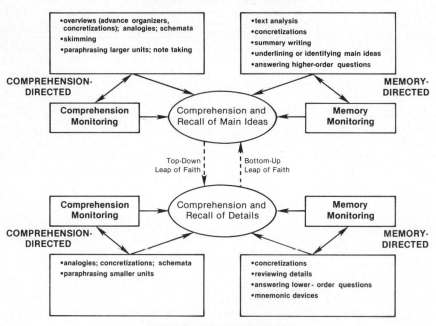

Figure 1
Prose-Learning Strategies Classified According to Level
of Text Information and Primary Cognitive Function Served

prose-learning strategies. Thus, for example, the strategy of rendering
unfamiliar prose concepts more familiar through the use of analogy is
viewed primarily as a comprehension-directed strategy, whereas the
strategy of rereading (as a form of repetition) is viewed primarily as a
memory-directed strategy. In short, comprehension-directed strategies
are those designed to enhance a student's conceptual understanding of a
text's propositions and the relationship among those propositions; memory-
directed strategies are those designed to facilitate a student's later
retrieval of text information, assuming that it has initially been
adequately understood.

A few additional comments bearing on the comprehension/memory distinction
are in order. First, and related to the "nonmutual exclusivity" point
mentioned above, sorting popular prose-learning strategies into either
comprehension-directed or memory-directed categories is not a straightforward process. As a result, the subjective criteria adopted by the
present author can certainly be expected to yield both inter- and intra-
judge placements that are less than perfectly reliable. Second, it is

readily acknowledged that strategy distinctions along other lines are
possible. For example, one could view a prose-learning strategy as
directed primarily at processing individual propositions (as in paraphrasing sentences or answering separate and unrelated questions), in
contrast to a strategy that is directed primarily at structuring or inter-
relating those propositions (as in text analysis or in summary writing).
Such an alternative formulation may prove similarly useful with respect to
the issues raised in this paper.

Specific Strategies Included in Figure 1
Each of the four main corner boxes of Figure 1 includes exemplars of the
kind of strategy represented by combining categories of the just-discussed
text information (macro- versus microstructure) and cognitive function
(comprehension- versus memory-directed) factors. Brief mention will now
be made of the specific strategies included in the figure.

Comprehension-directed macrostructure strategies. In the upper left box of
Figure 1 are strategies that ostensibly impact directly on one's understanding of a passage's theme, main ideas, major conceptual structures, or
interrelationships among the main ideas. Selected from Levin and
Pressley's (1981) stage-setting strategies are overviews such as advance
organizers (to provide a more general framework for the upcoming passage
information) and pictorial concretizations (to provide a more concrete
framework). In this box are also included analogies (to render unfamiliar
or difficult-to-comprehend conceptual structures more familiar), and
schemata (where one's prior knowledge is activated with respect to unfamiliar major concepts within the passage). Whereas the overview
strategies are, by definition, exploited prior to passage presentation,
capitalization on analogies and schemata can occur during passage
presentation as well.

Skimming for upcoming main ideas and concepts is another macrostructure
strategy that has been proposed for improving text comprehension. The
same can be said for paraphrasing larger units of text (i.e., paragraphs
and major sections), as well as its sister strategy, note taking. Placing
these latter two strategies on the "comprehension-directed" side of
Figure 1 implies that the primary purpose of saying things in one's own
words is to force understanding. The rationale for this placement is
further bolstered if the paraphrasing/note-taking activity takes place
during processing with the text in full view--in contrast to, say, con-
cocting summaries, which typically is attempted following processing, in
the text's absence. As such, I regard summary writing as a storage/
retrieval (memory-directed) strategy (see the upper right box of Figure 1).
I wouldn't think of quibbling with one who argued otherwise, however.

Memory-directed macrostructure strategies. In the upper right box of
Figure 1 are strategies that are directed at coding the text's macropropositions for efficient retrieval. Text analysis, for example, is
based on the assumption that constructing a hierarchical structure for the
text will furnish the constructor with a systematic retrieval plan. That
is, the text is coded in terms of a series of higher-to-lower-level nodes,
and the most important text information is prominently displayed at the top
of the hierarchy. Assuming that the information associated with these
nodes is familiar enough (through either prior knowledge or sufficient
text processing), then the constructed retrieval hierarchy should indeed be
helpful. Yet, even though this may be true for the higher-level

propositions in the text, whether or not command of higher-level propositions invariably leads to recall of the lower-level propositions is one of
the major issues confronted in this paper.

Concretizations here include pictorial representations of the macrostructure to make it more memorable. The use of maps, graphs, flowcharts
and other visual depictions of the superordinate concepts in the text--or
the relationships among these concepts--would certainly fill a concretiza-
tion-of-macrostructure bill. Reliance on the initially encoded
concretizations for furnishing information-retrieval cues would, in
addition, qualify such entries as memory-directed.

The technique of summary writing was discussed previously, along with my
rationale for viewing it primarily as a memory-directed strategy. By
placing it in the "macrostructure" category, I am assuming that a good
summary results in a considerable reduction of the original text content,
and that the reduction contains the most important passage information
(see Brown, Campione, & Day, 1981). Underlining or identifying main ideas
is basically a form of rereading rehearsal, in which important concepts
are stored for future use. A similar type of memory-storage strategy
consists of answering higher-order questions (i.e., questions directed at
main ideas or those requiring inferences involving main ideas).

Comprehension-directed microstructure strategies. In this category (lower
left box of Figure 1) are included techniques that serve to elucidate
factual information within a passage. As was stated in regard to
macropropositions, providing analogies (or alternatively mobilizing a
learner's schemata) can serve this function well. Concretizations
typically involve pictorial representations of abstract or otherwise
difficult-to-comprehend factual information. Political cartoonists make
habitual use of such comprehension-enhancing tactics. Whereas analogies
are regarded as translations involving a vehicle that is removed from the
actual text content, other concretizations of the comprehension-directed
microstructure kind rely heavily on the use of conventional symbols and
other pictorial auto-translations of the information being conveyed. For
example, in one study to be reported later, we translated a high level of
literacy into a picture of numerous books, advances in technology into a
picture of a computer terminal, abundant natural resources into a picture
of an oil well, etc.

Paraphrasing smaller units of text (i.e., individual details and sentences) is regarded as another technique for enhancing one's comprehension
of a passage's micropropositions. As was mentioned previously, the case
for calling paraphrasing a "comprehension-directed" strategy would appear
to be strengthened if the activity takes place during processing, with
the text in view.

Memory-directed microstructure strategies. The final set of strategies
appears in the lower right box of Figure 1. Concretizations here
include direct pictorial representations of the text's factual details.
Most experimental investigations of the efficacy of visual illustrations
and visual imagery have employed this kind of strategy (see Levin, 1981b;
and Levin & Lesgold, 1978).

Reviewing details, as a rereading activity, is a form of rehearsal in the
service of memory, and answering lower-order questions (i.e., questions

directed at factual details) is regarded as another form of information storage/retrieval activity. As will be argued here, however, the most effective techniques for remembering a passage's factual information are those based on the application of mnemonic devices. Whether or not such devices can be applied with similar success to a text's macrostructure is an issue that will be examined as we progress.

Strategy Monitoring
An additional component of Figure 1 consists of students' metacognitions about how successfully they are processing a text, reflected by students' monitoring of their comprehension of and memory for what they are studying. "Do I or don't I understand this information?" and "Will I be able to remember it?" are the relevant questions here (see, for example, Baker & Brown, in press; and Flavell, 1978).

Strategy monitoring is viewed as a cybernetic process, with effective monitoring providing information concerning the effectiveness of strategy implementation. That is, the degree of strategic processing of text segments is regulated by one's own monitoring behavior. This regulatory activity is reflected by the solid bidirectional arrow between each strategy box and its respective monitoring box. Note also that the degree of effective monitoring is assumed to have a direct effect on the amount of text information comprehended and remembered.

Relationship Between Strategy Implementation and Text Information Processed
In Figure 1, the solid unidirectional arrows between the strategy boxes and the performance ovals indicate the direct effect that the degree of effective strategy implementation is assumed to have on one's level of comprehension and recall of text information at the same level of structure. This last qualifier is extremely important, and central to the arguments advanced in this paper. Thus, prose-learning strategies that focus on a text's macrostructure can reasonably be assumed to have a direct facilitative effect on students' comprehension and recall of text macrostructure information (i.e., a passage's higher-level propositions). A similar statement can be made for microstructure strategies and microstructure information (i.e., a passage's lower-level propositions). But surely it is a considerable leap of faith to assume that a strategy suited for one type of information processing (either "macro" or "micro") will have a direct facilitative effect on the opposite type of information. This skepticism is reflected in both the extant empirical data that adequately address the issue and the dashed arrows of Figure 1. Expecting that the implementation of macrostructure strategies will directly facilitate students' storage and retrieval of microstructure information is viewed here as a top-down leap of faith, whereas the reverse strategy/ performance expectation is viewed as a bottom-up leap of faith. Of course, indirect facilitative effects might be posited in each case, but the associated cognitive processes and mechanisms responsible for such facilitation are far from obvious, as is discussed in more detail later in the paper. For now, suffice it to say that there is no compelling reason to expect that increased comprehension of a text's macrostructure (say, through the provision of a coherently and transparently structured text, or by casting the appropriate anchors to a student's schemata) will facilitate one's subsequent recall of specific micropropositions within the text. Yet, such facilitation has indeed been implied (e.g., Pearson & Spiro, 1980), if not regarded as fact.

PICTORIAL PROSE-LEARNING STRATEGIES

Having considered all the various ingredients of Figure 1, I will now
attempt to mix in a dash of picture theorizing. In particular, I will try
to fit some recently posited "functions" of prose-learning pictures
(Levin, 1981b) into the conceptual framework just developed. Throughout
the discussion, pictorial strategies will include both text-embedded
visual illustrations (on the page) and student-generated visual imagery
(in the head).

Summary of Pictures' Major Functions

Levin (1981b) ascribed eight different functions of prose-learning
pictures, four of which were deemed interesting from a cognitive-
psychological perspective. These "interesting" functions will be briefly
reviewed.

Representation function. It is often the case that a verbal text can be
equivalently expressed as a sequence of pictures. Consider, for example,
a concrete narrative passage, where it is possible to construct parallel
verbal and pictorial forms (e.g., Baggett, 1979). When the pictures accompanying a prose passage are virtually redundant (i.e., overlapping) with
the verbal information contained in that passage (Levin & Lesgold, 1978),
then pictures are serving a representation function. Verbal information
represented via pictures is assumed to be more concrete, and more concrete
representations are known to be more memorable (Paivio, 1971).

Organization function. With certain types of passages, pictures are
called on to do more than simply represent the text information as given.
Rather, restructuring or reorganizing that information may be accomplished
through a map or graph. Similarly, a single integrated illustration can
conveniently expose a text's interpropositional relationships. Integrating
propositions is critical for establishing efficient retrieval structures,
and all too often such integration is either lacking in, or only implicitly
provided by, the text itself (see Gagné & Bell, 1981). Moreover, even
when propositional connections are adequately signaled in a text, pictures
may facilitate the perception of those connections by individuals who
lack the comprehension skills necessary to benefit from the provided
passage structure (see, for example, Levin, 1973). Pictures that enhance
the relatedness of the textual elements are said to be serving an
organization function.

Interpretation function. Text information that is abstractly or complexly
presented can clearly profit from the provision of pictures. Picture
yourself, for example, in an experiment where the following excerpt
is presented:

> The presence of a foreign particle or impurity
> in the chemical composition of the metal also
> reduces the efficiency of heat transfer in the
> medium. This is because the particle produces
> a distortion in the structural symmetry of the
> crystalline lattices. The result is that some
> of the molecules in the medium will be moved
> into oblique positions, with a resultant loss
> of thermal agitation transfer. The impurity
> produces this loss of efficiency in two ways.

> It absorbs some of the energy instead of
> passing it on, and because of the fact that
> the impurity is not as structurally bonded as
> the crystal lattices, it moves erratically,
> thereby disturbing the normal transfer of
> energy (Royer & Cable, 1976, p. 207).

This is not one of John Bransford's passages that is written expressly to
be ambiguous and uninterpretable. The meaning is in the message as
presented. All one needs is an electrochemistry major to crack the code!
Or, as Royer and Cable (1976) found, providing students with either concrete analogies or pictorial translations also serves to enhance comprehension. For the above passage, the analogy of inserting a cigarette
package into a sequence of toppling dominos was used as a comprehension-
enhancing vehicle; as were conventional illustrations of the concepts
described (e.g., the internal structure of metals and nonmetals, heat
transmission, and disruption due to pressure and impurity). When pictures
are used to increase the meaningfulness of the information that is being
processed, the interpretation function of pictures is being served.

Transformation function. Finally, and as represented by the title of this
paper, pictorial mnemonic devices can also be summoned up to operate on
a text. The chief application of such devices to date has been with
comprehensible texts containing unfamiliar terminology (e.g., various
technical passages) or with texts containing a good deal of factual
information, as in the following social studies passage:

> The southern area of Mala can best be described
> as a desert. Rainfall is less than 2 inches per
> year in southern Mala. The soils in the southern
> area of Mala are either rocky or sandy. In the
> summertime temperatures have been recorded as
> high as 135 degrees in southern Mala.
>
> The history of Mala has been marked by exploitation.
> The first slaves were forcefully taken from Mala
> to Europe in 1610. When Europeans came over to
> Mala to settle there, they never paid the Malans
> for the land they occupied. Prior to the coming
> of the Europeans, Arab nomads frequently plundered
> villages in Mala (Rickards & DiVesta, 1974, p. 355;
> adapted from Bruning, 1970).

Unlike the Royer and Cable (1976) excerpt presented to illustrate relative
uninterpretability, in the passages referred to here interpretability is
not the problem. New terms are adequately defined or exemplified, and the
factual information presented in the form of names, dates, events, event
sequences, etc., is straightforward enough. The problem with such
passages, however, is one of how to store that information in the most
efficient manner for later retrieval. In a text loaded with definitions
and facts, this information-storage/retrieval problem is certainly not a
trivial one. By taking the text as presented and mnemonically operating
on it to produce a physically different text as encoded, one can exploit
the transformation function of pictures. Such pictorial transformations
are assumed to enhance directly the memorability of the text content.

Relationship of Picture Functions To Strategy Classifications
We will now examine the four picture functions just discussed, in relation to the four main strategy boxes of Figure 1. A distilled version
of Figure 1 is presented as Table 1. As was indicated in our earlier
discussion of Figure 1, it must be pointed out that: (a) the distinctions made here should be regarded more as predominant than as exclusive
labels; and (b) the particular boxes to which the picture functions have
been assigned could be contested. With these caveats in mind, let
us proceed.

On the comprehension-directed side of Table 1 are located pictures that
satisfy the interpretation function. Note that such pictures can be
devised to clarify aspects of a text's macrostructure (e.g., pictorial
overviews and pictorial analogies), as well as to clarify the micropropositions themselves (e.g., pictorial interpretations of abstract
concepts and details, as in the previously presented Royer & Cable,
1976, excerpt).

In contrast, the three picture functions located on the right side of
Table 1 are seen as memory-directed. As mentioned at the outset,
however, the distinction is certainly not cut-and-dried. For example,
it has been shown that enhanced concreteness (à la the representation
function) results in enhanced comprehension per se (e.g., Johnson,
Bransford, Nyberg, & Cleary, 1972). Yet, in Table 1 the primary

Table 1
Picture Functions Classified According to Level of Text Information
and Primary Cognitive Function Served

Primary Cognitive Function

	Comprehension-Directed	Memory-Directed
Macrostructure	Interpretation[a]	Organization[b]
Microstructure	Interpretation[a]	Representation[c] Transformation[d]

(Level of Text Information)

[a]Enhanced meaningfulness
[b]Enhanced relatedness
[c]Enhanced concreteness
[d]Enhanced memorableness

beneficiary of pictorial representations is assumed to be memory. The
case for such a placement is strengthened by the numerous studies in which
it has been found that even easily comprehended text is more memorable in
the company of pictures (see Levin, 1981b; and Levin & Lesgold, 1978).
On the other hand, arguing for memory over comprehension is less
persuasive with respect to, say, complex procedural ("How To...") texts,
where pictorial representations undoubtedly serve to enhance one's
initial understanding of the component operations (e.g., Stone & Glock,
1981).

Satisfying the representation function are pictures that overlap with a
text's micropropositions (e.g., illustrated factual details); satisfying
the organization function are pictures that operate on the text's
macrostructure (e.g., maps, flowcharts, graphs), as well as those that
provide explicit interproposition integrations where these are lacking.
Finally, pictures that permit efficient mnemonic codings of a text's
factual information satisfy the transformation function. Rather than
simply to list examples of the uses to which transformational prose-
learning pictures have been put, I will consider these in detail in the
remainder of the paper. Consideration will also be given to the possibility of elevating the transformation function to the "level" of various
macrostructure strategies--either through its own efforts or on the
coattails of currently existing macrostructure strategies.

PICTORIAL PROSE-LEARNING MNEMONIC STRATEGIES

Mnemonic Versus Nonmnemonic Strategies
Numerous prose-learning studies have been conducted in which the effects
of "mnemonic" pictorial materials and strategies have been scrutinized.
When the studies themselves are scrutinized, however, it becomes clear
that the materials and strategies employed are not "mnemonic" at all, in
the sense intended in this paper. Thus, researchers who have either
provided text-related illustrations or instructed students to generate
visual images of a passage's content are not exploring the "mnemonic"
domain. Constructing pictures of the text as presented--either through
illustrations or imagery--is exploiting the representation function of
pictures. The construction of additional pictorial elaborations and
connections brings the organization function into play. Finally, the
anchoring of such pictures onto familiar schemata, analogies, or symbols
is to involve the interpretation function.

In contrast, being "mnemonic" implies a physical recoding of the text as
presented--not just displaying, extending, or "hypostatizing" (Davidson,
1976) it in picture form. Simply stated, mnemonic pictures implicate the
transformation function. A characteristic of mnemonic pictures is that
they prominently display objects or events that are not even mentioned in
the text--and that may, indeed, be semantically unrelated to the prose
content. These prominently displayed objects or events are representations of the recoded or transformed text, which provide efficient
retrieval paths back to the corresponding text content.

To help concretize these notions, let us consider a factual prose passage
in which one or more names, terms, labels, etc., is accompanied by one
or more attributes, facts, concepts, etc. In this section, we develop
some mnemonic picture constructs for simple passages of this type. In

the final section of the paper, extensions are made to more complexly structured texts (i.e., multilevel texts with multiply-connected propositions).

Table 2 contains a summary of pictorial strategies that could be applied to simple factual prose passages of two types. Single-name passages are those that define or describe the attributes of only one subject label. An example of this type of passage is the previously presented Rickards and DiVesta (1974) excerpt, where several attributes were to be associated with the name concept, Mala. In that passage, a number of specific attributes are described within each of two general attribute domains (geography/climate and exploitation history). The second type of factual prose passage represented in Table 2 is the multiple-name passage, where two or more different name concepts are each accompanied by a set of attributes. An example of this type of passage will be provided shortly.

Single-Name Factual Passages

Let us begin with single-name passages and, in particular, the first paragraph of the Rickards and DiVesta (1974) excerpt. Essentially we are given four geography/climate attributes to associate with a place by the name of southern Mala:

1. It is a desert.
2. It receives less than two inches of rain per year.
3. Its soil is either rocky or sandy.
4. Its temperature can reach 135° in the summertime.

Suppose that one's goal is to store these four characteristics of southern Mala, so that they can be recalled or recognized at a later time.[3]

Table 2
Pictorial Strategies for Factual Prose Passages

A. Single-Name Passages
    1. Nonmnemonic pictorial strategies
        • separate pictures of attributes
          (representation function)
        • integrated picture of attributes
          (organization function)
        • meaning-enhancing pictures of attributes
          (interpretation function)
    2. Mnemonic pictorial strategies
       (transformation function)
        • ordered mnemonic pictures
          (loci, pegword, digit/symbol variations)

B. Multiple-Name Passages
    1. Nonmnemonic pictorial strategies
        • meaning-enhancing pictures of name/attribute
          associations (interpretation function)
    2. Mnemonic pictorial strategies
       (transformation function)
        • unordered mnemonic pictures
          (keyword variations)

Illustrations serving each of the four picture functions could be constructed to capture various aspects of the southern Mala attributes.
Representational pictures would, where possible, afford literal depictions
of the separate attributes. For example, a desert could be displayed
(Attribute 1), as could the two soil types (Attribute 3). Attributes 2
and 4 could only be represented in a rough way through, say, arid-looking
conditions and the sun shining brightly, respectively. Depicting all
four of the above in a single integrated picture would fulfill the
organization function. Capitalizing on the interpretation function could
take several different forms here. Were the student already familiar with
certain aspects of the name concept being discussed (through prior
knowledge or instruction), the newly presented attribute information could
be pictorially anchored to the old in a variety of ways. In other cases,
where the student has no existing schemata for the name concept, one
could exploit a student's prior knowledge of the attribute concepts. For
example, one could provide illustrations and graphs in which the
attributes of southern Mala are juxtaposed with those of some other
place(s) with which the student is presumably familiar. One could also
use pictorial analogies to provide students with an answer to the question,
"How hot is it?" In addition, one-step-removed symbolic representations
could show a rain gauge recording less than 2" of precipitation and a
thermometer registering at 135°. Finally, it should be mentioned in
regard to pictorial interpretations that they can be combined with
pictorial organizations to produce memorial benefits likely to be greater
than those associated with either separately. More will be said later
about such pictorial strategy combinations.

The just-discussed pictorial approaches are, by definition, nonmnemonic
inasmuch as they do not involve the transformation function. It will
also be argued--as a point for subsequent empirical challenge--that none
of these nonmnemonic approaches is as memorially potent as are the true
mnemonic approaches to be discussed now. Of course, not all mnemonic
techniques can be expected to be equally effective. And given the large
number of candidate techniques available (see Bellezza, 1981), I am forced
to be selective here. Thus, excluded from present consideration are the
first-letter-mnemonic method and other verbal-based procedures. Also
excluded temporarily is the link method, which will surface in a subsequent context. Three mnemonic pictorial strategies will be considered:
the method of loci, the pegword method, and the digit/symbol method.
Each of these is specialized for storing and retrieving a list of information, as is desired for the southern Mala attributes of present concern.
All of the techniques make use of pre-established concrete "codes", "pegs",
or "hooks" and, because they all involve variations of the same theme, all
three techniques will be described first before adapting them to our
southern Mala example.

The method of loci. With this approach, one hooks new information onto an
overlearned set of ordered locations (loci). Commonly used loci are rooms
in one's house, stores along a neighborhood street, and campus landmarks,
as one proceeds along a familiar route from Point A to Point B. As
alternative "loci", we have constructed scene settings out of the four
seasons, as well as out of the 26 letters of the alphabet (Levin, 1981a).
To use the latter system, for example, one simply pictures the first to-
be-acquired piece of information in an airplane scene, the second in a
bank scene, the third in circus scene, the fourth in a doctor's office
scene, etc.

The pegword method. Here, the pre-established codes are simple picturable words that are rhyming proxies for various numbers. Thus, 1 is a bun, 2 is a shoe, 3 is tea, 4 is war, etc. Each incoming piece of information is pictorially related to a specific numerical peg, and these pegs later serve as information-retrieval cues. A limitation of this method is that convenient rhyming words have been devised for only the first 10 (or, in some systems, for the first 20) integers. A similar limitation is associated with the previously discussed alphabet-scene loci method, where only 26 different scenes can be constructed. Note, however, that these two methods can be combined to yield an efficient retrieval system for up to 260 pieces of information. The first ten pieces of incoming informa- tion (1-10) are coded by imagining an airplane scene with one of ten ob- jects in it (1 = bun, 2 = shoe, ... , 10 = hen), the next ten pieces of information (11-20) by imagining a bank scene with one of these same ten objects in it, etc., all the way to the 251st through 260th pieces of information by imagining a zoo scene. A more complex system, whose capability for storing serially presented information is virtually limitless, will now be described.

The digit/symbol method. With this method, the digits 0-9 are each represented by a consonant sound. Specifically, 1 is represented by a t or d sound, 2 by an n sound, 3 by an m sound, 4 by an r sound, 5 by an l sound, 6 by a j, ch, sh, or soft g sound, 7 by a k, hard c, or hard g sound, 8 by an f, v, or ph sound, 9 by a p or b sound, and 0 by an s, z, or soft c sound. Each of these sounds or sound combinations is then coded as a picturable word. Vowels, unvoiced consonants, and the conso- nants w, h, and y are not associated with any numerical values in the resulting words. In one system, for example (Lorayne & Lucas, 1974), 1 = tie, 2 = Noah, 3 = ma, 4 = rye, 5 = law, ... , 13 = tomb, ... , 25 = nail, ... , up to 100 = disease. Beyond 100, one can always invent something, such as 135 = tamale, etc., up to a wordsmith's infinity. Each of these number ➡ consonant ➡ word pictures is then associated with the corresponding piece of new information.

Examples of the three mnemonic techniques just described have been constructed for the four geography/climate attributes of the Mala excerpt. These are displayed in Table 3. Note, as well, that there are two obvious attribute distillations in that table: Attribute 2 (less than two inches of annual rainfall) was "gisted" as little rainfall, and Attribute 4 (summer temperatures as high as 135°) was "gisted" as very hot tempera- tures. Suppose, instead that the student thought it important to remember exactly how much rainfall and how much heat were associated with southern Mala. Using, say, the pegword method to represent the four attributes, one could add specific digit/symbol recodings where appropriate. Thus, to represent "less than two inches of rain", Noah (2) could be wearing the shoe that is collecting rain droplets; and to represent "temperatures as high as 135°", a war among Mexican soldiers (or Mexican waiters) over a priminently displayed tamale (135) would do the job.

Before moving on to multiple-name factual passages, I would like to make two additional comments about pictorial mnemonic strategies in the present single-name context. First, and as may have been inferred from the examples presented in Table 3, mnemonic pictures clearly make use of all three other picture functions. The airplane landing in the desert combines the pre-established airplane scene with a literal desert representation. All of the mnemonic techniques involve the organization

Table 3

Sample Mnemonic Pictures for the Single-Name Mala Excerpt

Mnemonic Technique	Pre-established Codes	Distilled Attribute: 1. Desert	2. Little Rainfall	3. Rocky or Sandy Soil	4. Very Hot Temperatures
Method of Loci	1 = a = airplane 2 = b = bank 3 = c = circus 4 = d = doctor's office	An airplane landing in the desert	A tiny puddle of rain droplets forming inside a bank vault	Two circus elephants, one atop a big rock pile and the other atop a big sand pile	A doctor taking a patient's temperature that is at the high end of the thermometer
Pegword Method	1 = bun 2 = shoe 3 = tea 4 = war	Lawrence of Arabia eating a hamburger bun in the desert	A shoe filling with tiny droplets of rain	A tea party, where one group of people is sitting on a rock pile and another group is sitting in a sand box	A war in which soldiers are wiping their brows as a result of the hot sun beating down on them
Digit/ Symbol Method	1 = t or d = tie 2 = n = Noah 3 = m = ma 4 = r = rye	Lawrence of Arabia putting on a flashy tie in the desert	A very confused Noah looking up to see only a few droplets of rain!	One's mother stacking a Toad of rocks around a sand pile	A delicatessen, where customers in a line to purchase rye bread are wiping their brows because of the heat

function to some degree, inasmuch as the various picture components that
are produced (from either external- or internal-to-text sources) must be
integrated in some meaningful fashion. Finally, pictorial interpretations
based on schemata (e.g., Noah's flood) and once-removed-from-text
symbolic representations (e.g., a doctor's thermometer) are often included
in one's mnemonic transformations.

A second point of interest is that any of the three mnemonic methods
represented in Table 3 could very easily be extended to encompass the
additional information in the second paragraph of the Rickards and DiVesta
(1974) excerpt, namely information documenting Mala's history of
exploitation. Another four attributes, distilled from that paragraph, can
be extracted and added to the four of the initial paragraph. A simple way
to do this would be just to label them Attributes 5-8 and continue using
any of the three counting systems described. Or, if one preferred, these
could be regarded as Attributes 1-4 of a new attribute category, and then
the same loci, pegwords, or digit/symbols that were applied in the first
paragraph could be reused in the second. That multiple applications of
the same mnemonic codes is an easily managed, noninterfering process has
been well-documented in the literature (see for example, Bellezza, in
press). Of course, it might be desirable to tag the two superordinate
attribute categories (geography/climate and exploitation history) in some
distinctive fashion. Such tagging could be considered from either a
mnemonic or nonmnemonic perspective--the subject of this paper's final
section.[4]

Multiple-Name Factual Passages
The strategies for enhancing students' recall of information in single-
name, multiple-attribute passages are general strategies for enhancing
free or serial recall. These include semantic categorization, organization, and association strategies; that is, strategies designed to increase
the integration or connectedness of the attributes presented. An important
characteristic of such strategies is that they are directed exclusively
toward the attributes themselves.

In contrast, with multiple-name passages one cannot ignore which names go
with which attributes. Thus, for example, even though one may remember
perfectly the set of attributes for southern Mala, it does no good if one
believes that these attributes are associated with the arctic community
of northern Pola (see also Bower, 1973, p. 70). Appropriate connections
between specific names and specific attributes (or attribute clusters)
are essential for multiple-name passages and, consequently, facilitative
strategies are those that strengthen not just the inter-attribute links
but especially the name/attribute links.

As may be seen in Table 2, nonmnemonic pictorial strategies for achieving
name/attribute integrations depend on the interpretation function. And,
as was mentioned in the case of single-name passages, the activation of
a student's relevant schemata would be a primary ingredient. Note,
however--and this is critically important--that such pictorial interpretations will be helpful only to the extent that the student has some prior
knowledge about the particular name concept being considered. Consider,
for example, the difference between acquiring new information for somewhat
familiar places [i.e., places whose names are already stably encoded in
memory, along with schema rubrics (e.g., Transylvania, Oz, or Camelot)],

as opposed to completely novel ones (e.g., Tergomania, Od, or Cumuland).
With the former familiar places, there are anchors there to which new
information can be attached; with each of the latter unfamiliar places,
however--and as Gertrude Stein would have said--there is no there there.
In contrast, it will now be shown that mnemonic pictorial strategies can
be effectively applied even to name concepts that are lacking a "there."

The keyword method. Based on the age-old mnemonic notion of recoding
unfamiliar terms into familiar picturable ones, the keyword method
(Atkinson, 1975) has been successfully applied to a variety of educationally relevant tasks containing an associative element (see Levin, 1981a;
and Pressley, Levin, & Delaney, Note 2). The keyword method includes the
two basic components of associative mnemonic devices, phonetic recoding
and semantic relating (Levin, Note 1). Thus, for example, to remember
that a woman named McKune was famous for owning a cat that could count:
(1) In the phonetic recoding stage, one would recode the unfamiliar name
McKune into an acoustically similar, more concrete representation, such as
raccoon. (2) Then, in the semantic relating stage, one would integrate
the recoded name with either a literal or figurative representation of the
attribute associated with that name (in this case, what the person was
famous for). Thus, to link raccoon with counting cat, one could picture,
say, a cat standing beside a tally board, counting raccoons as they jump
over a fence. Each other unfamiliar name would be recoded and related in
similar fashion.

Multiple-Name Applications Based on the Keyword Method
We have conducted just such a names-and-accomplishments adaptation of the
keyword method, embedding it in a prose-learning context. I will only
briefly discuss the results of that particular effort here, however,
in that more detailed information about it has been recently provided
(Levin, 1981b; Shriberg, Levin, McCormick, & Pressley, in press). The
names-and-accomplishments study will illustrate application of the keyword
method to multiple-name factual passages containing only one attribute
per name. Two other very recent investigations out of our laboratory will
then be detailed to illustrate application of the keyword method to
multiple-name factual passages containing multiple attributes per name.
As will be seen shortly, the collective results of the three studies
provide us with interesting information concerning the benefits to be
expected from various pictorial strategies accompanying factual prose
passages. In all of the studies to be discussed, the subjects were junior
high school students. Each of these studies will be organized around the
major question it was designed to address.

Can the keyword method be successfully applied to factual prose passages?
In the Shriberg et al. (in press) study, 12 short paragraphs were written
to describe the accomplishments of "famous" people (actually fictitious
accomplishments paired with names randomly drawn from the phone book).
Thus, one paragraph described Charlene McKune and her counting cat;
another described Douglas Rice, the inventor of a disappearing potion;
a third described Vicki Poulos, who achieved fame by floating across the
Atlantic on her back; etc. Keyword subjects were provided with a keyword
for each surname (e.g., McKune = raccoon; Rice = rice; Poulos = pole)
and either actual illustrations that related the keyword to the
accomplishment or instructions to create such a relationship via visual
imagery. Three experiments were conducted to address different practical
and theoretical issues surrounding use of the keyword method in this

context, including an empirical assessment of the transformation vs.
representation functional distinction that was made earlier in this paper.
The major results (based on cued-recall questions) can be summarized as
follows:
      1. The keyword method (as manifested through pictorial transforma-
tions) greatly facilitated students' name/accomplishment recall in all
three experiments.
      2. This was true whether actual keyword illustrations were provided
by the experimenter or whether the students generated their own keyword
images. It was found, however, that--at least for students of junior
high school age--experimenter-provided illustrations were more effective
(over 200% facilitation) than subject-generated images (over 100%
facilitation).
      3. Incorporating keyword pictures into more detailed (representation-
al) illustrations did not materially diminish the just-noted facilitative
effects. At the same time, these representational pictures tended to
improve students' memory for the passage details that were pictured.
      4. This latter result, along with the finding that pictures that
simply represented the literal (untransformed) text information did <u>not</u>
facilitate name/accomplishment recall, provided solid evidence for the
transformation-representation distinction. In particular, simple
pictorial <u>representations</u> might be expected to enhance recall of the
information depicted, but pictorial <u>transformations</u> are required to
enhance recall of the critical name/accomplishment associations.

<u>Can the keyword method be successfully applied to relatively abstract
prose information?</u> Linda Shriberg, Jill Berry, and I have recently
completed four experiments in which students were given prose passages
containing the distinguishing attributes of various fictitious
communities such as Hammondtown, Pleasantville, Fostoria, etc. Each of
the 20 attributes generated was randomly assigned to a particular
community. Consider, for example, the following paragraph about Fostoria
and its four attributes:

> Fostoria has a lot to offer its people.
> People have <u>considerable wealth</u>, and
> everyone lives comfortably. Many of the
> townsfolk also become quite prosperous
> because the land has <u>abundant natural resources</u>.
> In addition, the town is especially well known
> for its <u>advances in technology</u>, for just
> about everything is run by computer. This
> progress has attracted many new residents, and
> statistics show a <u>growing population</u>.

After studying several such paragraphs, students in two experiments were
required to match community names with their attributes (associative
recognition), and students in the other two experiments had to list the
characteristics for each community name (associative recall). In one of
the recognition experiments, there were ten community paragraphs with
two attributes per community. In the other recognition experiment and
in the recall experiments, there were five community paragraphs with four
attributes per community.

Unlike the Shriberg et al. (in press) attributes, most of those mentioned
in the present study were considerably less concrete, in the sense of their

not being amenable to direct pictorial representation. Contrast, for
example, the means of depicting a counting cat or someone floating on one's
back in the ocean vs. considerable wealth and abundant natural resources.
Clearly, one-step-removed pictorial interpretations are needed in the
latter case, in the form of symbolic representations (e.g., a stack of
dollar bills for considerable wealth) and specific concretizations (e.g.,
an oil well for abundant natural resources). One of the major questions
in this series of experiments was, Would the keyword method be adaptable
to relatively abstract attributes of this kind?

In these experiments, the comparative effects of pictorial interpretations
per se, interpretations plus organizations, and interpretations plus
organizations plus transformations, were respectively examined in the
following manner: (i) in the Control condition, after studying each
paragraph students were presented a page on which the attributes for that
paragraph were summarized; (ii) in the Picture condition the summary page
following each paragraph contained separate pictorial symbols to represent
the attributes (see Figure 2 for the four symbolized Fostoria attributes);
(iii) in the Organized Picture condition, the pictorial symbols on the
summary page were presented in the context of an integrated illustration,
as in Figure 3; and (iv) in the Organized Keyword Picture, a picture of
the keyword for the particular community (e.g., Fostoria = frost) was
incorporated into the integrated illustration, as in Figure 4.

Whether or not pictorial interpretations per se (Picture condition) would
facilitate students' acquisition of community/attribute associations was
not known. It was predicted, however, that whereas both picture organization conditions (Organized Picture and Organized Keyword Picture) would be
facilitative with respect to associating the appropriate attributes with
one another, the Organized Keyword Picture condition would be additionally
facilitative with respect to associating the attribute clusters with their
appropriate community names. An additional question of interest in the
recall experiments was, How well would picture subjects be able to recall
verbatim the previously listed attributes? That is, it is one thing to
remember a frosty scene with a mass of people clutching dollar bills and
watching a computer terminal operator beside an oil well. It is quite
another, however, to decode these pictorial symbols into their appropriate
attribute labels.

The results may be summarized as follows:
    1. Organized keyword pictures did indeed facilitate students'
associative memory for the community attributes, and by a substantial
amount. In the two recognition experiments, keyword subjects outperformed
controls by 70 to 90 percent; in the two recall experiments, the facilitation exceeded 100%. It should be noted, however, that the figures in the
recall experiments are based on a liberal scoring system, which accepted
appropriate paraphrases and concretizations. Nonetheless, even according
to a strict verbatim criterion, the increase amounted to over 60%
facilitation. The level of verbatim recall was low in all conditions.
However, requiring verbatim responses neither eliminated the positive
keyword effects nor placed keyword subjects at a disadvantage, as might
have been aniticipated on the basis of the previously mentioned difficulty-
of-decoding conjecture.

Research now in progress is investigating the possibility of elevating
students' level of verbatim recall through the use of additional keywords

FOSTORIA

Figure 2
Sample Illustration for the Picture Condition

to represent the attributes themselves. Thus, for example, rather than
provide pictorial <u>symbols</u> for the Fostoria attributes, one could provide
pictorial <u>keywords</u> to represent the key words in the attributes, such as
<u>well</u> for <u>wealth</u>, <u>race horses</u> for <u>resources</u>, <u>tacks</u> for <u>technology</u>, and <u>pop</u>
for <u>population</u>. An integrated visual scenario, based on this compound-
keyword approach, appears as in Figure 5. Would students be able to keep
each set of integrated attribute keywords distinct from, yet relatable
to, the corresponding community keyword (here, <u>frost</u>)? If so, this
type of compound mnemonic strategy may be just what is needed to
facilitate retrieval of <u>both</u> the higher- and lower-level propositions of
more complexly structured factual prose passages. This possibility will
be returned to shortly. Another question associated with a compound
keyword strategy is, Would the greater acoustic correspondence between

FOSTORIA

Figure 3
Sample Illustration for the Organized Picture Condition

the key attribute terms and their pictorial representations result in more efficient verbatim recall of the attributes, in comparison to verbatim recall in the combined keyword/symbol condition? Verbatim responses may be desired in certain situations and, thus, the answer to this question is important.

2. As predicted, organized pictures without keywords produced the same level of attribute organization as did organized keyword pictures, but the level of correct attribute/community pairings was considerably lower. In fact, with the ten-community paragraphs, the number of attributes and communities correctly associated by organized picture subjects approximated that of control subjects.

3. Simple symbolic representations of the attributes (i.e., non-integrated pictures without keywords) were totally ineffective with respect to either acquiring attribute/community associations or grouping

FOSTORIA

Figure 4
Sample Illustration for the Organized Keyword Picture Condition

together appropriate attributes. Thus, for this particular task, separate
pictorial interpretations were insufficient to boost performance.

Are there differences associated with different prose-learning variations
of the keyword method? In the Organized Keyword Picture condition of the
study just discussed, each name concept was integrated (via its keyword)
with all of its associated attributes, in a single picture. Clearly, this
is not the only kind of keyword approach that could have been taken, as
Christine McCormick recently demonstrated in her doctoral dissertation
(McCormick, Note 3).

As in the just-described study, McCormick's paragraphs contained multiple
attributes per name. The passage content, however, consisted of brief
biographies of four fictitious individuals. Five pieces of biographical
information were associated with each person: the kind of environment
in which the person was raised, what (s)he did as a child to earn spending

FOSTORIA

Figure 5
Sample Illustration for the Organized Compound Keyword Picture Condition

money, and his or her present occupation, major hobby, and aspirations. In addition, rather than providing students with actual keyword illustrations, McCormick simply described the particular images to be generated by the students themselves. In each of these images, a keyword for the "famous" individual's name was to be related to a representation of the corresponding biographical data, in one of three ways:

1. Separate Keyword Pictures, where each piece of biographical information was separately related to the keyword. Thus, for each biography, five discrete scenes were to be imagined, each containing the same keyword paired with a different biographical attribute. The theoretical notion here is that the person's name will re-evoke each of the five keyword attribute scenes.

2. Linked Keyword Pictures, where the keyword is related to the first piece of biographical information, then the first piece of

information (sans keyword) is related to the second, the second (sans first) is related to the third, etc. As in the Separate Keyword Pictures condition, five discrete scenes are to be produced. However, each biographical attribute (except the last one mentioned) is involved in two of the scenes. The theoretical notion here is that of a scene-linked chain: The person's name will re-evoke the scene involving the keyword and the first attribute, recall of the first attribute will then re-evoke the scene involving the second attribute, etc.

3. <u>Cumulative Keyword Picture</u>, where the student starts with the keyword and first biographical attribute, and cumulatively incorporates each new attribute into a <u>single</u> integrated image. This condition resembles the Organized Keyword Picture condition of the previous study, except that the components of the resulting picture are built up successively rather than presented simultaneously. The theoretical notion is that the ultimate scene will afford a thematic integration of the keyword and set of corresponding biographical attributes.

An example of each of these keyword approaches is provided in Table 4 for the ubiquitous Charlene McKune. Two control conditions were also employed, one with once-repeated biographical attributes (as in the Separate Keyword Pictures and Linked Keyword Pictures conditions), and one with multiply-repeated biographical attributes (as in the Cumulative Keyword Picture condition). Performance was based on 20 cued-recall questions, with each question relating to a specific piece of information about a specific individual. Two different question orders (sequential and scrambled) were also incorporated.

Let me now attempt to summarize the major findings:
1. All three keyword approaches resulted in increased levels of biographical-information recall (anywhere from 25-40 percent increases). The smaller effects in this study, in comparison to the others, may have been due in part to the finding that in each of the keyword conditions, story information was often confused with other information about the same individual. For example, Charlene McKune may have been remembered as being a painter rather than as painting for a hobby. Such a finding is of considerable interest in that: (<u>a</u>) four of the five attribute categories had conceptual overlap to some extent (i.e., type of work while younger, present occupation, present hobby, and aspirations all relate to types of activities); and (<u>b</u>) the experimenter did not provide students with a specific strategy (mnemonic or otherwise) for relating passage information to its appropriate question category. Subsequent mnemonic prose investigations--including extensions to more complex prose types--will take these issues into consideration.

2. The preponderance of control subjects' overt errors consisted of confusing different pieces of different individuals' biographies. More-over, control subjects' recall of one piece of biographical information was virtually unrelated to the probability of their recalling the next piece of information about the same person. The same tended to be true for separate keyword subjects. In contrast, the recall of linked and cumulative keyword subjects was highly dependent on the correctness of their immediately preceding response. That is, they were much more likely to remember a biographical fact if they had remembered the preceding fact about the same person than if they had forgotten it. Interestingly--and consistent with the theoretically different processes

Table 4

Example of Three Different Keyword Variations for Factual Prose
(From McCormick, Note 3)

			Condition	
Sentence	Separate Keyword Pictures	Linked Keyword Pictures	"Make up a picture in your head of..."	Cumulative Keyword Picture
1. While Charlene McKune was growing up, she and her family led an interesting life traveling on their houseboat.	a RACCOON standing on the deck of a houseboat	a RACCOON standing on the deck of a houseboat		a RACCOON standing on the deck of a houseboat
2. During her school years, McKune earned extra money delivering newspapers.	a RACCOON throwing newspapers onto a doorstep	newspapers being thrown to the shore from the deck of a houseboat		a RACCOON standing on the deck of a houseboat throwing newspapers
3. McKune was always interested in whatever was happening around her, and so she eventually became a TV news reporter.	a RACCOON being interviewed by a TV reporter	a TV reporter throwing newspapers onto a doorstep		a RACCOON standing on the deck of a houseboat throwing newspapers to a TV reporter on shore
4. In her spare time, McKune loves to paint.	a RACCOON painting a picture	a TV reporter painting a picture		a RACCOON standing on the deck of a houseboat throwing newspapers to a TV reporter on shore who is painting a picture
5. Although McKune is not particularly athletic, she still dreams of some day winning an Olympic gold medal.	a RACCOON with an Olympic gold medal around its neck	an Olympic gold medal hung on a painting		a RACCOON standing on the deck of a houseboat throwing newspapers to a TV reporter on shore who is painting a picture of an Olympic gold medal

associated with the various keyword approaches--when the questions were asked in a scrambled order (i.e., different from the original order within a paragraph), the response-dependency pattern was reduced considerably in the linked, though not in the cumulative, keyword condition.

Thus, as with the two other recent investigations, the results of the McCormick (Note 3) study are very encouraging with respect to the potential for applying pictorial mnemonic strategies to factual prose passages. As will now be argued, however, the ultimate versatility of a mnemonic approach depends on how successfully it can be adapted to passages containing a variety of connected propositions at different levels of structural importance.

PICTORIAL MNEMONIC STRATEGIES FOR COMPLEX PROSE

Unlike what was written in the immediately preceding section, which was based on empirical fact, what is written here is based largely on speculation and should be recognized as such. Hopefully, at least fragments of this speculation will have been put to empirical test within the next few years. We consider here strategies and strategy combinations that are likely to enhance students' comprehension and retention of both a text's main ideas and its details. This statement implies that we will need to concentrate simultaneously on a text's macropropositions, its micropropositions, and its inter-propositional relationships. Let us now examine three possible approaches for doing this.

Nonmnemonic Strategies
I will have little to say about this approach. Many examples of popular nonmnemonic prose-learning strategies have been provided throughout the paper and elsewhere. These include strategies designed to increase understanding of a text's structure, as well as important concepts described in the text. Such strategies typically involve a distillation of the details in favor of themes and major ideas communicated by the text. Other strategies operate within the text structure to provide hierarchically-ordered retrieval cues. To date, however, there is little evidence that these retrieval cues really do help one to retrieve the specific details that are waiting at the end of the path. That is, getting to a newly learned piece of information does not guarantee getting it. And to the extent that the gotten-to information is non-obvious--in the sense of it not being easily relatable to an individual's prior knowledge--there is no reason to expect that nonmnemonic prose-learning strategies will be effective.

A simple example will be offered from the area of vocabulary learning. In three recently completed studies (Levin, McCormick, Berry, Miller, & Pressley, in press; Pressley, Levin, & Miller, in press; and Pressley, Levin, Kuiper, Bryant, & Michener, Note 4), we have examined a host of strategies deemed by reading theorists and practitioners as "effective" for vocabulary instruction. The strategies consist of a variety of semantic-, contextual-, and schema-based approaches. In none of the approximately ten experiments that we have conducted have such non-mnemonic strategies improved subjects' (both adults' and children's) acquisition of new vocabulary items. In contrast, adaptations of the mnemonic keyword method have substantially facilitated performance.

It is not that nonmnemonic semantic alternatives are inherently poor strategies; rather, they are poor strategies when it comes to coding unfamiliar terms for later retrieval. That is, interacting with a new word and its definition on a semantic level may well enhance <u>certain</u> types of performance--as Pressley et al. (Note 4) found out--but not performance in which vocabulary item/definition <u>associations</u> are critical, such as when having to recall or recognize a definition in response to a vocabulary item. The keyword method does provide the needed <u>direct link</u> between a vocabulary item and its definition and, consequently, associative performance is facilitated.

I think that one can extend the same argument to the acquisition of new information within a prose passage. The keyword method experiments reported in the preceding section suggest that one should at least listen to--if not embrace--the argument. The bottom line is that I do not believe that exclusively <u>nonmnemonic</u> prose-learning strategies will as effectively deal with our <u>dual</u> "macro"/"micro" concerns as will strategies that do contain a mnemonic component.

<u>Compound Mnemonic Strategies</u>
Note, however, by the way I worded the last sentence, that I am not saying that all texts should be exclusively processed mnemonically at all times. What I am saying is that at least some parts of some texts should at some times. It is too soon yet to say whether or not <u>all</u> parts of certain prose passages should be mnemonically processed. The relevant data have not yet been collected, but that is the topic of speculation for this subsection.

We know by now that factual information in a prose passage can be mnemonically coded in an efficient manner. But what about a passage's higher-order content (information) and structure (connections)? Actually, we <u>can</u> say something about mnemonic strategies and higher-order passage content. The Shriberg et al. (in press) "famous" people passages contained both higher-order information (main accomplishments) and lower-order information (additional details about the accomplishments). The mnemonic keyword method facilitated students' recall of the higher-order information. This example is offered simply to point out that "higher-order" and "lower-order" propositional information must always be defined relative to the passage at hand. Thus, although a specific accomplishment for a specific person may well represent a trivial detail in one passage, it may represent another passage's raison d'être (as, for example, in a biography).

More complex factual prose passages differ from the above "famous" people example in at least three ways. First, greater dependence on <u>text/schema interactions</u> is required in order for new information to be related to existing knowledge. Moreover, in comparison to lower-level text information, higher-order information is generally stated at a <u>higher level of abstraction</u> and is <u>associated with a greater number of inter-propositional connections</u>. The text/schema interaction issue must be considered with respect to <u>any</u> prose-learning strategy employed, be it mnemonic or nonmnemonic. If one cannot bring one's prior knowledge to bear on at least some aspect of the text content (either as presented or as recoded), then the strategy will be ineffectual.

What is of concern here, then, is whether or not <u>exclusively</u> mnemonic strategies can be devised to permit an efficient coding of a passage's micropropositions, while at the same time permitting an efficient coding of the more abstract, multiply-connected macropropositions. Enough research has been done to expect success at the "micro" level. Moreover, the limited research on mnemonically-coded abstract prose concepts (reported earlier) also bodes well for combining pictorial representations and pictorial transformations. What has yet to be touched upon is the propositional-connection issue. Can this be effectively dealt with strictly from a mnemonic perspective? And if so, can one use the same mnemonic system to represent passage content and passage structure, or can different mnemonic systems be combined to serve unique functions? In addition, are there limits to the amount of mnemonic content and structure that can be coded for a given passage? Finally, even if such exclusive mnemonic processing of text were to prove to be effective relative to a no-strategy control condition, how would it fare relative to either alternative nonmnemonic strategies or mnemonic/nonmnemonic strategy combinations? My own hunch is that neither exclusively non-mnemonic strategies nor exclusively mnemonic strategies will prove to be as effective as mnemonic/nonmnemonic combinations, the topic with which this paper comes to a close.

Combined Mnemonic/Nonmnemonic Strategies
An interesting series of demonstrations by Snowman, Krebs, and their associates (Krebs, Snowman, & Smith, 1978; Snowman, Krebs, & Lockhart, 1980; Snowman, Krebs, & Kelly, Note 5) will be used to indicate some promising research avenues. These investigators have shown--in the context of actual college-level courses on "study skills"--that inefficient prose processors can be taught combined mnemonic/nonmnemonic strategies to improve their prose-learning performance substantially. The basic instructional procedures, which are developed over several weeks, combine a text-analysis macrostructure strategy with a mnemonic microstructure strategy. The text-analysis strategy is essentially a four-tiered simplification of Meyer's (1975) system. Its primary purpose is to get students to focus on the text structure, abstracting themes and coding propositions with respect to their importance and relationship to other propositions. The mnemonic strategy is the method of loci applied to the details at the lowest level of the prose hierarchy, which enables students to remember the facts and examples associated with the higher-level propositions.

The Snowman and Krebs approach merits scrutiny, and it clearly invites additional research. Based on the work out of our laboratory, reported here and elsewhere (e.g., Levin, 1981a), it would certainly appear that mnemonic strategies other than the method of loci: (<u>a</u>) would prove useful for certain types of to-be-coded passage information; (<u>b</u>) would be better suited to cued-recall performance measures (rather than the free-recall measures employed by Snowman and Krebs); and (<u>c</u>) could be used in conjunction with the loci method as a compound mnemonic strategy (see, in particular, Levin, McCormick, & Dretzke, in press). Regarding the last point, strategy combinations involving the loci method and other mnemonic systems could be applied to higher-order passage content and structural connections, as was suggested in the immediately preceding subsection.

A concluding excursion. Although I do not have a firm fix on how these notions could be "systematized", either within or across passages, let me conclude by taking an N=1 voyage into the target paragraph of Meyer's (1975) _Parakeet_ passage, which is reproduced here:

> The wide variety in color of parakeets
> that are available on the market today resulted
> from careful breeding of the color mutant off-
> spring of light green-bodied and yellow-faced
> parakeets. The light green body and yellow
> face color combination is the color of parakeets
> in their natural habitat, Australia. The first
> living parakeets were brought to Europe from
> Australia by John Gould, a naturalist, in 1840.
> The first color mutation appeared in 1872 in
> Belgium; these birds were completely yellow.
> The most popular color of parakeets in the United
> States is sky-blue. These birds have sky-blue
> bodies and white faces; this color mutation
> occurred in 1878 in Europe. There are over
> 66 different colors of parakeets listed by the
> Color and Technical Committee of the Budgerigar
> Society. In addition to the original light
> green-bodied and yellow-faced birds, colors of
> parakeets include varying shades of violets,
> blues, grays, greens, yellows, whites and multi-
> colored variations (Meyer, 1975, p. 201).

What follows now is a personalized account of an effort after understanding and remembering the content of this paragraph. In the account, I will indicate the specific strategies employed, as well as the relevant self-monitoring activity that accompanied these strategies (see Figure 1).

The superordinate concept in this paragraph--and in the passage from which the paragraph was taken--is _parakeet_. Yes, I know that a parakeet is a small bird, but that's about all. A check in the dictionary shows that a parakeet is actually a member of the parrot family, and I think I have a better-developed schema of _parrot_. What is more, _keet_ could be thought of as a diminutive, and so the "small parrot" analogy may indeed serve me well. The specific topic of the paragraph is the _color_ of parakeets and, in particular: (i) the many varieties of color that there are today; and (ii) the history of their evolution.

● _Comment_: The above illustrates use of a variety of nonmnemonic strategies (including text analysis, rereading, summarizing, self-questioning, and schemata activation) and the potential use of the mnemonic keyword method (i.e., _parakeet_ = _parrot_ + _keet_; _keet_ resembles _kid_, or someone _small_).

Concerning _history_, the most important place is _Australia_, the most important date is _1840_, and the most important name is John _Gould_. I can well imagine parrots in Australia, and of course they have green bodies and yellow faces. I can also see them flying wild in the midst of kangaroos and koala bears. I can also focus on or draw a map of Australia to help cement the Australia-parakeet connection. In addition, I can see a ship sailing from Australia to Europe. The ship has a bunch of deep sea divers on it. They're trying to dive, but can't; their feet are glued to the ship boards. The divers are important

because via the mnemonic digit/symbol method, that gives me d-v-r-s =
1840, the critical year of John Gould, the naturalist. Why John Gould?
Two reasons: 1. The divers' feet were glued to the deck. Remember?
2. The connection in my mind is also mediated by an Australian-swimmer
connection, which elicits the name Shane Gould, an Aussie Olympic
swimmer of years gone by. Why John? Why not?

● Comment: The above illustrates use of the nonmnemonic strategies of
concretizations (here, maps) and schemata activation (including idiosyncratic associations, such as Shane Gould), as well as the mnemonic
digit/symbol (1840) and keyword (glued-Gould) strategies.

Having gotten to Europe, we learn that two dates and two places are
significant. One date is 1872, when an all-yellow color variation
appeared in Belgium. Because I already know that we're in the 1800s
(from my divers), life is made simpler by focussing on just the 72, which
is coded as coin according to the Lorayne and Lucas (1974) digit/symbol
method. As our ship comes into port, I can see an old man with a beard
coming on board ship. He is carrying a bright yellow coin, which he
offers the captain in exchange for the ship's yellow bell (= Belgium).
I also remember my map, which shows a route from Australia to southeastern
Europe, through Gibraltar, and up to Belgium--realizing full well that I
have fabricated this particular route just to get from "somewhere" in
Europe to Belgium. The old man (a hermit?) then takes the ship's bell to
his cave (= 78), "who knows where" in Europe. The bell hangs from the
cave entrance while the hermit sits there just gazing at the bright
blue sky and white puffy clouds. This of course, tells me that in 1878,
a blue-and-white color variation of parakeet appeared "somewhere" in
Europe.

● Comment: The above illustrates use of nonmnemonic maps and schemata
once again (including a plausible scenario of a route traveled by), as
well as the mnemonic digit/symbol method, keyword method (Belgium = bell),
and link method (in the form of an integrated story, to get from one
critical date to the next).

Finally, concerning colors of parakeets today: Of course there are
green and yellow varieties, from their parrot ancestors. Also, in
encountering the unfamiliar term, buderigar, I hear a familiar budgie
bell ring inside. Budgie must either be a derivative, or the informal
term [a dictionary check confirms the latter]. At least some budgies
I know are blue and white, and so I make either the inferential or
synonymic leap to parakeets [a dictionary check confirms the
latter]. Thus, we have green, yellow, blue (and its relative, purple
or violet), white (and its neighbor, gray), and--as the passage said--
numerous other variations (including multi-colored ones). But how many
exactly? I can't tell exactly, but I do see a "Miss Parakeet" contest,
with a very important-looking judge perusing a long list of entries. The
judge is, of course, more than just important looking; he tells me via
his j-g that there are 66 (= j-g) names on a "Society" list. But, then,
there must be more than 66, because someone has just handed him a list of
late entrants.

● Comment: The above illustrates the application of nonmnemonic schemata
yet again, including inference generation through self-questioning. The
mnemonic digit/symbol numbering system is applied again as well.

As should have been apparent, in performing this exercise I had to make repeated use of both existing nonmnemonic schemata and appropriate mnemonic systems. I was even able to combine the two in places (e.g., Shane Gould, as a link between Australia and John Gould). Note also, that in order to organize my mnemonic strategies in an effective manner, I was forced into performing a nonmnemonic text analysis of sorts. The product of this analysis could have taken shape in any number of forms, structured either propositionally, cartographically, or historically, with the last either in proper or reversed sequence.

Having spent considerable time with the paragraph applying the various analyses and devices, I am now willing to risk the following conclusions:
   1. It is indeed possible to devise combined mnemonic/nonmnemonic prose-learning strategies that "work".
   2. Getting strategies that "work" requires work, and work in this case involves both effort and time. One might be further disheartened to learn that the paragraph dissected here was only one of four that comprised the Meyer (1975) Parakeet passage. Thus, more work lies ahead for the serious student.
   3. Such strategies, when presented to students in an optimally structured form, should be effective. Consistent with the theme of this paper, pictures represent a class of prose adjuncts that should be exploited when one's goal is to enhance students' comprehension or memory.
   4. The strategies offered and taught to students should be geared appropriately to their prior knowledge and skill levels. The complexity of strategies such as the ones illustrated here can quickly get out of hand, with the result of frustrating or "turning off" the student.
   5. It is unlikely that the facts surrounding the color evolution of the parakeet, as we know it today, will soon be forgotten by the present author. The question of how to differentiate between the "real" and "imagined" information that I now have dancing around in my head is an interesting one, as is the question of what will become of that information as time goes by.

ACKNOWLEDGMENTS

This research was funded by the Wisconsin Research and Development Center for Individualized Schooling, supported in part as a research and development center by funds from the National Institute of Education (Center Grant No. OB-NIE-G-81-009). The opinions herein do not necessarily reflect the position or policy of the National Institute of Education and no official endorsement by the National Institute of Education should be inferred. I am grateful to Lynn Sowle for typing the manuscript, and to artist Robert Cavey for his pictorial devices.

REFERENCE NOTES

1. Levin, J. R. Pictures for school learning: Practical illustrations (Theoretical Paper No. 90). Madison: Wisconsin Research and Development Center for Individualized Schooling, 1980.
2. Pressley, M., Levin, J. R., & Delaney, H. D. The mnemonic keyword method (Theoretical Paper No. 92). Madison: Wisconsin Research and Development Center for Individualized Schooling, 1981.

3. McCormick, C. B. The effect of mnemonic strategy variations on
    students' recall of potentially confusable prose passages.
    Unpublished doctoral dissertation, University of Wisconsin,
    Madison, 1981.
4. Pressley, M., Levin, J. R., Kuiper, N. A., Bryant, S. L., &
    Michener, S. Mnemonic versus nonmnemonic vocabulary-learning
    strategies: Putting "depth" to rest (Working Paper No. 312).
    Madison: Wisconsin Research and Development Center for
    Individualized Schooling, 1981.
5. Snowman, J., Krebs, E. W., & Kelly, F. J. Enhancing memory
    for prose through learning strategy training. Paper presented
    at the annual meeting of the American Educational Research
    Association, Boston, April 1980.

REFERENCES

Atkinson, R. C. Mnemotechnics in second-language learning. American
    Psychologist, 1975, 30, 821-828.
Baggett, P. Structurally equivalent stories in movie and text and the
    effect of the medium on recall. Journal of Verbal Learning and
    Verbal Behavior, 1979, 18, 333-356.
Baker, L., & Brown, A. L. Metacognitive skills and reading. In P. D.
    Pearson (Ed.), Handbook of reading research, New York: Longman,
    in press.
Bellezza, F. S. Mnemonic devices: Classification, characteristics,
    and criteria. Review of Educational Research, 1981, 51,
    247-275.
Bellezza, F. S. Updating memory using mnemonic devices. Cognitive
    Psychology, in press.
Bower, G. H. Analysis of a mnemonic device. American Scientist,
    1970, 58, 496-510.
Bower, G. H. Educational applications of mnemonic devices. In K. O.
    Doyle (Ed.), Interaction: Readings in human psychology.
    Lexington, Mass.: Heath, 1973.
Brown, A. L., Campione, J. C., & Day, J. D. Learning to learn. On
    training students to learn from texts. Educational Researcher,
    1981, 10(2), 14-21.
Bruning, R. H. Short-term retention of specific factual information in
    prose contexts of varying organization and relevance. Journal of
    Educational Psychology, 1970, 61, 186-192.
Davidson, R. E. The role of metaphor and analogy in learning. In
    J. R. Levin & V. L. Allen (Eds.), Cognitive learning in children:
    Theories and strategies. New York: Academic Press, 1976.
Flavell, J. H. Metacognitive development. In J. M. Scandura &
    C. J. Brainerd (Eds.), Structural/process theories of complex
    human behavior. Alphen a.d. Rijn, The Netherlands: Sijthoff &
    Noordhoff, 1978.
Gagné, E. D., & Bell, M. S. The use of cognitive psychology in the
    development and evaluation of textbooks. Educational Psychologist,
    1981, 16, 83-100.
Higbee, K. L. Recent research on visual mnemonics: Historical roots
    and educational fruits. Review of Educational Research, 1979,
    49, 611-629.

Johnson, M. K., Bransford, J. D., Nyberg, S. E., & Cleary, J. J. Comprehension factors in interpreting memory for abstract and concrete sentences. Journal of Verbal Learning and Verbal Behavior, 1972, 11, 451-454.

Kintsch, W., & van Dijk, T. A. Toward a model of text comprehension and production. Psychological Review, 1978, 85, 363-394.

Krebs, E. W., Snowman, J., & Smith, S. H. Teaching new dogs old tricks: Facilitating prose learning through mnemonic training. Journal of Instructional Psychology, 1978, 5, 33-39.

Levin, J. R. Inducing comprehension in poor readers: A test of a recent model. Journal of Educational Psychology, 1973, 65, 19-24.

Levin, J. R. The mnemonic '80s: Keywords in the classroom. Educational Psychologist, 1981, 16, 65-82. (a)

Levin, J. R. On functions of pictures in prose. In F. J. Pirozzolo & M. C. Wittrock (Eds.), Neuropsychological and cognitive processes in reading. New York: Academic Press, 1981. (b)

Levin, J. R., & Lesgold, A. M. On pictures in prose. Educational Communication and Technology Journal, 1978, 26, 233-243.

Levin, J. R., McCormick, C. B., & Dretzke, B. J. A combined pictorial mnemonic strategy for ordered information. Educational Communication and Technology Journal, in press.

Levin, J. R., McCormick, C. B., Miller, G. E., Berry, J. K., & Pressley, M. Mnemonic versus nonmnemonic vocabulary-learning strategies for children. American Educational Research Journal, in press.

Levin, J. R., & Pressley, M. Improving children's prose comprehension: Selected strategies that seem to succeed. In C. M. Santa & B. L. Hayes (Eds.), Children's prose comprehension: Research and practice. Newark, Del.: International Reading Association, 1981.

Lorayne, H., & Lucas, J. The memory book. New York: Ballantine, 1974.

Meyer, B. J. F. The organization of prose and its effects on memory. Amsterdam: North-Holland, 1975.

Paivio, A. Imagery and verbal processes. New York: Holt & Co., 1971.

Pearson, P. D., & Spiro, R. J. Toward a theory of reading comprehension instruction. Topics in Language Disorders, 1980, 1, 71-88.

Pressley, M., Levin, J. R., & Miller, G. E. The keyword method compared to alternative vocabulary-learning strategies. Contemporary Educational Psychology, in press.

Rickards, J. P., & DiVesta, F. J. Type and frequency of questions in processing textual material. Journal of Educational Psychology, 1974, 66, 354-362.

Royer, J. M., & Cable, G. W. Illustrations, analogies, and facilitative transfer in prose learning. Journal of Educational Psychology, 1976, 68, 205-209.

Shriberg, L. K., Levin, J. R., McCormick, C. B., & Pressley, M. Learning about "famous" people via the keyword method. Journal of Educational Psychology, in press.

Snowman, J., Krebs, E. W., & Lockhart, L. Improving recall of information from prose in high-risk students through learning strategy training. Journal of Instructional Psychology, 1980, 7, 35-40.

Stone, D. E., & Glock, M. D. How do young adults read directions with and without pictures? Journal of Educational Psychology, 1981, 73, 419-426.

Tuinman, J. J. Determining the passage dependency of comprehension questions in 5 major tests. Reading Research Quarterly, 1973-74, 9, 206-223.

FOOTNOTES

[1]Although the term "mnemonic" can be applied to anything that
enhances one's memory, in this paper the term will be used exclusively
as an abbreviation for "mnemonic devices" (i.e., systematic techniques
that physically transform the to-be-processed stimuli into more memorable
representations). For additional discussion of the characteristics
of mnemonic devices, see Bellezza (1981) and Levin (Note 1).

[2]Baker and Brown (in press) have recently distinguished between
comprehension and memory purposes for reading, which differs from the
strategy function issue discussed here.

[3]To be sure, this particular four-attribute cluster is one that
likely could be easily constructed from a general desert schema and
in that sense, the particular attributes listed are not "passage
dependent" (Tuinman, 1973-74). Yet, even though this excerpt contains
a particularly easy-to-recall set of attributes, we continue to use
the example to illustrate a variety of pictorial strategies. Note, as
well, that the specific numerical values mentioned in the passage (less
than 2 inches of rain per year and summer temperatures of up to 135
degrees) could not be produced exclusively from a general desert schema.

[4]For those few who may care: Using the digit/symbol method, one
would recode the critical year of 1610 as "two jets", "two sheets",
"tee shots", "digits" (among others), and then incorporate the
corresponding literal or figurative representation into one's picture.

DISCOURSE PROCESSING
A. Flammer and W. Kintsch (eds.)
© *North-Holland Publishing Company, 1982*

INSTRUCTIONAL VARIABLES IN TEXT PROCESSING

Richard E. Mayer

Department of Psychology
University of California
Santa Barbara, California 93106
U.S.A.

This paper explores five techniques for increasing the
novice's understanding of scientific prose. Novices
are defined as readers who have little or no prior experience with the subject matter in the passage. Understanding is defined in terms of the reader's ability
to use information from the passage to solve transfer
problems. The five techniques reviewed are: (1) organizing the passage around familiar principles, (2)
using concrete advance organizers, (3) providing pretraining in prerequisite knowledge, (4) encouraging
use of elaboration strategies, (5) inserting meaningful adjunct questions within the passage.

INTRODUCTION

Sometimes a person can read a new scientific passage and then use the information creatively to solve problems. In other circumstances, a person
can read the same information, retaining much of it, and yet cannot solve
problems. This paper provides examples from a program of research concerned
with increasing the novice's understanding of scientific or technical prose.
Novices are readers who are not familiar with the subject matter in the
passage; understanding of a scientific text is measured by the reader's
ability to use information from the passage in creative problem solving.

This paper reports on five manipulations that have produced reliable effects in our lab on increasing the novice's understanding of science prose:
(1) organization of prose, (2) concrete advance organizers, (3) pretraining in prerequisite knowledge, (4) elaboration strategies, (5) adjunct questions. Implications for a theory of meaningful learning from
prose include the following: the reader must pay attention to relevant
material in the passage, the reader must possess appropriate anchoring
ideas in memory, and the reader must actively assimilate the presented information to these anchoring ideas. Instructional manipulations, such as
those cited in this paper, tend to enhance these three processes and thus
tend to increase the reader's understanding of science prose.

LEARNING BY UNDERSTANDING

Why should anyone be concerned with the issue of understanding? The concept of learner understanding is a rather vague and difficult idea (White
& Mayer, 1980). Isn't it enough to establish clear behavioral objectives

and then to measure performance? As long as students can perform on a set
of target behaviors, why should we be concerned with whether or not they
understand, or whether or not the material was meaningful for them?

Let me give you an example, a rather traditional one, which conveys some
of the argument for emphasis on learning by understanding. The Gestalt
psychologists, working in the 1930's and 1940's, provided an early attempt
to study the role of understanding in learning (see Wertheimer, 1959;
Katona, 1940; Duncker, 1945; Luchins, 1942). For example, Wertheimer (1959)
provides an example of two ways to teach children how to find the area of
a parallelogram. The first method--which he called the rote, mechanical
method--is to teach children the procedure of dropping a perpendicular,
measuring the height, measuring the base, and then multiplying height times
base to get area. The formula, Area = Height x Base, is emphasized from
the start. A second method--which he calls the meaningful or understanding
method--is to allow children to see that you could cut off a triangle from
one side and move it to the other in order to change a parallelogram into
a rectangle. This realization is called "structural insight" because the
learner can see how the structure of a parallelogram can be related to what
he already knows concerning a rectangle. Since the learner already knows
how to find the area of a rectangle, his structural insights about the
parallelogram allow him to find that area also.

What are the advantages of learning by understanding? According to
Wertheimer, if you gave performance tests to children in both groups you
would find that both groups perform quite well on problems like those used
in instruction. However, suppose you give unusual problems such as a tall
narrow parallelogram or other peculiar shapes. The rote group children
give the familiar refrain known to all teachers, "We haven't had this yet."
However, the meaningful group children are able to solve the problem. Thus,
according to Wertheimer, and the Gestalt claims in general, when children
understand a mathematical or scientific procedure they will be better able
to transfer what they have learned to new situations. In other words, the
payoff for meaningful instruction is not in immediate retention of the just
learned information but rather in creative transfer to novel situations.

INFORMATION PROCESSING FRAMEWORK FOR PROSE LEARNING

The traditional approach to instructional research summarized in Table 1
is to conduct some instructional manipulation (e.g., producing method A
and method B) and then to measure the performance of students who learned
under each method. The performance measure is generally "amount recalled"
or "amount correct" on a retention test. Thus, under this approach, the
goal of research is to determine the effects of some observable manipulation on some observable behavior. In general, the results of such studies
may be summarized as "more (or less) is learned under method A than method
B."

Table 1

Research Variables for Studying "How Much Is Learned?"

INSTRUCTIONAL ————————————————————————————————⟶ PERFORMANCE
METHOD   MEASURES

One problem with this approach is that it does not provide an understanding of why or how method A is better than method B. We could have a much more powerful and useful psychology of instruction if we understood the general principles or mechanisms which mediate between the instruction and the test performance. This is where the "cognitive point of view" (see Farnham-Diggory, 1977) is relevant. In the cognitive approach to instructional research the goal is to determine how instructional procedures influence internal information processing events and the acquired cognitive structure.

Some of the major cognitive variables in instructional research are summarized in Table 2. As you can see, the table includes the two observable variables--the instructional method and the test performance. In addition, I have added some internal variables--<u>subject characteristics</u> such as what the learner already knows; <u>learning processes</u> such as paying attention or actively using existing knowledge during learning; <u>encoding processes</u>, such as assimilating new incoming information with old or adding new information to memory as presented.

Table 2

Research Variables for Studying "What is Learned?"

INSTRUCTIONAL METHOD →	(SUBJECT FEATURES & LEARNING PROCESSES) →	(ENCODING PROCESSES) →	(LEARNING OUTCOME) →	PERFORMANCE MEASURES
	Availability Reception Activation	Assimilation Addition	Integrated Isolated	

In this paper I will employ an information processing framework for describing the three "internal" variables in Table 2, with special focus on how people learn scientific information from text. The information processing view of learning and memory proposes that people may be thought of as processors of information (see Farnham-Diggory, 1976). In order to make some general comments about the "internal" variables in Table 2, allow me to introduce a simple information processing system. The system consists of short term memory, working memory, and long-term memory.

First, students may vary with respect to the cognitive structures (i.e. knowledge) and cognitive strategies that they bring to a learning situation. Some knowledge may be conceptually prerequisite to the to-be-learned information. In this case, we may evaluate learners as to the degree to which they possess conceptual knowledge. Let's call this an evaluation of <u>availability</u>--for meaningful learning one of the conditions that must be met is that the learner has relevant prerequisite knowledge available in his/her long term memory.

Second, subjects may vary with respect to the cognitive processes they use for meaningful learning. One obvious information processing event concerns whether or not students pay attention to the presented material. In this case, we may evaluate learners as to the degree to which they pay attention to the presented material. Let's call this an evaluation of <u>reception</u>--for meaningful learning one of the conditions that must be met is that the learner receives the presented information and transfers it to working memory.

Another basic information processing event involves the degree to which subjects transfer their prerequisite knowledge from long term memory to working memory. In other words, students may vary with respect to how actively they search long term memory and consciously think about that existing knowledge during learning. Let's call this activation--for meaningful learning one of the conditions that must be met is that the learner actively transfers relevant knowledge from his long term memory to active consciousness (i.e. working memory).

In short, I have presented three information processing conditions for meaningful learning---(a) reception of the presented material in working memory, (b) availability of prerequisite knowledge in long term memory, (c) transfer of prerequisite knowledge from a long term memory to working memory. If all three conditions are met, then, the presented information can be integrated within the context of existing knowledge--let's call this assimilative encoding. The outcome of this series of events will be an integrated learning outcome, i.e., the acquisition of cognitive structure with many connections to past experience. However, if condition (a) is not met there will be no learning, and if condition (b) or (c) is not met the learning process will involve addition learning. While these three conditions of meaningful learning and the possible learning outcomes represent very general characterizations of the learning process, it is useful to keep them in mind when assessing the impact of various instructional methods.

Table 3 presents predictions concerning the relation between learning outcomes and performance measures. For problem solving tests, subjects who acquired integrated learning outcomes should excel on problems requiring creative applications in new situations while subjects who have acquired isolated learning outcomes should excel on computing answers to problems like those given in the original passage. For recall, recognition, and retention tests, subjects with integrated learning outcomes should excel on recall of conceptual principles and related intrusions while subjects with isolated learning outcomes should focus on technical and formal information as well as the first few items in the passage. In addition, subjects with integrated learning outcomes will be more likely to recall information in a reworded format and in a reorganized order, while subjects with isolated learning outcomes will be likely to perform better on tests of verbatim memory and retention of information in its original presentation order. It should be noted that one learning outcome is not better than the other for all dependent measures; when the test involves specific retention of details and near transfer, subjects with isolated learning outcomes may perform best; when the test involves retention of conceptual principles or creative problem solving, subjects with integrated learning outcomes may perform best.

The literature on instructional psychology is replete with grand claims and conflicting results. However, there has been extensive research attention paid to a number of potentially important instructional techniques for influencing meaningful learning. In this paper I will examine five major types of instructional techniques. This paper is not meant to be an extensive review of the literature, but rather to provide the reader with examples that represent the state of the field. Further, my goal is to provide you with a perspective--e.g., the information processing framework outlined above--for making sense out of instructional research and claims. For example, I have chosen five instructional techniques

which should have an effect on one of the three major processes I listed
earlier--paying attention to the material, possessing a rich set of
existing concepts, actively using that knowledge to integrate the incoming
information. For each of the instruction techniques, I will try to point
out how these information processing events will be involved in determining what is learned.

Table 3

Predictions for Differences in Performance by
Subjects with Different Learning Outcomes

Performance Measure	Integrated Learning Outcome	Isolated Learning Outcome
Problem Solving Test	Excel on Far Transfer	Excel on Near Transfer
Recall Test (Content)	Focus on Conceptual Units	Focus on Technical & Formal Units
	Include Intrusions	Focus on Primacy Information
Recall Test (Structure)	Reword Information	Retain Verbatim Information
	Reorganize Sequence of Units	Retain Presentation Order

ORGANIZATION OF PROSE

Problem. This section deals with the role of prose organization. In
particular, this section examines the effects of organizations that
emphasize the conceptual principles vs. organizations that emphasize the
formal rules and facts. For example, in science and mathematics prose,
one organizational problem is to determine when the "formula" should be
presented: is it better to use a "formal-to-familiar" organization by
presenting the formula first, or is it better to use a "familiar-to-formal"
organization by giving concrete examples that build up to the formula?
Another related technique is to clearly organize the passage around
conceptual principles, or around the basic facts and actions. Based on
our information processing framework, we can predict that "conceptually
organized" or "familiar-to-formal" passages provide the learner with
familiar statements of the principles that can be used to interpret the
rest of the passage; thus, these techniques are more likely to lead to
meaningful learning outcomes with performance as predicted in Table 3.

Examples. As an example, suppose you wanted to teach someone the concept
of binomial probability. This rule allows one to compute answers to
questions such as, "What is the probability of flipping a coin five times
and getting heads to come exactly three times?" You could begin by presenting the formula in its abstract form, and then explaining how to use the
formula. I call this the formula method. Alternatively, you could begin
by presenting familiar, concrete background such as discussing what a
trial is, what an outcome is, what a success is, and so on. Examples such
as batting averages, probability of rain, and others could be used to
demonstrate each of the background concepts. Only when the learner

understood the underlying concepts, the instruction would go on to build up to the formula. I call this the general concepts method.

In order to investigate the effects of these two methods, we devised two instructional booklets--formula versus general concepts method--and asked students to read them. On a posttest we found that the formula group performed better than the general concepts group on a straightforward performance test involving problems like those given as examples. Thus, if we had stopped our assessment with a simple performance test we would have concluded that the formula method is best. However, we also included transfer problems. The general concepts group performed much better on unusual problems and on recognizing when the formula did or did not apply. Thus, there was an interaction in which formula subjects performed better on straightforward retention but general concepts performed better on transfer. A typical patter of results is shown in Table 4 (Mayer & Greeno, 1972, Exp. 1). These results, coupled with an extensive series of follow-up studies lead us to conclude that the groups differed not only in "how much" they learned, but also in the way they structured the information in memory (Mayer & Greeno, 1972; Mayer, Stiehl & Greeno, 1975; Mayer, 1974; Mayer, 1975a). In these studies an instructional sequence which moved from concrete underlying concepts to the formula (rather than starting with the formula) lead to better performance particularly for students with poor mathematics and science backgrounds and particularly on transfer questions.

Table 4

Proportion Correct on Near and Far Transfer Problems
for Two Text Organization Groups

Text Organization Group	Near Transfer	Far Transfer
Formula	.75	.43
General Concepts	.48	.73

More recently, Bruce Bromage and I (Bromage & Mayer, 1981) became interested in books which explain how technological devices work. For example, suppose you wanted to write a short manual to explain how to use a 35mm camera. We produced such a manual by trying to employ the same general information and style as in popular books on the topic. Our text consisted of the following types of information: descriptions of each part of the camera such as the "focus knob" or the "shutter speed dial"; descriptions of how adjusting one of the parts of the camera would affect the final picture such as "adjusting the focus knob will affect whether the picture is blurry"; and descriptions of the internal workings of the camera such as the idea that "turning the focus moves the film away or towards the vertex of the image inside the camera." Notice that knowing about the latter category--what we call "internal principles"-- is not essential for operating the camera, while the first two types of information are essential.

We asked non-camera users to read our manual, take a cued recall test, and then try some problem solving transfer items. The problems involved determining how to set the camera for an unusual situation, designing a special camera, etc. As you might expect some of our people performed quite well

on the problems while others performed poorly. We compared the recall
protocols of people who were able to perform well on the transfer problems
to those who were not. Good problem solvers did not differ from poor problem solvers in their ability to recall essential facts--i.e., how manipulating one part of the camera influences how the picture turns out--but
they did differ greatly in memory for internal principles. Although they
seem extraneous, the internal principles seem to be related to good problem
solving.

Armed with this new information we designed two versions of the manual--
one structured around the internal mechanisms of the camera and one
structured around the features of the outcome picture. Both contained the
same basic information but differed in organization and emphasis. On a
subsequent problem solving application test, the test organized around
internal mechanisms resulted in much better performance; however, the
groups did not differ on measures of simple retention of facts. Typical
results are shown in Table 5 (Bromage & Mayer, 1981, Exp. 2). Thus, these
results again exemplify the idea that the same content can be structured
differently, with drastically different learning outcomes as a result (see
Bromage & Mayer, 1981).

Table 5

Proportion Correct on Near and Far Transfer Problems
for Two Text Organization Groups

Text Organization Group	Near Transfer	Far Transfer
Standard	.68	.60
Conceptual	.68	.77

In another set of experiments, conducted by Nancy Loman, high school
students were asked to read a short passage about "How Cities Began" or
"The Mystery of Red Tides." The passages were presented either in their
standard version, or in a "signalled" version. The signalled text gave
headings to each of the major paragraphs so that the main principle was
made clear, and the signalled text provided additional cues to spell out
the causal chain such as "as a result of this." After reading the passage,
subjects were asked to take recall, retention, and problem solving tests.
Subjects in the signalled group tended to recall conceptual information
better than the non-signalled group, and tended to produce more creative
answers on the problem solving test, but the groups did not differ in
retention of details. Typical results for a group of "college preparatory"
readers are given in Table 6.

Table 6

Proportion Recalled by Type of Information, Proportion Correct
on Fact Retention, and Mean Number of Creative Problem
Solutions for Two Text Organization Groups

Text Organization Group	Recall		Fact Retention	Problem Solving
	General	Conceptual		
Non-Signalled	.32	.41	.93	.47
Signalled	.33	.66	.96	.90

Conclusion. The foregoing section provided three clear examples of
manipulations in text organization that lead to superior problem solving
performance on tests of far transfer: familiar-to-formal sequencing for
a passage on binomial probability, organization by underlying principles
for a passage on cameras, and signalled organization for a passage on red
tides. Each of these techniques serves to cue the reader at the beginning
of each section; the techniques encourage the reader to focus on ideas
and to use them to integrate the passage. Thus, each technique encourages
availability, reception, and activation, as described earlier in this
paper. In conclusion, these organizational techniques should be used when
the goal of instruction is meaningful learning that can support creative
problem solving; however, more standard techniques (e.g. formal-to-familiar,
or non-signalled) should be used when the goal of instruction is straight
retention of presented information.

CONCRETE ADVANCE ORGANIZERS

Problem. This section of the paper deals with the role of concrete models
as advance organizers in learning from science text. In particular, this
section investigates instructional situations in which an unfamiliar scientific text is preceded by a description of relevant concrete models which
are familiar to the learner. Since the early work of Brownell (1935),
mathematics instructors have noted the importance of using concrete models;
for example, manipulatives such as Dienes' blocks have been used to concretize computational algorithms. However, the use of concrete models and
analogies in prose instruction has not been as well documented.

One major research battleground concerns the role of advance organizers in
learning from prose (Ausubel, 1960, 1968; Mayer, 1979b). More recently,
new studies have been conducted in which the advance organizers involved
concrete, specific models rather than the abstract principles suggested
by Ausubel (Royer & Cable, 1975, 1976).

Similarly, we have conducted a series of studies in which subjects are
asked to read an elementary manual on computer programming (Mayer, 1975b,
1976, 1978, 1979a; Mayer & Bromage, 1980). A concrete model of the computer was presented either before or after reading the passage. The model
represented input as a ticket window, memory as an erasable scoreboard,
executive control as a shopping list, output as a message pad. Subjects
in the advance organizer group excelled on creative use of the presented
information in problem solving; subjects in the post-organizer group
performed as well or better than the advance organizer group on test items
involving simple retention of the presented information. In addition,
subjects in the advance organizer tended to recall more of the conceptual
information in the passage while subjects in the post-organizer group tended
to recall more of the technical facts. These results are consistent with
the idea that advance organizers provide an assimilative context to which
new information may be systematically integrated. Typical results are shown
in Table 7 (Mayer, 1976, Exp. 1) and Table 8 (Mayer & Bromage, 1980, Exp. 1).

Table 7

Proportion Correct on Near and Far Transfer Problems for Two Groups

Treatment Group	Near Transfer	Far Transfer
Model After Text	.70	.24
Model Before Text	.53	.37

Table 8

Mean Number of Recalled Idea Units by Type for Two Groups

Treatment Group	Technical & Format Idea Units	Conceptual Idea Units	Appropriate Intrusions
Model After Text	8.7	4.9	1.2
Model Before Text	6.9	6.6	4.3

Similar results were obtained using a manual for a different computer programming language and a different concrete model (Mayer, 1980). For example, a short manual was devised to teach a file management language; the model for this language consisted of file cabinets, in-baskets, save-baskets, discard-baskets, memory score board, and output pad. Results were similar to those obtained above: subjects who were given no model performed well on tests of recall for technical information and on very short problems like those in the booklet, while subjects who received the model prior to learning excelled on recall of conceptual information and on creative problem solving (far transfer). Typical results are shown in Table 9 (Mayer, 1980, Exp. 4 and 5).

Table 9

Proportion Recalled by Type of Information and Proportion Correct on Near and Far Transfer Problems for Two Groups

Treatment Group	Recall Test		Problem Solving Test	
	Technical & Format	Conceptual	Near Transfer	Far Transfer
No Model	.23	.16	.62	.27
Model Before Text	.15	.21	.67	.63

More recently, we conducted a study in which subjects listened to a tape recording about "how radar works" or about "Ohm's Law." Before listening to the tape, some subjects were given a simple diagram that symbolized the main principles of radar (e.g., transmission of pulse, reflection of pulse off a remote object, reception of returning pulse at source, measurement of time and angle, conversion to distance and location) or the main principles of Ohm's Law (e.g., a circuit, including battery, wire, and bulb). Following the passage, subjects took a variety of tests including recall, verbatim recognition, and creative problem solving. The subjects given no model before the passage recalled the technical facts and easily visualizable idea units well and excelled on verbatim recognition, while the subjects given the model before the passage excelled on recall of conceptual information and on creative problem solving. Typical results based on the radar passage are shown in Table 10.

Table 10

Proportion Recalled by Type of Idea Unit and Proportion Correct on Recognition and Problem Solving Tests for Two Groups

Treatment Group	Recall Test		Recognition Test (Verbatim)	Problem Solving (Far Transfer)
	Facts & Visual Idea Units	Conceptual Idea Units		
No Model	.31	.21	.59	.30
Model Before Text	.28	.31	.51	.55

There has been a great deal of additional research in this area. For example, in a recent review, I analyzed about 50 advance organizer studies (Mayer, 1979b). In general, advance organizers tend to have their strongest effects when the material is unfamiliar--so that the learner does not already possess his/her own model--or when the subject is a novice--again, so that the learner is unlikely to possess his/her own model--and when the dependent measure is creative problem solving. Some reviews which did not pay attention to these factors such as Barnes & Clawson's (1977) recent review conclude that the support for advance organizers is thin. However, when one pays attention to the conditions listed above, the case for advance organizers in prose learning becomes much stronger (Mayer, 1979b).

Conclusion. The foregoing section provided several clear examples of concrete advance organizers leading to superior far transfer performance; for a computer programming manual, for a file management manual, and for a lesson on how radar works. In each case, presenting a concrete model prior to the passage led to superior performance on recall of conceptual and superior far transfer, as predicted earlier in this paper. When the text presents information that is unfamiliar or technical and when the learner is not likely to possess or use his existing relevant analogies for comprehending the material, it is useful to carefully construct relevant analogies and to show the learner how elements in the text map into elements in the model. Procedures for model construction are discussed elsewhere (Mayer, 1979a, 1979b).

ELABORATION STRATEGIES

Problem. Another class of techniques that have been suggested as a way of increasing meaningful learning are elaboration techniques such as "note-taking." Rothkopf (1970) has used the term "mathemegenic activity" to refer to an overt behavior which influences learning. In addition, Wittrock (1974) has suggested that activities such as writing summaries and paraphrases of prose material are "generative activities" that serve to broaden learning. This generative hypothesis may be summarized within the context of our information processing framework presented earlier in this paper; notetaking may encourage the learner to search long-term memory for relevant underlying concepts and the act of writing down notes encourages an active integration of presented information with existing concepts. An alternative conception is that notetaking forces that the learner pay more attention, and thus should result in better learning overall.

Example. Suppose we asked our students to watch and listen to a short video-taped lecture on statistics or on how to use a computer. Some subjects are allowed to take notes as they watch the screen while others are not. Then, we give our students a test consisting of retention questions and problems which requre creative transfer. Will there be any difference in how notetakers and non-notetakers perform?

According to the generative theory, students who take notes are actively integrating the newly presented material with their own past experience; this should result in broader learning outcome which will support creative problem solving. According to the attention theory students who take notes simply pay more attention overall and thus should show better performance on all measures. In a recent series of experiments (Peper & Mayer, 1978), subjects who took notes performed better on far transfer test items but non-notetakers performed better on near transfer or retention

455 INSTRUCTIONAL VARIABLES IN TEXT PROCESSING

items. This pattern was particularly strong for low ability subjects, thus suggesting that high ability subjects have learned strategies for integrating the material even when notetaking is not allowed. Typical results are given in Table 11 (Peper & Mayer, 1978, Exp. 2).

Table 11

Proportion Correct on Near and Far Transfer Problems for Two Groups

| Treatment Group | Problem Solving Test | |
	Near Transfer	Far Transfer
No Notes	.46	.32
Notes	.36	.46

These results suggest that notetaking can result in a broader learning outcome. In order to get a better description of what is learned by notetakers and non-notetakers, another study was conducted in which students were asked to take a recall test rather than a problem solving test. Notetakers tended to produce more conceptual ideas and more intrusions from other information while non-notetakers produced more technical facts in their recall protocols. This pattern is consistent with the earlier results since it seems likely that creative problem solving is best supported by the conceptual ideas in the passage.

Past research on notetaking has been far from unanimous. However, in general the goal of previous research has been to determine whether or not notetaking helped overall retention. If we had limited our analysis simply to retention of presented information we also would have concluded, as many other studies, that notetaking does not affect learning. However, basing our description of notetaking on an information processing model, we were able to predict that notetaking should have its strongest effects on transfer problems, and that the effects should be strongest for subjects who do not possess the natural strategy of trying to integrate new information.

In order to bridge the gap between laboratory studies with word pairs and large scale development effects involving elaboration techniques (Dansereau, 1978; Weinstein, 1978; Levin, 1976; Pressley, 1977), we recently conducted a series of studies (Mayer, 1980). Subjects read a manual about computer programming either with elaboration activities after each unit or no elaboration activities. Elaboration activities consisted of telling how two ideas in the manual were alike and how they were different (comparative elaboration), or in telling how an idea in the manual related to a concrete example (model elaboration). Elaboration students performed much better than the other students particularly on transfer tests and on recall of major concepts, thus giving a pattern of results similar to notetaking and advance organizers. Apparently, the elaboration activity served to encourage students to integrate the information in the booklet with other knowledge.

In another study (Mayer & Cook, 1981) we used an elaboration technique which could interfere with the process of integrating new incoming information with existing knowledge. We asked students to listen to a 10-minute lecture on how radar works; half the subjects were asked to repeat back each phrase during short pauses in the tape while the other half were asked simply to listen carefully. According to our information processing model, the group that was forced to repeat the phrases would put more time into the attention process (reception of the material) but would have less time for finding available pre-requisite concepts and actively integrating the new material with those concepts. Thus, by forcing our students to repeat what we say, we were discouraging them from understanding the information.

The main principles in the passage were that a pulse is transmitted, it strikes remote object and is reflected back, and the time between trans- mission and return can be converted into a measure of distance. This principle was stated in several contexts in the text, as well as much technical and historical information. On a subsequent test, both groups performed equally well on retention of facts (as measured in true-false test) but the listen only group performed much better than the repeat group on problems requiring creative problem solving. In addition, in another study we asked subjects to recall all they could remember. Sub- jects, in the two groups performed equally well on recall of technical and historical facts but the listen only group recalled twice as much information about the underlying principles as described above. Typical results are shown in Table 12 (Mayer & Cook, 1981, Exp. 1 & 2). These results suggest that when students cannot give their full interest to a passage--either due to a distraction as in this study or due to anxiety or speed pressure--they are less likely to find the underlying principles.

Table 12

Proportion Recalled by Type of Information and Proportion Correct
on Near and Far Transfer Problems for Two Groups

Treatment Group	Recall Test		Problem Solving Test	
	Nonconceptual Idea Units	Conceptual Idea Units	Retention of Facts	Far Transfer
Nonshadow	.29	.26	.82	.81
Shadow	.24	.11	.79	.49

Another processing strategy that a reader can use is to repeat a passage. For example, on the first reading of technical passage a reader may not be able to locate the major concepts and structure but after several repetitions the reader may be able to organize his/her reading around the major principles. In order to investigate this idea, Bruce Bromage and I asked subjects to listen to a passage (such as radar, Ohm's Law, or exposure meters) either one, two or three times. Then, subjects took tests such as recall, verbatim recognition, and problem solving (far transfer). In general, subjects' performance was much different after one presentation than after three presentations: the one presentation group per- formed better on verbatim recognition and recall of specific facts but the three presentation group performed better on verbatim recognition and recall of princi- ples. Typical results based on the radar passage are summarized in Table 13.

Table 13

Proportion Recalled by Type of Information and Proportion Correct
on Recognition and Problem Solving Tests for Three Groups

Treatment Group	Recall Test		Recognition (Verbatim)	Problem Solving (Far Transfer)
	Facts & Visual Units	Conceptual Idea Units		
One Presentation	.28	.18	.59	.30
Two Presentation	.32	.18	.43	.37
Three Presentation	.35	.39	.28	.62

Conclusion. These results show that it is important that students be encouraged to actively process prose material. Exercises such as putting the information in one's own words, as in notetaking, encourage an active learning process in which new information is integrated with existing knowledge. However, action per se, such as shadowing where a student blindly copies the material, does not normally result in meaningful learning. Instructions should involve activities which encourage the learner to actively search for relevant past experience and to integrate the presented information with that past experience.

PRETRAINING IN PREREQUISITE KNOWLEDGE

Problem. If a learner lacks appropriate prerequisite knowledge, then meaningful learning cannot take place. In order to enhance the reader's understanding, pretraining can be given in which relevant prerequisite knowledge is learned. Then, this knowledge will be available during acquisition of new material, and can be used for integrating the new incoming information.

Example. In order to test this idea, Linda Cook asked subjects who had no prior coursework or experience in natural science to read a passage on "density." Some subjects were given pretraining concerning the prerequisite concepts--mass and volume--while other subjects were given no pretraining. After reading the passage, subjects took a recall and problem solving test. Subjects given pretraining were more likely to produce the density principle in words or sentences and subjects given no pretraining were more likely to recall the density formula in formal symbols. In addition, the pretraining group performed more poorly on verbatim recall but better on far transfer than the no pretraining group. Typical results are given in Table 14.

Table 14

Mean Number of Idea Units Recalled by Type, Mean Verbatim Recall Score and Proportion Correct on Near and Far Transfer Problems for Two Groups

Treatment Group	Recall Test		Verbatim Score	Problem Solving	
	Words	Symbols		Near Transfer	Far Transfer
No Pretraining	.9	5.4	2.3	.72	.54
Pretraining	2.2	2.4	1.7	.68	.78

In an earlier study, subjects read a booklet about probability theory (Mayer, Stiehl & Greeno, 1975). Some subjects were given pretraining in the underlying concepts such as "trial" and "outcome" while others were not. Instructional methods that fostered meaningful learning were far more effective for pretrained subjects than the no pretraining group. However, instructional methods that emphasized the formula and did not foster meaningful learning were equally effective regardless of pretraining. These results suggest that "availability" of prerequisite knowledge is important only when the passage attempts to teach in meaningful way, such as the familiar-to-formal sequencing discussed earlier.

Conclusion. These results suggest that meaningful learning requires that the learner have specifically relevant knowledge available at the time of learning. For students who lack this knowledge, one alternative is to provide text that is non-conceptual. However, another alternative is to provide appropriate pretraining in specific knowledge that is prerequisite,

INSTRUCTIONAL IMPLICATIONS

and then use meaningful instructional passages.

INSERTED QUESTIONS

Problem. Another technique which has been suggested to influence meaningful learning is the use of adjunct or inserted questions. In general, summaries of the inserted question literature (Frase, 1968; Mayer, 1977), show that when questions are inserted in a passage performance on a final test which covers the same material is improved. There have been two basic theories to account for this inserted question effect--a backwards theory and a forwards theory. The backwards theory states that students use the question as a chance to review the specific material in the question; thus students have an extra exposure to the material that is involved in the question. The forwards theory states that the questions serve to direct the readers' attention on subsequent portions of the passage; based on previous questions, students develop expectations concerning which type of information is important in the text.

Examples. Suppose you wanted to teach students about set theory and the laws of probability. In order to accomplish this task, I (Mayer, 1975c) developed eight sequential lessons. Each lesson had the same general form in that it presented a formula with definitions of each variable, it presented an example of how to compute a value using the formula, and it presented a concrete example of the principle underlying the formula. I then constructed three sets of the questions for each lesson--questions on definitions, questions on computing an answer, and questions about the concrete model. Students read each of the first six lessons in order, with questions as part of each lesson; on each of the first six lessons a student received solely definition questions, solely computation questions, solely model questions, all three or none.

Imagine yourself as the learner in this task. For each six lessons you are asked the same type of question. How would this influence your infor- mation processing strategy on the seventh and eighth lesson? Would you pay more attention to that part of the text that contained the type of information you expected to be tested on? Students in our study tended to behave as if previous tests influenced how they studied new material. In our study, we gave all three types of questions after lesson seven and after lesson eight. Students who had expected only definition questions performed well on definition questions but poorly on the other questions; students who expected model questions performed quite well on model ques- tions and also performed well on the other questions. A particularly inter- esting aspect of the result is that we obtained the same pattern when the questions were given before each of the first six lessons (without students having to solve them) as when they were given after each of the first six lessons (with students actually having to solve them).

These results are consistent with the idea that previous test questions influence processing of new material. Thus, inserted questions have a "forward effect" of drawing students' attention to particular parts of the material. Related studies by Watts & Anderson (1971) and by McConkie, Rayner & Wilson (1973) have provided complementary evidence that the type of question you ask influences the information processing strategy of stu- dents on subsequent reading.

Conclusion. Inserted questions can have both desirable and undesirable effects. For example, telling a student in advance of learning that he or she should be able to answer a given set of questions may have the effect of encouraging the student to ignore incidental material. Further, giving students questions which emphasize computation may limit the students' learning strategy. Questions may serve as road signs telling the learner what to pay attention to and what to ignore. If the goal of instruction is the acquisition of a well defined set of responses to a well defined set of questions then explicit emphasis on these questions before and during the text is appropriate. However, if the goal of instruction is the production of students who will be able to creatively solve novel problems and who will be able to build new learning on old, then more consideration must be paid to using a balanced set of questions--questions which will not serve as blinders.

SUMMARY

In this paper I have attempted to summarize five instructional techniques for increasing the meaningfulness of technical or scientific information. Each technique has received much research attention, with less than perfectly consistent results. However, when we take the point of view of our students, and try to describe how these techniques influence information processing events during learning, we are better able to make sense out of the literature. The examples I have presented are representative of much of my own research in this field. Based on this work it seems clear to me that instructional techniques influence the learning process in systematic and predictable ways. The goal of research on the psychology of learning and instruction must be to continue to develop precise descriptions of the mechanisms involved. I hope that this paper has encouraged you that such work will have increasing relevance not only for cognitive theory but also for the difficult task of developing instructional procedures in science.

REFERENCES

Ausubel, D. P. The use of advance organizers in the learning and retention of meaningful verbal material. Journal of Educational Psychology, 1960, 51, 267-272.
Ausubel, D. P. Educational psychology: A cognitive view. New York: Holt, Rinehart and Winston, 1968.
Barnes, R. R. & Clawson, E. U. Do advance organizers facilitate learning? Recommendations for further research based on an analysis of 32 studies. Review of Educational Research, 1975, 45, 637-659.
Bromage, B. & Mayer, R. E. Relationship between what is remembered and creative problem solving in science learning. Journal of Educational Psychology, 1981, 73, 451-461.
Brownell, W. A. Psychological considerations in the learning and teaching of arithmetic. In The teaching of arithmetic: Tenth yearbook of the National Council of Teachers of Mathematics. New York: Columbia University Press, 1935.
Dansereau, D. The development of a learning strategies curriculum. In H. F. O'Neil, Jr., (Ed.), Learning strategies. New York: Academic Press, 1978.
Duncker, K. On problem solving. Psycholopical monographs 1945, 58:5. Whole No. 270.
Farnham-Diggory, S. The cognitive point of view. In D. J. Treffinger, J. K. Davis, & R. E. Ripple (Eds.), Handbook on teaching educational psychology. New York: Academic Press, 1977.

Frase, L. T. Some data concerning the mathemagenic hypothesis. _American Educational Research Journal_, 1968, _5_, 181-189

Katona, G. _Organizing and memorizing_: New York: Columbia University Press, 1940.

Levin, J. R. What have we learned about maximizing what children learn? In J. R. Levin & V. L. Allen (Eds.), _Cognitive learning in children_: _Theory and strategy_. New York, Academic Press, 1976.

Luchins, A. S. Mechanization in problem solving. _Psychological Monographs_, 1942, _54:6_ Whole No. 248.

Mayer, R. E. Acquisition processes and resilience under varying testing conditions for structurally different problem-solving procedures. _Journal of Educational Psychology_, 1974, _66_, 644-656.

Mayer, R. E. Information processing variables in learning to solve problems. _Review of Educational Research_, 1975, _45_, 525-541. (a)

Mayer, R. E. Different problem solving strategies established in learning computer programming with and without meaningful models. _Journal of Educational Psychology_, 1975, _67_, 725-734. (b)

Mayer, R. E. Forward transfer of different reading strategies evoked by testlike events in mathematics text. _Journal of Educational Psychology_ 1975, _67_, 165-169. (c)

Mayer, R. E. Some conditions of meaningful learning for computer programming: Advance organizers and subject control of frame order. _Journal of Educational Psychology_, 1976, _68_, 143-150.

Mayer, R. E. The sequencing of instruction and the concept of assimilation to schema. _Instructional Science_, 1977, _6_, 369-388.

Mayer, R. E. Advance organizers that compensate for the organization of text. _Journal of Educational Psychology_, 1978, _70_, 880-886.

Mayer, R. E. Can advance organizers influence meaningful learning? _Review of Educational Research_, 1979, _49_, 371-383. (a)

Mayer, R. E. Twenty years of research on advance organizers: Assimilation theory is still the best predictor of results. _Instructional Science_, 1979, _8_, 133-167. (b)

Mayer, R. E. Elaboration techniques that increase the meaningfulness of technical text: An experimental test of the learning strategy hypothesis. _Journal of Educational Psychology_, 1980, _72_, 209-225.

Mayer, R. E. & Bromage, B. Different recall protocols for technical text due to advance organizers. _Journal of Educational Psychology_, 1980, _72_, 209-225.

Mayer, R. E. & Cook, L. Effects of shadowing on prose comprehension and problem solving. _Memory and Cognition_, 1981, _8_, 101-109.

Mayer, R. E. & Greeno, J. G. Structural differences between learning outcomes produced by different instructional methods. _Journal of Educational Psychology_, 1972, _63_, 165-173.

Mayer, R. E., Stiehl, C. C. & Greeno, J. G. Acquisition of understanding and skill in relation to subjects' preparation and meaningfulness of instruction. _Journal of Educational Psychology_, 1975, _67_, 331-350.

McConkie, G. W., Rayner, K. & Wilson, S. J. Experimental manipulation of reading strategies. _Journal of Educational Psychology_, 1973, _65_, 1-8.

Peper, R. J. & Mayer, R. E. Note taking as a generative activity. _Journal of Educational Psychology_, 1978, _70_, 514-522.

Pressley, M. Imagery and children's learning: Putting the picture in developmental perspective. _Review of Educational Research_, 1977, _47_, 585-622

Rothkopf, E. Z. The concept of mathemagenic activities. _Review of Educational Research_, 1970, _40_, 325-336.

Royer, J. M. & Cable, G. W. Facilitated learning in connected discourse. _Journal of Eduational Psychology_, 1975, 67, 116-123.

Royer, J. M. & Cable, G. W. Illustrations, analogies, and facilitative transfer in prose learning. _Journal of Educational Psychology_, 1976, 68, 205-209.

Watts, G. H. & Anderson, R. C. Effects of three types of inserted questions on learning from prose. _Journal of Educational Psychology_, 1971, 62, 387-394.

Weinstein, C. E. Elaboration skills as a learning strategy. In H. F. O'Neil (Ed.), _Learning Strategies_, New York: Academic Press, 1978.

Wertheimer, M. _Productive thinking_. New York: Harper & Row, 1959.

White, R. T. & Mayer, R. E. Understanding of intellectual skills. _Instructional Science_, 1980, 9, 101-127.

Wittrock, M. C. Learning as a generative process. _Educational Psychologist_, 1974, 11, 87-95.

FOOTNOTE

Preparation of this paper was supported by Grant SED-80-14950 form the National Science Foundation. Program of Research in Science Education (RISE). The following people conducted some of the research described in this paper: Bruce Bromage, Linda Cook, Nancy Loman.

DISCOURSE PROCESSING
A. Flammer and W. Kintsch (eds.)
© North-Holland Publishing Company, 1982

CONCRETE ANALOGIES AS AIDS IN LEARNING FROM TEXT[1]

P.RobertJan Simons
Department of Instructional Psychology
Tilburg University
Tilburg
The Netherlands

Various theorists have proposed different reasons for the
usefulness of concrete analogies in written texts. Some stress
a concretizing function, others a structurizing function, and
still others suggest that analogies induce a more active
processing of the text. The main question which we tried to
answer in a series of six experiments were: (a) Does the addition of concrete analogies lead to higher performances and
longer reading-times in subjects of different ages? (b) What
are the effects under restricted time conditions? (c) Why are
concrete analogies effective? (d) Are there aptitude-treatment
interactions? In general, the results showed that subjects,
when confronted with analogies, not only studied longer, but
learned more and different things. However, if the study time
was limited, these effects disappeared. Furthermore some aptitude-treatment interactions were found, especially in the case
of the visualizer-verbalizer dimension. All three of the above
mentioned functions of analogies were supported by the data.

LEARNING VIA ANALOGIES

In the past few years, there has been a revival of interest in the role of analogies in human learning, thinking and development. Some examples of this renewed
interest can be seen in the study of Sternberg (1977a) and Gick and Holyoak (1980)
who studied the process of analogical reasoning, Billow (1977) and Ortony, Reynolds
and Arter (1978) who studied developmental aspects of analogical reasoning and
Pask (1976) who looked at the use of spontaneous analogies in learning. This paper
concerns learning via analogies. General conclusions are reported from six experiments on effects of experimenter-provided analogies.

Analogical reasoning was defined by Sternberg (1977b) as follows: "We reason analogically whenever we make a decision about something new in our experience by
drawing a parallel to something old. When we buy a goldfish because we liked our
old one, or when we listen to a friend's advice because it was correct once before,
we are reasoning analogically" (p. 353). Likewise, we learn via analogies whenever
we draw a parallel between to be learned information and old information we already
learned before. Learning via analogies may proceed in at least three different
ways. First, learners may spontaneously search for comparable old information
(Pask, 1976). Second, learners may be stimulated to search for comparable information in their cognitive structure (Wittrock, 1979). Third, comparable information
may be presented to the learner. This last category is discussed in this paper.

When we present analogical information to learners with the hope of beneficially
affecting their learning-processes, at least one of the following conditions should
be met: (a) the analogical information is already known to the learner but his or
her knowledge should be refreshed; (b) the analogical information is already known
to the learner but his or her knowledge should be integrated and pointed at the

known information; (c) the analogical information is new, but is easier to
learn (or understand) than the to be learned information (for instance,
because it can be easily assimilated to prior knowledge, or because it is
familiar to the learner); (d) the analogical information is more concrete
than the to be learned information (for instance, because it can be demonstrated, pictured or taken apart). The analogies we used in our experiments
met the last three conditions, thus as far as the information presented was
known to the subjects, this knowledge was directed at the task at hand. As
far as it was not known, it was easier to learn because it was more concrete
and more familiar to the learners.

The analogies we used were of a rather broad type. In some experiments we
compared several electricity concepts (current, voltage, resistance, conduc-
tionity, etc.) to several water-flow concepts. In other experiments, we
compared the behavior of electrons in a wire to the behavior of a group of
children entering a restaurant, each searching for a chair. In another experiment the structure of a computer was compared to the structure of a
post-office. Finally, assimilation and accomodation in cognitive structures
were compared to adaptation processes in a football-team.

FUNCTIONS OF CONCRETE ANALOGIES

Various theorists have proposed different reasons why the presentation of
analogies might be an effective learning-aid. Some theorists stress that
analogies make abstract information imaginable, concrete and vivid (Davidson,
1976; Ortony, 1975). Others, however, stress a completely different function,
that being a structuring function (e.g. Norman, 1978; Rumelhart and Ortony,
1977). This second group stresses that in learning via analogies an existent
schema is used as a kind of formal structure in which new information is
absorbed. The existent schema may aid students in comprehending the structure of the new text. A third function of analogies stems from the assimi-
lationintegration theory of Mayer (1979a,b) and from the generative meaning
theory of Wittrock (1979). According to Mayer, analogies may induce an integrative assimilation process (at least under some conditions) which lead to
qualitatively different learning-outcomes (Mayer and Bromage, 1980). Likewise Wittrock (1979) stated that the effectivity of learning depends on the
number and kind of transformations which a learner performs. In some cases
analogies may stimulate learners to transform information more deeply and
more actively.

Apart from these possible positive functions of analogies, in our view,
several possible drawbacks of their use can be discerned. These drawbacks
have been distilled from discussions with practicing teachers and, occasionally, from the educational literature (e.g. Miller, 1976; Davidson, 1976).
Drawbacks of analogies in texts seem to be of the following nature: (a) they
may confuse pupils, especially younger ones; (b) they may create cognitive
distortion (Davidson, 1976); (c) they may be superfluous (cf. Parkhurst,
1975); (d) they may require the use of extra learning-time; (e) they may
block real understanding of abstract information causing pupils to get stuck
on a concrete level without ever reaching the level of abstract insight; and
(f) they may strengthen a concrete attitude of pupils.

PRIOR RESEARCH

Most of the prior research on concrete analogies as aids in learning has

been directed at the effectivity question: "Does learning with the aid of
analogies cause better learning results?". Results of these studies were,
in general, rather clear. The majority of the investigators found significantly higher results for learning with than without analogies (Scandura and
Wells, 1967; Lesh (cited in Mayer, 1979b); Mayer, 1975, 1976, 1978, 1979a,b;
Rigney and Lutz, 1976; Royer and Cable, 1975, 1976). Exceptions were the
studies of Bell and Gagné (1979) and Devine-Hawkins (cited in Davidson, 1976).
Some investigators (particularly Mayer) found support for the contention
that analogies also bring qualitatively different results (especially Mayer
and Bromage, 1980). Furthermore some aptitude-treatment-interactions with
intelligence as aptitude were found (Mayer, 1975; Bell and Gagné, 1979).

When compared to results of other fields of research in educational psychology (i.e. advance organizers, Barnes and Clawson, 1975), the results of
these studies on analogies seem rather consistent and clear. The number of
studies, however, was rather small and the research was in some ways limited.
For one thing, almost all of the studies employed college students (exception:
Rigney and Lutz, 1976). Furthermore, no research was done on the efficiency
question (cf. Faw and Waller, 1976), nor did any investigator take reading-
time effects into account (exception: Scandura and Wells, 1967). Finally, in
most studies very short texts were used. Many prior studies have been directed at questions raised by Mayer's assimilation theory (see for a review
Mayer, 1979a, b). No research, however, has been directed at the other two
discerned theoretical functions of concrete analogies, that being their concretizing and structurizing functions. Our research, described in this paper,
aimed at filling in the described gaps. Thus, our experiments were carried
out with younger subjects and relatively long texts. Furthermore, the two other
functions of analogies were investigated (see below) and much attention was
given to reading-time and efficiency.

A VIEW ON READING-TIME

Analogies (and other reading aids) may exert three different kinds of
influence on reading-time. Analogies may directly influence reading-time
because of the extra words involved. Analogies should be read by the subjects
and this reading will take time. Though this direct effect on reading-time
was investigated in research on other reading aids (i.e. advance-organizers
cf. Faw and Waller, 1976), as yet no research on direct reading-time effects
of analogies has been done. Apart from these direct effects, however, one
can discern two kinds of indirect effects. These indirect effects were
neither controlled for nor measured in prior research on analogies or reading aids in general. This omission is a very serious one, because indirect
effects may confound results (this view is exposed more fully in my dissertation (Simons, 1980) and in Simons (in preparation)).

The first indirect effect may be called an indirect lengthening-effect.
Reading aids may cause subjects to study the text longer (this apart from
the direct effect). For example, because analogies may stimulate a different
kind of processing behavior in the reader (i.e. more actively, more deeply,
in a comparative way), the text as such may be processed in a slower tempo
than a text without analogies. The second indirect effect is an indirect
shortening of reading-time. Reading aids may facilitate the reading of the
text as such (this is exactly why they are constructed!), causing an increase
in the reading-tempo. For example, because of the presence of an analogy a
subject might understand a text sooner than when this analogy is lacking and
thus be able to read the text more quickly and easily.

One might object that these two indirect effects are controlled in normally used experimental designs, in which experimental and control groups are allotted the same (nominal) amount of time. This objection, however, is wrong. Equal-time-allotment is no guarantee that indirect effects are controlled for when time-limits are broad. In almost all prior experiments on reading aids (for good reasons) broad time-limits were imposed. Therefore, many subjects will not have used all of the permitted time. Thus, results of prior experiments may have been confounded by indirect effects: significant differences in results may have been caused by an indirect lengthening of reading-times and non-significant differences by an indirect shortening. All of this leads to the proposition that it is better not to try to control indirect effects, but rather that one should carefully measure reading-times under free-time-conditions and take them into account.

RESEARCH QUESTIONS AND HYPOTHESES

The experiments, summarized here, were directed at answering the following questions:
(1) Does the addition of concrete analogies to texts lead to higher performances in elementary and secondary school pupils?
(2) Does this addition of analogies lead to longer reading-times (direct and indirect effects)?
(3) What are the effects under restricted-time conditions?
(4) Are there aptitude-treatment-interactions?
(5) What functions do analogies have in learning from texts? Or stated differently: "Why are analogies effective?"
As to the last question (why?) the following hypotheses were formulated:
(a) If concrete analogies function to make texts more imaginable, then an interaction-effect as to a visualizer-verbalizer dimension should show up.
(b) If concrete analogies help subjects to get a better impression of the (formal) structure of subject-matter, then an interaction-effect as to a structurizing-style should be significant and subjects should have a better view of the structure of the subject matter. (c) If concrete analogies lead to a different kind of processing (i.e. more actively, more deeply), then the following effects will appear: (1) an interaction-effect as to general intelligence and advance-knowledge; (2) differences in reading-times (different processing might take different time); (3) effects on certain dependent variables (comprehension, transfer).

METHOD

In each of the six experiments 80 - 100 subjects participated. Subjects were from secondary schools (3 experiments), elementary schools (1 experiment) and college students (2 experiments). All experiments consisted of 3 or 4 sessions of 2 hours each. During the first session a pretest was administered consisting of items from the posttest. Furthermore, subjects were administered certain "background gathering" tests (different per experiment). Structurizing style, for example, was measured via the use of Pask's Spy Ring History Test (Pask, 1976) and via the Hidden Figure Test. The visualizer-verbalizer dimension was measured via procedures designed by Boekaerts (1979) and Richardson (1978). Intelligence was measured via an analogical-reasoning-ability-test.

In the next session(s) subjects studied (read) texts of approximately 20 pages on electricity (3 experiments), the theory of Piaget, computer-programming

and the human blood system. Subjects were assigned randomly to either of two
or three conditions. In one or two conditions, texts were extended with concrete analogies (see the introduction). The other condition was a text only
control condition. In some experiments subjects were required to read the
text several times, registering their reading-times each time they finished
a reading. Sometimes direct effects of analogies were measured separately
by presenting them apart from the text. At other times the analogies were
woven into the texts. In other experiments the so called efficiency method
was used (Peeck, 1977). In this method experimental subjects are allowed the
same amount of time to study a text plus analogies as control subjects have
for the text only. After the learning-phase different achievement-tests were
administered (comprehension, transfer, knowledge) and different control-tests
(use of analogies, knowledge of analogies). In one experiment a relation-test
was given to the subjects (Lodewijks, 1981). In this test subjects must rate
all possible pairs of concepts as to their relatedness. These ratings are
compared to expert ratings. Two scores emerge from this test, a reproductive
(rep) and a productive (prod) score. Rep denotes the extent to which a subject reproduced the relations exposed in the text. Prod relates to the extent
to which a subject produced relations between concepts that were not stated
explicitly in the text, but were considered important by the experts. The
last session was devoted to a long-term-retention-test and to the debriefing
of the subjects. Data were analysed by way of regression-analyses (Kerlinger
and Pedhazur, 1973).

RESULTS

PERFORMANCE EFFECTS
As to the first question (higher performances under unlimited time conditions?), results indicated on all dependent variables differences in favour
of the learning with analogies, though these differences were not always
significant. (See the results of one experiment in Figure 1).
In this experiment significant results were obtained on the first comprehen-
sion-test (F=6.79; p<.05) and on the factual-detail-test filled in after
three weeks (F=4.72; p<.05). Results on the other two dependent measures
were not significant (F-values of 2.28 and 2.65).

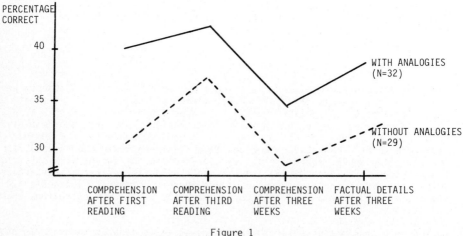

Figure 1
Results on 4 dependent variables in an experiment
with 61 secondary-school-children learning science

There was no support for the contention that analogies only lead to higher far-transfer and comprehension results and not to higher factual-knowledge. On all three kinds of performance-measures significant and non-significant differences were found. Subjects learning with the help of analogies had a significantly better view of the structure of the concepts, as measured by the relation-test (F(1,80) = 7.05; p <.01; 8.1% variance).

TIME-EFFECTS
Results as to time-spending were different for younger and older subjects. Secondary-school-pupils spent both time to read the extra text on the analogies (direct effect) and more time on the text as such (indirect effect). Indirect lenthening of reading-time occured during the first-reading of the text (significant in one experiment, not in a replication-study). Also indirect shortening of reading-time occurred during the second and third reading (non-significant in the first experiment, significant in the replication-study). These indirect effects are illustrated in Figure 2 (first experiment). The first reading took significantly more time in the condition with analogies (F=33.06; p<.01). No significant differences were found on the second and third reading (F=1.10, n.s.).

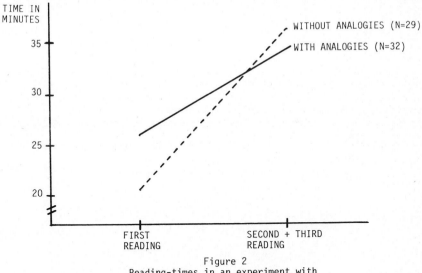

Figure 2
Reading-times in an experiment with
61 secondary-school-children learning science

With college students different results as to time spending appeared. Experimental subjects used approximately the same amount of time to study the analogies (400 words) and the text as the control subjects did for the text only. Thus, an indirect shortening of reading-time compensated for direct and/or indirect lengthening effects.

RESTRICTIVE TIME CONDITIONS
In two experiments restrictive time-limits were imposed. In these cases no significant differences between learning with and without analogies were

found. Thus, learning with analogies does not seem to be more efficient than learning without. These results, however, contrast with the results of the other experiments where no time-limits were imposed. In these cases, statistical control of time-variations by way of regression-analysis did not make performance-differences disappear (see further the discussion section).

APTITUDE-TREATMENT-INTERACTIONS
Several significant aptitude-treatment-interactions were found. In two experiments (interestingly enough these were the experiments with time-limits) interactions of the treatment (with or without analogies) and visualizer-verbalizer-dimensions were significant (F=6.69; p<.05). These interactions accounted for 10-15% of the variance (see Figure 3).

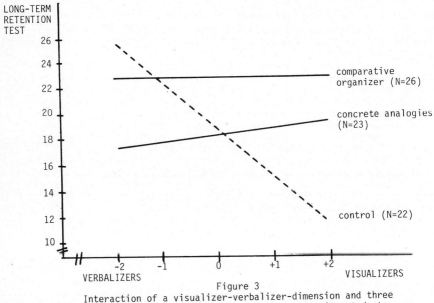

Figure 3
Interaction of a visualizer-verbalizer-dimension and three treatments in an experiment with 71 university students

Also, interactions with the structuring-style dimension proved to be significant (14.5% of the variance; F(1,57) = 10.62; p <.05). This last interaction, however, did not reappear in a replication-study. Inconsistent results were also found in reference to general intelligence: In one experiment a significant interaction was found (elementary school subjects), in other experiments, however, this result was not replicated. The following characteristics of subjects did not interact with the treatments: field(in)dependence, age, pretest, type of school and attitude towards mathematics.

WHY ARE CONCRETE ANALOGIES EFFECTIVE?
All three of the hypotheses on the why-questions found support in the data. The concretizing explanation was given credence through the appearance of

the significant interactions with the visualizer-verbalizer dimension. The structurizing explanation was supported by the (inconsistent) interaction with the structurizing-style and by the results on the relation-test presented above. Several of the results were in agreement with the different-processing-hypothesis (assimilation-integration-theory and generative meaning theory). Both results on reading-time (analogies caused slower reading in secondary-school children) and results on comprehension and transfertests (not elaborated here) support this hypothesis. Furthermore, all of our subjects had no advance-knowledge of the subject matter. That significant main-effects of analogies were found with subjects without advance-knowledge, agrees with the different processing explanation (cf. Mayer, 1979).

DISCUSSION

Though it has been shown that concrete analogies are effective learning aids, their efficiency appears to be questionable. In the experiments with time-limits, no differences between learning with and learning without analogies could be shown. On the other hand in two of our experiments without time-limits, differences remained significant after partialing out time-variance. This discrepancy may be solved in the following two ways. First, one should realize that results under restrictive time conditions depend upon arbitrarily chosen time-limits. In most cases one has no argument as to why a certain time-limit should be chosen above another. Yet results may be different under different time-conditions. Perhaps the particularly chosen time-limit may have been too short to make performance differences possible. This dependence of results on time-limits, forms a serious argument against the use of time-limits (see Simons, in preparation). Second, it might be possible that, especially with younger subjects, concrete analogies may only be effective when there is enough time available for both the direct effect (time to read the extra text) and the indirect lengthening of reading time (time to compare the concepts with their analogs). Important questions become then: "Is this extra time-investment worthwhile?"; "Is it worthwhile that subjects are willing to spend more time?" and "How much time is normally available?"

Three explanations were discerned for the effectivity of concrete analogies as reading aids. Results of our experiments do not make it possible to point to one best explanation. The only thing we may conclude is that all three explanations may be operating. This forms an important extension of the current theories on analogies. One should in the future not restrict theorizing on analogies to the different-processing-view alone, but should also consider the concretizing and structurizing views. In future research, analogies might be designed in such a way that they may trigger one of the three functions specifically (concretizing analogies vs structurizing analogies etc.).

The conclusions as to the "why" question should be viewed in proper perspective. Necessarily, these conclusions should be made cautiously because of the distance between data and conclusions. We only found indications, not firm evidence. The conclusions, for instance, that analogies make a text more imaginable because the interaction with a visualizer-verbalizer-dimension was significant remains to be checked against an imagery-control: Is this interaction indeed to be explained in terms of better imaginability of phenomena or concepts? This could be checked by way of a questionaire. Finally, we would like to discuss a practical implication of all of this. Because analogies were effective under some conditions (e.g. time) and for some types of students (visualizers), but uneffective under other conditions and for other types of students, differentiation seems necessary. It does not makes sense to make special books with analogies for visualizers and others without them for verbalizers. The data-base for such an implication is still too weak. Furthermore, it is not as yet possible to measure these individual differences in a practical setting. Instead, more concrete analogies should be included in text books than is done thus far, but these analogies should be placed in such a way that subjects are free to either use them or not.

NOTES

1) I wish to thank drs. P. Kirschner for useful comments on substance and style of the manuscript.

REFERENCES

Barnes, B.R., & Clawson, E.U., Do advance organizers facilitate learning? *Review of Educational Research*, 1975, *45*, 637-659.
Bell, M.S., & Gagné, E.D., *Individual differences and the use of analogies in technical text*. Paper presented at the meeting of the American Educational Research Association, San Francisco, april 1979.
Billow, R.M., Metaphor: A review of the psychological literature. *Psychological Bulletin*, 1977, *84*, 81-92.
Boekaerts, M., *Towards a theory of learning based on individual differences*. Ghent (Belgium): Communication and Cognition, 1979.
Davidson, R.E., The role of metaphor and analogy in learning. In J.R. Levin, & V.L. Allen (Eds.), *Cognitive learning in children*. New York: Academic Press, 1976, 135-162.
Faw, H.W., & Waller, T.G., Mathemagenic behaviours and efficiency in learning from prose. *Review of Educational Research*, 1976, *46*, 691-720.
Gick, M.L., & Holyoak, K.J., Analogical problem solving. *Cognitive Psychology*, 1980, *12*, 306-355.
Kerlinger, F.N., & Pedhazur, E.J., *Multiple regression in behavioral research*. New York: Holt, Rinehart & Winston, 1973.
Lodewijks, J.G.C.L., *Leerstofsequenties: van conceptueel netwerk naar cognitieve structuur*. Doctoral dissertation, Tilburg University, 1981.
Mayer, R.E., Different problem-solving competencies established in learning computer programming with and without meaningful models. *Journal of Educational Psychology*, 1975, *67*, 725-734.
Mayer, R.E., Some conditions of meaningful learning of computer programming: Advance organizers and subject control of frame sequencing. *Journal of Educational Psychology*, 1976, *68*, 143-150.
Mayer, R.E., Advance organizers that compensate for the organization of text. *Journal of Educational Psychology*, 1978, *70*, 880-886.
Mayer, R.E., Can advance organizers influence meaningful learning? *Review of Educational Research*, 1979, *49*, 371-383.
Mayer, R.E., Twenty years of research on advance organizers: Assimilation theory is still the best predictor of results. *Instructional Science*, 1979, *8*, 133-167.
Mayer, R.E., & Bromage, B.K., Different recall protocols for technical texts due to advance organizers. *Journal of Educational Psychology*, 1980, *72*, 209-225.

Miller, R.M., The dubious case for metaphors in educational writing. *Educational Theory*, 1976, *26*, 174-181.

Norman, D.A., Notes toward a theory of complex learning. In A.M. Lesgold, J.W. Pellegrino, S.D. Fokkema, & R. Glaser (Eds.), *Cognitive psychology and instruction*. New York: Plenum Press, 1978.

Ortony, A., Why metaphors are necessary and not just nice. *Educational Theory*, 1975, *25*, 43-53.

Ortony, A., Reynolds, R.E., & Arter, J.A., Metaphor: Theoretical and empirical research. *Psychological Bulletin*, 1978, *85*, 919-943.

Parkhurst, P.E., Generating meaningful hypotheses with aptitude-treatment interactions. *AV-Communication Review*, 1975, *23*, 171-183.

Pask, G., *Conversation theory: Applications in education and epistemology*. Amsterdam: Elsevier, 1976.

Peeck, J., Preinstructional strategies and extra reading time in learning from text. *Tijdschrift voor Onderwijsresearch*, 1977, *2*, 202-207.

Richardson, J.T.E., Mental imagery and memory: Coding ability and coding preference? *Journal of Mental Imagery*, 1978, *2*, 101-116.

Rigney, J.W., & Lutz, K.A., Effect of graphic analogies of concepts in chemistry on learning and attitude. *Journal of Educational Psychology*, 1976, *68*, 305-311.

Royer, J.M., & Cable, G.W., Facilitated learning in connected discourse. *Journal of Educational Psychology*, 1975, *67*, 116-123.

Royer, J.M., & Cable, G.W., Illustrations, analogies and facilitative transfer in prose learning. *Journal of Educational Psychology*, 1976, *68*, 205-209.

Rumelhart, D.E., & Ortony, A., The representation of knowledge in memory. In R.C. Anderson, R.J. Spiro, & W.E. Montague (Eds.), *Schooling and the acquisition of knowledge*. Hillsdale: Erlbaum, 1977.

Scandura, J.M., & Wells, J.N., Advance organizers in learning abstract mathematics. *American Educational Research Journal*, 1967, *4*, 295-301.

Simons, P.R.J., *Onderzoek naar de invloed van metaforen op het leren*. Doctoral dissertation, Tilburg University, 1980.

Simons, P.R.J., How we should control time on task - or should we? (in preparation).

Sternberg, R.J., *Intelligence, information processing, and analogical reasoning: The componential analysis of human abilities*. Hillsdale: Erlbaum 1977.

Sternberg, R.J., Component processes in analogical reasoning. *Psychological Review*, 1977, *84*, 353-378.

Wittrock, M.C., The cognitive movement in instruction. *Educational Researcher*, 1979, *8*, 5-11.

DISCOURSE PROCESSING
A. Flammer and W. Kintsch (eds.)
© *North-Holland Publishing Company, 1982*

SUBJECTIVE VERSUS OBJECTIVE PRE-INFORMATION AS A
DETERMINANT OF STUDENTS' CHOICES OF INSTRUCTIONAL
TEXTS AND THEIR SUBSEQUENT LEARNING THEREFROM

Karl Josef Klauer

Department of Education
Technical University of Aachen
West Germany

In a series of three experiments the effects of
subjective versus objective pre-information about
instructional texts on choice behavior and learning was investigated. Subjective pre-information
connected the subject matter of the text to the
learner's future life whereas the objective pre-
information consisted of a summary. Choice behavior
was strongly influenced by the different types of
pre-information but neither the amount nor the
quality of the learning was affected by it.

INTRODUCTION

Nineteenth century Herbartean educational tradition has paved the way for
modern cognitive psychology and education. Wilhelm Rein (1847 - 1929) is
our most recent scholar professing this tradition. He is known for having
introduced the use of the goal statement ("Zielangabe") as a pre-instructional technique to be regularly employed before commencing with a lesson.
In modern terms, he took a cognitive and action-oriented point of view when
he argued as to why it should be preferable to make the objective known to
the student.

His orientation toward action theory becomes evident when he shows that an
advance statement of the objective is an important part of effective teaching (Rein, 1906, 509-513): "Without goal, no will", without an orientation
toward an objective, without a goal to anticipate, there is no active involvement of the student. Thus, an advance statement of the objective has
a general motivating effect on the student. Accordingly, Rein would predict
that pupils given a goal in advance will be more motivated when learning,
and consequently will learn more effectively (prediction 1).

But Wilhelm Rein was also a forerunner of modern information-processing
theory. He stated that the learner's attention would be better directed by
informing him of the goal. According to Rein, the directing of attention is
a double process: (a) directing attention away from the mental ideas which
are momentarily present in the consciousness and which could interfere with
the new ideas, and (b) the directing of attention to ideas which are related
to the topic stated. Thus, Rein would predict that the statement of an objective, (a) depresses incidental learning, i. e., the learning of material
irrelevant to the goal, and (b) enhances intentional learning, i. e., the
learning of goal-relevant material (prediction 2).

Experiment I and II are concerned with prediction 1. In order to test such
a prediction it is necessary to write a statement of the objective conforming to
Rein. His guidelines for constructing such a statement are not very precise,
but an inspection of the numerous examples he gives (in connection with F.
Lehmensick) reveals a common feature in most of them: Nearly all of them
constitute a relationship between the new subject matter and the student
himself, his actual or future life, or interests, or problems. Thus, a
statement of the objective might produce a sort of ego involvement on the part
of the student. I shall call this kind of goal statement a subjective one,
that is, in contrast to an objective one, which is conceived as merely a
summary stated in advance of a lecture. One might expect that a subjective
kind of introducing technique would produce a higher learning motivation
than the objective one. As a consequence of this hightened motivation, choice
behavior and learning might be influenced.

EXPERIMENT I

Along this line of reasoning the influence of the pre-information types upon
choice behavior and subsequent learning is to be investigated.

METHOD

Materials. For the instructional texts two chapters in a textbook of educational psychology were chosen. The text concerning "Cooperation and Solidarity" (C) consisted of 2378 words, and the text concerning "Receptive Learning"
(R) contained 1900 words. For each text a test was constructed. The tests
consisted of 23 items, each of the short-answer type. The reliabilities of
the test were sufficient: Cooperation and Solidarity, $\alpha = 0.91$; Receptive
Learning, $\alpha = 0.81$.

Stating the objectives. The statement took the form of short texts with a
length of 65-85 words. For each of the instructional texts two statements of
the goal were formulated, an objective one and a subjective one. The objective
statement consisted of a summary of the subject matter found in the instructional
text. The subjective statement related the content of the text to the learner's
own life. In the case of "Cooperation and Solidarity", the instructional text
was introduced as being of some use in the student's future life in so far as
he/she might be interested in teaching his/her own students or even children
about the subject of being able to cooperate or being able to show solidarity. In reference to "Receptive Learning", the statement reminds the student that
he/she has to learn a lot for exams. The instructional text was introduced as
an opportunity to lern how to learn effectively using the research results
of modern Learning Psychology.

Procedure. Each subject received a manila envelope containing four smaller
envelopes, one for each of the two texts and one for each of the corresponding
tests. On the outside of the envelopes containing the instructional texts there
was only information about the text in the envelope. The subject had to choose
between the two texts, and the choice had to be based upon the informational
text on the outside of the envelopes. The informational text consisted of (a)
the objective statement of the goal mentioned above, or (b) the subjective
statement of the goal, or (c) the heading of the respective chapter. Consequently, three types of choices were possible:

Choice 1: Text I   introduced subjectively, or
          Text II introduced objectively

Choice 2: Text I   introduced objectively, or
          Text II introduced subjectively

Choice 3: Text I   introduced by heading, or
          Text II introduced by heading.

Choice 3 was a mere control condition which took into account that the two texts might interest the subjects differently.

Provisions were made for the subjects to be randomly alloted three possible choices.

Each test was reproduced in two versions of different item sequences. The distribution of the tests was made in such away that two subjects sitting side by side never had the same test version.

At the beginning of the session, subjects were told that the research was aimed at optimizing instructional texts and self-instructional procedures. After the content of the envelopes had been explained, the subjects made their choices from the texts mentioned above. After this, they took the text and read it at their own pace. Most subjects took 20 to 30 minutes for reading. After reading the text, they put it back into the envelope and took the tests for both texts, once again at their own pace. Most students required 40 to 45 minutes for answering the test items.

Subjects. An attempt was made to estimate the number of subjects needed for medium effect sizes, power = 0.8, α = 0.05, and three groups (Cohen, 1977, p. 252, resp. 377). For the choice experiment, the number of subjects needed was 117, for the learning experiment 108.

N = 111 subjects participated in the experiment. Most of the subjects were students preparing to become teachers for the secondary II level (grades 11 - 13), some were studying for the secondary I level (grades 5 - 10). The subjects were participants in five typical courses in Education or Educational Psychology. The experimental sessions had not been previously announced.

Hypotheses. If the type of advance pre-information has an influence on the student's motivation, two outcomes are to be expected.

H_1: In a choice situation between a subjectively introduced and an objectively introduced instructional text, students prefer the subjectively introduced text.

H_2: Students learn more from an instructional text if they have chosen the subjectively instead of the objectively introduced text version.

RESULTS

According to hypothesis 1, the subjects' choice behavior was to be compared. This was accomplished through the comparison of conditioned relative frequencies. Choice group 1, the control condition, had to choose between text C, introduced by its heading, and text R, introduced by its

heading, too. Two thirds of all the subjects preferred text C to text R.
This preference is irrelevant to the point in question but it was to be
accounted for later through further comparisons.

choice group 1 N = 36	choice group 2 N = 36	choice group 3 N = 39
p (C|h) = 0.67 p (R|h) = 0.33	p (C|o) = 0.36 p (R|s) = 0.64	p (C|s) = 0.82 p (R|o) = 0.18

In choice group 2 the subjects had to choose between the texts, which were introduced either objectively or subjectively. This time, about two thirds preferred
text R to text C. The kind of introduction produced a reserval in preference.
The differences between the observed frequencies of group 2 and the expected
frequencies, the frequencies of the control group taken as expected values,
were significant (χ^2 = 15.1, df = 1, p < 0.05).

In choice group 3, the preferences are shifted back again, due to different
pre-information. The text which was originally their favorite one was more
attractive after having been subjectively introduced. The difference between choice group 3 and the control group was significant (χ^2 = 4.2, df = 1,
p < 0.05). Needless to say, the difference between the two experimental
groups was significant, too.

The hypothesis that choice behavior is not influenced by the kind of introduction is to be rejected.

Next the amount of learning under the different conditions was compared.
Before doing so, it had to be proven whether the subjects had learned something or not. As each subject had to take the tests for both texts it was
possible to compare the means of the number of items correct for those
subjects who had read the respective text and for those subjects who had
not read it.

Test R	N	$\bar{x}$	s	
with text	42	13.30	4.46	p < 0.01
without text	69	3.32	2.91	

Test C				
with text	69	11.97	3.65	p < 0.01
without text	42	3.42	2.07	

It was evident that learning had taken place after having read the text.

The next table shows that learning was not influenced by the method in which
the pre-information was presented.

	Pre-information	N	$\bar{x}$	s	
	by heading	24	11.4	3.6	F = 0.315
Text C	objectively	13	12.4	3.4	df (2;66)
	subjectively	32	12.0	4.0	p > 0.05

	Pre-information	N	$\bar{x}$	s	
	by heading	12	14.3	3.6	F = 0.30
Text R	objectively	7	13.7	5.6	df (2;39)
	subjectively	23	13.2	3.8	p > 0.05

This was the case with both texts.

DISCUSSION

The results of this experiment can be quickly summarized. The kind of pre-information determines the choice of a text to a large extent but it does not influence the amount of subsequent learning. One might ask if a failure to demonstrate the effect of a goal statement on the amount of learning can be accounted for through special conditions inherent in the experiment.

If we take the following into consideration, this might be the case. The effects of the subjective type of pre-information could be expected to lie in the future, e. g.,when the student is learning for an examination, or when he or she is acting as educator or teacher. For that reason, a difference in long-term memory storage might be expected due to the kind of pre-instructional statement involved. Possibly in the present experiment only the subjects' working memory was required. In Experiment II an attempt was made to demonstrate expected learning effects on a delayed dependent variable.

EXPERIMENT II

This experiment was a perfect replication of Experiment I except for the following: Insofar as it has already been shown that learning had taken place, the second test was not given. Instead the subjects were given a test in verbal analogies (Amthauer, 1970) after having read the text but before answering the text-related test, thus subjects were prevented from solving the test items through immediate recall, i. e.,by means of their immediate working memory. N = 141 subjects participated in Experiment II.

RESULTS

With regard to choice behavior, the results of Experiment I were replicated. Again, text C was preferred in the control group (choice group 1).

choice group 1 N = 46	choice group 2 N = 47	choice group 3 N = 48
p (C|h) = 0.65	p (C|o) = 0.37	p (C|s) = 0.77
p (R|h) = 0.35	p (R|s) = 0.63	p (R|o) = 0.23

And once again, this preference was reversed in choice group 2 due to the kind of pre-information given. And again, the control group preferences were exceeded by those of choice group 3 due to the pre-information. Once more, the differences between the same groups were significant ($p < 0.05$).

The learning phase led to the following results.

	Pre-information	N	$\bar{x}$	s	
Text C	by heading objectively subjectively	30 18 37	13.2 13.9 14.2	3.6 3.8 3.6	F = 0.66 df (2;82) p > 0.05

	Pre-information	N	$\bar{x}$	s	
Text R	by heading objectively subjectively	16 11 29	16.7 14.6 15.4	3.2 3.6 4.3	F = 0.75 df (2;53) p > 0.05

With regard to the learning data, Experiment II is also a perfect replication of Experiment I.

DISCUSSION

Evidence has been accumulated that the subjective statement of a goal has a considerable impact on choice behavior. But it has also been confirmed that this pre-information does not influence the amount of learning - at least not to any remarkable degree. Finally, comparing the results of Experiment II with those of Experiment I, one must conclude that the conditions of immediate or delayed recall have no influence on achievement.

Four reasons might explain why the learning data failed to meet our expectations.

(1) Possibly, the theory derived from Wilhelm Rein is not an adequate one.
(2) The size of the experimental effect is considerably smaller than assumed.
(3) The choice might have influenced learning data in that the choice of the text itself leads to the subjects placing themselves into the particular experimental groups. Under the circumstances given, it is possible that the subjects in the different text groups were almost equally well motivated with regard to the subject matter they had chosen. This would preclude any learning differences produced by motivational variance simply because there are no motivational differences.
(4) It cannot be excluded that different goal statements do not influence

the quantity but the quality of learning. A recently performed meta-analysis on intentional and incidental learning with instructional texts revealed a considerable enhancing effect of goal statements on goal-relevant items and a equally considerable negative effect on goal-irrelevant items (Klauer,1981). This explanation would be in line with Wilhelm Rein's reasoning, i.e., that the advance statement of a goal has a directing effect on the learner's attention (prediction 2).

Experiment III was performed to throw some light on alternatives (2), (3), and (4).

EXPERIMENT III

This experiment was run as a pure learning experiment without the choice phase.

In order to facilitate the detection of a possible small experimental effect, (a) the number of advance statement types was reduced from three to two which led to a higher number of subjects in each group; (b) the total number of subjects was raised; and (c) an attempt was made to strengthen the experimental effect. This was done by replacing the ten original headings of the paragraphs with subjectively oriented headings in the text which was subjectively introduced.

If the different advance statements (objective versus subjective) directed the learner's attention differentially, then one would expect the subjective condition to promote learning what is relevant to the learner's personal life and actions. Correspondingly, one would expect that the objective condition would encourage subjects to learn the gist of the information inherent in the text. In accordance with this consideration, a knowledge-oriented test and an action-oriented test were constructed. The expectation was that the subjectively pre-informed group would outperform the corresponding group in the action-oriented test and conversely the objectively pre-informed group would outperform the corresponding group in the knowledge-oriented test.

METHOD

Materials. Text C ("Cooperation and Solidarity") of the former experiments was used. Some smaller paragraphs from the text containing information on special facts was deleted in order to optimize the text itself. Thus, the text was reduced to 1877 words.

This instructional text was made in two versions. The subjective version consisted of a text with ten headings above paragraphs which were replaced with headings that were expected to instigate some ego-involvement. For instance, the first heading was originally "Education leading to cooperation and displaying solidarity". It was replaced by "This is how you can educate your pupils to be cooperative and to show solidarity".

The objective version was identical to the original one.

Test. The knowledge-oriented test was identical to test C of the former experiments. With regard to Experiment III its internal consistency was reduced to $\alpha = 0.66$. The action-oriented test was constructed, using items of the shortanswer type. It consisted of 12 educational problems, and the testee had to explain how to solve them. Unfortunately, the internal consistency of this test was low ($\alpha = 0.39$).

Procedure. In the manila envelope were two smaller envelopes. One the them contained the text, the other the test. On the outside of the enevelope containing the text stood the pre-instructional statement. It was either of the subjective or the objective statement type which the subjects first read before they opened the envelope and took out the instructional text. After 20 minutes (which was reading time enough for the majority of them) they were allowed to take the test. The test contained the two different items types in a random order.

Subjects. N = 229 students of the same background as in Experiment I and II served as subjects.

RESULTS

Before turning to the chief results we should clarify whether reading the text induces better performance in the newly constructed action-oriented test. Otherwise, one would not be justified in speaking of learning at all. To answer this question N = 141 subjects took the test, namely N = 113 after having read the original (objective) version of the text, and an additional group of N = 28 subjects who had not read the text. The two groups differed significantly from one another ($\bar{x}_1 = 6.0$, $s_1 = 1.9$, $\bar{x}_2 = 4.8$, $s_2 = 1.6$, $t = 3.18$, df = 139, $p < 0.05$) indicating that learning has taken place by reading the text.

The results of Experiment III are shown in the table. They indicate that the kind of pre-information - advance statement plus paragraph headings - had

Knowledge-	Pre-information	N	$\bar{x}$	s	t	=	-.18
oriented	objective	113	8.7	3.2	df	=	226
test	subjective	115	8.8	3.1	p	>	0.05
		228					
Action-					t	=	-.88
oriented	objective	113	6.0	1.9	df	=	226
test	subjective	115	6.3	1.9	p	>	0.05
		228					

no influence on learning. Especially, the expected interaction " type of pre-information x type of test" was not significant ($p > 0.05$).

COMPREHENSIVE DISCUSSION

The present series of three experiments failed to demonstrate that an advance statement of the instructional objective had any effect on subsequent learning. The special pre-instructional technique being explored had been derived from a cognitive theory of Wilhelm Rein (1906). From this theory it was predicted that a subjective statement as opposed to an objective one would produce more learning motivation and hence more learning. Further it was hypothesized that the subjective pre-instructional statement would lead to emphasizing action-oriented items while the objective type of statement would lead to emphasizing knowledge-oriented items, both due to different attention directing processes.

None of these predictions were confirmed. It is assumed that this failure cannot be explained by technical reasons, e. g., by insufficient power in the experimental design. Furthermore, there is no reason for speculating that the Yerkes-Dodson law played any role, where an increase in motivation might have taken place but where the motivational optimum might have eventually been surpassed. Finally, when comparing the results of Experiment III to the previous experiments, one has to conclude that the self-selection of texts by the subjects did not alter the learning results.

Should the early cognitive theory of Wilhelm Rein be abandoned? I think not. The special operationalization I have given to Rein's concept of advance statement for the instructional objective has turned out to have no influence on learning. This operationalization followed Lehmensick's examples and consisted of connecting the material to be learned with the learner's future at least with regard to learning.

A study of Ross & Bush (1980) is in some respects comparable to the present one. The authors gave a self-instructional programm on probability to pre-service teachers. The treatments differed with regard to the different types of examples and explanations, which were either abstract-symbolic or education-related or medicine related. The subjects showed an increase in the number of education-related test items but not in the number of abstract-symbolic or medicine-related items. Relating the instructional material to the subjects' future lives as was done by Ross & Bush failed to produce a general learning effect. This results is in line with the results of the present study.

Not only the quantity but also the quality of learning was independent of the pre-information types used in this study. The conclusion is that the types of pre-information do not direct the learner's attention in the way we had assumed.

Another point deserves consideration. In the choice experiments, strong evidence was accumulated showing that subjective type of pre-information has a remarkable impact on choice behavior. Subjects who have the opportunity to choose prefer, to a large extent, subjectively introduced texts rather than objectively introduced texts. Again, the subjectively type of introduction relates the text to the learner's future life whereas the objective type is merely a summary.

In order to explain all the results obtained we can assume the following: Telling students that a text is important and why it is important for their future lives stimulates their interest in that text but does not alter the

way the text information is processed. Information processing can be modified by telling the subjects which specific parts of the text should be important to them.

This interpretation is in line with experiments showing that specific objectives have a greater influence on learning than general objectives (e. g.
Kaplan & Rothkopf, 1974). Telling the subjects that the text as a whole is
important for them might be equivalent to telling them that they should learn
all that is being presented. But this latter procedure has been the control
condition in a great number of studies in intentional and incidental learning where it turned out to be inefficient compared with giving specific
objectives (Klauer, 1981).

REFERENCES

Amthauer, R. Intelligenz - Struktur - Test. Göttingen: Hogrefe, 1970.
Cohen, J. Statistical power analysis for the behavioral sciences. New
    York: Academic Press, 1977.
Kaplan, R., and Rothkopf, E. Z. Instructional objectives as directions to
    learners: Effect of passage length amount of objective-relevant content.
    Journal of Educational Psychology, 1974, 66, 448-456.
Klauer, K. J. Intentionales und inzidentelles Lehren und Lernen bei Lehr-
    texten. Eine Metaanalyse. Unterrichtswissenschaft, 1981, 9, 300-318.
Rein, W. Pädagogik in systematischer Darstellung: Die Lehre von der Bil-
    dungsarbeit. Vol. 2. Langensalza: H. Beyer und Söhne, 1906.
Ross, S. M., and Bush, A. J. Effects of abstract and educationally oriented
    learning contexts on achievement and attitudes of preservice teachers.
    Journal of Educational Research, 1980, 84, 19-22.

DISCOURSE PROCESSING
A. Flammer and W. Kintsch (eds.)
© *North-Holland Publishing Company, 1982*

EFFECTS OF ELABORATION ON RECALL OF TEXTS

Heinz Mandl and Steffen-Peter Ballstaedt

Deutsches Institut für Fernstudien
an der Universität Tübingen
Tübingen
Federal Republic of Germany

Elaboration processes are an important component in any
theory of comprehension. Their quantitative investigation
and qualitative categorization, however, present us with
a number of methodological difficulties. In a preliminary
investigation it could be shown that elaborative processes
can be influenced by task orientation. The data also indicate an inverted u-shaped relationship between the number
of elaborations and recall performance: A subject who elaborates very little and one who elaborates a great deal
both perform less well than a subject with an average
number of elaborations.

PROBLEM

Some time before the development of cognitive psychology, it was already
known that new information can only be registered and comprehended through
the mediation of previously stored knowledge. Herbart (1824/25) for example,
described the process of apperception as the integration of new ideas resulting from perceptual processes into the apperceptive mass already
available. Hermeneutics, too, being the classic theory of text comprehension, stresses the importance of prior knowledge for the way readers assimilate texts (Dilthey, 1957; Gadamer, 1960). This ancient idea, fundamental
to any theory of comprehension, only entered the associationistic theory of
verbal learning and cognitive psychology through the back door. On the
assumption that learning processes are all based on the association of elementary units, experiments with lists of meaningless syllables, words, and
word pairs were conducted to discover the rules governing the acquisition
of associations. It soon became apparent that in learning the lists, subjects did not confine themselves merely to creating associative links based
on temporal contiguity as postulated, but that a lot of organizational and
integrative processes went on (Bredenkamp and Wippich, 1977). Let us take
the experimental paradigm of paired-associate learning as an example. During
the learning phase the experimenter presents the subjects with pairs of
words, the first word of each pair having the function of stimulus, and the
second the function of response. Efficient learners not only make connections between the paired words, but also integrate them into a semantic relationship with each other. Or, they may generate non-verbal images in
which the concepts presented are imaginatively united. These processes of
mediation represent a simple example of elaborative encoding: in addition
to the material that has been presented, prior knowledge has been activated
into which the new information is embedded. Treiber and Groeben (1976) give
an extensive review of the transition from associative learning theory to

the elaboration model of learning.

Further development of the elaboration model can be found within the levels-of-processing approach (Craik and Lockhart, 1972; Cermak and Craik, 1979). According to this theory, information processes are supposed to be located on a continuum reaching from perceptual to semantic analysis, whereby each level is supposed to have its specific memory traces (Kintsch, 1977). The concept of processing depth refers to the level that has been reached in each case. At the highest level of semantic processing, however, the concept of processing breadth would be more adequate (Craik and Jacoby, 1979), since a number of different kinds of inferences occur at this level during reading (Crothers, 1979; Frederiksen et al., 1978). All these inferences are due to the influence of schemata which have been activated either by the text or by other schemata. Basically, two types of inferences can be discerned, even though in some actual cases it may not always be possible to draw a clear line between them (Reder, 1980):
(1) Slot-filling inferences are based on schemata that have been activated by the text. This type of inference is obligatory for any kind of sentence or text comprehension. Hence, a sentence like *Peter drank too much again last night* can only be understood if the DRINKING-schema becomes activated containing the information that in everyday language "too much" usually refers to alcoholic drinks. In other words the empty argument slot of the DRINKING-schema is filled in by prior knowledge. In many texts coherence may only be established by inferring arguments. The short passage *The car went around the corner. The tires squealed* needs the activation of a CAR-schema containing the information that tires represent a part of a car, in order to become coherent and, hence, understandable. This kind of inference represents minimal conditions for comprehension. It is also called an intended inference since the author of the text thinks that he/she may rely on the fact that the reader will infer this information with the help of his/her prior knowledge (Clark, 1977).
(2) There are other inferences, however, which go beyond slot-filling, when activated schemata have the effect of enlarging and supplementing the information in the text. For example, if the text contains the sentence *Many plants contain substances which are of pharmaceutical use* the activation of the two schemata PLANTS and ILLNESS could evoke the idea *Some people drink herb teas when they feel sick*. These optional inferences are elaborative processes. Through elaborations relations are created that go beyond those present in the text and that relate the text to the various knowledge structures the reader possesses. Elaborations help to make his/her knowledge coherent. This happens as follows: One content unit of the text activates a schema or a group of schemata with the help of which conclusions going beyond the information in the text may be drawn. By means of elaborations the knowledge structure realized in the text may be enlarged in a number of ways. Thus, elaborative inferences can be regarded as the creative aspect of reading, for they relate the novel information to knowledge (semantic memory) and to experience (episodic memory) in a number of idiosyncratic ways. The number of such inferences can vary considerably from one reader to another, depending on his/her prior knowledge, interests, reading time, etc. Although the reader may understand a text without elaborations, these can still be regarded as a help towards deeper understanding.

Herbart was also aware of the educational advantages of elaborative processes. Learning can be facilitated by activating prior knowledge and experience through various learning and teaching techniques. Starting from Rothkopf's (1970) theory of mathemagenic behavior, Mayer (1980) developed a theory of assimilation corresponding to Herbart's approach. According to this theory, learning of meaningful material is affected by the following two conditions:

(1) the learner must possess a meaningful pattern of past experiences that he/she can use as an "assimilative context";

(2) the learner must make active use of such an assimilative context during reading.

Mayer (1980) assumes that this second condition can be supported by elaborative techniques. If the novel information is embedded in a broader pattern of past experiences, this should result in a more comprehensive and better integrated structure. In interpreting his own findings, he stresses the importance of learning activities such as the search for relevant past experiences and the active application of this available knowledge to key-concepts appearing in the text. If these two conditions are met, new information can be assimilated and integrated.

Some elaboration techniques such as generating mental images, integrative sentences, or questioning oneself, can be successfully trained (Ballstaedt, Mandl, Schnotz and Tergan, 1981). They play an important part in most memory techniques. Weinstein (1978), Weinstein, Underwood, Wicker and Cubberly (1979) developed and conducted a complete elaboration training program for ninth graders. Learning performance proved to be better in the experimental group, trained in elaboration techniques, than in the control group.

The findings so far suggest that elaborative processes can help to improve learning and memory performance. However the question of whether or not they are always helpful under any circumstances is still open.

Anderson and Reder (1979) as well as Reder (1980) developed a so-called script-elaboration model based on the approach of Schank and Abelson (1977). In this model, elaborative inferences are made on the basis of activated scripts i.e.,very complex schemata containing knowledge about stereotyped sequences of actions and events in well-defined situations. The best-known example is the famous RESTAURANT-script comprising all information necessary for a successful visit to a restaurant. Reder (1980) identifies three functions that elaborations may have in the process of comprehension:

(1) securing coherence between the passages and within the memory structure;

(2) generating expectations concerning further developments in the text;

(3) discovering and resolving ambiguities in the text.

Especially the first of these three functions all of which facilitate understanding, is of great importance because it helps to integrate new knowledge into the knowledge base. According to Anderson (1980) there are two theoretical reasons why elaborations lead to better recall. His argument is based on the assumption that knowledge is represented in memory in the form of semantic networks:

(1) Because of their greater number, a node available in an elaborated network is more likely to be retrieved, since it is related to a great number of other nodes. These connections may serve as alternate retrieval routes.

(2) If one node is missing in the memory structure, an elaborated network still leaves the possibility of inferring or reconstructing the missing node from the neighboring nodes.

As a rule, information seems to be better retained in an elaborated network structure because there are more cues to refer to, if reconstruction is necessary. Such a positive interpretation of the influence of elaborations bears a close relationship to a reconstructive theory of recall. A theory

concerned exclusively with retrieval of stored information could not explain
why an increase in stored information should lead to better recall. Following this approach, Anderson and Reder assume that recall performance is
particularly affected by the number of elaborations: the probability of
reconstruction appears to increase as a function of elaborative connections.
This quantitative hypothesis seems plausible at first sight, but there is
reason for caution. For one thing, there certainly is an upper limit to
the number of elaborations that may be considered useful. If someone elaborates endlessly, he/she will be considered a very distractive rather than
an integrative learner. His/her performance at reconstruction would probably be worse than that of a learner with less elaborative processing. Perhaps
the relationship between the number of elaborations and recall performance
follows an inverted u-shaped curve. Theoretically, this could be explained
as follows: If someone makes few or no elaborations, the new information is
not sufficiently "woven into" his knowledge structures and consequently,
he has few cues to reconstruct the information of the text. Recall performance will accordingly be poor. Someone who elaborates very broadly, on the
other hand, will have difficulties in reconstructing the original text information because she/he has to choose among an enormous number of activated
schemata. The second criticism concerns the purely quantitative approach.
It is possible that elaborations may be "good" or "bad" for the process of
learning, depending on their quality. Some elaborations may distract too
much from the text and, hence, contribute very little to the construction
of a coherent knowledge structure. This is the aspect Bransford and his
coworkers focussed upon.

The research team around Bransford performed a few experiments showing
quite clearly that not all kinds of elaborations are equally efficient as
regards learning facilitation (cf. review by Bransford, Franks, Morris and
Stein, 1979; Bransford, 1979). Stein, Morris and Franks (1978) used the
method of cued recall of target words with three experimental groups.
Group 1 listened to a list of base sentences such as *The tall man bought
the crackers*. Each sentence in the list was understandable and semantically consistent. During the testing phase, a sentence frame was presented in
which the adjective, as the target word, was omitted and had to be recalled:
The _____ man bought the crackers. Groups 2 and 3 also listened to
the base sentences, but in addition they were given some elaborative phrases
as context. Group 2 listened to the phrase: *The tall man bought the
crackers that were on sale*. Group 3 received a different elaborative context: *The tall man bought the crackers that were on the top shelf*. Both
elaborative contexts constitute semantically congruent continuations of the
base sentence. The differences lies in the fact that the elaborative context
for Group 3 describes a situation which has a specific and non-arbitrary
meaning for the target concept.
The findings showed excellent cued recall scores for Group 3 while the
scores of Group 2 were bad. In part, the scores of Group 2 were even lower
than those of Group 1, showing that elaborations may even reduce recall
performance. It follows that elaborations are only efficient to the extent
that they produce a relevant context for the integration of new information.
A series of experiments by Auble and Franks (1978) shows that for difficult
sentences, elaborations conducive to better understanding improve recall
performance, whereas postcomprehension elaborations reduce performance.
However, we must not forget that these findings refer to elaborative contexts provided by the experimenter and not generated by the subjects. The
same principle might apply to spontaneous elaborations nonetheless. These
findings support the theory of comprehension by Bransford and McCarrell
(1974); Bransford (1979). According to this theory, text comprehension con-

sists of a series of active construction processes. The linguistic input serves as a basis for "semantic descriptions" integrating information from preceding sentences (linguistic context), from the reader's prior knowledge, and information from the communicative situation (extralinguistic context). Elaborative inferences are effective to the extent that they contribute to the integration of these informational sources. Thus, in the end, the quality of elaborations may be said to be of greater importance than their quantity.

We began with a series of experiments intended to further clarify the effects of elaboration on the comprehension process, with regard to both quantitative and qualitative aspects. In the following section the results of the first experiment are reported.

Based on the theoretical approaches and results presented above, the influence of an instruction to elaborate aloud during reading and the influence of a task expectation, namely, that a text will have to be recalled after reading, are to be investigated. In particular, the following three questions will be studied:

(1) Is the recall performance of a group which receives the elaboration instruction and the task orientation concerning future reproduction of the text better than that of a group which reads the text without this instruction or task orientation?

(2) Does an inverted u-shaped relationship exist between the number of elaborations and recall performance?

(3) Do specific types of elaborations affect recall performance?

METHOD[1]

Experimental design and procedure. Four experimental groups were formed. The first group received no task orientation, i.e., no instruction that they would have to reproduce a text after reading it, and no instruction to elaborate aloud during reading. The second group also received no task orientation, but they were instructed to elaborate. The third group received the task orientation, but no instruction to elaborate. The fourth group received instructions concerning both task orientation and elaboration. All four groups were told to read the text carefully, sentence by sentence or in self-chosen units. Before the subjects commenced with their intensive work on the text, they were asked to skim over it for one or two minutes and to form an idea of its content (prestructuring phase). The two elaboration groups were particularly requested to connect these parts of the text concerning its subject or topic with anything they already knew, had read, or had heard about that subject or topic. All subjects were also asked to say aloud what went through their heads during processing. They were also asked to verbalize any feelings, moods, or judgments which occurred to them in the process. The procedure was carefully explained using an example. It must be particularly noted that the subjects themselves determined which portions of text, sentences, or other units they wanted to elaborate upon aloud. As control variables and as intervening tasks between text processing and recall, three subtests of the Intelligence Structure Test by Amthauer (1971) on verbal intelligence (word selection, finding common attributes, analogies) and one memory subtest were presented to all four groups. No significant differences were found between the groups on this intelligence test (cf. Table 2). The written recall of the previously processed text took place after the intelligence tests, approximately 20 minutes later.

Subjects and experimental text. In order to obtain a group of subjects with relatively homogeneous prior knowledge regarding the text, the investigation was carried out with 24 law students. The experimental text was taken from an introduction to anthropology by Nachtigall (1974) and contained 453 words.

Analysis of verbal protocols. The text, verbal protocols, and the written text reproductions were divided into so-called content units (cf. Schnotz, Ballstaedt and Mandl, 1981). One content unit approximately corresponds to a superordinate proposition in Kintsch's model (Kintsch, 1978). The experimental text, thus transformed, consisted of 38 content units.

Coding categories for elaborative content units. Qualitative classification of elaborations from verbal protocols proved to be very difficult. The first attempt was to select five categories supposed to have an effect on learning processes, the direction of which was still unspecific in some cases. Referring to personal experiences shows that the reader explicitly resorts to the context of his own personal experiences. Perhaps the activation of personal experiences improves recall performance due to ego-involvement. The problem still is that it also depends on the communicative context whether personal experiences will be stated or not. Not all subjects will actually verbalize all their personal elaborations, but rather disquise them as general knowledge as the surface level of the text. The fact that generation of images may also enhance learning in text processing seems to be well established (e.g., Yuille and Paivio, 1969). But the same argument applies here with reporting personal contexts. The utterances may not necessarily reflect the images that underlie it. In a follow-up study.the question concerning imagery will be replaced by a measure for concreteness or imagery. The category critical comments refers to the extent to which the reader interacts with the text in a critical and interested way. It is to be expected that this kind of interaction will result in deeper or broader processing and, hence, will have a positive influence on recall. Paraphrases frequently occur in verbal protocols. Whether they reflect superficial or thorough processing is hard to determine. But the very fact of repeating a meaning unit in the sense of maintenance rehearsal will probably have a positive effect on recall. The last category refers to so-called metastatements usually representing statements concerning the structure or style (organization) of the text. So-called metacognitions, with which a subject refers to his/her own cognitive processes in a form of self-reflection, were not counted as elaborations. The justification for this procedure is derived from the fact that metacognitions of this kind make no direct reference to the content of the text. In Table 1 the labels for each category are presented and illustrated with some examples drawn from our material. It should be emphasized once again that we are dealing here with a preliminary system of categories still in need of revision.

Table 1. Categories for elaborative content units

Context of personal experiences: explicit reference to some context, autobiographical data

Last week I went to an exhibition about the Chinese in Zürich.

When I hear Julius Cesar or Tacitus, I am reminded of my Latin course.

Imagery: explicit reference to mental imagery: color descriptions, shape descriptions, reference to spatial constellations

Now I'm visualizing some people living in a small rural community.

I'm seeing a map of the world in my mind and I'm trying to imagine what kind of people they are.

Critical comments: explicit value judgments, implicit value judgments through the use of evaluative words, statements of agreement or disapproval, criticism, questions on the content

I think this definition isn't very precise.

This view is too limited in my opinion.

Paraphrases: reproduction of contents in own words

Text: This classification results from the history of science- for after the philologists had started research on the written sources of non-European cultures, what was left for ethnology were in the main non-literate peoples.

Paraphrases:
Ethnology is concerned with non-literate peoples.

So Ethnology is merely concerned with non-literate peoples.

Metastatements: Statements concerning the structure and organization of the text

I consider this at the beginning as the introduction.

The sentence reads as if this was the point to come.

RESULTS AND DISCUSSION

Question 1. In order to obtain an answer to the question of whether instructions about elaboration and task orientation improve recall performance, a two-factorial analysis of variance was carried out. It showed no significant effects - as suggested by a simple inspection of the means: elaboration instruction: $F_{(1.20)} = 1.2$ ns; task-orientation: $F_{(1.20)} = 1.85$ ns; interaction: $F_{(1.20)} = 1.35$ ns. The results show (cf. Table 2) that recall performance in Group 4 (elaboration instruction, task orientation) was no better than that in Group 1 (no elaboration instruction, no task orientation) and in Group 3 (no elaboration instruction, task orientation).

Table 2. Means and standard deviations of elaboration units, metacognitions, recall units and intelligence (IQ: $\bar{x}$ = 100; s = 10)

	Group 1 no elaboration instruction/no task-orientation		Group 2 elaboration instruction/no task-orientation		Group 3 no elaboration instruction/task-orientation		Group 4 elaboration instruction/task-orientation	
	$\bar{x}$	s	$\bar{x}$	s	$\bar{x}$	s	$\bar{x}$	s
elaboration units			96.0	73.0			155.2	106.6
elaboration categories:								
personal experience			1.5	1.9			4.7	5.2
imagery			1.3	2.4			5.0	8.9
critical comments			25.5	31.5			44.2	40.1
paraphrasing			17.5	10.3			18.5	20.4
metastatements			21.3	15.0			27.5	37.3
metacognitions			4.0	3.5			7.7	10.4
recalled content units	18.5	6.8	12.8	6.7	19.0	5.6	19.2	5.3
recalled content units/minute of processing time	2.9	1.4	0.9	0.4	3.1	1.5	1.0	0.6
verbal intelligence (IST/IQ)	111.0	8.8	109.6	3.6	107.9	4.4	110.4	4.4
memory (IST/IQ)	113.3	7.9	110	9.4	107.7	10.2	110.5	4.9

Group 2 (elaboration instruction, no task orientation) produced even lower scores than Group 1 (no elaboration, no task orientation) and Group 3 (no elaboration, task orientation). However, the differences were not significant. These results do not support the assumption by Reder and Anderson (1979) that elaborative processing always improves recall performance. However, there are two possible explanations of our findings which would leave this assumption untouched. First of all, it is impossible to control the extent to which the groups without an elaboration instruction nevertheless actually did elaborate. Furthermore, the quality of elaborations in the elaboration groups was not considered. Following the investigation by Bransford, it can be assumed that there are effective and ineffective elaborations with respect to the task.

Also the variable "recalled content units/minutes of processing time" showed no significant differences between the experimental groups. This variable will not be used for the following questions.

Question 2. The relationship between the number of elaborations in Group 4 (elaboration, task orientation) and recall performance showed an inverted u-shaped distribution (cf. Figure 1). Curve fitting yielded the following theoretical equation: (Bortz, 1978, p. 238, 6.51): $y = 1.62 + 0.55x - 2.12x^2 + 0.3x^3$. The relationship between the theoretical and the empirical distribution was $R^2 = .91$.

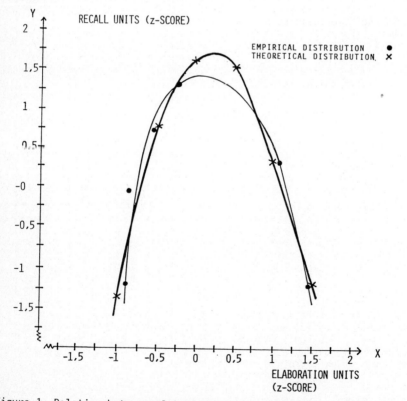

Figure 1. Relation between elaboration units and recall units

These findings suggest the following explanation: If just a few elaborations take place, the novel information is only minimally integrated into existing knowledge structures. Therefore, recall is based on very few clues. A person who elaborates extensively creates an intricate interweaving of new and old knowledge, but then has difficulty discerning the original text information during recall. In Group 2 (elaboration, no task orientation) the relationship between elaboration and recall performance has a bimodal distribution and thus appears to us to be uninterpretable. Elaborating without task orientation seems to lead not only to inferior recall performance, but also to a less clear relationship between elaboration and reproduction.

Question 3. The verbalization data were evaluated according to the categories described above: context of personal experiences, imagery, critical comments, paraphrases, metastatements. Inspection of the individual categories of elaboration for Group 4 (elaboration, task orientation) reveals that they occur in very different amounts. The most frequent categories are critical comments, metastatements, and paraphrases; least frequent are personal experiences and imagery. It is also striking that,quantitatively speaking, there are very large interindividual differences within each elaboration category. The category critical comments ranges from 8 to 109 elaborative content units, metastatements from 5 to 102, paraphrases from 3 to 55, imagery from 0 to 23, personal experiences from 0 to 14. If we look at the relationship between the categories of elaboration and recall performance for Group 4, we find for the category paraphrases an interpretable inverted u-shaped relationship. This finding appears plausible, as paraphrasing is the reformulation of the presented text in one's own words, meaning that elaborations are formed which stand in close connection to the given text. All other types of elaboration showed no significant correlation with recall data. The present categorization of elaborations appears to us to be still unsatisfactory, both with regard to its theoretical foundations and its empirical results.

DISCUSSION

There is no doubt that a complete model of text comprehension must include elaborations as a decisive component in information processing. There are, however, a number of theoretical and even more methodological problems which turn elaborations into a difficult object of investigation. We would like to briefly present a few of these problems here.

(1) Elaborations are only accessible via the verbalizations of subjects. This method, however, only reveals the tip of the iceberg because, out of the immense number of elaborative processes actually taking place, subjects select only those elaborations that meet certain selection criteria. For example, the following criteria are plausible:
Verbalizability: Can the subject find a suitable word to express an elaboration?
Task orientation: How does the subject view the task which is demanded of him/her in the experimental situation?
Evaluation: Which elaborations does the subject consider worth communicating? How is verbalization controlled by communicative conventions?
Thus, a verbal protocol only offers a selective look at the elaborative processes occurring during reading.
(2) Another problem arises in the analysis of verbal protocols. How does one determine the size of the unit of analysis? We chose relatively comprehensive content units which, roughly speaking, correspond to a high level proposition, encompassing subordinate propositions (Schnotz, Ballstaedt and

Mandl, 1981). A different suggestion with smaller units was put forward by
Chafe (1980). Using paralinguistic and syntactic criteria, he divided the
text surface into idea units roughly corresponding to phrases. In a forthcoming investigation we will compare our approach to forming content units
to that of Chafe (Ballstaedt and Mandl, 1982).

(3) Previous attempts at categorization of inferences by Crothers (1979)
and Frederiksen et al. (1978) are certainly useful for some types of
questions. They are hardly practical for work with longer texts however,
as they require an analysis of the original text, of verbalization, and of
recall on a propositional level. On the other hand, our category system
appears to us to be too coarse as yet, and its theoretical foundation too
sketchy.

(4) If recall performance is related to processing time, then the elaboration instruction has little economizing effect on immediate recall: elaboration requires time (Table 2). However it remains to be tested whether the
effort is not worthwhile after all, as elaboration may improve long-term
retention and/or cause broader processing to take place, as specific comprehension tests could show. They seem to be more suitable to test effects of
elaborations than simple recall tasks. It is furthermore conceivable that
elaborations produce specific effects on tasks other than the recall of a
text. For instance, elaboration may facilitate access to more creative
solutions in problem-solving tasks. This question, too, will be further
investigated.

---

1) The data were collected by cand.rer.soz. Gerhard Walsken under instruction of the authors. The verbal protocols and the recall data were categorized with assistence of cand.rer.soz. Manfred Maikler and cand.rer.soz.
Rainer Kluza.

REFERENCES

Amthauer, R. Intelligenz-Struktur-Test 70. Göttingen: Hogrefe, 1971.

Anderson, J.R. Cognitive psychology and its implications. San Francisco:
    W.M. Freeman and Co., 1980.

Anderson, J.R. and Reder, L.M. An elaborative processing explanation of
    depth of processing. In L.S. Cermak and F.I.M. Craik (Eds.). Levels of
    processing in human memory. Hillsdale, N.J.: Erlbaum, 1979.

Auble, P.M. and Franks, J.J. The effects of effort toward comprehension on
    recall. Memory and Cognition, 1978, 6, 20-25.

Ballstaedt, S.-P. and Mandl, H. Problems in quantitative and qualitative
    research on elaborations in text processing. In H. Mandl, N. Stein and
    T. Trabasso (Eds.). Learning and text comprehension. Hillsdale, N.J.:
    Erlbaum, 1982, in press.

Ballstaedt, S.-P., Mandl, H., Schnotz, W. and Tergan, S.O. Texte verstehen,
    Texte gestalten. München: Urban und Schwarzenberg, 1981.

Bortz, J. Lehrbuch der Statistik. Berlin: Springer, 1979.

Bransford, J.D. Human cognition, understanding and remembering. Belmont,
    California: Wadsworth, 1979.

Bransford, J.D. and McCarrell, N.S. A sketch of a cognitive approach to comprehension: some thoughts about understanding what it means to comprehend. In W.B. Weimer and D.S. Palermo (Eds.). Cognition and the symbolic processes. Hillsdale, N.J.: Lawrence Erlbaum, 1979.

Bransford, J.D., Franks, J.J., Morris, C.D. and Stein, B.S. Some general constraints on learning and memory research. In L.S. Cermak and F.I.M. Craik (Eds.). Levels of processing in human memory. Hillsdale, N.J.: Erlbaum, 1979.

Bredenkamp, J. and Wippich, W. Lern- und Gedächtnispsychologie. Bd. 2. Stuttgart: Kohlhammer, 1977.

Cermak, L.S. and Craik, F.I.M. (Eds.), Levels of processing in human memory. Hillsdale, N.J.: Erlbaum, 1979.

Chafe, W.L. The flow of thought and the flow of language. In T. Givon (Ed.). Discourse and syntax. New York: Academic Press, 1979.

Clark, H.H. Inferences in comprehension. In D. LaBerge and S.J. Samuels (Eds.). Perception and comprehension. Hillsdale, N.J.: Erlbaum, 1977, 243-263.

Craik, F.I.M. and Jacoby, L.L. Elaboration and distinctiveness in episodic memory. In L.S. Cermak and F.I.M. Craik (Eds.). Levels of processing in human memory. Hillsdale, N.J.: Erlbaum, 1979.

Craik, F.I.M. and Lockhart, R.S. Levels of processing: A framework for memory research. Journal of Verbal Learning and Verbal Behavior, 1972, 11, 671-684.

Crothers, E.J. Paragraph, structure, inference. Norwood, N.J.: Ablex, 1979.

Dilthey, W. Die Entstehung der Hermeneutik. In Gesammelte Schriften. Bd. 5. Göttingen: Vandenhoeck and Ruprecht, 1957.

Frederiksen, C.H., Frederiksen, J.D., Humphrey, F.M. and Ottensen, J. Discourse inference: Adapting to the inferential demands of school texts. Paper presented at the meeting of the American Educational Research Association. Toronto, 1978.

Gadamer, H.-G. Wahrheit und Methode. Grundzüge einer philosohpischen Hermeneutik. Tübingen: Mohr, 1960.

Herbart, J.F. Psychologie als Wissenschaft. Erster und zweiter Teil. Königsberg, 1824/25.

Kintsch, W. Memory and cognition. New York: Wiley, 1977.

Kintsch, W. Comprehension and memory of text. In W.K. Estes (Ed.). Handbook of learning and cognitive processes. Vol. 6. Linguistic functions in cognitive theory. Hillsdale, N.J.: Erlbaum, 1978.

Mayer, R.E. Elaboration techniques that increase the meaningfulness of technical text: An experimental test of the learning strategy hypothesis. Journal of Educational Psychology, 1980, 72, 770-784.

Nachtigall, H. Völkerkunde. Eine Einführung. Frankfurt/M.: Suhrkamp, 1974.

Reder, L.M. The role of elaboration in the comprehension and retention of prose: a critical review. Review of Educational Research, 1980,50,5-53.

Rothkopf, E.Z. The concept of mathemagenic activities. Review of Educational Research, 1970, 40, 325-336.

Schank, R.C. and Abelson, R.P. Scripts, plans, goals and understanding. An inquiry to human knowledge structures. Hillsdale, N.J.: Erlbaum, 1977.

Schnotz, W., Ballstaedt, S.-P. and Mandl, H. Kognitive Prozesse beim Zusammenfassen von Lehrtexten. In H. Mandl (Ed.). Zur Psychologie der Textverarbeitung. Ansätze, Befunde, Probleme. München: Urban und Schwarzenberg, 1981.

Stein, B.S., Morris, C.D. and Bransford, J.D. Constraints on effective elaboration. Journal of Verbal Learning and Verbal Behavior. 1978, 17, 707-714.

Treiber, B. and Groeben, N. Vom Paar-Assoziations-Lernen zum Elaborationsmodell. Zeitschrift für Sozialpsychologie, 1976, 7, 3-46.

Weinstein, C.E. Elaboration skills as a learning strategy. In H.F. O'Neil, jr. (Ed.). Learning strategies. New York: Academic Press, 1978.

Weinstein, C.E., Underwood, V.L., Wicker, F.W. and Cubberly, W.E. Cognitive learning strategies: Verbal and imaginal elaboration. In H.F. O'Neil and C. Spielberger (Eds.). Cognitive and affective learning strategies. New York: Academic Press, 1979.

Yuille, J.C. and Paivio, A. Abstractness and the recall of connected discourse. Journal of Experimental Psychology, 1969, 82, 467-472.

DISCOURSE PROCESSING
A. Flammer and W. Kintsch (eds.)
© *North-Holland Publishing Company, 1982*

ARGUMENT IN TEXT AND READING PROCESS

Peter Whalley

The Open University
Institute of Educational Technology

Measures of reading rate have conventionally been held to relate
to the syntactic structure of text. Eye movement studies directed
at the level of recognition find reading rate to be a function of
syntactic and lexical complexity. However experiments focusing on
comprehension, and therefore using longer texts, indicate a relation between the reading process and the macro propositional
structure of text. The author's *assigned relevance* (in van Dijk's
terms) appears to be the major determining factor of reading
rate. The implications of the predictive potential of the
author's argument structure for the study of active, flexible
reading of book length texts is discussed, and a general
methodology for experimentation at this level is put forward.

Introduction

It is the intention of this paper to briefly review some of the inherent
problems of text processing research, and to put forward an experimental
methodology for the investigation of long term study strategies under
naturalistic reading conditions. The principal topic concerns the role of
process measures of reading behaviour in text research, and in particular
the use of *macro* level reading protocol recorders. The function of such
devices is to provide a reading protocol for studies above the level of the
sentence; without artificially constraining the choice of text material or
the reader's study pattern. The three main sections deal with the analysis
of text, the ways in which it may be used, and how it is understood.

Analysing text

Many psychologists in the past have accepted rather naive ideas concerning
the complexity and range of text, but it is now generally admitted that it
is not possible to regard texts as mere sequences of sentences; the notion
of the unity of text must be taken into account. Once the text linguists
had made it acceptable to consider the relationships that exist beyond the
sentence, many of the worst constraints on choice of experimental material
and methods that had followed on from adopting sentence level linguistics
disappeared. Table one summarises the main text analysis methodologies to
be found in the text processing literature. Although there is insufficient
space here to review them all in detail, the subjective representational
analyses of texts will be discussed later in their complementary role as
measures of comprehension.

The most neglected aspect of text analysis relates to the role of the author's argument structure. Texts should be seen as the embodiment of an author's intention, and not simply as a neutral list of undifferentiated facts. The consequence of thinking of them in this way, as a design rather than a map, is that rhetoric and presentation, how the author arrives at a whole organized text, then have to be taken into consideration. A useful framework for the creation of discourse, as it relates to studies of prose comprehension, is Clement's (1975) *staging* analysis, with its explicit model of text production. Van Dijk's (1979) analysis of *relevance assignment* may also be used to explicate the author's intentions both in terms of linguistic aspects of text and also its presentation. This wide ranging analysis encompasses typographical signalling, conventional linguistic analysis of the connectives and the analysis of argument structure. Waller (1980) develops an analytic approach to the presentational aspects of text. This is necessary for studies concerned with the use of parallel arguments or explicit cross referencing within texts.

Table 1. Methods of text analysis

Surface

* 'Readability' formulae

* Vocabulary analysis
  Range
  Particular: Evaluative, Assertive, Indefinite
  Reference
  Connectives: Relevance assignment, Argument, Parallelism

Computer
analysis
possible

* Reverse parsing (e.g. Rieger)

* Propositional depth (e.g. Meyer)

* Staging (e.g. Clements)

* Coherence graphs (Kintsch)

* Reader structuring (Thomas)

* Reader scaling (e.g. Bisanz)

* Clustering (e.g. Pollard-Gott)

Personal

Another important and yet neglected aspect of text analysis in text processing research concerns the issue of *text types*. Most text linguists have developed their own taxonomies and table two exemplifies the wide range identified; and also indicates the source of the interrelations between the different text genres. Often it may be necessary for researchers to develop their own more specialized taxonomy. For instance the author found it necessary to develop a finer grain analysis of the *didactic* text type, when attempting to relate reader's perceptions of course structure to a computer analysis of the incidence and patterns of referential links (Whalley, in press).

A detailed discussion of what are essentially overlapping categories is not relevant here. The important point is the wide range of possible text types in relation to the very narrow range that have received attention in the prose learning literature. Psychologists have studied the representation and understanding of descriptive and narrative prose in far greater detail than any of the other text genres. Very few studies have examined the other types, and these have most often been in the educational research field where only fairly simple analyses of texts are made. There are obviously several reasons why this has come about. Descriptive and narrative texts fit in particularly well with the currently popular ideas of frames and schemas. Also, well developed models of story grammars have been worked out for some time, although these too are not without their critics.

Table 2. **A taxonomy of text types** (Derived from de Beaugrande, 1980)

Descriptive	Concerns objects and situations (frames).
Narrative	Concerns events and actions (schemas).
Conversational	An especially episodic and diverse range of sources for admissible knowledge. Changes of speaking turn.
Literary	Events and situations portrayed as exemplary elements. Linkages with real world events are problematized.
Poetic	Organization of the real world and the organization of discourse about that world are problematized.
Scientific	Linkages of events and situations are deproblematized via statements of causal necessity and order.
Argumentative	Entire propositions assigned values of truthfulness and reasons for belief as facts.
Didactic	Textual world presented via a process of gradual integration. Linkages of established facts are problematized and eventually deproblematized.

This unbalanced emphasis would perhaps not matter if it were not that the data available indicates that the recall for narrative prose is nearly twice that for expository prose. Studies with scientific texts usually result in a very poor level of understanding, and an ability to make inferences that is no better than control groups. Graesser (1981) has pointed out that this effect is unlikely to be due to the surface structure of the passages, in terms of linguistic or rhetorical organization. The difference is much more likely to be due to problems at a deeper level of understanding; and is probably a consequence of the studies being controlled laboratory experiments, as against the students' normal experience of self-induced reading. It is self-evident that equally complex material can be successfully mastered when the students are studying for course credits.

One of the main differences between narrative and expository texts is that the latter are fundamentally non-sequential. Events, participants and settings are not the main concern, although they may be used to illustrate the dominant explanatory information. The argument structure and presentation of such expository texts therefore becomes central to any text analysis. A possible consequence is a more dominant role for the reader in non-sequential texts, which would result in a greater variability in experimental studies (a point that will be developed later in terms of field studies).

In summary then, it is not obvious how solving *all* the problems concerned with the comprehension of one text type, and in particular narrative text, would solve many of the problems associated with the other (and perhaps more important) text types. However, the problems of linguistic analysis awaiting anyone who might wish to work with the higher order text types, and particularly if they are of any length, are quite complex. The way that texts presuppose other texts, has been shown by the text linguists to be quite different from the way that sentences presuppose other sentences. Even within texts the intertextuality of summaries, conclusions and overviews has to be taken into account. There are no 'off the shelf' analytic methods for problems at this level of text complexity, although several text linguists now include subheadings, summaries and other such *access devices* (Waller, 1980) as part of their description of the macrostructure of text.

One idea which may be applicable in this context is Grimes' (1975) theory of *overlays*. Although this was originally developed to cope with the more complex story structures of languages other than English, it may be used to examine the development of topics in long educational texts. The author is currently attempting to apply it to the analysis of Open University course material, which typically may consist of 30 *units* each fifty pages in length. When working with such material, it is obviously difficult to make detailed linguistic analyses of the whole text and in many cases these would be inappropriate anyway. In the area of literary criticism, computer analysis at the statistical level has been used for some time to identify aspects of style. If the text is available in a suitable form. it is possible that a 'guided' computer analysis will be useful. Several researchers have recently made use of computers to analyse the development of the logical connectives within texts, and it is also possible to make statistical evaluations of the use of assertive and evaluative expressions by authors in relation to important themes within the text.

Process measures of reading

A central argument of this paper is that process measures of the reader's interaction with the text may be useful in text processing research. The focus of such research is a concern with how readers react to complex text structures and is not simply to do with knowledge outcomes; such as might be measured by pre- and post-testing. Records of eye movement patterns have appeared to offer an attractive measure of information acquisition. This section is intended to outline an analysis of why it has been so difficult to learn about language processes by recording eye movements, and to put forward a partial solution to the study of lengthy texts by means of a macro-level reading recorder.

The main criticisms of eye movement methodologies are outlined here only in summary form, but are dealt with at greater length in a parallel paper (Whalley, 1981):

- We don't know what part of the text is actually being 'seen' during a fixation, if any (Shebilske, 1981).
- The basic nature of the relationship between eye movements and cognitive processes is not understood.
- Researchers have inadequately specified aspects of text that might be relevant to the way readers control their eye movements.
- The 'discovery problem'; the data is not rich enough to discover new aspects of the comprehension problem (Graesser, 1981).
- Inferences, expectations and tacit knowledge are dealt with inadequately.
- The technology available leads to the generation of self-selecting stimulus material.

The essential problem for the reader is not the acquisition of information but its meaningful manipulation. The 'discovery problem' noted by Graesser is therefore the most important methodological issue. Like many other researchers, Graesser considers that the simple response measures such as reading times and eye movement data cannot provide the *critical* data required to test models of complex processes, such as comprehension, that are not already well understood. The argument of this paper, however, is that behavioural records of reading protocols *can* play a useful role in reading research, provided that eye movements are seen as being only the most accessible sub-skill in a very complex process. In which case, it is only possible to make sense of such process records (or for them to be of any real use) within the coherent framework of a thorough analysis of the text, the reader's understanding of it, and the intentions behind the reader's study.

The question of the best method for acquiring process measures of reading is still open. The technical ingenuity of the eye movement monitoring techniques has to be balanced against the often unacceptable constraints that they place on text and reader. However, the alternative process measures that researchers have attempted to use in their place such as simple measures of reading time, protocol analysis of 'think aloud' data or relative interference with some secondary task as a measure of attention, are themselves not without problems. These are matters for the individual researcher's judgement, and we will move on to some concrete examples of attempts to study text usage under realistic study conditions.

An 'effective' eye movement recorder

After initial attempts to use the available techniques for recording eye movements, most text researchers conclude that too much is lost in order to obtain a precision of record that is often more trouble than it is worth. Research is often now concerned with the time spent on ideas and themes within the text, and in terms of analysing the sequence in which ideas are read, rather than concentrating on processing at the word level (Thomas, 1977; Shebilske, 1981). Given that the concern of the research is focused at a higher level such as 'meaning units', or hierarchical versus heterarchical argument structure, then there is no longer any need for precise measurement, with all the restrictions that it imposes on the form of text presentation and reading task. Experiments are often conducted using micro-level recording devices and the data is then averaged up to the macro-level analysis made of the text. Of course this means that fewer experimental restrictions are overcome than is possible.

However, several recording systems exist that have been specifically designed to operate at the level of macro-level reading. Some employ a 'window' arrangement permitting only a few lines of a continuous text to be viewed. This is either organized mechanically, as with the old programmed learning machines, or on a computer screen using control buttons to scroll forwards and backwards (e.g. Alessi, 1979). Another method is to employ a half-silvered mirror, and monitor the reader's eyes with a TV system (e.g. Schumacher, 1981). This has the advantage of permitting the use of conventional text material containing diagrams, tables, etc., but necessitates a rather laborious analysis of video tape data.

Figure 1. An 'effective' eye movement recorder

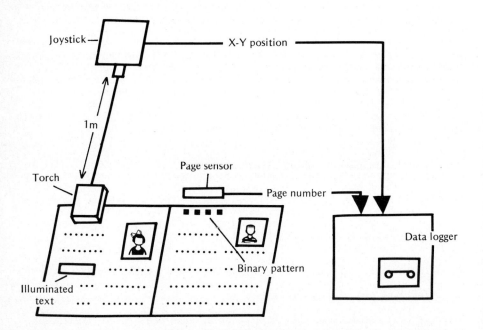

The author's simple if rather inelegant contribution to eye movement recording methodology is shown in figure one. It was preferred to trade off a dim lighting regime for the ability to work with proper book-like texts. Essentially the reading record is obtained by tracking the movements of the 'torch' about the page, which makes automated analysis fairly simple. The beam of light is arranged to brightly illuminate three lines of text and yet permit sufficient 'peripheral' vision for the reader not to become disorientated. In practice, hand-eye coordination develops rapidly and readers move the torch smoothly; keeping the centre of the beam on the line currently being read. Comparison studies with a conventional eye movement recording camera indicated that readers were not being constrained in terms of sentence and paragraph level regressions, in the way that they are with 'rolling text' systems. Of course the deleterious effect of diagrams being 'over the page' from their point of reference is similar to that found with ordinary texts (Whalley, 1975).

Reading a structured exercise

This trial study was intended to evaluate one component of an Open University science foundation course. It took the form of a six page structured exercise containing text, questions, diagrams, charts and data tables. The 'structured' aspect of the design involved the students forming and testing hypotheses concerning the evolution of the species; given the information that Darwin had at his disposal about the Galapagos Islands and their various populations of finches. The text was intended to encourage a scientific mode of thought and it was envisaged that students would find it an interesting activity. However, many students on the course found it a rather disconcerting experience, and trials with five students who were used to studying Open University course material suggested at least one reason for this.

Table 3. Proportion of time spent on relevant information when answering questions in a structured exercise

Question no.	1	2	3*	4	5**
'Hit-rate' %	30	33	10	45	78

*Main source of information in the answer to the previous question
**Main source of information in a data table

A 'dependency' analysis was made of the text in terms of where the most important information needed to answer each question could be found. From this analysis a 'hit-rate' of the time spent on relevant information was calculated for each question and is shown in table three. From their previous experience of instructional texts, the students appeared to have well formed views concerning the superficiality of inserted questions. Much of the difficulty that the students were experiencing was brought on by them not paying adequate attention to the answers, and moving on before they had really understood their implications. As a consequence they had great difficulty in locating the appropriate information to answer the following question. (The important topic of when and how the reader might use inferred knowledge to *avoid* having to re-read portions of the text involves tapping the students' perceptions and understanding, and is not dealt with here.)

These problems might have been avoided by the use of appropriate study instructions or even by better typographic signalling of the importance of the answers. However, it must be mentioned that there were other deeper problems with the text concerned with conceptual development, and this must have contributed to the students' confusion. Although the original intention of this trial had been only to evaluate the structural aspects of the text, there is always the danger in text processing research of 'significant' results being the consequence of a superficial text analysis.

Other related studies have been reported examining the way in which students react to conventional in-text questions (Alessi, 1979). Schumacher's (1981) study revealed that although subjects who received questions went back into the text to check relevant information, this more active interaction did not result in a better test performance. Such a result could be predicted from Marton's (1976) work concerned with the deleterious effects of the narrow focusing of attention produced by conventional inserted questions.

Propositional depth and reading rate

In this trial, two of Meyer's (1975) texts were used. These dealt with nuclear power as an energy resource, and were about one page in length. The main text manipulation is to have the same block of text embedded high or low in the propositional structure. It was assumed that the relation between propositional depth and reading rate found at the sentence level would be confirmed, and that it would be possible to generalise the patterns of reading rates to other texts.

However no relation was found between reading rate and propositional depth and there was also none with the surface readability measures either. Although the expected difference in recall scores between the two texts was found, inspection of the protocols in terms of intrusions, revealed several problems. After their recall of the text, some students were requested to make a subjective analysis in terms of what *they* considered to be 'main themes', 'side themes' and 'embellishments' within the texts. This 'flow-charting' technique is described by Thomas (1976). Others were asked to indicate the important elements of the text that would be recalled by other readers, as in Johnson's (1974) studies. Although there was broad agreement with the 'levels' of the propositional analysis, it was immediately apparent that some students had taken a very strong engineering issues perspective, whilst others had seen ecological issues as being most important. Such problems of individual interpretation are taken up in the next section.

Table 4. Average reading rates for the Meyer Texts

	Main text	Target paragraph	Meyer's results*
Fast breeder (high)	212	249	106
Future energy (low)	317	370	140

*Note   These are derived rates calculated from total reading times. The other data represents the subjects' 'first read' through the texts and does not include regressions and rereading.

The pattern of reading records did not appear to have any significance until an analysis in terms of how authors signal their argument structure was made. As well as the legitimate differences in perspective, there appeared to be an extra confounding factor in that one of the texts was apparently far more interesting to read. The text with the target paragraph embedded high in the propositional structure contained twice as many assertive and evaluative expressions and this appeared to dominate the

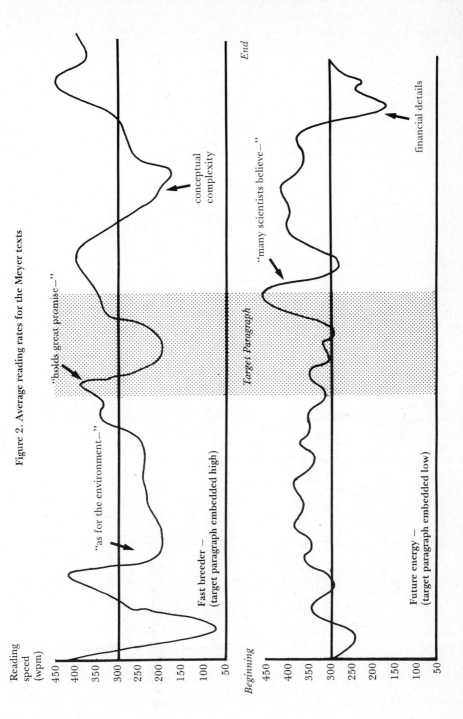

Figure 2. Average reading rates for the Meyer texts

students' reading rate and their pattern of re-reading parts of the texts.
Pronounced changes in reading rate were found after the few phrases in
these texts signalling argument structure e.g. 'while at the same time',
'as for the' etc., as shown in figure two. Such expressions have a focusing
function and tend to occur in topic sentences of paragraphs. They establish
a centre of interest for the reader and signal the structural relationships
amongst the sentences.

Table four indicates the average reading rates of the five subjects in each
group. Although the target paragraph is read more slowly in the 'high' text,
that text is itself read more carefully as a whole. However it should be
noted that these results do not directly invalidate Meyer's finding of
better recall for material high in the propositional structure, as equivalent recall scores were reported for a different set of texts where the
'high' text was read more quickly than the 'low' text; they just indicate
the importance of a thorough analysis of the text.

A study protocol recorder

Open University texts are specifically written for distance teaching. In
order to be able to monitor the developmental testing of these texts in
students' homes, the 'page' element of the torch recorder was further
developed as a separate device. Figure three indicates the form of this
version, which also incorporates the facility to monitor key depressions on
a micro-processor kit or computer keyboard.

Figure 3. The study protocol recorder

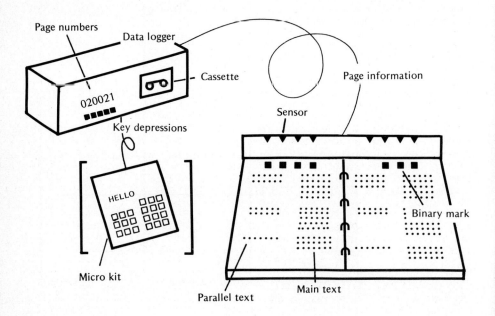

The data logger has an internal clock for date and time and can store several weeks worth of data. A folding version has now been developed that plugs into an 'Apple' microcomputer, and makes it possible to study the use of interrelated texts such as revision or statistical units. Texts not being read may be shelved out of the way. Details of an evaluation study made with this recorder of the use of algorithms in a one day micro-computer course are described elsewhere (Whalley, 1981).

The reader's understanding of the text

If it is accepted that process measures of reading only make sense in the context of the readers' intentions, then we must confront the problem of eliciting these intentions and the changes in understanding that result from their interaction with the text.

Free recall and multiple choice questioning tasks have dominated the prose learning experimental methodology, with several unfortunate consequences. They have imposed an additional bias towards experimentation with simple descriptive and narrative texts, and encouraged the imposition of fairly artificial study styles upon subjects. "Read through once slowly", is the last thing that students on study skills courses would be advised to do, and yet it is still probably the most common instruction given to subjects. The alternative of allowing a free study style leads to enormous varia-bility between subjects, *and* without some process measure makes reading times uninterpretable. This relates back to the previous section. If a text manipulation is made which might be expected to bring about changes in reading strategy, then any simple temporal measure is almost certain to be too confounded to be useful. A record of the *sequence* in which text el-ements are read, combined with some measure of the *reader's* perception of the text structure is necessary.

A more important bias they encourage though is *against* any conception of tapping the reader's interpretive knowledge. This involves categorizing, classifying, predicting and making inferences; activities which are all too often regarded as intrusion effects and ignored because they are so diffi-cult to evaluate. The dangers inherent in missing differences in interpret-ation, the sum of the text and what the reader brings to it, were apparent in the trial study with the Meyer texts described earlier. If a sub-set of readers are taking a much more reflective attitude towards the text (e.g. commenting on the author's style) then it may totally confound simple recall scores. This is all part of the general problem that any study in-volving large amounts of text will have to confront, namely that psychology does not have a really coherent framework for understanding the growth of knowledge. Notions of *reconstruction* and *tuning* of frames are floated, but it is usually only the simplest associative knowledge that is tested for. Theories are required that can cope with the accommodation of new and possibly conflicting information. It could be contended that in contrast to the ideal world of prose learning studies, *most* knowledge derived from text involves the assimilation of inconsistent and incomplete information.

However there are some hopeful signs in the literature of attempts to use multidimensional scaling (Bisanz, 1978) and related clustering techniques (Pollard-Gott, 1979) to elicit the reader's perception of concept relations and text structure. It is possible using these methodologies to bring out the development of the readers' ideas as they progress through a course, and to show how originally naive ideas or misconceptions can be changed. A recent study by the author used scaling techniques to try and elucidate readers' interpretations of the arguments put forward by different authors dealing with the same topic. The idea was that within the framework of a fairly stable pattern of concept relations it should be possible to explore the effects of text manipulations such as argument and emphasis. The texts in this study were concerned with the educational role of 'play' in the junior school and depending on the relative perspective of the reader and the text it was possible to obtain 'movements' on the various dimensions as the readers accepted or rejected different viewpoints, as in figure four.

Figure 4. Changes in the perception of play in an educational context.

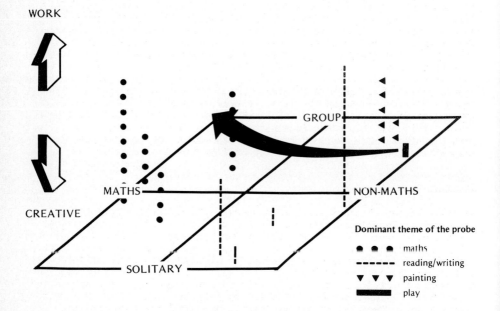

Another related issue now being referred to in the text processing litera- ture is that of 'meta-comprehension', the readers' subjective perceptions of their own comprehension. These ideas have been considered for some time in the *learning-to-learn* literature (Thomas, 1977), but is another sign of research into text processing moving away from simple notions of total recall; which of course is often not what the reader requires of a text. In many instances it is only necessary to 'know' the contents of the discourse at a very general level, it may well be more important to know how it relates to other texts in terms of topics and arguments; perhaps for later study. To sum up then, experimental results indicating no significant difference in terms of propositions recalled or multiple choice scores may often undervalue real improvements in text design which *can* be successfully brought out by more sensitive subjective measures of understanding or adjudged text complexity.

Conclusion

The most appropriate conclusion to this paper is a consideration of laboratory versus field experimentation in text processing studies. Although
models of reading are generally moving towards the view of the adaptive
flexible reader, in the vast majority of studies, texts are read in task-
induced situations where the readers are extrinsically motivated to read.
This must of course be a factor in the lower scores obtained for the less
intrinsically interesting expository texts. Studies have shown that field
trials of newspaper reading indicate a much greater selectivity than is
generally found in experimental settings (Graesser, 1981). Several researchers have tried to create more realistic laboratory reading situations
by requiring students to come in and read their own course texts. The study
mentioned previously by Schumacher (1981) is particularly interesting in
this context, as it involved students coming into the laboratory to read
texts that they were studying for course credits. This of course would
ensure a more uniformly realistic task perception and motivation. However,
this form of experimentation is difficult to set up, and is still unlikely
to tap the more reflective study activities of the flexible reader, e.g. the
selective use of complementary texts.

Comprehensive text research should involve as few compromises as possible
in the choice of text and the reader's study activities. A realistic self-
induced reading environment will almost certainly involve some element of
field trial; tapping into an extended period of study as adequately as
possible. This should be seen as complementing the more sophisticated
manipulations that may be made in the laboratory.

References

Alessi, S.M. et al. An investigation of lookbacks during studying.
  Discourse Processes, 1979, 2, 197-212.
Bisanz, G.L. et al. On the representation of prose: new dimensions. *Journal
  of Verbal Learning and Verbal Behavior*, 1978, 17, 337-357.
Clements, P. The effects of staging on recall from prose. PhD Dissertation,
  Cornell University, 1975.
de Beaugrande, R. *Text, discourse, and process: Toward a multidisciplinary
  science of texts*. London: Longman, 1980.
Graesser, A.C. *Prose comprehension beyond the word*. New York: Springer-
  Verlag, 1981.
Grimes, J.E. *The thread of discourse*. The Hague: Mouton, 1975.
Johnson, R.E. Learners' predictions of the recallability of prose. *Journal
  of Reading Behaviour*, 1974, 6(1), 41-52.
Kintsch, W & van Dijk, T.A. Towards a model of text comprehension and
  production. *Psychological Review*, 1978, 85(5), 363-394.
Marton, F. On non-verbatim learning II. The erosion effect of a task-
  induced learning algorithm. *Scandinavian Journal of Psychology*, 1976,
  17, 41-48.
Meyer, B.J.F. *The organization of prose and its effects on memory*.
  Amsterdam: North-Holland, 1975.
Pollard-Gott, L. et al. Subjective story structure. *Discourse Processes*,
  1979, 2, 251-281.
Rieger, C. GRIND-1: First report on the magic grinder story comprehension
  project. *Discourse Processes*, 1978, 1, 267-303.

Schumacher, G.M. & Young, D. The effects of inserted questions on studying
    processes in normal textbook materials. American Educational Research
    Association Annual Meeting, Los Angeles, 1981.
Shebilske, W.L. & Fisher, D.F. Eye movements during the reading of extended
    discourse. Conference of the European Group for Eye Movement Research,
    Bern, 1981.
Thomas, L.F. & Augstein, E.S. Harri-. Learning to learn: the personal
    constructs and exchange of meaning. In Howe, M. (Ed.), *Adult Learning*.
    New York: Wiley, 1977.
van Dijk, T.A. Relevance assignment in discourse comprehension. *Discourse
    Processes*, 1979, 2, 113-126.
Waller, R.H.W. Graphic aspects of complex texts: Typography as macro-
    punctuation. In Kolers, P.A. et al (Eds.) *Processing of Visible
    Language 2*. New York: Plenum Press, 1980.
Whalley, P.C. Macro level recording of reading behaviour. Conference of the
    European Group for Eye Movement Research, Bern, 1981.
Whalley, P.C. A partial index of text complexity involving the lexical
    analysis of rhetorical connectives. *Journal of the Association of
    Literary and Linguistic Computing*, (in press).
Whalley, P.C. & Fleming, R.W. An experiment with a simple recorder of
    reading behaviour. *Programmed Learning and Educational Technology*, 1975,
    12(2), 120-123.

DISCOURSE PROCESSING
A. Flammer and W. Kintsch (eds.)
© *North-Holland Publishing Company, 1982*

SELF-REGULATED VERSUS TEACHER-PROVIDED SEQUENCING OF
INFORMATION IN LEARNING FROM TEXT

HANS G.L.C. Lodewijks

Department of Instructional Psychology
Tilburg University
Tilburg
The Netherlands

Three experiments are discussed in which differential effects
of self-regulated and teacher-provided subject matter sequences were examined. In all experiments secondary school children
took an introductory course in physics, which was presented to
them in written format. In general, data revealed that subjects
performed better on achievement tests (post- and retention
tests) under self-regulated conditions, than under teacher-
provided ones. Furthermore, subjects under self-regulated conditions were better able to construct an internal representation of the subject matter. In addition, several disordinal
aptitude-treatment interactions were detected for inductive
and deductive reasoning ability, field independence and analogical reasoning ability. Learners scoring high on these
characteristics had an advantage under conditions of self-sequencing and were held back under teacher-provided sequences.
The opposite, however, was true for learners judged as low on
these aptitudes.

INTRODUCTION

During the last two decades a considerable amount of research has been done on
text learning (e.g., McConkie, 1977). After abandoning nonsense syllable and
paired-associate learning tasks in the research laboratories, researchers started
to study more meaningful learning tasks and found texts to be feasible material
for experimental research. In these twenty years, we have gained reasonable insights into the more fundamental text processing activities of readers. Nevertheless, there is still much to be learned, primarily because most research done
on text learning has been restricted to only short passages of text. As a result of
this we know practically nothing about the processes which take place in learning
more comprehensive texts. How, for instance, do learners build up knowledge structures about more substantial subject matter domains while reading about them?
Answering questions like this one require longer range studies and the use of more
comprehensive written materials than those used up till now.

We did several studies in which pupils had to acquire a considerable amount of
knowledge from texts with regard to some school relevant subject matter domain. In
this research we dealt mainly with the question of whether variations in the order
in which textual information is presented influences the reader's processing and
storing of that information. We attempted to find out what kind of presentation
order (sequence) is optimal in learning from written materials. However, we were
also interested in exploring more basic information-, or text-processing activities
of learners.

In instructional psychology, a great diversity of text structures has been distinguished. Some of these are used in experimental research, others have only been
suggested in the literature. Though terminology appears not very consistent, among
the most frequently mentioned types of structures one will find the following:

logical, hierarchical, random, analytical, synthetic, inductive, deductive, cumulative, concentric, temporal and thematical (Klauer, 1974; Tennyson, 1972; Lodewijks, 1981). In addition, more general approaches to sequencing verbal material are related to Ausubel's notion of "assimilation to schema" and Berlyne's "cognitive conflict" view. Examples of these latter approaches may be found in Mayer (1977) and Groeben (1972). More recently, Posner & Strike (1976) presented an integrative model for deriving text-sequencing principles.

It appears that, in spite of the importance attached to the problem of sequencing learning materials, relatively little empirical research has been done with respect to the differential effectiveness of possible sequences. One possible reason for this may simply be a question of conviction such as the following from Gagné in 1973: "Naturally, many subjects have their own 'sequence', implied by the content itself. ...Most other subjects that are held together by a complex of verbal knowledge obviously contain logical relations, as well as superordinate and subordinate categories of concepts. Whether the stimulus materials are displayed in a conventional textbook or in the form of programmed instruction, one can do little better than follow either common sense or Skinner's (1958, p. 974) prescription that the content be arranged 'in a plausible development order'. If in fact such an order is not followed, there is an absence of evidence that this will make much difference. ...The sequencing of events within a single exercise or lesson is a different problem. ...If designed for the learning and retention of *verbal information*, the evidence again suggests that the sequence of presentation has no strong effect". (Gagné, 1973, p. 26-27). In carrying out some earlier experiments on this topic (Lodewijks, 1978) we also found rather small differences in what pupils learned under different sequencing conditions. With respect to these results Gagné's general conclusions seem quite correct. But, we also found that learning outcomes were consistently higher under sequencing conditions in which pupils could mentally rearrange the order of presentation. If pupils had the opportunity to take notes, to make summaries and such, their performance was better. In so doing, pupils disrupted the preplanned order of the materials and followed, mentally, a different route. These results directed our attention to the question of what learners will do if they are allowed to plan the sequence of presentation on their own. To study this we performed several experiments in which we compared the effectiveness of self-regulated sequencing modes with pre planned, teacher-provided ones.

SEQUENCES IN WRITTEN MATERIALS

We started our research with the development of an introductory course on basic electricity concepts. This course consisted of 16 or (depending on the particular experiment) 18 units. Each unit represented one of the concepts covered by the course. These concepts are listed in Table 1. The course was presented to secondary school children, ranging in age from 13 to 15 years. All instruction was given in written format. A total of approximately seven hours was necessary to learn the subject content in these units.

Presentation order of the units was varied in six different ways. First we asked a group of experts (physics teachers) to construct a sequence which was, according to their experience and opinion, most appropriate for teaching the concepts. Inter-expert reliability was high (with different groups of experts Kendall's coëfficiënt of concordance W varied from 0.83

to 0.92; p≤.001) and thus we could design a general sequence which we called the *communal sequence*. Furthermore, we analyzed the content of the
learning materials and searched for logical-prerequisite relations. A logical-prerequisite relation was, following Posner & Strike's (1976) description, defined as a relation between two subject matter elements, one of
which must be known to the learner before the other can be understood. Sequences in which these prerequisite relations were taken into account were
called *hierarchical sequences* and formed the second type of sequencing.

ampere	potential
atom	tension
coulomb	siemens
electricity	specific conductance
electro-motor-power	specific resistance
electron	tension source
conductance	strength of current
molecule	volt
ohm	resistance

Table 1
Overview of course concepts

Also based on content analysis of the learning materials, we constructed
a third kind of sequence, the so-called *referential sequences*. These sequences were based on a model initially proposed by Flammer (1974) and later
formalized by Flammer, Büchel & Gutmann (1976). In the latter article formulas are presented for predicting which subject matter element a pupil
will choose under conditions of self-sequencing. For every element of the
to-be-learned units a so-called "Dringlichkeits-" (in English: urgency-)
index can be computed. The value of this index depends on the number of
subject matter elements a learner has already mastered. For example,
given three units (A,B,C) and three relations between these units (AB, AC
and BC), and assuming furthermore that a learner has already mastered the
elements B and C (as depicted in Figure 1), then the urgency to choose to
learn next the relation BC must be greater than to learn element A, or the
relations AB or AC. The reason for this is, that in the case of
BC, two of the adjacent parts of the mini-content-structure

B ⟵——BC——⟶ C are already known to the learner. In the case of the other two
relations only one, and in the case of element A no part of the content
structure is known.

Figure 1
Hypothetical content structure, consisting of three
elements (e.g. concepts) and three relations between
these elements. Elements known to the learner are
italicized; dotted lines indicate unknown relations.

This model has in our opinion a certain amount of validity. Therefore, we started to develop sequences in which learners could go their own way through the materials, with the restriction that they could choose only between those elements which had the highest urgency-indices at the moment of choice.   For various reasons, the formulas which Flammer et al. (1976) proposed had to be modified, but we were able to preserve the key notions of their proposal. Elsewhere, (Lodewijks, in preparation), we discuss this topic in more detail. In addition, we had to change Flammer et al.'s "Dringlichkeits-model" in some respects and developed what we called the CUEING-model (Lodewijks, 1981). In the CUEING-model relations are defined in terms of the references between the subject matter concepts. Urgency indices are a function of these references. According to the model, a sequence is considered optimal if the subsequent steps in that sequence follow the direction of the inter-concept references (e.g., the value of the urgency indices).

The construction of sequences in which these conditions are taken into account is, however, quite a problem. To solve this problem we reasoned as follows: Learners, when reading a particular text, will encounter *references to other concepts* which they do not know yet. Encountering these yet-unknown concepts may mean that the learner has detected gaps in his/her knowledge of the subject matter. In order to get a closer understanding of the subject matter, the best thing a learner can do now is to proceed to study materials which relate to the detected gaps in that knowledge. That means that he/she can best select those parts of the learning materials which fill these gaps. By way of illustration, in Figure 2 a part of the referential structure of the subject matter is displayed. This figure can be read as follows: In reading about the concept *electrical current* there will be mention of concepts such as *electron, molecule and atom*. If a learner has not yet studied these three concepts, the best thing he/she can do is to select one of these concepts to proceed with in studying the learning materials. Suppose the text about the concept molecule has been selected, then after learning this unit the next choice to be made must be atom, because there is mention of that concept in the text on molecule.

To construct these kinds of sequences an analysis of the subject matter was necessary. In this analysis we searched for cross-references between the subject matter elements. The resulting referential structure of the learning materials was fed into a computer. Use of a computer in this kind of sequencing was necessary because sequencing depended on previously made individual choices by the learners. Thus, in the referential sequencing mode, the succession of elements was in the direction of the references.

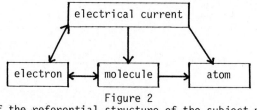

Figure 2
Part of the referential structure of the subject matter.
Direction of arrows indicate direction of references.

Finally, the last teacher provided sequence was a *random sequence*. Here, the subject matter elements were arranged and presented in alphabetical order.

All of these sequences we called preplanned because the construction principles underlying them were developed in advance. The communal and the random sequence had to be studied in the order in which they were presented to
the learners. Under the conditions of hierarchical and referential sequencing
learners were allowed to choose the unit to begin with, but in their subsequent learning their freedom was limited by the underlying construction
principles.

We compared the effectiveness of these preplanned, teacher-provided sequences with sequences which were developed by the learners themselves.
Under conditions of *self-sequencing*, pupils received a "table of contents"
in which the to-be-learned concepts were presented in alphabetical order.
From this index they had to choose the unit which they wished to begin with,
and after they completed studying this unit they chose the next and
so on. Thus, under these conditions subjects were allowed to construct their
own preferred sequences.

In some experiments we, additionally, gave some pupils supplementary written
instructions. These instructions specified how to take maximal advantage
of self-sequencing. In this condition, pupils received a structural overview of the subject matter, in which co-ordinate, superordinate and subordinate relations between elements were indicated. Furthermore, these pupils
were advised to look for those elements in the table of contents that
could clarify passages in the text which remained unclear. (Table 2 summarizes the sequences we used and the construction priciples underlying them).

TEACHER-PROVIDED	CONSTRUCTION PRINCIPLE
1. Communal	. Expert ordering
2. Hierarchical	. Logical prerequisite relations
3. Referential	. Inter-concept references
4. Random	. Alphabetical
SELF-REGULATED	
5. With supplementary instructions 6. Without supplementary instructions	Pupils preferences

Table 2
Types of sequences and the underlying construction
principles used in the experiments

LEARNING OUTCOMES

In most of our experiments we assessed learning outcomes with (1) a post test,
(2) a retention test and (3) a relations test. With the post and retention
tests we assessed the *amount of information* students *retained* from studying one

week and three weeks after completion of the course, respectively. The relations test was used in an attempt to assess the *quality of the structural
representation* of the subject matter present in the learner. A learner who
has a good overview of the structural properties of the subject matter can
do at least two things: (a) he/she can validly discriminate between relations which exist and which do not exist; (b) he/she can infer relations
between elements, which, though not explicitly described in the texts, are
a sensible inference from the knowledge acquired. We used reproductive responses to discriminate between existing and non-existing relations.
In contrast, a productive response was an inferred relation betwee two
subject matter elements which we deemed to be sensible.

We expected a reproductive response to be an indication of the amount of in-
ternalization of the text-bound structure and a productive response to be
a measure of the active building up of the more general conceptual content
structure. Using the relations test we could calculate two scores: a so-called REP (reproductivity)score and a PROD (productivity)score. The way these
scores could be determined can best be illustrated by Figure 3.

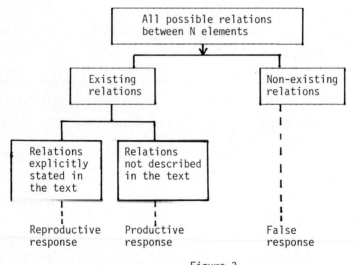

Figure 3
Deduction of productivity and reproductivity scores
from the relations test

The relations test consisted of all possible relations between the N (16
or 18) subject matter concepts. Respondents had to rate the degree of rela-
tednes of every pair using five-point scales. First we administered this
test to a group of 10 physics teachers in order to determine which of these
pairs indicated existing and non-existing relations. After having done this,
we analyzed the texts to find out which of the existing relations were explicitly described in the texts and which were not. After completion
of the course this test was administered to the learners. The ratings of
the learners were scored as reproductive whenever the learner indicated a high degree of relatedness between terms of a relation explicitly
stated in the course. The response was scored as being productive

when relatedness was rated high for a concept pair which indicated an existing relation, but not one that was explicitly described in the text. A response was scored as false if the learner indicated a high degree of relatedness on a non-existing relation. Finally, the REP-score was calculated as the percentage of correct reproductive responses minus a correction factor for guessing. The PROD-score was determined along similar lines for the percentage of productive responses.

EXPERIMENTAL RESULTS

Experiment 1

In the first experiment we compared the effectiveness of communal, random and self-constructed sequences. In the last condition learners received *no* supplementary instructions. The results of this experiment are summarized in Table 3.

LEARNING OUTCOMES				
CONDITION		RETENTION TEST	REP- TEST	PROD- TEST
Communal sequence	M SD	14.96 3.90	31.52 16.62	22.04 17.07
Self-regulated sequences	M SD	20.57 3.45	46.22 16.50	42.04 11.86
Random sequence	M SD	14.41 3.39	24.73 11.83	19.18 16.95

Table 3
Means and standard deviations in Experiment 1 for scores on three learning outcome measures under three sequencing conditions (N=68).

Surprisingly, at first glance we did not find significant differences between the communal and the random sequence conditions. (In all cases F-ratio's did not exceed the value of .80). This means that pupils learned both as well and as much under sequence conditions in which the order of presentation was rather illogical as when carefully planned. These results can, in our opinion, best be interpreted as an indication of the importance of active structuring by the learners. Active structuring is obligatory under random sequence conditions in order to get an adequate overview and representation of the relations between the subject matter elements. By actively structuring these elements, pupils can compensate for the handicap caused by the random sequence.

Furthermore, we found in this experiment strong superiority for the self-regulated sequences. Table 4 summarizes the F-ratio's and the associated probabilities found for retention, reproductivity, and productivity test scores in a comparison of the three conditions.

CRITERION	F	P
Reproductivity	4.15	<.02
Productivity	14.77	<.0001
Retention	20.52	<.0001

Table 4
F-values and associated probabilities in comparing
the three sequence conditions (Df=2; N=68)

These significant differences are completely attributed to the effectiveness
of the self-regulated sequence condition. When compared with communal and
random sequence conditions, the results of the self-sequencing conditon were
much better. This appeared to hold for the retention test scores (in comparing communal with self-regulated sequence conditions: $F(1;65) = 28.08$;
$p<.001$), as well as for both our indices of quality of internal representation (comparing self-regulation with communal sequencing we found for productivity: $F(1;65) = 19.24$; $p<.001$ and for reproductivity: $F(1;65) = 3.81$;
$p<.06$).

Experiment 2

The design of the second experiment was very similar to that of the first one.
Here we compared referential, hierarchical and self-regulated sequences.
With respect to the self-regulated sequences, a distinction was made between
a condition in which pupils received supplementary instructions for self-se-
quencing and a condition in which no further instructions were given.
The results of this study are summarized in Table 5.

Again, the learning outcomes were highest under self-regulated sequencing
conditions. More precisely, the effects of self-sequencing were highest
under conditions in which supplementary instructions were given. Self-sequencing without these further instructions was as effective as learning
under the referential sequence condition. In contrast, the effectiveness
of the hierarchical sequences was very poor. Again, these results hold for
both the achievement measures (post and retention test), as well as the
relation test scores (productivity and reproductivity of relations).

These results lend credence to the proposition that, among other things, the
effectiveness of self-sequencing can be further maximized by giving learners
adequate general "attack" instructions. Furthermore, it appears that sequencing written learning materials in accordance with the referential network
which underlies these materials may be a very effective sequencing mode.

CRITERION	CONDITION	MEAN-SCORE	STANDARD-DEVIATION
Post test	hierarchical	12.89	3.63
	referential	17.50	3.82
	self-regulated $+^{a)}$	19.53	3.54
	self-regulated $-^{b)}$	16.36	3.32
Retention test	hierarchical	12.12	4.15
	referential	14.17	3.82
	self-regulated $+^{a)}$	15.12	4.18
	self-regulated $-^{b)}$	13.94	3.90
Reproductivity	hierarchical	24.87	21.89
	referential	39.14	24.18
	self-regulated $+^{a)}$	49.08	17.31
	self-regulated $-^{b)}$	35.62	17.37
Productivity	hierarchical	10.54	31.91
	referential	24.21	16.57
	self-regulated $+^{a)}$	35.75	12.74
	self-regulated $-^{b)}$	30.34	17.53

Table 5
Means and standard deviations for four measures of learning outcomes
under four conditions of sequencing (N=70).
a) + means: with supplementary instructions
b) - means: without those instructions

Experiment 3

In the third experiment we were primarily concerned with looking for individual differences. To this end we designed an aptitude-treatment interaction study in which a selection of learner characteristics was included. This selection was done by using a heuristic strategy "correspondence analysis", which is specially devised for ATI research (Lodewijks & Simons, 1979).

With regard to the treatments, we again compared two preplanned sequence conditions and two self-regulated ones. In order to replicate Experiment 2, the preplanned conditions were again hierarchical and referential sequences. For self-sequencing, we again used conditions with and without supplementary instructions. The results obtained here were practically the same as those found in Experiment 2. With the exception of the retention test scores, achievement was consistently and significantly better under self-regulated, than under preplanned sequence conditions. Furthermore, several interesting effects were found with regard to the learner caracteristics.

Individual differences: some puzzling aptitude treatment interactions.

Using the correspondence analysis strategy student characteristics were derived which were presumed to interact with different sequencing conditions. These characteristics were: inductive and deductive reasoning ability, subjective prior knowledge (indexed as the degree to which a learner judges the different subject matter elements to be easy and familiar prior to instruction). In addition, achievement motivation and analogical reasoning ability were studied. With respect to these latter aptitudes main effects were expected.

Using multiple regression analysis the following was found with regard to learner characteristics. Data showed that learner's judgements of easiness and familiarity ('subjective prior knowledge') of learning materials were good predictors of learning outcomes. About 10% of the variance on all four learning measures can be accounted for by this factor. Significant main effects were further found for deductive reasoning ability (with regard to post test scores only), and for achievement motivation (exclusively with regard to productivity scores). A significant ordinal interaction was found for "facilitating minus debilitating anxiety", this with respect to productivity scores.

With respect to all four dependent variables significant and *disordinal* interactions were found for inductive and deductive reasoning ability, field independence and analogical reasoning ability. For ease of survey, only one general figure is presented here (details are to be found in: Lodewijks, 1981), which illustrates the kind of disordinal interactions that were found for these learner characteristics.

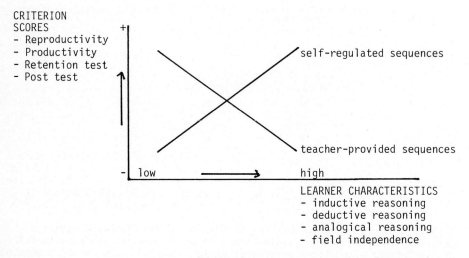

Figure 4
General ATI-figure, illustrating the kind of relations found for inductive, deductive, and analogical reasoning ability and field-independence with regard to all four criterion measures (N=69).

Interestingly enough, these interactions are quite puzzling. The nature of the interaction indicates that learners with high scores on field-independence, inductive, deductive, and analogical reasoning take maximal advantage of working under free, self-regulated, sequencing conditions. In contrast, learners with low scores on these measures do not do very well under self-regulated conditions. This is, however, not the puzzling part of the interaction. What, in fact, needs further clarification is the question of why students with high scores on the aforementioned measures perform so much more poorly under teacher-provided sequences than pupils with low scores on

these measures.
There is good reason to assume that less talented learners and learners with
low levels of field-independence may be helped by letting the teacher construct a sequence for them. This may compensate for their lack of ability in
effectively planning the learning of a sequence of information. However, it is
more difficult to understand why highly talented and high field-independent
learners are so handicapped by teacher-provided sequences. Obviously, some
sort of interference effect must be present here. The nature of this
interference effect is still unclear, but there is some reason to
believe that such an effect may show up under certain circumstances, as for
example, the ones described by Snow (1977, p. 69-75). In this review Snow
discusses several experiments in which interference effects were active for
highly talented students under conditions of strongly structured instruction.

CONCLUSIONS

The main conclusions to which our research on self-regulated versus teacher-
provided sequencing of written learning materials led us, can be summarized
as follows:
(1) In general, self-regulated sequences appear to be more conducive to
    learning than teacher-provided sequences.
(2) The effectiveness of self-sequencing depends to some degree on the availi-
    bility of "self-sequencing schemes". When these schemes are lacking or
    not adequate, specific sequencing instructions can compensate for this.
(3) Self-sequencing is not advantageous for all learners and may even be
    detrimental for some of them. Less talented and more field-dependent
    learners are most handicapped by self-sequencing. In contrast, highly ta-
    lented pupils with high levels of field independence profit greatly from
    this kind of sequencing of learning materials.
(4) With teacher-provided sequences however, this conclusion, needs to be
    reversed. In this case, the more talented and more field-independent
    learners are severely handicapped in learning, whereas the less talented
    and more field-dependent learners profit most.

The research we are doing now is directed towards *analyzing the learning processes* which take place when learners are allowed to regulate their own
learning. In so doing we hope to find out *why*, generally speaking, self
regulation is as effective as it appears to be here.

NOTE

The author wishes to express appreciation to Paul Kirschner for his helpful
comments on substance and style of the manuscript.

REFERENCES

Flammer, A., *Kognitive Struktur und Lernsequenz*. Forschungsbericht.
      Universität Freiburg, Schweiz. 1974.
Flammer, A., Büchel, R., & Gutmann, W., Wissensstruktur und Wahl von Infor-
      mationstexten. *Zeitschrift für Experimentelle und Angewandte Psycholo-
      gie*, 1976, *23*, 1, 30-44.
Gagné, R.M., Learning and instructional sequence. In: F.N. Kerlinger (Ed.),
      Review of Research in Education, *Volume I*, Itasca, Ill.: Peacock
      Publishers, 1973, 3-35.

Groeben, N., *Die Verständlichkeit von Unterrichtstexten: Dimensionen und Kriterien rezeptiver Lernstadien*. Münster: Aschendorf Verlag, 1972.

Klauer, K., *Methodik der Lehrzieldefiniton und Lehrstoffanalyse*. Düsseldorf: Pädogogischer Verlag Schwann, 1974.

Lodewijks, J.G.C.L., Over het aanleren van conceptuele netwerken door middel van uiteenlopende leerstofstructuren. (Teaching conceptual networks by different subject matter structures.). *Nederlands Tijdschrift voor de Psychologie*, 1978, *33*, 85-104.

Lodewijks, J.G.L.C., *Leerstofsequenties: van conceptueel netwerk naar cognitieve structuur*. (Subject matter sequences: From conceptual networks to cognitive structures.). Doctoral Dissertation, Tilburg University, Prinsenbeek: Perfekt, 1981.

Lodewijks, J.G.L.C., *Sequencing subject matter based on urgency-indices* (in preparation).

Lodewijks, J.G.L.C., & Simons, P.R.J., Een heuristische strategie ten behoeve van aptitude-treatment-interactie onderzoek: Correspondentie-analyse. (A heuristic strategy for aptitude-treatment interaction research: correspondence analysis.). In: W.J. Nijhof, & J. van Hout (Eds.), *Differentiatie in het onderwijs*. 's-Gravenhage: Staatsuitgeverij, 1979.

Mayer, R.E., The sequencing of instruction and the concept of assimilation-to-schema. *Instructional Science*, 1977, *6*, 369-388.

McConkie, G.W., Learning from text. In: L.S. Shulman, *Review of Research in Education, Volume 5*. Itasca, Ill.: Peacock Publishers, 1977, 3-49.

Posner, G.J., & Strike, K.A., A categorization scheme for principles of sequencing content. *Review of Educational Research*, 1976, *46*, 665-690.

Simons, P.R.J., Klerk, L.F.W. de, & Lodewijks, J.G.L.C., Aptitude-treatment-interacties tussen veld(on)afhankelijkheid en instructiekenmerken. (Aptitude-treatment-interactions between field(in)dependence and characteristics of the instruction.). *Nederlands Tijdschrift voor de Psychologie*, 1981, *36*, 317-326.

Snow, R.E., Research on aptitude for learning: A progress report. In: L.S. Shulman (Ed.), *Review of Research in Education IV*. Itasca, Ill.: Peacock Publishers, 1977.

Tennyson, R.D., A review of experimental methodology in instructional task sequencing. *AV-Communication Review*, 1972, *20*, 147-159.

DISCOURSE PROCESSING
A. Flammer and W. Kintsch (eds.)
© *North-Holland Publishing Company, 1982*

TEXT PROCESSING : A COMPARISON OF READING AND LISTENING

Marcel L. Goldschmid, Pierre Moessinger, Tamar Ferber-Stern,
André Koerffy and Jan Rozmuski

Chaire de Pédagogie et Didactique
Ecole Polytechnique Fédérale de Lausanne
Lausanne, Switzerland

This article describes an experiment on learning by listening
versus learning by reading. Two main variables were introduced,
the structure of the text and the expressiveness of the
lecturer. Students were tested on their recall of the material
and given questionnaires on their personality. Results reveal
that after hearing a non-expressive lecture, conformist students
perform better than independent ones. There is, furthermore, an
interaction between social orientation of the students and the
treatment, namely expressive lecture and non-structured text.

Within the framework of the evaluation of teaching methods, we shall treat
the comparison between learning by reading versus learning by listening.
It seems that merely comparing reading and listening to the same text is
insufficient. In fact, such a comparison does not reveal any conclusive
advantage of one method over the other (Costin, 1972). Therefore, we
chose to vary other factors in each oral and written treatment. One is the
expressiveness of the teacher, the other, text structure. We further
hypothesized that differences in learning are related to the student's
personality and study skills, and that there is an interaction between
personality and the treatment. This study is thus placed within the
methodological context of the ATI (Aptitude-Treatment-Interaction).

Listening

One of the most important variables in oral transmission seems to be the
expressivity of the lecturer. Frequently, when students evaluate their
teachers among themselves, the expressiveness of their professors has a
major influence on their judgment. This has been illustrated in a more
extreme context by the "Dr. Fox" experiments where an actor replaced the
teacher and gave an expressive but poorly-structured lecture. The would-
be teacher was not only highly evaluated but it was found that students
learned better than with a non-expressive but well-organized lecture
(Ware & Williams, 1975).

In our study, expressivity is defined as variation of intonation, the
presence of gestures which complement the speech (hand movements, eye
contact, movements between the desk and the blackboard), and the attempt

to establish a personal rapport with the audience by demonstrating
enthusiasm and interest in the subject presented. Non-expressivity is
defined as the absence of these gestures, a lack of enthusiasm and a
rather monotonous intonation. It is indeed difficult to define
expressivity very precisely. Yet a clearer behavioral description is
possible since the speaker was filmed on video during both the expressive
and monotonous lectures.

Reading

Extensive research has shown that text structure plays an important role
in the transfer of knowledge (Mayer, 1979; Rothkopf, 1971; Nelsson, 1976).
Most of this research deals with written texts which are read by the
students rather than oral ones. The experiment defined structure as the
presence of a small introduction, underlining of sentences (or italics),
learning objectives before each chapter, titles, sub-titles, and a
summary. In the non-structured text, all of these elements were absent,
except for the main title.

Content of text

The text chosen was a collection of ideas written for this experiment by
one member of the research team on the subject of obedience and
conformism. There were three reasons for the choice of this text :

1) Students were expected to be motivated by the confrontation with a
   moral dilemma,
2) the content was remote from their fields of study (in order not to
   interfere with attitudes towards the discipline studied), and
3) differences of knowledge of the subject were likely to be randomly
   distributed in the population studied.

These three points were not tested, but a small group of students was
questioned in a pilot stuly concerning their previous knowledge and their
interest in the theme to be presented.

Population

120 first-year students were taken from an introductory class of mathematics at the Swiss Federal Institute of Technology in Lausanne. Only
the answers of those students participating in the two stages of the
experiment were considered (N = 90).

Experiment

The students were divided into four groups. One group listened to the
expressive speaker, another to the non-expressive speaker. The two other
groups read the text; one read the structured text, the other the non-
structured text. A time limit was fixed which corresponded to a slow
reading. The content of the text was the same in the four instances.
Students were told that they were participating in an experiment, but the
purpose of the experiment was not explained. Immediately after this
learning session, a first questionnaire was distributed.

First questionnaire

In the first part of this questionnaire, students were asked to give their opinions regarding their interest in the theme presented, and their reactions to the manner in which it was presented. The questionnaire was given in three versions, one for the two oral presentations, one for the non-structured text, and one for the structured text.

Students were then presented with an immediate recall test which consisted of both multiple-choice and short-answer questions. These questions were prepared on precise points which were present in the text, and also on inferences which the students were asked to make from the content listened to or read, based upon an adaptation of Bloom's taxonomy (1956) and included 3 levels : comprehension, application, and analysis.

Ten days after the first session, students were asked to answer a second questionnaire in order to test their retention of the material presented as well as to obtain some information on their personalities, study habits, and work methods.

The learning test was of the same format as the recall test. It also contained four questions which were included in the recall test given immediately after the first learning session.

The personality test was divided into 4 parts : a test of values, a questionnaire on the "locus of control", two scales of the California Psychological Inventory (Gough, 1956) concerning the achievement via independence or conformity, and a shortened version of the Adjective-Check-List (Gough, 1952). The four personality tests were translated into French and adapted by F. Gendre (1974).

Our choice of these tests was influenced by previous research on the effects of personality or learning. First, we wanted to test Entwistle's (1975) hypothesis according to which students who believe in external control of their behavior learn better by lectures than by independant study, whereas students who believe in an internal control, learn better by independent study (reading). The choice of the CPI and the "Locus of control" was influenced by Domino's (1971) study who found that independent students are better at learning by reading whereas conformist students are better at learning by listening. According to Domino, there is an interaction between pedagogical treatment and the conformity-independence dimension of personality.

In the last test (study and work methods), students were asked about their methods of reading and listening, their home-work habits and the role of lecture courses in their study program.

Results

The following results are merely preliminary; the projected statistical analyses have yet to be completed and interpreted. It is also planned that the study be expanded and used as a basis for further experiments.

1) The study failed to show statistically significant differences in learning with respect to the manner in which the text was presented. However, of the four groups, the structured text group produced the best results.

2) The immediate recall test and retention test were found to be significantly correlated ($p \leqslant .05$) with the different personality measures. The following were principally retained :

   V_{59} CPI   Score - Achievement via conformity scale

   V_{60} CPI   Score - Achievement via independence scale

   V_{61} ACL   Score - Realist scale

   V_{62} ACL   Score - Independence scale

   V_{63} ACL   Score - Artistic scale

   V_{64} ACL   Score - Social scale

   V_{65} ACL   Score - Entrepreneurial scale

   V_{66} ACL   Score - Conventional scale

3) When the lecture was non-expressive, conformist students performed significantly better than independent students (CPI) on both the immediate recall and the learning tests. There was a positive correlation ($p = .038$) between the learning outcome of the non-expressive lecture and the achievement via conformity dimension. There was a strong negative correlation between the learning outcome for the non-expressive lecture and the achievement via independence scale of the CPI ($p = .006$). It was also found that the entrepreneurial score (V_{65}) on the ACL correlated negatively in the learning outcome with non-expressive subjects ($p = .034$). However, contrary to what was shown above, there was a negative correlation ($p = .010$) between lack of expressiveness and the ACL scale of conventionality (V_{66}) for the learning tests.

4) With the expressive lecturer, socially oriented students (according to V_{64}, the ACL social attitude scale) performed better than the non-socially-oriented students on both the immediate recall and the learning tests. When the lecture was expressive, there was a positive correlation between internal control (Rotter test) and the immediate recall test ($p = .022$) and the learning test ($p = .005$). With respect to the scales of the Adjective-Check-List, there was no significance between these and the different learning tests. As for the other dimensions of personality studied, no significant correlation was found with the learning tests (V_{59}, 60, 61, 62, 63, 65, 66).

5) When the text was unstructured there was a negative correlation with V_{64}, social orientation on the recall test ($p = .034$). For all the other variables no significant correlation was found.

6) With regard to the structured text, no correlation between either one of the learning tests and the above-mentioned personality dimensions was found.

Discussion

This experiment failed to show that a structured text produces a better learning outcome than a non-structured text, somewhat contrary to current research (Mayer, 1979; Nelsson, 1976; Ausubel, 1978). Expressiveness in a lecture was not found to be more conducive to learning than a non-expressive presentation. However, one should remember that our hypothesis was based upon Williams and Ware's (1975) experiment in which an expressive lecturer led the students to learn better than a non-expressive one. Moreover, this experiment has been frequently criticized (Frey, 1979; Goldschmid, 1978). Furthermore, there is a study by Bligh (note 1) showing results which seem to conflict with those of Williams and Ware. In fact, the simple presence of the lecturer was found to distract the students : those students who merely listened to the taped lecture were better able to learn than those who also viewed it.

The performance of the conformist students with a non-expressive lecturer is a new result. This could lead to elaborate Domino's (1971) hypothesis according to which conformists are better at learning by listening, than non-conformists.

The expressive lecture and the non-structured text produced opposing results with socially-oriented students. One can observe an interaction here between the treatment and personality. Thus this study is to be placed among the rather few experiments which corroborate the Aptitude-Treatment-Interaction hypotheses.

Among our projected analyses, we expect to emphasize significant effects of study habits on learning, and possible interactions between personality and study habits.

REFERENCE NOTE

Bligh, D. A pilot experiment to test the relative effectiveness of three kinds of teaching methods. University Teaching Methods Unit, University of London, Institute of Education.

REFERENCES

Ausubel, D.P. In defence of advance organizers : A reply to the critics. Review of Educational Research, 1978, 48, 251-257.

Bloom, B.S. (Ed.) Taxonomy of educational objectives : Handbook 1, cognitive domain, New York : David McKay, 1956.

Costin, F. Lecturing versus other methods of teaching : a review of research. British Journal of Educational Technology, 1972, 41, 1-31.

Domino, G. Interactive effects of achievement orientation and teaching style on academic achievement. Journal of Educational Psychology, 1971, 62, 427-431.

Entwistle, N.J. How students learn : information processing, individual developement and confrontation. Higher Education Bulletin, 1975, 3, 129-148.

Frey, P.W. The Dr. Fox effect and its implications. Instructional Evaluation, 1979, 3 (2), 1-5.

Gendre, F. L'évaluation de la personnalité à l'aide de l'inventaire psychologique de Californie de H. Gough. Revue de Psychologie Appliquée, 1974, 24, 159-179.

Goldschmid, M.L. The evaluation and improvement of teaching in higher education. Higher Education, 1978, 7, 221-245.

Gough, H.G. The Adjective Check List. Palo Alto : Consulting Psychologists, 1952.

Gough, H.G. California Psychological Inventory. Palo Alto : Consulting Psychologists, 1956.

Mayer, R.E. Twenty years of research on advance organizers : Assimilation theory is still the best predictor of results. Instructional Science, 1979, 8, 133-167.

Nelsson, O. Mathemagenic activities and teaching : A review. Higher Education Bulletin, 1976, 4, 159-197.

Rothkopf, E.Z. Experiments on mathemagenic behavior and the technology of written instruction. In E.Z. Rothkopf & P.E. Johnson (Eds) Verbal learning research and the technology of written instruction, New York : Teachers' College Press, 1971.

Ware, J.E. & Williams, R.G. The Dr. Fox effect : A study of lecture effectiveness and ratings of instruction. Journal of Medical Education, 1975, 50, 149-156.

DISCOURSE PROCESSING
A. Flammer and W. Kintsch (eds.)
© *North-Holland Publishing Company, 1982*

THE INFLUENCE OF WITHIN- AND BETWEEN-SENTENCE VARIABLES
ON THE COMPREHENSION OF NEWSPAPER ARTICLES BY TWO READER GROUPS

Marianne Tauber & François Stoll

Psychologisches Institut
der Universität Zürich
Zurich, Switzerland

The relative contribution of readability (within-sentence variables) and text organization (between-sentence variables) on the comprehension of newspaper articles
by two reader groups is examined. Three articles on
foreign politics were rewritten according to readability
(high, low) and organization (optimal, impaired). 76 job
trainees and 28 students were tested for reading time
and free recall. The trainees' recall performance was
affected by readability, but not by text organization.
While the students' recall performance was not affected
by text version, their reading speed was faster when the
texts showed high readability as well as optimal organization. It was concluded that the within- and the between-sentence dimension influenced text processing in an
interactive way.

INTRODUCTION

Reading-ease formulas continue to be the most practical procedure for measuring text comprehensibility. However, one criticism of this method is that
it is limited to sentence and word variables, i.e., within-sentence variables,
and neglects sentence bridging variables, i.e., between-sentence variables
(e.g., Groeben, 1976; Langer & Schulz von Thun & Tausch, 1974; Wieczerkowski
& Alzmann & Charlton, 1970). Langer et al. (1974) have developed a rating-
procedure to also measure sentence bridging variables. In an earlier study
(Tauber & Stoll & Drewek, 1980) we contrasted the reading-ease formula of
Dickes & Steiwer (1977) with the four rating dimensions of Langer. Among
other results a factor analysis revealed that the rating dimension called
'text organization' was not correlated with the constituents of the reading-
ease formula. If it is true that within- and between-sentence variables
measure two individual and mutually independent text dimensions, then their
relative contribution to text comprehension is of particular interest.

The object of this study was therefore to modify text readability on the one
hand and, on the other hand, text organization, to test their relative contribution to comprehensibility. Because comprehensibility is considered to
be the product of a reader-text-interaction (Mandl & Tergan & Ballstaedt,
1981, Note 1; Tauber & Gygax, 1980, Note 2) we were further interested in
the influence of the two text dimensions on the comprehension of two groups
of readers.

For our text sample, we selected newspaper articles dealing with foreign news because these articles use a particularly difficult writing style in Swiss-German newspapers (Amstad, 1978; Stoll, 1975). Furthermore newspaper articles are addressed to a large population and it is therefore worthwhile to examine them with regard to their comprehensibility for different groups of readers. As our subject samples, we selected job trainees and students from the 'Mittelschule'. Without making any claim for representativeness, we wanted to include samples from two populations which vary in social and economic status, level of education, and personal interests. Readability was measured with the Dickes & Steiwer formula, containing a word-length factor, a sentence-length factor and the type-token ratio. Text organization was defined on the basis of a text grammar specifically developed for this type of text. An example is given in Fig. 1, showing the macrostructure of the 'Afghanistan' article used in the experiment.

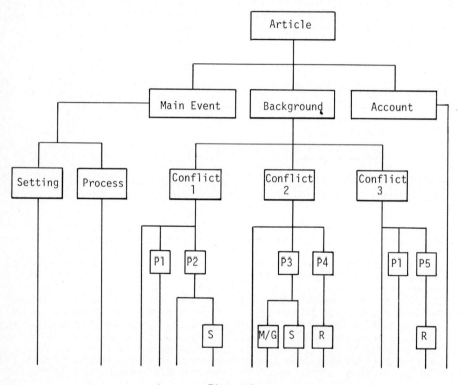

Figure 1
Macrostructure of the article 'Afghanistan'

With the term main event we mean the event that gave rise to a report in the news. Background elements are those factors that caused the main event: the conflicts which led up to the outbreak of the main event. Conflicts occur between parties (P) who manifest different motives and goals (M/G), strategies (S), and reactions (R). In his account, the journalist draws certain conclusions or makes predictions about continued development of the

situation in that country. According to this schema optimal organization
was achieved first by arranging the statements in the order of succession,
as can be read in Fig. 1, from left to right. And secondly, by dividing the
paragraphs according to their macroelements of main event, background conflict 1, 2, 3 and account.

METHOD

Materials. Three newspaper articles, entitled 'Afghanistan', 'Peking' and
'Holland', were taken from either the Neue Zürcher Zeitung or the Tages-
anzeiger. These articles appeared in the newspapers approximately 18 months
before the experiment took place and dealt with an overthrow of the govern-
ment in Afghanistan, a strike in Holland and a demonstration in Peking. For
each of the original articles, an improved and an impaired version was
written in accordance with the criterion 'readability' (high and low readability) and 'text organization' (optimal and impaired organization), so
that four versions of each content resulted (Table 1).

| | | ORGANIZATION | |
		optimal	impaired
READABILITY	high	A	B
	low	C	D

Table 1
The Four Text Versions

In the version employing high readability the shortest words possible were
used, foreign words were replaced by more common ones, sentences were shortened and the sentence construction was simplified. The optimal organization version was already described. In the impaired organization version,
the sentences were so arranged that the five macroelements were no longer
distinguishable. Nevertheless, a meaningful, random ordering of sentences
was avoided. The beginning and end of the original text versions were left
unchanged. The readability measures of the high and low readability versions
and the cluster indexes of the optimal and impaired organization versions
are represented in Table 2.

Subjects. The experiment was carried out once with 76 job trainees and once
with 28 'Mittelschule' students, all were males, between the ages of 17 and
18. The experiment required 90 minutes and took place during the subjects'
work or school time.

Design. A 2 x 2 x 3 factorial design with repeated measures was employed.
This included two organization levels (optimal and impaired) and two readability levels (high and low). The subjects were randomly assigned to the
four treatment groups, each group consisting of 19 job trainees and 7 students. Each subject was given all three articles, Afghanistan, Peking,
Holland, to be read one after the other. All three were read in the same
version, because we were also interested in learning by transfer which
might be caused by the text version. The third factor, called content, had

VERSION	CONTENT		
	Holland	Peking	Afghanistan
Readability[1]:			
low readability version	2.1	8.0	14.6
high readability version	10.3	13.9	22.1
Clusterindex[2]:			
impaired organization version	.77	.80	.75
optimal organization version	1.00	1.00	1.00

[1] Readability Formula of Dickes & Steiwer (1977)

[2] Adjusted Ratio of Clustering (Roenker & Thompson & Brown, 1971)

Table 2
Readability Measures and Cluster Indexes of the Text Versions

repeated measures and included three levels: Afghanistan, Holland, Peking. The order in which the articles were to be read was also balanced out.

Procedure. Subjects were tested in groups of 10. They were instructed to read the passages through with the same speed that one reads with interest. Each subject recorded his own reading time by means of a stop watch. After reading each article, the subjects were instructed to write down, to the best of their ability, what they could recall of it. Exact verbatim recall was not required, but to give the gist of the articles as accurately as possible. Unlimited recall time was provided. The subjects were also asked to rate the articles for comprehensibility according to a five-point scale.

RESULTS

For the scoring of the recall protocols, the original articles were segmented into propositions in accordance with the rules set down by Thorndyke (1977). The recall protocols were then scored for gist reproduction of propositions. First, we will present the results of the trainees, then the results of the students.

Trainees

The mean reading speed, i.e., the number of letters read per second, and the mean recall performance, i.e., the percent of correctly recalled propositions, are shown in Table 3. Both measures could be analyzed separately since a trade-off between reading speed and recall did not occur. The two measures correlated even positively ($r = .28$, $df = 74$, $p < .05$). If not otherwise mentioned, all the following results are based on 2 x 2 x 3 factorial analyses of variance for the factors organization, readability, and content, the last being a factor with repeated measures.

Reading speed. In the analysis of the reading speed data, the factors orga-

	CONTENT		
VERSION	Holland	Peking	Afghanistan
Reading Speed (Letters/Second)			
Optimal Organization			
High Readability	13.2	14.7	12.1
Low Readability	13.4	14.2	12.6
Impaired Organization			
High Readability	12.0	13.6	11.8
Low Readability	12.2	12.9	13.3
Recall Performance (Percent of Repr.Prop.)			
Optimal Organization			
High Readability	29.7	26.6	31.2
Low Readability	25.1	23.1	19.4
Impaired Organization			
High Readability	27.7	18.6	27.2
Low Readability	28.8	19.7	19.5

n per Group = 19
Total N   = 76

Table 3
Means for Reading Speed and Recall Performance of the Job Trainees

nization and readability each obtained significance only in a two-by-two interaction with the factor content (interaction between organization and content: $F(2,144) = 4.56$, $p < .05$; interaction between readability and content: $F(2,144) = 4.30$, $p < .05$). It is hardly possible to interpret the two interactions, since, depending on the article content, improving readability either raised or lowered the reading speed of the trainees, and improving organization either left unchanged or raised their speed. The trainees' reading speed seems to have been unsystematic with respect to both text manipulations. The factor content finally was highly significant ($F(2,144) = 13.45$, $p < .001$) and showed that 'Peking' was read faster than 'Afghanistan' and 'Holland'. The three way interaction remained above the significance threshold of .05.

Free recall. In the analysis of the recall data, the factor readability obtained a significant main effect ($F(1,72) = 5.75$, $p < .05$) and also interacted significantly with the factor content ($F(2,144) = 4.72$, $p < .05$). The factor organization, however, did not reach a significant main effect ($F(1,72) = 1.17$, $p > .10$) nor did it interact with the content ($F(2,144) = 2.42$, $p < .10$). The factor content was again highly significant ($F(2,144) = 8.97$, $p < .001$). The three-way interaction again remained above the threshold of significance. Improving readability benefited the trainees, the effect being highest in the Afghanistan article. Improving the organization, however, did not raise their recall performance.

Effect of position. In a two-factorial analysis of variance for the factors position of the articles (first, second, or third position) and text version (4 levels corresponding to the two organization versions and the two readability versions), position evidenced a significant effect on recall performance ($F(2,144) = 14.24$, $p < .001$) in the direction of improved performance with each progressive position. Text version did not interact significantly with position ($F(6,144) = .48$, $p > .10$), so that the conclusion must be made, that an equivalent learning effect took place with all text versions.

Subject ratings. Did the trainees' comprehensibility ratings correspond to their recall performance? The analysis of the subject ratings did not reveal any significant main effects for either readability or organization, but the factor content reached significance ($F(2,142) = 19.21$, $p < .001$). All the interactions remained above the threshold level of significance. The trainees rated the comprehensibility of the three contents in the same order of succession as their recall performance (Table 4).

	CONTENT		
	Holland	Afghanistan	Peking
Subject Ratings[1]	3.99	3.21	2.97
Free Recall	27.8	24.3	22.0
Text Length (Words)	266	331	416

[1] 5 is easy to understand
1 is difficult to understand

Table 4
Subject Ratings and Recall Performance of the Job Trainees
as a Function of Content or Text Length

'Peking' was ranked as the most difficult article, followed by 'Afghanistan' and then 'Holland'. The order of the three contents corresponded to that of the recall performance and also to that of text length. The shorter the article, the better it was recalled and judged as understandable.

Summary of the trainees' results. Improving readability led to better recall performance. Optimal organization had no effect on reading performance. The trainees' reading performance and their comprehensibility ratings were strongly influenced by article content or text length.

Students

In this instance, reading speed correlated slightly negatively with recall, however, the correlation was not significant ($r = -.19$, $df = 26$, $p > .10$). Thus, both measures could again be analyzed separately. The mean reading speed and the mean recall performance are shown in Table 5. At an average of 17 letters per second, the students read better than the trainees at 13 letters per second, and brought forth better recall performance with 35% reproduced propositions as compared with the trainees' 25%.

VERSION	CONTENT		
	Holland	Peking	Afghanistan
Reading Speed (Letters/Second)			
Optimal Organization			
High Readability	19.2	21.0	19.7
Low Readability	14.6	15.8	16.0
Impaired Organization			
High Readability	14.7	19.0	14.1
Low Readability	16.4	19.6	16.0
Recall Performance (Percent of Repr.Prop.)			
Optimal Organization			
High Readability	35.3	32.7	32.9
Low Readability	47.5	40.2	42.1
Impaired Organization			
High Readability	30.3	29.5	31.8
Low Readability	37.4	36.7	29.3

n per Group = 7
Total N   = 28

Table 5
Means for Reading Speed and Recall Performance of the Students

Reading speed. The versions optimalized according to both criterions were read fastest. Unlike the trainees, the students reacted systematically, i.e., they adjusted their reading speed in the same way to the text manipulations of all three contents. In the analysis of variance, the factors readability and organization interacted significantly ($F(1,24) = 4.42$, $p < .05$) without having any main effects (readability: $F(1,24) = .91$, $p > .10$; organization: $F(1,24) = .60$, $p > .10$). The content factor did reach a significant main effect ($F(2,48) = 4.76$, $p < .05$) but did not interact with readability ($F(2,48) = .22$, $p > .10$) nor with organization ($F(2,48) = 2.07$, $p > .10$). As with the trainees, Peking was read faster than Afghanistan and Holland.

Free recall. In the analysis of variance for recall performance not one source of variance approached significance. In contrast to the trainees, the students reproduced equally well all three articles and text versions.

Effect of position. The students also evidenced a learning effect with the progressive position ($F(2,54) = 9.18$, $p < .001$). Because of the small sample, a possible interaction between position and text version could not be clarified.

Subject ratings. In the analysis of variance neither the factor content nor the factor readability nor organization reached any significant main effects, and of all possible interactions only the one between readability and content reached significance ($F(2,48) = 3.44$, $p < .05$). In contrast to the trainees, the students judged the three contents as comparable in their comprehensibility. Not only that, their ratings revealed an interesting phenomenon: as was to be expected, the low readability version of the Afghanistan article was judged poorer than the high version, but the 'Holland' and 'Peking' articles were rated exactly the opposite. Even the recall means were somewhat higher for the low versions than for the high versions, although this effect was not significant. Nevertheless, the ratings revealed that the students found the more demanding, low readability version more comprehensible in two of the three articles.

Summary of the students' results. In contrast to the trainees, the students' recall performance was not affected by low text comprehensibility. They even judged the low readability version in two of the three articles as more comprehensible than the high readability version. However, the students adjusted their reading speed to text comprehensibility. Where one or both dimensions of comprehensibility were impaired, their reading speed was slower than in the high readable and optimally organized versions, and this phenomenon remained the same for all three articles.

DISCUSSION

It is not astonishing that the students, with their academic orientation, were less impeded by low text comprehensibility than the trainees (see Klare, 1976, for the influence of prior knowledge and intellectual level of the readers on the validity of readability formulas). As Rothkopf (1972) already observed in situations with unlimited reading time, the students adjusted their reading speed to the text difficulty and exhibited no loss of information in their free recall. This study, however, showed, that readers with lower intellectual level may not achieve this adjustment of reading speed and manifest a loss in their recall performance due to low text readability.

The main conclusion of this study is that the within- and the between-sentence dimensions did influence text processing in an interactive and not in an additive way. This conclusion is based on two arguments: First, students' reading time was reduced only by improving readability and organization, but not by improving only one of these dimensions. The second argument for an interactive influence is based on the interpretation as to why text organization did not affect the trainees' recall performance. The result that the trainees reproduced worse with increased text length suggests that their memory was overtaxed since they could only recode or 'chunk' units on a within-sentence or microstructure level of analysis and not on a sentence-bridging or macrostructure level. For readers who do not recode text information through units of a macrostructure level - maybe because they encounter too many difficulties in the microstructure - optimalizing text organization cannot have any facilitating effect. Improving text organization seems therefore to aid text processing only if the text readability is reader-adjusted, i.e., if the reader's recoding on the microstructure level occurs without difficulty.

REFERENCE NOTES

Mandl, H., Tergan, S.O.,and Ballstaedt, S.-P. Textverständlichkeit - Text-verstehen. Forschungsbericht Nr. 12 des Deutschen Instituts für Fernstudien an der Universität Tübingen, 1981.

Tauber, M. and Gygax, M. Psychologie der schriftlichen Kommunikation. Standortbestimmung und Ausblick. Bericht Nr. 12 der Abteilung Angewandte Psychologie der Universität Zürich, 1980.

REFERENCES

Amstad, T. Wie verständlich sind unsere Zeitungen? Universität Zürich: Dissertation, 1978.

Dickes, P. and Steiwer, L. Ausarbeitung von Lesbarkeitsformeln für die deutsche Sprache. Zeitschrift für Entwicklungspsychologie und pädagogische Psychologie, 1977, 9, 20-28.

Groeben, N. Verstehen, Behalten, Interesse. Unterrichtswissenschaft, 1976, 2, 128-142.

Klare, G.R. A second look at the validity of readability formulas. Journal of Reading Behavior, 1976, 8, 129-152.

Langer, I., Schulz von Thun, F., and Tausch, R. Verständlichkeit. Basel: Reinhardt, 1974.

Roenker, D.L., Thompson, C.P., and Brown, S.C. Comparison of measures for the estimation of clustering in free recall. Psychological Bulletin, 1971, 76, 45-48.

Rothkopf, E.Z. Structural text features and the control of processes in learning from written materials. In: R.O. Freedle and J.B. Carroll (Eds.). Language Comprehension and the acquisition of knowledge. Washington, D.C.: Winston, 1972.

Stoll, F. Le score de la lisibilité de Flesch appliqué à quelques textes de langue allemande. Schweizerische Zeitschrift für Psychologie und ihre Anwendungen, 1975, 34, 275-277.

Tauber, M., Stoll, F., and Drewek, R. Erfassen Lesbarkeitsformeln und Textbeurteilung verschiedene Dimensionen der Textverständlichkeit? Zeitschrift für experimentelle und angewandte Psychologie, 1980, 27, 135-146.

Thorndyke, P.W. Cognitive structures in comprehension and memory of narrative discourse. Cognitive Psychology, 1977, 9, 77-110.

Wieczerkowski, W., Alzmann, O., and Charlton, M. Die Auswirkung verbesserter Textgestaltung auf Lesbarkeitswerte, Verständlichkeit und Behalten. Zeitschrift für Entwicklungs- und pädagogische Psychologie, 1970, 2, 257-268.

DISCOURSE PROCESSING
A. Flammer and W. Kintsch (eds.)
© *North-Holland Publishing Company, 1982*

DEVELOPMENT AND EVALUATION OF A
TEXT MAPPING STRATEGY

Donald F. Dansereau
Texas Christian University

Charles D. Holley
Texas College of Osteopathic Medicine

Networking is a content-independent text learning
strageqy that requires the student to transform
text material into two-dimensional maps. Key ideas
(nodes) are related to one another by a set of six
empirically derived relationships (links). This
chapter consists of a presentation of the historical and theoretical foundations of networking, a
description of the empirical assessments, a comparison of networking with spatial text strategies developed in other laboratories, and a discussion of
the future of networking.

INTRODUCTION

Until recently educational research and development efforts have been directed almost exclusively at the improvement of teaching. As has been
argued previously, this endeavor has been only marginally effective in
improving student learning (Dansereau,1978). In addition, it is clear that
an exclusive focus on improving teaching methods may lead to inadvertent
reinforcement of inappropriate and nontransferable learning strategies.
For example, many teaching and testing methods implicitly encourage rote
memorization by specifying exactly what must be learned, rewarding verbatim answers on tests, and putting little emphasis on the development of
relationships between incoming and stored information. Rote memorization
usually involves multiple readings of the material with little or no effort
devoted to assimilating the information. Therefore, the material learned
through this method usually is not meaningfully related to other stored
information, which limits the facility with which such information can be
retrieved at a later date. Such a strategy, although perhaps useful in our
present educational environments, is maladaptive in many job situations,
where understanding is more important than mere storage. Although the
limitations of rote memorization have been emphasized, the same arguments
probably apply to a large number of other strategies developed by students
to cope with a teaching-oriented education.

By not stressing learning strategies, educators, in essence, discourage
students from developing and exploring new strategies, and, in so doing,
limit students' awareness of their cognitive capabilities. For example,
the results of the administration of an extensive learning strategy inventory (Dansereau, Long, McDonald, & Actkinson, 1975a) indicate that even
good college students have very little knowledge of alternative learning
techniques. This lack of awareness obviously limits an individual's

ability in a situation requiring new learning strategies. In addition, if the strategies that individuals have spontaneously adopted do not match their cognitive capabilities, the emotional toll may be very large. Most of us know individuals who spend inordinate amounts of time memorizing college or high school text materials and are still barely "getting by." Such an individual's personal, intellectual, and social development must certainly suffer from the pressures created by this use of a relatively inefficient learning strategy.

In summary, exclusive emphasis on teaching methods may lead to ineffective instructional manipulations, force students to develop nontransferable and inefficient strategies, limit a student's cognitive awareness, and, consequently, extract a large emotional toll. The solution to this problem is clear: Educators and researchers should redirect at least some of their efforts to the development and training of appropriate learning strategies and skills.

Over the last four years there has been substantial progress made in this redirection of efforts. Two major volumes on learning strategies have been published (O'Neil, 1978; O'Neil & Spielberger, 1979) and the National Institute of Education has established a separate granting program focused on cognitive strategies.

To provide further information on the present utility and future potential of learning stragegy research, this paper describes the development and evaluation of a specific text processing strategy (networking) that has emerged from a programmatic effort to create a learning strategies curriculum.

Over the past four years the authors and their colleagues have developed, evaluated, and modified components of an interactive learning strategy system. This system is composed of both primary strategies, which are used to operate on the text material directly (e.g., comprehension and memory strategies) and support strategies, which are used by the learner to maintain a suitable cognitive climate (e.g., concentration strategies). Assessments of the overall strategy system and system components indicate that strategy training significantly improves performance on selected text processing tasks (Collins, Dansereau, Holley, Garland, & McDonald, 1981; Dansereau, 1978; Dansereau, Collins, McDonald, Holley, Garland, Diekhoff, & Evans, 1979a; Dansereau, McDonald, Collins, Garland, Holley, Diekhoff, & Evans, 1979b; Holley, Dansereau, McDonald, Garland, & Collins, 1979).

The major component of the support strategies is concentration management. This component, which is designed to help the student set and maintain constructive moods for studying and task performance, consists of a combination of elements from systematic desensitization (Jacobsen, 1938; Wolpe, 1969), rational behavior therapy (Ellis, 1963; Maultsby, 1971), and therapies based on positive self-talk (Meichenbaum & Goodman, 1971; Meichenbaum & Turk, Note 1). The students are first given experiences and strategies designed to assist them in becoming aware of the negative and positive emotions, self-talk, and images they generate in facing a learning task. They are then instructed to evaluate the constructiveness of their internal dialogue and are given heuristics for making appropriate modifications.

In preparing for studying or testing sessions students report that they usually spend little or no conscious effort establishing constructive moods. To remedy this situation the student is trained on a technique that forms the basis of systematic desensitization: imagination of the target situation during relaxation. Specifically, the students are instructed to spend 2 to 3 minutes relaxing and then imagining their actions as they proceed through a productive study or test session. To help them maintain the resulting mood they are given experiences and techniques to assist them in determining when, how, and why they get distracted, the duration of their distraction periods, and their typical reactions to distraction. They are then trained to cope with distractions by using relaxation and positive self-talk and imagery to reestablish an appropriate learning state.

This particular combination of concentration management strategies has been shown to lead to significantly better performance on text processing tasks in comparison to students using their own methods (Collins et al., 1981). These strategies have been supplemented by training on goal-setting, scheduling, and other monitoring strategies to form the support strategy component of the program (see Dansereau, 1978).

NETWORKING AND RELATED SPATIAL STRATEGIES

Networking forms the basis for the primary strategies in the learning strategy system. During acquisition the student identifies important concepts or ideas in the material and represents their interrelationships and structure in the form of a network map. To assist the student in this endeavor s/he is taught a set of named links that can be used to code the relationships between ideas.[1] The networking processes emphasize the identification and representation of (a) hierarchies (type/part), (b) chains (lines of reasoning/temporal orderings/causal sequences), and (c) clusters (characteristics/definitions/analogies). Figure 1 is a schematic representation of these three types of structures and their associated links and Figure 2 is an example of a summary map of a nursing textbook chapter. Application of this technique results in the production of structured two-dimensional maps. These cognitive networks provide the student with a spatial organization of the information contained in the original training materials. While constructing the map, the student is encouraged to paraphrase and/or draw pictorial representations of the important ideas and concepts for inclusion in the network.

When faced with a test or a task in which the learned information is to be used, the student is trained to use the named links as retrieval cues and the networking process as a method for organizing the material prior to responding. Assessments of networking (Dansereau et al., 1979b; Holley et al., 1979) have shown that students using this strategy perform significantly better on text processing tasks than do students using their own methods.

---

[1]
Earlier versions of networking contained thirteen experimenter-provided links. However, students found it unwieldy to remember and apply this number of relationships. A subsequent version of networking used four experimenter-provided links, but this system did not appear to provide the students with sufficient detail in their networks. The six-link system appears to be a satisfactory compromise between generality and specificity.

Structure	Link	Description	Key Words
Hierarchy	Part (of) hand ↓p finger	The content in a lower node is part of the object, idea, process or concept contained in a higher node.	part of segment of portion of
	Type (of)/ Example (of) school ↓t public	The content in a lower node is a member or example of the class or category or processes, ideas, concepts, or objects contained· in a higher node.	type of category example of kind of Three "x" are
Chain	Leads to practice ↓l perfection	The object, process, concept, or idea in one node leads to or results in the object, process, idea, or concept in another node.	leads to results in causes is a tool of produces
Cluster	Analogy T.C.U. ↓a factory	The object, idea, process, or concept in one node is analogous to, similar to, corresponds to, or is like the object, idea, process, or concept in another node.	similar to analogous to like corresponds to
	Character- istic sky ↓c blue	The object, idea, process, or concept in one node is a trait, aspect, quality, feature, attribute, detail or characteristic of the object, process, concept, or idea in another node.	has characterized feature property trait aspect attribute
	Evidence broken arm ↓e x-ray	The object, idea, process, or concept in one node provides evidence, facts, data, support, proof, documentation, or confir- mation for the object, idea, process, or concept in another node.	indicates illustrates demonstrates supports documents proof of confirms evidence of

Figure 1
Link Types and Structure Types
Employed with the Networking Technique

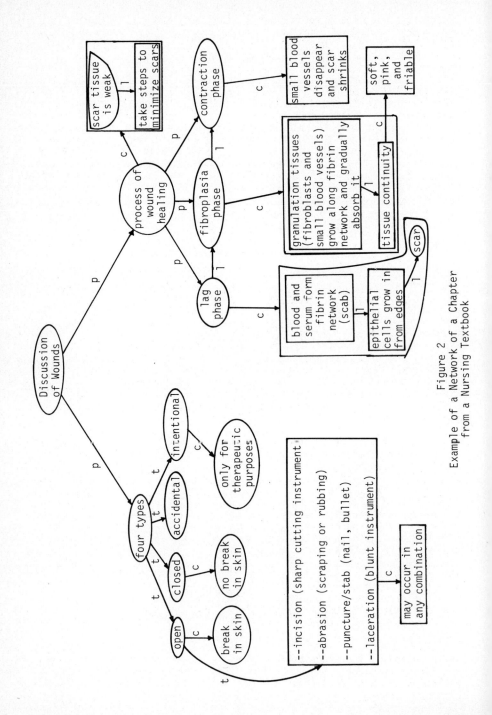

Figure 2
Example of a Network of a Chapter
from a Nursing Textbook

Concomitant with the development of networking, two other laboratories were also embarked on longitudinal research projects to develop similar spatial strategies. These laboratories are the University of Illinois (Urbana-Champaign) which developed a technique called mapping and the University of Amsterdam which developed a technique called schematizing.

Like networking, each of these techniques requires the students to convert prose material into two-dimensional node-link diagrams. The nodes represent important ideas or concepts and the links represent the relationships between ideas. These techniques, along with networking, are particularly noteworthy in that they provide a formal, easily learned, flexible system for re-representing text material. Unlike more content dependent techniques (e.g., matrixing, flow charting, constructing pictures), these systems can be used with a wide variety of text. Further, they can potentially be used to enhance not only learner activities, but teaching and testing activities as well. Before discussing networking in greater detail a brief description of the mapping and schematizing strategies and their supporting evidence will be presented.

MAPPING AND SCHEMATIZING AS SPATIAL STRATEGIES

Mapping was developed at the Center for the Study of Reading, University of Illinois (Urbana-Champaign) by T. H. Anderson and his colleagues (e.g., T. H. Anderson, 1979; T. H. Anderson & Armbruster, 1981; Armbruster, Note 2; Armbruster & T. H. Anderson, Note 3; Armbruster & Schallert, Note 4). T. H. Anderson (1979) credits Hauf (1971) and Merritt (Merritt, Prior, Grugeon, & Grugeon, 1977) as precursors to mapping. In particular, Hauf (1971) used an elementary approach to mapping which involved placing the central idea of a passage near the middle of a note page and attaching the subsidiary ideas in a concentric fashion, thus producing a product resembling a road map. T. H. Anderson (1979) argued that any mapping scheme "should have the flexibility and simplicity of the one discussed by Hauf (1971), but also should be capable of succinctly representing a variety of relationships" (pp. 93-94).

In mapping, the student learns a set of relational conventions or symbols. These experimenter-provided symbols provide for depicting seven fundamental relationships between two ideas, e.g., A and B. These relationships are: (a) B is an instance of A; (b) B is a property or characteristic of A; (c) A is similar to B; (d) A is greater than or less than B; (e) A occurs before B; (f) A causes B and (g) A is the negation of B. Additionally, two special relationships identify A as an important idea or a definition; the connectives and and or are also used. Application of mapping results in the production of structured two-dimensional diagrams such as the example shown in Figure 3.

The experimental support for mapping is sparse, but the few studies that have been conducted indicate that the technique facilitates delayed recall of short narrative prose (e.g., Armbruster, Note 2; Armbruster & T. H. Anderson, Note 3). One important aspect of these studies is that they employed middle school students as subjects vis-à-vis the traditional college sophomore.

The principal differences between mapping and networking appear to be that the former strategy: (a) emphasizes local organization rather than abstraction of an overall framework or schema, and (b) employs spatial repre-

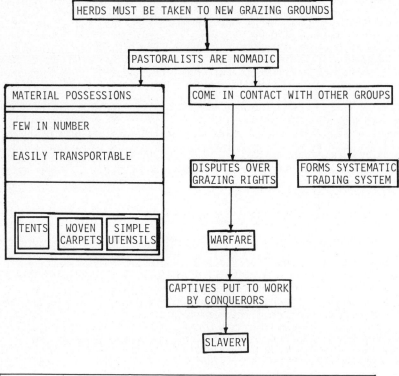

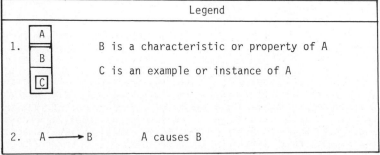

Figure 3
Example of a Map of a
Sociology Passage

sentation of relationships rather than labeled relationships. With respect to the first difference, T. H. Anderson (1979) argued that application of mapping to entire text chapters was too time consuming and recommended that the strategy be employed for each important task outcome (e.g., potential test item on a chapter test). However, Holley et al. (1979) argued that the abstraction of an overall framework (macrostructure) for ecologically oriented passages (e.g., textbook chapters) was an important feature of a mapping strategy (i.e., networking). With respect to the second difference, whether the relationships are depicted graphically or labeled may be irrelevant--as long as they are depicted. Whichever method is eventually demonstrated to be simpler for students to comprehend and apply would probably determine which (if either) method is superior.

Schematizing was developed at the Center for Research into Higher Education (COWO), University of Amsterdam (e.g., Breuker, Note 5; Camstra, Note 6; Mirande, Note 7; van Brugger, Note 8). According to Brueker (Note 5), the theoretical underpinnings for schematizing are an eclectic blend of node-arc representations (e.g., Frijda, 1972), schema notions (e.g., R. Anderson, Spiro, & Montague, 1977; Winograd, 1975), macrostructure (e.g., van Dijk, 1977), episodic-semantic memory distinctions (e.g., Tulving, 1972); and artificial intelligence (e.g., Winston, 1977).

Schematizing involves the labeling (and, where appropriate, the clustering) of concepts and the depiction of relationships between concepts via lines which are annotated to reflect seven types of relationships (Mirande, Note 7). These relationships and annotations are presented in Table 1. Application of the technique results in the production of serially-organized (left to right), two-dimensional diagrams of a passage.

Schematizing is similar to networking, and different from mapping, in that it uses annotated lines to depict relationships between concepts and emphasizes the extraction of an overall framework or macrostructure. It is different from networking in the types of relations depicted, the method of annotation that is used (as previously argued, such differences may be irrelevant), and the organizational structure of the resulting diagrams (serial vis-à-vis hierarchical). The importance (if any) of this latter difference has not been demonstrated.

As with mapping, little experimental evidence is available to support (or refute) the effectiveness of schematizing. The majority of studies that have been conducted are of a "field study" nature and are more along the lines of formative rather than summative evaluations. Nonetheless, the technique has been shown to be an effective processing aid in the context of a general study skills course (Camstra, Metten, & Mirande, Note 9).

During the remainder of this paper we will present the foundations of networking, more detail on the empirical evaluations and a discussion of future directions.

FOUNDATIONS OF NETWORKING

Dansereau, Long, McDonald, Actkinson, Ellis, Collins, Williams, and Evans (1976) explored the utility of imagery (drawing), paraphrasing, and questioning as techniques for students to use in re-representing textbook material. On a delayed (1 week after study) essay test over four 1,000-

Table 1

Relationship Symbols Employed with
the Schematization Technique[a]

Relationship	Symbol
Similarity	═══════════
Interaction	───────────▶
Denial of Similarity	═══════/═══
Denial of a Static Relation	───────/───
Denial of a Dynamic Relation	──────/──▶
Negative Influence	──────────▶⊖
Positive Influence	──────────▶⊕

[a]
 Lines represent static relationships (e.g., classifications, properties,
 time/space, comparisons); arrows represent dynamic relationships (e.g.,
 conditional, cause-and-effect).

word passages, the order of mean performance from best to worst was:
paraphrase, imagery, question-answer, and control students using their own
study methods. The performances of the paraphrase and imagery groups were
significantly better than those of the control group. Studies conducted
by other investigators have also indicated positive findings for paraphrasing (Andre & Sola, 1976), imagery/drawing (Kulhavy & Swenson, 1975;
Levin & Divine-Hawkins, 1974; Rasco, Tennyson, & Boutwell, 1974), and self-
generated questions (Frase & Schwartz, 1975). In general, research along
these lines has used relatively short bodies of prose material (usually
1500 words or less). With this amount of material, abstraction of an
underlying organization may not be as difficult or as critical as it is
for longer passages. A number of researchers have suggested that the
identification of an organizing framework or schema is necessary for complete understanding, and may aid in the retention of details (e.g.,
Bransford & Johnson, 1974; Rumelhart, 1975). Consequently, with longer
bodies of material processing strategies that emphasize the identification
and utilization of an organizing framework or schema may be more effective
than localized strategies such as paraphrasing, imaging, and questioning.

In response to this state of affairs the networking technique was developed. This technique was designed to assist the student in reorganizing passage information based on principles abstracted from relationship based models of long term memory. Quillian (1968) suggested that
human memory may be organized as a network composed of ideas or concepts
(nodes) and named relationships between these concepts (links). For example, the relationships (links) between the concepts (nodes) bird, parrot,
and colorful can be expressed as, "A parrot is a type of bird" and "A

parrot can be <u>characterized</u> as colorful." These node-link relationships can be represented spatially as follows:

Since Quillian's early work, a number of network models of memory have been proposed and tested (e.g., J. R. Anderson, 1972: J. R. Anderson & Bower, 1973; Bobrow & Winograd, 1977; Rumelhart, Lindsay, & Norman, 1972). The results of these efforts indicate that at least some aspects of human memory can be functionally represented as networks.

In addition to providing an alternative representational system that may be closer to the way information is stored in human memory, the networking procedure requires the learner to engage in a number of activities which have been hypothesized to facilitate text processing. These activities include:

1. Visual representation of the ideas presented (e.g., R. Anderson & Kulhavy, 1972; Dansereau, Long, McDonald, Actkinson, Collins, Evans, Ellis, & Williams, 1975b; Kulhavy & Swenson, 1975; Lesgold, McCormick, & Golinkoff, 1972; Levin & Divine-Hawkins, 1974; Nelson, 1979; Paivio, 1976).

2. Increased processing to determine key ideas and their relationships (e.g., J. Anderson & Reder, 1979; Craik & Lockhart, 1972; Craik & Tulving, 1975; Jacoby & Craik, 1979; Reder, 1980).

3. Establishment of schemata or organizers for subsequent encounters with the text (e.g., R. C. Anderson, 1977; R. C. Anderson, Spiro, & M. C. Anderson, 1978; Ausubel, 1963; Bransford, 1979; Rigney & Munro, Note 10; Rumelhart & Ortony, 1977).

4. Reorganization of the text information (e.g., DiVesta, Schultz, & Dangel, 1973; Frase, 1969; Holley et al., 1979; Myers, 1974; Perlmutter & Royer, 1973; Shimmerlik, 1978).

5. Development of a cuing system to facilitate subsequent retrieval (e.g., Craik & Jacoby, 1975; Jacoby, 1974; Tulving, 1974; Tulving & Thompson, 1973).

Improved performance due to the use of networking is probably the result of some combination of these and other factors. To provide a basis for improving this strategy, one would like to know which factors are primarily responsible for the present level of success. Consequently, studies should be designed to evaluate versions of networking which have been modified to eliminate or amplify sets of the previously listed activities.

It should be noted that such an approach can capitalize on the potential reciprocal relationships between strategy application and basic cognitive/educational theories. On the one hand, notions derived from these theories can provide heuristics for selecting effective manipulations of the strategy. On the other hand, the training and implementation of the strategy can serve as an arena for the collection of information relevant to the development of basic theories of text processing.

In addition to its role as a text learning strategy, networking also appears to have potential for facilitating communication (e.g., teaching and writing) and problem-solving (personal as well as objective) processes. Networks are potentially more amenable to a variety of manipulations (e.g., problem-solving processes) than are natural language representations. If these speculations are accurate the students can be taught the basic concepts of networking and then given training on applying this general purpose tool to text, communication, and various types of problems. These possibilities will be discussed further in a subsequent section. Prior to that, however, we will present a brief review of the networking research that has been conducted to date.

EVALUATIONS OF NETWORKING

One aspect of the initial study in this domain compared a combined para-phrase/imagery strategy with normal study methods on a 3,000-word text-book passage (longer material than typically used in prior learning strategy experiments) and showed no significant differences (Dansereau, McDonald, Collins, Garland, Holley, Diekhoff, & Evans, 1979b). In that same study a planned comparison between performance of a group using net-working and performance of a group using their own methods was significant (Holley, Dansereau, McDonald, Garland, & Collins, 1979); on the portion of the test designed to tap retention of the main ideas the networking group performed approximately 42% higher than the control group.

Holley et al. (1979) conducted a more controlled assessment of a network-ing strategy using a 3,000-word passage extracted from a geology textbook. Treatment students received 5.5 hours of networking training prior to studying the passage and were compared to a "no-treatment" control group which used their normal study methods on the passage (see Holley & Dansereau, 1981, for elaboration of the control procedure). Five days after studying, the students were given the following sequence of tests over the material: essay (free recall), short-answer, multiple-choice, and a summary-oriented concept cloze (see Battig, 1979, for an elabora-tion of this testing sequence).

A Hotelling T^2 test indicated that the networking group significantly outperformed the control group on the dependent measures. Further analyses showed that the major differences between groups were attribu-table to the concept cloze and essay exams, both of which were designed to assess performance on "main ideas." This pattern of results suggests that the strategy is valuable in assisting the student in the extraction and retention of main ideas but does not appear to affect the extraction and retention of details; this finding is consistent with other less well-controlled evaluations of networking (e.g., Dansereau et al., 1979a and b). Additionally, post hoc 2 x 2 factorial analyses of high and low grade point average (GPA) subgroups indicated that the strategy may be more beneficial for low GPA students.

Vaughn (Note 11) and Vaughn, Stillman, and Sabers (Note 12) have de-veloped a strategy (Concept Structuring) which is conceptually similar to networking and argued that, in two studies, students who used this

procedure had better immediate and delayed recall of general ideas, mid-
level ideas, details, factual information and inferential information.
However, due to methodological flaws in the experimental designs, Vaughn
(Note 11) cautioned against over-generalizing these findings.

Vaughn's procedure appears to lack the structural emphasis of the original
networking strategy and also leaves the links unlabeled. With respect to
the first difference, Holley et al. (1979) argued that this structural
emphasis was important with longer passages of text. While Vaughn (Note
11) employed longer passages and obtained positive results, the methodological limitations of the studies do not allow definitive conclusions
to be drawn. With respect to the second difference, T. H. Anderson (1979)
argued that an important characteristic of spatial strategies was that
students could "record ...the relationship among ideas" (p. 93). Whether
or not the student uses experimenter-provided or student-generated
"labels" is probably irrelevant (except for initial training purposes),
but identification of specific relationships would seem to be essential,
particularly for delayed review of the spatial aids.

Long (Note 13; Long, Hein, & Coggiola, Note 14) has successfully employed
networking as a spatial strategy with hearing-impaired students.[2] However,
his modification of networking also lacks the structural emphasis of the
original approach. Since Long's evaluations generally employed short,
narrative passages this modification probably did not affect the results.

To date, the empirical work supporting the efficacy of the networking
strategy and spatial strategies in general has been relatively sparse.
To provide a basis for subsequent evaluation and improvement of these
techniques, studies should be conducted to determine the critical aspects
of the strategies. Experimentation with spatial strategies, and to a
large extent learning strategies in general, poses a unique set of
problems and concerns that require resolution. The major concerns can
be subdivided into those associated with the following:

1. Strategy training -- This involves selection of effective and economical training methods, durations, and incentives.

2. Measurement of effects -- Multiple measures are needed to converge
on the locus of strategy training effects (cf. Jenkins, 1979).

3. Experimental design and analyses -- Appropriate empirical and
statistical controls are necessary to disambiguate alternate interpretations of treatment effects (cf. Holley & Dansereau, 1981).

These problems, and potential solutions, have been examined in detail
elsewhere (e.g., Dansereau, 1981; Holley & Dansereau, 1981). Future research in this domain should be based on careful consideration of these
issues.

---

[2]
  Dr. Long was a member of the research team at Texas Christian University
which developed the earlier versions of networking. After his transfer
to Rochester Institute for the Deaf, he developed his own modifications
to networking and applied the technique with hearing-impaired students.

THE FUTURE OF NETWORKING

To a large extent the comments made in this section apply to other spatial
strategies as well as networking. In addition to the basic empirical work
that is needed to establish parameters and boundary conditions relevant to
networking as a text processing strategy, the following potential applications of networking appear to warrant serious consideration.

1. Evaluation of students. Surber and his colleagues (Surber, Harper, &
Smith, Note 15; Surber, Smith, & Harper, Note 16) have begun work on a
project for using mapping (the technique developed at the University of
Illinois) as a vehicle for testing and diagnostics. Early results from
this project have shown moderate validity with respect to traditional objective tests, and high interrater reliabilities.

Conceptually, it seems reasonable to expect that ability to network (i.e.,
to discover and organize meaningful relationships among ideas, objects,
and actions) should be related to general reading comprehension ability.
If this expectation is borne out, networking may serve as an alternative
assessment and diagnostic device. In fact, the noun phrases in a body of
text can be replaced by nonmeaningful symbols. A student's ability to
network this material would seem to reflect a type of comprehension skill
that is separable from vocabulary level and prior knowledge.

2. Text analysis. Since it identifies the organization and interrelationships of the underlying concepts, networking may be a valuable tool
for evaluating content and content organization. For example, are the
ideas in the text logically organized? Are the relationships between
ideas unambiguous? Since the networking type of analysis would be generally at a more macro level when compared to analytical schemes such as
those of Meyer (1975) or Kintsch and van Dijk (1978), it may provide a
valuable supplement to these existing approaches. Further the ease and/
or accuracy with which a text can be networked may provide a more valid
index of comprehensibility (readability) than is presently available.

3. Facilitation of teaching/communicating. From the teacher's perspective networking can be used in the preparation of lectures as an alternative to outlining. Also, teacher-prepared networks can be presented
as advance and post organizers. Additional benefits may be derived from
using networks in teaching students who are employing networking as a
learning strategy.

Networking can be used to facilitate group communications by providing a
mechanism for systematically organizing and manipulating the task space.
This approach has been used in the context of a graduate psychology seminar at Texas Christian University. Subjective reactions to the approach
indicate that it has substantial promise as a communication facilitator.

4. Problem solving. Research is being conducted to determine the value
of networking as a tool for creating manipulable problem spaces. Informal evaluations of this approach have indicated that it has substantial
potential in assisting the individual in comprehending problems and determining potential corrective actions.

We have just barely scratched the surface in examining the utility of
networking and other similar spatial strategies. Major systematic research and development efforts are needed before the promise of these
techniques can be fully realized.

Reference Notes

1. Meichenbaum, D. H. & Turk, D. The cognitive-behavioral management of anxiety, anger, and pain. Paper presented at the Seventh Baniff International Conference on Behavioral Modification, Canada, 1975.

2. Armbruster, B. B. An investigation of the effectiveness of "mapping" text as a studying strategy for middle school students. Unpublished doctoral dissertation, University of Illinois, 1979.

3. Armbruster, B. B., & Anderson, T. H. The effect of mapping on the free recall of expository text (Tech. Rep. 160). Champaign, Ill.: Center for the Study of Reading, University of Illinois, February 1980.

4. Armbruster, B. B., & Schallert, D. L. Understanding text through mapping. Paper presented at the annual meeting of the National Reading Conference, San Diego, Ca., December 1980.

5. Breuker, J. A. Theoretical foundations of schematizations: From macrostructures to conceptual frames. Paper presented at the EARDHE International Conference, Klagenfurt, Austria, January 1979.

6. Camstra, B. Empirical research with "learning by schematizing." Paper presented at the EARDHE International Conference, Klagenfurt, Austria, January 1979.

7. Mirande, M. Schematizing: Techniques and applications. Paper presented at the EARDHE International Conference, Klagenfurt, Austria, January 1979.

8. van Brugger, J. M. Personal communication, June 11, 1979.

9. Camstra, B., Metten, A., & Mirande, M. Effectonderzoek van enn studievaardigheidscursus. Manuscript available from the first author, Center for Research into Higher Education (COWO), University of Amsterdam, Amsterdam, The Netherlands.

10. Rigney, J. W., & Munro, A. On cognitive strategies for processing text (Tech. Rep. 80). Los Angeles: University of Southern California, Behavioral Technology Laboratories, March 1977.

11. Vaughn, J. L. The construct procedure fosters active reading and learning. Manuscript available from the author, College of Education, East Texas State University, Commerce, Texas.

12. Vaughn, J. L., Stillman, P. L., & Sabers, D. L. Construction of ideational scaffolds during reading. Manuscript available from the first author, College of Education, East Texas State University, Commerce, Texas.

13. Long, G. L. Dissecting prose passages through semantic mapping: Procedures for training. Paper presented at the annual meeting of the National Reading Conference, San Diego, Ca., December 1980.

14. Long, G. L., Hein, R. D., & Coggiola, D. C. <u>Networking: A Semantic-based learning strategy for improving prose comprehension</u> (Tech. Rep., R & D Paper Series No. 26). Rochester, N. Y.: National Technical Institute for the Deaf, Department of Research and Development, September 1978.

15. Surber, J. R., Harper, F., & Smith, P. L. <u>Training students to take tests written in text-map format</u> (Tech. Rep. 2). Milwaukee: University of Wisconsin-Milwaukee, Department of Educational Psychology, 1980.

16. Surber, J. R., Smith, P. L., & Harper, F. <u>A practical method of assessing memory organization in instructional settings</u>. Paper presented at the annual meeting of the American Educational Research Association, Los Angeles, Ca., April 1981.

References

Anderson, J. R. A simulation model of free recall. In G. H. Bower (Ed.), <u>The psychology of learning and motivation</u> (Vol. 5). New York: Academic Press, 1972.

Anderson, J. R., & Bower, G. H. <u>Human associative memory</u>. Washington, D. C.: Winston, 1973.

Anderson, J. R., & Reder, L. M. An elaborative processing explanation of depth of processing. In L. S. Cermak & F. I. M. Craik (Eds.), <u>Levels of processing in human memory</u>. New York: Wiley, 1979.

Anderson, R. C. The notion of schemata and the educational enterprise. In R. C. Anderson, R. J. Spiro, & W. E. Montague (Eds.), <u>Schooling and the acquisition of knowledge</u>. Hillsdale, N. J.: Erlbaum, 1977.

Anderson, R. C., & Kulhavy, R. W. Learning concepts from definitions. <u>American Educational Research Journal</u>, 1972, <u>9</u>, 385-390.

Anderson, R. C., Spiro, R. J., & Anderson, M. C. Schemata as scaffolding for the representation of information in connected discourse. <u>American Educational Research Journal</u>, 1978, <u>15</u>, 433-440.

Anderson, R. C., Spiro, R. J., & Montague, W. E. <u>Schooling and the acquisition of knowledge</u>. Hillsdale, N. J.: Erlbaum, 1977.

Anderson, T. H. Study skills and learning strategies. In H. F. O'Neil, Jr., & C. D. Spielberger (Eds.), <u>Cognitive and affective learning strategies</u>. New York: Academic Press, 1979.

Anderson, T. H., & Armbruster, B. B. Studying. In P. D. Pearson (Ed.), <u>Handbook on reading research</u>. New York: Longman, 1981.

Andre, T., & Sola, J. Imagery, verbatim and paraphrased questions, and retention of meaningful sentences. <u>Journal of Educational Psychology</u>, 1976, <u>68</u>, 661-669.

Ausubel, D. P. The psychology of meaningful verbal learning. New York: Grune & Stratton, 1963.

Battig, W. F. The flexibility of human memory. In L. S. Cermak & F.I.M. Craik (Eds.), Levels of processing in human memory. New York: Wiley, 1979.

Bobrow, D. G., & Winograd, T. An overview of KRL, a knowledge representation language. Cognitive Science, 1977, 1, 13-46.

Bransford, J. D. Human cognition: Learning, understanding and remembering. Belmont, Ca.: Wadsworth, 1979.

Bransford, J. D., & Johnson, M. K. Considerations of some problems of comprehension. In W. G. Chase (Ed.), Visual information processing. New York: Academic Press, 1973.

Collins, K. W., Dansereau, D. F., Holley, C. D., Garland, J. C., & McDonald, B. A. Control of concentration during academic tasks. Journal of Educational Psychology, 1981, 73, 122-128.

Craik, F.I.M. & Jacoby, L.L. A process view of short-term retention. In F. Restle, R. M. Shiffrin, J. J. Castellan, M. R. Lindman, & D. B. Pisoni (Eds.), Cognitive theory (vol. 1). Hillsdale, N. J.: Erlbaum, 1975.

Craik, F.I.M., & Lockhart, R. S. Levels of processing: A framework for memory research. Journal of Verbal Learning and Verbal Behavior, 1972, 11, 671-684.

Craik, F.I.M., & Tulving, E. Depth of processing and the retention of words in episodic memory. Journal of Experimental Psychology: General, 1975, 104, 268-294.

Dansereau, D. F. The development of a learning strategies curriculum. In H. F. O'Neil, Jr. (Ed.), Learning strategies. New York: Academic Press, 1978.

Dansereau, D. F. Learning strategy research. Proceedings of the NIE-LRDC conference on thinking and learning skills. Washington, D.C.: National Institute of Education, 1981.

Dansereau, D. F., Collins, K. W., McDonald, B. A., Holley, C. D., Garland, J. C., Diekhoff, G., & Evans, S. H. Development and evaluation of a learning strategy training program. Journal of Educational Psychology, 1979a, 71, 64-73.

Dansereau, D. F., Long, G. L., McDonald, B. A., & Actkinson, T. R. Learning strategy inventory development and assessment (AFHRL-TR-75-40). Lowry Air Force Base, Colo.: Technical Training Division, June 1975a. (NTIS No. AD-A014 721).

Dansereau, D. F., Long, G. L., McDonald, B. A., Actkinson, T. R., Ellis, A. M., Collins, K. W., Williams, S., & Evans, S. H. Effective learning strategy training program: Development and assessment. Catalog of Selected Documents in Psychology. 1976, 6, 19.

Dansereau, D. F., Long, G. L., McDonald, B. A., Actkinson, T. R., Collins, K. W., Evans, S. H., Ellis, A. M., & Williams, S. Learning strategy training program: Visual imagery for effective learning (AFHRL-TR-75-47). Lowry Air Force Base, Colo.: Technical Training Division, June 1975b. (NTIS No. AD-A014 724).

Dansereau, D. F., McDonald, B. A., Collins, K. W., Garland, J. C., Holley, C. D., Diekhoff, G. M., & Evans, S. H. Evaluation of a learning strategy system. In H. F. O'Neil, Jr., & C. D. Spielberger (Eds.), Cognitive and affective learning strategies. New York: Academic Press, 1979b.

DiVesta, F. J., Schultz, C. B., & Dangel, I. R. Passage organization and imposed learning strategies in comprehension and recall of connected discourse. Memory & Cognition, 1973, 6, 471-476.

Ellis, A. Reason and emotion in psychotherapy. New York: Lyle Stuart, 1963.

Frase, L. T. Paragraph organization of written materials: The influence of conceptual clustering upon level and organization of recall. Journal of Educational Psychology, 1969, 60, 394-401.

Frase, L. T., & Schwartz, B. J. Effect of question production and answering on prose recall. Journal of Educational Psychology, 1975, 67, 628-635.

Frijda, N. H. The simulation of long term memory. Psychololog- ical Bulletin, 1972, 77, 1-31.

Hauf, M. B. Mapping: A technique for translating reading into thinking Journal of Reading, 1971, 14, 225-230.

Holley, C. D. An evaluation of intact and embedded headings as schema cuing devices with non-narrative text (Doctoral dissertation, Texas Christian University, 1979). Dissertation Abstracts Inter- national, 1979, 40, 4491A. (University Microfilms No. 80-02, 220)

Holley, C. D., & Dansereau, D. F. Controlling for transient motivation in cognitive manipulation studies. Journal of Experimental Education, 1981, 49, 84-91.

Holley, C. D., Dansereau, D. F., & Fenker, R. M. Some data and comments regarding educational set theory. Journal of Educational Psychology, 1981, 74(4), 494-504.

Holley, C. D., Dansereau, D. F., McDonald, B. A., Garland, J. C., & Collins, K. W. Evaluation of a hierarchical mapping technique as an aid to prose processing. Contemporary Educational Psychology, 1979, 4, 227-237.

Jacobsen, E. Progressive relaxation. Chicago: University of Chicago Press, 1938.

Jacoby, L. L. The role of mental contiguity in memory: Registration and retrieval effects. _Journal of Verbal Learning and Verbal Behavior_, 1974, _13_, 483-496.

Jacoby. L. L., & Craik, F.I.M. Effects of elaboration of processing at encoding and retrieval: Trace distinctiveness and recovery of initial context. In L. S. Cermak & F.I.M. Craik (Eds.), _Levels of processing in human memory_. Hillsdale, N. J.: Erlbaum, 1979.

Jenkins, J. J. Four points to remember: A tetrahedral model of memory experiments. In L. S. Cermak & F.I.M. Craik (Eds.), _Levels of processing in human memory_. Hillsdale, N. J.: Erlbaum, 1979.

Kintsch, W., & van Dijk, T. A. Toward a model of text comprehension and production. _Psychological Review,_ 1978, _85_, 363-394.

Kulhavy, R. W., & Swenson, I. Imagery instructions and the comprehension of text. _British Journal of Educational Psychology_, 1975, _45_, 47-51.

Lesgold, A. M., McCormick, C., & Golinkoff, R. M. Imagery training and children's prose reading. _Journal of Educational Psychology_, 1972, _67_, 663-667.

Levin, J. R., & Divine-Hawkins, P. Visual imagery as a prose-learning process. _Journal of Reading Behavior_, 1974, _6_, 23-30.

Maultsby, M. _Handbook of rational self-counseling._ Madison, Wisconsin: Association for Rational Thinking, 1971.

Meichenbaum, D. H., & Goodman, J. Training impulsive children to talk to themselves: A means of self-control. _Journal of Abnormal Psychology_, 1971, _77_, 115-126.

Merrit, J., Prior, D., Grugeon, E., & Grugeon, D. _Developing independence in reading_. Milton Keynes: The Open University Press, 1977.

Meyer, B.J.F. _The organization of prose and its effect upon memory_. Amsterdam, The Netherlands: North Holland, 1975.

Myers, J. L. _Memory for prose material_. Amherst, Mass.: University of Massachusetts, 1974. (Eric Document Reproduction Service No. ED 094 360)

Nelson, D. L. Remembering pictures and words: Appearance, significance, and name. In L. S. Cermak & F.I.M. Craik (Eds.), _Levels of processing in human memory_. Hillsdale, N. J.: Erlbaum, 1979.

O'Neil, H. F. _Learning strategies_. New York: Academic Press, 1978.

O'Neil, H. F., & Spielberger, C. D. _Cognitive and affective learning strategies_. New York: Academic Press, 1979.

Paivio, A. Imagery in recall and recognition. In J. Brown (Ed.), _Recall and recognition_. London: Academic Press, 1976.

Perlmutter, J., & Royer, J. M. Organization of prose materials: Stimulus, storage and retrieval. Canadian Journal of Psychology, 1973, 27, 200-209.

Quillian, M. R. Semantic meaning. In M. Minsky (Ed.), Semantic information processing. Cambridge, Mass.: M.I.T. Press, 1968.

Rasco, R. W., Tennyson, R. P., & Boutwell, R. C. Imagery instructions and drawings in learning prose. Journal of Educational Research, 1975, 67, 188-192.

Reder, L. M. The role of elaboration in the comprehension and retention of prose: A critical review. Review of Educational Research, 1980, 50, 5-53.

Rumelhart, D. E. Notes on a schema for stories. In D. Bobrow & A. Collins (Eds.), Representation and understanding: Studies in cognitive science. New York: Academic Press, 1975.

Rumelhart, D. E., Lindsay, P. H., & Norman, D. A. A process model for long-term memory. In E. Tulving & W. Donaldson (Eds.), Organization of memory. New York: Academic Press, 1972.

Rumelhart, D. E., & Ortony, A. The representation of knowledge in memory. In R. C. Anderson, R. J. Spiro, & W. E. Montague (Eds.), Schooling and the acquisition of knowledge. Hillsdale, N. J.: Erlbaum, 1977.

Shimmerlik, S. M. Organization theory and memory for prose: A review of the literature. Review of Educational Research, 1978, 48, 103-120.

Tulving, E. Episodic and semantic memory. In E. Tulving & W. Donaldson (Eds.), Organization of memory. New York: Academic Press, 1972.

Tulving, E. Cue-dependent forgetting. American Scientist, 1974, 62, 74-82.

Tulving, E., & Thompson, D. M. Encoding specificity and retrieval processes in episodic memory. Psychological Review, 1973, 80, 352-373.

van Dijk, T. A. Macro-structures and cognition. In P. Carpenter & M. Just (Eds.), Cognitive processes in comprehension. Hillsdale, N. J.: Erlbaum, 1977.

Winograd, T. Frame representations and the declarative-procedure controversy. In D. A. Bobrow & A. M. Collins (Eds.), Representation and understanding. New York: Academic Press, 1975.

Wolpe, J. The practice of behavior therapy. New York: Pergamon, 1969.

Winston, P. Artificial intelligence. Philippines: Addison-Wesley, 1977.

DISCOURSE PROCESSING
A. Flammer and W. Kintsch (eds.)
© *North-Holland Publishing Company, 1982*

QUEST FOR AN "A": A CASE STUDY OF A UNIVERSITY
STUDENT'S TEXT PROCESSING

Anthony M. Owens

State College of Victoria, Coburg
Australia

A student who had a previous history of two years of
class grades in the C-D range on the A-B-C-D-F system
and who in the current class was scoring at a D level
agreed to use a study method which included reading
for meaning, generating her own questions about the
text, testing her own knowledge in various ways, and
using devices such as mnemonics, modal shifts, and
overlearning to develop easily accessible cognitive
structures of the two chapters of examinable material.
All procedures used were based on understanding, maximal attention, and time. The initial assignment was to
read four pages of text and to develop an open question
about each of the paragraphs. Her early questions were
found to require little more than rote citation of
factual material and to omit much of the content. This
discovery was followed by training in ways to find the
central ideas of each paragraph and the level of subsequent questions improved substantially. Methods of
revision and recall facilitation were followed and the
60 pages of text were eventually reduced to two small
file cards containing a series of one to three word recall cues. On subsequent class tests the student
achieved A grades and even topped the class on one of
them; she also reported improvement in other subjects.
Later her performance fell to a B level which she explained in terms of having made a compromise with the
use of her time.

Judy, a 20 year-old female undergraduate in her third year at a midwestern
university in the U.S., proposed to become a teacher when she graduated.
She was a nondescript student in most ways: blonde hair, light complexion,
about five foot nine, a friendly student of medium intelligence who did
nothing in class to distinguish herself except that she once said that she
had come from a family of fifteen children. Since she had been at the university her class grades had hovered around the low "C" range in an A-B-C-
D-F system; her few "B" grades had been more than offset by the proponder-
ance of "C" and "D" grades she had achieved. At that rate she appeared to
be destined to graduate at the lower end of her class in a little more than
one year's time.

For the first four weeks of Spring term, Judy had scored at a "D" level on
the bi-weekly multiple-choice tests in my Child Psychology class. At the
end of a class in which we had discussed a previous test, Judy came to see
me in response to my offer to help the students raise their grades; she
was the only person to respond to the offer from a class of 35 students.

FIRST MEETING

During that first meeting, which lasted about one hour, Judy told of her
previous study methods and I outlined the bases for the practices I was
going to ask her to follow in the coming weeks. Up until that time Judy
had studied for exams by skimming the relevant text sometime during the previous two weeks and trying to read it thoroughly one or two nights before
the test. Sometimes she used a coloured felt-tip pen to underline the
text. She would also read her relevant class notes before taking a test.
When asked what went through her mind while she was reading in preparation
for the test, Judy replied that she understood what she read quite well
the first time she read it properly but that if she tried to read it again
she found herself just staring at the words and daydreaming, and this usually resulted in dozing off. She said she was puzzled by the contradiction
in that she could completely understand something she read the previous
night but not know it when she tried to answer questions on the test the
next day. When asked her opinion of her dilemma she said that "maybe I'm
a bit too dumb" or that she "hadn't studied hard enough."

She was then given a very brief sketch of some of the then current research
into the determinants of learning from text by skilled readers. The bases
of the sketch included work by many researchers, especially Anderson (1970),
Ausubel (1968), Bugelski (1970), Carroll (1963, 1971), Carver (1970, 1972,
1973), Cooper and Pantle (1967), Frase (1975), Frase and Schwartz (1975),
Owens (1980), Rothkopf (1965, 1970), Wittrock (1974), and Wittrock, Marks
and Doctorow (1975). She was told a paraphrase of the following: To be
able to correctly answer questions about a unit or chapter of text the
reader must first of all understand what is read. This does not mean that
he should know names, places, and other associations by rote. Rather, it
means that the reader should have a grasp of the general basic ideas that
the author was attempting to convey. So one of the major bases of successful reading is to read while purposefully trying to understand what the
author means.

The second basis of successful reading concerns the amount of time spent
reading and thinking about the content of the text. Researchers have shown
that for simple learning tasks such as poetry (Lyon, 1917) and word lists
(Bugelski, 1962) there is an almost perfect linear relationship between
length of task and the length of time required for mastery. There is good
reason to believe that although other variables enter prose learning, the
total time hypothesis is a plausible heuristic once reading and learning
ability are accounted for.

The third important variable concerns attention. Most people become bored
when they repeatedly perform the same behaviour unless there is some element of the task to keep their interest. For instance, we quickly lose
interest in reading a mystery story once we have discovered that we have
read it before. To combat this drop in attentiveness while studying, we
keep changing the mode of our learning. First of all we read for meaning

and try to glean the author's main ideas. We then convert these ideas into questions which we can use to continually challenge ourselves.

Once we have adequate questions over the whole chapter or two we list the questions on the left side of a page leaving room for the answers on the right. Then without looking at the text, we answer our questions in pencil. Later we check our answers with the text and write in the correct answers in pen. Once we have a full set of questions and answers we will start to build up the amount of time we spend thinking about these questions and answers. To do that we will have to rehearse in a number of different ways to keep up our interest and be as efficient as possible in our learning.

The ways in which this questioning technique continues to be varied to stimulate our attention is only limited by the extent of the learner's imagination. Social involvement is highly motivating and is an excellent way to change the mode of learning. Question "bees" with roommates, fellow students or cooperative family members can give a learner a rewarding event to work towards while learning material that could otherwise become deadly boring very quickly. Exchanging questions with fellow students can be a useful way to keep a cross check on one's answers and add to the pool of questions at the same time.

The question-answer method is included for three important reasons. Firstly, it is a sure way to make us resymbolize the information in the text while using only our memory as an aid. This process, when coupled with added rehearsals, increases retention. Secondly, when we construct questions using the ideas and facts from the text, it is good chance that we are devising questions which will be on the upcoming examination. So our study method can become a simulation of the method by which our knowledge is to be evaluated. If other testing methods are used, we would be wise to change our study methods accordingly. Thirdly, question-answer exercises are extremely amenable to variety and modification. They can be done alone, in groups of all sizes, using dramatic or comic settings, on the telephone, and even between computer terminals. Any method of information transmission can be used for this study method.

Judy left the first meeting after voicing a committment to give the plan a chance and to fully cooperate. Her first task was to read four pages of her textbook for meaning and to construct one open question about each paragraph and bring them to our next meeting in two days time.

SECOND MEETING

The initial quality of Judy's questions was, as expected, of a reasonable low level. Most questions did not tap the central idea of the paragraph but asked simple associational questions which concerned only peripheral parts of the idea unit, e.g., "Who dismisses the genetic/environment argument of sex-role development?" This question missed the major idea of the paragraph and the answer elicited was of a very low level of meaningfulness. The major part of this meeting was devoted to demonstrating to Judy that each paragraph had a central idea and that her task was to find the idea and frame a question around it. Judy caught on to this idea rather quickly and after devising some higher quality questions she left confident about devising better questions for the next seven pages, or 24 paragraphs of text.

THIRD MEETING

Judging from the questions that she had constructed since our last meeting, two days ago, Judy appeared to be well on her way to understanding paragraph meanings. The question which replaced the example given during the second meeting was: "Describe Lewis and Weinraub's active organismic approach to the origins of early sex-role development." The question itself carries a wealth of information and the answer elicited could contain most of the information from the paragraph. Judy appeared quite elated with her progress and admitted that she had never known that paragraphs were developed from only one central idea. She agreed to finish constructing questions for the remaining 10 pages of the chapter over the weekend and to begin work on the next chapter.

FOURTH MEETING

I was in for a very pleasant surprise, when at 10:30 the next Monday morning, Judy presented me with a great sheaf of pages of questions and answers on the two chapters which we were currently studying. The questions were generally of pretty good standard. After examining a sample of her questions, it was evident that Judy was still having trouble devising questions which subsumed an entire paragraph. The remainder of the hour was spent identifying questions that required revision and after we had redeemed some of them, Judy left with her homework for the evening, i.e., further revision of questions.

FIFTH MEETING

The next morning a quick look at a few sample questions and their answers convinced me that Judy now had an adequate notion of how to construct questions which elicited most of the information in a paragraph. We spent the majority of that hour finding and discussing how we could devise questions which related to several parts of the text. Her next assignment was to develop two questions on each chapter which required integrating several theories or research findings. Before she left I folded one of her many pages of questions and answers down the dividing line so that the questions were visible with their respective answers on the back. Judy smiled and said, "Yes, I know what you're suggesting." She said that she would try to get her roommate, a music major, to help her test her knowledge in the next two days.

SIXTH MEETING

Judy, for whatever reason, did not develop the four integrating questions promised; she did, however, devise one on each chapter. One of them was: "In what way is Kohlberg's notion of sex-role development inconsistent and/ or compatible with the active organismic approach of Lewis and Weinraub?" Although the question was basically on the same topic, it did cover six neighbouring paragraphs of the text. When I fired a succession of questions about the text at her, she was able to answer most of them quite well. For her last assignment before the test the following day, I gave her two white four by six inch file cards and asked her to use key words to summarize all the information in her question-answer sheets at one card per chapter. With an incredulous look and without a word she took the cards and left the room.

SEVENTH MEETING

Before the test the next day Judy, with a triumphant smile, showed me the two file cards which were quite full of words and diagrams that probably wouldn't make much sense to most people. However, Judy did acknowledge that she had found them quite handy and a lot less cumbersome than her question/ answer sheets, although while studying she occasionally had found it neces- sary to refer back to them or to the textbook. After the test, a quick manual check showed that Judy had scored 87%, enough to put her at the "A" level for that test. (After machine scoring and the elimination of one faulty item her score was raised slightly). She was elated and I was quite pleased. We arranged an appointment for the following Friday, one week away, for her to show me questions and answers on the next two chapters.

EIGHTH MEETING

Judy did not arrive at our next appointment. Instead she telephoned to say she was going quite well and would be doing note cards on the weekend. She apologized for not coming to my office but didn't want to waste time walking down the hill and up to her dormitory again.

On the next test Judy topped the class with a score of 96%. Weeks and tests passed with her scoring 90%, 84%, and 82% on the last bi-weekly test of the quarter. Toward the end of that term, we happened to meet in the corridor near the psychology laboratory. I congratulated her on her success and her overall "B" grade for the quarter, and questioned her about her scores fall- ing off at the end of the term. She explained this is terms of having to compromise between four courses and her boyfriend. Nevertheless she said she had encorporated rudiments of our study method with her other classes and achieved three "B" grades (including Child Psychology), one "A" in Modern History, and was planning to go skiing with her boyfriend during the term break. In a later conversation, Judy admitted that she had really wanted to get an "A" but once she realized that she was able to do "A" level work in Child Psychology, she was quite content to use the basics of the study method to ensure a "B" grade and forego all the extra effort that "A" level work required.

The following plan has been used (and usually modified) by several students with success. The basic principles are:

1.   Understand what you read.
2.   Maintain total attention however you can.
3.   Build the amount of time you attend to ideas even after you know them well.

BASIC PLAN

1.   Skim. Take particular note of headings, charts, highlights.
2.   Read for meaning.
3.   Frame a question(s) that covers a unit or paragraph of text.

4. Try to answer questions without peeking. Pencil.
5. Score them (honestly).
6. Modify answers with reference to text in pen.

7. Read content units to check that questions cover all content.
8. Modify questions or add as required.

9. Answer questions aloud. Ask aloud too. Check questions having trouble with.
10. Read correct answers aloud.
11. Do same from memory.

12. Exchange questions and answers with friend. Friend asks you your questions and you answer without peeking. (Reciprocate).
13. Friend asks you his questions. Answer aloud.
14. Practice A & A as above together after break.

15. Precis answers to all questions with key words.
16. Looking at precis respond to questions.

17. As above without looking at precis. Peek when wrong and correct.

18. Further precis to letter mnemonics.

19. Reduce all answers to one 3 x 5 index card.

    (Modify all Q/A sessions. Aloud, silent, with friend(s), on telephone, play acting esp. when alone. e.g. court witness answering magistrate).

20. Check answers with text. Amend.

21. Enjoy your success.
22. While using the principles of understanding the main points, maintaining your attention by using a variety of study modes, and building up the amount of time spent processing the topic (preferable in Q-A form, esp. if that is to be the examination method), change and prune these steps to suit your own circumstances, preferences, and imagination.

REFERENCES

Anderson, R. C. Control of student mediating processes during verbal learning and instruction. Review of Educational Research, 1970 40, 349-370.

Ausubel, D. P. Educational psychology: A cognitive view. New York: Holt, Rinehart and Winston, 1968.

Bugelski, B. R. Presentation time, total time, and mediation in paired associate learning. Journal of Experimental Psychology, 1962, 63, 409-412.

Carroll, J. B. A model of school learning. Teachers College Record, 1963, 64, 723-733.

Carroll, J. B. Learning from verbal discourse in educational media: A review of the literature. Princeton, New Jersey: Educational Testing Service, 1971.

Carver, R. P. A critical review of mathemagenic behaviours and the effect of questions upon the retention of prose material. Journal of Reading Behaviour, 1972, 4, 93-119.

Carver, R. P. A test of an hypothesized relationship between learning
    time and amount learned in school learning. Journal of Educational
    Research, 1970, 64, 57-58.
Carver, R. P. Understanding, information processing, and learning from
    prose materials. Journal of Educational Psychology, 1973, 64, 76-84.
Cooper, E. H., and Pantle, A. J. The total-time hypothesis in verbal
    learning. Psychological Bulletin, 1967, 68, 221-234.
Frase, L. T. Advances in research and theory of instructional technology.
    In F. N. Kerlinger (Ed.), Review of Research in Education 3, Itasca,
    Illinois: F. E. Peacock, 1975.
Frase, L. T. and Schwartz, B. J. Effect of question production and
    answering on prose recall. Journal of Educational Psychology, 1975, 67,
    628-635.
Lyon, D. O. Memory and the learning process. Baltimore: Warwick and York,
    1917.
Owens, A. M. Generative and passive questions in learning from text.
    Perceptual and Motor Skills, 1980, 51, 714.
Rothkopf, E. Z. Some theoretical and experimental approaches to problems
    in written instruction. In Krumboltz, J. D. (Ed.), Learning and the
    educational process. Chicago: Rand McNally, 1965, 193-221.
Rothkopf, E. Z. The concept of mathemagenic activities. Review of Educa-
    tional Research, 1970, 40, 325-336.
Wittrock, M. C. Learning as a generative process. Educational Psychologist,
    1974, 11, 87-95.
Wittrock, M. C., Marks, C., and Doctorow, M. Reading as a generative pro-
    cess. Journal of Educational Psychology, 1975, 67, 484-489.

EXTENSIONS

DISCOURSE PROCESSING
A. Flammer and W. Kintsch (eds.)
© North-Holland Publishing Company, 1982

PROCESSING DREAM TEXTS

Ruedi Seitz

Institute of Psychology
University of Zurich
Zurich
Switzerland

A text processing approach is applied to the study of
dream interpretation. Specific problems in relation
to this approach are being raised. Proceeding from
working hypotheses, a dream text processing system
(DTPS) is outlined. DTPS postulates three subsystems
and operates on an understanding and an interpretation
level.

THE STATE OF DREAM RESEARCH

Dream research is currently in a state of conceptual and methodological re-
orientation. The psychophysiological research paradigm that has ruled the
field for the past three decades seems about to have run its course.

The psychophysiological paradigm followed from the discovery of apparent
physiological correlates of dreaming in 1953. Initially, it gave rise to
the enthusiastic conviction that by controlling physiological variables it
would become possible to clarify the mysterious nature of the dream process.
But this enthusiasm gradually receded. Finally, in the seventies, experimental dream research entered a period of relative stagnation.

Today, dream research reevaluates the simple fact that dreaming is a psychological process with some physiological concomitants and not vice versa.
One of the most prominent dream researchers, David FOULKES (1981), puts it
in the following way: "Dreaming is a mental process, and it must be studied
as we now study other mental processes." (p. 250) Time has come to get into
contact with what now is called 'cognitive science'.

FOULKES (1978) himself made an effort towards developing cognitive methods
for investigating dreams. In his ingenious book "A grammar of dreams" he
presents a scientific tool for detecting latent structures of dream contents. Another cognitive approach to the study of dream phenomena was made
by MOSER et al. (1980). Their method of model building is via computer
simulation. Even more decidedly than FOULKES the group around MOSER tries
to integrate some features of psychoanalytic dream theory into an information processing model of dream formation.

THE NEED TO APPLY TEXT PROCESSING MODELS TO DREAM RESEARCH

The view that dreaming is an information processing and reprocessing act is widely accepted nowadays. Problems arise with the question: what kinds of systems operate on what kind of information?

FREUD (1900), as pioneer of modern dream interpretation, recognized the textual character of dreams from the beginning. Dreams are not mere transformational products of sensory and memory inputs, but below the sometimes loosely connected manifest content there is one coherent latent meaning, a global structure.

The notion of the textual character of dreams has been a stimulating factor in clinical dream interpretation. However, in experimental dream research this factor has made things considerably more complicated. Experimental effects are to be found not as a clear-cut reaction consisting of a single sentence but as rather dispersed residuals throughout a whole text. A typical substitute for a textual analysis are overall ratings, e.g., of dream mood or of activity of dream characters. As long as there is no conception of textual dream structures, dream research cannot cope with the efficiency of clinical dream interpretation.

There are three areas in dream research where a text processing approach can be useful: dream formation, dream reporting, and dream interpretation. Dream formation can be considered as a process of retrieving text-like information stored in episodic memory and transforming it into a rather coherent sequence of visual information. - Dream reporting or dream text production can be considered as a process of retrieving structured experiential information and transforming it into coherent verbal information, a narration of the dream. A particular problem is the difference between immediate and subsequent dream reports. - Dream interpretation or dream text comprehension surely is a text processing problem. It   presents an operational approach to the complex problem of dream meaning. Dream interpretation is the issue on which I am focusing now.

PROBLEMS WITH PROCESSING DREAM TEXTS

The central problem in dream text processing is meaning. The meaning problem divides into four subproblems. They appear in a text processing design as the aim, the text, the subject and the task problem.

The aim problem: *latency*. - As mentioned above, FREUD (1900) differentiated between manifest content and latent content of a dream. Strictly speaking this means two levels of meaning. The manifest content refers to a literal meaning. The latent content or meaning is on a lower level and is the one we are aiming for. If text processing procedures are concerned with semantic or pragmatic representation of texts, they do not reach the latent meaning level.

The text problem: *ambiguity*. - One of the findings of experimental dream research is that systematically recorded dream reports are far less bizarre than commonly believed. Nevertheless, people may interpret a dream text in many ways. One of the reasons for this is the fragmentary and vague character often found in dream texts.

The subject problem: *involvement*. - Subjects asked to process a dream text
are highly motivated and become emotionally involved with this task. A
purely cognitive point of view misses the effect on the subject. Dream text
processing presupposes a great deal of evaluative and participative processes.

The task problem: *interpretation*. - It follows that the usual procedures
for studying text processing, such as reproducing, paraphrasing, summarizing or completion techniques, are not appropriate for the study of dream
text processing. They may help to detect text processing operations related
to the manifest meaning of texts. As far as processing operations related
to latent meaning are concerned, they must be studied by a text interpreting procedure.

SOME WORKING HYPOTHESES RELATED TO THE MEANING PROBLEM

How should the specific meaning problem inherent in dream text processing
be handled? Related to each subproblem there is a working hypothesis supposedly functioning in everyday dream understanding and interpretation. In addition, a general working hypothesis may be formulated.

The general working hypothesis: *A dream is a message*. - This is one particular way to say that dreams are meningful. They are not only relevant experiences but contain a message. A dream text, as a communication about a
dream experience, is consequently a communication about a communication.

The latency hypothesis: *A dream is a message from an unknown author*.   With
dream texts we are faced with the strange phenomenon that the text producer
can give us only limited information about text meaning. Moreover, he sometimes expects us to tell him the meaning of his report. We assume that the
dream text producer, i.e., the dreamer, is speaking of somebody else whom
nobody knows. However, we may construct hypotheses about the intention of
the unknown author. This intention is called 'latent meaning'.

The ambiguity hypothesis: *A dream is an open message*. - It is difficult to
find the latent meaning of a dream text even if the manifest meaning is easy
to understand. This is because the same manifest meaning may lead to different latent meanings. The only way to cope with this problem is to look for
hints given in the text which favour one single latent meaning. And texts
are full of hints.

The involvement hypothesis: *A dream is a personal message addressed to the
dreamer*. - The set of possible latent meanings is restricted by the criterion of personal relevance. It may be beneficial for the dreamer when he
recognizes the latent meaning of his dream. Non-dreamers processing a dream
text participate either through assisting the dreamer or through assuming
it to be their own dream.

The interpretation hypothesis: *A dream is an encoded message*. - Interpretation of a dream text is a decoding task. The latent meaning is seldom directly accessible through the manifest meaning. On the other hand, it is not

necessary to assume intentional disguise of the latent meaning, as FREUD (1900) did. Maybe the unknown author is polyglot and communicates simultaneously in different codes.

PRELIMINARY NOTES ON A MODEL OF DREAM TEXT PROCESSING

If we assume a *dream text processing system* (DTPS), we may say that DTPS operates on two levels:
(a) on the level of manifest meaning, i.e., the content of dream text as told by the dreamer,
(b) on the level of latent meaning, i.e., the intention ascribed to the unknown author.

Processes concerning manifest meaning of dream texts shall be called *understanding* processes; processes concerning latent meaning of dream texts will be called *interpretation* processes. Interpretation processes are based on understanding processes; understanding processes are guided by interpretation processes. Thus, DTPS operations on the two levels are circularly interrelated: starting with an understanding step, an interpretation schema is activated which in turn controls understanding information. Starting with an interpretation step, understanding information is analyzed in order to validate the interpretation schema. Theoretically, the text processing cycle may run until the interpretation schema is found that fits best. Practically, the cycle may stop already after one turn.

What are the *interpretation schemata* available in DTPS? This is a core question. Following the involvement hypothesis mentioned above the criterion of personal relevance applies here. It seems that at this point cognitive and emotive/motivational processes are converging.

Generally, DTPS considers three types of communication called 'listen', 'look' and 'take'. 'Listen' is concerned with instructive information, with the issue: what is there to do? This type of communication is action-related. - 'Look' is concerned with expository information, with the question: what is the state of the world and of the self? This type of communication is situation-related. - 'Take' is concerned with expressive information, with the issue: what is there to get? This type of communication is motivation-related.

Corresponding to the three types of communication DTPS postulates *three subsystems* called likewise LISTEN, LOOK, and TAKE. The subsystems work independently but may cooperate if needed. Each subsystem disposes over a set of interpretation schemata: LISTEN over the instructive schemata, LOOK over the expository schemata, and TAKE over the expressive schemata.

The subsystem LISTEN treats a dream text as a narrative text. On the level of manifest meaning LISTEN organizes textual information by applying a (chronological) story structure, thereby constructing a DREAM STORY. On the level of latent meaning LISTEN evaluates the DREAM STORY by instructive interpretation schemata: it processes the DREAM STORY into an instructive meaning called DREAM MORAL.

The subsystem LOOK treats a dream text as a descriptive text. On the level
of manifest meaning LOOK organizes textual information by applying a (topo-
logical) image structure, thereby constructing a DREAM IMAGE. On the level
of latent meaning LOOK evaluates the DREAM IMAGE by expository interpretation schemata: it processes the DREAM IMAGE into an expository meaning
called DREAM MOMENT.

The subsystem TAKE treats a dream text as a fictional text. On the level of
manifest meaning TAKE organizes textual information by applying a (ontological) creation structure, thereby constructing a DREAM CREATION. On the
level of latent meaning TAKE evaluates the DREAM CREATION by expressive interpretation schemata: it processes the DREAM CREATION into an expressive
meaning called DREAM MOTIVE.

Each subsystem disposes over a set of three interpretation schemata, most
of which have a positive and a negative variant. The instructive schemata
are conceptualized as DO, LET, and EXPECT. Correspondingly, LISTEN produces
latent meanings of the types MORAL (DO), MORAL (LET), and MORAL (EXPECT). -
The expository interpretation schemata are conceptualized as EXPERIENCE,
IMAGINE, and FEEL. Correspondingly, LOOK produces latent meanings of the
types MOMENT (EXPERIENCE), MOMENT (IMAGINE), and MOMENT (FEEL). - The expressive interpretation schemata are conceptualized as WISH, NEED, and
CHANCE. Correspondingly, TAKE produces latent meanings of the types MOTIVE
(WISH), MOTIVE (NEED), and MOTIVE (CHANCE).

Figure 1 represents the structure of DTPS as far as outlined here.

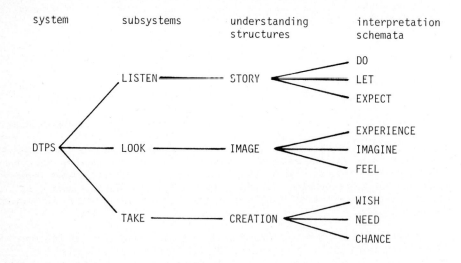

Figure 1
Structure of Dream Text Processing System (DTPS)

In this limited context it is not possible to give further specification
of the functioning of DTPS. Some empirical work has been done in order to
test the model. On the whole, our observations reveal that experts in dream
interpretation often use the subsystems LOOK and TAKE in processing dream
texts but rarely the subsystem LISTEN. Non-experts, however, do not seem to
prefer any subsystem. This result is preliminary and has not been tested
statistically. Further empirical investigations will follow.

REFERENCES

Foulkes, D. *A grammar of dreams*. New York: Basic Books, 1978.
Foulkes, D. Dreams and dream research. In W.P. Koella (Ed.), *Sleep 1980*.
          Basel: Karger, 1981.
Freud, S. *Die Traumdeutung*. Wien: Deuticke, 1900.
Moser, U., Pfeifer, R., Schneider, W., Zeppelin, I.v., & Schneider, H.
          Computer simulation of dream processes. Zurich: Interdiszipli-
          näre Konflikforschungsstelle, Soziologisches Institut der
          Universität Zürich, Report 6, 1980.

DISCOURSE PROCESSING
A. Flammer and W. Kintsch (eds.)
© *North-Holland Publishing Company, 1982*

COMPREHENDING THE DISCOURSE OF POETRY

W. John Harker

Department of Communication and Social Foundations
University of Victoria
Victoria, British Columbia
Canada

This paper provides a description of the comprehension of poetry which is based on current knowledge of text processing and recent theories of reader response to literature. While the reader of prose seeks goodness of fit between schemata represented in text and schemata brought to text based on his experience in the world, the reader of poetry encounters a separate reality from the real world. The result is that the reader of poetry alters his world view as his mind moves through the text recreating the separate reality represented there.

> A poem's existence is somewhere between the writer and the reader.
>
> T.S. Eliot (1933, p.30)

The purpose of this paper is to describe text processing when the text is in the form of poetry.[1] This description will proceed from the dual perspectives of current knowledge of text processing taken from psychology, and recent theories of reader response to poetry taken from literary criticism. It will be shown that during the past several decades, in both psychology and literary criticism, a fundamental shift has occurred in the way in which the reader's relationship to the text is conceived. This shift has appeared as a movement away from the belief that meaning resides in text and that the reader's task is to extract this meaning, to the belief that during reading there is an interactive process between reader and text in which the reader contributes to meaning. The first part of this paper will trace the development of this shift in terms of conceptions of text processing and reader response to literature; the second part will provide an exploratory description of the processing of poetic text.

TEXT PROCESSING AND READER RESPONSE TO LITERATURE

TEXT PROCESSING

If one lesson emerges from the study of intellectual history, it is that, while one climate of opinion may prevail during a given period, its opposite or near opposite often coexists in some subordinate form awaiting its turn for emergence and dominance. So it is, for example, that the pre-eminence of neo-classicism in English intellectual life during the early and mid-eighteenth century never entirely suppressed romanticism: thus we have with Pope, Blake. But following them both there was released the suppressed energy of romanticism which swept through English thought for decades after.

So too does the history of psychology during the twentieth century reveal an ebb and flow of interest in cognition. During the predominance of behaviorism, exemplified by Watson's (1920) expression of annoyance with psychologists "who try to introduce a concept of 'meaning' into behaviour" (p.103), there appeared Bartlett's (1932) work on remembering and associated aspects of mental life. Bartlett's conclusion that "all the cognitive processes...are ways in which some fundamental 'effort after meaning' seeks expression" (p.227) was as atypical of his time as were Blake's transcendental meditations in the man-centered universe of Pope and the neo-classicists.

Yet Bartlett's interest in cognition and language foreshadowed the emergence of an intense interest in these areas during the 1950s (notably in the work of Bruner and his associates, 1956), and increasingly during the 1960s (as seen in the work of Chomsky, 1965; Katz & Fodor, 1963; Katz & Postal, 1964). As a result of the work of this latter group of researchers in transformational linguistics, sentences were conceived to have both surface and deep structures. While surface structure gave sentences their phonological shape, deep structure carried their meaning. Typical of this view was the statement of Katz and Postal (1964) that the semantic interpretation of the deep structural relations underlying a sentence provided "a full analysis of its cognitive meaning" (p.12). On the basis of this view, the comprehension of text was seen as a process of deriving meaning from within the deep structure of the text itself. Extra textual sources of meaning were not to be admitted because they were not seen to be necessary.

This notion of "meaning in text" came under attack during the 1970s, particularly in the work of Bransford and his associates (Bransford, Barclay, & Franks, 1972; Bransford & Johnson, 1972). Through a series of experiments, these researchers demonstrated that the determination of meaning from text, rather than being a process of finding meaning within text, was a process of constructing meaning from information found both within text and brought to text by the comprehender. In reviewing this research, Bransford and McCarrell (1974) concluded that "a person may...have knowledge of a language and yet fail to comprehend an utterance because he is unable to make the necessary cognitive contribution" (p.215).

Current interest in the schema theory approach to text processing has resulted from a remarkable resurgence of interest in Bartlett's (1932) book combined with a growing general acceptance of the notion of text comprehension as a constructive process involving an interaction between the reader's knowledge of the world and the information he finds in text. Bartlett borrowed the term "schema" from the British neurologist, Sir Henry Head. Although Bartlett expressed dislike for Head's term, finding it "at once too definite and too sketchy" (p.201), he adopted it and defined a schema as "an active organization of past reactions, or of past experiences" (p.201).

The use of the term "schema," particularly in the recent writing and research of Anderson (Anderson, 1977; 1978) and Rumelhart (Rumelhart, 1980; Rumelhart & Ortony, 1977) and their colleagues shows a clear line of descent from Bartlett's earlier formulation. The key element in current schema theory is the structural quality of schemata. Schemata are conceived to be abstract knowledge structures which represent generic concepts stored in memory. Because they are abstract, schemata give general representations of objects, events, and situations in the world of human experience rather than particular ones.

The structures of schemata delineate their components and the network of typical relations which can normally be expected among these components. Anderson (1978) suggests that schemata contain "slots" for each component in the network. For example, the schema for "house," which would be an abstract mental structure representative of all houses and no particular house, would contain slots for such generalized components as "bedroom," "kitchen," "dining room," and so on. While these components are generic in the sense that they represent rooms in no particular house and therefore accommodate a wide variety of particular instances, they are also con- strained. Rumelhart (1980) calls this characteristic of schemata "variable constraint" (p.35). For example in the house schema one could expect to find a bedroom, a kitchen, a dining room, and even perhaps a dark room, but one would not normally expect to find a boardroom because knowledge of the world indicates that boardrooms are rarely found in people's houses. This quality of normalcy, of what can be ordinarily expected, is an essential characteristic of schemata.

It is in this way that schemata provide conceptual knowledge structures of abstracted reality. This is what they are. The next question is how they function during text processing. The application of schema theory to explain text processing is at once lucid and elusive. The lucidity derives from the fact that, according to schema theory, text processing is simply a matter of matching the semantic elements found in a particular text to the semantic elements represented as generic components of schemata stored in memory. When this occurs, the knowledge structures carried by schemata are "instantiated" in particular texts (Anderson, 1978, p.68). Put another way, comprehension occurs when the components of schemata brought to bear on a text provide a good fit with the components found in the text. The elusive part is how this happens.

Recent research on schema theory (for a review, see Spiro, 1980) has served to confirm the early conclusions of Bartlett (1932) and the later research of Bransford and his colleagues (Bransford, Barclay, & Franks, 1972; Bransford & Johnson, 1972) that comprehension results from a constructive interactive process which takes place between the reader and the text. During this process the reader uses both information he brings to the text (schemata held in his memory) and information found in the text (the print on the page) to determine meaning. Rumelhart (1980, pp. 37-38) likens this process to hypothesis testing. The reader is conceived to be engaged in selecting schemata which will provide the optimal interpretation of the text before him. If a selected schema is found to provide an inadequate inter- pretation, either it is modified or another schema is selected and its good- ness of fit to the text data is tested. Rumelhart (1980) describes this process as follows:

> Thus a reader of a text is presumably constantly evaluating hypotheses about the most plausible interpretation of the text. Readers are said to have understood the text when they are able to find a configura- tion of hypotheses (schemata) that offers a coherent account for the various aspects of the text. To the degree to which a particular reader fails to find such a configuration, the text will appear dis- jointed and incomprehensible. (p.38)

Because texts do not always contain all the information readers expect to find, comprehension often involves building inferential bridges between schemata and texts. It is not necessary for a reader to identify the pres- ence of every component of a schema in a text before the schema can be instantiated since schemata provide for the prediction of components beyond those actually identified. For example, in reading about a house, a reader could predict the existence of a kitchen even though a kitchen was not specifically mentioned. (Conversely, the introduction of a kitchen schema alone permits the inference of a superordinate house schema since kitchens are normally found in houses.) Rumelhart and Ortony (1977) describe this process as making plausible guesses and the inferences which result as "default values" (p.104). They argue that readers are able to infer these components through the influence of variable constraints which both suggest the components yet limit their possibilities. For example, in the house schema, a kitchen may be normally inferred, but a boardroom may not be.

It can be seen that comprehension, as represented by schema theory, results from a highly interactive process involving both reader and text. Schema theory permits the representation of this process in two basic ways. First, by depicting the structural organization of knowledge in memory, schema theory provides insights into the nature and organization of the reader's knowledge which is brought to bear on a text when meaning is sought. But schema theory goes beyond this to provide an explanation of the way in which this knowledge is activated. Thus schema theory describes not only static knowledge structures, but also the active cognitive processes which generate meaning from text.

READER RESPONSE TO LITERATURE

It would be difficult to find a more persuasive argument for the notion of prevailing intellectual climates than the parallel development of concepts of text processing and theories of reader response to literature. Corresponding to the prevalence of behaviorism in psychology and the later emphasis on meaning in text, there developed in the 1930s, particularly in North America, the hegemony of the New Criticism.[2] As psychology had denied meaning beyond what could be extracted from texts, the New Criticism argued that the essence of poetic meaning lay in "the structure and harmonious tension" (Wimsatt & Beardsley, 1954, p.239) of poems, and that this meaning could be determined through close textual analysis. Therefore a poetic text could be described as a "verbal icon" (Wimsatt & Beardsley, 1954) or "a well wrought urn" (Brooks, 1947), to use the titles of two statements of New Critical principles, a repository of meaning, visible, decipherable, yet inviolate. To consider the reader's response to a poem, to go beyond the text, was to commit "the affective fallacy" which Wimsatt and Beardsley (1954) described as "a confusion between the poem and its results (what it is and what it does)" and to invite "impressionism and relativism" (p.21).

The denial of the reader's response was not to prevail indefinitely, however. In recent years, critical theory has reassessed the role of the reader with the result that it has taken on new significance. Critical theories which embrace reader response range from psychoanalytic criticism (see, for example, Bleich, 1978; Holland, 1973, 1975, 1978; Lesser, 1962), which views reader response as a process through which the reader's personality is projected onto the text and the meaning derived is uniquely shaped by the reader's personality, to the criticism of the "Geneva critics" (see, for example, Miller, 1965, 1970; Poulet, 1969), which views reader response as a process through which the meaning of the text takes over the consciousness of the reader and allows the reader "to think what it thinks and feel what it feels" (Poulet, 1969, p.54).

Between these two poles lies the criticism of the "Reader Response School" in the United States represented by Stanley Fish, and the Rezeptionsästhetik[3] in Europe centered at the University of Constance and represented by Wolfgang Iser. The conclusions of these two critics, especially in the areas of common agreement between them, bear striking similarities to certain aspects of current psychological theories of text processing and therefore provide a basis for a theory of poetic text processing which has both psychological and aesthetic validity.

STANLEY FISH. Rather than seeking to avoid the affective fallacy of Wimsatt and Beardsley (1954), in his preface to the paperback edition of his study of Milton's Paradise Lost, Fish (1971) openly embraces it. He writes, "making the work disappear into the reader's experience of it is precisely what should happen in our criticism, because it is what happens when we read" (p.ix). The unifying theme in Fish's criticism is his elaboration of this reading process. In describing the reading of Paradise Lost, Fish contends that "the reader is drawn into the poem not as an observer who coolly notes the interaction of patterns..., but as a participant whose mind is the locus of that interaction" (1967, p.11). In his most recent book (1980), Fish reiterates this position by stating that "interpreting is not the art of construing but the art of constructing" (p.327).

Fish's method for describing this constructive process is to analyze the reader's emerging response to the text as reading progresses. In direct contradiction of the New Critics, the question Fish asks is not what the text means to the reader but what the text does to the reader. Fish contends that comprehension results from the reader's cumulative experiencing of the text and not from his attempt to unlock some meaning contained in the text itself. For example, in Surprised by Sin (1969, 1971), his analysis of the reading of Paradise Lost, Fish conceives the reader, through interacting with the text, to gradually experience in his own mind the Fall of Man. Thus for Fish both the analysis of the reading process and the objective of critical inquiry are the same -- to trace "the temporal flow of the reading experience" (1971, p.27) in the mind to the reader as the reader develops expectations and makes predictions only to have them upset and modified as the meaning of the poem is constructed through his cognitive experience. So it is that what a poem "does" -- its cumulative effect in the mind of the reader -- is also what it means. For Fish, literary criticism becomes essentially a study of the psychology of literary response.

Thus the meaning of a poem may be described as an "experience" (1970, p.131), or an "event" (1970, p.128). It follows that Fish questions the objectivity of poetic texts since different readers will experience the event of poetic meaning in different ways.[4] He rejects the notion of structural descriptions of poems as accounts of their meaning since it is only through the inter-action of the text with the mind of the reader during the temporal act of reading that meaning can result. Close textual analysis, which of necessity excludes the dynamics of the reading act, is for Fish an exercise in futility.

WOLFGANG ISER. For Iser (1974, 1978), as for Fish, the reader's response defines meaning. It is through the interaction between the reader and the text and the resulting aesthetic event that meaning is produced. For Iser, "meaning is no longer an object to be defined, but is an effect to be experienced" (1978, p.10).

In his most recent book, The Act of Reading (1978), Iser gives a detailed account of how meaning is experienced in poetry.[5] Influenced by the Polish

philosopher Roman Ingarden (1973a, 1973b), Iser maintains that a literary
text offers "'schematized aspects'" which permit the work to be interpreted
by the reader through a process of "concretization" (1978, p.21). Reading
is conceived as a "performance": "As the reader passes through the various
perspectives offered by the text and related the different views and patterns to one another he sets the work in motion and so sets himself in
motion" (1978, p.21). This motion results in the reader's continually
changing viewpoints, each becoming modified by the one succeeding it. It
is through this process that the reader comes to comprehend the poem by
accommodating constantly to changing viewpoints and altering perspectives
as reading progresses.

Although the structure of the text gives direction to the wandering viewpoint of the reader, the text does not provide a full account of the reality
it portrays. It is this quality of literary texts which Iser calls their
"indeterminancy" (1978, p.24). The gaps in meaning -- or "blanks" as Iser
calls them (1978, p.182) -- left in poetry provide the impetus for the
imaginative response of the reader. The reader must fill in these blanks if
he is to make sense of the poem, and it is this essentially constructive
process of the reader's imagination entering into the text that produces
comprehension. Thus, for Iser "the meaning of a literary text is not a
definable entity, but...a dynamic happening" (1978, p.22). He writes (1978):

> As we read, we react to what we ourselves have produced, and it
> is this mode of reaction that, in fact, enables us to experience
> the text as an actual event. We do not grasp it like an empirical
> object; nor do we comprehend it like a predicative fact; it owes
> its presence in our minds to our own reactions, and it is these
> that make us animate the meaning of the text as a reality. (pp.128-129)

COMPREHENDING POETIC TEXT

Any attempt to draw together concepts from psychology and literary criticism
is bound to encounter difficulties. The most obvious one is the difference
in intellectual orientation implicit in each discipline. The standards of
proof for psychology are those of scientific method while those of literary
criticism are largely the power and logic of argument derived from the
intuitions and individual experience of the critic. This difficulty is
clear in the juxtaposition between the current concepts of text processing
and recent understandings of reader response to literature outlined above.
While the concepts of Anderson and Rumelhart are supported by a growing body
of empirical research, those of Fish and Iser are based on essentially
impressionistic responses to literature experienced by themselves and their
students. Differences exist in the texts analyzed as well. Psychologists
have generally conducted their research and based their theoretical formula-
tions on rather commonplace prose material which deals with such subjects
as having a meal in a restaurant (Anderson, Spiro, & Anderson, 1977) or the
contents of a house (Pichert & Anderson, 1976). The extent to which conclusions about text processing based on this kind of material can illuminate
the nature of poetic text processing is certainly open to question.

Despite these differences in methodology and the standards of proof, striking
similarities are apparent between the findings of text processing research
and theories of literary response. The most fundamental similarity is the
manner in which comprehension is represented from both perspectives as a

constructive process. For both psychologists and literary critics, the reader is as important as the text. More specifically, what information what schemata -- the reader applies to the text is as important as the information the reader finds there -- the representation of the author's schemata in the text. Not only does the importance of a goodness of fit between these two sources of information constantly emerge as a requisite for comprehension, but both psychologists and literary critics are in close agreement as to the reader's role in making this happen. It is through a process of accommodation to the text -- a process involving expectation, prediction, and the redetermination of meaning as text is processed through time -- that meaning is seen to evolve. The mind of the reader moves through the text in a constant effort to find consistency between the meaning expected and the message encountered. When this effort is frustrated by incomplete or inconsistent information, the reading process becomes even more active. The "slots" needing filling but for which meaning is not provided by the text are filled inferentially by the reader and the schematic network of the text is completed. This general model of text processing is essentially the same whether one reads the work of psychologists or literary critics.

Is one to conclude then that the comprehension of poetic texts is generally the same as the comprehension of prose? Is poetry just an aberrant form of prose, transformed in appearance and syntax by the creative vicissitudes of poets but from the perspective of psychological reality having little difference from the processing of "normal" prose texts? The answer is "yes" and "no". Yes because, as has been seen, striking similarities are found between psychological and critical descriptions of text processing even when the nature of the texts varies widely. But these same descriptions point to a basic difference as well, even though this difference has not been made explicit in either the psychological or critical literature owing to the exclusive focus of the two disciplines.

In order to understand the nature of this difference it is first necessary to understand the basic difference between poetry and prose (although fiction should be excluded from this definition of prose). As the poet Allen Tate (1959) once observed, "in poetry all things are possible...because in poetry the disparate elements are not combined in logic" (pp.251-252). The significance of this observation is that, while prose seeks to represent the conventional world, poetry does not. The validity of a prose description of a restaurant meal or a house will be determined by the extent to which this description seems "real" -- the extent of its perceived accuracy or logic (its goodness of fit) when compared with similar events observed in the world of everyday experience. But poetry does not work this way. The world of a poem is a separate reality from the world of everyday affairs and is therefore unconstrained by the conventions of normal reality. How it is different will vary from one poem to another and from one poet's canon to the canon of another. But it will be different since a poem is a conscious representation of a separate reality conceived in the mind of the poet.

This separate reality has direct implications for the comprehension of poetry. Schema theory and the tradition of psychological research upon which it is founded hold as a basic tenet the importance of the information the reader contributes to the reading act. It is this prior knowledge -- the schemata stored in memory -- which provides the reader with the basis for understanding. The source of this prior knowledge is the reader's experience in the real world -- the schemata he has learned in response to his need to know how the real world works, what he can expect from it, and which predications

he can make successfully in it. But in poetry none of this holds. The
worlds encountered in poetry are not the world the reader has learned to
expect through his experience in everyday life. The result is confusion, a
confusion which T.S. Eliot (1933), with characteristic insight, described
this way:

> There is the difficulty caused by the author's having left out
> something which the reader is used to finding; so that the
> reader, bewildered, gropes about for what is absent, and
> puzzles his head for a kind of "meaning" which is not there,
> and is not meant to be there. (p.144)

The result for the reader of poetry is that comprehension is doubly difficult. In order to comprehend poetry, the reader must first participate in
the creation of the poem in his own mind to an extent equal to the poet,
although not necessarily with the same result. Literary critics have empha-
sised the temporal nature of the processing of poetic texts although with
little specificity as to the psychological process involved. If the schemata
represented in poems are at variance with those of conventional reality, then
the task of the reader is to develop new schemata so that the ideational
landscape of the poem becomes more predictable and the poem's meaning more
accessible. As the mind of the reader moves through the poem, this process
takes place. The schemata of conventional reality are set aside or at least
modified and the differing ones of the poetic world being encountered are
established in their place. It is only when this happens that poetic understanding results. The landscape of the poem loses its strangeness, the
imagination of the reader moving through the poem (and being all the while
guided by the text which imposes constraints on the possible meanings allowed)
fills in with increasing consistency the gaps in the poem's schematic structure and meaning is constructed. Thus the reader encounters not the meaning
of the poem in the sense of this meaning being something implanted in the
poem to be discovered and extracted, but rather a meaning of his own creation
resulting from a reformulation of schemata brought from the conventional
world or from previous literary experience. In this way, not only does the
reader change the text by acting on it, but he himself is changed by the
text as a result of his comprehension of it.

Seen in this light, the structure and tension found in poetry by the New
Critics take on an importance for the view of poetic understanding presented
here. The reader, if he is to comprehend poetry, will require a structural
density and complexity in text for his response to be impelled and guided to
a full realization of meaning. That the meaning realized will be the reader's
own and not a meaning deposited in the text for him to find and extract does
little to detract from the value of many of the insights into the structure
of poetry provided by the New Critics. There would therefore seem to be less
conflict between reader response criticism and the New Criticism that either
side has admitted. That the psychological research into text processing has
provided a basis for a reconciliation is less important, however, than that
this research has provided a basis for a clearer understanding of the comprehension of poetic texts, an understanding which this brief discussion, if it
has achieved its purpose, has only begun to reveal.

FOOTNOTES

[1]The question of "What is poetry?" will not be debated here. Perhaps
Stanley Fish ("How To Recognize a Poem When You See One," 1980) is correct
when he argues that a poem is any linguistic representation which a group
of readers decides is a poem. Certainly Yeats' arrangement of Walter Pater's
(1910) prose description of the Mona Lisa in free verse, and his inclusion
of it in his edition of the Oxford Book of Modern Verse (1936), provides one
example to support the notion that prose and poetry are not set categories.
To add to this, Louise Rosenblatt (1978) has recently used the term "poetry"
to designate "the whole category of aesthetic transactions between readers
and texts without implying the greater of lesser 'poeticity' of any specific
genre" (p.12). In this paper, the latitude permitted by Rosenblatt will be
limited so that "poetry" will be used as a term to designate any language
arranged in verse form.

[2]A corresponding movement in Europe, although one having little or no
direct contact with the New Critics, was Russian Formalism (see Erlich, 1965).

[3]For a summary of the work and direction of Rezeptionsasthetik, see
Segers (1975).

[4]Fish has recently (1976, 1980) addressed the implicit criticism of his
method, that it invites unrestrained subjectivity in interpretation, by
introducing the notion of "interpretive communities." He argues that,
because of common cultural constraints shared by poets and readers, the
meanings constructed by readers cannot be wholly independent of either the
intent of the poet or of the meanings derived by other readers.

[5]Although Iser's examples are taken largely from English prose fiction,
his theoretical position has clear application to poetry.

[6]This is an unfortunate choice of adjective in the translation from
German to English since it implies an aimlessness in the reader's response
which is the antithesis of Iser's position.

REFERENCES

Anderson, R. C. The notion of schemata and the educational enterprise. In
    R. C. Anderson, R. J. Spiro, & W. E. Montague (Eds.), Schooling and
    the acquisition of knowledge. Hillsdale, New Jersey: Erlbaum, 1977.

Anderson, R. C. Schema-directed processes in language comprehension. In
    A. Lesgold, J. Pelligreno, S. Fokkema, & R. Glaser (Eds.), Cognitive
    psychology and instruction. New York: Plenum, 1978.

Anderson, R. C., Spiro, R. J., & Anderson, M. C. Schemata as scaffolding
    for the representation of information in connected discourse (Tech.
    Rep. No. 24). Urbana-Champaign: Center for the Study of Reading,
    University of Illinois, March 1977.

Bartlett, R. C. Remembering: A study in experimental and social psychology.
    London: Cambridge University Press, 1932.

Bleich, D. Subjective criticism. Baltimore: Johns Hopkins University
    Press, 1978.

Bransford, J. D., Barclay, J. R., & Franks, J. J. Sentence memory: A
    constructive versus interpretive approach. Cognitive Psychology, 1972,
    3, 193-209.

Bransford, J. D., & Johnson, M. K. Contextual prerequisites for understanding:
    Some investigations of comprehension and recall. Journal of Verbal
    Learning and Verbal Behavior, 1972, 11, 717-726.

Bransford, J. D., & McCarrell, N. S. A sketch of a cognitive approach to
    comprehension: Some thoughts about understanding what it means to
    comprehend. In W. B. Weimer & D. S. Palermo (Eds.), Cognition and
    the symbolic process. Hillsdale: Erlbaum, 1974.

Brooks, C. The well wrought urn. New York: Harcourt, Brace and World, 1947.

Bruner, J. S., Goodnow, J. J., & Austin, G. A. A study of thinking. New
    York: John Wiley, 1956.

Chomsky, N. Aspects of the theory of syntax. Cambridge, Mass.: MIT Press,
    1965.

Eliot, T. S. The use of poetry and the use of criticism. Cambridge, Mass.:
    Harvard University Press, 1933.

Erlich, V. Russian formalism. The Hague: Mouton, 1965.

Fish, S. E. Interpreting the Variorum. Critical Inquiry, 1976, 2, 465-485.

Fish, S. Is there a text in this class. Cambridge, Mass.: Harvard
    University Press, 1980.

Fish, S. E. Literature in the reader: Affective stylistics. New Literary
    History, 1970, 2, 123-162.

Fish, S. E. Surprised by sin: The reader in Paradise Lost. London:

Macmillan, 1967.

Fish, S. E. Surprised by sin: The reader in Paradise Lost. Berkeley: University of California Press, 1971.

Holland, N. 5 readers reading. New Haven: Yale University Press, 1975.

Holland, N. Poems in persons: An introduction to the psychoanalysis of literature. New York: W. W. Norton, 1973.

Holland, N. A transactional account of transactive criticism. Poetics, 1978, 7, 177-189.

Ingarden, R. The cognition of the literary work of art (R. A. Crowley & K. R. Olson, trans.). Evanston: Northwestern University Press, 1973. (a)

Ingarden, R. The literary work of art (G. B. Grabowicz, trans.). Evanston: Northwestern University Press, 1973. (b)

Iser, W. The act of reading: A theory of aesthetic response. Baltimore: Johns Hopkins University Press, 1978.

Iser, W. The reading process: A phenomenological approach. In The implied reader: Patterns of communication in prose fiction from Bunyan to Becket. Baltimore: Johns Hopkins University Press, 1974.

Katz, J. J., & Fodor, J. A. The structure of a semantic theory. Language, 1963, 39, 170-210.

Katz, J. J., & Postal, P. M. An integrated theory of linguistic descriptions. Cambridge, Mass.: MIT Press, 1964.

Lesser, S. O. Fiction and the unconscious. New York: Vintage Books, 1962.

Miller, J. H. Poets of reality. Cambridge, Mass.: Belknap Press of Harvard University Press, 1970.

Pater, W. The renaissance. London: New Library Edition, 1910.

Pichert, J. W., & Anderson, R. C. Taking different perspectives on a story (Tech. Rep. No. 4). Urbana-Champaign: Center for the Study of Reading, University of Illinois, 1976.

Poulet, G. The phenomenology of reading. New Literary History, 1969, 1, 53-68.

Rosenblatt, L. M. The reader, the text, the poem: The transactional theory of the literary work. Carbondale and Edwardsville: Southern Illinois University Press, 1978.

Rumelhart, D. E. Schemata: The building blocks of cognition. In R. J. Spiro, B. C. Bruce, & W. F. Brewer (Eds.), Theoretical issues in reading comprehension. Hillsdale, New Jersey: Erlbaum, 1980.

Rumelhart, D. E., & Ortony, A. The representation of knowledge in memory.

In R. C. Anderson, R. J. Spiro, & W. E. Montague (Eds.) Schooling and the acquisition of knowledge. Hillsdale, New Jersey: Erlbaum, 1977.

Segers, R. Readers, text, and author: Some implications of Rezeptionsästhetik. In Yearbook of comparative and general literature, No. 24. Bloomington: Indiana University Press, 1975.

Spiro, R. J. Constructive processes in prose comprehension and recall. In R. J. Spiro, B. C. Bruce, & W. F. Brewer (Eds.), Theoretical issues in reading comprehension. Hillsdale, New Jersey: Erlbaum, 1980.

Tate, A. Narcissus as narcissus. In Collected essays. Denver: Alan Swallow, 1959.

Watson, J. B. Is thinking merely the action of language mechanisms? British Journal of Psychology, 1920, 11 (1), 87-104.

Wimsatt, W. K., & Beardsley, M. C. The verbal icon. Lexington: University of Kentucky Press, 1954.

Yeats, W. B. (Ed.). Oxford book of modern verse. Oxford: Clarendon Press, 1936.

ABSTRACTS OF THE REMAINING CONTRIBUTIONS TO THE
INTERNATIONAL SYMPOSIUM ON TEXT PROCESSING IN FRIBOURG 1981

Those papers not included in this volume are to be published in a second volume. The reference information is as follows: "In S. R. Mathews II (Ed.) Supplementary Proceedings of the International Symposium on Text Processing: An International Perspective, The Educational Research and Development Center, The University of West Florida, 1982, in press." Information regarding order for the volume may be obtained from

> The Educational Research and Development Center
> The University of West Florida
> Pensacola, Florida 32504
> U.S.A.

Avshalom Aderet and Paul J. Hoffman: COGNITION AND LEARNING IN THE DESIGN OF PROCESSING SYSTEMS

The features of three major groups of word processing systems are outlined in terms of their human interface design. A number of psychological aspects of performance on word processing systems are described, and the appropriateness of mnemonics devices in word processing systems is discussed. Studies underway at COGITAN have been designed to compare various systems with regard to their ease of learning and ease of use, and to investigate underlaying psychological factors. Tentative results from these studies are presented and discussed.

Urs Aeschbacher: LOOKING FOR EMOTION IN THE READING-THINKING PROCESS

Has the phenomenon of "intellectual satisfaction in reading" just been overlooked in psychology or does it not exist? It is argued that the information theoretical paradigm in research on intrinsic motivation has kept it out of sight. In order to gain research hypotheses, a schema theoretical approach to the conjectured phenomenon is developed. The conception of motivationally cathected cognitive schemas calls upon differential psychology in that it relates possible "intellectual emotion" in reading to general style of thinking.

Thomas Chacko: "CONNECTION", "CONTIGUITY" AND THE CONSTITUTION OF "COHERENCE"

This paper seeks to achieve two things: (1) presenting and defending "coherence" as an intuitive notion, an undefined term referring to the defining property of natural language texts, (2) estabishing "connection" and "contiguity" as two concepts necessary to account for, or, equivalently, to identify the mechanism with which language users effect and perceive, the coherence of natural language texts. Number (1) leads to a justified equation between text-processing and the working out of the relations of coherence, which are spelt out by number (2).

Philippe C. Duchastel: TESTING TO AID TEXT PROCESSING

Taking a test over a passage one has just studied can greatly increase later recall of information from the passage (on a delayed retention test), even without feedback or further review of the passage. This important phenomenon, known as the testing effect, is analyzed in this paper for both its practical instructional implications and for its theoretical ones related to text processing. The cognitive process involved in this phenomenon is called consolidation. Also considered is the relationship of this effect with the effects of adjunct questions in text (mathemagenics). The applicability of each type of processing aid to practical instructional situations is examined. The analysis concludes with a view of text processing which emphasizes text in its instructional setting.

(not published in the Mathews' volume)

Eric Espéret and Daniel Gaonac'h: WHAT DOES "STORYTELLING" MEAN FOR CHILDREN: NARRATIVE SCHEMA REPRESENTATION AND STORYTELLING AT DIFFERENT AGES

The purpose of this paper is to investigate a metacognitive dimension of storytelling, the representation of what is a story for children. Therefore, we use the following theoretical framework: in order to succeed, when asked to make up a story, children must first possess an abstract mental representation (a narrative schema), which they activate; then, this representation will structurally organize the content, caused by other factors. We consider the different features of this schema and their genesis in children. Results, from different researches, illustrate this analysis.

Peter M. Fischer: THE ROLE OF SYNTACTIC AND SEMANTIC FACTORS IN SENTENCE
PROCESSING

About two decades ago psycholinguistic research of the transformational/
derivational grammar type started its rise within the framework of reading
research. Since the paradigm of syntactic phrasing/chunking in speech
processing soon faced serious problems, the approach has been abandoned in
the meantime. Semantically or meaning based approaches were following, which
were replaced again by more global, text-oriented approaches. Recent models
of reading either make tacit assumptions about the very first stages of
meaning extraction from the written page, or fall back onto quite
elementaristic assumptions concerning word-by-word processing. Some
questions about the interplay of syntactic parsing with meaning access are
raised in the light of recent experimental findings.

Philip Greenway: MAKING SENSE OF PERSONAL DOCUMENTS: A PHENOMENOLOGICAL
FRAMEWORK FOR PSYCHOLOGICAL INTERPRETATION

This paper examines some of the methodological principles necessary for a
phenomenological theory of the interpretation of personal documents. A
number of hermeneutic rules are put forward on the basis of Jacobson's
notion of the two axes of language, the metaphoric and the metonymic.

Mathias Gygax and François Stoll: LINE BY LINE ANALYSIS OF SILENT AND
ORAL READING TIME

A total of 12 subjects silently read 25 lines of political newspaper text
that was presented on a screen. After this first trial the same text was
again presented with the request that it be read aloud. On both trials eye
movements were registered for the measurement of reading time for each line.
Thereby, two reading profiles were obtained for each subject. A comparison
of these two reading profiles reveals that reading behavior varies widely
among readers. Individual reading times are discussed in terms of their
dependence upon the number of syllables and the number of words per line.

Gay Lyons Haley: CHILDREN'S STORY COMPREHENSION AS A FUNCTION OF
SOCIOECONOMIC STATUS, PROBLEM SOLVING TRAINING, AND THE ORDER OF FREE RECALL

Story understanding was described as a personalized comprehension whose
quality and fluency depended on the nature of deletions and intrusions in
free recall. Semantic and structural components of the underlying structure
of a story were described using procedures for analyzing expository texts
and applied to the oral recall of children. Children's internal

representation of a story was affected by factors related to characteristics
of the preschool child during a sensitive period for psycholinguistic
development: socioeconomic status, active encoding, and construction in free
recall.

Ronald E. Johnson: PROSE LEARNINGS: HOW ESCAPETH THEE FROM THE POROUS
STORAGE VAULT?

According to Gomulicki (1956), as passages lengthen, the abstractive process
in forgetting results in deletions or "omissions that progress from single
adjectives, through short descriptive phrases, to longer phrases which are
only incidental to the main theme". Here, two experiments are reported which
test the idea that the unit of omission in longer passages is the phrase
rather than the individual word. In Experiment I, 83 learners heard the
final 459 words of O'Flaherty's "The Sniper". Prior to this target segment,
half of the learners heard the earlier 907 words of the story. Either
immediately or after 48 hours, learners received an I00-item forced choice
test that probed the accuracy of their knowledges of two individual words
within each of 50 phrases in the target section. In Experiment II, 84
learners attempted either immediate or delayed recalls of the I00 target
words from a skeletonized completion form that contained the remaining 359
words. Conditional probability analyses of the remembering of words within
a phrase, as compared with word pairings drawn from two different phrases,
provided little support for Gomulicki's hypothesis. The experiments thus
provide evidence that the forgetting of phrases occurs primarily on a
fragmentary basis rather than as wholistic units.

Guntram Kanig, Klaus Weltner, and Karl W. Hoffmann: DIAGNOSIS AND
COMPENSATION OF STUDENTS' PERFORMANCE IN SELF REGULATED STUDY OF SCIENCE
TEXTS

A test System and a questionnaire were developed to assess the competency
to learn with science tests. Four different learning activities are
assessed by four different tests: "Information scanning within time limits",
"Comprehension of text and self-control", "Tendency to use information
retrieval facilities", "Ordering and grouping". The tests are based on real
learning tasks. The correlation between results of learning tasks and data
of questionnaires was negligible. Interventions to improve the learning
performance were successful., but depended on the complexity of the learning
activity. The most effective intervention was by the method of content
related programmed study guides.

Gerald Knabe: A SYSTEM FOR COMPUTERGUIDED ANALYSES, CONCENTRATION AND
STORING AND RETRIEVAL OF SCIENTIFIC INFORMATION

The efficiency of scientific research is based on the complement and
precision of the analysis of prior theoretical models and empirical findings.
Retrieval and analysis of scientific information can be improved by an
extended text processing system.

Components:

- a manipulating system to develop a highly structured thesaurus
- a concentration system for highly structured scientific information
- a retrieval system
- facilities for analysing selected information
- facilities for editing a manuscript with correct citations,
  index etc.

This paper describes an extended text processing system developed for these
purposes.

Paolo Leonardi: ON IMPRECISELY SPEAKING

The fact that texts often, if not always, suffer from indeterminacy has been
looked at, most frequently, as a defect of overcome. Here an attempt is made
to show that sometimes, in natural conversation, indeterminacy can be looked
for and be positively exploited by conversationalists. It seems that text in
determinacy can be used by conversationalists (i) to make relevant how
recipients interpret it, (ii) to codetermine what they mean, (iii) to
suggest possible understanding.

Nancy Marshall: THE EFFECTS OF TEMPORALITY ON RECALL OF EXPOSITION

A temporal and nontemporal version of a passage were written as were two
context passages (relevant and irrelavant). Subjects read one or each and
wrote free recalls. Results show that subjects who read the temporal version
recalled more; however, subjects who received the relevant context processed
the other text less efficientely. The implications of these results are
discussed, and some suggestions for future research are made.

Maria Materska: THE EFFECT OF TEXT DIFFERENTIATION ON INFERENCES AND
CHOICE IN PROBLEM SOLVING SITUATIONS

The problem presented in this paper derives from studies on productive
utilisation of kowledge in the process of aquiring new information. The
experimental situation assumed learning a text which consisted of 27 core
sentences and eight additional sentences containing logical expansion of
the core information or supplementing it with discordant elements
The subjects were solving problems related in their content with the text,
namely producing ideas (inferences) and evaluating of ideas (choice). The
level of performance of these tasks was controlled during the mastery and
forgetting stages of learning the text.
The interpretation of the result includes an explanation of interaction
between the manner of text differentiation, the stage of learning and the
kind of task which requires processing of the information found in the text.

Michael Metzeltin and Harald Jaksche: A MODEL FOR REPRESENTATION OF
SEMANTIC TEXT STRUCTURE

On the basis of re-definition of the concepts "proposition" (basic semantic
unit of a text of clearly defined size), "textoid" (sequence of interrelated
propositions), and "isosemia" (isotopic thread of identical/partly identical
concepts in the text) the authors sketch out a model for assessment of the
semantic substance of texts integrating various older and more recent
findings in this field.

Jules M. Pieters and Gijs Beukhof: DESIGNING INSTRUCTION FOR VERBAL
INFORMATION PROCESSING

Ideas about verbal information processing within the field of cognitive
instructional psychology and ideas about designing in technical engeneering
are used in combination to design instruction of textual material. The
quality of instruction depends, for the main part, on the quality of the
design phase. In that phase evidence about verbal information processing
must be made operational for instruction. The elaboration theory (Merill,
Reigeluth) can serve for this purpose. The elaboration theory synthesizes
various principles and theories about learning and instruction. A cognitive
elaboration theory can deliver a basis for designing instruction for verbal
information processing.

Anthony K. Pugh and Jan M. Ulijn: SOME APPROACHES TO STUDYING REALISTIC
READING TASKS

Linguists and psycholinguists have increasingly stressed that interaction
is involved in reading a text. However, the nature of the interaction and
the factors likely to affect it have not been fully examined. Indeed, even
recent studies have often not involved realistic reading tasks and hence
have inhibited normal interaction. This contribution reviews, mainly from a
methodological perspective, studies made by the authors in which realistic
tasks were given to readers. Criteria for assessing reading tasks are
suggested and note is also made of research in progress to which these
criteria are applied.

Rob Rombouts: ON SOME INTONATIONAL FEATURES OF NATURALLY OCCURRING
CONVERSATIONS: COGNITIVE VERSUS INTERACTIONAL APPROACHES

This study reports on those acoustic features of the speech performed in
naturally occurring conversations, known as 'intonation'. Two different
functions of intonation, viz. cognitive and conversational, will be
discussed and demonstrated. The main point of this study is to integrate
both approaches into a discourse oriented framework; the analysis of
naturally occurring conversations within such a framework is more promising
as it is within either of the mentioned approaches individually. Therefore,
the study of intonational features - more than any other linguistic feature
of the speech performed in naturally occurring conversations - urges one to
integrate both approaches into a broader analytic framework.

Benny Shanon: DESCRIPTION OF ROOMS

Verbal descriptions of rooms were collected and analyzed. The analyses
examine the global structure of the descriptions, and they suggest one
optimal representation of rooms. On all levels of analysis, correspondeces
are noted between the underlying cognitive structure and the particular
linguistic forms in which they are expressed. Together, the different
analyses indicate that the act of describing is not based on a naive-
realistic mapping of things and words. Rather, descriptions presuppose a
cognitive structuring of the world which may not be expressed by simple
recursive algorithms.

Shane Templeton: READABILITY, REAL KIDS, AND REAL WORLD: THE RELATIONSHIP
BETWEEN SURFACE AND UNDERLYING STRUCTURE ANALYSES IN PREDICTING AND
MEASURING THE DIFFICULTY OF STORIES

The prediction and measurement of readability is extended to the underlying
structure of stories. Comparison of surface and underlying prediction
indices suggest there is not a systematic relationship between surface
and underlying levels. Based on texts intended for grades two through five
and the results of students' recall as a function of underlying text
complexity, implications for the measurement of readability are presented.
Application of these findings to the use of current basal reading selections
are discussed.

Beat Thommen: TEXT - EVERDAY KNOWLEDGE - COMPREHENSION - CONTENT ANALYSES

In the field of everyday-psychological knowledge the application of content
analysis turned out to be especially complex. The relationship between text,
everday knowledge, comprehension and content analysis proved to be intricate.
In the first part of this essay, the methodological assumptions of content
analysis are discussed. In the second part, new tendencies of the research
in psycholinguistics and cognitive psychology concerning the problem of
comprehension and meaning are summarized. Part three suggests some solutions
for the problems outlined. Content analysis will be redefined as a method
for the controlled reconstruction of communicative meaning. The propositions
made are partly illustrated by examples of a content analysis the author
performed to investigate everyday-psychological knowledge.

Harm Tillema and Nico Verloop: ASSESSING STUDENTS' UNDERSTANDING OF TEXTS.
A CONCEPTUAL AND METHODOLOGICAL FRAMEWORK

This paper presents a conceptual and methodological framework for understanding the processes of text-comprehension in the classroom. The analysis
of text comprehension could be facilitated by improving the measurement of
resulting cognitive structures after reading/processing. In the paper
attention is given to the problems of analysing cognitive structures on a
conceptual level (i.e. the role of expert-analyses and the construction of
ideal or formal information structures) and on a methodological level (i.e.
the method of multi-dimensional scaling and network analysis). An experiment
is described which compares the effects of two organizational structures of
a text on the cognitive representations of students. The different
organizational structures of the text refer to the way in which the main
concepts are spread across the text the students study in the course of the
experiment: webstructure and linear structure.
This is measured by various methods for analysing cognitve structures; these
methods differ in the characteristics they measure. A procedure for research
is proposed for analysing the differential effects of text comprehension.

Gerrit van Dam and Michèle Brinkerink-Carlier: THE PROCESS OF FREE RECALL OF TEXTS

The general outline is presented of a research program on text learning and recall. The program is based upon the suggestion that text learning results in the storage in memory of functionally differentiable types of information. During subsequent free recall retrieval of these different types of information has to be integrated in order to arrive at an acceptable reproduction.

Claes-Göran Wenestam: TEXT CONSIDERED AS MEANINGFUL ACTION

In most research investigating verbal learning and cognition the semantic and/or structural properties of the text are considered to be basic not only for the assessment of learning but also for the researcher's inferences about cognitive processes involved. It is argued in this paper that the empirical data resulting from comparison between the properties of a text and the learning of a person is invalid for any inferences about cognitive processes. Instead another framework is suggested, which is founded on a qualitative approach, in which the researcher investigates qualitative changes within individuals at different points in time.

Anca G. Manoliu-Dabija: INTEGRATION OF KNOWLEDGE FROM TEXTS IN CAUSAL FRAMES

The problem of drawing appropriate causal inferences and of integrating verbal material in logical causal frames is investigated in the present study. The method permitted the control of inferences during the reading and the retrieval of two texts (one narrative and the other expository) with a deficit of explicit causal information. The main results of the two experiments are: 1) Only a very small percentage of the readers seemed to make the inferences during reading, most of them making the inferences at the time of retrieval, while a considerable proportion of the readers did not integrate the material at all in logical causal frames; 2) In general, professional academics produced appropriate inferences significantly more often than high school students; 3) The results based on the verification task raised some doubts about the reliability of this task for the testing of inferences. Conclusions about the spontaneity of causal inferences and some methodological considerations about the testing of inferences are presented.

AUTHOR INDEX

McGaw, B., 232,236
McKoon, F., 192,204,267,313,381,390
Mees, U., 357,359
Meichenbaum, D.H., 537,549,553
Melton, A.W., 364,375
Merritt, J., 541,553
Metten, A., 543,549
Metzeltin, M., 588
Meyer, B.J.F., 72,75,87,89,97,178,
    183,199,204,214,217,218,221,222,
    237,251,262,293,294,304,305,307,
    308,313,347,363,375,381,390,400,
    401,403,404,405,407,409,438,439,
    441,442,496,502,503,504,505,507,
    548,553
Mialeret, G., 149
Michener, S., 436,442
Micko, H.C., 29,36,38,41
Miller, G.E., 17,28,351,436,443
Miller, J.H., 573,580
Miller, J.R., 163,164,165,187,188,
    202,204,314,324
Miller, R.B., 381,390
Miller, R.M., 463,471
Milton, 574
Minsky, M.A., 76,86,153,165,326,337,
    364,375,554
Mirande, M., 543,549
Mistler-Lachman, J.L., 226,238
Moessinger, P., 521
Montague, W.E., 96,165,217,336,337,
    350,376,471,543,550,554,579,581
Moore, P.J., 261
Moore, T.E., 110
Morgan, J.L., 109,136,149
Morris, C.D., 221,232,234,238,485,
    493
Morris, P.E., 217,313,375,390
Morton, J., 263,267
Moscovitch, M., 380,391
Moser, U., 564,569
Müller, G.E., 191,204
Müller-Bouquet, P., 390
Mullet, R.L., 233,237,381,390,393,
    398
Munro, A., 545,549
Murdock, B.B., 186,204
Myers, J.L., 88,97,234,238,545,
    553
Myrow, D.L., 219,236

Nachtigall, H., 487,493
Navon, D., 292
Neame, R.L.B., 326,337
Neisser, U., 207,209,216,217
Nelson, D.L., 240,250,545,553
Nelson, L., 240,250
Nelsson, O., 522,525,526
Neufeld, V.R., 326,337
Newell, A., 164,165
Nezworski, T., 63,75
Nicholas, D.W., 166,171
Nickerson, R.S., 110,250,324
Niegemann, H.M., 392
Nijhof, W.J., 520
Nikolaus, K., 16
Nisbett, R.E., 340,351
Nitsch, K., 221,236
Norman, D.A., 76,86,172,183,215,217,
    307,313,351,363,376,463,471,545,554
Nyberg, S.E., 420,443
Nystrand, M., 277

Olivier, D.C., 38,41
Olson, D.R., 269,274,277,278
Olson, K.R., 580
Oltman, P.K., 312,313
Omanson, R.C., 49,52,115,117,122
O'Neil, H.F., 358,459,493,537,550,551,
    552,553
Ortony, A., 153,165,228,232,236,326,
    332,337,364,376,462,463,471,545,554,
    571,573,580
Ottensen, J., 493
Otto, W., 277,278
Owen, G., 398
Owens, A.M., 555,556,561
Owens, J., 222,223,224,234,238
Owings, R.A., 358

Pace, A.J., 401,408,409
Pachella, R.G., 119,123
Paivio, A., 227,228,231,232,237,238,
    418,443,487,493,545,553
Palermo, D.S., 493,579
Palmer, R.E., 159,165
Pantle, A.J., 556,561
Paris, S.G., 279,289
Parkhust, P.E., 463,471
Pask, G., 462,465,471
Passerault, J.-M., 53
Pater, W., 578,580

ADDRESSES OF CONTRIBUTORS

Avshalom ADERET, Consulting and Research, 151 University Avenue, Suite 307, Palo Alto, CA 94301, USA

Urs AESCHBACHER, Psychologisches Institut, Universität Fribourg, 14 Rue St. Michel, 1700 Fribourg, Switzerland

Richard C. ANDERSON, Center for the Study of Reading, University of Illinois, 51 Gerty Drive, Champaign, IL 61820, USA

William ˙BAIRD, Ontario Institute for Studies in Education, 252 Bloor Street West, Toronto, Ontario M5S 1V6, Canada

Gijs BEUKHOF, Department of Educational Technology, Twente University of Technology, P.O. Box 217, 7500 Enschede AE, The Netherlands

Steffen-Peter BALLSTAEDT, Deutsches Institut für Fernstudien, Universität Tübingen, Bei der Fruchtschranne 6, 7400 Tübingen, West Germany

Gordon H. BOWER, Department of Psychology, Stanford University, Stanford, CA 94305, USA

Michèle BRINKERINK-CARLIER, Psychological Laboratory, University of Utrecht, Varkenmarkt 2, 3511 Utrecht BZ, The Netherlands

Fredi BUECHEL, Institut für Psychologie, Universität Basel, Missionsstr. 24, 4055 Basel, Switzerland

Thomas CHACKO, Department of Humanities and Social Sience, Indian Institute of Technology, Kanpur 208016, India

Hans COLONIUS, Institut für Psychologie, TU Braunschweig, Spielmannstr. 19, 3300 Braunschweig, West Germany

Donald F. DANSEREAU, Department of Psychology, Texas Christian University, Box 29880A, Forth Worth, TX 76129, USA

Eddy M. DEGRYSE, Psychology Department, University of Leuven, Tiensestraat 102, 3000 Leuven, Belgium

Philippe C. DUCHASTEL, Research and Evaluation Department, The American College, 270 Bryn Mawr Avenue, Bryn Mawr, PA 19010, USA

Stephane EHRLICH, Laboratoire de Psychologie, Université de Poitiers, 95 Avenue du Recteur Pineau, 86022 Poitiers, France

Eric ESPERET, Laboratoire de Psychologie, Université de Poitiers, 95 Avenue du Recteur Pineau, 86022 Poitiers, France

Tamar FERBER-STERN, Chaire de Pédagogie et de Didactique, Ecole Polytechnique Fédéral de Lausanne, Centre Est, 1015 Lausanne, Switzerland

Peter M. FISCHER, Deutsches Institut für Fernstudien, Universität Tübingen,
    Bei der Fruchtschranne 6, 7400 Tübingen, West Germany

August FLAMMER, Psychologisches Institut, Universität Fribourg, 14 Rue
    St. Michel, 1700 Fribourg, Switzerland

Daniel GAONAC'H, Laboratoire de Psychologie, Université de Poitiers, 95
    Avenue du Recteur Pineau, 86022 Poitiers, France

Simon GARROD, Department of Psychology, University of Glasgow, Adam Smith
    Building, Glasgow, G12 BRT, U.K.

Ulrich GLOWALLA, Institut für Psychologie, TU Braunschweig, Spielmannstr.
    19, 3300 Braunschweig, West Germany

Marcel L. GOLDSCHMID, Chaire de Pédagogie et de Didactique, Ecole Poly-
    technique Fédéral de Lausanne, Centre Est, 1015 Lausanne, Switzerland

Philip GREENWAY, Faculty of Education, Monash University, Clayton, Victoria
    3168, Australia

Mathias GYGAX, Psychologisches Institut, Universität Zürich, Schmelberg-
    str. 44, 8044 Zürich, Switzerland

Gay L. HALEY, Division of Educational Studies, Emory University, Atlanta,
    GA 30322, USA

John HARKER, Department of Communications, University of Victoria,
    Victoria BC, V8W 2Y2, Canada

Suzanne HIDI, Applied Psychology Department, Ontario Institute for Studies
    in Education, 252 Bloor Street West, Toronto, Ontario M5S 1V6, Canada

Angela HILDYARD, Office of Research and Development, Ontario Institute for
    Studies in Education, 252 Bloor Street West, Toronto, Ontario M5S 1V6,
    Canada

Eugen HINDER, Paedagogisches Institut, Universität Fribourg, Place du
    Collège, 1700 Fribourg, Switzerland

Karl W. HOFFMANN, Institut für Didaktik der Physik, Universität Frankfurt
    Grafstr. 39, 6000 Frankfurt a/M, West Germany

Paul J. HOFFMANN, Consulting and Research, 151 University Avenue, Suite 307,
    Palo Alto, CA 94301, USA

Charles D. HOLLEY, Texas College of Osteopathic Medicine, Texas Christian
    University, Forth Worth, TX 76129, USA

Harald JAKSCHE, Institut für Slawistik, Heinrichstr. 26, 8010 Graz, Austria

Ronald E. JOHNSON, Department of Education, Purdue University, West
    Lafayette, IND 47907, USA

Gregory V. JONES, Department of Psychology, University of Bristol, 8-10
     Berkeley Square, Bristol BS8 1HH, England

Guntram KANIG, Institut für Didaktik der Physik, Universität Frankfurt,
     Grafstr. 39, 6000 Frankfurt a/M, West Germany

Walter KINTSCH, Department of Psychology, University of Colorado, Boulder,
     COL 80309, USA

John R. KIRBY, Faculty of Education, University of Newcastle, Newcastle NSW
     2308, Australia

Karl J. KLAUER, Lehrstuhl für Pädagogik III, Institut für Erziehungswissen-
     schaft, RWTH Aachen, Eilfschornsteinstr. 7, 5100 Aachen, West Germany

Gerald KNABE, Organisationspsychologischer Dienst, An der Blankstr. 33 B,
     4052 Korschenbroich, West Germany

André KOERFFY, Chaire de Pédagogie et de Didactique, Ecole Polytechnique
     Fédéral de Lausanne, Centre Est, 1015 Lausanne, Switzerland

Steen F. LARSEN, Institute of Psychology, University of Aarhus, Asylvej 4,
     8240 Risskov, Denmark

Paolo LEONARDI, Instituto di Storia della Filosofia, Università di Padova,
     35100 Padova, Italy

Joel R. LEVIN, Wisconsin Research and Development Center, University of
     Wisconsin, 1025 W. Johnson Street, Madison, WIS 53706, USA

Hans J. LODEWIJKS, Instructional Psychology, Tilburg University, Postbus
     90153, 5000 Tilburg LE, The Netherlands

Heinz MANDL, Deutsches Institut für Fernstudien, Universität Tübingen, Bei
     der Fruchtschranne 6, 7400 Tübingen, West Germany

Anca MANOLIU-DABIJA, Psychological Laboratory, University of Utrecht,
     Varkenmarkt 2, 3511 Utrecht, The Netherlands

Nancy MARSHALL, Montgomery County Public School 13500 Dowlais Drive,
     Rockville, MD 20853, USA

Maryanne MARTIN, Department of Experimental Psychology, Oxford University,
     South Parks Road, Oxford OX1 3UD, England

Maria MATERSKA, Instytut Psychologii, Uniwersytet Warszawski, Warszawa
     00-183, Poland

Samuel R. MATHEWS II, Educational Research and Development Center, Uni-
     versity of West Florida, Pensacola, FLA 32504, USA

Richard E. MAYER, Department of Psychology, University of California,
     Santa Barbara, CA 93016, USA

Michael METZELTIN, Grote Kruisstraat 2/1, 9712 Groningen TS, The Netherlands

Hans Christoph MICKO, Institut für Psychologie, TU Braunschweig, Spielmann-
    str. 12A, 3300 Braunschweig, West Germany

Pierre MOESSINGER, Chaire de Pédagogie et de Didactique, Ecole Polytech-
    nique Fédéral de Lausanne, Centre Est, 1015 Lausanne, Switzerland

Helmut M. NIEGEMANN, Fachrichtung 6.1: Allgemeine Erziehungswissenschaften,
    Universität des Saarlandes, Bau 15, 6600 Saarbrücken, West Germany

Kurt NIKOLAUS, Fachbereich Linguistik, FU Berlin, Habelschwerdter Allee 45,
    1000 Berlin 33, West Germany

Anthony M. OWENS, Faculty of Education, Monash University, Clayton,
    Victoria 3168, Australia

Jean-Michel PASSERAULT, Laboratoire de Psychologie, Université de Poitiers,
    95 Avenue du Recteur Pineau, 86022 Poitiers, France

Martin S. PAYNE, Department of Psychology, University of Bristol, 8-10
    Berkeley Square, Bristol BS8 1HH, England

Georges PERSONNIER, Laboratoire de Psychologie, Université de Poitiers,
    95 Avenue du Recteur Pineau, 86022 Poitiers, France

Jules M. PIETERS, Department of Educational Psychology, Twente University
    of Technology, P.O. Box 217, 7500 Enschede AE, The Netherlands

Ruediger POHL, Institut für Psychologie, TU Braunschweig, Spielmannstr. 19,
    3300 Braunschweig, West Germany

Anthony PUGH, Faculty of Educational Studies, Open University Walten Hall,
    Milton Keynes MK7 6AA, U.K.

Uta QUASTHOFF, Fachbereich Linguistik, FU Berlin, Habelschwerdter Allee 45,
    1000 Berlin 33, West Germany

Gert RICKHEIT, Fakultät für Linguistik und Literaturwissenschaften, Univer-
    sität Bielefeld, 4800 Bielefeld, WestGermany

Margret RIHS-MIDDEL, Fenetta 3, 1752 Villars-sur-Glâne, Switzerland

Rob ROMBOUTS, Department of General Literary Studies, University of Amster-
    dam, Spuistraat 210, 1012 Amsterdam, The Netherlands

Jan ROZMUSKI, Chaire de Pédagogie et de Didactique, Ecole Polytechnique
    Fédéral de Lausanne, Centre Est, 1015 Lausanne, Switzerland

Anthony J. SANFORD, Department of Psychology, University of Glasgow, Adam
    Smith Building Glasgow G12 8RT, U.K.

Machiko   SANNOMIYA, Department of Psychology, Faculty of Human Siences, Osaka University, Suita, Osaka 565, Japan

Henk G.   SCHMIDT, Department of Educational Development, Rijksuniversiteit Limburg, P.O. Box 616, 6200 Maastricht MD, The Netherlands

Wolfgang SCHNOTZ, Deutsches Institut für Fernstudien, Universität Tübingen, Bei der Fruchtschranne 6, 7400 Tübingen, West Germany

Ruedi   SEITZ, Psychologisches Institut, Universität Zürich, Schmelzbergstr. 40, 8044 Zürich, Switzerland

Benny SHANON, Department of Psychology, Hebrew University, 91999 Jerusalem, Israel

Robertjan SIMONS, Instructional Psychology, Tilburg University, Postbus 90153, 5000 Tilburg LE, The Netherlands

Murry   SINGER, Department of Psychology, University of Manitoba, Winnipeg R3T 2N2, Canada

François   STOLL, Psychologisches Institut, Universität Zürich, Zürichbergstr. 44, 8044 Zürich, Switzerland

Norbert   STREITZ, Institut für Psychologie, Rheinisch-Westfälische TH Aachen, Krämerstr. 20-34, 5100 Aachen, West Germany

Hans   STROHNER, Fakultät für Linguistik und Literaturwissenschaften, Universität Bielefeld, 4800 Bielefeld 1, West Germany

An   SWERTS, Psychology Department, University of Leuven, Tiensestraat 102, 3000 Leuven, Belgium

Marianne   TAUBER, Psychologisches Institut, Universität Fribourg, 14 Rue St. Michel, 1700 Fribourg, Switzerland

Shane   TEMPLETON, Division of Educational Studies, Emory University, Atlanta, GA 30322, USA

Beat   THOMMEN, Psychologisches Institut, Universität Bern, Gesellschaftsstr. 49, 3012 Bern, Switzerland

Harm   TILLEMA, Vakgroep Onderwijskunde, Heidelberglaan 1, 3508 Utrecht TL, The Netherlands

Jan M.   ULIJN, Eindhoven University of Technology, Postbus 513, 5600 Eindhoven MB, The Netherlands

Gerrit   VAN DAM, Psychological Laboratory, University of Utrecht, Varkenmarkt 2, 3511 Utrecht BZ, The Netherlands

Nico   VERLOOP, National Institute for Educational Measurement, Oeverstraat 65, 6011 Arnhem JD, The Netherlands

Yvonne WAERN, Psykologiska Institutionen, Universitet Stockholms, Box 6706,
    11385 Stockholm, Sweden

Ruediger WEINGARTEN, Fakultät für Linguistik und Literaturwissenschaften,
    Universität Bielefeld, 4800 Bielefeld 1, West Germany

Klaus WELTNER, Institut für Didaktik der Physik, Universität Frankfurt,
    Grafstrasse 39, 6000 Frankfurt a/M, West Germany

Karl F. WENDER, Institut für Psychologie, Technische Universität Braun-
    schweig, Spielmannstr. 19, 3300 Braunschweig, West Germany

Claes Göran WENESTAM, Department of Education, University of Göteborg,
    Box 1010, 431 26 Molndal, Sweden

Peter WHALLEY, Institute of Educational Technology, The Open University,
    Witzton Hall, Milton Keynes MK7 6AA, U.K.

Gery d'YDEWALLE, Psychology Department, University of Leuven, Tiensestraat
    102, 3000 Leuven, Belgium

Vanda L. ZAMMUNER, Instituto di Psicologia, Università di Padova, Piazza
    Capitaniato 5, 35100 Padova, Italy